W9-BWV-027

Big Deal

Big Deal

The Battle for Control
of America's Leading
Corporations

Bruce Wasserstein

WARNER BOOKS

A Time Warner Company

Warner Books, Inc., 1271 Avenue of the Americas, New York, NY 10020
Visit our Web site at http://warnerbooks.com

W A Time Warner Company

Printed in the United States of America
First Printing: April 1998
10 9 8 7 6 5 4 3 2 1

Library of Congress Cataloging-in-Publication Data

Wasserstein, Bruce.
    Big deal : the battle for control of America's leading
corporations / Bruce Wasserstein.
        p.   cm.
    Includes index.
    ISBN 0-446-52268-6
    1. Consolidation and merger of corporations—United States.
2. Conglomerate corporations—United States. 3. Corporate
reorganizations—United States. 4. Corporations—United States.
I. Title.
HD2746.55.U5W37 1998
338.8'3'0973—dc21   97-39165

To my wife, Claude,
my love and inspiration

Research Director:
Burke Smith

Acknowledgments

This is the culmination of many people's helpful insights and assistance. In particular, I wanted to thank the Herculean efforts of my research director, Burke Smith, my colleagues at Wasserstein Perella, my clients and the law firms who have shared so much of their wisdom.

Lucie Longworth, Lisa Desmond, Crissy Kerr and Allison Mahler have worked tirelessly to support the effort, and Mort Janklow, my agent, and Larry Kirshbaum, my publisher, were always generous with their time. Most of all, the tolerance and love of my children, Pam, Ben and Scoop, the inspiration of my parents and sisters and the support of my wife, Claude, were essential to writing the book. I will forever miss the love and assistance of my deceased sister, Sandra W. Meyer.

Bruce Wasserstein
East Hampton
January 1998

Contents

Introduction

The swirl of mystery and controversy surrounding the deal business continues to spiral. Recent big deals—ITT; MCI; SBC-UBS; Dean Witter–Morgan Stanley; Disney-ABC; NYNEX–Bell Atlantic; the breakup of AT&T; and Chemical-Chase—suggest a seismic shift in the structure of the American economy. Perhaps we are at the dawn of a post-industrial age, a world of microchips, services and outsourcing. At the least, the tide of globalization will continue to rise.

The movement and restructuring of assets—mergers, acquisitions and divestitures—are currents in this evolutionary whirlpool. Front-page news and trends are inexorably reflected in a deal.

Indeed, growth by merger has been a part of American economic history since the coming of the Industrial Revolution. Over the years, the rationale, style and intensity of successive merger waves have varied, and a rich assortment of knaves and fools, heroes and winners, have played cameo roles. Millions of people and thousands of companies have felt the reverberations.

Change of this sort has been inherent in business since the Age of Discovery. But the image of the merger process is clouded by technical jargon and the premise that somehow the structure of business is static, gray, unchanging and unfathomable. The key barrier to comprehension is that changes in the structure of the economy have not come smoothly. Cycles of recession, depression and growth have battered our experience. By 1932, the stock market declined over 70 percent from its 1929 highs. Yet from the Crash of 1987 to 1997, the market appreciated by over 400 percent.

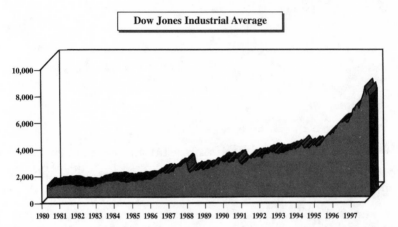

Dow Jones Industrial Average

Further, the wisdom of the moment often is misleading. The last decade has seen a breathtaking bull market, as stock market valuations of companies have soared. As a result, the 1980s turned out in hindsight to have been a time of relative bargain shopping. Curiously, little is said today of the fact that the carping at the end of the 1980s about prices paid in deals being too high turned out in hindsight to have been wrong. Today, the scope of the bull market is hard to comprehend as it unfolds, obscuring the fact that companies are being bought at all-time highs in the sensible 1990s.

Nor are hustlers anything new. In 1720, shares in the glamorous English conglomerate, the South Seas Company, were hot: its interests in whaling, exploration and the slave trade were a window on the future. The bubble eventually burst, and the company passed into history.

The process of change can also bring pain and destruction, a reflection of the cruel face of capitalism. That is why it is easy to attack mergers and acquisitions on an anecdotal basis. Such criticism calls to mind what Samuel Johnson once said about London: "When a man is tired of London, he is tired of life; for there is in London all that life can afford."

Similarly, the mergers business reflects the hubbub of our society with all its bustling and pretense. It is at the edge of change and fashion, and yet a minefield for the unwary. Mistakes are common. Still, good, bad or indifferent, mergers and acquisitions are an essential vehicle for corporate change, and the pace of change is increasing.

The patterns of industrial development through mergers, like those of economic activity, are crude and imperfect. However, there do seem to be elemental forces, Five Pistons, which drive the merger process. They are regulatory and political reform, technological change, fluctuations in financial markets, the role of leadership, and the tension between scale and focus.

Regulatory and Political Change   Many of the most active M&A sectors over the past few years—media and telecommunications, financial services, utilities, health care—have been stimulated by deregulation or other political turmoil.

Before deregulation, a number of industries owed their very existence to regulatory boundaries. In the financial services sector, for example, specific rules carved up the world into commercial banking, investment banking, insurance, mutual funds, credit unions, and so forth. These rules defined everything from the role of the local bank to that of the largest financial institution. Competition across the metaphysical regulatory boundaries was forbidden. However, lately these barriers have been relaxed, and in some cases completely removed. An Oklahoma land rush of deals has ensued, as companies struggle to make sense of this new competitive landscape.

Likewise, Congress literally rewrote the rules for the media and telecommunications businesses in the Telecommunications Reform Act of 1996. In the past, the various telecommunications players had defined realms. Local and long-distance companies were not allowed to compete against each other; cable television companies generally had monopoly status. By contrast, the 1996 legislation eventually will allow local and long-distance phone companies to compete in each other's markets. Cable companies also will be permitted to offer local service. Television and radio broadcasting companies may now own more stations. Though the regulations to implement this vision are currently tied up in litigation, the churning of the economic structure of the industry has already begun.

Technological Change Technology creates new markets, introduces new competitors and is intertwined with regulatory change. Changes in technology make old regulatory boundaries obsolete and sometimes silly. For example, the media and telecommunications business is an industry shaken by technological change and by regulatory reform. Technology has created industries like wireless telephony and satellite television, and promises a convergence of voice, video and data transmission that will dissolve the boundaries between market participants. The emergence of thousands of new businesses in the last decade based on new technologies assures a heated merger pace in the future.

Financial Change Financial fluctuations have a similar catalytic effect. A booming stock market encourages stock deals. A low market with low interest rates can have an especially strong effect after a period of high inflation in which the cost of hard assets has increased more rapidly than stock prices. In this environment, it may be cheaper to buy hard assets indirectly by purchasing companies on the stock market. Falling interest rates and available capital lubricate the process.

This was the story of the early 1980s. After a decade of relatively steep inflation, the replacement cost of assets had appreciated considerably. Yet, the stock market remained flat into the early part of the decade. As a result, a company's breakup value often exceeded its stock market value. The gap provided a powerful incentive for takeover entrepreneurs and financial buyers. On the other hand, tight money chokes the deal flow.

Leadership   Of course, corporate combinations do not occur in a mechanistic fashion. A human element is involved—the man on horseback who leads a company to seminal change. Jack Welch at GE, Louis Gerstner at IBM, Philip Purcell at Dean Witter, make a difference, just as J.P. Morgan or Harold Geneen made the difference. As in political history, one can come up with a lot of rationales about economic determinism, but people have an impact.

The Size-Simplicity Vortex   Scale matters, and bigger seems to mean better to most managers. Maybe it's critical mass, or technology and globalization, or integration, or sheer vanity and ego, but there is a natural imperative toward scale. However, just as some companies keep getting bigger, others shed their skin and become smaller. The imperative toward focus and simplicity is as strong as that for size. The two competing elements create a vortex of change.

This book is an attempt to put the deal business in context. Part One surveys the broad sweep of merger history, from the nineteenth century to the 1980s. Part Two focuses more closely on the strategy and tactics behind some active industries in the 1980s and 1990s and the deals that transformed them. Part Three describes the implementation of the modern transaction.

The emphasis here is on the structural forces, tactics and personalities that shape the deal process. My hope is that the spirit emerges in these clashes of corporate will, the uncertainty, fear and emotion, the failure and the triumph.

Of course, this book reflects many prejudices and experiences. Some twenty years ago, I wrote a book on corporate finance law from a young lawyer's point of view. I have since worked on well over 1,000 deals, including many of the larger transactions. With the inflation of asset values during this period and the dramatic rise in the Dow

Jones Average, most deals have worked well, but there certainly have been disappointments.

My perspective today is influenced by a particular combination of five experiences in this field. While at Harvard law and business schools, I worked for Ralph Nader examining government merger policy. Mergers were the natural intersection of my interest in law, business, economics and public policy.

After Harvard, I studied economics and British merger policy at Cambridge University and wrote an article for the *Yale Law Journal* on the subject. When I went to work as a young lawyer at New York's Cravath, Swaine & Moore, I was sent off to specialize in mergers partly because of the article. At the time, mergers were less exciting to many of my colleagues than the booming public offering practice.

After five years of lawyering, one of my clients, First Boston, convinced me to become an investment banker. I stayed there for over ten years, eventually as Co-Head of Investment Banking. Then for the past ten years at Wasserstein Perella & Co., I have continued to advise clients on deals as well as investing in businesses directly as a principal.

Because the scope of this book is so broad, it cannot purport to be exhaustive. The intent is rather to provide a sensitivity and a context for an appreciation of the traits of an important part of our economic history and an inevitable phenomenon.

Part One | # Past as Prelude

"Go where you will on the surface of things, men have been there before us."

Henry David Thoreau,
A Week on the Concord and Merrimack Rivers

The Battle
for Paramount

*"A billion here, a billion there, and pretty soon
you're talking about real money."*

Former U.S. Senator Everett Dirksen

A host of lawyers and investment bankers trooped into the dark
granite Manhattan office tower on the corner of Sixth Avenue
and 52nd Street in January 1994. Known to New Yorkers as "Black
Rock," the building houses the main executive offices of CBS Television. However, the lawyers and bankers were in the building to
visit the new offices of Wachtell, Lipton, Rosen & Katz, a powerhouse takeover law firm, which in a typically shrewd move had
leased space at the bottom of the real estate cycle from the downsizing CBS network.

QVC chairman Barry Diller arrived last in the thirty-third-floor
Wachtell, Lipton conference room. The epic battle for control of Paramount Communications, pitting home shopping channel QVC against
Sumner Redstone's Viacom, had dragged out over months. Now it
came down to this one moment. As the clock ticked toward the impending February 1 deadline for final bids, Barry Diller and his partners
had to decide whether to raise QVC's $10 billion bid for Paramount.

When Diller arrived in the conference room, he found a small
crowd that included Marty Lipton, one of Wachtell, Lipton's found-

ing partners, and high profile media banker Herb Allen of Allen & Co. A bevy of advisers including a team from Wasserstein Perella & Co. represented Diller's partners in the bid.

The meeting opened with a description of the situation. Viacom had just raised its bid from $104 to $107 a share for 50.1 percent of Paramount's stock. Media mogul Sumner Redstone was a tenacious and skilled adversary. Earlier, hoping to craft a "Diller killer," Viacom had added a contingent value right (CVR) to the complicated package of securities it was offering in exchange for the remaining 49.9 percent of Paramount's stock. The rest of the Redstone package was easy to beat. Consequently, the CVR was the main topic of Diller's conversation with his advisers.

The CVR provided that Paramount shareholders would receive additional Viacom securities if Viacom's stock failed to reach a specific price target within three years. Although there were substantial loopholes in Viacom's CVR, a consensus quickly developed among Diller's advisers. In light of the CVR and the downside protection the CVR provided, the view was that the arbitrageurs, or professional speculators, who held a majority of Paramount's stock would favor Viacom over QVC. QVC would lose the bidding war unless it offered a similar security.

The debate raged. Was gaining Paramount worth taking the additional risk inherent in a CVR? If QVC added such a right to its bid, QVC's existing shareholders might be forced to pay a steep price. Should QVC's stock not hit the price target, new QVC shares would have to be issued to the former Paramount stockholders, diluting the interest of the other QVC shareholders. Was the price for Paramount so high that the winner of the bidding would really be the loser?

Diller closed the debate and asked his friends to make their personal recommendations to him in private. Lipton, Allen and all the others realized that a "win" was within grasp and that Diller's destiny was to run Paramount. They all strongly endorsed the raise. Diller said he needed time to think the issue over and would be back shortly. While Diller's advisers waited, he walked the halls.

Finally, Diller returned and in a soft voice told the exhausted entourage his decision—he would not let the emotional momentum of the contest push him; QVC would not raise. He would rather lose than overpay. The battle for Paramount was over.

Before the Storm

The Paramount epic foreshadows many of the themes of this book: the dominant roles of personalities, the changing strategies of major corporations, the importance of the courts, and issues of pricing and takeover tactics.

While the contest for Paramount raged on, it dominated the financial news. Newspapers, television, radio, online information services—all were filled with the latest word on the bidding. In fact, the back-and-forth received so much attention for so long that at least one reporter openly professed to be "sick of writing about Paramount."

However, many Americans were captivated with the struggle. One reason for this interest was the nature of Paramount's business. Paramount was, as then–Viacom president Frank Biondi described it, one of the great American "dream machines."

Paramount Communications—the company being fought for— had not always been a sexy, sought-after media company that could command a steep price in the market. Not long before, the company called Paramount Communications had been Gulf + Western, a plodding corporate conglomerate. Of course, the Paramount movie studio—one division of Gulf + Western—had a long and compelling history. Founded in 1916 by Adolph Zukor, Paramount Pictures was a Hollywood powerhouse in the 1930s and 1940s. The studio boasted a stable of stars that included the Marx Brothers, Gary Cooper, W.C. Fields, Claudette Colbert, Bob Hope and Bing Crosby.

In those early days, Paramount not only made movies, it also owned a captive chain of theaters. To the politicians of the late

1940s, this arrangement smacked of a dangerous monopoly. Eventually, in something called the "Paramount Decrees," the government forced Paramount and other movie studios to sell off their captive theater chains.

By the 1950s, however, Paramount was wounded and dying. Along came the highly controversial Charles Bluhdorn—dubbed the "Mad Austrian" by *Life* magazine—and his company Gulf + Western. Even before it bought Paramount in 1966, Gulf + Western was a corporate menagerie. Starting from a car bumper business, Bluhdorn built one of America's largest conglomerates. His company made building products, owned racetracks, marketed consumer products and cigars, ran a publishing company, held land in the Dominican Republic, mined titanium, peddled panty hose and so on. The various operations were known as "Charlie's cats and dogs."

In the end, Gulf + Western's performance was lackluster. The sudden death of Bluhdorn in 1983 and rise of Martin Davis to the position of CEO only underscored what had been clear for several years—Gulf + Western needed to slim down and refocus.

On taking the helm, Davis, a tough former publicist with an instinct for survival, quickly assessed the situation. In a radical departure for a company once known as "Engulf & Devour," he launched Gulf + Western on a campaign to sell off more than 100 unrelated businesses. By 1989, this effort was largely complete. In that year, the company sold its large finance division to Ford Motor Company for $2.6 billion, rechristened itself Paramount Communications and made an unsuccessful $12 billion hostile bid for Time Inc.

Having failed to win Time, Davis and Paramount sat in the early 1990s on a large slug of cash and looked for another strategic partner. Potential acquisitions reportedly included Geffen Records, Thorn EMI and even MCA. Rumors also periodically circulated of an impending Paramount-Viacom merger. In talks with Viacom's Sumner Redstone, as well as with other potential partners, Davis reportedly insisted that he control the surviving entity as CEO. Redstone initially found this demand unacceptable, as did other potential partners. A match failed to materialize, and the pressure began to mount.

A New Kind of Rumor

In the summer of 1993, Martin Davis heard a new rumor. Word on the street had QVC's Barry Diller preparing a bid for Paramount. Davis and Diller knew each other well. Their shared history traces back to when they worked together under Bluhdorn in the old Gulf + Western days. A clash of wills after Davis took over had led Diller to leave Paramount.

Naturally, given the antipathy between Diller and Davis, Davis viewed the prospect of a QVC bid with alarm. Early in 1993, Davis heard from John Malone, the leader of both Tele-Communications Inc. (TCI), a cable company, and Liberty Media, an affiliated owner of cable television channels and QVC's largest shareholder. Malone told Davis that QVC intended to purchase Paramount. At the time, Malone was regarded by his enemies as the Darth Vader of the cable industry, an all-powerful, brilliant overlord with his fingers grasping for every media opportunity. According to court papers filed in later litigation, Malone recalls Davis responding that the Liberty Media boss should keep Diller "on a leash."

In July, Davis had a tense lunch with Diller at Paramount headquarters. According to Davis, Diller denied the rumors of QVC's interest in Paramount, but only in a "vacant" fashion. Diller, who claims he was noncommittal when asked about his intentions, describes the meeting differently. In a later deposition, he testified that the lunch was cut short when Davis became incensed, yelling "I know you're coming after me."

Meanwhile, Redstone and Davis had been in serious discussions since June 1993. The negotiations were at times difficult. The two sides squabbled over the total price and the amount of cash to be paid for Paramount. Governance issues were also debated, everything from who would be CEO to the name of the surviving entity.

However, the approaching shadow of Diller apparently motivated the Paramount side to come to terms. A little over a month after Davis' lunch with Diller, Davis took a proposed merger with Viacom to the Paramount board. The deal called for Viacom to pay Paramount shareholders $9.10 a share in cash plus Viacom stock then valued at $60. The entire package valued Paramount at roughly $8.2 billion.

To facilitate the merger, Paramount agreed to amend its existing "poison pill," a takeover defense device. Moreover, as approved by the Paramount board, the deal also contained two lockup provisions designed to keep other bidders from busting apart the Viacom-Paramount marriage: first, Paramount granted Viacom an option to acquire 20 percent of its stock, and second, Paramount agreed to pay Viacom a $100 million fee if it backed out of the deal. Finally, for Davis, the deal had another important feature—he would be CEO of the proposed Paramount Viacom International, though Redstone would control the company.

PROFILE

Barry Diller

Barry Diller is regarded as unique in Hollywood, a cut above the rest. He retains a genuine creative capability while having outstanding business management and leadership skills.

Diller was born and raised in California. Lured by the world of show business, he dropped out of UCLA at age nineteen and convinced neighbor Danny Thomas to secure him an interview at the

William Morris Agency. Eventually, Diller landed a job in the famed William Morris mail room. He rose from there to become an agent and then, at age twenty-four, an executive at ABC.

Diller spent ten years at the television network, cementing his reputation as a creative force. In those years, he launched ABC's popular and successful *Movie of the Week* format and the first successful miniseries.

In 1974, Diller left ABC to become the head of Paramount and, with a highly successful team that included Michael Eisner, Frank Mancuso and Jeffrey Katzenberg, drove the studio to renewed success. The studio produced such hits as *Saturday Night Fever* and *Raiders of the Lost Ark*. However, when Martin Davis succeeded Charles Bluhdorn in 1983, Davis and Diller clashed.

Diller then moved to Twentieth Century Fox. He arrived at the studio during a period of instability under owner Marvin Davis (who is unrelated to Martin Davis) and created "the comeback studio of the year." Diller, along with the next Fox owner, Rupert Murdoch, built Fox Television into a successful fourth network with popular series such as *The Simpsons*.

In February 1992, Diller stunned the entertainment industry by abruptly resigning his post at Fox. His explanation for leaving the studio was simple: "It's not mine," he said. He landed at QVC with the express desire to own a major entertainment property and started eyeing Paramount.

Watching Diller, both during the Paramount battle and since, he dazzles with his ability to take on different roles for different crowds. When appropriate, he can be as emotional as any director. The fire blazes from his eyes. Other times, he is as businesslike and efficient as a button-down IBM executive. Diller has learned all the parts and is in total control.

Stroke, Counterstroke

On Sunday, September 12, 1993, the Viacom and Paramount boards approved a merger agreement. The transaction would bring the two companies together into a combined entity with a market capitalization of roughly $18 billion. Two days later, papers were filled with the news, heavily sprinkled with words like "mega," "mogul" and "giant."

"We think we've created the number one software company in the world," Sumner Redstone told reporters at a press conference in Viacom's cafeteria. "Only a nuclear attack" would break the deal. When asked, he dismissed the notion that Davis had agreed to the deal only to stave off Diller. "Martin has never had any fear of those people," he said. "We're not concerned about them."

Redstone's confidence in the Viacom-Paramount deal stemmed largely from his assessment of developments in the media business. While distributors of programming, in particular cable providers, currently had a powerful position as access providers, content, according to Redstone's vision, would soon reign supreme. New technologies promised to allow phone companies to transmit video over phone lines. Cable providers would have to share their distribution monopoly with telephone companies and satellite dishes. In a 500-channel world, content manufacturers like Viacom and Paramount would have a sought-after commodity.

From this perspective, the Viacom-Paramount combination made compelling strategic sense. Viacom brought cable channels MTV, Nickelodeon, VH-1 and Showtime to the table. Paramount produced movies and television shows, owned a successful publishing house, and had a library of over 850 films. The distribution boom—digital cable, movies on demand, global satellite television and hot international movie and videocassette markets—dramatically increased the leverage and value of content.

However, as soon as the deal was announced, it became clear

that the market doubted Redstone's confident assertions that no other bidder would emerge. Arbitrageurs—speculative investors who buy up the stock of merger targets in the hope a deal will go through at a higher price—elbowed to buy up Paramount stock. The price was bid up from the mid-50s to the high 60s. The arbs were betting a higher bidder would top Viacom.

There was good reason for the arbs to hope. On a breakup basis, most observers valued Paramount's treasure chest of media assets at between $9 and $10 billion. A buyer could easily outbid Redstone— say by $500 million—and make up the difference with asset sales. Paramount's theme parks, Madison Square Garden, which owned the Knicks and Rangers sports teams, and seven TV stations were likely candidates for easy sale.

Eight days later, with the stroke of a pen, Barry Diller indicated his intention to break up the deal. In a letter that began "Dear Martin," Diller proposed a merger of Paramount and QVC "on terms far more attractive to Paramount stockholders than the transaction proposed with Viacom." In the merger, Diller continued, each share of Paramount stock would be converted into $30 cash and .893 share of QVC stock. The package was valued at $80 a share, or $9.5 billion in the aggregate, based on QVC's market price at the time. When compared to Viacom's offer, by this time valued at around $63 a share, Diller's bid was compelling. In essence, Diller thought the Viacom deal was vulnerable because they had low-balled their bid.

According to Diller, QVC would finance the generous offer, which included $3.5 billion in cash, with the help of several equity investors. At the time of his letter, cable operators Liberty Media and Comcast already had agreed to invest $500 million each in QVC. Another $1 billion would come from Paramount itself. When asked about the final $1.5 billion, Diller responded with a question: "Is there anybody in the world who doesn't think we can borrow $1 billion, $1.5 billion? I'm not paying for any bank commitments . . . until we know more." True to form, Diller soon had another $1 billion of equity commitments, $500 million each from Cox Enterprises, a cable and newspaper company, and Advance Publications, the New-house family's publishing company.

Like Redstone, Diller had a compelling strategic vision to back his offer. A combination of QVC—with support from cable providers Liberty and Comcast—and Paramount would create a vertically integrated media company. In addition, Diller brought a strong creative history, running both Paramount and other studios, and a demonstrated ability to turn a flagging media company around.

Diller's bid naturally threw the Viacom-Paramount deal into great turmoil. Paramount shareholders were not likely to tender shares to Viacom in light of QVC's steep premium over the existing Viacom offer. Still, Paramount management stuck to its position that a combination with Viacom represented the "best fit for growth" of its businesses. The Paramount board slowly considered the QVC offer but continually put off discussions with Diller. First, Paramount required QVC to provide information on its financing. Then, when that condition was satisfied, Paramount delayed signing the confidentiality agreement needed before QVC could safely share further information with Paramount.

Finally, Diller tired of the foot-dragging. He launched a public tender offer for Paramount stock, contingent on the removal of both Paramount's poison pill and the costly termination fees provided for in the Viacom deal.

Viacom responded by renegotiating its deal with Paramount, raising the total consideration to $80 per share in cash for 51 percent of Paramount's stock plus a package of securities for the remaining 49 percent. The total package was worth roughly $9.4 billion. Even with the raise, however, the lockup provisions were left in place.

On November 16, the Paramount board met and rejected QVC's offer as unduly conditional. Even though the most recent QVC bid remained appreciably more valuable than Viacom's best offer to date, the board urged shareholders to favor the Viacom merger. In support of this stance, a company spokesman pointed out that QVC's tender offer was contingent on the removal of Viacom's lockup provisions, which had escalated in value and were now worth more than $600 million.

Sumner Redstone

Sumner Redstone—most recently ranked as one of the 400 wealthiest Americans by *Forbes* magazine—has built an estimated $3.1 billion fortune on the strength of shrewd judgment and a tough competitive spirit. He was born on May 27, 1923, in a Boston, Massachusetts, tenement. An entrepreneurial spark was bred into Redstone from the start—he watched his father transform a single drive-in movie theater into a small but profitable chain.

Though the seeds of a business career were planted early, Redstone didn't return to the family business until the mid-1950s, after graduating from Harvard College and Harvard Law School and spending a number of years as a Washington lawyer. In 1954, Redstone joined his father and brother in the family's chain of twelve drive-ins, known then as Redstone Management.

Redstone soon spotted the trends that would reshape the movie business. People were moving out of the cities into booming suburbs. Land was becoming increasingly scarce and more valuable. Redstone put these two trends together, and realized that drive-in theaters were not the future. He recognized the value of clustering more screens at single indoor locations. So the multiplex was born—a concept and a term that Redstone is credited with creating.

In time, Redstone expanded the family chain from fifty-nine to 129 theaters. He carefully picked sites and bought the underlying land, giving his company a hedge on the volatile movie business.

By his fifties, Redstone was a wealthy movie exhibitor with a reputation for an unyielding negotiating style.

However, the course of Redstone's life changed dramatically in
1979. Caught in an early morning hotel fire, he barely survived.
This near-death experience seems to have sharpened Redstone's
drive. He continued to expand the family business, now known as
National Amusements, but became increasingly concerned at the
lack of further growth potential. Good theater locations near
major highways were scarce. Looking for growth, Redstone began
investing in the content side of the movie business, just as the
1980s deal frenzy took off.

In 1986, Redstone made a toehold investment in Viacom, a
cable television and movie company then the subject of takeover
rumors. Sparked by what he viewed as a low-ball management
bid to buy the company, Redstone subsequently launched his
own takeover offer. He ultimately won Viacom after a heated
round of bidding. The original management offer had been $2.7
billion; Redstone agreed to pay $3.4 billion.

Some observers scoffed at Redstone's initial foray into the
big-deal business. He was portrayed in the media as a novice
dealmaker who got caught up in the zeal to win and seemed to
have overpaid. Yet, very soon after the deal closed, Redstone
looked like a genius. Viacom's MTV and Nickelodeon channels
continued to captivate young audiences around the world, while
the value of Viacom's cable system doubled very quickly in a rising market. This growth allowed the company to service its debt,
and the value of Redstone's stake multiplied, providing the capital to launch his Paramount bid.

On a personal level, Redstone exudes congeniality and charm.
He almost gurgles with enthusiasm about his business in every
technical aspect. Yet the sunshine fades rapidly when Redstone is
crossed. In such circumstances, he displays the bulldog tenacity
of a former litigator.

The Battle Shifts

Both sides in the Paramount fight soon ran to court. Not surprisingly, Redstone, a litigator by training, was first out of the gate. Two days after Diller announced his bid, Viacom filed suit in New York federal court challenging QVC's offer on antitrust grounds. In a press release, Viacom claimed that the lawsuit, which was broadly focused on the allegedly anticompetitive practices of John Malone's Liberty Media and Tele-Communications Inc., had been in the works even before the QVC bid. In light of its Paramount bid, however, QVC was added to the complaint.

Redstone had repeatedly used litigation in his career as an integral part of business strategy. He shrewdly judged that Diller's glass jaw was his Malone connection. As CEO of TCI and chairman of Liberty, Malone controlled the largest cable operator in the country as well as a number of cable channels. Critics charged Malone made a practice of using to unfair advantage his status as a gatekeeper to millions of cable subscribers.

Liberty Media's partial ownership of QVC gave Redstone an opening, and he pounced. According to Viacom's complaint, Diller was nothing more than a front man for Malone. Diller's offer was just another manifestation of Malone's "conspiracy to monopolize" the cable television business. Malone was painted in stark terms, as a buccaneer, a "bullyboy" monopolist, who used his company's dominance in the cable market to exact tolls from content providers like Viacom.

By November 12, the Malone connection cracked. Facing mounting scrutiny and political pressure, QVC had dropped Malone's Liberty Media from its group of financial backers. A week later, John Malone announced a settlement with the Federal Trade Commission that required Liberty Media Corporation to sell its interest in QVC within eighteen months if QVC bought Paramount.

But the resourceful Diller bounced back. He scrambled and replaced Liberty Media's planned $500 million investment with a much larger $1.5 billion commitment from regional telephone company BellSouth Corporation, our client. BellSouth had been lying in wait, hoping for a crack in one side or the other so that it could acquire a relatively low-cost window on expertise for video content. Meanwhile, NYNEX, the New York regional Bell phone company, took a position backing the Viacom bid.

Notwithstanding Viacom's initial success, the central litigation took place in Delaware courts as Diller mounted a counterattack masterminded by Herb Wachtell, the senior litigator at Wachtell, Lipton. Delaware prides itself on, and profits from, its position as the leading legal home for corporations. Because of this role, takeover litigation most often involves the Delaware courts, where the fiery Wachtell was a star, smooth, articulate and yet passionate. He proceeded to cut Paramount's board to ribbons.

From a technical legal standpoint, the case *Paramount v. QVC* revolved around whether the Paramount board had treated its shareholders fairly: by agreeing to merge with Viacom, did the Paramount directors effectively put their company up for sale? Wachtell maintained that the company was on the auction block, and the process the directors followed was unfair. The Paramount-Viacom deal was not a strategic marriage, according to Wachtell. Rather, Paramount had sold itself to Viacom. Under that circumstance, according to an earlier case involving industrialist Ronald Perelman's hostile bid for the Revlon Corporation, the Paramount board had a responsibility to open the sale to all bidders and conduct a fair auction.

Ironically, Paramount and its lawyers were in the awkward position of relying on the case they had lost three years earlier in Paramount's effort to split apart the Time-Warner merger. The *Time* case, won in part by Herb Wachtell, stands for the proposition that a board of directors is not required to cancel a planned "strategic" merger when faced with a higher cash bid.

After hearing arguments, the Delaware lower court sided with QVC. In his November 24 opinion, Vice Chancellor Jack Jacobs lambasted the lockup provisions in the Viacom-Paramount merger agreement as "draconian" and enjoined Paramount from modifying its poison pill to favor the Viacom deal or honoring the lockup option. Instead, an auction would have to be held consistent with the *Revlon* case.

Fifteen days later, after a hearing broadcast live on Court TV, the Delaware Supreme Court affirmed the lower court. The court sided with Diller—the proposed Viacom-Paramount merger was a sale of control that triggered the *Revlon* duties. The Paramount board should have focused single-mindedly on securing the highest price for Paramount shareholders. This conclusion rested in part on the fact that Redstone would control 70 percent of Viacom's voting stock after a Viacom-Paramount merger, and in part on the court's distaste for the Paramount board's and advisers' procedures.

To the court, the board was too swift to act and too generous to Viacom. The court proceeded to rap the board and its advisers on the knuckles. Moreover, the Paramount board could not hide behind the "no-shop" provision in its agreement with Viacom, which prohibited Paramount from seeking other offers, for the board had originally given "insufficient attention to the potential consequences of the defensive measures demanded by Viacom," and the measures were therefore unenforceable.

Barry Diller now had a level playing field.

The Auction

Reacting to the Delaware Supreme Court, the Paramount board met into the evening of December 13, 1993. The deliberations were in one sense a formality—in light of the court's decision, Paramount would be auctioned to the highest bidder. Still, a long, heated debate ensued. Certain directors felt a committee of independent, non-management directors should be appointed to oversee the bidding procedures, especially in light of the court's concerns. However, Davis argued that the entire board could administer a fair auction.

Ultimately, Davis carried the day and the entire board approved a set of auction procedures.

Under the procedures, each bidder was required to submit a closed "final" bid by 4:00 P.M. on December 20, 1993. Paramount agreed to drop its poison pill defense with respect to the bidders so that shareholders would be free to select either offer. In addition, the bidders were required to hold their offers open for at least ten days after gaining enough stock to complete the acquisition. This stipulation would allow stockholders who had tendered to the losing bidder to switch sides, thereby eliminating the incentive to tender early. Without this rule, only those shareholders who tendered to the winner prior to its deadline would receive a share of the cash consideration offered.

When the auction opened, QVC had a decided edge over Viacom. QVC's latest offer for Paramount was a $9.8 billion package of cash and securities. Viacom, with the help of a $600 million investment from Blockbuster Entertainment and a $1.2 billion investment from NYNEX, had cobbled together a $9.6 billion counteroffer. However, even this offer threatened to overwhelm Viacom's resources. The combined Viacom-Paramount entity would barely have enough cash flow to cover its massive debt unless both companies performed far better than they had over the past few years.

On December 20, the parties submitted their bids. However, reflecting Viacom's cash crunch, its bid remained unchanged from its last offer. QVC, on the other hand, raised the cash portion of its new bid to $92 per share for 50.1 percent of Paramount. At the same time, the stock portion of the bid was reduced, so that the shift did not raise the total value of the offer. A day later, in a blow to CEO Martin Davis, the Paramount board adhered to the Delaware Supreme Court's admonition and endorsed the higher QVC bid. Putting the best face on these developments, Davis emphasized that Viacom could still raise its bid.

Davis' wish came true during the first week in January. Sumner

Redstone announced an $8.4 billion merger with cash-rich Block-buster Entertainment. By paying stock for the acquisition, Redstone acquired new fuel for his battle with Diller and, with this new part-ner, dramatically raised the cash portion of his bid to $105 a share. However, like Diller, Redstone adjusted the stock portion of his bid, so that the total value of Viacom's offer was around $9.4 billion, still well short of QVC's $9.8 billion bid. Redstone, it seemed, was count-ing on the greater cash pool to entice the arbitrageurs who now held most of Viacom's stock.

In an angry response to Viacom's new bid, QVC charged that its rival had violated the bidding procedures by entering a new bid with the same value as the old bid. Earlier, QVC had charged Redstone with attempting to manipulate the price for Viacom stock higher to keep the Paramount purchase price down.

The New York Times sparked these claims when it reported in De-cember that Redstone's National Amusements Inc., Viacom's parent company, had been buying Viacom stock in July and August and that WMS Industries, a company 25 percent owned by Redstone, made similar purchases around the time of QVC's original bid. The WMS Industries purchases amounted to about 20 percent of the volume in Viacom Class B shares, at the time a large component of Viacom's acquisition currency. For his part, Redstone insisted that he was ig-norant of the purchases by WMS Industries. Meanwhile, both com-panies had secret talks as to a compromise settlement with no success.

Despite the strong feelings on either side, Barry Diller refused to raise his bid in response to Viacom's new offer. At a January 11 media conference in Los Angeles, he told reporters, "The bids are in. The public, the shareholders, should decide. As for me, I'm finished."

Finally, with parties on either side weary from the long fight, Red-stone's camp came up with their "Diller killer." The bid was raised to $107 per share in cash on the front end, and stock and securities on the back end, with a blended value of around $82 a share, roughly

$9.8 billion in total. The important contingent value right was added to protect Paramount shareholders should Viacom's stock price decline. Though QVC raised the cash portion of its bid once more, to $104 a share, Diller's decision not to include a CVR meant the battle was over.

The bidding had reached the upper limit of Paramount's breakup value. To some degree, Redstone's fierce competitive reputation was an asset to him. No matter the obstacle, Redstone seemed determined to overcome it. Redstone was betting that efficiencies and the opening of new windows for the use of creative content would leave room for adequate returns on Viacom's $10 billion investment. Diller disagreed. Rather than overpay, he pulled back.

Implicit in Diller's thinking was a relatively high value for Paramount's movie studio and a relatively low value for both Paramount's publishing businesses and Madison Square Garden and its sports teams. The studio business was pegged at between $3.5 and $4.0 billion, roughly 15 times cash flow from operations. The publishing business was valued at between $2.5 and $3.0 billion, or roughly 10.5 times cash flow from operations. The Garden, the sports teams and the theater chains together were valued at between $800 million and $1.0 billion. This was about 15 times operating cash flow. Adding all Paramount's assets up, Diller couldn't get to a number higher than he had already bid. Redstone was in a different position because he already had a large asset base in Viacom. Diller also had to bring along his partners in a complex and difficult situation.

Diller, however, was not just concerned about the Paramount purchase price and persuading his partners; he also was thinking ahead to life after the deal. Additional money would need to be invested in Paramount to realize his vision. If QVC paid much more than $10 billion for Paramount, Diller would be hard-pressed for capital. Improvements would be difficult. Diller refused to parachute into what he saw as an untenable situation.

On February 15, Viacom announced it had enough shares to complete the deal. The evening before, with the "cruel, abusive and sometimes ridiculous battle for Paramount" (as Redstone described it) winding down toward a midnight resolution, Redstone, Viacom CEO Frank Biondi and two other Viacom executives dined at Manhattan's "21" Club. At around 8:30 P.M., a call came in from Viacom's proxy solicitor. Viacom already had the 50.1 percent it needed to complete the deal. A few weeks later, Redstone described his reaction: "I picked up a champagne glass and said, 'Here's to us. We won.' It was not said in arrogance. The frustration, the stress, the meanness that had taken place all disappeared."

Diller, on the other hand, was philosophical about losing the biggest takeover fight of the year. He told the *Los Angeles Times,* "One of the things I learned long ago about auctions . . . you have to remember it's not ego or talent. It's simply raising your hand for the next bid. You don't always get to win."

Postscript

In the aftermath, Sumner Redstone felt like the winner, Barry Diller expected to be a winner and the rest of the world was waiting to see.

Diller's official statement about the Paramount contest—"They won. We lost. Next."—turned out to be prophetic. Diller soon bounced back and made a run at a QVC-CBS merger with himself as chief executive. But Comcast and Liberty Media, his major shareholders, had little interest in being minority holders in CBS and bought the home shopping channel's remaining stock. Diller found himself out of a job but with a tidy profit for his efforts.

A year later, Diller became chief executive officer and part-owner of Silver King Productions. His company then acquired a majority stake in both Home Shopping Network and Savoy Pictures in a deal designed to give him the raw materials to build a new television network and an edge in the field of electronic commerce. Diller has since added controlling stakes in Ticketmaster and the television operations of Universal Studios, and continues to make progress in his search for empire. He is on the edge of a breakout.

In the immediate aftermath of the Paramount deal, Viacom professed to be happy with its purchase. The huge hit *Forrest Gump,* which came right on the heels of the purchase, filled Paramount's coffers, hinting at a promising future. Subsequently, the financing mechanism, Blockbuster, has had deep problems due to a slump in its core video rental business, dragging down Viacom's performance.

Ironically, the hidden jewels in the company turned out to be publishing and the Madison Square Garden assets—not the forecasted movie business. In 1994, Redstone sold the Garden—with the Knicks, Rangers and cable channel but without the theater chains— to ITT and Cablevision for just over $1 billion. Two years later, Cablevision bought ITT's half interest for $650 million, valuing the whole at $1.3 billion. Clearly, the Garden and the theater chains together were worth more than the combined $1 billion value commonly quoted in 1993.

Likewise, Paramount's publishing business has been on a roll and is probably worth significantly more than the $2.5 to $3.0 billion figures quoted in 1993. In late 1997, Simon & Schuster was rumored to be on the market. Analysts speculated a purchaser might pay over $4 billion.

At these prices, Redstone in fact may have gotten a solid deal in Paramount. However, the strength of the Paramount purchase will continue to be obscured until the problems with Blockbuster are resolved.

History's Shadow

2

"The best of prophets of the future is the past."

Lord Byron, *Journal*

T he Five Pistons—regulatory change, technological developments, fluctuations in financial markets, the role of leadership,
and the tension between scale and simplification—run throughout
the Paramount story. However, the merger dynamic is by no means
new; these themes carry through the long history of mergers and acquisitions.

Mergers in the Iron Horse Age

The Fight for the Erie

In 1868, "Commodore" Cornelius Vanderbilt faced the same
dilemma that would torment Barry Diller over a century later. Vanderbilt had been trying to gain control of the Erie Railroad for more
than two years, but had been stymied at every turn. The Erie
Three—Daniel Drew, Jay Gould and Jim Fisk, the incumbent managers—had skillfully defended their positions. In the process, Vanderbilt had lost about $5.5 million, a phenomenal sum in those days.
Vanderbilt faced a quandary: Raise or fold?

Daniel Drew—titular head of the Erie—received Vanderbilt's cryptic answer late in the summer of 1868. "Drew," wrote Vanderbilt, "I'm sick of the whole damned business. Come and see me."

Old "Uncle Daniel," the "Sphinx of the Stock Market," as he was popularly known, could only have been relieved to read those few words. This is not to say the seventy-one-year-old former cattle driver was meek, for Drew was no stranger to aggressive business tactics. He had made his first fortune in the rough-and-tumble cattle business, bringing herds to market. Along the way, Drew reputedly fed salt to the cows, keeping them thirsty during the trip, then let them drink their fill right before reaching the scales at market. The scheme, called "watering stock," later became a metaphor for the issuance of corporate securities with an inflated value, a strategy used by Drew in his later incarnation as a stock market player.

Still, by the time he received Vanderbilt's note, even the pugnacious Drew had wearied of the constant back-and-forth battle over the Erie. Of course, Drew, who had been both a Vanderbilt ally and an enemy in years past, knew that everything—most especially peace—had its price with the Commodore.

The struggle for the Erie had started in 1866. Vanderbilt, at the time seventy-two years old, was a master of corporate growth through timely acquisitions. The gruff old man had parlayed a smallish shipping company into a massive transportation empire. The New York Central Railroad was the linchpin of his operations. An amalgamation of the New York & Harlem, the Hudson River and the old New York Central railroads, the reconstituted New York Central had lines running from New York City to Buffalo. Vanderbilt also owned an interest in the Lake Shore line, which gave him connections as far west as Toledo, Ohio.

But Vanderbilt saw the need for a further link with the bustling hub of Chicago. The Michigan Southern line possessed such a link. Vanderbilt wanted it. There was a problem, though. Another suitor, Drew's Erie Railroad, was after the Michigan Southern.

For a shrewd corporate acquirer like Vanderbilt, the answer was clear—he would pursue Erie itself. Vanderbilt thought himself well positioned. His agents were given orders to buy up Erie shares in the market, but as they did the stock price rose dramatically. Still, the Commodore kept buying, paying a hefty premium in the process.

Unbeknownst to Vanderbilt, many of the Erie shares he was buying in the market were coming directly from the Erie Three. Their main strategy was both simple and probably illegal (notwithstanding its validation after the fact by corrupt public officials). Fundamentally, it was very similar to the poison pill defense adopted by Paramount and others in the 1980s. As Vanderbilt feverishly tried to corner the market in Erie shares, management kept the printing press whirling, issuing more and more new shares.

Exasperated at the Erie Three's tenacity, Vanderbilt again commanded his brokers to buy, but to no avail. Each time they waded into the market, the printing press spun out a new batch of certificates, and Vanderbilt's ownership interest was diluted. Finally, Vanderbilt understood that he would not wrest control of the Erie in the market. Vanderbilt then resorted to a common raider's tool—he went to court. These were the days of Boss Tweed and Tammany Hall, when corrupt politicians controlled the New York political infrastructure. Not surprisingly, Vanderbilt was able to find a friendly judge, who complied with Vanderbilt's request and issued a warrant for the Erie gang's arrest.

Fortunately for the Erie Three, sources at the courthouse warned them of the impending arrest. Gould and Fisk hurriedly stuffed $6 million from the Erie treasury into several suitcases and fled with Drew across the river to New Jersey. They settled in at Jersey City's Taylor Hotel. Then, as now, the press loved the dramatic. They dubbed the hotel "Fort Taylor" after the Erie incumbents installed a stout antitakeover defense—fifteen policemen and three small cannons mounted on the waterfront.

Finally, after some time, Vanderbilt tired of "kicking a skunk," as he is reputed to have characterized the battle. He sent the note to

Drew, offering to meet and come to terms. Drew responded favorably, and the two men met at Vanderbilt's house. The Commodore was not, however, in the mood to give up quietly. He demanded in excess of $4.5 million as partial repayment for his losses from the fight. This was an early case of a spurned raider seeking a payment to go away—what became known as "greenmail" in the 1980s.

Vanderbilt was not without a negotiating position. If one believes Jim Fisk's description, Vanderbilt threatened to continue his legal assault: "He said . . . he would keep his bloodhounds (the lawyers) on our track; that he would be damned if he didn't keep them after us if we didn't take the stock off his hands." Though Vanderbilt's price was steep, Drew and his compatriots accepted.

PROFILE

Cornelius Vanderbilt

Cornelius Vanderbilt was a man governed by instinct and an uncommon drive to succeed who parlayed $100 into an immense fortune. An ability to spot and capitalize on new technologies was the essence of his success.

Vanderbilt was born on rural Staten Island, New York, in 1794 and cared little for schooling. When pressed to attend, he would instead volunteer to work on his father's farm or ferry passengers to New York City in the family boat. Noting her son's passion for his father's ferry business, Mrs. Vanderbilt agreed to lend him $100 to buy his own small ferry boat.

Vanderbilt began his ferry service at an opportune time. He was able to repay his parents within the first year, and gave them an additional $1,000. Then came the War of 1812 and boom times. With British ships blockading the harbor, vessels like Vanderbilt's were the only means to transport goods up and down the seaboard.

By the end of the war, Vanderbilt had a small fleet of sailing ships at his command. When new steamboat technology threatened to make his wind-powered vessels obsolete, Vanderbilt jumped on the technology and slashed prices to keep out competition.

When the Civil War broke out, Vanderbilt was in his late sixties and, again, saw the rise of a new technology—railroads. He realized that the United States must "span its imperial distances . . . or else crumble apart from the dead-weight of its size."

Once more, Vanderbilt adapted to change. He divested his shipping company for $3 million and bought railroads. By the time Commodore Vanderbilt died in 1877, he had built a railroad empire and an estate valued at more than $100 million.

The Consolidation of the Railroads

Railroading was the high tech of the nineteenth century, promising to open the great American expanses to commerce and development. From the founding of the Baltimore and Ohio Railroad in 1828, the craze for railroads spread. Most of the early roads were built between cities along the Eastern seaboard and carried passengers. Starting in 1849, though, freight revenue exceeded passenger revenue. Entrepreneurs recognized the railroad's promise and began to build a massive coast-to-coast network. By the 1880s, iron and steel tracks crisscrossed the country.

This massive expansion was funded partly with federal land grants, but also absorbed a considerable amount of capital. Almost $300 million was invested in the railroads in the 1840s, and $840 million more was invested in the 1850s, mostly from foreign investors. By 1890, the railroads were both overbuilt and overleveraged. Then, the Panic of 1893 hit, and the economy sagged badly from 1893 to 1897.

A mess ensued in the railroad industry. Out of the companies on the New York Stock Exchange, roughly 60 percent were railroads. Many were unable to pay their creditors. The Interstate Commerce Commission counted 192 insolvent railroad corporations, with roughly 25 percent of the country's combined railroad capitalization. Thousands were thrown out of work. Those companies that survived barely limped along. The industry was chaotic.

Investment banker J.P. Morgan stepped into the breach. Over the next several years, working in the interests of his many European clients who had loaned money to the railroads, he played a large role in merging together and restructuring their operations.

Morgan was a man of few words. Though notorious for a sharp tongue and booming baritone, his physical appearance was perhaps his most recognized feature. A recurring skin disorder left his face, and particularly his nose, swollen, gnarled and scarred. Business acquaintances struggled to keep from staring. A reputed mistress said: "I have never met anyone so attractive. One forgets his nose entirely after a few minutes."

In the late nineteenth century, Morgan controlled one of the main crossroads of American finance. His dominance derived from the intersection of America's burgeoning need for capital and Europe's concentrated supply of wealth. J.P. Morgan & Company grew by mediating between this European supply and American demand. With developed European contacts, especially among wealthy Britons, Morgan earned his commissions floating American bonds in Europe.

Most of the American demand was from railroads. Given their immense fixed costs, the railroads required fantastic amounts of start-up money. By 1893, Morgan's clients held a large quantity of American railroad bonds. Naturally, then, when the railroads began to default on their obligations, Morgan became quite concerned.

To Morgan, the railroads' grief seemed self-inflicted. There were just too many competing lines, which led to harrowing competition.

In Morgan's time, the brutal environment left competitors with anemic profits, vulnerable to every economic downdraft. Morgan and his father had both devoted their lives to developing a mature capital market, which depended on preserving the trust of European investors. The idea that sniping competition between the railroads could destroy this trust incensed Morgan.

Rather than sit by and watch this happen, Morgan set about restructuring the roads in a process that came to be known as "Morganization."

In the usual Morgan restructuring, the stockholders placed their shares in a voting trust to be controlled by Morgan until the railroad's debts were paid. Then, fixed costs were slashed, and Morgan's people carefully projected the railroad's future cash flow. New replacement debt was issued to bondholders. These instruments required payments in line with the railroad's projected cash flow. New stock, of only speculative value, was also issued to the stockholders and bondholders. If the railroad survived, this new stock might be quite valuable. Finally, because Morgan was overseeing many different railroads at once, he was able to reduce the warfare that had so debilitated the industry. He minimized the overlap between railroads by shutting down some lines and, when possible, merging companies together.

Though Morgan thought he was doing a public service by saving the railroads, critics saw his activities differently. He was, they argued, too powerful. By dominating the railroads, he reduced competition and forced higher prices upon consumers. Morgan also made himself and his firm incredibly wealthy in the process.

The essence of Morganization became the reorganizations and distressed securities practices of today. By 1900, the survivors were returning to economic health. Railroad bonds, which had been anathema to investors during the lean years, became a glamour investment once more.

Steel and Oil

Many other industries developed along lines similar to railroading. Steel and oil are prominent examples. The steel industry was born from the centuries-old iron business. In 1860, over 250 firms produced almost one million tons of iron. However, iron is a product of limited strength and was costly to produce. Steel, an alloy of pure iron and a controlled amount of carbon, is a stronger product.

In 1856, Henry Bessemer and William Kelly each independently discovered a cheap and effective method for purging iron of its impurities. A series of subsequent discoveries improved the process, and a new industry was born. Large mills were built throughout the 1850s and again in the 1870s and 1880s. Output increased accordingly.

Andrew Carnegie was perhaps the best known steel man. Starting from a company founded to make iron railroad bridges, Carnegie built an enterprise that in 1899 produced 75 percent of all U.S. steel exports and more than 50 percent of the plate steel made in America. He accomplished this feat through a two-tiered strategy. First, he drove his subordinates in a relentless pursuit of technological innovations and cost savings. Second, he retained a considerable portion of earnings in his company and bought his competitors at bargain prices when times were hard.

In the oil business, John D. Rockefeller followed a similar path in building his Standard Oil. He began in 1862 with an investment in a small Cleveland refinery. By 1870, the company was reorganized as Standard Oil and boasted the world's largest refining capacity. Much like Carnegie, Rockefeller detested the unremitting competition in the oil industry. Rockefeller's motto was "pay a profit to nobody." Vertical integration was his strategy, and acquisitions his tactic to accomplish that goal.

By the spring of 1872, about 80 percent of all Cleveland refineries had sold out to Rockefeller. Standard Oil's capacity increased to 12,000 barrels a day, or about one third of all U.S. production.

Rockefeller then repeated his Cleveland pattern in other cities— Pittsburgh, New York, Philadelphia and Baltimore. As his empire spread, transportation and distribution became critical. Still committed to vertical integration, he bought into pipeline projects and pipeline companies.

Rockefeller's strategy worked well, and by 1880, Standard Oil controlled at least 90 percent of the nation's oil business. Standard Oil was everywhere. At this point, more than forty stockholders held interests in the company and its various subsidiaries.

Rockefeller rationalized the ownership structure in 1882 with the formation of the Standard Oil Trust. In exchange for their shares, each stockholder received trust certificates. The trust was governed by a board, which was controlled by Rockefeller. The arrangement was ordered broken apart by an Ohio court on the ground that it violated the state's monopoly statute, but Rockefeller simply remade the trust into a New Jersey holding company that survived until 1911.

Economic Rhythms

The evolution of the railroad, steel, and oil industries, from the rapid pre–Civil War expansion to the turn-of-the-century consolidation, followed a pattern common to most American industries. Initially, as a promising new technology was first commercialized, certain producers experienced rapid growth and investors thronged to support the industry. This growth eventually resulted in overcapacity, and a period of retrenchment followed. While some market participants thrived in this more difficult environment, others collapsed under the weight of new competition. The strong bought the weak. Companies combined in the race to gain new efficiencies, to curtail competition or just to survive.

This evolutionary process sparked a great leap toward industrialization between the end of the Civil War and the turn of the twentieth century. With the close of the war, more than a million men returned from service on either side and threw themselves into the workforce. This influx, together with the pent-up demand for industrial expansion, sparked an economic boom. Heavy industry in particular grew at a breakneck speed. Great railroad and shipping empires were pieced together, the steel mills of Pennsylvania took shape, and the immense meat-packing yards of Chicago blossomed. The boom period lasted for almost ten years.

Then, in September of 1873, financier Jay Cooke's once powerful Philadelphia bank failed. The shock waves of this collapse toppled related business firms and eventually pushed the country into the Panic of 1873, the most serious depression yet experienced by Americans. More banks teetered and, in an effort to stave off failure, called in loans. This in turn forced many debtor firms into bankruptcy.

America came out of depression in the late 1870s, only to sink back again in 1893. By the turn of the century, though, the country was well on the road to industrialization and was becoming a nation of large enterprises. Around this time, a merger wave took off, with the peak period of activity between 1898 and 1902. Combinations in this period were a function of the Five Pistons—changes in regulation, technology, financial markets, personal leadership, and scale.

Statutory revisions in New Jersey and elsewhere contributed by creating the legal framework for the modern holding company. Prior to that, corporations were required to be operating entities and had been restricted in what they could do. Whether cause or effect, this new legal structure provided a mechanism for consolidation.

By some measures, this turn-of-the-century wave was more consequential than any merger boom since then. During the period, companies with roughly 40 percent of the nation's manufacturing capital participated in a combination of some sort. The boom ended with the stock market crash of 1904 and the Bank Panic of 1907.

More than three quarters of the mergers during the first wave were horizontal combinations that involved companies in the same industry, including concentrations in oil, sugar, tobacco, chemicals and canning. These mergers often left one or two concerns with an overwhelming majority of market share within a given industry. As a result, over 3,000 companies disappeared.

However, numbers alone cannot give a full sense of the first merger wave. Many of the individuals and corporations who proved most dominant attracted the ire of social critics, who found the financial workings of the age needless and harmful. The cruel side effects of industrialization and monopoly power were attacked and sometimes curbed, but the deals went on.

The Great American Steel Deal

Andrew Carnegie's high-tech, consolidation-based strategy ultimately paid off with the landmark deal of the first merger wave—the formation of U.S. Steel. The transaction netted Carnegie more than $225 million, over $4 billion in 1997 dollars.

On a cold December evening in 1900, eighty guests gathered at Manhattan's elegant University Club. Chiefly industrialists and investment bankers, the men came to honor one of their own, Charles Schwab, the president of Carnegie Steel, the largest and most prosperous steel company in the country. J.P. Morgan, the leading banker of the day, sat to Schwab's right. Others in attendance included Andrew Carnegie, railroad magnate E.H. Harriman, Standard Oil president H.H. Rogers and investment bankers August Belmont and Jacob Schiff.

After dinner, the honoree—a smooth, energetic orator—rose and gave a short speech. Being a steel man, he talked about steel. The industry faced tough times ahead, he told the group. Every last production efficiency had been wrung out of Carnegie Steel's operations. Foreign competition loomed on the horizon. The economic future was uncertain.

But all was not gloom, Schwab told the audience. He suggested an alternative. If several firms banded together, substantial savings could be achieved in distribution. These cost savings could be significant. Overlapping sales forces could be eliminated. Shipping costs could be slashed. New, low prices would result and the market for steel would expand accordingly.

By December of 1900, Schwab's boss, Carnegie, was sixty-five years old and growing impatient to begin a stage of more active philanthropy. Schwab's speech may have been a loosely disguised sales pitch.

At the same time, the steel business was entering a new age. A series of mergers had already consolidated the production of raw steel into the hands of Carnegie Steel, the Morgan-controlled Federal Steel Company and the Moore brothers' National Steel Company. While the market for steel had been booming for a number of years, demand had recently softened. As a result, steel processing firms, which turned the raw product into finished goods, were beginning to feel the pinch. The Morgan and Moore camps, each of which controlled a number of processors, had recently announced their intention to stop purchasing steel from Carnegie. Carnegie had countered with an ambitious plan to build a series of fabricating facilities, an area he had previously left to other companies. Difficult competitive times lay ahead for everyone involved.

Morgan was clearly intrigued by Schwab's vision and arranged a follow-up meeting. Four weeks later, a deal creating the nation's largest steel company was inked.

The formation of U.S. Steel, which combined Carnegie Steel and nine other companies, was valued at $1.4 billion. Taking inflation into account, the transaction easily ranks in the top five U.S. mergers of all time.

Trust-Busters Win a Round

The first merger wave left many industries highly consolidated. However, shifting regulatory winds soon reversed some of the earlier combinations.

At the start of the twentieth century, Standard Oil and U.S. Steel dominated their respective industries. The American Cottonseed Oil Trust, the National Linseed Oil Trust and the National Lead Trust each controlled a large portion of the market for their particular commodities. At its peak, the American Sugar Refining Company controlled nearly the entire refining business. The Pullman Palace Car Company held 85 percent of the market for passenger cars; the International Harvester Company held 85 percent of the market for farm machinery. The American Tobacco Company was formed in 1890 through the merger of the five leading cigarette manufacturers and at one time produced 80 percent of the nation's tobacco.

Business leaders justified the trusts, and later holding companies, as a necessary means to increase efficiency and gain economies of scale. In addition, they sought the elimination of unrestrained competition, which many saw as the cause of the successive depressions of 1873 and 1893. Critics, on the other hand, condemned the combinations, arguing that the concentration of market power in the hands of one or two producers left consumers vulnerable to price gouging. Politicians such as President Theodore Roosevelt fueled the fear by playing on the populist sentiment against the great concentrations of wealth and power represented by the leading industrial combinations.

As a result, Congress passed the Sherman Antitrust Act of 1890. However, the law at first proved largely ineffectual. In 1895, the Supreme Court ruled in favor of the American Sugar Refining Company, holding that it was not a monopoly in restraint of trade.

It was Roosevelt's successor, President William Taft, who succeeded in breaking apart several important trusts. His administration vigorously prosecuted U.S. Steel, American Sugar Refining, General Electric and International Harvester. In 1911, Taft's Justice Department won a huge victory in the Supreme Court, forcing the breakup of Standard Oil.

Even in pieces, Standard Oil dominated the oil industry. The former holding company, Standard Oil of New Jersey—which later became Exxon—ended up with close to half the aggregate net value. The second largest piece, Standard Oil of New York, later renamed Mobil, had 9 percent of the total net value. The laundry list of the remaining pieces, and the companies they eventually became, illustrates the magnitude of the original Standard Oil: Standard Oil (California) became Chevron, Standard Oil of Ohio became the American subsidiary of British Petroleum, Standard Oil of Indiana became Amoco, Continental Oil became Conoco, and Atlantic became part of ARCO.

Before the Fall: The Roaring Twenties

In the early years of the twentieth century, the business cycle continued its dramatic rise and fall, but the secular trend with regard to capacity and wealth was decidedly upward. The nation's real wealth, placed at $88.5 billion in 1900, more than doubled by the end of World War I. The war itself spurred a considerable expansion in productive capacity. The country experienced a brief postwar depression in the early 1920s, then boomed again—industrial output nearly doubled over the remaining course of the decade.

Industries established in earlier periods, such as oil, steel and electricity, continued to expand. At the same time, several new industries were born. Automobiles, airplanes, movies and radio all became commercial realities in the 1910s and 1920s. The number of radio stations went from 30 in 1922 to 500 in 1924. The number of registered cars went from 8.1 million in 1920 to 23.1 million in 1929. Meanwhile, on Wall Street, the stock market boomed. Volume climbed from 143 million shares in 1918 to 460 million in 1925, 920 million in 1928, and 1,125 million in 1929. The Dow Jones Industrial Average nearly quadrupled, from 100 in late 1924 to over 380 five years later.

The rising market and strong industrial growth combined to fuel a second merger movement, which ended with the Great Crash of

1929. Over 4,600 mergers were announced during the most hectic years, between 1926 and 1930. During that period, between 500 and 1,000 companies disappeared annually as a result of mergers or other consolidations. At the end of the 1920s, the nation's top 200 companies controlled an estimated half of the nation's corporate wealth.

Baby Blue Chips Grow by Merger

The volcanic activity of the second merger boom spawned many of the great creations of American industry. Dozens of today's major, established companies were formed during this period. These were the start-ups of the age, often pieced together with the help of funding from the overcharged stock market. General Motors' history illuminates the dynamic nature of the period.

General Motors founder William Durant got his start selling wagons and carriages. Then, in 1904, the car company of his neighbor, David Buick, ran into difficulties, and Durant took over. He reorganized the business, and in 1908 produced more than 8,000 cars. In that same year, after an aborted attempt at merging Buick together with Reo, Ford and Maxwell-Briscoe—together the four leading automakers—Durant instead formed General Motors as a New Jersey holding company. Buick was its main subsidiary. He then used $8.75 million in GM stock and the cash dividends from Buick to go on a massive buying binge. He had two goals in mind. First, he would broaden General Motors' product lines. Second, he would arrange a guaranteed supply of parts.

Durant quickly fulfilled both goals. He purchased the W.F. Stewart Body Company, the supplier of Buick's bodies, and 49 percent of Weston-Mott, the supplier of Buick's axles. Durant also established a joint venture with Albert Champion, a promising young Frenchman who produced spark plugs. GM and Champion formed a new company, which became the maker of AC spark plugs. Then, in November of 1908, GM purchased the Olds Motor Works for roughly $3 million in stock and in the process acquired a second line of cars. However, the intervening deals all paled when compared with Durant's coup—GM's acquisition of the Cadillac Motor Car Company for $4.75 million, mostly in cash. After a long courtship, Durant had finally succeeded in putting together two of the five largest carmakers.

All these acquisitions ultimately left GM with considerable indigestion. In 1910, Durant was ousted as president of GM in favor of a team selected by the company's creditors. The bankers controlled GM through 1915, when enough of the company's debts were paid down to warrant a return to stockholder control. Durant, still a major owner of GM stock, in the interim had co-founded the Chevrolet Motor Company. Though Chevrolet was becoming successful in its own right, Durant badly wanted to regain control of GM. So he launched a raid on his own company.

Durant began by feverishly buying GM shares in the market. The price, which stood around $80 at the start of the year, rose to a high of $558 by December 1915. Durant funded his buying spree first with cash from a massive $50 per share dividend he forced the bankers to pay on GM stock and second with the proceeds from a public offering of Chevrolet stock. In this fashion, by the end of the year, Durant owned 44 percent of the outstanding GM stock.

However, Durant sought an absolute majority. Ever the tactician, he devised a clever scheme. He and the other Chevrolet shareholders met on Christmas Eve in 1915. A tender offer resulted—Chevrolet would exchange five shares of its stock for each tendered share in GM. The offer, which represented a premium on GM's current stock price, would remain open for just a month. To make the offer more attractive, Durant and a syndicate of backers began buying Chevrolet stock in an effort to force its price higher. When the price responded, Durant cut his offer to GM shareholders from five to one to four to one.

For the bankers who controlled GM, the situation was dire. The smaller Chevrolet, which Durant had unsuccessfully offered to sell to GM, now threatened to gobble the larger GM. The bankers, who still had visions of controlling GM, fought Durant's effort, but were unsuccessful. By May 1916, Chevrolet—and indirectly, Durant—owned 54.5 percent of GM.

With control assured, Durant brought in the DuPont Company as a financial partner and shareholder. By the end of 1919, DuPont controlled roughly 28 percent of GM. Assured of a stable shareholder base, Durant launched a second acquisition tear. In 1918, GM acquired Chevrolet, reversing the corporate hierarchy so that GM again sat at the top. The following year, GM purchased 60 percent of the Fisher Body company, a major supplier. Numerous other acquisitions were added to the fold, including what later became the Frigidaire Division.

Then, in 1920, history repeated itself for Durant. Personal reverses in the stock market forced him to sell the large majority of his interest in GM to DuPont, and he was again pushed out of his management position. Though this was not the most ceremonious way for Durant to exit, his acquisition strategy had positioned GM for the future. As Alfred Sloan—who served as CEO of GM for twenty-three years starting in 1923—later wrote, "General Motors had then the makings of a great enterprise."

However, ultimately, Durant was a creative high-wire artist who operated without a net. He simply lacked the discipline to transform the hodgepodge of companies he brought together into a large industrial enterprise. That role fell to Sloan.

Between 1923 and the Great Depression, Sloan made a few additions to the GM enterprise through acquisition. The remaining 40 percent of the Fisher Body Corporation was purchased in 1926 in a stock deal designed to assure supply and harvest economies of scale.

Primarily, though, Sloan spent the years between 1923 and the Great Depression installing a set of financial and operational controls at GM. He created committees and a command-and-control structure. Inventories were closely managed. Cash flow was tracked.

Though now standard, these developments were highly innovative at the time. Sloan essentially created the American management structure that would be replicated by other industrial companies.

GM's management structure and the strength of its fundamental business allowed it to ride out the Great Depression extremely well. Sales dropped off dramatically. Yet the company still earned $248 million between 1929 and 1933. Even more astonishing, GM paid out more than $343 million in dividends over the same period.

The command-and-control structure also had a wider impact. In the words of legendary management guru Peter Drucker, this structure was "a foundation for America's economic leadership in the forty years following World War II."

Frenzy, Then Collapse

During the 1920s, Wall Street achieved new highs, both in financial terms and in social standing. This was the Jazz Age, the time of Gatsby, and the booming stock market. Between the end of 1924 and the end of 1925, the Dow Jones Industrial Average jumped from 120 to 159. The market jumped another 22 percent in 1927. Then, the real boom began—up 48 percent in 1928.

Individual stocks performed even more amazing feats. Radio Corporation of America—at the time a speculative flier—jumped from 85 to 420 in 1928. DuPont almost doubled. Montgomery Ward went from 117 to 440.

However, the upward progression was not smooth, the markets wild. RCA would jump 20 points one day, open up another 20 the next, then crash back 30 by the market close. The volatility was widely attributed to the manipulations of the big-money players. Trying to piggyback on these anonymous market insiders, investors fixated on the tape, the strip of paper churning out current prices. The hope was to spot a big move in the early stages and jump on for the ride.

There was certainly an element of truth to the feeling that insiders had an advantage over Middle America when it came to stock trading. Corporate reporting was relatively unregulated, and accurate data on companies was often hard to come by. Insider trading had not yet been made illegal. As a result, board members, corporate insiders and bankers often had access to information before it became disseminated in the market.

The presumption of inside information was a powerful force, the thirst for inside information strong. The classic example is the market reaction to comments made by J.P. Morgan partner Thomas Cochran. Cochran, on his way to Europe, granted an interview aboard ship. The Dow Jones ticker flashed a quote from Cochran while he was at sea. Cochran reportedly said that General Motors was due for a 100 point increase. J.P. Morgan and its ally DuPont owned large stakes in GM. Traders presumed Cochran knew what he was talking about and bought the stock in bulk. It soared 25 points in two days.

While Cochran's comments appear to have been offhand and innocent enough, touting stocks was not an uncommon practice in the 1920s. Stock pools and syndicates, later outlawed, were commonplace, even fashionable. A group of investors would pool capital and appoint a manager. The manager would buy heavily into a company, trade back and forth, and generally attempt to create the impression of strong market activity. Some pools planted rumors in the press. Public relations men were hired to flog the stock. Then, when investors piled in, driving up the price, the pool would sell out at a large profit. Without the support of the pool, the price often fell back dramatically.

Though now viewed as unethical, in the 1920s pool membership was not restricted to shady market operators. Rather, prominent bankers, partners of J.P. Morgan, the presidents of large banks, corporate heads, all participated.

Of course, in October 1929, the boisterous market came to a screeching halt. The broader market had been depressed for a period of months. On Black Thursday, October 24, pessimism spread to the stocks of companies in the Dow Jones Average. Within a matter of weeks, stocks listed on the New York Exchange lost almost 40 percent of their value. The market would continue to slide downward for years thereafter.

Following the Crash, America's bankers were the object of scornful Senate hearings. Ferdinand Pecora, a fiery assistant district attorney from New York, was deputized by the Senate Banking Committee to lead the charge. Over a period of months, this public servant, on a salary of $12.75 a day, went toe-to-toe with America's most powerful bankers and most able corporate lawyers. He dragged John Pierpont Morgan Jr. (known as Jack), the son of the first J.P. Morgan, before his tribunal and battered the sixty-six-year-old banker with tough questions and sardonic asides. A senator with pro-Morgan leanings decried the spectacle. "We are having a circus," he said, "and the only things lacking now are peanuts and colored lemonade."

The remark spawned one of the humorous oddities of history. A Ringling Brothers press agent, hearing of circuses and lemonade, thought to bring Lya Graf, a thirty-two-year-old midget, to Capitol Hill for the next day's hearings. During an intermission, an enterprising photographer put Ms. Graf together with Jack Morgan, and a classic photo was born. The image of Graf, perched on Morgan's lap like a doll, went out to newspapers around the world. Here was the proof—the Pecora hearings had become an out-and-out circus.

Still, in the end, Pecora caught his prey. Other Morgan partners followed Jack. Each was forced to answer publicly for the speculative excesses of the previous decade. Eventually, it came out that, during the feverish 1920s, the house of Morgan made a practice of selling stock to those on its "preferred list" at a bargain. The list included prominent politicians, bankers, corporate executives and friends of the Morgan partners. The press and public reacted with disbelief. Despite protestations from the Morgan partners, this looked and smelled like influence peddling. As a result of these and other revelations uncovered by the Pecora hearings, banks in general became one of the scapegoats for the 1929 stock market collapse.

Whether the banking industry deserves the brunt of the blame for the Crash is hotly contested. Regardless, banks certainly played some role in fueling the preceding speculative binge. The stock market run-up in the late 1920s sparked considerable demand for new securities. Companies responded by raising funds directly in the capital markets rather than by borrowing from banks. Deprived of this income stream, many of the nation's largest banks set up securities affiliates to participate in the booming brokerage business.

For example, the National City Bank, the largest American bank and the predecessor of Citibank, was a wholehearted purveyor of securities through its National City Company. City had 1,900 fast-talking brokers spread around the country. They concentrated on selling to Middle America, and took on a carnival barker's tone. In addition to stocks, they hawked foreign bonds, mostly from Latin American countries. Only later would it be revealed that many of these bonds were repackaged bank loans that had gone sour.

PROFILE

Charles Mitchell

Charles Mitchell, president of the National City Bank, shattered the image of bankers as gray-haired conservative types. He was a bear of a man, a glad-handing salesman who traveled the country in a specially outfitted luxury railroad car. Mitchell thought of National City as a manufacturer. Stocks and bonds were its product, and they had to be pushed out the door.

Mitchell did all he could to whip his sales force into a frenzy. He organized rallies and contests, awarded points for each share sold and paid prizes to top performers. The National City sales force was built in Mitchell's image, filled with talkative salesmen who could charm average citizens into buying Peruvian bonds or shares in Anaconda Copper. When the Crash came, many of the shares pushed by National City proved worthless—the Peruvian bonds hyped only a few years before became a popular metaphor for foolishly speculative investments.

At his height, Mitchell was both famous and rich. National City paid him over $1 million in bonus for 1928, and again in the first half of 1929. However, like his customers, Mitchell would not emerge from the Crash unscathed.

Mitchell's problems stemmed largely from the planned merger of National City and the Corn Exchange Bank. Under the terms of the deal, Corn Exchange stockholders could take either cash or stock. The exchange ratio was such that, before the Crash, holders would undoubtedly opt for stock, but the Crash reversed the incentives. National City would have to come up with $200 million to complete the deal. Seeking to avoid this unpleasant prospect, Mitchell first tried to support National City's stock by buying shares in the market. He borrowed $12 million from J.P. Morgan for the purchases. His efforts were unsuccessful and the deal fell apart, but in the process Mitchell had mortgaged himself to the hilt.

Mitchell's larger problems came in 1933, when he was arrested on charges of tax evasion. Toward the end of 1929, he had "sold" a block of National City shares to his wife in order to generate a tax loss that would offset his large income. The shares were later "repurchased" from his wife. Mitchell resorted to this wash-sale tactic—which was then fairly common—rather than sell the shares in the market because the shares were tied up as collateral on the J.P. Morgan loan. Though he was ultimately acquitted on the criminal charges, a large civil tax liability was entered against him. Mitchell retired from the National City Bank a broken man.

Though National City was perhaps the most unabashed when it came to selling securities, it was not alone. The Chase National Bank, the nation's second largest bank, opened brokerage offices coast to coast. Together with securities dealers, the banks encouraged average Americans to invest in stocks, oftentimes on margin. At the time, the margin rules allowed customers to purchase a dollar of stock for as little as 10 cents. The remaining 90 cents would be borrowed from the bank.

This leverage, responsible for stellar returns in an up market, left investors extremely vulnerable to a downturn. When the crash came, many investors were ruined. The inability of investors to pay their loans in turn contributed to the hundreds of bank closings during the Depression years.

Part of the problem, as perceived after the fact, was that banks had acted on conflicting incentives. On the one hand, they were charged with safeguarding customer deposits. On the other hand, as the underwriters of securities offerings, they wanted to sell securities. As a result, they were motivated to encourage customers to make sometimes quite risky investments. The banks then made margin loans to these same customers, secured by the stock purchased. With banks borrowing funds from the Federal Reserve at 5 percent, and loaning them out at 10 percent, the whole process was quite lucrative.

Pyramids and the Power of Leverage

The stock market collapse of 1929 naturally brought with it a good deal of recrimination. One chief target of criticism was the prominent use of debt to fuel the recent acquisition boom. From a post–Great Depression vantage point, many companies had clearly over-borrowed in the years before. Like the railroads after the Panic of 1893, these highly leveraged companies were unable to service their debt and collapsed as a result.

Both the significant use of debt and problems of debt service during downturns have been recurring aspects of American economic life. The 1920s spawned a unique capitalization structure known as the pyramid holding company, which allowed a small group of investors to control large companies with relatively little invested capital.

The basic structure involved the creation of a holding company with layered subsidiaries. Stock and debt of the second-, third- and fourth-tier subsidiaries was offered to the public, but always in such a way that the ultimate parent company retained control.

The Van Sweringen Brothers

For a time, the Van Sweringen brothers were two of the most prominent financiers in America. They started in real estate and soon discovered the power of leverage. With time, they discovered its downside.

Otis and Mantis Van Sweringen were born in Wooster, Ohio, in 1879 and 1881. When their father died in 1893, they left school to enter the workforce. By 1900, the brothers decided to branch out on their own in the real estate business. They bought an acre of land with their life savings and resold it at a profit.

Inspired by their early success, Otis and Mantis took more options, sold more land, then borrowed enough capital to purchase 4,000 acres. The brothers also extended the scope of their vision; they planned to utilize a railroad line that would run from their development to the center of Cleveland. They realized this vision in 1916 with the acquisition of the Nickel Plate Railroad for $8.5 million. The deal was financed with borrowed cash and bank notes.

Subsequent to their purchase, the Van Sweringens founded a holding company, Nickel Plate Securities, to hold their railroad, property and debts.

Pleased with the now thriving Nickel Plate line, the Van Sweringens continued buying up properties. Borrowing against the Nickel Plate, the brothers bought the Lake Erie & Western from the New York Central, as well as the Toledo, St. Louis & Western line. The three lines were consolidated in 1923, and the brothers pushed onward. By late 1925, Otis and Mantis' holdings included control of 9,200 miles of railroad and assets of about $1.5 billion.

However, this empire was short-lived. In October 1930, the prices of the Van Sweringens' securities began to fall as a result of the stock market crash. The majority of their holdings were pledged to banks as securities for loans. As a result, the pyramids came tumbling down. The end came in September 1935, when the Van Sweringen holdings went up for sale. The brothers were wiped out.

The pyramid structure was the foundation of many acquisition programs carried out in the 1920s, especially among public utilities. Power company executives like Sidney Mitchell of the Electric Bond and Share Company and Samuel Insull of Middle West Utilities pieced together dozens of small power companies through the use of highly leveraged holding company structures.

Insull's empire, for example, had as many as six layers of sub–holding companies. At the apex of the pyramid was Insull Utility Investments, Inc. The Corporation Securities Company of Chicago occupied the next tier, though it owned part of Insull Utility in a circular relationship. Beneath this were Insull's four operating systems—Middle West Utilities (holding 111 subsidiaries), People's Gas, Light & Coke (eight subsidiaries), Commonwealth Edison Company (six subsidiaries) and the Public Service Company of Northern Illinois.

When the Great Depression hit, the results among the utility holding companies were somewhat mixed but generally negative.

Mitchell's company, one of the stronger utilities, continued to pay dividends on its common stock through the mid-1930s. Insull's companies, on the other hand, collapsed into bankruptcy, with investors losing between $500 million and $2 billion. After a period of flight, Insull was eventually tried and acquitted on charges of mail fraud.

Depression, War, the 1950s

From the perspective of business and industry, the 1930s were a lost decade. The stock market crash of 1929 ushered in a long, three-year economic slide. While the economy bottomed out in 1933, it didn't really bounce back until 1939 and the onset of World War II in Europe. Merger activity was scant during the Depression, but picked up slightly in the war years.

The late 1940s and 1950s were largely a period of organic industrial growth. This growth, like the broad expansion following the Civil War, set the stage for yet another major merger wave, during the "Go-Go Years" of the 1960s.

The Rise and Fall of the Conglomerate

3

"A man lives not only his personal life, as an individual, but also, consciously or unconsciously, the life of his epoch and his contemporaries."

Thomas Mann, *The Magic Mountain*

The 1960s witnessed the full emergence of the American postwar industrial economy. These were the Go-Go Years of the stock market, with the increased power of professional institutional money managers and their emphasis on the leading, "Nifty Fifty" stocks.

The decade began with the optimism of Kennedy's Camelot and the extolling of professional management. The "Whiz Kids" and numbers men were in style in Washington and on Wall Street, and Robert McNamara and Harold Geneen were revered as the best and the brightest.

By the end of the decade, the nation was deeply divided, and disillusionment eroded the government's monopoly on truth. The Vietnam War was a fiasco, and the numbers boys were discredited.

The Third Merger Wave

The 1960s spawned a third merger wave. By the end of 1968, the 200 largest industrial corporations controlled more than 60 percent of the total assets held by all manufacturing firms—a share equal to that held by the 1,000 largest firms in 1941. In 1968 alone, twenty-six of the nation's 500 largest corporations were swallowed in mergers or acquisitions, sometimes with much smaller acquirers. However, since many of the surviving firms were widely diversified, market concentration did not materially increase.

Much of the deal activity of the mid-1960s now looks strange: the pairing of RCA, a defense, technology and broadcasting company, with Banquet frozen foods; Jimmy Ling's golfball, goofball and meatball combination of sporting goods, pharmaceuticals and meat packing; Textron's crazy quilt of companies making zippers, chain saws, fountain pens, rocket engines and helicopters. In fact, a lot of the activity of the 1980s and 1990s involved undoing the deals of the 1960s. The lessons to be learned are important and as universal as the South Sea Bubble of the eighteenth century.

Diversification, not concentration, was the goal; targets operated in unrelated industries. Four factors drove this trend. First, federal regulators heightened antitrust scrutiny of horizontal and vertical mergers. As a result of these restrictions, executives who wished to grow by acquisition needed to diversify for acquisition candidates.

Second, the intellectual fabric of the early 1960s deified management science and business schools. The "best and the brightest" could manage anything. Management skills were assumed to be easily transferable between companies in unrelated industries. The conglomerates of the 1960s were partially justified by this theory. Consequently, as the conglomerates spread into seemingly incongruous industries, investment analysts and other stock watchers began to hear from executives about "critical mass" and "free-form management." Jargon aside, the basic theory was that each unit of a larger enterprise could draw as necessary on a central management pool, generating operating efficiencies.

Third, in the heated stock market of the 1960s, there was a need for growth in earnings per share and a higher stock price. The institutional market was raw and naive. Numbers seemed so scientific; common sense and strategy were out of fashion.

Fourth, the men running these companies had both a financing and a personal imperative toward the manifest destiny of corporate growth. The 1960s were the decade of large diversified conglomerates like ITT, Litton Industries, Teledyne and Textron. The heads of these companies—Harold Geneen, Royal Little, Henry Singleton and Charles "Tex" Thornton—and their peers molded their own legacy.

Ling: The King and His Realm

Of all the conglomerators, Jimmy Ling's career is among the most colorful. A high school dropout and Navy veteran, Ling's management career began in 1947 with the creation of an electrical contracting business in Dallas. Ling raised an initial $2,000 and founded the Ling Electric Company.

The early days were anything but glamorous. Ling hustled for wiring jobs in homes and small office buildings. However, frenetic energy, salesmanship and a chugging Dallas economy combined to make Ling a success. After a period of steady earnings growth, Ling embarked on the acquisition campaign that would make him famous.

Again, the first steps were relatively small—Ling Electric bought a series of small electronic and defense contractors—but the combination of deals bulked Ling up significantly. Then, in 1958, Ling found an investment bank willing to underwrite an offering of convertible bonds. With this burst of fresh capital, Ling began to hunt for bigger companies. Results came quickly. A stock-for-stock merger of Temco Electronics into Ling Electric, followed by a stock-for-convertible-debt hostile takeover of Chance-Voight Aircraft, transformed Ling Electric into Ling-Temco-Voight, which became LTV. The combined entity earned 158th place on the Fortune 500.

For several years after the Chance-Voight acquisition, Ling bus-
ied himself shifting LTV's capital structure. First, he reduced the
company's debt load by swapping equity for debt at opportune times.
Then in 1965, in a restructuring dubbed Project Redeployment, Ling
created something like the pyramid holding structures of the 1920s.
He first separated LTV's operations into three affiliated subsidiaries.
A portion of the stock in each subsidiary was then swapped with
LTV shareholders for their LTV stock and some cash. In this fashion, Ling created a public market for the subsidiaries' stock, boosting their value, which consequently increased the value of LTV
stock.

Thus repositioned and recapitalized, Ling reenergized his acquisition campaign with the hostile takeover of Wilson & Company.
This acquisition was structured as a two-tier offer of just over $81
million in cash for 53 percent of the company and $115 million face
value of preferred stock for the remainder. The transaction underlined Ling's willingness to range far afield. Wilson's operations were
divided into three primary areas—meat packing, sporting goods and
pharmaceuticals.

The Wilson acquisition was well received in the market. En-
thused with the momentum, Ling next acquired GreatAmerica, a diversified company that owned an insurance operation, Braniff
Airlines, a bank, the National Car Rental Company and real estate.
Finally, Ling acquired a majority stake in the Jones & Laughlin Steel
Company for $425 million in cash. At the time, this was the largest
cash tender offer ever. In 1969, LTV placed fourteenth on the Fortune 500 list.

But Ling's last acquisition would bring his downfall. The Justice
Department challenged the deal on antitrust grounds. As a result,
Ling was unable to recapitalize and restructure the company. In the
general downturn that affected all conglomerates, LTV's stock price
eventually fell from $170 to $16. LTV shareholders lost a lot of
money, and Ling lost his job.

James Joseph Ling

The bulk of Jimmy Ling's personal history is tied up in the history of LTV. In the company's heyday, Ling received glowing press. Business publications referred to him as "Jimmy Ling, the Merger King." He spun one complicated restructuring plan after another, and his prowess as a financier became legendary.

A self-starter, Ling got his introduction to high finance hawking shares in his company at the 1955 Texas state fair. In short order, he became a master of the "Chinese paper" financings of the 1960s. LTV was built on a foundation of complicated deals—paper swaps, triangular mergers, debt restructurings and so on. Each deal brought some new variation of complex securities.

Ultimately, Ling became the magician of the deal business. Attention to the fundamentals was only of secondary concern. He seemed consumed by an insatiable desire to fashion a larger and larger enterprise.

As LTV's financial health worsened, so too did Ling's. He had over the years pledged most of his assets, including his stock in LTV, as security for personal loans. Nervous bankers tightened the screws when LTV's stock price tanked in the early 1970s. Ling's personal finances were thrown into a shambles.

Eventually, Ling made several comeback attempts. The first—Omega-Alpha—was a small-fry conglomerate which Ling hoped to convert into a major company. The second—Xenerex—was an oil services company. Ling's convoluted financial structures, which captivated the market in the 1960s, did not play well in the 1970s and 1980s. Both efforts failed. His companies collapsed into bankruptcy, and Ling receded into retirement.

ITT Diversifies

Another continuing tale of the 1960s was ITT. International Telephone & Telegraph was created in 1920 through a combination of telegraph, telephone and communications equipment manufacturers. The company, with operations around the world, was largely international in focus until 1959, when Harold Geneen became president.

Geneen left the presidency of Raytheon to join ITT. His résumé included time at several other old-line industrial companies, including Jones & Laughlin Steel and American Can. In the process of hopscotching his way up the corporate ladder, he had developed a reputation for strong and disciplined management—Raytheon's stock, trading at 64, dropped 6¼ points the day his departure was announced. Yet, in retrospect, Geneen's previous experiences only prefaced the dramatic transformation he would work at ITT.

The forty-nine-year-old Geneen brought an established management style to ITT, but, more importantly, he came with a preexisting strategic vision. At each of his previous jobs, he had unsuccessfully pushed diversification as a corporate goal. Geneen favored growth through acquisition for a number of reasons, but saw it primarily as a matter of prudence. Building a new business from scratch was inordinately risky when compared to taking over an established business. Buy, then build was his philosophy. Now ITT would be the laboratory for this vision.

If Geneen had any doubts about the virtues of his plans, they were soon eliminated. In 1960, ITT's operations in Cuba were privatized by the new Castro regime. This experience highlighted the international phone company's vulnerability. Shortly thereafter, Geneen began his drive to reshape ITT. He sought a greater mix of income from the United States and diversification across industries.

After nine years of voracious merger activity, with more than 100 deals consummated, Geneen had achieved his goal. Included in the

ITT fold were operations like Sheraton Corporation, Avis Rent-a-Car, Bobbs-Merrill publishers, and Levitt & Sons. ITT then made a failed bid to take over the American Broadcasting Company. Despite this and a few other setbacks, Harold Geneen compiled an impressive record during his first decade in office. In the span of years between 1959 and 1970, ITT grew from a company with $766 million in sales to a company with $6.4 billion in sales and became one of the twenty largest industrial companies in America.

PROFILE

Harold Geneen

Unlike many other conglomerators, Harold Geneen was known as much for the way he ran companies as for the pace of his acquisition program. Tales of Geneen hustling to his plane, staff in tow, with multiple briefcases full of financial statements and memoranda for his review, defined his popular image. He was legendary for his fourteen-hour days, incredible memory and inquisitorial management style.

Geneen believed that information was the key to good management. "Facts" was his favorite word. After one 1965 meeting, he wrote a memo blasting those present for playing fast and loose with the term. In Geneen's mind, facts were incontrovertible, an expression of "final and reliable reality." "Apparent facts" or "reported facts" were not facts at all. However, once "true" facts were uncovered, management decisions became easy.

Geneen designed the entire ITT management structure around his passion for uncovering facts. Monthly General Management Meetings (GMMs) were at the heart of the process. In advance of the meetings, managers would prepare monthly reports. These were the documents that filled the numerous suitcases shepherded around by Geneen's personal staff. He would review several reports each evening, on weekends, even on vacations.

However, this was all just preparation for the GMMs. The meetings took place in a specially designed, Orwellian conference room atop the ITT Americas Building in New York City. The giant windowless room had an oval table that could seat ninety-two, with sophisticated microphones and screens to project slides of the data being discussed. Geneen would sit at the midpoint of the table. Company executives would fill the other ninety-one chairs, with their own staff in even more chairs behind them.

Ostensibly, the GMM provided a forum for management interaction and centralization. A manager in one division might raise a problem that a manager from a different division had dealt with in the past. Really, though, the managers who presented their monthly reports at the meetings had an audience of one—Harold Geneen.

The questions—sometimes picayune, but always discerning—would start shortly after a manager launched into a presentation. Woe to the manager who was not on top of his or her data. Geneen would ask four, five, ten or more follow-up questions on the same point. For example, as described by Robert J. Schoenberg in *Geneen:*

> If you presented Geneen with what might seem an elementally simple fact—say, the value of physical assets in your unit—his first question might be, How do you know? If you told him, Our controller told me, his next questions would be, How does he know? Did you ask? Or have you uncritically accepted his statement and passed it along as fact without bothering to determine whether it is a fact, an opinion, or a guess? (p. 193)

Some participants found Geneen's confrontational style demeaning. Others found his attention to small details a waste of time, especially with more than 100 people often in attendance at

> the GMMs. Yet for Geneen, his questions, and the lessons they
> taught, were a critical part of knitting together the diverse units
> under the ITT umbrella. He wanted all his managers to be tough
> detectives capable of uncovering problems before they mush-
> roomed.

In the early years, the Geneen system seemed to work almost in-
fallibly. ITT sailed along. Then, in 1969, problems began to surface.
Geneen agreed to acquire the Grinnell Corporation, the leading
maker of fire protection sprinkler systems, and the Hartford Fire Insurance Company. Richard McLaren, the government's antitrust
chief, opposed both acquisitions. The attack had little grounding in
existing antitrust law—McLaren seemed more concerned with ITT's
burgeoning size than any actual anticompetitive effects. Both a federal district court and an appeals court ruled in ITT's favor.

Still, on the eve of the government's Supreme Court appeal, Geneen settled the case. He agreed to divest Avis, Levitt and certain
other businesses in exchange for the right to retain Hartford. For a
time, Geneen put the turmoil surrounding Hartford behind him.
But, in 1972, Washington political correspondent Jack Anderson uncovered a memo from Dita Beard, a lobbyist for ITT. The memo
linked the Nixon administration's willingness to settle the antitrust
case against ITT and a $400,000 contribution from ITT to the city of
San Diego to support its bid to host the 1972 Republican convention.
Anderson alleged a political bribe.

Though ITT had violated no laws, the company's image suffered
as a result of the Dita Beard affair. But that fallout paled in comparison to the problems for ITT—and Geneen—when Anderson made
his next revelation. About a month after he published the Beard
memo, Anderson ran a series on a link between ITT and the CIA,
again supported with memos from ITT lobbyists. ITT, the CIA and
other American business interests had apparently been working to-

gether in an effort to forestall socialist Salvador Allende Gossens' election to the Chilean presidency.

Several high-ranking ITT executives were indicted for perjury as a result of the Chilean affair. Charges ultimately were dropped on "national security" grounds. Geneen escaped prosecution entirely. Critics alleged a cover-up. Even without being directly implicated, Geneen's reputation was severely damaged. As a company, ITT became associated in the public mind with questionable practices.

The damage was only exacerbated when the IRS challenged the tax-free status of the Hartford merger. ITT successfully appealed the case, but for a time former Hartford shareholders faced a potential $100 million tax liability.

While Geneen and ITT weathered the political problems of the early 1970s, the company's acquisition program cooled. The next decade would be spent repairing the damage.

The Earnings-per-Share Game

Although it may seem hard to fathom from the perspective of the 1990s, conglomerates such as LTV and ITT were actually thought of as high-growth companies during the third merger wave. At the time, many investors placed great emphasis on a company's earnings per share and price/earnings ratio. At their peak, the P/E ratios of hot conglomerates like Litton Industries and Teledyne soared to over 40, well in excess of the market average. Of course, to keep these high P/E ratios, the companies had to keep growing—and growing. When Litton in 1968 announced its first earnings decline in fourteen years, conglomerate share prices collapsed. The game was over.

The conglomerates often maintained earnings growth by acquiring firms which had lower price/earnings multiples, paying a premium in the process. These deals typically were funded with common stock. Under the right circumstances, this strategy provided an easy mechanism both to create instant growth in earnings per share and to boost an acquirer's stock market price.

As an example, take a diversified growth firm selling at 20 times earnings. If it were to acquire a firm equal in earnings which was selling in the market at 8 times earnings, it might have to pay a premium, perhaps 10 times earnings. Earnings would have mathematically doubled for the firm as a whole, assuming that no write-down of the purchase price is required by accounting principles under the particular circumstances. But the total number of shares outstanding would not have doubled because of the difference in price/earnings ratios. For example, if the acquiring firm had 1 million shares outstanding, it would only have to issue an additional half a million shares to make the deal. As a result, the earnings per share would dramatically rise because of the acquisition: an increase of 33 percent, as the following table illustrates.

GROWTH IN EPS BY ACQUISITION

	Acquirer	Target	Merged Firms
P/E	20X	8–10X	20X
Earnings	$1 million	$1 million	$2 million
Shares outstanding	1 million	1 million	1.5 million
EPS	$1	$1	$1.33
Market valuation per share	$20	$10	$26.67

This effect could become even more pronounced if securities other than common stock were offered. For example, companies such as LTV specialized in devising hybrid securities to be issued in connection with mergers. Debt convertible into common stock was a frequent choice. For an acquiring company, convertible debt was advantageous because the tax laws permitted a company to deduct the interest on convertible debt issued in an acquisition, while dividends on stock were not deductible. This rule was later changed in reaction to the perceived abuse of convertible debt.

In addition, stodgy, old-line companies often are replete with opportunities for discovering buried earnings. For example, depreciation or capitalization policies might be very conservative and can be altered to produce more beneficial results. A revaluation of optional accounting policies to a new system which yields higher earnings is very attractive. The possibility that some assets might be understated was an additional inducement.

Therefore, a company could maintain high growth in the short run by acquiring low-growth firms. Deals could bring favorable earnings-per-share growth results, even though the separate firms may not, in fact, have been growing. As a result, the acquiring firm at first impression seems even more deserving of a high multiple, which allows it to make future acquisitions to perpetuate its growth record.

This earnings game had obvious weaknesses. First, in order for the game to work, it had to go on in perpetuity. When the string of earnings increases stumbled, the price/earnings multiples crashed. Acquisitions became difficult and expensive, and the mass of all the so-called Chinese paper, the innovative hybrid securities issued to target-company stockholders, began to impose a heavy burden because of their dividend or yield features.

Second, a key presupposition was that the stock market would treat the growth in EPS from acquisitions as being the same as if it were from internal growth. If a company merited a high P/E because of internal growth, the acquisition of more slowly growing companies would only dilute its long-term momentum. Gradually, the P/Es of the conglomerates began to shift downward.

Third, the use of the leverage of hybrid securities became less efficacious. Again, analysts began pinpointing the effect undue leverage was having on earnings and began discounting the results. Meanwhile, the government began to limit the tax deductibility of interest on certain debentures issued in merger transactions, and, as will be discussed, accounting authorities began to reform the treatment of acquisitions to reflect costs more realistically.

Fourth, in the mad rush to make deals, some were necessarily rotten. Companies began to sag under the weight of interest costs and low internal growth from ill-thought-out acquisitions.

This focus on earnings growth, which set the stage for the conglomerate boom, was driven in part by the return of institutional investors as a key governing force. Professional money managers had not played a major role in the market since the highly popular and eventually disastrous investment trusts of the 1920s. However, between 1949 and 1960, the amount of money managed by institutional investors went from $9.5 billion of NYSE-listed investments to about $70 billion. The 1960 total constituted roughly 20 percent of all NYSE-listed securities.

The money management business was highly competitive in the 1960s. As is now the case, performance was the key. Fortunately for money managers, the 1960s were a time of almost uninterrupted growth in stock prices. Significant returns were not difficult to achieve in this environment, and the reputation of money managers in general soared. They were christened the "gunslingers" in a popular book titled *The Money Game*, written under the pseudonym "Adam Smith." The gunslingers earned their reputation by jumping quickly on hot stocks. They followed the market closely, traded regularly and were generally considered to have a significant edge over individual investors.

Many money managers lived and died on their quarterly performance and needed short-term gains to maintain momentum. Consequently, they became frequent supporters of corporate takeovers and were quick to accept hostile cash offers that included a premium to the previous market price. Investment bankers therefore often focused on a company's ownership structure as a key in advising on takeover strategy. Of course, these were early days in the development of the institutional market, and the judgment can look crude in hindsight. But all bull markets seem overwrought with the 20/20 perspective of history.

RCA: A Case of Mission Creep

The hot-blooded markets of the 1960s caused even the most established American companies to rethink corporate strategy. Some resisted diversification, others did not. RCA—the Radio Corporation of America—was one company that fully embraced the concept.

RCA had been founded in 1919 at the encouragement of Franklin Roosevelt. At the time assistant secretary of the Navy, Roosevelt asked General Electric to help set up RCA. Roosevelt wanted an American firm in the radio business for national security reasons. In 1922, RCA began selling its first crystal radio sets. Four years later, RCA, GE and Westinghouse established the National Broadcasting Company. RCA also pioneered in the record industry and was the first company to commercialize television sets.

Reversing course in the 1930s, government authorities forced GE to end its partial ownership of RCA. Free of GE, RCA developed into a major competitor with operations in electronics, communications and aerospace technology. However, RCA lost its way in the 1960s and 1970s, purchasing Hertz Car Rental, Gibson Greeting Cards and CIT Financial. Other new businesses included frozen food and carpeting.

The acquisition program added debt to the balance sheet and increased RCA's annual interest burden. By the early 1980s, the company had almost $3 billion in debt and dramatically rising interest costs. CIT and Hertz were largely the culprits—both were capital-intensive businesses, odd partners for an already cash-hungry electronics and technology firm.

While these new businesses consumed capital, RCA largely ignored its core markets. The lack of capital spending arguably gave Japanese competitors the opening to develop lucrative markets. The core consumer electronics business was left to shrivel on the vine. RCA had once been an industry leader, with an edge in radios, tape recorders, record players and TV sets. By the early 1980s, RCA made little other than TV sets and was losing out in that market. The company's famed Princeton, New Jersey, research center had focused for too long on a failed attempt to get into computers, leaving RCA with dated TV technology. Meanwhile, the company's main new product—the videodisc—flopped badly.

NBC also struggled for want of attention. The network's ratings fell off badly, and NBC became an also-ran in the three-way ratings wars.

Nor did the newcomers to the corporate fold make up for failings in the old core businesses. CIT proved a disaster. RCA had wildly overpaid—ponying up an 80 percent premium to snare the lackluster unit. RCA's management compounded the problem by agreeing to leave enough cash in the CIT business to maintain a favorable credit rating.

Hertz had its own problems. The company made an aggressive effort to move into commercial truck rental. The program floundered, and RCA was forced to write off the investment. At the same time, sudden oil price increases forced Hertz to shift its fleet over to compact and subcompact cars. Management was stuck with an overstock of costly gas guzzlers.

Some of RCA's problems can be attributed to financial fluctuations, chiefly steep jumps in interest rates and the price of oil. However, RCA's diversification program, compounded by management turmoil, certainly contributed to its problems.

The Collapse of Penn Central

Though diversification was the central theme of the 1960s merger boom, some horizontal mergers would also turn sour. The Penn Central merger is perhaps the most famous example of a poorly executed deal.

The 1968 combination of the New York Central and Pennsylvania railroads essentially was an effort to remake two unprofitable operations into a successful unit. The great trunk lines of the Middle Atlantic had, by the late 1950s, become moribund and weak. With the increasing orientation toward the automobile and the airplane, passenger traffic declined precipitously. Meanwhile, both the Pennsylvania and the New York Central competed for business. Each company had lines linking New York City with the Midwest.

As far back as the late 1950s, management of the Pennsylvania and the New York Central had explored a merger as the potential answer to mounting competitive difficulties. The respective managements agreed to terms in 1961. After years of delay, the merger was finally completed in 1968. In the interim, the Pennsylvania had made a number of diversifying acquisitions, primarily in real estate development. Still, the resulting entity—dubbed the Penn Central—first and foremost was a railroad, with lines stretching from New York City west to Chicago and combined revenues in 1967 of nearly $2 billion.

Just two years later, Penn Central was insolvent with a loss of $500 million, one of the largest bankruptcies in American history. Among other factors, the failure was attributed to mismatched management styles, excess debt and ill-advised diversification. However, the fundamental factor in the decline appears to have been the failure to plan for the operational integration of the two roads—plain bad management.

Hints of trouble at Penn Central began leaking out in the spring of 1968 and into 1969. The stock price fell from the post-merger high of 86 to under 30. Meanwhile, David Bevan, the company's chief financial officer, and other executives were struggling to finance the company. The railroad operations were burning through cash. Assets were sold off and cash squeezed out of subsidiaries. Interest rates were high in light of the Nixon administration's efforts to control inflation. But the Penn Central could not afford to wait out the market.

Bevan raised as much capital as he could from banks, but they were wary. In March 1968, Bevan turned to investment bank Goldman, Sachs & Co. He had a personal relationship with Gustave Levy, the firm's managing partner. Over the next several months, Goldman raised $200 million for the Penn Central in the short-term commercial paper market. This was a risky source of funding for the railroad's long-term capital needs. The paper, with a maximum nine-month term, would have to be rolled over on a regular basis. If the railroad was unable to do so, it would face a huge, immediate cash liability. However, Bevan could not afford to be conservative. He did the best he could, backstopping half of the commercial paper with standby bank loans.

These precautions proved inadequate. The Penn Central turned in an awful performance for the first quarter of 1970. Institutional investors dumped its commercial paper, which the railroad was forced to repurchase. Bevan attempted to secure additional bank loans, even help from the government. Neither was forthcoming. On June 21, 1970, the railroad collapsed into bankruptcy.

Clearly the Penn Central had problems. Still, the Pennsylvania and New York Central lines were strong strategic assets, and would be reorganized with government help as part of Conrail, the successor to Penn Central and the centerpiece of a 1996 takeover battle.

The Air Goes Out of the Conglomerates

Of course, like all fads, the conglomerate era was destined to end. Starting in 1968, the conglomerates were battered with a string of bad news. Litton Industries announced an earnings decrease for the first time in fourteen years. Trust-buster McLaren was busily making war on the conglomerates, both in the press and in the courts. Ling was hamstrung over the Jones & Laughlin purchase, and Geneen struggled with the Hartford deal.

In part reflecting this bad news, a major bear market swept the Street in 1968, taking the Dow from 1,000 down to 631 in May 1971. With their stock prices deflated, the conglomerates could no longer play the P/E game that had fueled all those earnings increases.

Then, Penn Central collapsed, striking the final nail into the coffin. The conglomerate movement was dead.

The flaws in the conglomerate financial model had been exposed. The model didn't account for the possibility of financial fluctuations in the marketplace. Ling, Geneen, Tex Thornton and their compatriots needed a strong and increasing stock market to keep their companies' inflated stock prices aloft. Without valuable stock as a currency, the acquisition spree came to a crashing halt. Without acquisitions, the conglomerates went from high-fliers to humdrum plodders.

Indeed, most diversified companies suffered through the next decade along with the nation. Watergate, war in the Middle East and two major Oil Shocks diverted attention from the economy. The conglomerates struggled with anemic earnings and share prices and were ultimately dismantled.

The Early Evolution of Hostile Takeovers

During the 1970s, the deal business was in something of a recession, recovering from the collapse of the conglomerate merger wave. Yet, here and there, inklings of the future were apparent. For example, it was during this era that the hostile takeover in its modern form first moved from the corporate fringes to become an establishment practice.

The hostile takeover was part of the 1960s corporate landscape. Though not successfully used against major American companies, medium-sized companies like Wilson were the subject of hostile bids. These bids were blitzkrieg affairs, largely unrestrained. Federal securities laws only stipulated that an offer be left open for at least seven days. A potential acquirer could make an exploding cash tender for enough shares to control its target. The target would have little time to respond to such a "Saturday Night Special" offer, and shareholders were put under intense pressure to decide quickly.

By the late 1960s, blue-chip corporate America was given an

inkling of the hostile battles to come. At the close of the decade, in 1969, three major companies were targeted—Olympian Pan American World Airways by upstart Resorts International, Chemical Bank by Leasco Data Processing, and B.F. Goodrich by Northwest Industries.

Each attempt failed, but corporate executives got an early taste of the no-holds-barred tactics necessary to fight off an unwanted suitor. B.F. Goodrich, for example, fired out negative ads against Northwest and successfully lobbied the state and federal governments to block the deal on antitrust grounds. In addition, Goodrich completed two defensive mergers and altered its accounting method to pump up reported earnings. In the end, the company remained independent.

Five years later, in 1974, the tide turned. The raider was the International Nickel Company of Canada, a large, established corporation with a long history. On July 18, 1974, representatives of Inco met with Frederick Port, the president of ESB. In the meeting, Inco offered to buy ESB. More importantly, Inco made clear that it would go ahead with a public tender offer whether or not ESB agreed to the proposition.

Inco's offer for ESB stemmed from its desire to diversify away from its exposure to fluctuations in nickel prices. In the early 1970s, it began looking for a different business to enter, one that was less cyclical and more likely to experience growth. After the Oil Shock of 1973, Inco management settled on energy as an attractive sector. Eventually, a management committee selected the subcategory of "packaged energy" as strategically attractive. A failed attempt was made to acquire a British car battery maker. ESB, formerly the Electric Storage Battery Company, the world's largest battery maker and Philadelphia's eleventh largest company, seemed a good second choice.

When Port turned down Inco's offer, Inco was encouraged to proceed with a hostile bid by its banker, Morgan Stanley, which saw an opportunity to carve out a leadership position in aggressive offers.

The day of the meeting between the parties, ESB's stock closed at $19.50 a share. After the close, Inco announced a $28 per share cash tender offer, and the fight for control began.

With the large differential between ESB's stock price and Inco's offer, ESB soon concluded that public relations and other defensive measures would not be sufficient to keep ESB independent. Very quickly, the company began to look for a more friendly acquirer—what came to be known as a "white knight"—to take Inco's place. United Aircraft—later renamed United Technologies—was approached and by Sunday, July 21, had agreed to terms. Sometime after 6:00 P.M. the following day, United announced a $34 per share counteroffer for ESB shares. ESB management endorsed the offer as fair. Thinking he had fended off Inco, Port was jubilant.

His happiness was short-lived. Two days later, Inco upped its offer to $36 a share. Thereafter, United matched Inco's bid twice. Each time, Inco topped United, first by $2 a share, then by $3 a share. When the price reached $41 per share, United dropped out. A few weeks later, the tender offer closed. Inco received 90 percent of the shares. So, in the space of less than a month, Inco had fought and won the first takeover contest initiated by a major strategic buyer. The purchase price came to roughly $227 million.

With hindsight, the ESB acquisition turned out to be a bellyflop for Inco and vastly overpriced. Inco suffered through a replay of Jimmy Ling's Pyrrhic Jones & Laughlin acquisition. Antitrust authorities attacked the ESB deal as anticompetitive because Inco dominated the nickel market, then a raw material for batteries. The process dragged out for over three years. In the interim, Inco exercised little direct control over ESB. The same CEO who had tried to fight off Inco was left in place.

More fundamentally, Inco simply seemed ill-matched to managing a consumer goods business. The miniaturization revolution that would bring portable calculators and Sony Walkmans to America swelled battery usage. However, Inco was conditioned to thinking in terms of selling raw materials in a commodity market. Duracell and others thrashed ESB's Ray-O-Vac line at the checkout counter.

ESB also made two technology bets which later proved losers. First, the company was slow to develop its alkaline battery alternative. Duracell was not so shy, and its copper-topped batteries became the prototype. Similarly, in the market for automotive batteries, ESB stuck with its low-maintenance battery rather than getting on the no-maintenance bandwagon. Competitors again came to market with better alternatives, and consumers shifted away from ESB's products.

The failure to capitalize on growing segments of the battery market was not entirely an oversight. People inside ESB saw the way the market was moving and wanted to invest in new technologies. Unfortunately, in the mid-1970s, Inco suffered through a major down market for nickel. The company's earnings plummeted and ESB became something of a poor stepchild when it came to getting cash for investment.

Nine years later, Inco gave up. ESB had been thoroughly trounced by Duracell and Eveready in the race to develop the long-life dry-cell batteries used today. Sears, Delco and others owned the automotive battery category. Having already poured another $300 million into the ESB business, Inco saw little room for a turnaround and decided to divest ESB. The parts were sold off piecemeal. Inco lost more than $200 million on the failed diversification attempt.

The Deal Decade: 4
Early Years

"For now I stand as one upon a rock, / environed with a wilderness of sea, / who marks the waxing tide grow wave by wave, / expecting ever when some envious surge / will in his brinish bowels swallow him."

William Shakespeare, *Titus Andronicus*

The cauldron of American economic activity in the 1980s resulted in the cresting of America's fourth merger wave. Death throes of mature industries, the spawning of new engines of economic growth, and innovation in financial markets all swirled to create the surge. It was an awkward and raw time because the mechanisms of economic change were imperfect and subject to abuse. The bubble burst, the wave collapsed and the critics smirked. They missed the point. America had fundamentally revamped its corporate economy and was poised for an unprecedented boom.

The decade began as a period of retrenchment for many of America's large companies. Between 1979 and 1988, the Fortune 500 shed more than 3 million jobs. While some of these cuts were associated with a merger, buyout or other transaction, the majority were not. The job loss at big companies reflected a trend that had begun in the 1960s and 1970s. American industry faced increasing foreign competition where none had existed before. At the same time, several key industries were weighed down by relatively mature markets, such as steel and automobiles.

Balanced against the trend among the very large companies was a phenomenal growth among small and midsized companies and the emergence of new growth industries. Even accounting for the layoffs and restructurings among major corporations, America gained millions of jobs in the 1980s. Entire new industries were born, creating new opportunities. Cable television, wireless communications, consumer electronics, computers and overnight courier services, to name just a few examples, all grew into major industries.

This juxtaposition of growth in new industries and the maturation of others created powerful incentives for mergers and acquisitions—entire industries were in need of restructuring and building. During this period—from 1981 to 1989—over 22,000 deals were announced.

TEN LARGEST U.S. DEALS OF THE 1980s

Rank	Buyer	Seller	Approximate Equity Value (Millions)	Year Announced
1.	Kohlberg Kravis Roberts & Co.	RJR Nabisco Inc.	$24,561.6	1988
2.	Beecham Group PLC (U.K.)	SmithKline Beecham Corp.	$16,082.4	1989
3.	Chevron Corp.	Gulf Corp.	$13,205.5	1984
4.	Philip Morris Companies, Inc.	Kraft Inc.	$13,099.8	1988
5.	Bristol-Myers Co.	Squibb Corp.	$12,001.8	1989
6.	Time Inc.	Warner Communications Inc.	$11,650.3	1989
7.	Texaco Inc.	Getty Oil Corp.	$10,128.9	1984
8.	DuPont Co.	Conoco Inc.	$8,039.8	1981
9.	British Petroleum Co. (U.K.)	Standard Oil Co. (remaining 45%)	$7,762.2	1987
10.	U.S. Steel Corp.	Marathon Oil Corp.	$6,618.5	1981

Source: *MergerStat*

The 1980s represented three distinct trends: first, strategic purchases by corporate buyers, second, going-private transactions funded by financial buyers, and third, the move by foreign multinationals into the U.S. merger market.

Strategic deals predominated during roughly the first half of the 1980s and became less important toward the end of the decade. These were mergers or acquisitions involving major corporate acquirers. The goal was to satisfy a strategic imperative, such as the desire to build critical mass or diversify into a new industry. Both horizontal and diversifying mergers became more common. Part Two of this book is about the strategy and deal implementation of these strategic mergers in the 1980s and 1990s.

Financial buyers—entities and individuals in the business of buying and selling companies—also emerged as major factors in the early part of the 1980s. Kohlberg Kravis Roberts & Co. (KKR), one of the early financial buyers, became particularly visible starting in 1984, when it took part in three of that year's top thirty announced transactions. In the late 1980s, though, the financial buyers rose to even greater prominence. KKR, for example, became a household name in 1988 with its $24 billion purchase of RJR Nabisco. More broadly, three of the top ten deals in that year involved financial buyers.

International acquisitions were another significant part of the late 1980s merger dynamic. Foreign multinationals had a spotty U.S. presence in the early part of the decade. Reflecting the pace of the larger merger market, many early cases involved targets in the oil business. However, foreign acquirers had not really found their footing and many attempted acquisitions failed to go through. For example, Seagram of Canada bid for Conoco in 1981, only to have its target snatched away by DuPont. Similarly, Rupert Murdoch's Australia-based News Corporation made a run at Warner Communications but was rebuffed.

By the second half of the decade, though, foreign acquirers were

a force in the market. Their presence was wide-ranging, from pharmaceuticals to consumer goods, from retailing to insurance, from
publishing to movie studios.

Backlash

Hostile takeovers were another visible sign of the 1980s merger
boom. These struggles still were relatively few in number. Even the
peak year of 1988 saw only forty-six contested tender offers. Yet these
contested deals often involved very large companies such as Time,
Inc., Sterling Drug and RJR Nabisco and, as a result, received a good
deal of press and captured the public imagination. Terms like "corporate raider," "greenmail," "white knight" and "arbitrageur" or "arb"
entered the common lexicon.

As the profile of hostile deals increased, so too did the political
heat directed toward the individuals involved. The Business Roundtable, a lobbying group for the Fortune 500's corporate management,
along with labor unions decried what they saw as the negative impact of hostile deals.

The campaign against takeovers had a pronounced effect. During
the 1980s, Congress considered hundreds of bills aimed at curbing
the merger market. While no general antitakeover laws were enacted
on the federal level, various changes in the tax code were used to reduce the incentive to merge. The Securities and Exchange Commission meanwhile appointed an Advisory Committee on Tender
Offers on which I served, along with Bob Rubin, Marty Lipton and
Joe Flom, among others. The committee's report, released in 1983,
adopted a hodgepodge practical approach that failed to please either
side in the debate but was meant to achieve a fairer process. Fifty
different specific recommendations were made, but few were
passed.

While the federal government did not enact specific legislation
on takeovers, antitakeover laws were passed at the state level.
Delaware passed such a law in 1988. Not coincidentally, the law was

made retroactive to December 1987, when corporate raider Carl Icahn began buying stock in Texaco Inc. and commenced a hostile takeover attempt. The law generally bars an unwanted bidder who buys more than 15 percent of a company's stock from acquiring the company. The three exceptions allow a takeover if the acquirer buys 85 percent or more of the target's stock, if two thirds of the stockholders approve the acquisition, or if the board of directors and stockholders waive application of the statute. Several other states have adopted similar laws.

The Role of the Courts

Litigation played a key role in almost every boisterous takeover battle of the 1980s. Like any other fight, these corporate struggles needed a referee. The courts filled this role, with raiders and defenders fighting hard to tip the rules in their favor. Takeover litigation generally fell into two broad categories—antitrust litigation and fiduciary obligation litigation.

The large majority of the legal battles took place in the paneled courtrooms of Delaware. Because many major American companies are incorporated in that state, its judges often hear corporate cases and consequently have developed a reputation and expertise in the area.

From the perspective of those in the deal business, the Delaware courts have another key advantage. Delaware has a well-oiled system in place that allows a complex takeover case—often involving billions of dollars—to be heard and resolved in an extremely short time. Other state and federal courts now have similar procedural systems, but Delaware remains the key forum. The result is a rapid-fire brand of legal sparring. Lawyers on either side work around-the-clock to build documentary evidence. Hearings are short, jury trials are nonexistent.

The six weeks or less needed to resolve a Delaware case must be contrasted with the months or years that pass before a general civil dispute is resolved in the courts.

In the heyday of takeover litigation, a single situation would sometimes generate multiple suits in various jurisdictions. The target would challenge the bidder in federal court on antitrust and other grounds. The acquirer would challenge the target's board of directors in state court on fiduciary obligation charges. Forum shopping was common, with targets tending to favor hometown courts and acquirers looking more often to the specialized Delaware courts.

Though the legal mudslinging at times got quite ferocious in heated takeover battles, litigation rarely proved an effective defense to a well-funded takeover offer. Over time, the federal courts wearied of antitrust challenges to takeovers, which seemed to have more to do with delay than actual competitive effects. The U.S. Supreme Court consequently raised a number of roadblocks to such antitrust challenges. Fiduciary obligation litigation, on the other hand, tended to be used more as an offensive weapon with the intent of forcing the hand of a target company's board. Here too the courts developed a number of impediments to legal assault.

Milken, Drexel and the Emergence of Junk Bonds

A distinctive element of the 1980s was the development of a liquid market for debt obligations below investment grade. This market was created largely by Michael Milken.

Fresh out of the Wharton School, Milken joined the firm Drexel Harriman Ripley in 1970 as its director of research for low-grade bonds. The firm had a distinguished name, but had become weak. Despite Drexel's shaky standing, Milken's new job matched his interests. While in school, he had become fascinated with the idea of investing in what would eventually come to be known as junk bonds.

In 1970, a thin, but established market for low-grade debt existed. The securities fell into two main categories: "fallen angels" and original issuances. The fallen angels, greater in number, were bonds that had lost their original investment-grade rating due to the issuers' poor performance. Original issuances below investment grade, on the other hand, were rare instances. The issuers typically were small companies, or sometimes acquisitive conglomerates like LTV.

Milken first became interested in low-grade bonds—what later became known as junk bonds—while helping out his father, an accountant, with some work for a client. Milken pursued the topic in school and eventually discovered a 1967 study by Professor W. Braddock Hickman. Hickman's analysis showed that lower-rated bonds actually outperformed higher-rated bonds over certain periods of the economic cycle. Hickman's work had received little attention when published, but Milken found it inspirational.

In his early years at Drexel, Milken traveled the country, speaking to money managers and wealthy individuals. He tried to interest them in investing in the higher-yielding junk bonds and assured them Drexel would make a market in the securities. If they ever wanted to sell, he would buy. Slowly, he developed a following. Milken focused on the prior issues of conglomerates and the fallen angels. As it turned out, these securities performed quite well through the volatile economic times of the mid-1970s.

Milken prospered as his audience grew. In 1974, he was permitted to organize a separate junk bond unit within Drexel. The unit was at first comprised of salesmen, traders and research analysts, and had a $2 million capital base. Milken was also given the freedom to distribute a third of his unit's profits to whomever he liked.

The success of Milken's junk bond unit drove Drexel to incredible success. However, until the late 1970s, the group was primarily a sales and trading operation. Then Milken made the shift into original issuance, which would transform Drexel into a household name.

Drexel was not the first firm to issue junk bonds. Goldman, Sachs and Lehman Brothers underwrote a series of junk securities for LTV,

Zapata and Pan American World Airways in early 1977. However, Milken's strong network of loyal customers gave him a decided advantage over other firms. Drexel managed seven issues worth $124 million in 1977.

The added business was extremely profitable for Drexel. By the mid-1980s, close to $50 billion in new junk bonds were in the market. Drexel dominated the new issuance business, with a market share in the 60 percent range. Entrepreneurs were the primary customer for Drexel's corporate finance services. Milken financed MCI, Ted Turner, Craig McCaw, Ron Perelman and many other creative but cash-poor managers. Cable television, cellular phones and casinos were big Drexel-backed issuers of junk bonds.

Drexel profited from the expanded market for junk securities in a number of different ways. First, the firm charged an underwriting fee to issue junk bonds for a borrower. The fee generally amounted to about 3 percent of the total issuance. Drexel also often demanded equity in an issuer—usually in the form of warrants—as an additional fee.

On top of these investment banking fees, Drexel made a considerable profit trading junk bonds. The business of making a market in junk securities allowed Milken's traders to set spreads between the price at which they would buy the security and the price at which they would sell it. Because Drexel dominated the market, it had a strong position and could set fairly broad spreads.

In 1984, Milken decided to expand Drexel's burgeoning empire even further—into the world of mergers and acquisitions (M&A). The first step was to use the firm's financing capability to back leveraged buyouts (LBOs) and corporate takeovers. With this beachhead, Milken then hoped to get Drexel into the M&A advisory business. In other words, Milken looked to strike up an alliance with financial buyers, an alliance that eventually would propel Drexel into the center of some of the decade's largest deals.

Michael Milken—The Glory Years

In 1978, against the wishes of his nominal superiors at Drexel, Milken moved the bulk of his operation—traders, salesmen, research analysts and investment bankers—from New York to Beverly Hills. A native of California, Milken wanted to return home. Part of the motivation was that his father had recently been diagnosed with cancer; part was that he hoped to spend more time with his children. Beyond the personal reasons, Milken felt that a presence in California would give him a competitive advantage precisely because it was far from New York. He would be able to operate away from the watchful eyes of competitors.

Milken did not slow down once he left New York. Rather, he took advantage of the time difference between the two coasts. He would arrive in Drexel's high-tech office at 4:00 A.M. Milken could then work two hours before the markets opened in New York and still be out of the office in time to see his children.

With Milken's staff matching his dedication, Drexel's Wilshire Boulevard offices became the center of the junk bond world. Chief executives would gladly agree to 5:00 A.M. meetings, just for the opportunity to pitch Milken on their companies. Invitations to the annual High-Yield Bond Conference, later dubbed the "Predators Ball," were sought after as a prized ticket.

The eagerness with which potential issuers approached Drexel and Milken was a reflection of the junk bond market's dynamic. There was no shortage of companies and individuals who wanted to sell junk bonds. Buyers were the scarce commodity, and Milken controlled access. Drexel's primacy in those glory years was a reflection of the strength of Milken's network. At his peak, Milken acted as a kind of gatekeeper.

Amidst all the glory and glitter was also hustle and sleaze. Anyone could sense the exuberance, only the naive could miss the recklessness. Milken himself sounded like a reasonable man, even soft-spoken, always playing with ideas. Some disciples were among the brightest on Wall Street. But the tone of the organization was out of control and some of the staff inappropriate for a major firm. The tragedy of Drexel was that the excess and illegality weren't necessary to its success.

The Financial Buyers Come to the Fore

The withering of the 1960s conglomerates, the fashionability of divestitures and the availability of financing spawned a boom in financial buyers in the 1980s.

Financial buyers were beneficiaries of a new market orthodoxy, which favored slimmed-down, pure-play companies with a single line of business. Time and again, the financial buyers teamed with managers to purchase a moribund division from a conglomerate. If all went as planned, the leveraged acquisition would be followed by a period of debt reduction. Operations would be streamlined and costs slashed. Within a couple of years, the cleaned-up company would be sold for a substantial gain.

The financial buyers filled a vacuum in the relatively inefficient market for corporate control. Many major public companies focused on return on assets ("ROA") as the appropriate measure of whether an acquisition would pay off. The assets involved included the total purchase price, both debt and equity. So, for example, if a company with a 20 percent ROA threshold paid $100 for an acquisition, it would need to be comfortable that the target would return $20 in the first year, taking into account both earnings and appreciation of asset value.

Financial buyers took a different view. They focused more narrowly on return on equity. The same $100 acquisition might be funded with $20 of equity and $80 of debt. Assuming a 10 percent interest rate on the debt, the debt holders would be entitled to the first $8 of return. If the target returned $20 in the first year, the stockholders would receive the remaining $12, for a 60 percent return on invested equity.

By financing an acquisition largely with debt, a financial buyer could pay a substantial premium over current public market value. Success came from both performance improvement and simple financial arbitrage. In inflationary times with cheap stock market prices, the formula was stunningly successful.

Jerome Kohlberg Jr. was one of the early practitioners of the leveraged acquisition. He began arranging small leveraged deals in the mid-1960s as a partner at Bear, Stearns & Co. Leveraged transactions were not a specialty of the firm, but so-called bootstrap acquisitions, featuring the use of a company's own borrowing capacity to finance its purchase price, intrigued him.

In 1965, Kohlberg arranged a $9.5 million buyout of Stern Metals, a dental supply company owned by its seventy-one-year-old founder. Stern wanted to sell the business, but couldn't bear to see it swallowed by a larger company. Finally, Kohlberg and his associates came up with another alternative—a bootstrap acquisition financed with some equity from Bear, Stearns and members of the Stern family, and considerable debt.

The Stern Metals transaction proved extremely profitable. The success led to more deals. In the early 1970s, Kohlberg added two new associates—cousins Henry Kravis and George Roberts—to help with the effort. By then, Kohlberg and others had developed a profile of the kind of company most susceptible to a successful LBO. A stable cash flow stream which could support leverage and ultimately pay down acquisition debt was key. Cyclical or speculative growth companies were therefore eliminated as possibilities. Rather, the typical LBO company was like Stern Metals—in a mature industry, steady, almost boring.

As a corollary, an LBO target—whether currently public or private—should be undervalued. Here, value is a relative term. For a financial buyer like Kohlberg, a company's ability to service its debt was a measure of its value. A company with $1 million of operating cash flow (before interest payments and taxes), for example, might be able to support $5 million in borrowings. If payments on a portion of the debt could be delayed, even more debt capital might be raised. A financial buyer then would add a sliver of equity—generally 10 to 20 percent of the purchase price.

A motivated seller was another important piece in the LBO puzzle. There were two primary paradigms. In the first category were privately held companies, like Stern Metals, where the owners wanted to cash out their investment. Many times, a generational change was involved. The senior member of a family was ready to retire, but worried about handing over control to younger family members. This concern was understandable because the company often represented the senior family member's retirement savings. Junior family members, on the other hand, often ached to get out on their own. An LBO promised to satisfy both parties.

Large companies were a second category of motivated seller. They were being pressed to maximize shareholder value. Selling off underperforming subsidiaries was part of the process. From the perspective of managers in the subsidiaries, an LBO was the most attractive alternative because such a transaction would allow them to run an independent company.

The Leveraged Acquisition Model

Mastery of the leveraged acquisition model was the cornerstone of the financial buyers' initial success. Stripping away the technical and legal jargon, the leveraged acquisition process is quite simple—the acquisition of a company is financed largely with borrowed money. The company's own cash flow or assets serve as the main security for the loan.

A legendary early LBO involved Gibson Greeting Cards. In 1981, Wesray, an investment partnership owned by former Treasury Secretary William E. Simon and investment manager Ray Chambers, purchased Gibson Greetings from a stumbling RCA. Debt financing provided $79 million of the $80 million purchase price. Gibson's existing managers, who stayed on to run the company, owned 20 percent of the common equity.

A year later, Bill Simon looked like a genius. The country was coming out of recession, operation profits were up dramatically, and the bulls began to charge on Wall Street. On May 19, 1983, Wesray took Gibson Greeting Inc. public, selling about 30 percent of the company for just over $96 million. The IPO (initial public offering) valued the whole company at $330 million. Wesray had earned a $250 million pretax paper profit on its $1 million equity investment.

Some observers wrote off Wesray's success as a fluke, a case of a pair of sophisticated investors who outwitted a dense conglomerate. Others attributed Wesray's phenomenal profit to opportune timing. A strong economy, a booming stock market—a confluence of unpredictable events—allowed the partners to cash out quickly.

However, other early LBOs proved equally remarkable. The vitality of this transaction structure eventually became widely recognized. Over time, the nature of the typical LBO evolved through three stages. Generally, each of the three models has worked out well in the long bull market of the last decade, but each variation on the theme has its own risks and pressure points which may be exposed in a less exuberant market.

The Classic LBO   The classic LBO capital structure is a device to buy the maximum assets with the least amount of cash invested. By borrowing against the assets and cash flows of an acquisition target, an LBO buyer can put up one dollar of equity and buy five or six dollars of business.

The effect of this leverage is striking. Simply shifting the capital structure allows the buyer to more than double the return on equity. So, while the classic LBO structure reigned during the late 1970s and early 1980s, financial buyers didn't need to perform any miracles to earn excellent returns on equity.

Of course, if a financial buyer did manage to improve the acquired business, the added appreciation in value would only compound the effects of leverage. Financial buyers recognized this effect and developed a typical approach to maximize the likelihood of positive results. As a rule of thumb, existing corporate management was encouraged to participate in most early LBOs. The top managers generally were allowed to purchase a significant portion of the common equity, often at a discount.

Management participation was part carrot, part stick. The carrot came in the form of promised riches should the company meet its financial plan. Naturally, the hope was that the company would be sold after a few years of hard work. As part-owners, the managers would share in the gains. The stick came from the fact that managers had a significant portion of their net worth tied up in the typical LBO. Failure had a steep price, and this prospect tended to concentrate the mind.

The classic LBO was not without complexities and potential pitfalls. For example, the debt-equity dichotomy obscures the layering and texture of the classic LBO capital structure. In fact, the classic LBO capital structure is sliced into various pieces, spanning a spectrum between common equity and "pure" debt.

The capital structure is fractionated for financial marketing reasons to appeal to different investors. A bank might want a more secure, lower paying instrument. An insurance company may have more appetite for risk if it means getting a higher yield. Junk bond investors would take on even more risk to get a better payoff.

At the top of the LBO capital structure is the senior debt provided by banks or other more traditional lenders. The essential defining feature of senior debt is that it stands first in line to be paid in case of bankruptcy. Senior debt also can be "secured" in the sense that it can be given a claim on specific assets of the debtor, similar to a mortgage on a house. These two features—seniority and security—make senior secured debt a low-risk, low-yield instrument.

In the classic LBO, the space between the common equity and the senior debt is filled with successive layers of increasingly senior capital sources—for example, preferred stock, subordinated debt or senior unsecured debt. Because such instruments occupy an intermediate space, they are often referred to as "mezzanine financing."

Like senior debt, the mezzanine financing offers some fixed return. This return generally declines as an instrument becomes more senior. Lenders also frequently demand an equity "kicker"—an option to buy equity at a favorable price—as an inducement to provide financing.

The layered architecture of the classic LBO capital structure cannot be designed in isolation. Lenders who provide each tranche of debt generally require a certain amount of cash flow to support each dollar of debt. Generally, in the classic LBO structure, the debt is scheduled to be paid off within seven years. Cash flows, not earnings, are the focus because the LBO loans are collateralized only by the purchased company's assets. The purchased company's cash flow is the sole means to service the debt.

During the 1980s, there was a tension to projecting cash flows. A financial buyer only profited to the extent it was able to buy and sell target companies. As the market became more crowded, the competition for target companies became more fierce. This environment put pressure on the cash flow model because the higher the projected cash flows, the more a financial buyer could afford to pay for a business.

Yet cutting the cash flow margin too closely could cause problems later. The business might be unable to service its debt burden, which could force it into bankruptcy. Of course, this is why early financial buyers selected businesses with stable cash flows as LBO candidates. Even so, projecting the future is art not science, and errors were bound to be made.

A firm grasp of tax law was also essential to the classic LBO model. By focusing on cash flow, financial buyers magnified the perceived capacity of a business to carry debt. Tax rules made the levered capital structure even more palatable. Unlike dividends on stock, interest on debt generally is tax-deductible. Increasing a company's leverage therefore reduces its tax bill. The resulting cash can be used to pay down the additional debt.

However, nothing in the federal tax law is simple. Reacting to the outcry over hostile takeovers and leveraged acquisitions, politicians and regulators built a thicket of interlocking rules regarding the deductibility of corporate interest expense. As a result, financial buyers spent considerable time coming up with creative structures to maximize tax benefits.

The Breakup LBO   The vitality of the classic LBO structure depended on both leverage and the ability to pay existing target company shareholders an acquisition premium. As prices were bid up, the model became less tenable. By the mid-1980s, when financial buyers looked at potential targets, projected cash flows often weren't sufficient to pay interest on the desired level of debt. Something had to give.

Over time, a second-stage LBO model developed, built on breakup values. The second-stage LBO featured a similar leveraged financial structure. However, the company was not expected to service its debt solely from operating cash flow. Divestitures of businesses were planned from the outset, with the proceeds to be used to pay down the debt, typically by half within seven years. Though depending on asset sales for survival opened an LBO company to additional risk, the tactic generally worked well in the hot merger market of the mid-1980s.

The new importance of asset sales required increased attention to underlying asset values. Diversified conglomerates—which often traded at a discount—became favorite targets.

In 1987, the attraction of the breakup LBO was severely limited by tax law changes. Specifically, a 1987 change in the applicable tax rules eliminated the popular "mirrors" liquidation technique, which had allowed an acquirer to split up a target company on purchase.

The basic technique involved three steps. First, the acquirer would purchase the target company in a cash-for-stock deal. Second, the acquirer would have the target company, now a wholly-owned subsidiary of the acquirer, distribute as a dividend the target company assets that the acquirer wished to retain. Finally, the target company (which now would hold only unwanted assets) would be sold to a third party. Due to a quirk in the tax rules, any gain on the distribution of the desired target company assets would be mirrored, or offset, by a loss on the stock sale.

Unwanted assets could thus be sold off with little or no resulting corporate tax liability. The death of mirrors was also the death of many breakup LBOs because the tax impact on value was so large.

The Strategic LBO   A third-stage LBO model has developed in the 1990s. This approach has two variants. The common elements are that an initial public offering is the anticipated exit strategy, and the fact that the gain comes from increased earnings and higher growth.

In the first variant, a private company or division of a public company is bought. The operations and finances of the company are then improved. More glamorous management might be installed. Then, when the time is right, the company is taken public in an IPO.

The second, similar strategy involves a buildup of small units which wouldn't receive a favorable public-market value standing on their own. An attractive IPO candidate is created by rolling up a number of these smaller pieces into a larger whole, with top-notch management again key to the process. The larger business is then taken public.

In either case, the strategic LBO is a departure from the leverage-driven models of the 1980s. Given the investor emphasis on earnings per share, the focus on a public-market exit means that financial buyers can no longer ignore earnings as a measure of a company's financial health. Leverage is therefore not the key determinant of success. Rather, the financial buyers provide the managerial expertise and capital necessary to dress companies for market in a way that will appeal to investors.

Managing the LBO   The variety of LBO pursued determines not only capital structure and investment focus. Management style also is impacted. Very different approaches are necessary in a classic LBO versus a strategic LBO. In the former case, management must squeeze cash flow to pay down debt. However, if the public market is the anticipated exit, as in a strategic LBO, management may want to do the opposite. The ultimate stock market value and investment return might be maximized by investing cash to build future earning potential.

Catalysts

The basic LBO structure may not have been an innovation of the 1980s, but the dollar volume of deals during the decade was unprecedented. About $2 billion of LBO transactions were completed in 1980. In 1988, 239 deals were executed for a total purchase price of $81.2 billion.

A number of factors, financial, regulatory, market and technological, help explain the dramatic growth in LBO volume. On the financial front, the availability of credit was a critical spark. Easier lending terms began to appear in the late 1970s. Successive Oil Shocks generated immense wealth for the oil-producing nations. Many of these dollars flowed into New York's money-center banks. The banks needed to recycle the petrodollars into income-producing loans. However, at the same time, many of banks' traditional lending markets were being closed off.

Faced with this dilemma, financing LBOs—which were known in the banking community as highly leveraged transactions, or HLTs—was extremely attractive to the banks. HLTs gave banks the potential to earn high interest rates and up-front fees. The risks involved were reduced through syndication, the practice of getting other banks to make part of a loan for a cut of the fees. Credit standards loosened further when Japanese banks made a major push into the U.S. lending market with vast pools of capital to invest.

Even more liquidity was added to the market in the mid-1980s, when financial buyers began to issue junk bonds to finance acquisitions. Previously, Drexel had concentrated on financing entrepreneurs and operating businesses. This changed when Milken decided to open the junk bond market to financial buyers and began to underwrite takeover entrepreneurs and LBO firms.

Meanwhile, regulatory changes increased the flow of equity capital into the buyout business. In the early 1980s, many states allowed their massive public employee pension funds to spread money among a broader range of investments. This change marked a break from the past, when the funds generally were restricted to investing in conservative stocks and bonds. State pension funds consequently began to invest heavily in LBO investment pools.

Capital may have been the spark for the LBO boom, but market factors provided the kindling. The stock market began the 1980s at a level seen in the early 1960s. Diversified large companies faced a particularly unforgiving environment and were pressured by the market to divest subsidiaries. Financial buyers simply stepped into the void created by this market imbalance.

The Financial Players

KKR—The Early Years   In 1976, Kohlberg, Kravis and Roberts left Bear, Stearns to pursue leveraged buyouts full-time. Kohlberg, then in his fifties, radiated a sense of solidity and prudence and was the elder statesman of the group. His wire-rim glasses gave him a stern countenance, offset by bursts of droll humor. Cousins Kravis and Roberts were in their early thirties and hungry.

There was little fanfare when KKR opened its doors. Not sure how long it would take to find a first deal, Kohlberg, Kravis and Roberts husbanded their $120,000 start-up capital where they could. Kohlberg and Kravis leased space in a shabby Manhattan office suite, using the metal furniture left behind by the previous tenant. Roberts, who had worked out of Bear, Stearns' San Francisco office, found similar space.

By the time they started KKR, Kohlberg, Kravis and Roberts had honed their approach. The CEO in transition was the ideal target audience. A takeover loomed, ornery investors threatened or estate tax issues pressed. KKR had a viable option. The firm would join with existing management in a leveraged buyout. After the buyout, the CEO and his team would have considerable autonomy to run things as they saw fit, so long as they hit their financial plan. Top management, KKR and its investors would share in any gains.

As it turned out, Kohlberg, Kravis and Roberts opened KKR at an opportune time. The stock market was in a swoon, and mature companies in particular received relatively low valuations. Executives who once had rushed to go public began to question the merits of that decision.

In the fall of 1976, KKR financed a $26 million management buyout of a small conglomerate. Three more deals were closed during the next year. Then, in 1978, KKR broke into the big time, financing the acquisition of its first Fortune 500 company, Houdaille Industries.

Houdaille manufactured steel, machine tools, pumps and car bumpers. Spurred by rumors of an impending takeover, Kohlberg approached CEO Gerald Saltarelli.

Saltarelli's aversion to debt could be seen on Houdaille's balance sheet. In 1978, the company had $40 million in cash and $22 million in debt. The conservative Saltarelli needed convincing, but, urged on by his subordinates, he ultimately signed off on a leveraged buyout. KKR's investment group bid $40 a share for the company's stock, then trading at around $25. The total purchase price—about $350 million—was more than three times larger than any KKR had previously financed. Financed with 85 percent debt, the deal closed in April 1979.

Over the next few years, Houdaille struggled. KKR's projections proved too rosy. Faced with strong foreign competition in its core business, Houdaille was forced to shed operations and redeploy capital. However, despite these problems, KKR and its investors still earned a healthy 22 percent return on common equity over a seven-and-a-half-year period.

LBOs in the Early 1980s   News of the Houdaille purchase put the LBO on the map. A few other players already were in the LBO business. Gibbons, Green & van Amerongen actually preceded KKR, having been formed in 1969 to do leveraged acquisitions. Forstmann Little was formed in 1978 by the two Forstmann brothers—Ted and Nick—and Brian Little. The firm pioneered the practice of raising pools of equity and subordinated debt capital from pension funds. Clayton & Dubilier, which had started as a firm specializing in turnaround situations, switched to LBOs in the same year. Martin Dubilier, CEO of the firm, had been exposed to bootstrap acquisitions as chairman of Stern Metals.

After the Houdaille deal, Wall Street was abuzz. Copies of the public documents for the deal were passed around like trading cards, and people began to see the profit potential in leveraged acquisitions. Within the space of a few years, many of the major investment banks, including Morgan Stanley, First Boston and Merrill Lynch, jumped into the business.

Still, KKR benefited from its position as an early entrant, and the Houdaille deal opened a lot of doors. Executives began to return calls, the business press took notice, deals came more easily. As a result, the firm dominated the business: in dollar terms, KKR accounted for 40 percent of all leveraged buyouts in 1981.

KKR Moves into Billion-Dollar Territory   Things accelerated dramatically for KKR when the country came out of recession in 1983. Over the next two years, the firm acquired seven companies, spending in excess of $2.8 billion. Awareness of KKR, previously more or less limited to readers of the business press and investment professionals, began to spread. Then, in 1986, the $6.2 billion Beatrice transaction thrust KKR fully into the limelight.

Beatrice was a hodgepodge collection of food and consumer products businesses that was staggering under the eccentric leadership of CEO James L. Dutt. Dutt's increasingly autocratic style led the Beatrice board to remove him. An interim chief executive was appointed, but the company's situation was unstable.

Beatrice was a company KKR had studied for years. In addition, Donald P. Kelly, a flamboyant but savvy executive who had run Esmark, a minor conglomerate itself bought by Beatrice, had told KKR that he could materially improve Beatrice.

On October 16, 1985, KKR made a $5.6 billion offer to the Beatrice board. Though friendly, the offer amounted to a "bear hug," an attempt to pressure the company into a deal. The board refused the offer as inadequate, but the company was in play. Very quickly pressure mounted on the directors from shareholders irate at Beatrice's record. A number of Beatrice executives tried to arrange an alternative LBO, but they lacked credibility. KKR upped its bid and persuaded the board to accept.

The capital structure—including money for working capital and $248 million of fees—called for $4 billion of bank loans, $2.5 billion of junk bond financing and $407 million of equity. These sums seemed phenomenal at the time, but Beatrice was operationally strong and had easily salable assets. The company owned a long list of major brands: Tropicana orange juice, Playtex, Hunt-Wesson grocery products, Orville Redenbacher popcorn and dozens of others.

The energetic Kelly promised to dedicate himself to restructuring the company's operations. He would slash frivolous expenses, like the millions spent on auto racing by Dutt, a racing enthusiast. Kelly also would sell $1.5 billion of Beatrice's noncore businesses and grow the remainder.

The banks' and bondholders' faith in KKR paid off. Kelly kept his word. He trimmed more than 15 percent out of a $975 million marketing budget, a budget that had included ad spending in markets where the company didn't sell the products being advertised. He reduced corporate overhead and initially sold off more than $3 billion in assets—Wesray bought Avis for $275 million, Coke bought the Los Angeles bottling business for more than $1 billion, and a group of managers bought Playtex in a leveraged buyout. With the cash from these transactions, debt was reduced to manageable levels.

Soon, it became apparent that a frothy stock market and frenzied takeover environment would allow KKR to sell the remaining 75 percent of Beatrice for a healthy gain. First, the nonfood businesses— with Kelly at the head—were sold to the public in a stock offering which raised $420 million. After the intervening Crash of 1987, Seagram bought Tropicana for $1.2 billion. ConAgra then bought the remaining businesses in 1990 for $1.3 billion in cash and stock, plus the assumption of over $1 billion in debt.

In the final tally, after paying down Beatrice's debt, KKR and its co-investors retained net proceeds of approximately $2.2 billion. Over the four years of the investment, KKR had earned an annual return of roughly 50 percent on the $407 million equity invested. Beatrice was a triumph.

Henry Kravis

Today, Henry Kravis is probably the most visible embodiment of the LBO movement. The son of a wealthy Oklahoma oilman, he started working at Bear, Stearns with Kohlberg after graduating from Columbia Business School.

Kravis had the advantage of a keen analytical mind honed by Kohlberg's training and a natural gift for persuasion. He understood early on that the LBO business had four equally important elements: raising money, investing it well, running the company, and selling well. Much of his early days in the business involved wooing investors and persuading companies to sell.

The firm's annual investor conference was an important forum to bond with investors, and Kravis exerted great efforts to ensure that the presentations were unusually thorough. Although West Coast cousin George Roberts never quite got the glare of attention, he was equally important in spotting deals and in persuading the large state pension plans of the wisdom of investing in this new "alternative investment" category.

When Kravis and Roberts parted with Kohlberg, the business continued to expand. Kravis received unrelenting attention, both professionally and socially. Inevitably, his success created resentment and criticism when the deal business stumbled in the early 1990s and RJR Nabisco became a controversial deal. Kravis managed to retain his stamina and his calm. His large investors gave him complete support, mainly because they remembered past gains, and Roberts and Kravis excelled at communicating with investors.

Today KKR is more successful than ever. The cumulative years of business experience and social contacts give Kravis a clear edge in the business, but also his tight organization has mel-lowed and gained patina. Based in wood-paneled suites with a stunning view of Central Park, the operation is highly professional.

Kravis' success has brought wealth and power. With an estimated net worth of over $500 million, Kravis has become a major philanthropist, contributing tens of millions of dollars to museums, universities and other causes. The shock of his success has worn off, and KKR is accepted as the senior partner of the LBO business.

Tapping the Money Source   Few if any other buyout shops pursued acquisitions on the scale of Beatrice. However, all buyout shops had a considerable thirst for capital. They needed debt, both senior and subordinated, and equity capital.

For equity capital, KKR initially relied on a group of passive investors. These were primarily wealthy individuals who agreed to pay a portion of KKR's expenses in exchange for the opportunity to invest alongside KKR's partners. KKR typically would form a separate investment vehicle for each deal. Kohlberg, Kravis and Roberts would put in 1 or 2 percent of the equity; the passive investors would supply the remainder.

As KKR's deal flow began to multiply, its need for equity outgrew the capacity of a handful of wealthy individuals. In 1978, Kravis, Roberts and Kohlberg raised their first "blind pool" of $30 million. The money, supplied mainly by insurance companies and banks, could be invested in deals as KKR saw fit. This arrangement gave the firm the flexibility to act quickly.

From then on, KKR's capital needs grew with the size of the deals it pursued. The Houdaille deal took a large chunk out of the first fund. Another $316 million blind pool was raised in 1982, a $1 billion pool in 1984 and a $5.6 billion pool in 1987.

As the pools got bigger, KKR was forced to expand its fund-raising efforts. Picking up on a practice adopted by Forstmann Little in the late 1970s, KKR began to look to pension funds as a major capital source. State pension funds were the most receptive. The list of KKR limited partners eventually included the state employee pension funds of Washington, Oregon, Michigan, Massachusetts and several other states.

LBO firms make money in a number of different ways under the blind pool arrangement. First, they sometimes charge investors a management fee. This amounts to an average 1.5 percent of committed capital up until the funds are invested, and then a lesser percentage.

Second, LBO firms usually charge a transaction fee for arranging a deal, whether purchase or sale. These fees range as high as 1 percent of the purchase price, but generally are lower in large transactions. KKR's 1996 sale of Duracell to Gillette, where KKR was paid $20 million on a $7 billion deal, provides a recent example.

Third, firms retain any director's or monitoring fees paid to their professionals, who often sit on the boards of acquired companies. A typical director's fee might be in the range of $25,000 to $50,000 per year.

Fourth, firms earn a 20 percent share of the profits realized by the pool. This arrangement gives the firms a huge performance incentive. Usually, the profit override doesn't kick in unless the fund has achieved a return over a set threshold, for example 8 percent.

Though the blind pools eventually became quite large, they only provided one tranche in the leveraged acquisition capital structure. LBO firms also must raise the two remaining tranches—the senior debt and the mezzanine financing. For senior debt, financial buyers generally went to banks. Mezzanine financing, on the other hand, generally came from insurance companies. However, as the junk bond market developed, KKR and other financial buyers increasingly turned to Michael Milken and Drexel Burnham Lambert for junior debt.

During the early 1980s, there was a cachet to investing with KKR or one of its competitors. Proximity to the glamorous world of big-dollar deals was part of the attraction. Glamour was not enough, however, to keep investors coming back. Hundreds of millions of dollars were at stake, and the people directing these sums were sophisticated and demanded substance.

The first few generations of buyout funds delivered. Investors in KKR's early funds, for example, earned annual returns in the range of 30 to 50 percent, even after deducting KKR's fees. Other funds showed similar results. Of course, timing is important. A leveraged investment in the S&P 500 also showed a handsome return. However, that wasn't a feasible alternative for most investors.

As news of past successes spread, more and more money flowed into the buyout funds. Over 200 buyout firms had crowded into the field by 1988. The funds controlled an estimated $30 or $40 billion in equity capital. With the power of leverage, this gave the funds the ability to spend over $200 billion on acquisitions.

The Takeover Entrepreneurs

The new financing techniques of the 1980s also spawned a second category of financial players—the takeover entrepreneurs, men who used the liquidity of the 1980s to build empires or amass fortunes. Many were self-made, others inherited their initial table stakes. The takeover entrepreneurs also were more likely to entertain hostile takeovers as a strategic alternative. Some put up a large percentage of the equity in their deals, and for this reason, captured the lion's share of any profits.

The takeover entrepreneurs—Carl Icahn, T. Boone Pickens, Sir James Goldsmith, Nelson Peltz, Oscar Wyatt, Saul Steinberg, Ronald Perelman—all initially relied on the junk bond prowess of Drexel to finance their efforts. Some profited immensely by acting as financial stalking horses that put companies in play. Others actually took control of major industrial empires.

Ronald Perelman   From an early age, Ronald Owen Perelman had no question his objective was to be an industrialist. He began his professional life working for his father, who owned a number of medium-sized companies. Together, the two men built the family holdings with a string of acquisitions. Perelman learned the mergers and acquisitions game on the job.

Perelman struck out on his own in 1978 at the age of thirty-five. He moved to New York and began scouting for deals. The first came together within a matter of months. Perelman bought 40 percent of a small jewelry company for $1.9 million, borrowing the entire amount on his personal credit and assets. He rapidly set about liquidating nonproductive stores. Then, he threw himself into marketing the company's products. A year later, Perelman had repaid the original acquisition loan, netted a $15 million profit and still had a large stake in the remaining business.

In 1980, Perelman acquired MacAndrews & Forbes, a supplier of licorice extract and chocolate. The deal was originally financed by a syndicate of banks, but Perelman soon convinced Bear, Stearns and Drexel Burnham to float $35 million in junk bonds. Perelman paid considerable attention to the company's operations, taking sales trips to meet executives at cigarette companies, which were major consumers of licorice extract. He also broadened his company's supply base of licorice beyond the politically unstable Iran and Afghanistan.

Perelman next added Technicolor to his budding empire. He sold off its unproductive one-hour developing labs and refocused the company on servicing entertainment clients. This business was bulked up with $150 million in add-on acquisitions of other film and video processing companies. Less than five years later, Perelman sold Technicolor for $780 million (added to the roughly $300 million in operating profits he earned while owning the company).

In 1984, Perelman took MacAndrews & Forbes private in a Milken-financed deal. The transaction gave Perelman new freedom to continue his acquisition program. Consolidated Cigar was added the same year, grocery chain Pantry Pride in 1985. The grocery company had been poorly run, but had a valuable tax loss carry-forward. Perelman liquidated its business but retained the shell company so that he could later use its loss carry-forwards to shelter other business income from taxation.

At this point, Perelman had a diversified, highly leveraged business empire. MacAndrews & Forbes was in jewelry, cigars, licorice and film processing. Perelman had fashioned a minor conglomerate, but he wanted more.

Perelman used Drexel to advance to the next step. In 1985, the firm underwrote a $761 million Perelman junk bond offering. The money, investors were informed, would be used to finance future, as yet unidentified acquisitions. Perelman needed this blind pool of capital to step up to the big leagues.

With money in hand, Perelman could pursue a much larger acquisition. Revlon soon caught his eye. The cosmetics company—which had diversified into health products, pharmaceuticals and eye care—was in a slump, both operationally and in the stock market. Yet, in Perelman's judgment, the Revlon brand name remained powerful. He could buy the company, divest the noncore assets for a substantial premium over their original purchase price, and rejuvenate the cosmetics operation.

Perelman met with Revlon CEO Michel Bergerac, hoping to negotiate a friendly deal. The negotiations never got off the ground, though. Bergerac made little effort to conceal his disdain for Perelman and his team. Perelman responded on August 20, 1985, with a $1.8 billion public offer for the company.

A drawn-out takeover contest ensued. LBO shop Forstmann Little tried to lock up the company in a white knight bid, but the Delaware court ruled in the landmark *Revlon* decision that once a company was for sale, the board had to deal fairly with the highest bidder. With superior tactics and an intense hunger to win, Perelman outbid Forstmann Little and won his prize. A key factor in his success was preselling part of the Revlon assets and knowing on an operating basis the changes he needed to make at Revlon.

Within a few months of taking over, Perelman sold off various health and pharmaceutical operations, raising over $1 billion. He moved to shore up Revlon's cosmetics core with two acquisitions. First, he bought Max Factor and Almay from Playtex Products; then, he added a group of top-line cosmetics brands. The pieces were in place. Perelman set about improving them. He increased research and development, modernized factories and refocused advertising.

While MacAndrews & Forbes had some trouble digesting Revlon, after a number of years Perelman managed to first turn the cosmetics giant around and then engineer a marketing triumph with Revlon's Colorstay long-lasting cosmetics line.

PROFILE

Ronald Perelman

Ronald Perelman has evolved from being a small businessman in Philadelphia to being one of the richest men in America. Part of the explanation is, of course, his intense drive and operational skill.

We watched Perelman closely in the Revlon deal when representing two buyers of assets he would presell. His personal energy level is kinetic and exhausts those around him. However, it is his intensity about operational details that sets him apart from other leveraged buyers. He thinks and breathes industrial strategy and operations, peppering his conversations with statistics and questions.

Another strength is his ability to lever off skilled people. Perelman's internal team is probably as capable as any group of investment bankers and more focused. His chief lieutenants are Bruce Slovin, a lawyer turned chief operating officer, Howard Gittis, his chief financial strategist, who was once the senior partner

of a distinguished Philadelphia law firm, and Don Drapkin, Perelman's longtime lawyer at Skadden, Arps who was induced to join
MacAndrews & Forbes. The acquisition company in the Revlon
deal, Nicole, was named after Drapkin's daughter.

The Perelman team is like a brotherhood, sharing breakfast
and lunch. Key meetings are held at their art-filled headquarters
in a town house in Manhattan's East Sixties. Calling on one officer
is like calling on all as each wanders in and out of the meetings.

Similarly, Perelman has been able to hire all-star managers to
run his investments, and today, despite some setbacks, he is
worth an estimated $4 billion.

After the Revlon deal, Perelman's coterie of companies kept him
increasingly occupied. Still, he continued to pursue major deals. He
made unsuccessful runs at Gillette and investment bank Salomon
Brothers. Then, at the end of 1988, he snared a particularly favorable
acquisition. MacAndrews & Forbes put up about $160 million in eq-
uity to buy a group of failed savings and loans. In return, as part of a
larger program, the government granted the company a number of
lucrative—and later controversial—incentives.

By the end of 1988, Perelman had assembled an impressive group
of businesses. As was the case with KKR, the leveraged acquisition
model was the foundation of Perelman's success. This, together with
a deft understanding of how to turn around an ailing business, gave
him the ability to magnify a relatively small equity stake across increasingly larger deals.

Today, Perelman's empire includes Revlon, camping equipment
manufacturer Coleman, First Nationwide Bank and Consolidated
Cigar, as well as a substantial financial services empire. Of course,
things go wrong, even for the most able managers. Recently, Perelman's Marvel Entertainment Group collapsed into bankruptcy.
Perelman had bought the company in 1989 for an estimated $83 mil-

lion. He installed a top manager—William Bevins, formerly Ted Turner's right-hand man.

In 1988, Marvel earned a lackluster $2.3 million, mainly from publishing its comic books. Perelman had a larger vision for the company. He saw a valuable library of characters which could be licensed for everything from toys to movies.

Perelman initially had great success with his strategy. A booming market for comic books, new TV shows and licensing deals pumped revenues up to $415 million by 1993. Flush with success, Marvel bought out two trading card companies—Fleer and Skybox.

Perelman took Marvel public in 1991. Over the next few years, his stake rose to be worth more than $2 billion. Perelman sold bonds secured by his stock interest and used part of the money to fund other parts of his empire.

Starting in 1994, two of the markets for Marvel's products—comic books and trading cards—took dramatic turns for the worse. Demand for comic books fell off a cliff and a number of competitors crowded into the trading card business. Then the 1994 baseball strike stopped interest in trading cards cold. By early 1997, Marvel was in deep trouble. Perelman attempted a restructuring, but Carl Icahn and other investors—who had bought up the distressed Marvel bonds—didn't like the terms. They took control of the company in bankruptcy proceedings.

Measured from the market peak, the collapse of Marvel cost Perelman over $2 billion. However, he had already had his initial investment returned through the stock and bond offerings. Further, the paper loss on Marvel was offset by his dramatic sale of New World Entertainment Group—a company on the rocks when Perelman took over—to Rupert Murdoch for $2.7 billion. Meanwhile his other companies kept prospering.

Carl Icahn Of course, Perelman was not the only takeover entrepreneur who actually bought a major company. Nelson Peltz bought National Can, Sir James Goldsmith bought Crown Zeller-bach, Oscar Wyatt's Coastal Corporation bought American Natural Resources. As the merger boom of the 1980s matured, more and more dealmakers became corporate managers. Not all found the role an attractive one. Carl Icahn's stint as the owner-manager of TWA is a cautionary tale.

After college, Icahn gravitated toward the excitement of Wall Street and became a successful options trader. Then, in 1979, he made the shift from his small brokerage operation into a new business. He was going to invest in and take over undervalued companies.

Tappan, a company that made stoves, was Icahn's first target. He took a position in the company's stock and launched a proxy contest. A white knight swooped in to acquire the company within a few months. Icahn netted $2.7 million on his stock.

Over the course of the coming decade, Icahn would go after increasingly larger companies such as Marshall Field and American Can. He fueled these efforts at the outset with the help of a group of limited partners. These wealthy individuals chipped in $100,000 or $200,000 apiece. Buying on 50 percent margin, Icahn leveraged the money into large stakes in his target companies.

Once Icahn had a stock position, he would approach management, present a plan to improve the company and ask for a board seat. The request was generally denied. Icahn would then threaten a proxy fight or an outright takeover, exciting interest in the company among other acquirers.

Icahn's early takeover efforts were not always successful. In 1980, for example, Icahn and his investors took a large position in Hammermill, a paper company. He met with CEO Albert Duval soon after the group's ownership stake was disclosed in a federal filing. Icahn asked for two board seats, telling Duval he wanted to see Hammermill sold to the highest bidder.

Duval and the Hammermill board rejected Icahn and initiated a number of defensive maneuvers. Icahn countered with a proxy fight.

The parties exchanged lawsuits. After an acrimonious battle, Icahn lost the proxy vote. Ultimately, though, Duval wanted Icahn to go away and eventually agreed that Hammermill would pay part of his expenses. In return, Hammermill received an option to purchase Icahn's shares. Icahn's investors eventually made a profit on the Hammermill stake when the option was exercised.

In 1984 Icahn transitioned from hostile raider to leveraged industrialist. In June of that year, he followed through on his $405 million offer to buy ACF Industries. The acquisition came as a surprise. Icahn had been after the railcar and automotive products manufacturer for months. After a period of hostilities, Icahn had agreed to a standstill agreement to give management time to arrange financing for an LBO. When management came back with a rich offer, market observers expected Icahn to accept and take his profits. Instead, Icahn topped the management bid, not once but twice. Icahn was no longer content to put companies in play, he wanted to run the company.

ACF was to Icahn what Houdaille had been to KKR. The deal brought a measure of respect that had eluded him. More important, Drexel Burnham began returning his calls. By the end of 1984, Milken's troops had refinanced ACF and provided Icahn with his own $150 million "blind war chest." A few months later, he played a cameo role in the Phillips Petroleum takeover fight initiated by T. Boone Pickens.

Then, in early 1986, Icahn completed what he hoped would become his signature deal, the acquisition of TWA. The preceding takeover fight, which had dragged out over many months of 1985, had been particularly bruising. It had featured the usual litigation and public relations attacks on Icahn. In addition, TWA management unsuccessfully attempted to lobby Congress to block an Icahn bid and searched for a white knight.

Frank Lorenzo of Texas Air turned out to be the most promising prospect from management's perspective. Lorenzo was, however, deeply flawed in the eyes of TWA's unions. He had only recently taken Continental Airlines through voluntary bankruptcy to force concessions from its employees. TWA's unions were viscerally opposed to a Lorenzo bid. Their willingness to negotiate concessions with Icahn ultimately swung the contest in his favor.

The TWA Icahn took over had a proud tradition but was a poor financial performer. Howard Hughes, who owned the airline after World War II, had set it back considerably with a foot-dragging transition to jet aircraft. In the 1960s, management had diversified, buying Canteen Corporation and Hilton International Hotels. The airline, deemed a cyclical dog, was spun off in 1983.

Despite a promising start, Icahn's days as an airline CEO were a disaster. The airline had a few profitable years. However, months after the takeover, a terrorist hijacked one of TWA's planes. At roughly the same time, TWA's flight attendants, the one group which had not agreed on a contract in advance of the takeover, walked out in a bitter strike. Icahn moved to replace the attendants with nonunion employees. He broke the union, but was tarred in the press with the same brush previously applied to Lorenzo.

In 1988, Icahn took TWA private. First, the company issued junk bonds through Drexel Burnham. Then, TWA bought out the public shareholders with this cash plus debt securities. Icahn also cashed out his original investment in the process.

After the restructuring, matters went steeply downhill. Critics argued Icahn failed to invest in the airline's planes or employees. Service was dismal. Finally, the recession of the early 1990s crippled TWA. Notwithstanding the problems, though, Icahn continued to press potential merger partners or acquirers for top dollar. No savior emerged.

TWA eventually went through bankruptcy. Icahn suffered a few harrowing months during which it looked like he might be on the hook for the airline's underfunded pensions. When those issues were settled, Icahn gladly gave up his position as a failed industrialist and returned to the life of a takeover entrepreneur.

Today, Icahn remains active in the financial markets. He lately has focused on investments in distressed bonds and real estate. One such investment, a large position in the bonds of Marvel Entertainment, put him at odds with Ron Perelman over a reorganization plan for the troubled company. Icahn won in bankruptcy court and emerged as chairman of Marvel. Icahn also for a time had a large position in RJR Nabisco and agitated on several occasions in favor of splitting the company's food and tobacco operations apart.

In retrospect, the activities of financial entrepreneurs and financial buyers have come to define the pace, rhythm and scope of the 1980s merger boom. The irony is that many of these financial entrepreneurs and financial buyers were able to vastly expand their horizons because of financing by Drexel. Yet, after Drexel's fall, most of these players survived and prospered.

M&A Goes Global

Large cross-border deals were another significant part of the 1980s merger dynamic. Though relatively uncommon in the early 1980s, a rush of deals in the latter part of the decade broke the boundaries of geography.

Like the domestic merger market, the international merger market went through cycles. The factors at play in the domestic market also affected the international. However, there were also a number of additional drivers—currency fluctuations, politics and home-country regulatory attitudes.

Companies from different countries were active at different times. For the obvious reasons associated with a common language, British and Canadian companies were consistently active in the United States. Japanese companies on the other hand enjoyed a window of opportunity in the second half of the decade. Both the Japanese home market and the Japanese currency were strong. Rich with cash, a number of Japanese companies made large U.S. acquisitions

TEN LARGEST CROSS-BORDER DEALS OF THE 1980s

Rank	Buyer	Seller (Unit sold, if applicable)	Approximate Equity Value (Billions)	Year Announced
1.	Beecham Group PLC (U.K.)	SmithKline Beecham Corp.	$16.1	1989
2.	British Petroleum Co. (U.K.)	Standard Oil Co. (remaining 45%)	$7.8	1987
3.	Campeau Corp. (Canada)	Federated Department Stores, Inc.	$6.5	1988
4.	Grand Metropolitan PLC (U.K.)	Pillsbury Co.	$5.6	1988
5.	Royal Dutch/Shell Group (Netherlands)	Shell Oil Co. (remaining 30.5%)	$5.5	1984
6.	BAT Industries PLC (U.K.)	Farmers Group Inc.	$5.2	1988
7.	Société Nationale Elf Aquitaine (France)	Texasgulf Inc.	$4.3	1981
8.	Amoco Corp.	Dome Petroleum Ltd. (Canada)	$4.2	1987
9.	Exxon Corp.	Texas Canada Inc. (Canada)	$4.1	1989
10.	Private Group—Led by Alfred Checchi/KLM Royal Dutch Airlines	NWA Inc. (Northwest Airlines)	$3.5	1989

Source: *MergerStat*

in the last several years of the decade. Then the cycle turned, and the Japanese pulled back.

In the 1980s, U.S. companies also began to look internationally for acquisition candidates. From autos to financial services, from entertainment to pharmaceuticals, industries became increasingly global. As Japanese and European manufacturers pushed into the U.S. market, many American companies began to see acquisitions as a way to hammer back.

Troubled Years | 5

"Each organic being is striving to increase in a geometrical ratio . . . each at some period of its life, during some season of the year, during each generation or at intervals, has to struggle for life and to suffer great destruction. . . . The vigorous, the healthy and the happy survive and multiply."

Charles Darwin, *On the Origin of Species*

The leveraged acquisition business was itself rocked by changes in the second half of the 1980s. By 1986, the business had matured. More and more financial buyers had crowded into the field. Longtime market participants had immense pools of capital at their fingertips and faced pressure to invest the money.

RJR Nabisco

The new realities in the buyout market were highlighted in 1988, when a bidding war erupted over giant RJR Nabisco. Company chief executive F. Ross Johnson triggered events with a management buyout bid. The ensuing auction was the Roller Derby of deals, an imperfect process cloaked in sanctimonious phrases. Outside board members never fully got control of the situation; management continued to make access to information difficult and relied on leaks from the boardroom to target their own bid.

The press had a field day lampooning everyone involved and fictionalized some events to protect favored sources. Two *Wall Street Journal* reporters even became best-selling authors based on their well-written burlesque, *Barbarians at the Gate*, although their credibility was injured when one of the reporters subsequently had to write an article attacking a key source as a congenital liar. Nevertheless, the HBO movie based on the book was all hilarious and made everyone involved look like a fool.

Johnson set the bidding war in motion on October 13, 1988. An able manager with a taste for the perks of office—jets, golf tournaments and club memberships—Johnson proposed a management buyout of RJR Nabisco. He, a small group of top managers, and investment banks Lehman Brothers and Salomon Brothers offered to buy the company for $75 a share. The stock—which closed at about $56 the day before the announcement—recently had been trading in the 40s. Meanwhile, stock analysts put the breakup value of the company at about $100 per share.

Many members of the board felt blindsided by Johnson's offer. Rather than endorse his offer or give management exclusive rights to negotiate, the board appointed a committee of nonmanagement directors to consider his proposal and made the details public. This effectively put the huge company into play.

When news of the bid came out, Henry Kravis was surprised. KKR had approached Johnson a few months earlier to discuss the possibility of a buyout, but had been turned away. Now, Johnson had advanced what Kravis considered to be a low-ball bid. KKR responded within a few days with a higher offer, $90 a share for 87 percent of the company.

The board now faced a pressured situation. Should it accept one of the buyout offers or adopt some other form of restructuring? No matter which way they came down, a lawsuit would inevitably result. The special committee members needed a defensible alternative and asked for final bids.

KKR and Johnson were not the only potential bidders involved in the RJR process. A number of other bidders had expressed some interest in a deal. Forstmann Little pulled together a bidding syndicate, but ultimately dropped out. First Boston cobbled together a proposal, but it wasn't regarded as a serious offer.

After working through the three bids, each of which was different from the others, the board committee opted for the old auctioneer's ploy. It asked for another round of bids. Curiously, again the bids were leaked. In the middle of the bidding process, our Tokyo office called to tell us that the "secret" bids were being described in minute detail on the Asian feed of the Dow Jones News Service.

Both Johnson and KKR—the two strongest bidders—had reacted to the board's request by coming back with complicated packages of cash and securities. The board's investment bankers valued the two bids roughly equally. At a climactic meeting in the Manhattan offices of law firm Skadden, Arps, the board finally picked KKR's offer as the winner, basically because management's strong-arm tactics had ultimately backfired. Things being equal, the outside board members didn't like the image of backing management.

From start to finish, the RJR transaction consumed less than three months. The deal was both negotiated and closed in that time. Nearly $20 billion in debt capital was raised, $15 billion from a large syndicate of banks and $5 billion in junk bonds. The $25 billion price paid for the company represented almost a 100 percent premium over RJR's recent market valuation.

Although the dollars involved were huge, the valuation was not excessive based on the facts known at the time. During the deal, there had been a series of times when a compromise was possible. A joint bid could have been fashioned. However, the underwriters for the rival bidders were too busy fighting for territorial turf to make it happen.

In hindsight, the RJR deal turned sour. The public visibility was simply too much, and the deal's doings became too easy to equate with the excesses of an overheated market. However, the most immediate threat to the deal came from a security Drexel had designed to finance the purchase. Called an increasing-rate note, these instruments were designed to reset periodically to trade at face value. Before the widespread liquidity crisis of 1990, Drexel had considered the bonds—which were used in several deals—an aggressive marketing innovation. By assuring selling shareholders that the paper they were to receive would be worth face value, Drexel managed to dispel the unsavory image associated with the packages of securities often included in buyout offers.

However, RJR's $6 billion of increasing-rate notes boomeranged in 1990. Confidence in the tobacco company's ability to service its debt plummeted on January 26, when Moody's downgraded the company. In this environment, the rate on the notes would have to be reset at sky-high levels for them to trade at face.

Often these notes have a cap, a limit on the top interest rate, but RJR's advisers and Drexel had not included that term. RJR wasn't able to handle the interest payments. To avert this result, KKR negotiated a difficult recapitalization. KKR agreed to put $1.7 billion of additional equity capital into RJR and refinance the outstanding junk bonds.

Disaster was averted in the reset crisis, but competitor Philip Morris was relentless in attacking RJR on the pricing side, and the tobacco liability threat didn't die. Perhaps the only heroes of the RJR deal were Kravis and Roberts, who remained calm throughout and, when adversity hit, handled it with dexterity and dignity.

Eventually, KKR's investment was liquidated in an exchange for Borden stock at a low rate of profit. Ironically, after KKR sold, RJR stock rose as its prospects improved.

Teddy Forstmann and the Anti–Junk Bond Crusade

Teddy Forstmann and his partners at Forstmann Little were troubled by the junk-bond-fueled buyout wars sweeping the market. The RJR circus just reinforced their view. Forstmann was so troubled that he became an outspoken critic of junk bonds in the press and on the editorial pages. In the process, he earned a reputation on Wall Street as something of a Cassandra.

Forstmann had three principal complaints regarding junk-financed deals. First, he argued that many companies were being overleveraged. Heavy cash interest obligations were one part of the problem. In the typical LBO, a tough principal repayment schedule would be layered on top of interest payments. As a result, an LBO company had little margin for error.

Second, Forstmann argued that the easy credit provided in the junk bond market allowed financial buyers to bid unreasonable amounts for target companies. Junk bonds were mere "funny money" in Forstmann's eyes. For this reason, Forstmann Little, which on average bought two companies a year in the early 1980s, curtailed its efforts in the late 1980s, sitting on a good part of its $2.7 billion fund. When the firm did make an offer, it was often outbid by Drexel-financed acquirers. Perelman snatched Revlon away. Kravis took RJR Nabisco. To Forstmann, his competitors were using wampum with high risks of default.

Finally, Forstmann complained that junk bonds were an expensive capital source. Drexel and its competitors took an up-front percentage of any money it raised by underwriting junk bonds. They also typically demanded a piece of the equity in the issuer. Even once the capital was raised, junk bond investors charged relatively steep interest rates that ate into potential LBO returns.

Rather than rely on junk bonds for subordinated debt financing, Forstmann turned to the same pension funds that provide the lion's share of LBO equity. Starting in the late 1970s, Forstmann Little raised mezzanine debt funds as companions to its equity funds. The investors in the debt funds were promised a fixed return on the loans plus a portion of the equity upside. This proved to be an extremely lucrative combination—in the mid-1980s, the mezzanine funds were averaging total returns of roughly 25 percent a year.

The fund arrangement allowed Forstmann to commit debt capital extremely quickly. In addition, the current cash interest liability on the debt generally was 2 to 4 percentage points lower than on comparable junk bonds. The principal repayment schedule associated with the captive financing was similarly favorable. Moreover, Forstmann Little LBO companies benefited from greater flexibility because the debt would be issued by a Forstmann-controlled fund.

Theodore Forstmann

During the 1980s, Ted Forstmann and his partners matched the success of KKR, though on a smaller scale. Forstmann Little broke into the big time in 1984 with the purchase of Dr. Pepper. Observers tagged the $650 million purchase as too high; the deal earned the distinction as the 1984 LBO "most likely to fail." Within two years, Forstmann Little confounded the critics. The firm sold off some assets, then the remainder, netting more than eight times its investment.

The Dr. Pepper buyout and similar investments earned Forstmann Little's investors very high returns. As of 1996, Forstmann Little boasted 60 percent annual returns on invested equity and 20 percent on debt. Of course, competitors point out that it is more sensible to take a blended return.

The son of a wealthy industrialist who went bust, Forstmann graduated from Yale University and Columbia Law School. By his own admission, his performance in school was mediocre. He practiced as a lawyer for a few years, then worked at a number of Wall Street jobs. At the age of thirty-five, he was trying to broker deals on his own, but was fast running out of money.

Summing up his own background, Forstmann told a reporter, "I never went to business school. I was basically never in an investment banking firm worthy of mentioning. I've always been a guy who had ideas."

The LBO caught his fancy in the late 1970s. His younger brother Nick was working at KKR at the time. As a favor, Ted arranged a meeting between Henry Kravis and Gerald Ruttenberg, a president of an industrial company whom Ted had met in his early days as a dealmaker. Forstmann had heard of bootstrap acquisitions before, but had never done one. Ruttenberg liked the buyout idea, but wondered why he and Ted couldn't carry it out on their own. Forstmann jumped at the chance. With initial funding from Ruttenberg and his friends, Forstmann, his brother Nick and Brian Little set up their firm.

In those early days, Forstmann Little thrived by concentrating its efforts on performing the classic LBO deal, where "reasonable prices [were] paid for mature companies with steady cash flows and with dominant positions in industries that were less volatile than the economy."

Forstmann Little carved out its unique niche by targeting the pension funds. In the early days, Brian Little, who had a reputation as one of the nicest guys on Wall Street, charmed clients while Ted ran the shop. Eventually, Ted became more dominant and driven. Sleek and silver-haired, he dives right into the Forstmann Little investments personally. For example, when Gulfstream, a maker of corporate jets, was sputtering with indifferent sales, Forstmann became chairman and started moving sales along himself.

The Insider Trading Scandal

In May 1985, a compliance officer at Merrill Lynch in New York opened an anonymous letter from Caracas, Venezuela. The letter alleged that two brokers in the firm's Caracas office were engaging in insider trading. As it turned out, the letter set off a chain of events that resulted in the arrest of Drexel investment bankers Dennis Levine and Martin Siegel, and ultimately to guilty pleas on unrelated charges by Ivan Boesky and Michael Milken.

Levine was the first to fall. An affable fellow, he was regarded as a mediocre professional who lacked the analytical skill to be an effective deal strategist. He began his career at Citibank, but being on the inside of large deals was his dream. After several attempts, he finally landed a spot at Smith Barney. His jocular nature eventually paid off with a spot in the firm's M&A department.

Despite Levine's aggressive self-promotion, his superiors at Smith Barney ultimately were unimpressed with his abilities. They passed him over for promotion a few years after he joined the firm. Incensed, Levine moved to Lehman Brothers. His habit of paying cash for expensive meals and his flashy cars raised some eyebrows at the firm, but Levine prospered in a boom environment from his penchant for knowing deal stories. He joined Drexel in 1984 as part of the firm's push into M&A.

Of course, the source for many of Levine's tips turned out to be a ring of insiders he had cultivated to provide information. The loose circle of lawyers and investment bankers provided Levine tips on unfolding transactions. Levine also developed a relationship with arbitrageur Ivan Boesky. Under the arrangement, Levine agreed to provide tips to Boesky in exchange for a share of Boesky's trading profits.

This web began to unwind in 1986. Merrill Lynch, and later the SEC, had followed the anonymous letter of 1985 to an account under the name Mr. Diamond at a bank in the Bahamas. It later came out that Levine had opened the account in 1980 to conduct insider trading. Impatient for wealth and prestige, Levine had found what he saw as an easier road. The success of his trades, which were made by a bank executive through various brokers, lured the executive and a New York broker to begin mirroring Levine's trades on their own behalf. Eventually, the circle of people involved widened to the two brokers in Merrill Lynch's Caracas office.

In the spring, federal officials finally were able to crack the bank secrecy laws that hid Mr. Diamond's true identity. On May 12, 1986, Levine was arrested on charges of insider trading. The charges stemmed from his use of information on pending corporate takeovers, gleaned from his position as an M&A banker. Less than a month after the arrest, Levine pled guilty to four felonies and agreed to forfeit his $11.6 million in trading profits. Despite his downfall, Levine failed to see anything wrong with his trading. He likened his behavior to that of a worker in a deli who "take[s] home pastrami every night for free. It's the same with information on Wall Street."

PROFILE

Rudolph Giuliani

At the time of the insider trading scandal, Rudolph Giuliani was the United States attorney responsible for federal prosecutions in New York City. He had already earned a reputation as a bulldog prosecutor, primarily for his pursuit of the New York Mafia, and had demonstrated a thirst for publicity. When the SEC unearthed the Levine case, Giuliani and his staff turned their attention to insider trading.

Once incited, Giuliani's staff members pursued the new brand of criminals with zeal. They used broad racketeering statutes, which had been written to break the Mob, against defendants. As well, Giuliani made headlines by supporting longer prison sentences for those convicted of insider trading and a stricter definition of the insider trading law in order to eliminate any potential ambiguities.

Critics complained that Giuliani was engaged in a reign of terror designed to boost his own image and political career. They pointed to the constant press conferences and leaks to the news media regarding ongoing investigations. Giuliani's staff appeared to have adopted a strategy of using media pressure to force suspects to plea-bargain.

Even worse to civil libertarians, Giuliani seemed to delight in treating white-collar criminals with particularly draconian measures, even though his actual conviction record was mixed. In 1987, he had three arbitrageurs arrested—Tim Tabor, formerly of Kidder, Peabody, Richard Wigton, head of arbitrage at Kidder, and Robert Freeman, head of arbitrage at Goldman, Sachs. Tabor was arrested in the evening so that he would have to spend a night in jail. Wigton and Freeman were dragged off their trading floors, handcuffed and led away while forewarned television crews looked on. Two years later, Giuliani was forced to drop charges against the first two men. Freeman pled guilty to a single charge and was sentenced to four months' jail time.

In 1993, Giuliani was elected mayor of New York City, where he has achieved considerable popularity, and during his tenure the overall crime rate has, in fact, fallen. He won a sweeping victory for a second term in 1997.

Feeling the heat, Levine decided to cooperate with government prosecutors. He implicated the members of his information-gathering ring, all relatively minor figures in the takeover business. Then, in a stunning revelation, Levine also pointed a finger at Ivan Boesky. Boesky was a prominent figure, an arbitrageur who had made millions trading on takeover rumors. United States Attorney Rudolph Giuliani and his allies at the SEC salivated at the prospect of bringing Boesky down.

Unfortunately, Levine could not provide ironclad proof that Boesky had been trading on inside information. He did, however, lay out the tips he had provided to Boesky, which were a road map for authorities. They subpoenaed Boesky for records of all his trades.

As it turned out, Boesky was extremely vulnerable to the threats of prosecution. Not only had he traded on information from Levine, he also had other relationships with investment bankers. Most prominent were Michael Milken and Martin Siegel, the latter formerly at Kidder, Peabody before he joined Drexel. Boesky and his lawyers discounted the government's ability to build a case around Levine—who had previously lied under oath and had admitted to orchestrating his insider trading ring. But Boesky feared one of his other sources might make a deal with the government. He raced to cut a deal before it was too late.

On November 14, the SEC made the stunning announcement that Boesky had agreed to become a government witness. He would pay $100 million in fines and plead guilty to a single felony count. Giuliani and Gary Lynch, the head of enforcement at the SEC, thought the government had struck a tough bargain. However, shortly after the announcement, *The Wall Street Journal* reported that Boesky had made more than $200 million on tips from Levine alone.

Criticism mounted when it later came out that Boesky had been allowed to sell some of his firm's stock positions in advance of the announcement, which drove the price of many takeover stocks down. To some, this seemed like government-sanctioned insider trading. Furthermore, allowing Boesky to plead to just one count, as compared to Levine's four counts, seemed out of proportion to their relative wrongdoing. Boesky's three-year sentence—of which he served a bit more than half—seemed light in view of his wide-ranging involvement.

PROFILE

Ivan Boesky

Ivan Boesky was born on March 6, 1937, the son of a Russian immigrant milkman turned pub owner. He grew up in an upper-middle-class neighborhood in Detroit, Michigan. A hyperactive youth with a short attention span, Boesky jumped around a number of different high schools and colleges. Though he never graduated from college, he eventually earned a degree from the Detroit College of Law, which did not require an undergraduate degree for admission. Boesky married Seema Silberstein—the daughter of a wealthy real estate developer—at about the time he graduated from law school.

Intrigued by Wall Street, Boesky used his law degree to secure a position as a securities analyst, but found the work unappealing. His dissatisfaction led him to discover arbitrage, a business more in tune with his energetic nature and lust for quick results. After several false starts, brokerage firm Edwards & Hanley hired Boesky to do professional arbitrage work.

At Edwards & Hanley, Boesky was an overnight sensation. Like other arbitrageurs, Boesky typically bought on margin, which allowed him to take larger positions. Edwards & Hanley had modest capital, but Boesky nonetheless invested as much as $2 million in single situations. His tactics, however, grew too daring, and eventually contributed to the ruin of the firm. When Edwards & Hanley went out of business, Boesky opened his own arbitrage boutique—Ivan F. Boesky & Corporation. The development of his firm fortuitously coincided with the beginning of the takeover boom.

The new Boesky firm opened for business in late 1975, backed by $700,000 of his in-laws' money. Again, Boesky demonstrated a talent for the business. In the 1980s, Boesky made large sums by placing heavy bets on pending takeovers. He reportedly made $50 million on Getty stock when it was taken over by Texaco and $65 million on Chevron's purchase of Gulf.

Not all of Boesky's bets were winners. He lost considerable sums on the busted Cities Service and Phillips Petroleum takeovers in the middle 1980s—transactions which reportedly triggered his increased interest in inside information.

Information is the lifeblood of arbitrage. Before placing a large bet on a particular merger or acquisition, Boesky needed to develop a judgment that the transaction would proceed. Boesky cultivated the image of an expert information gatherer. In the heat of a contest, he would have people posted at courthouses, legislative hearings and companies' headquarters. Only later did it become apparent that his success had come at least partly by building a network of informants, eager to get cash payoffs for their tips.

With the help of Siegel and others, Boesky won far more often than he lost. By 1985, he was on *Forbes'* list of America's 400 wealthiest individuals. As Boesky became more successful, he thrilled in the attention. He set himself up as the icon of arbitrage, preaching the glories of greed as a mantra. While the exposure helped Boesky raise money, his practices invited severe criticism from his fellow risk arbitrageurs, who were horrified by his tactics.

In retrospect, Boesky's punishment was light. He was released from prison in April 1990.

Of course, the merit of the Boesky plea agreement also depended on Boesky's value as a witness. Once allied with the government, Boesky in turn implicated others, including both Siegel and Milken.

In February of 1987, Martin Siegel pled guilty to two felonies. His was perhaps the most troubling story to come out of the insider-trading scandal. Siegel was a golden boy, a capable professional with movie-star looks and an appealing personality. He had come to prominence at Kidder, Peabody & Co., where he built a reputation in takeover defense, promoting himself as the "Secretary of Defense." He moved to Drexel Burnham Lambert in 1986, where he was guaranteed a $3.5 million salary and a $2 million bonus.

Siegel's downfall stemmed from an earlier arrangement with Boesky. Kidder, Peabody was having a rocky time financially, and seemed in danger of being pushed to the edges of the M&A business. At the same time, Siegel felt pressure to maintain an expensive lifestyle. He had already developed a professional relationship with Boesky. In 1982, Boesky proposed a different kind of relationship. Siegel would pass tips on pending takeovers to Boesky, and Boesky would pay Siegel a "consulting" fee.

Siegel's first tip came sometime later that year. Boesky made $120,000 trading on the information. From then on, Siegel exchanged tips with Boesky in return for a share of Boesky's trading profits. Boesky made good on the deal by having messengers deliver suitcases full of $100 bills to Siegel in the lobby of Manhattan's Plaza Hotel. Siegel received between $700,000 and $800,000 in cash. Finally, in 1984, the pressure of dealing with Boesky got to Siegel. He stopped taking Boesky's calls. However, the damage had already been done.

Following Boesky's lead, Siegel plea-bargained his way out of serious jail time. He agreed to pay a $9 million penalty, keeping only his two residences and pension contributions, and ultimately was sentenced to a light two months in prison, even though the information he provided proved of dubious value. The main outgrowth of Siegel's cooperation were the flawed arrests of arbitrageurs Freeman, Wigton and Tabor.

Unlike Giuliani's other targets, Tabor, Wigton and Freeman refused to roll over. They asserted their innocence and prepared to fight the charges against them. Nine days before the trial was to begin, the government was forced to admit it was not ready. Then, in a highly unusual move, the charges against the three were dropped. Wigton and Tabor were not reindicted. Unwilling to admit complete defeat, the government pursued Freeman.

After fighting for two and a half years, Freeman pled guilty to a single charge of mail fraud and was sentenced to four months in prison. The charge related to a bizarre series of events. Before his arrest, Freeman had been head of arbitrage at Goldman, Sachs. Freeman had taken a large position in Beatrice during KKR's takeover of the company. At some point, rumors began to circulate that the deal was about to collapse. A failed deal would mean a big loss for Goldman, Sachs.

As was customary, Freeman called around the Street looking for confirmation. A fellow arb named Bernard "Bunny" Lasker told Freeman the deal was indeed in trouble. Freeman's next call was to Siegel, who had been talking to Freeman on and off for some time. Siegel was working for KKR on the deal. Freeman asked if the rumor relayed by Lasker was true. Siegel responded, "Your bunny has a good nose." Freeman promptly dumped his position. Of course, Siegel's information soon proved to be false. KKR's Beatrice deal went through. Freeman would have earned a big profit if he had held on.

The most significant personal fallout from the 1985 letter to Merrill Lynch was the 1989 indictment of Michael Milken on ninety-eight counts of mail fraud, securities fraud, tax evasion and racketeering. Milken eventually pled guilty to just six counts, none of which involved insider trading or stock manipulation.

Several of the counts related to stock parking arrangements with Boesky. These arrangements were designed to put companies in play or support the prices of Drexel clients' stock. In one case, Milken encouraged Boesky to buy stock in the Fischbach Corporation. Milken wanted to create the appearance that Boesky was after Fischbach so that a Drexel client would be freed from an agreement not to pursue Fischbach. As an inducement, Milken agreed to guarantee any losses Boesky might incur while he held the Fischbach stock.

Other charges against Milken related to an arrangement to charge one client slightly more for certain stock trades rather than taking that amount as commission, and to an arrangement to help a client evade taxes by creating current losses to be offset by guaranteed future gains.

Milken and his staff clearly broke a number of rules. However, while stock parking arrangements involved regulatory violations, they had never been the subject of criminal convictions. In past cases, the defendants had been permitted to plead guilty to lesser civil charges.

Ultimately, in an effort to make a statement against perceived Wall Street excesses and to pressure Milken to finger others, federal judge Kimba Wood sentenced Milken to a stiff ten years in prison. Wood later reduced Milken's sentence in 1992. He served twenty-four months in prison and forfeited over $1 billion to settle various criminal and civil charges.

Drexel Implodes

Allegations against Drexel as an institution began to surface soon after the Boesky plea bargain. For a time, the firm's management considered fighting the charges. However, in December 1988, Giuliani threatened to indict the firm on federal racketeering charges.

Drexel management was in a tight spot. If they fought the charges, legal proceedings might drag on for months, or even years. In the interim, the firm's clients likely would flee, fearing the associated uncertainty. The firm decided to settle and came to terms with the government.

Drexel agreed to plead guilty to six counts and to pay a $650 million fine, the largest ever for a securities violation. Three outside directors, appointed by the SEC, would be added to Drexel's board in an effort to address the fundamental problems with the culture of Drexel. The firm also agreed to place Milken on a leave of absence and withhold $200 million of his earnings for 1988. The settlement was a calculated gamble. Drexel management traded the short-term pain of the penalty, and the loss of the firm's star, for a chance at survival. As it turned out, the gamble failed to pay off.

Drexel survived through 1989, and actually had a number of successes. The firm raised $5 billion in a junk bond offering for KKR's purchase of RJR Nabisco. That single deal—a strong statement of the firm's continuing distribution capabilities—brought Drexel a fee of $250 million.

Yet, without Milken at the helm, Drexel began to unwind. The first hint of real trouble came in June 1989. Drexel was unable to refund $40 million of commercial paper for Integrated Resources. These short-term securities were used by Integrated to finance its working capital needs. Companies generally roll over commercial paper when it comes due, replacing the old paper with new. The failure to raise just $40 million for Integrated forced the company into default on $1 billion of junk bonds. Market observers wondered whether the failure would have happened with Milken still on the job. In the past, he had managed to find creative solutions to similar problems.

Drexel's lackluster defense of Integrated Resources becomes more understandable when seen in the context of the time. The firm was reeling. Its own credit rating was lowered to the point where it could not refund outstanding commercial paper. Still, to have any hope of survival, Drexel felt it had to defend its junk bond franchise. As the $200 billion junk bond market tanked, Drexel continued to act as a buyer of last resort. The firm's inventory of troubled securities grew to over $1 billion.

By the start of 1990, it was becoming clear that Drexel had been forced into a classic mistake—funding its long-term cash needs, primarily to carry its junk bond inventory, with short-term borrowings. Drexel was facing a major liquidity crisis and was on the brink of bankruptcy.

Fred Joseph, CEO of the firm, spent the fall and winter months looking for someone willing to put up the money needed to save Drexel. There was precedent for a rescue. E.F. Hutton had a near-death experience in 1987, only to be resuscitated by the coordinated efforts of the government and other financial institutions.

But when Joseph called around to other investment banks, none was willing to buy equity in Drexel, not even to gain the firm's once vaunted junk bond operation. The potential for liability was just too great. Furthermore, there was little goodwill toward Drexel on the Street. The other big investment banks had been bullied by Drexel over the years. Now they turned their backs on the former upstart.

As Drexel struggled, its client base evaporated. Employees began to sense trouble and circulated résumés. The firm lost a number of stars. Rumors flew around the Street about the impending failure of the once-proud firm.

Joseph turned to the government. He kept the heads of the Federal Reserve, SEC and Treasury Department informed about Drexel's problems. The hope was that the government would lead a rescue effort. However, Federal Reserve Chairman Alan Greenspan and Treasury Secretary Nicholas Brady declined to act.

Greenspan and Brady apparently decided the financial markets could withstand the failure of Drexel. There would be no government bailout. In fact, on the evening of February 12, the Fed and the Treasury told Joseph that Drexel would either have to file for bankruptcy or go into liquidation.

The next day, February 13, 1990, Drexel announced its bankruptcy.

Tough Times

Drexel was not alone in facing difficulties in 1989 and 1990. The second half of 1989 ushered in a rocky period for the financial markets in general. The RJR Nabisco deal was a high-water mark for the 1980s buyout boom. In the remaining months of 1989, a series of negative events rocked the financial world. Tough times followed, a dramatic shakeout period during which many financial buyers struggled for economic survival.

Milken's 1989 indictment and resignation from Drexel were major blows to the junk bond market on which so many financial buyers relied for liquidity. A further blow came in October 1989 when a management buyout of United Airlines deal fell apart.

UAL, the airline's parent company, had announced a $6.75 billion employee-led buyout only a month earlier. The United pilots had agreed to team up with management and British Airways to buy the airline. The deal was to be funded with cash from British Airways and management, and wage concessions from the pilots. In addition, $7.2 billion would be borrowed by the company to fund both the deal and operating cash flow needs.

Reflecting the turmoil in the junk bond market, UAL intended to raise the money entirely from a syndicate of banks led by Citicorp and Chase Manhattan. These two lead banks promised $3 billion, and agreed to raise the remaining $4.2 billion from other banks.

However, only a few weeks after the deal was first announced, Citicorp and Chase gave the market a jolt. The two banks could not raise the additional $4.2 billion. The major Japanese banks, to which they had looked for most of the money, had blanched at the deal's financial and fee structure. The buyout collapsed in disarray. Both the stock and junk bond markets reacted sharply downward.

The problems in the credit markets were exacerbated by a nascent economic recession. Companies struggled at the operational level, and a number of junk-financed LBOs slipped into default. KKR was in the market attempting to refinance $624 million of debt issued by its Hillsborough Holding Company. The Southland Corporation, owner of the 7-Eleven chain, was on the ropes after a 1987 buyout. Gibbons, Green & van Amerongen was unable to refinance a $450 million bridge loan related to its purchase of Ohio Mattress, popularly known on the Street as the "burning bed" bridge. As the economy slumped further into 1990, bad news kept coming. KKR's re-funding crisis at RJR Nabisco opened the year.

For a time, the credit markets were almost nonexistent. Banks were extremely hesitant when it came to issuing any new loans. The market for new junk bond issuances dried up almost completely. Even the secondary market for junk bonds almost disappeared.

Financial buyers were particularly vulnerable to the credit crunch that ensued. Capital was the oxygen that gave life to the leveraged acquisition structure. Moreover, in the late 1980s, the larger financial buyers had holdings to match the conglomerates of the 1960s.

When tough times came, the financial buyers were forced to pull back, to retrench. KKR was consumed for a time with reshuffling the capital structure at RJR Nabisco. Forstmann Little had its problems with Gulfstream. Others faced similar difficulties, compounded by the fact that the market for corporate control was relatively quiet, making it extremely difficult to sell portfolio companies at a favorable price.

Retailing was another extremely troubled industry of the late 1980s. Robert Campeau's Federated and Allied Stores chains collapsed into bankruptcy in 1990. Carter Hawley Hale followed suit the next February. Macy's, which had been taken private by CEO Edward Finkelstein in a 1986 LBO, lingered on life support for several years. Finally, in 1992, the chain also entered Chapter 11.

Bankruptcy did not spell the end for most of the troubled retailers. They possessed valuable brand names which, despite tough competition from discounters, remain strong. After difficult years of restructuring and debt reduction, the retail industry has come back.

The problem for Finkelstein, Campeau and other retailers was not that they overpaid. Indeed, in hindsight today, these late-1980s deals were good asset values. Rather, they didn't finance well, taking on too much debt. Campeau funded his Federated acquisition with a $1 billion short-term bridge loan. The granting of this bridge loan allowed First Boston to replace Wasserstein Perella in the future as adviser, which they demanded. Then First Boston correctly advised Campeau to refinance his bridge or sell assets. Campeau balked when he had the opportunity to take on long-term financing because he thought he could get better terms later. He also became enamored of several assets, such as Bloomingdale's, and refused to divest them as part of a previously planned delevering of the company. As a result, Federated had a classic mismatched book. The short-term Federated and Allied Stores debt was financing long-term obligations.

A highly leveraged capital structure of this sort is particularly precarious in retailing, a cyclical business financed by flighty trade debt. When the economy stalled in 1989 and 1990, retail sales fell off. Then, as is common in retailing, suppliers began to get jittery and called in their trade credits. The stores used these credits as a crucial source of funding for inventory. This calling of trade credits accelerated the downward spiral.

The Legacy

The abrupt pricing of the 1980s bubble led to an explosion of common wisdom about the mergers process: merger deals were overpriced, junk bonds dead and the stock market too frothy. In time, all of these insights would be proven wrong in the remarkable 1990s.

The Merits of Mergers: 6
The Good, the Bad
and the Ugly

*"[Should] . . . large corporations . . . be treated like
artichokes and simply torn apart without any
regard for employees, communities, or customers,
solely in order to pay off speculative debt?"*

Felix G. Rohatyn,
investment banker and diplomat

During the 1980s, the debate about the merits of mergers raged
not only in New York and Washington, but also in towns like
Bartlesville, Oklahoma. For Bartlesville in particular, the issue hit
home on February 22, 1985.

Rain lashed the city's streets that day, and the unpleasant weather
matched the mood among Bartlesville's 38,000 residents. In the coffee shops and at the meat counters, everyone focused on the same
thing. For nearly three months, the town had been hunkered down
in what many saw as a life-or-death fight. Now, in an auditorium
filled with lawyers, shareholders and bankers—out-of-town folk—
Bartlesville's fate would be decided.

"Corporate raiders" had targeted Phillips Petroleum, the economic anchor of this small company town forty miles north of Tulsa.
In Bartlesville, Phillips was a whole lot more than a faceless corpo-

ration—it was the heart of the town. The company employed about 7,700 of the town's residents, a fifth of the community. Countless other small business owners depended on some of that Phillips money trickling into their cash registers each year.

Everything came down to this shareholder vote. The Phillips shareholders were being asked to approve a management plan designed to turn back the raiders. If Phillips lost the vote and was taken over, many Bartlesville residents feared the entire town would be shuttered. Bartlesville would become a run-down, post-industrial shell.

The last few months had been a stressful, roller-coaster ride. First came T. Boone Pickens, the flamboyant independent oilman who had been shaking up Big Oil for the past several years—making a hefty profit for his Mesa Petroleum in the process. Late in 1984, Pickens, his company and a group of investors had bought up a large chunk of Phillips stock. Pickens argued that the company's management had been wasting shareholders' money.

Management disagreed with Pickens' assessment, but was over a barrel. If Phillips didn't get rid of Boone, another more powerful company might bid. Phillips bought Pickens' stock for $53 a share and paid his $25 million of expenses. At the same time, the company would buy back 38 percent of its stock in the market and carry out a recapitalization designed to give shareholders the same $53 a share in value.

Boone had, once again, "greenmailed" a company to buy out his stock position for cash, although the recapitalization was a thin attempt at covering his tracks. The widely held view was that the securities offered by Phillips to the rest of its shareholders were worth less than $45 per share. The deal was announced just before Christmas, and Bartlesville breathed a sigh of relief.

Other shareholders, however, were not pleased, especially speculators who were betting on a takeover of Phillips at a higher price. Carl Icahn—one of the leading speculators—took up the assault on

Phillips. Icahn announced he would lobby shareholders to reject the Phillips recapitalization. He instead suggested a $55-a-share leveraged buyout and Bartlesville was back on the ropes. Still, as a local car dealer told a reporter, "We're tired, but we're not ready to quit."

The fight over Phillips, first between Pickens and management, then between Icahn and management, centered on two very different images. On the offense, Pickens and Icahn cast their actions as a campaign for shareholder rights. Shareholders, they argued, owned Phillips, and management ought to do whatever was necessary to maximize shareholder value. Instead, by their reckoning, management had been depleting Phillips' holdings of natural resources while living a perk-filled life, with private planes and fishing lodges—all at the considerable expense of shareholders. The insurgents purported to speak for all shareholders, including retirees and pensioners, the little people who indirectly owned a majority of Phillips through institutional money managers. For their sake, Phillips was in need of restructuring, with or without the blessing of incumbent management.

Ranged against this image, management had the people of Bartlesville. The fight for Phillips was about jobs and community, about preserving the American middle class from grasping, money-hungry financiers. Sure, the company's stock price was down a bit. But management was working hard to correct the situation. They just needed a couple years, time to take the long-term view. Of course, that would be impossible without freedom from Pickens and Icahn, "speculators" out to make a fast buck.

This latter vision certainly carried the day in and around Bartlesville. "I doubt that I could be elected mayor of Bartlesville," Pickens joked to a television reporter. And Icahn was no more loved. In fact, a few days before the stockholder meeting on that rainy February day, people had gathered for a pep rally of sorts. They stood around a bonfire and burned proxy solicitations from Icahn. "Burn, Icahn, burn," they chanted in unison.

But the shareholders, not the town, had the final vote. By the time of the vote, Phillips stock was held mostly by institutions and arbitrageurs—an unsentimental lot who wanted to keep the company in play. A majority voted against the recapitalization.

The company scurried in desperation to placate Icahn and his fellow-traveling institutional friends. Finally, Phillips came up with a sweeter but riskier recapitalization plan. The new package of securities offered was valued by the Street in the $53 to $56 range. Icahn withdrew his tender offer, but only after Phillips also agreed to pay him $25 million for expenses.

Bartlesville again celebrated. The barbarians had been turned back at the inner wall, but at a steep cost to Phillips' balance sheet. Ultimately, the town would not emerge unscathed. To service its debt, Phillips planned to cut its workforce by 10 percent and sell off assets.

PROFILE

T. Boone Pickens

The life of Boone Pickens is full of irony. Oil was in his blood from the start. Born and raised in the small town of Holdenville, he grew up in the oil patch of the Oklahoma panhandle. His father was a land man, an itinerant broker who put together deals between farmers and oil companies.

Coming out of college with a geology degree, Pickens got his start in the oil business at Phillips Petroleum, the same company he would later bring to its knees. He chafed in the world of Big Oil. Within four years, he had set out on his own as an independent oilman. He founded Mesa Petroleum in 1964 and built an initial $2,500 investment into a company with $400 million in sales. By the early 1980s, he was a rich man. Yet, by the standards of the oil business, Pickens was a fairly small player.

That all changed when he realized oil companies were under-valued relative to the worth of their proven reserves. Further-more, his experience working for Phillips had left Pickens with a lack of respect for the bureaucratic tendencies of Big Oil. He felt the companies were dramatically undermanaged. Executives were more concerned with perks than performance.

Pickens may not have been the first to recognize the value of prospecting for oil on Wall Street, but he was certainly one of the most enthusiastic promoters of the practice. Though he never succeeded in actually buying a major oil company, his early hos-tile tenders were nonetheless successful. Following the Phillips model, Mesa profited in each case when a third-party suitor ap-peared.

In the process, Mesa became the "terror of the oil patch." Pickens soon became caught up in his campaign and the publicity it brought. He founded a group called the United Shareholders Association to lobby against entrenched management and for better governance provisions.

Then, in the ultimate irony, Pickens himself became a target of shareholder dissent. Mesa had a miserable performance starting in the late 1980s, largely because Pickens made a bad bet on nat-ural gas prices. He fought to keep control, but, in 1996, he was forced out of Mesa by a group of dissidents.

The Merger Movement

The press understandably loved the battle for Phillips. It offered such contrasting images: Boone Pickens, a direct descendant of Daniel Boone, fighting for the "little guy," the twenty-four-hour prayer vigils in Bartlesville, the children with heart-shaped Phillips balloons standing in the rain outside the shareholder meeting, the local women who brought "I love Phillips" cookies to a meeting in

New York City. The pictures and stories crystallized opposing views about the wave of mergers and acquisitions sweeping over the oil business, and America in general.

By now, the shibboleths have become familiar. Are mergers good because they restructure inefficient companies or allow good companies to continue to grow? Or do they strip-mine American communities for the benefit of Wall Street profiteers? Do mergers benefit or harm shareholders? The intensity of this debate flares whenever the periodic merger cycle booms. In fact, the discussion is usually clouded more by rhetoric than elucidated by penetrating thought.

A key problem with the quality of the debate is that the protagonists are usually self-interested advocates, proselytizing a point of view. In the 1980s labor unions and target corporations joined in an unholy alliance. Together, they had public relations and lobbying firms machine-gunning the deal process. A lot of that invective is still found in derivative press accounts. To stir up the political fires, pressure was focused on constituents who feared the loss of their jobs.

On the other hand, the investment banks led by Morgan Stanley went ahead and hired McKinsey & Co. and other consultants and their own string of lobbyists to defend the deal process. The politicians were more than pleased. They received donations from all and did very little.

Truth also is obscured by the fact that the M&A databank is itself defective as a basis for analysis. The temptation is to use anecdotal information: Ling went under, Macy's went bankrupt, RJR didn't work for KKR and so on. The stories are colorful and often funny, but they don't compel the conclusions for which they are cited.

However, with all their limitations, it is useful to summarize the arguments for and against mergers, first those from proponents:

- Mergers and acquisitions provide specific economic benefits;

- An active market for corporate control motivates incumbent management to act in the interest of shareholders;

- Mergers and acquisitions maximize overall shareholder wealth;

- Economic activity as a whole is benefited by the active acquisition and divestiture marketplace, which allows young companies to be bought and mature companies to adapt to changing circumstances; and

- The system of corporate change through mergers is inherently integrated into our capital markets system, which is the envy of the world.

Economic Benefits for the Target Company

Managers involved in a merger or acquisition, as well as takeover proponents, generally project economic benefits to justify such transactions. Particular benefits include enhanced operating and financial efficiency, or the need for critical mass and sheer size.

Operating Efficiencies   The combination of two companies into one presents the opportunity to achieve economies of scale, a common source of merger-related economic benefits. Such savings typically result from the elimination of redundant overhead or capacity, allowing the combined firm to service customers more efficiently.

For example, enhanced operating efficiency is often given as the reason behind bank mergers. Chemical Bank's 1991 acquisition of Manufacturers Hanover suggests why. At the time the deal was announced, the two banks projected $650 million in annual cost savings from reducing duplicative overhead. When the dust settled, the new Chemical had shed overlapping branches, cut back-office staff and reduced marketing expenses. The annual cost savings at the end of the day actually totaled more than $750 million. The new company did so well that it was poised for a similar combination, the recent merger with Chase, attaining similar benefits. Driven by these cost-cutting combinations, Chemical's (now Chase's) stock price has zoomed.

Obviously, not all attempts at reducing total costs through merger succeed. Meshing two complicated organizations into one can be incredibly complex. There may well often be economies of scale, the benefits of sheer size, but the reverse can happen as well, diseconomies of size. Of course, the real difficulty is that these efficiencies cost jobs in the short term.

Financial Efficiencies Financial scale is also a source for merger-related efficiencies. Many academics argue that such efficiencies in theory should not exist, but anecdotal evidence suggests otherwise. In the early 1990s, for example, small and medium-size firms had incredible problems trying to raise capital. The first problem was the expense. Banks charge a premium to smaller firms as compared to their larger competitors.

Money is not only expensive during crises; it may be unavailable. In times of really tight money, lenders will take care of the needs of larger firms first. The public market, which lately has been accessible to small companies, periodically dries up, as it did in the early 1970s. Indeed, the cyclical lack of money for financing results in a larger firm having more staying power in the face of adversity than a smaller concern. Unfortunately, even a well-managed small firm may find itself insolvent in a cash crunch.

Academics have argued that institutional investors should be able to get the diversification benefits of investing in larger firms by buying securities of many different smaller firms, and, therefore, money should not be scarce. Maybe so, but the world does not seem to work that way when money is short. Institutions are inclined to purchase securities in large blocks, and in smaller firms such an investment could be illiquid. Of course, when the public market is hot, there are lots of sources of liquidity. However, when the public market is cold, the only way for a small firm owned by a group of investors to achieve financing or liquidity is to sell out to another corporation.

The Merger Market and Management Incentives

The possibility of being taken over can also act as a necessary curb on management. The specter of runaway executives managing inefficient firms with no shareholder control has haunted academics. In the 1930s, Adolph A. Berle and Gardiner C. Means charged that in the modern corporation ownership and control were becoming separate: the shareholders bear the financial risk but the professional managers control the company. Disciples of Berle and Means for the next fifty years continued to rip into the performance and responsibility of America's managers.

The concept is that in large, publicly held companies, each individual investor has little incentive to monitor management carefully. Each individual investor likely will have a diversified portfolio and may have only a small portion of his net worth invested in a single corporation. In addition, even if an investor has the motivation and the time to follow a particular company, he has little power to effect change. Rather, a dissident investor must lobby a large group of fellow shareholders in order to build a sufficient base of support to challenge management. Such an endeavor is usually very costly, especially relative to the size of the dissident investor's holdings.

From the perspective of hostile takeover proponents, the situation recognized by Berle and Means has practical implications. First, ineffective managers have little incentive to perform and face few repercussions as a result of poor results, barring extreme crisis. Second, absent self-imposed restraint, managers have little reason to curb expensive perks. The saga of Ross Johnson is the critics' favorite. F. Ross Johnson was the flamboyant CEO of RJR Nabisco at the time it was purchased in 1989 by KKR. At shareholders' expense, RJR Nabisco maintained an "air force" of corporate jets, twenty-four country club memberships, and numerous sports stars on retainer as expensive "consultants."

Takeovers may address these two concerns. The mere possibility that an outsider will bid for corporate control forces management to be less complacent about poor results and limit perks. Moreover, takeovers provide a vehicle actually to oust particularly bad management.

Shareholder Wealth Effects of Mergers

Mergers also may make sense based on a simple dollars-and-cents analysis, by putting extra money in shareholders' pockets. Shareholders in target companies on average gain a considerable premium from selling their shares in a takeover, roughly 33 percent over the years but varying considerably in particular years depending on the pace of the takeover market. However, perhaps these gains could have been achieved anyway if the shareholders had not sold out, and the evidence is less clear regarding any benefits to acquiring shareholders.

Mergers and Economic Flexibility

Mergers also may have broader positive impacts. The ability to react to change through mergers and acquisitions may help to keep the American economic system from becoming sclerotic. Economic circumstances change over time. Change both creates new opportunities and makes old approaches obsolete. Mergers allow companies to respond quickly by shifting resources, reshaping our economy in the process. The pace and scope of change is fantastic. In the 1980s, for example, more than one third of all companies in the Fortune 500 were merged with other companies or taken private.

The importance of economic flexibility can be seen in comparing recent American experience with the French experience. America went through a painful recessionary period in the early 1990s. Companies cut jobs and slashed overhead. Now the American economy is performing well and companies have enjoyed record profitability. Innovative technologies and approaches are being developed on a wide-ranging scale.

France, on the other hand, is mired in an economic funk. The country suffers nearly 13 percent unemployment. State-owned enterprises are operating at massive deficits. Yet the country appears unable to react. Attempts to cut costs are greeted with labor unrest and the proposed sale of moribund state-owned enterprises to foreign entities is difficult.

It would be overly simplistic to say that an active merger market is the key differentiating factor between the United States and France. However, mergers and acquisitions may be one piece to the puzzle, providing an effective mechanism for economic change.

Mergers and the Capital Markets

This raises a related point. America's capital markets are the envy of the world. Each year billions of dollars are funneled into new ventures by private investors and large companies. Of course, this level of investment would not continue if the investors could not receive some return on their investment. Stock offerings are one mechanism for recovering investment; the availability of the merger or acquisition route is another. Even if a company does go public, most public venture companies are eventually bought. This merger takeout on an investment is an important motivation in starting and putting capital into a small business in the first place. If it were overrestricted, there might well be a disincentive for future venture capital transactions.

Against the Tide

Mergers have long been the target of populist rancor. The outraged reaction to J.P. Morgan's turn-of-the-century U.S. Steel amalgamation was a foreshadowing of the future. One critic, Yale president Arthur Hadley, an economist, argued that the continuing concentration of corporate power, if unchecked, would lead to the appearance of "an emperor in Washington within twenty-five years." *The Wall Street Journal* expressed "uneasiness" about the risky capital structure Morgan and his team had devised. "Would U.S. Steel ever be able to pay a dividend?" the newspaper wondered.

Then there were the phenomenal fees. Wall Street interests earned $57.5 million (somewhere north of $1 billion in today's dollars) for underwriting the issuance of various U.S. Steel securities. How could the mere reshuffling of corporate ownership earn so much money for so few? Unethical or dishonest practices were suspected.

Today's critics raise very similar issues. They put forward the following basic arguments:

- Mergers and acquisitions have induced the overleveraging of corporate America, with disastrous consequences;

- The premiums paid to target shareholders in corporate takeovers derive from inappropriate wealth redistribution;

- Management self-interest drives most strategic corporate acquisitions; and

- By and large, mergers destroy rather than create value and have serious social costs.

Naturally, proponents of corporate takeovers have attempted to counter these arguments. A look at the evidence objectively results in a statistical quagmire. There is a lot of rhetoric but few compelling facts.

The Overleveraging of America

According to takeover opponents, as the 1980s came to a close, America was drowning in a rising tide of speculative debt. People like Carl Icahn and Boone Pickens, with the help of funds raised in the junk bond market by Michael Milken and Drexel Burnham Lambert, were making assaults on some of the largest bastions of the Fortune 500. Meanwhile, Henry Kravis and his partners at KKR were taking public companies private in highly leveraged transactions.

When the 1980s merger wave picked up steam, so did the criticism of leverage. In a newspaper op-ed piece, investment banker Nicholas Brady, who later became treasury secretary under George Bush, warned of dire consequences. Under the heading "Equity Is Lost in Junk-Bondage," Brady predicted that "speculative, highly leveraged financing techniques involving junk takeover bonds, if unchecked, will leave misery in their wake."

Corporate executives, many of whom experienced firsthand the power of leverage when threatened with takeover, also complained. The campaign was carried out under the auspices of the Business Roundtable, a big-business lobbying group. Its spokesman, Andrew Sigler, the CEO of Champion International, called leveraged acquisitions "one of the most destructive phenomena of the twentieth century." Fred Hartley, CEO of Unocal (one of Boone Pickens' targets), concurred: "What this all comes down to is simply withdrawing the warm blood of equity and replacing it with the cold water of debt."

The debt-based criticism of takeovers has taken hold in the public consciousness. For example, in the 1980s, Marty Lipton, the dean of takeover defense lawyers, was able to play to the grandstands with his invectives against "Bust-up, junk bond deals" as management buyout specialist Ted Forstmann pilloried Henry Kravis for his leveraged deals. Fortune magazine reached the following verdict on the "deal decade" of the 1980s:

> Too often the debt-driven deals imposed suffocating interest charges and repayment schedules on once solid businesses. Scores of companies, unable to withstand this year's [1991] brief and mild recession, have defaulted in record numbers on their junk bond payments or have fled behind the shield of Chapter 11. Junk holders have watched a lot of their paper crumple in

value. . . . Turning corporations into Flying Wallendas is not what the U.S. economy needs.

A few years later, a *Business Week* cover story compared the "debt-laden" leveraged buyouts of the 1980s to the "thoroughly discredited" conglomerate mergers of the 1960s.

However, notwithstanding the popular appeal of the antidebt message, revisionists have begun to attack the underlying claims. Specific examples of companies taking on an excessive debt load can be identified, particularly in hindsight. However, some observers counter that average debt levels compared to market values or cash flow were actually declining or stable during the 1980s, a fact obscured by the headlines regarding major corporate bankruptcies.

Economist and law professor Daniel Fischel, for example, argues "there was no dramatic increase in corporate leverage during the 1980s." Fischel and others use market statistics to make this point. While companies added a good deal of debt to their balance sheets in the 1980s, they also experienced a considerable growth in market value. This growth outpaced the additions to debt. So, when calculated on a market-value basis, the ratio of debt to assets for the average U.S. company actually declined from a high of 37 percent in 1974 to 35 percent in 1978, and then to 30 percent in the years 1984 through 1988.

A large majority of the debt added to American balance sheets in the 1980s was taken on by companies in stable industries with predictable cash flows. Interest expense as a percentage of total cash flow for companies in risky, cyclical industries actually declined during the decade. Of course, mistakes were made. Overexuberance crept into the junk bond market after 1986 and the quality of new issues declined. When recession hit at the end of the decade, default rates increased.

The biggest weakness in the overleverage argument is that it applies only to financial player buyouts—not acquisitions by strategic partners, which account for the preponderance of 1990s M&As. With regard to most of the major deals that blew up, the deals themselves weren't bad; the use of short-term borrowing to cover long-term obligations was a mismatch.

Furthermore, as the market perceives debt in deals as more risky, financing will be harder to obtain, a natural protection against long-term abuse. Even with this effect, the overall risky-finance market is booming, and the allure of investing in leveraged buyout funds is higher than ever. The market clearly doesn't buy the concept that leveraged deals are bad.

According to critics, though, high levels of takeover-induced indebtedness have several unattractive side effects. These include an increased likelihood of bankruptcy, cost cutting that displaces workers and disrupts communities, and a management focus on the short term that leads to reduced competitiveness.

Bankruptcy Effects   Former SEC chairman John Shad, before he went to work at Drexel Burnham, stated the first criticism in a widely publicized 1984 speech: "The more leveraged takeovers and buyouts today, the more bankruptcies tomorrow." Mired in his fight with Pickens, Fred Hartley of Unocal used more apocalyptic imagery. "This speculative binge," he warned, "this chain letter, must eventually collapse, leaving wreckage of ruined companies, lost jobs, reduced U.S. oil production, failed banks and savings and loans, and government bailouts, not to mention unemployment and empty buildings." Takeovers, according to Hartley and others, allow fast-buck financiers to play high-risk games with America's big companies.

This vision gained validity during the early 1990s. Several major companies—Federated, Macy's, Revco, TWA, among others—that had been involved in highly leveraged transactions sank into bankruptcy. Moreover, in 1991, *Fortune* magazine reviewed the status of the forty-one companies that had been featured on its "Deals of the

Year" lists between 1985 and 1990. While nineteen companies had managed to pay down their debt, twenty-two were treading water or had added even more debt. One of the twenty-two had defaulted on outstanding bonds, three were in bankruptcy, two had been restructured out of court and one was liquidated.

Yet an active merger market can be a powerful source of economic rejuvenation. More often than not the target companies of the 1980s were troubled long before any takeover. The fact that some attempts were unsuccessful should be unsurprising. As Icahn put it during a 1985 congressional hearing, "Did any raider take over the railroads? And yet these companies had to be closed down. . . . Thousands and thousands of people, indeed a whole section of this country, has been closed down . . . not because raiders came in but because raiders did not come in."

Some academics point out that the frequency of failure, not the fact that some firms failed, should be the yardstick for measuring the success or failure of takeovers. Fischel's view is that the bankruptcy argument is nothing more than a red herring that relies on a few sensational failures to discredit the entire merger movement.

Community Impact   In addition to the bankruptcy issue, critics point to a second side effect of high leverage: companies with a high debt load are forced to close plants and cut jobs to meet interest payments. While such cutbacks may benefit the few investors who hold company stock, on a broader level, some find the associated social cost unacceptable. Stated in sensational fashion, the shorthand for this argument is that mergers result in "the strip-mining of communities."

These are the concerns that animated Bartlesville, Oklahoma, during the 1984–85 fight for Phillips Petroleum. It did not matter how often Boone Pickens—by now an adoptive Texan—professed in his drawl, "I'm from Holdenville," a little town just south of Bartlesville. Nor did it matter that he claimed to have no plans to move the company from Bartlesville. Residents remembered well what had happened at Cities Service, another Oklahoma company Pickens had targeted. The company had avoided selling out to Pickens only by agreeing to be acquired by Occidental Petroleum. In the aftermath, Cities Service's 22,500 employees had been reduced to 4,000.

Like Bartlesville, organized labor was strident in its opposition to takeovers, presumably on the basis of feared job losses. Lane Kirkland of the AFL-CIO lambasted "corporate raids" as "an outrage and a bloody scandal." By his estimate, mergers cost 90,000 union members their jobs during the 1980s. Such cutbacks, merger opponents argued, often had painful collateral effects beyond the few hundred, or few thousand, jobs lost. Entire communities suffered.

The dislocations from plant closings and layoffs struck a chord and generated political rumblings. In the 1988 presidential election, plant closings and layoffs became a political issue. Legislation was passed to require sixty days notice for certain closings.

The attention given to the layoffs that follow mergers is understandable. Naturally, when an entire plant with thousands of employees is closed as the result of a merger, the press and politicians pay attention. However, the overall employment effect of takeovers is, like most empirical questions surrounding the social impact of mergers, subject to debate. A 1989 government study found that less than 5 percent of major layoffs were related to a change in corporate control. Another study found that employment actually increased slightly at a group of companies involved in LBOs between 1980 and 1986. The impact of the downsizing of major corporations in the 1980s clearly overshadowed the effect of mergers.

Whatever the true numbers are, takeover proponents make an additional point about layoffs and restructurings. This goes back to Carl Icahn's congressional testimony. He and others have argued that mergers serve as a necessary catalyst to change. Or, as Michael Jacobs puts it in his book *Short-Term America:*

For a nation to be competitive, it is vital that labor—like capital—is deployed efficiently. Some layoffs may be appropriate if they involve nonproductive workers, or workers in nonproductive business units. In this sense, LBOs may expedite the painful but necessary process of restructuring noncompetitive or declining businesses by laying off unnecessary workers.

From this perspective, a vital and active merger market may be crucial to the ongoing evolution of a vibrant economy. Indeed, proponents argue that the health of the American economy versus the European economy in the 1990s was an outgrowth of the fact that our economy adjusted to reality earlier—the downsizing already had taken place.

Perhaps the biggest problem is a conceptual confusion. Many people include in the jobs-lost calculation the employees of subsidiaries sold by an acquirer. Of course, these jobs are not lost to the economy.

The Short-Term View Another major charge is that the need to pay down debt has a stultifying effect that leads to reduced investment in research, development and capital improvements.

The American news media repeated this shibboleth throughout the 1980s. A *Forbes* magazine story called the practice "mortgaging the future." "When companies start worrying about sharks," the story began, "practically the last thing they care about is tomorrow. As a result, one of the first items to go in corporate restructurings is the R&D budget."

People in the antitakeover camp label such behavior "managing for the short term," which they identify as a major cause of America's perceived lack of competitiveness in the 1980s. For example, Andrew Sigler made the point for the Business Roundtable: "This kind of game-playing imposes short-term attitudes and strategies on companies which are just the opposite of what is needed if this country is to remain competitive."

Empirical research on post-deal R&D and capital spending is generally inconclusive. The market price of companies that announce "strategic investments" with a projected long-term payoff appears to be slightly positive, suggesting that the market actually rewards managing for the long term. Obviously, whole industries such as biotech have been spawned by the market's belief in the worth of long-term development expenditures.

The real issue seems to be whether the market believes the management as to the wisdom of its investment. Some studies have found measurable cuts in strategic spending following takeovers, but the aggregate numbers were low and the definition of research and development is ambiguous. In fact, companies involved in takeovers and buyouts in the 1980s tended to be in industries with little emphasis on R&D. According to an SEC study, 77 percent of the companies involved in going-private transactions during the 1980s reported no R&D spending in the prior year.

Furthermore, critics seem to ignore that the existence of the merger market increases R&D at start-ups. Mergers are one take out of the venture capital process.

Wealth Redistribution

Critics also doubt whether takeovers in fact create wealth. Rather, critics claim, the premiums paid to target company stockholders represent a wealth transfer, not wealth creation, and have little if any social utility. In particular, critics have identified bondholders and the government (in the form of the federal treasury) as possible sources for the premiums paid to existing target shareholders. An additional possible wealth transfer—from stockholders to management—has also been singled out for concern.

Bondholders   Bondholders, and to a lesser extent preferred stockholders, complain that the premiums paid to common stockholders come at their expense.

On several occasions at least, the decrease in bond values triggered by a takeover was significant. The leveraged buyout of RJR Nabisco is perhaps the most cited example. Prior to the announcement of the deal, RJR Nabisco had outstanding A-rated bonds. The bonds qualified as investment grade, and were held largely by insurance companies and other institutional investors. This all changed when the deal was announced. The bonds were downgraded to BB, below investment grade, becoming fallen angels in the lingo of the market. As a result, they lost as much as 15 percent of their value.

Naturally, RJR Nabisco's bondholders were furious at the sudden turn of events. Metropolitan Life Insurance Company—holding a paper loss of $40 million on RJR Nabisco bonds—ultimately filed suit, arguing the company had made an implied promise not to do anything that would dramatically alter its credit rating. Metropolitan Life lost the case. Some creditors began to demand provisions that gave them the right to receive their principal back upon the occurrence of a takeover-related downgrading, but the concept has not had widespread support.

The Tax Man   The tax man is another potential victim of a negative wealth transfer. At the height of the 1980s merger wave, anti-takeover politicians and critics were fond of harping on this point. Mergers, they argued, took money out of the federal and state treasuries, money which was used to pay premiums to stockholders and profits to dealmakers and their financial backers.

The main source of complaint is that leveraged buyouts take advantage of the tax deductibility of interest payments. By increasing a company's debt load, a takeover can reduce the company's tax liability, sometimes to zero. But this analysis is incomplete. The target company in an acquisition is not the only relevant taxpayer. Individual shareholders who sell their stock, lenders receiving interest, all provide offsetting tax revenue.

Target Stockholders to Management　In management-led take-overs or marriages, another kind of wealth transfer has been singled out as troubling—from existing shareholders to management (and any financial allies). The perceived conflict of interest inherent in management's dual role as a custodian for shareholders and as a self-interested acquirer had real vitality in the mid-1980s.

A series of mishaps have made the courts leery of management self-dealing. The colorful Ross Johnson of RJR was accused of trying a low-ball steal of the company for his LBO investor group. In the auction of Macmillan, the management tipped off a group it was in-volved with as to another contender's bid. But these obvious conflict problems have been addressed by strict court cases on conflicts and the use of special committees of independent directors.

Management Self-Interest

Even in cases where managers do not have as obvious a direct economic stake in their company as a result of a management buy-out, opponents argue that management self-interest, not potential gains to the acquiring firm, drives most mergers. Critics argue that managers do deals simply because managing a larger business pro-vides greater prestige, as well as access to more perks and a higher salary.

A related hypothesis is that pride or ego causes managers to launch overpriced transactions. This hubris propels managers to pay steep premiums for target companies. Managers convince them-selves that a higher valuation is appropriate when that is objectively not the case.

Value Destruction

In perhaps the most direct attack on mergers and acquisitions, a constituency contends that takeovers simply do not make economic sense for the corporate buyer. More often than not, according to this view, mergers destroy rather than add value from the acquirer's perspective. Harvard Business School professor Michael Porter advanced this thesis in a famous 1987 *Harvard Business Review* article. He studied the diversification strategies of thirty-three major American companies, involving acquisitions, joint ventures and start-ups. As Porter put it, the data "paint a sobering picture." On average, Porter's subjects divested over half their acquisitions in new industries and over 60 percent of their acquisitions in entirely new fields.

In a 1995 article entitled "The Case Against Mergers," Phillip Zweig of *Business Week* reported the results of a similar study. *Business Week* measured the post-deal stock market performance of 150 deals from the 1990s against the S&P 500. Relative to this benchmark, half the deals reduced shareholder value, and another third added only marginal value.

By way of contrast, most studies generally show acquiring companies breaking even on mergers in terms of stock price. But all of these studies are misleading. First, the benefits of most deals are long-term, not immediate. Second, controlling the variables for data is impossible. What would have happened to companies that didn't do the transactions? Who knows? Third, the size of the deal relative to the company purchasing is key. Fourth, the stock price may already have included an assumption of growth that the deals provide. Fifth, the data is polluted by including takeover candidates in the sampling. When a potential target itself does a deal the speculative frenzy subsides.

More fundamentally, the problem with many academic studies is that one must make flawed assumptions to squeeze untidy data points into a pristine statistical model. For example, the assumption that the sale of an acquired company makes the original purchase a bad deal is misguided. Many acquirers exist to buy and sell companies—and make money in the process—including the diversified conglomerates, financial buyers and the companies they control. Furthermore, running a business is not like building a building. There is no defined structure which can be constructed brick-by-brick in a linear process. The process is more dynamic than that, and pruning former acquisitions is an assumed part of the dynamic.

Yet if one bought a random company on the stock exchange at, say, a 30 percent premium and then financed it with, say, 50 percent debt, generally a prudent level, on average an investor would do exceptionally well. In fact, you'd be laughing all the way to the bank. If you also improved the company or unlocked further good opportunities for investment or achieved some efficiencies from the combination, so much the better.

For example, the Dow average was at 1800 in 1987, the peak of the "deals are bad" hubbub. In 1997, the Dow was four times higher; therefore, even with a premium, the total return is at least three times the investment before debt, and four times including the cost of debt service. This understates the return because the ultimate takeout calculation doesn't itself assume a premium. Thinking about it differently, if deals are so bad for the buyer, why have Henry Kravis' investors done so well?

Thoughts on the Debate

Many, if not most, companies bought eventually do get resold, a fairly startling thought. This is the most searing indictment of the critics of mergers. My favorite example is Entenmann's Bakery, which my partner Bill Lambert has worked on four times. Lambert, whose career has centered on creating acquisition ideas for clients, figured that the New York City–centered regional specialty bakery, known for its chocolate donuts, could use the help of a major corporation to push for national expansion. Furthermore, the owners were aging and might be willing to sell. Bill first represented Warner-Lambert, then a food and drug company, in buying Entenmann's.

Then Warner-Lambert decided to focus on drugs, and Bill sold Entenmann's to General Foods. Bill later represented Philip Morris when they bought General Foods, including Entenmann's. Philip

Morris eventually decided to exit the baked-goods business, and Bill worked on selling Entenmann's to its proud, new buyer, CPC International.

Each time Entenmann's was sold, the company increased in value and quality. But the strategic needs of the buyers had changed over time. This churning of assets is not necessarily bad. It shows the adaptability of the American corporation.

The criticisms of mergers were much more stinging in the late 1980s than the mid-1990s. When the stock market is high and defaults low, much of the attack withers. Even the anecdotal evidence shrivels into the dust of history. Of course, there is also some learning from experience. Managers are increasingly motivated by their own stock price and are, therefore, unlikely to make an imprudent deal merely for the sake of empire. Leverage in deals is less and some have learned the lesson of not having a mismatched book—borrowing all short-term against the acquisition of long-term assets.

Of course, there is no guarantee for companies that attempt to move with the times, but there is a virtual certainty that those who rely on the past will fail. One of the envies of foreign companies and, especially, government-owned companies is the speed at which American businesses can change. There is both a silliness in the pace of change and a glory, a crudeness and a marvelous flexibility. It is quintessentially part of the American economic experiment.

Part Two | # The Strategic Challenge

"Everything in strategy is very simple, but that does not mean that everything is very easy."

Carl von Clausewitz, *On War*

The Strategic Dilemma | 7

" 'Would you tell me please
which way I have to go from here?'
" 'That depends a good deal on where
you want to get to,' said the cat."

Lewis Carroll,
Alice's Adventures in Wonderland

After dramatically declining in the late 1980s, M&A activity has exploded in recent years. Each of the last five years has seen a record dollar volume of announced deals. In the aggregate, between the start of 1993 and the end of 1997, more than $2 trillion of corporate assets changed hands. As a result, the 1990s will be remembered as the fifth merger wave of the twentieth century.

However, mergers in the 1990s have differed. Going-private transactions have decreased from 27 percent of all M&A transactions in 1988 to less than 3 percent in 1996; financial buyers participated in only 5 percent of announced deals in 1996 versus 35 percent in 1988; and major hostile takeover attempts have declined from forty-six in 1988 to eight in 1996.

Strategic buyers have been the driving force in the 1990s. Corporate managers view acquisitions and mergers as critical tools for positioning their companies in response to competitive dynamics. The resulting strategic combinations have been both horizontal, as in the banking and health care industries, and vertical, as in the media business, but rarely diversifying.

The merger wave of the 1990s parallels the boom at the turn of the century. In both periods, business has been rocked by the tremors of fundamental shifts in the business environment. The late nineteenth century was the brink of the industrial age. Managers groped for the appropriate strategic platform, the model of a successful industrial company. Now the search is for a post-industrial model appropriate to the digital age.

In this new environment, strategic thinking has taken center stage. Managers struggle with fundamental issues, such as how to compete in a world where the South Koreans can bend metal cheaper. After several lean years of downsizing and cost cutting, companies are now seeking to increase revenues in an environ-

TEN LARGEST U.S. DEALS OF THE 1990s

Rank	Buyer	Seller	Approximate Equity Value (Billions)	Year Announced
1.*	WorldCom	MCI Communications Corp.	$36.5	1997
2.	Bell Atlantic Corp.	NYNEX Corp.	$19.5	1996
3.	Walt Disney Co.	Capital Cities/ABC Inc.	$19.0	1995
4.*	First Union Corp.	CoreStates Financial Corp.	$17.1	1997
5.	SBC Communications Inc.	Pacific Telesis Group	$16.7	1996
6.	NationsBank Corp.	Barnett Banks	$14.9	1997
7.	WorldCom Inc.	MFS Communications Co.	$14.1	1996
8.	Boeing Co.	McDonnell Douglas Corp.	$13.3	1996
9.	Chemical Banking Corp.	Chase Manhattan Corp.	$13.0	1995
10.	American Telephone & Telegraph Co.	McCaw Cellular Communications Inc.	$12.6	1993

Source: *MergerStat*. As of December 31, 1997. Starred deals are pending.

ment of low U.S. population growth. "What kind of company do we want to be?" is the threshold issue.

The specifics driving each deal are different, but there is a common pattern to the process. Existing business strategies and structures ossify over time. These structures may survive for some period with the protection of systemic inertia. Eventually, however, external catalysts give a sharp jolt to the system. Outmoded practices become apparent. Mergers and acquisitions, a kind of rough-hewn evolutionary mechanism, then occur as companies react to the new business realities.

The financial buyers too increasingly have focused on strategic issues. As the 1980s came to a close, many of the financial buyers, with vast diversified holdings, ironically resembled the conglomerates they previously had dismantled. The 1990s began with a sharp economic recession, and the financial buyers experienced their own struggle for life. Changing economic circumstances dictated a new approach. Consequently, the financial buyers began to think and act more like strategic buyers, and the strategic LBO became the prototype.

In retrospect, the major financial buyers survived the test of the early 1990s. Debt was restructured; costs were trimmed. Portfolio companies returned to health as the economy came out of recession. The bull market for stocks, which began in 1994, created opportunities to take the companies public or merge them into public companies.

Still, precisely because so many financial buyers rode out the downturn, the competitive buyout environment remains. If anything, the number of buyout funds has multiplied. In 1996, KKR alone raised a new $5 billion LBO fund. Market observers estimate that buyout funds in the aggregate have more than $40 billion in uninvested equity capital at their disposal.

With a booming stock market, many financial buyers have concluded that the mechanistic application of financial leverage will not guarantee satisfactory returns on this money. By adopting the strategic LBO model, financial buyers expanded the range of potential acquisition targets. Stable, no-growth enterprises are no longer the primary target. Instead, there is a new interest in finding promising companies with the potential for revenue growth.

For example, Forstmann Little acquired General Instrument in 1990, a maker of cable set-top boxes and other electronics. Ted Forstmann was attracted to the company as a growth play. He believed technological advances—mainly the shift to digital systems—would greatly expand the market for General Instrument's products. The company would need to make a major investment in new technology to serve this market. As such, General Instrument was a break from the LBO norm.

The increasing emphasis on leveraged buildups is another by-product of the new strategic focus. This acquisition model begins with the initial leveraged acquisition of a company in a fragmented industry. The company is then used as a platform to acquire other companies through further leveraged purchases. K-III, a leveraged publishing company associated with KKR, provides a case in point. The company has assembled a portfolio of magazines and other interests through a series of leveraged acquisitions.

The new market environment—a booming stock market and relatively few cash deals compared to the mid-1980s—has also dictated a renewed emphasis on public-market exit strategies. Financial buyers lately have relied on IPOs and mergers with public companies as a means to cash out their investments. Consequently, some financial buyers have relaxed their former single-minded attention to cash flow and now consider revenue and earnings growth important considerations, compounding the strategic focus.

The Strategic Dilemma

The Five Pistons—regulatory reform, technological change, fluctuations in financial markets, the role of leadership and the tension between scale and focus—propel the dynamics of corporate transformation. What is a company's strategic dilemma and how should it be addressed? How should resources be deployed? Success depends on managing in the face of these uncertainties. This is the core of the merger business—the development of a sound and executable corporate strategy at a justifiable price.

Most companies face significant dilemmas in the evolution of their objectives. Buggy whips, slide rules, typewriters, adding machines—at different times the manufacture of each of these products represented a strong, attractive business. Yet technological volatility created different environments. The products slipped into obsolescence and manufacturers were forced to react.

We live, then, in a world of risks, contradictions and limited resources. Making the tough strategic choices with consistent tactical follow-up is the province of good management. Ambling along, oblivious of the need for change, is a prescription for trouble; inconsistency between strategy and tactics brings a fiasco.

The problems that constrain a company's growth can be described with a Rosen's Cube, named after our senior international partner, Jeffrey Rosen, who innovated work on the link between strategy and mergers. The three-dimensional Rosen's Cube shows a company inside the box anxious to burst out and achieve growth, but constrained by limitations and its resources. Breaking through the box of constraints is the obsession of top management. To do so requires taking a calculated but disciplined risk on one or more of the six barriers.

For example, in 1995, our client Aetna Life & Casualty wanted to expand its presence in the high-growth health care business, but CEO Ronald Compton was boxed in. Fundamental problems in Aetna's main property and casualty insurance businesses were a performance drag. Market earnings and dividends expectations, immediate cash needs and a low price/earnings ratio limited the company's flexibility to buy additional managed care businesses. Management constraints and a lack of broad managed care capabilities kept Aetna from expanding internally.

In other words, Aetna faced the following Rosen's Cube:

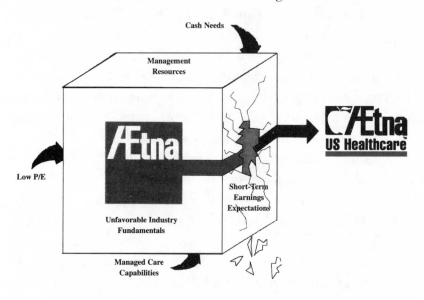

Compton broke through the constraints in 1996 with a transformative purchase of U.S. Healthcare. Part of the $8.9 billion purchase price was funded with cash from the sale of Aetna's property and casualty business to the Travelers Group. However, these proceeds fell short of the full purchase price. Determined to break out of Aetna's Cube, Compton and his board decided to buck short-term market expectations. He slashed Aetna's quarterly dividend and issued additional debt and new equity securities to buy U.S. Healthcare even though the purchase would dilute earnings per share in the near term.

Investors were convinced the calculated risk would pay off. Between April 1, 1996, when the deal was announced, and August 1997 Aetna's stock price zoomed from around $75 per share to a high of $114 per share. However, in the middle of August 1997, the initial market exuberance wore off. Aetna announced that post-closing integration was on plan but had created certain operating problems. The company had been aggressive in laying off claims processors and other employees. As a result, a backlog of claims built up. This backlog delayed the data gathering required for Aetna management to see the extent of rising health care costs. When earnings took a hit, the stock price fell back to the mid-70s.

Despite these problems, Aetna management remains confirmed in the strategic vision behind the U.S. Healthcare deal and the consensus on Wall Street is that, irrespective of short-term dislocations, the company has regained the long-term initiative in the managed care business.

Strategic Models

Of course, there is no magic answer to the "right" direction for a company. Giving advice on corporate strategy is an increasingly crowded cottage industry teeming with gurus of the moment. Old models regularly lose favor, and new ones gain faddish popularity. Fundamentally, though, all the models merely formalize the attempt to arrive at common sense.

Four of the more popular theories are:

- The McKinsey Formulation
- The Boston Consulting Group Model
- Michael Porter's Five Forces
- Hamel and Prahalad's Core Competencies

Each of these models has been ascendant in a different era. McKinsey's concepts were innovations in the Kennedy years. The Boston Consulting Group Model came to prominence during the conglomerate boom of the late 1960s. Michael Porter introduced his Five Forces in a seminal 1980 book. Gary Hamel and C.K. Prahalad popularized their strategic concepts in the early 1990s. In each case, I don't purport to do them justice as they would express their concepts, just to summarize their gut impact on CEO thinking.

The McKinsey Formulation   Company after company has brought in teams from McKinsey and learned the golden rule of corporate strategy: he who rules makes the gold. The derivative is simply that the leading companies in the leading industries will make more money and are, therefore, more attractive acquisitions. Of course, adding to market share is also encouraged because greater power yields higher profitability.

The obvious problem with this analysis is that it doesn't cover emerging industries and has no relationship to the price paid or the feasibility of merging the best companies. McKinsey's lack of practicality spawned the corporate guru industry and created a vacuum for investment bankers to assert a wider expertise as "practical" strategists.

The Boston Consulting Group Model   The Boston Consulting Group Model attacks the nondynamic nature of the McKinsey formulation. It is really an amalgamation of three different ideas: the experience curve, the product life cycle and portfolio balance. The experience curve theory maintains that as the total historical volume of output produced by a company increases, unit costs decline geometrically. Hence, the company with the most historical output should have the lowest unit cost. If the relationship holds, companies presumably should target early market entry and price products to maximize volume.

The product life cycle is a model for industry evolution. According to this view, each product or business line goes through four stages: development, growth, maturity and decline. The first two phases are marked by strong sales growth and low barriers to entry. In the later phases, entry becomes more costly and difficult as market participants move down the experience curve and volume growth slows. Once the business enters decline, unprofitable or marginally profitable firms are squeezed by falling prices and volume, sparking consolidation.

Conceptually, portfolio balance theory is related to movements along the product life cycle. The early stages of product development and growth often require considerable capital spending. Then, once capacity is on-line and the market matures, a business line typically generates more cash than is needed in that specific operation. Portfolio balance theory dictates that a company should attempt to fund cash-poor, high-growth opportunities with money from cash-rich, mature businesses. At the same time, a company should shut down or divest underperforming businesses. These theories were the intellectual foundation for conglomerate activity, which eventually was widely discredited in popular opinion.

Michael Porter's Five Forces   In his strategic model, Michael Porter blasts his predecessors for being too diffuse in not focusing on a company's specific competitive environment. For Porter, the environment is defined by Five Forces: potential entrants, suppliers, customers, product substitutes and industry competitors. Because the mix and relative strength of these forces vary by industry, strategy has to be tailored to the circumstances.

With regard to industry competitors, potential entrants and product substitutes, Porter emphasizes the threat posed to existing market participants. Any of these three forces can erode a company's strategic position dramatically. The issue with respect to a company's customers and suppliers is relative bargaining power. For example, customers may be able to dictate pricing in a saturated industry, whereas the reverse may be true in an industry dominated by a few major players.

Hamel and Prahalad's Core Competencies   Gary Hamel and C.K. Prahalad have popularized the concept that corporate strategy should be bold and based on leveraging a company's core competencies to achieve its goals. In their view, strategy should be about stretching to shift industry structure, or to develop an entirely new industry.

Of course, this concept should be grounded in a firm understanding of a company's limited core competencies or bundles of skills. By definition, this approach favors the more focused strategic deals of the 1990s and the divestiture of the excess baggage of 1960s diversification.

A company's core competence should not, however, be defined too narrowly. If a buggy whip company defines its competence as making really good whips, it will be out of business when the buggy disappears. Perhaps the business is better defined as the manufacture of small hand tools. Or maybe the focus should instead be on the company's branding power. The problem is that a good slide rule maker is not necessarily a competitive personal computer manufacturer.

Practical Reality

Each of these approaches has obvious elements of insight and can help a company conceptualize its strategic dilemma. Different approaches have been validated in the market at different times: the drive to expand revenues or earnings, the primacy of a purified business portfolio, or the advantages of diversification all have their time and place.

The practical reality is that the phenomenal bull market of the past decade has acted as a wide safety net for strategic acquirers. Whether the original strategic vision underlying a deal has played out as expected, the assets generally have appreciated. Tenacity and a rising stock market cure many ills. The risk for the future may be the impact of buying at a cyclical peak.

The interplay of the Five Pistons of the merger movement and the various strategies and tactics they engender is the theme of this section. Particularly active industries in the 1980s and 1990s—oil, the conglomerates, financial services, media and telecommunications, health care—illustrate the strategic dynamics of the M&A boom and the tactics employed to achieve success.

The Energy Wars | 8

"We're eyeball to eyeball,
and I think the other fellow just blinked."

Secretary of State Dean Rusk
on the Cuban Missile Crisis

T. Boone Pickens canceled his plans for the long weekend. On the Friday before Memorial Day, 1982, Cities Service, the nation's nineteenth largest oil company, announced a public tender offer to purchase all of Mesa's stock for $17 per share. At that price, Cities Service would pay a scant 25 cents above Mesa's latest closing price. Pickens' company, which itself had been contemplating a bid for Cities, was being Pac-Manned.

Takeover professionals had been discussing the possibility of a so-called Pac-Man defense for some time. The idea was relatively simple. When faced with a hostile bidder, a takeover target could tender for the shares in the hostile bidder. In this way, the hunted could swallow the hunter, eliminating the threat.

We represented Cities with Lehman Brothers, and all the bankers were having a great time. By instinct, our team and the Lehman bankers—Henry Breck, a former CIA agent with a sense of humor, and Jack Lentz, who had played a year of professional football—all had an instinct for the jugular and saw an unusual opportunity. We felt there was a good chance for the "pool shot"—to break up Pickens' assault before it could be mobilized.

At the time of the Cities bid, little Mesa Petroleum posed a very real threat to the larger company. On paper, this seemed unlikely. After all, in addition to being the nineteenth largest oil company, Cities was also the thirty-eighth largest industrial company in America with $8.5 billion of revenues in 1981. By way of comparison, Mesa had roughly $400 million of revenues, one third the assets of Cities and only 900 employees compared to 20,000.

However, Pickens possessed other assets. The press loved this twangy Texan. Pickens wrapped himself in the classic frontier spirit, and projected a David versus Goliath mentality. He was a master of spinning zippy quotes. For example, when asked by a *Wall Street Journal* reporter if his attack on Cities was a bluff, Pickens responded, "Well, we didn't come to town on a load of watermelons." This down-home homily threw the reporter, who asked for clarification. Pickens laughed. "I may not be from Wall Street," he said, "but I know what I'm doing."

Indeed, in Cities, Pickens had picked a vulnerable target. The company's main problem was a poor operating performance. In each of the prior ten years, it had depleted reserves more quickly than it discovered new oil. Over the previous five years, its reserves had fallen by about 20 percent. Meanwhile, to no avail, the company had been pouring more and more money into exploration.

Reflecting this track record, Cities' stock price lingered in the mid-30s. At that level, the company's market value was less than half the appraised value of its proven oil and gas reserves. The board was known to be upset with the company's performance, and sensitive to shareholder complaints. Consequently, Mesa could acquire oil in the ground at a below-market price even if it paid a large premium to Cities' shareholders.

Pickens had recognized this situation in 1979, when he began purchasing Cities stock for Mesa's account. By late May 1982, Mesa had acquired slightly more than 5 percent of Cities' outstanding stock. Pickens also had four partners waiting in the wings with another $1 billion to invest. Preparations were underway for a June 4 hostile tender offer. But word leaked to Cities, and it launched its surprise bid to the bankers' delight. As a backup, though, the board also deputized us to explore the interest of other bidders in Cities. If the price were high enough, the board would seriously consider selling, even if Boone were no threat.

While the Pac-Man defense was a well-known possibility, Cities had taken the idea one step further. Rather than passively waiting for the bid from Mesa, Cities attacked first. As a result, Cities gained an important tactical advantage. Federal law required that a tender offer remain open for at least twenty days. So, because Cities beat Mesa out of the blocks, the Cities offer would expire first. This time difference would allow Cities to buy Mesa before the opposite happened.

Pickens was in danger of being boxed in. It had taken months to find financial backers willing to throw in with Mesa. Now, in the face of the Cities bid, the lead investor backed out, taking $500 million with it. Pickens had to scramble to keep his other partners from following suit, or he might lose control of Mesa itself.

But Pickens was not about to give up. If Mesa walked away, it stood to lose $60 million. So, instead, Pickens shot back a classic bear hug letter—an offer made directly to Cities' CEO and announced to the world. Mesa was prepared to pay $50 a share for Cities stock, part in cash and part in securities. This was not a tender offer; the Cities board would have to give its approval for the deal to go forward. The likelihood of that happening was slim. However, that wasn't the point. Pickens just wanted to build pressure on Cities' incumbent managers and board of directors. The tactic was a failure.

Pickens and his advisers scrambled for a stronger counterattack. They kept coming back to the same stumbling block—where to get the cash for an all-out tender? Eventually, with the clock ticking on Cities' offer for Mesa, Pickens settled on an unusual partial tender offer. On June 7, Mesa announced the terms. It would pay $45 per share for an additional 15 percent of Cities stock, which would give Mesa more than 20 percent in total.

Given the steep premium over the market price for Cities stock, more than 15 percent of the shareholders might very well tender their shares to Mesa. If that happened, Pickens would have a powerful lever to raise additional cash. Moreover, Mesa would argue that the tender offer was a referendum on incumbent management's performance. Even if the Mesa bid were to be turned away, another predator might attempt to capitalize on the palpable shareholder discontent, and Boone would make a profit.

Meanwhile, Cities faced a dilemma. The strike against Boone looked like a winner. Boone would be knocked out before he could punch. But an insistent Gulf Oil wanted to make an offer. Gulf was told Cities didn't need a white knight rescue bid with the Boone situation under control. On the other hand, if Gulf bid a preemptive price, the board would listen. Basically, the board was a seller and was using Boone as a stalking horse.

On June 17, Gulf Oil took the bait and offered $63 per Cities share in a friendly deal. This was a slam-dunk bid at a price well above what Pickens could ever afford. We urged Gulf to continue the bid for Mesa and buy it too, but Gulf settled. Boone gave up the fight, and sold Mesa's shares in Cities back to the company for $55 a share, less than the other shareholders were to receive, but still a $30 million profit.

Though matters with Pickens were settled, the Cities story was not over. Less than two months after agreeing to its deal with Cities, Gulf backed out. The company cited irreconcilable antitrust problems. Observers on Wall Street found the explanation implausible. Gulf, they argued, could have settled its differences with the government by selling certain assets. According to this view, Gulf had just gotten cold feet over the price it was paying. The antitrust issue was a convenient way to save face, and Gulf was sued for its insincerity. After years of legal sparring, a Tulsa jury finally hit Gulf—now part of Chevron—for $742 million in damages. The 1996 judgment was still on appeal as of December 1997.

With Cities left at the altar, Dr. Armand Hammer's Occidental Petroleum stepped in and tried to scoop up the company at a bargain price. Although the board was anxious to sell, the directors all agreed that Hammer, as the culminating gesture of a long and controversial career, was even more anxious to buy. The board taunted Hammer by threatening to sell Cities' assets on a piece-by-piece basis. Hammer eventually overruled his staff and bought the wounded Cities Service for $53 a share, about $1 billion less than Gulf, but still higher than Boone's offer. The shareholders were also entitled to a slice of any proceeds received from the Gulf lawsuit. The Cities board members were thrilled. Cities was finally sold.

Early Landmark: Belridge

The Cities Service deal, as well as other oil megamergers of the period, was the incubation laboratory for modern merger tactics. Many of the devices and strategies that would become familiar over the next twenty years came from these often bitterly contested conflicts. For example, the evolution of the poison pill came about directly to curb Boone-like strategies. In addition, the deals indicate the role of macroeconomic developments in the creation of industry strategies.

The tide of oil megadeals began in 1979, when a little-known California producer named Belridge Oil was put on the auction block. Belridge, founded in 1911 by three land speculators, owned the rights to a large oil patch north of Los Angeles. Most of the company's 380 million barrels of proven reserves were heavy crude. Relatively undesirable, this gooey, viscous oil adhered to underground rock formations and was costly to extract.

Belridge was put on the market under pressure. Descendants of the company's three founders controlled 55 percent of the company's stock. Mobil and Texaco were the other major shareholders, with a combined 34 percent ownership stake. In July 1979, the two majors expressed an interest in buying out the other shareholders. They attempted to divide the founding families, hoping to buy the company on the cheap by negotiating with each shareholder individually.

The other shareholders didn't take kindly to the tactic. The members of the founding families, mostly in their sixties and seventies, would not be pushed around. Instead, they decided to run an auction. When the result was announced, Shell Oil had snatched Belridge away from Mobil and Texaco on the strength of a $3.6 billion offer.

The deal was stunning on several counts. Shell reportedly had topped the next highest bidder by $500 million. The transaction would be the then-largest corporate acquisition in American history with the purchase price valuing Belridge's reserves at roughly $9 a barrel, considerably higher than the going rate of $5 or $6 a barrel.

Shell CEO John Bookout had shocked the industry, but Bookout was betting that Shell possessed the technology, mainly steam injection, to capitalize on Belridge's reserves. Shell had been an innovator in the process, which pumps steam into oil reserves, causing the oil to flow more freely. While his competitors stumbled, Bookout was able to apply the steam injection technology and output from the California wells more than tripled. Mr. Bookout had bought himself a bargain and earned the reputation for being one of the smartest men in the industry.

ON THE BRINK OF THE OIL WARS

The main seeds of the 1980s Oil Wars were planted the decade before. The 1970s saw a worldwide shift away from reliance on politically secure oil from the United States. This development led to two major Oil Shocks—dramatic increases in the price of oil.

By the early 1980s, the world returned to overcapacity in the oil market, with important consequences for Big Oil.

For a time, Big Oil profited in the new environment created by the 1973 Oil Shock. The aggregate net income for these largest of oil companies had grown at an anemic pace in the five years prior to 1972. But, on the cusp of the shock, profits rose to $11.7 billion in 1973, almost double the $6.9 billion earned in 1972, and then $16.4 billion in 1974. These phenomenal cash flows were in need of investment.

The combination of this cash and predictions of continuing oil shortages led to an obvious result. A helter-skelter race to discover new supply took off in 1973 and continued into the next decade. Billions of dollars were invested in exploration and prices for everything related to the hunt for oil shot up dramatically. The oil cities of Houston, Dallas and Denver experienced boom times. The thrill of wildcatting and the independent oil business was popularized in the hit television series *Dallas*.

One of the main assumptions underlying the push for new capacity was an ever-increasing demand for oil products. The so-called Iron Law—an observed relationship between overall economic growth and the growth in demand for oil and energy— lay at the heart of this prediction. According to the Iron Law, energy consumption in general, and the demand for oil in particular, would grow at the same rate as the economy.

In fact, during the late 1970s and early 1980s, the major economies embraced conservation and efficiency as a new mantra. Demand actually shrank while the economy grew. Between 1973 and 1985, the United States became 25 percent more energy-efficient and 32 percent more oil-efficient. Measured in terms of demand, this translated to 13 million barrels of unneeded daily capacity.

Meanwhile, the fear was that the oil business was a sunset industry dying a slow death. Sooner or later, the world's supply of oil and gas would be depleted and new energy sources—solar, hydro, nuclear—would replace oil and gas. Diversification became the industry byword. Exxon spent roughly $500 million on a start-up office electronics business amid talk of taking on IBM. The company also spent $1.2 billion to acquire Reliance Electric Co. and invested heavily in the copper industry. Mobil Oil shelled out $1 billion for retailer Montgomery Ward. Standard Oil acquired copper producer Kennecott for $1.8 billion. As with almost all diversification by oil companies, these deals later would haunt the buyers.

The early 1980s—the brink of the Oil Wars—saw a growing buyers' market for petroleum and petroleum products. The deep recession that followed in 1981 and 1982 contributed to the erosion of demand for oil. At the same time, three major, non–Middle Eastern oil sources came on-line—in Alaska, Mexico and the North Sea. The Alaskan oil fields by themselves had an enormous impact. The project, completed in 1977, shipped over a million barrels per day in the following year, and would transport more than 2 million barrels per day by the early 1980s. At that time, the single field accounted for 25 percent of U.S. crude oil production.

With the advent of this new capacity, the price of oil came under pressure, which hit many of the big oil companies hard. They had poured billions of dollars into exploration and production, all premised on an oil price north of $30 a barrel. Exxon, for example, spent $1 billion on developing shale oil technology. But Exxon backed out of the project in 1982. It just no longer made sense in a world of $10-a-barrel oil.

The huge administrative staffs built up during the 1970s also began to look increasingly anachronistic as the price of oil continued its downward progression. Not only was this infrastructure incredibly costly to maintain, it created a built-in bias for further inefficient exploration and production.

Soon, as prices bottomed at around $10 a barrel, continuing

exploration on the traditional basis was hard to justify. A series of major exploration disappointments highlighted the issue, including the failure of a $2 billion Alaskan wildcat project called Mukluk, known in the industry as the most expensive dry hole in history.

The Mukluk disaster reinforced the notion that the cost of acquiring oil reserves was considerably below the cost of developing reserves. In 1982, for example, major oil companies spent an average of $14.22 a barrel to develop new domestic oil reserves. During that period, oil reserves could be purchased in the market for roughly $4 a barrel.

Measured against this benchmark, most major companies were priced on Wall Street at a steep discount to the underlying value of their proven oil and gas reserves. A company's share price often implied a value significantly below $4 a barrel for a company's oil in the ground. The differential between the market price for oil and the market price for stock allowed an acquirer to pay a premium for the stock without paying an above-market price for the oil. The big oil companies were ripe for consolidation.

The Conoco Brawl

Belridge set off a bruising competitive atmosphere. When in May 1981, Conoco—the nation's ninth largest oil company—became a target, the deal captured the public imagination. The battle would drag out over three months and involve four separate bidders. The tactical maneuvering was at a level of complexity that set precedents for years to come. With Conoco, the Oil Wars exploded, and the 1980s merger boom began.

The jousting began on May 6, 1981, when Canada's Dome Petroleum tendered for up to 20 percent of Conoco's stock. Dome offered to pay $65 a share. Conoco's stock opened at just under $50 on the morning of the announcement.

Dome, a much smaller company than Conoco, explicitly stated it was not out to gain control. Rather, Dome wanted to swap the Conoco stock it would purchase for Conoco's majority interest in its Canadian subsidiary, Hudson's Bay Oil & Gas. Dome suggested a stock swap, and not an outright cash purchase, because the swap structure would be tax-free to Conoco.

The Dome tender was not a complete surprise. Ralph Bailey, Conoco's chairman, had committed a classic error. He had listened to an earlier informal offer from his counterpart at Dome and responded in noncommittal fashion. Bailey's failure to be clear and forceful encouraged Dome to strike. In retrospect, Bailey simply had no sense of urgency over the Dome offer. The chairman believed that his company was worth more than $65 a share, and thought his shareholders would agree. They didn't. Nearly 53 percent of the company's shareholders tendered to Dome, a remarkable event. America's institutional shareholders had demonstrated a clear willingness to cash in on a takeover.

Meanwhile, Seagram's chairman Edgar Bronfman Sr. had been on the prowl for an acquisition for almost a year. His liquor company recently had sold its own oil and gas properties for $2.3 billion. Seagram needed to invest the cash, and Conoco looked like an intriguing possibility.

Bailey and Bronfman met to discuss a deal. Again Bailey had aimless conversations. He liked having Seagram as an offset to Dome but was afraid of Seagram's long-term intentions. Without telling Bronfman, Bailey rushed from Conoco's Connecticut headquarters to a waiting corporate jet. That same evening, he touched down in Oklahoma City, on his way to a meeting with Charles Waidelich, the CEO of Cities Service, to propose a merger.

The next day, Bailey was back at Conoco's headquarters. He hadn't made an agreement with Cities, but felt in a strong position. Meanwhile, Conoco's board protected its flanks by approving an agreement with Dome whereby the Canadian oil company would swap its Conoco stock plus $245 million in cash for Hudson Bay, roughly double the amount promised in its initial tender offer.

With Dome in hand, Bailey tried to pursue the Cities merger while keeping Seagram at bay. Feeling abused, Edgar Bronfman commenced a hostile tender offer for 41 percent of Conoco's stock at $73 a share.

The Seagram tender offer irretrievably put Conoco in play. Bailey had outsmarted himself in the sense that the offer shattered Bailey's hoped-for deal with Cities Service. The parties had been negotiating a defensive stock-for-stock merger. Even as the Seagram offer came across the wire services, Bailey and Waidelich had been preparing a press release to announce the merger of their two companies. The Seagram offer ripped the foundations out from under that deal.

Bailey reacted angrily to his new predicament and rushed to find a white knight. Blue-chip DuPont had been pondering the future of energy prices and had calculated that buying oil interests would be a sound hedge against the volatile costs for its vast chemical operations. Conoco seemed an ideal vehicle, and we were brought in to advise DuPont. A deal was put together at a breakneck pace over the July 4th weekend and announced the following week.

DuPont's bid was structured carefully, taking into account the opening left by Seagram's failure to tender for all of Conoco's stock. We knew we needed at least 51 percent of the stock, but didn't want to pay cash for fear of adversely affecting DuPont's debt ratings. The result was a two-tier package. DuPont offered to pay $87.50 per share in cash for 40 percent of the company and 1.6 DuPont shares per remaining Conoco share. Both parts of the bid were tied together so that one could not happen without the other. In effect, DuPont was offering for 50 percent of the company, 80 percent for cash and 20 percent in stock, and the remaining 50 percent of the company would be bought for stock in a back-end merger.

A bidding war ensued. Seagram was not willing to give up easily, but couldn't compete with DuPont's two-tiered package. However, as it turned out, all the maneuvering between DuPont and Seagram was just a prelude. On July 16, 1981, giant Mobil Corporation, a jilted Belridge suitor, weighed in with its own offer.

Finally, on August 5, three months after the initial Dome offer, top executives from DuPont gathered at the Hotel Dupont in downtown Wilmington, Delaware. When the clock struck midnight, the team lifted champagne glasses in a toast. Then DuPont began sending out payments to make good on its tender offer for shares in the Conoco Corporation.

The festivities that evening were not without reason, for DuPont had just done an unusual thing, purchasing America's ninth largest oil company for an average price of less than $100 per share. At the time, it was the largest takeover in history, but such records are made to be broken. The real surprise was that the Mobil Corporation had offered to purchase the stock for $120 per share, a more than 20 percent improvement on DuPont's price. So why did rational shareholders tender their stock to DuPont? Because DuPont had raised sufficient concern about Mobil's antitrust position to carry the day for DuPont.

In fact, from the moment Mobil bid, DuPont took the public position that price alone would not decide the winner. Mobil's offer, argued DuPont, had to be discounted for the risk that a merger between Mobil and Conoco would be blocked by the government on antitrust grounds. DuPont and Conoco continually stressed the antitrust implications of a Mobil-Conoco merger. As part of this strategy, when Mobil ultimately raised its bid to $120 per share (compared to DuPont's $98), DuPont consciously decided against a raise. The company instead relied on antitrust issues to carry the day.

Though the antitrust law is incredibly complex and typically involves sophisticated economic analysis, the DuPont antitrust strategy was simple—keep yelling "two and nine." This catchphrase pressed the fact that a Mobil and Conoco merger would combine the nation's number two and number nine oil companies, which, DuPont and Conoco argued, just had to have antitrust implications.

This tactic was targeted specifically toward the audience that really mattered—the institutional investors and arbitrageurs who held large blocks of Conoco stock. The idea was to play on these investors' fear that antitrust issues eventually would kill the Mobil deal, which would be a disaster for any investor who tendered to Mobil. To feed this fear, Conoco promptly sued Mobil on antitrust grounds. Meanwhile, the main action took place in Washington, D.C., at the Justice Department's Antitrust Division.

The government played such an important role because under the antitrust laws it had the power to delay any of the Conoco bids. In particular, the Hart-Scott-Rodino Antitrust Improvements Act required each bidder to file a notice with both the Justice Department and the Federal Trade Commission. The government then had a period to review the filings for antitrust implications.

In the case of the Conoco contest, the Justice Department antitrust review process was scheduled to end on a different date for each player. If both DuPont and Mobil got approval in the first round, DuPont would have to wait until August 7 to purchase shares, a week later than Mobil. DuPont would then either have to give up the fight or raise its bid enough to convince shareholders to forgo the Mobil offer and wait the extra week.

Even worse for DuPont, if it got an information request from the government, DuPont's offer would be delayed until at least August 27. On the bright side, however, if Mobil got an information request and DuPont did not, Mobil would be delayed until after August 10. Then, on August 7, institutional shareholders would either have to tender to DuPont or take the antitrust risk and wait for Mobil. The upshot of all this was that Conoco would likely go to whichever party first navigated the antitrust gauntlet.

With so much riding on the review process, DuPont's antitrust lawyers worked hard to satisfy the Justice Department. In fact, they did everything short of bringing the government lawyers coffee, and, as a result, DuPont sailed through the process three days early. The response—no further information request—played right into DuPont's bidding strategy.

On July 31, Mobil got an information request. Mobil's in-house counsel George Birrell, who received the call from the government, described the result this way: "With that phone call, it was over for us." Investors tendered to DuPont, and the battle ended. The Justice Department and the antitrust laws decided the outcome of the multibillion-dollar fight for Conoco.

Meanwhile, Seagram would end up purchasing 32 percent of Conoco's stock through its tender offer, but would not gain control. Instead, Seagram eventually tendered its Conoco stake to DuPont and received a 20 percent DuPont stake in return, which years later was sold back to DuPont and provided the equity for Seagram's purchase of movie studio MCA.

PRORATION POOLS

Among the confusing exotica of the public merger process is the proration pool. The effective price to an investor is what he will receive—not the average price paid to all investors. For example, if a company offers $100 in cash through a tender offer for half a company and $80 in stock for the remainder in a back-end merger, the average price paid is $90. However, if only 90 percent of shareholders tender, the results are that the 10 percent not tendering receive the $80 in stock, and the average price received by the 90 percent who do tender is a total of $91.11.

Because of the importance of the eligibility dates under the federal securities laws, which determine the pool of shareholders eligible for proration, a tender offer for less than 100 percent of shares has been called a coercive device. If a shareholder misses the pool eligibility date, he is at a disadvantage. Today, poison pills are used to prevent the coercive effect of hostile partial offers, but partial offers are commonplace in friendly deals and are a flexible tactical tool.

Always a Bridesmaid . . .

Mobil's defeats in Belridge and Conoco did not kill the large company's thirst for acquisitions. Heavily dependent on Saudi oil, Mobil desperately wanted to expand its U.S. reserves. In fact, the company had spent $4.3 billion on domestic exploration and production between 1976 and 1980. Yet U.S. reserves were down 6 percent over the period. Mobil chairman Rawleigh Warner and president William Tavoulareas sought to reverse the decline.

It didn't take long for the two men—who worked without the meaningful help of outside advisers—to find another target. In October 1981, about a month after Conoco slipped away, Mobil announced a $5 billion bid for Marathon Oil. Picking up on DuPont's two-tier bid for Conoco, Mobil offered $85 a share in cash for two thirds of Marathon's outstanding shares and bonds worth roughly the same amount for the remaining shares. Marathon stock was trading at $67 a share before the Mobil bid.

Marathon, the nation's sixteenth largest oil company, was a particularly inviting target for Mobil. The Ohio-based company was rich in U.S. reserves. It owned a 49.5 percent interest in the massive Yates oil field in West Texas. Marathon's other reserves also were mainly located in the United States. On the strength of these reserves, many oil analysts placed Marathon's breakup well above Mobil's bid.

We were brought in by Marathon's management to defend against the offer, building on our Conoco experience. The Marathon board was anxious to find a corporate white knight, a rescuer who ideally would be an industrial company that would protect the legacy of the company, its employees and the community, Findlay, Ohio, as well as offer a higher price. Mobil was one of the richest and toughest companies in the nation, but Marathon had learned from Conoco how to make them stumble—raise enough antitrust issues so that their bid was discounted while the white knight's bid was being consummated.

The list of companies that could absorb Marathon was not long, but within a matter of weeks, U.S. Steel expressed interest. Negotiations progressed quickly. U.S. Steel soon experienced the new realities of 1980s takeover contests. A company team flew into Ohio for meetings at Marathon's headquarters. They came aboard one of U.S. Steel's corporate jets, with the corporate logo emblazoned on the fuselage. Arbitrageurs and the local press had people stationed at the airport who saw the U.S. Steel plane. The market got wind of the visit, and rumors began to circulate.

Later, the Marathon team flew to Pittsburgh for the final negotiations at U.S. Steel's corporate headquarters. As our plane (without markings) touched down, it was quickly whisked directly into a separate hangar. The scene was out of a James Bond movie. Ground crew members, dressed in neon orange suits, stood all around the hangar along with security guards. We were ushered to the roof, where a helicopter was waiting to take the Marathon team to the U.S. Steel building. The helicopter landed on the top of the Pittsburgh skyscraper, we climbed down one flight of stairs, and were in the U.S. Steel executive offices.

The next day, the terms were announced. U.S. Steel offered $125 a share in cash for half the outstanding Marathon shares and securities worth about $86 for the remainder. U.S. Steel also agreed to keep Marathon intact as a separate subsidiary headquartered in

Findlay, Ohio. This clause is now famous as the "Findlay, Ohio" provision which is used in any negotiation where a seller is trying to protect the hometown offices from a shutdown.

When the U.S. Steel offer was announced, Mobil reacted and raised its bid. Meanwhile, Marathon won a valuable temporary injunction against Mobil on antitrust grounds. Mobil scrambled to respond. It negotiated a deal with another company to purchase the offending Marathon operations. Too little, too late.

Mobil had the higher bid by about $200 million, but again was thwarted by the perception of antitrust concerns. One can imagine Mobil's frustration. Unwilling to wait for the ambiguities regarding Mobil's offer to be resolved, shareholders overwhelmingly tendered into U.S. Steel's offer.

1984—The Year of the Megadeal

In 1984, the merger storm hit the majors with full force.

Superior Oil   First, a bitter feud between siblings Howard Keck and Wilametta Day Keck—son and daughter of the company's founder—led to the sale of Superior Oil, the country's largest independent.

Wilametta not only hated her brother, she chose to use Superior as a tool for revenge. Howard had just retired as CEO of Superior but was still on the board of directors. Angry at her brother's control of the company, she launched a proxy fight to make a change of control easier to accomplish. Around this time, spotting a potential profit, Boone Pickens had Mesa Petroleum buy into Superior. With the help of Pickens and others, Wilametta won the fight. Mobil eventually swooped in to buy the company for $5.7 billion. After years of searching, it finally had a willing partner.

Valuing Big Oil

Valuing a public oil company is a complicated task. The starting point is the SEC-required reports—known as the "standardized measure of discounted future net cash flows"—found in annual reports. However, for a number of reasons, the values derived in these reports cannot be taken at face value.

First, the SEC-required reports are misleading because they fail to include any reserves in excess of proved reserves, provide only a one-time snapshot based on constant price and cost assumptions (as of fiscal year-end), and employ a discount rate of 10 percent. Consequently, the reported figures must be supplemented with data from other sources.

With respect to reserves, oil companies routinely prepare engineering reports that show the total of proven, probable and possible reserves for internal use. Like the SEC reports, these engineering reports also must be read carefully. Each independent engineering firm is viewed differently, with some thought to provide higher estimates of reserves than others. The most well-known independent engineers include de Golyer & McNaughton and Ryder Scott.

In their reports, the engineers classify reserves as proven, probable or possible, but again, depending on the applicable recovery techniques and results on analogous or adjacent properties, the reports need to be adjusted to move reserves from one category to another. Similarly, assessment of raw undeveloped acreage can vary wildly. The Belridge auction proved that an engineer's report was the beginning—not the end—of inquiry.

Secondly, even if the reserve quantities are clear, differentiations between the quality and location of reserves are essential. "Oil quality" relates to the level of impurities (for example, sulfur), as well as specific gravity, with lighter being better, both of which have an impact on the cost of refining.

Finally, unlike other industrial assets, oil does run out. However, reserve lives can often be extended beyond the original estimate through the use of enhanced recovery techniques, which usually involve injecting water or a gas into the ground to push the reserves toward other well bores.

Similar concerns prevail in valuing natural gas. For example, natural gas values are enhanced if the gas is rich in liquids (such as propane, ethane or butane), which can be stripped out and sold, or its value can be reduced by the presence of impurities like hydrogen sulfide and other sulfur compounds, which necessitate costly processing.

To evaluate oil and gas reserves, the long-form method is to discount the future cash flows by multiplying the quantities available times the likely net sales price, after lifting costs. To do this, one needs a vision of the future price of oil, a "price deck." The resulting cash flows are discounted at the company's hurdle rate—the minimum rate of return required by the company.

As a matter of practical reality, however, companies seem to alter the price deck or their implicit hurdle rate when looking at large strategic deals. These adjustments in part reflect the buyer's sense of certainty as to the quality of reserves. Confidence in one's engineers, the level of familiarity with the particular field and recovery technology have a lot to do with the outcome.

Of course, this valuation method applies with most precision to proven reserves; the valuation of probable and possible reserves usually involves "haircutting" the quantities and is far more subjective, as is the evaluation of raw land.

Getty Oil   Getty Oil was the next big oil company to be bought. Again, Boone Pickens and Mesa Petroleum played a small role in the transaction. But billionaire Gordon Getty, son of Getty Oil's founder, J. Paul Getty, was at the center of the process. Gordon's passion was opera. He lived in a twenty-five-room San Francisco mansion, surrounded by his wife and four children, and passed many hours in a soundproof studio in the basement composing music.

Despite an apparent lack of interest in the details of day-to-day business management, Gordon retained considerable power over his father's company. His position as trustee of the Sarah C. Getty Trust, which held 40 percent of Getty Oil's shares, made his opinion very important to the company's future.

Over time, Gordon began to insert himself more forcefully in company affairs. He became increasingly disenchanted with the performance of CEO Sidney Petersen. Getty Oil was beset with the two main problems that plagued most of the majors. The company was depleting its reserves faster than it found new oil, and its stock was trading at a fraction of the value of the company's proven reserves.

Gordon Getty found this situation intolerable. He met with Boone Pickens and others, looking for ideas about what should be done. Sidney Petersen meanwhile attempted an unsuccessful boardroom coup, seeking to reduce Gordon Getty's influence. However, the efforts only increased the growing animosity on both sides. The hostilities broke out into the open, and Getty Oil was in play. Three weeks later, Pennzoil announced a $1.6 billion tender offer for 20 percent of the outstanding Getty Oil stock at $100 a share.

Pennzoil's partial tender represented an attempt by chairman J. Hugh Liedtke to become the swing voter who would decide Getty Oil's fate. Before the offer, the Getty Trust owned 40 percent of the company and the J. Paul Getty Museum another 12 percent. The museum, advised by takeover lawyer Martin Lipton of Wachtell, Lipton, Rosen & Katz, previously acted as a swing voter. As long as the museum sided with management, Petersen prevailed. However, at the end of 1983, the museum voted with Gordon to put down Petersen's coup. Liedtke jumped into the opening provided by this unrest.

The Pennzoil bid put both Gordon and the museum in a tough spot. If they allowed Pennzoil to proceed, its above-market tender offer might be oversubscribed—sending a clear signal of upheaval to the marketplace. They might lose control of Getty Oil in the process. After much public rumination about the future of Getty Oil, Gordon agreed with Liedtke that the trust and Pennzoil together would buy the 60 percent of Getty Oil not owned by the trust for $110 a share. But the agreement would survive only if approved by the Getty board at a meeting that same day. The insiders and independent members of the board resisted. They recessed the meeting in an effort to convince Gordon to auction the company to the highest bidder.

In the interim, investment bankers from Goldman, Sachs, representing Petersen and the company, had been canvassing for a white knight. One of these calls excited the interest of Texaco, which engaged a team to follow up, including us. Then the Getty board reconvened. After nudging a few extra dollars out of Liedtke, the board approved the Pennzoil agreement "in principle." A "definitive merger agreement" would have to be negotiated. An announcement was made to that effect.

With the cooperation of Lipton and Petersen, Texaco made a bid the very next day with options on the key holders' shares. Texaco ended up buying Getty for $10.8 billion. The deal made sense. Texaco had been depleting reserves at a rapid pace. The company's total reserves declined by 1.4 billion barrels between 1978 and 1983, leaving it with just 1 billion barrels in the ground. If the trend continued, Texaco would be out of business in a few short years. Furthermore, the company's finding cost had soared to roughly $21 a barrel. Even with the premium paid for Getty, Texaco was buying several billion barrels of oil for less than $5 a barrel.

Of course, any analysis of the Getty acquisition cannot overlook the huge impact of the subsequent Pennzoil litigation. Pennzoil claimed Texaco had induced a breach of contract. None of the New York or Delaware lawyers working on the deal thought there was any issue. However, due to a procedural blunder, Pennzoil was able to drag New York–based Texaco into a Texas court, removing the case from Delaware. Ultimately, the hometown jury ruled in Pennzoil's favor, concluding that Texaco had illegally intervened in Pennzoil's purchase of Getty. The jury awarded Pennzoil $10.5 billion in damages. Texaco eventually settled the case for $3 billion, but not before years of legal wrangling.

The Fight for Gulf   Ironically, by the summer of 1983, Mesa Petroleum was, by Pickens' admission, in trouble. Like other oil companies, it had overextended itself on a massive exploration program in the Gulf of Mexico.

In search of a quick fix, Pickens put his staff on the lookout for another Cities Service. Pickens and his team eventually settled on Gulf Oil, one of the Seven Sisters, as the world's seven largest oil companies were known. The company had $20 billion of assets, $30 billion in annual revenue and roughly 40,000 employees. However, Gulf was vulnerable because it traded at a huge discount to breakup value and had a history of poor management.

The size of Gulf did pose a problem. Mesa's plan was to make a major investment in Gulf and then agitate in favor of strategies to get Gulf's stock price up. Pickens planned in particular to advance a favorite proposal, one that he had put into action at Mesa. The idea was to spin off at least half of Gulf's oil and gas reserves into a royalty trust. Shareholders could then receive the cash flow from the reserves directly without first having to pay corporate tax on the money.

Before Pickens put his plan in motion, Mesa Petroleum invested $350 million in Gulf stock. To conceal Mesa's identity as the purchaser, the stock was bought through numbered bank accounts spread around the country. The initial stake equated to a roughly 4.9 percent ownership interest, just below the 5 percent threshold for a mandatory public filing. By investing heavily in Gulf, Mesa would profit on any increase in shareholder value resulting from its efforts.

By staying below the 5 percent threshold, Mesa was able to maintain secrecy long enough to raise the additional funds necessary to invest in Gulf stock. Today the tactic wouldn't work because of the Hart-Scott antitrust notification process required on purchases above $15 million.

In late September, Pickens set about the business of raising an additional $200 million of capital. He canvassed a small group of wealthy individuals. On October 4, a group of potential investors formed the Gulf Investors Group, a partnership with $550 million of equity (including the $350 million already invested by Mesa), for the express purpose of increasing Mesa's ability to pursue Gulf. This war chest provided Mesa $1.1 billion of purchasing power, taking margin loans into account. Pickens had learned a lesson from the Cities Service Pac-Man defense—the Gulf Investors Group agreement provided that voting control of the Gulf stock acquired would shift to one of the investors if Mesa were to experience a change in control.

Shortly after the meeting, Mesa returned to the markets and began buying more shares. Ten business days later, the Gulf Investors Group made the mandatory public filing with the Securities and Exchange Commission. At that point, the group owned almost 9 percent of Gulf's stock. But rather than indicating an intention to take over Gulf, the group characterized its holding of Gulf stock as "for investment purposes."

Though the statement was arguably accurate in light of Pickens' strategy of advocating management changes without assuming control, Gulf management was naturally skeptical and had reason to worry. Their company undeniably had problems, starting with a scandal in the 1970s involving illegal political contributions in the United States and questionable foreign payments. The ensuing purge of senior managers left Gulf indecisive during the tumultuous times following the first Oil Shock. In 1975, the company's oil rights in Kuwait—responsible for a large proportion of earnings—were nationalized. The company's United States reserves were in rapid depletion.

On the other hand, Gulf's incumbent managers, led by its new chairman, Jimmy Lee, had begun to address the existing problems. When the identity of Gulf's new large shareholder became known, they acted immediately to defend against Pickens. The company announced a special shareholder meeting in December 1983 to change Gulf's state of incorporation from Pennsylvania to Delaware, which state did not require cumulative voting, thereby minimizing the chance Mesa could elect a strong minority of the board.

Pickens turned the ensuing proxy contest into a referendum on Gulf's management. Management won the proxy contest, but only barely. The vote count was 52 to 48 percent, and Gulf was in play. ARCO jumped on the opportunity. It had been waiting on the sidelines anticipating Gulf's vulnerability. We were brought in to work with their team, and the tactical time to strike had come. ARCO offered $70 a share to buy out Gulf with the idea of cracking the Gulf board. The beleaguered board collapsed and announced an auction of the company. Immediately, a race broke out among three main bidders: ARCO, Chevron and KKR.

The auction was another watershed in the takeover business— the decided arrival of the financial buyer on the scene. KKR, with a few dozen employees, was bidding against two of America's largest and richest companies in a multibillion-dollar auction. Pickens was content to ride out his gain on the Gulf stock his group held.

On March 5, the Gulf board held a dramatic "one-shot" auction at the company's Pittsburgh headquarters. Each of the three bidders was given one opportunity to present its case and its highest offer. ARCO took a dive. It went first with a slightly sweetened $72 bid, knowing it was a loser. Having had the opportunity to conduct extensive due diligence, ARCO had enough concerns not to raise its bid materially. KKR followed with a mix of cash and stock valued, according to the buyout firm, at $87.50 a share. Chevron, third and last, offered $80 a share, all cash.

After hearing the presentations, the board debated the three offers. Very quickly, they settled on a choice between Chevron's all-cash offer and KKR's ostensibly higher package of cash and securities. The investment bankers advising the board could not put a precise value on the KKR securities. However, initially it appeared that KKR had an advantage. Under its proposal, management would stay in place.

However, some directors became concerned about this aspect of the KKR-led management buyout. They worried about the perception of impropriety that might result. Finally, after seven hours of debate, the board settled on Chevron. The deal would be valued at $13.2 billion. Mesa took home roughly $300 million after taxes.

Phillips Petroleum Under Siege   About six months after the Gulf transaction was approved by shareholders, three very interested observers were hunting in Spain. The trio—Fred Hartley, the CEO of Unocal, William Douce, the CEO of Phillips, and John McKinley, the CEO of Texaco—had been invited on the trip by the head of a construction company that worked with all three oil giants. But while they stalked around the Spanish countryside, two of the men, Douce and Hartley, must have felt something like the red-legged partridge they were hunting. Each of their companies' stock was under accumulation. Rumors swirled in the marketplace that Pickens was responsible.

Then, on December 2, the call came. At the time, Douce, Hartley and McKinley were having dinner. Someone interrupted to say Douce was wanted on the phone. It was urgent. Douce took the call. He learned from his company's treasurer that Mesa Petroleum had just filed Schedule 13D—a notice of over 5 percent ownership—with the SEC. Pickens already had purchased 6 percent of the outstanding Phillips stock. The day the filing became public, he also announced an intention to tender for an additional 14.9 percent at $60 a share. At the time, Phillips was trading at around $40 a share. With such a large difference between the tender and the market price, there likely would be a stampede to offer shares to Pickens.

Douce was on his way back to Bartlesville, Oklahoma, within hours, and we were called in with Morgan Stanley to fend off Mesa. Over the next four months, Douce would fight off first Pickens and then Carl Icahn.

Phillips was the quintessential hometown defense: the management and community cared enough to fight hard to keep the company intact, while protecting the shareholders. In the end, Phillips remained independent, but only after carrying out the complicated recapitalization plan that gave shareholders a package worth between $53 and $56 a share. The transaction put more than $4.5 billion of new debt on the Phillips balance sheet, but worked.

PROFILE

Fred Hartley

Fred Hartley earned his reputation as the toughest CEO in Big Oil long before Pickens came on the scene. He was born in Canada and trained as a chemical engineer. The consummate Organization Man, Hartley joined Union Oil in 1939 and worked his way up the ranks, spending his entire career at the company.

Over time, he also became known for an irascible nature, sharp tongue and fiery temper. He was fond of calling his financial advisers "bums." Proud of his tough reputation, he named his fifty-one-foot boat *My Way*.

Hartley rose to become president and CEO of the Union Oil Company of California in 1964. Within months, he presided over the then-largest oil deal in United States history: Unocal's acquisition of Pure Oil. The merger's success led Hartley to pursue an aggressive acquisition policy. He expanded Unocal into overseas exploration, chemicals and geothermal energy. In the process, Hartley transformed Unocal from a regional player to the nation's twelfth largest oil company. He accomplished that feat by plowing profits back into the company.

Even before the Oil Wars of the 1980s, Hartley often was in the press. After an oil spill coated the California coast in the late 1960s, he told a Senate committee, "I am always amazed at the publicity for the loss of a few birds." He also received considerable attention as an outspoken critic of early environmentalists.

In the early 1980s, Unocal suffered along with other members of Big Oil. Yet Hartley remained wedded to exploration and his expensive pet project—a massive oil shale mining effort in the Sierra Nevada mountains. To Hartley, his remaining in charge of Unocal was not just best for the company, it was best for the country. Exploration and R&D were a matter of patriotism and national security. American companies needed to search for more oil to "secure oil supplies for the United States and low energy costs for the free world."

Hartley held to his belief even as finding costs outpaced the market value of oil. This commitment, and its financial repercussions, eventually would lead Pickens to go after Unocal.

Unocal's Line in the Sand

Though Fred Hartley was spared in Spain, soon he too was under attack. On St. Valentine's Day 1985, he received the news. Pickens had filed another 13D with the SEC. Unocal was the target and Pickens already had 7.9 percent of the company's stock. Hartley came out with guns blazing. A bruising war ensued. Much of the action centered in Delaware court. Unocal would emerge bloodied, but Pickens would be beaten.

Unocal first turned to the courts. Pickens already had negotiated a $1.1 billion credit facility—a kind of standing agreement with a number of banks to provide loans. Security Pacific National Bank in Los Angeles, Unocal's traditional lead bank, was one of the banks in the syndicate. The bank was only a small player, to the tune of a $54 million commitment.

On March 12, Unocal filed a lawsuit against Security Pacific. The basis of the suit was that Security Pacific, with long-standing access to confidential Unocal information, had violated its contractual and fiduciary obligations. To maximize the impact of the suit, Unocal's public relations firm packaged a copy of the lawsuit with a letter from Hartley calling for an investigation of banks involved in take-overs and sent the material to Paul Volcker, chairman of the Federal Reserve. The same material was sent to every member of Congress and to every director at Pickens' banks. In the case of the banks, the documents arrived in unmarked brown envelopes on a Sunday morning, sent to the directors' home addresses.

Hartley decried raiders and the "merger mania" they had fashioned. People like Pickens left "ruined lives, corporate cadavers and poorer prospects for reserve replacement and future economic development for the nation" in their wake. The banks were also to blame. "Under the guise of 'protecting the small shareholders,' corporate raiders and their bankers and brokers are engaging in stock and bond and credit schemes reminiscent of those of the 1920s—but on a multibillion-dollar scale."

At times, Hartley became even more animated. Pickens was a financial barbarian and a "communist"; takeovers were "cannibalizing" the oil industry. Hartley hired squads of PR men and lobbyists to follow up. Hartley's antimerger shibboleths had some sticking power. A lot of antitakeover rhetoric was generated by his machine and is repeated even today.

Pickens struggled as the Unocal lawsuit began to have an effect. Security Pacific and two other banks pulled out of the Mesa credit syndicate. They were replaced, but Pickens worried that his vital loan capacity might be destroyed. On March 21, he struck back. Mesa filed suit against Unocal in a Los Angeles state court. The complaint alleged that Unocal had engaged in "unlawful efforts to interfere with the banking relationships" of Mesa.

To underline its commitment to the Unocal investment, Mesa then bought a huge block of stock, $322 million worth, and raised its ownership to over 13 percent. Pickens also began to consider a hostile tender offer. He met with investment bankers from Drexel and explored the possibility of raising capital through a junk bond offering. Drexel was enthusiastic.

On Good Friday, April 5, Pickens was in New York with a group of bankers, lawyers and other advisers. The decision was made to go forward with a tender offer for enough shares to give Mesa control of Unocal. Drexel would secure $3 billion in junk bond commitments to fund the offer. As a result, with the help of Drexel, Mesa offered $54 a share in cash for enough stock to give it over 50 percent of Unocal, and a package of securities for each additional Unocal share.

Unocal responded quickly. Its board rejected the Mesa offer as "grossly inadequate" despite the premium it would pay shareholders over the recent trading range of Unocal stock. Then Unocal announced a complicated self-tender offer under which Unocal would buy shares equal to 49 percent of its stock for a package of securities valued at $72 a share. The self-tender had two key features. First, it would only become active if Pickens succeeded in buying his 51 percent interest. Second, Pickens was excluded from the offer. So, if Mesa went forward with its takeover attempt, it would end up the only shareholder in a company with a huge amount of debt outstanding. Unocal would in fact be insolvent if Mesa went ahead.

Pickens denounced the Unocal offer as "just another poison pill in a new bottle." The offer, he argued, was illusory. If Mesa withdrew its planned purchase, Unocal would not be obligated to give shareholders anything. The shareholders would be back where they started, owning a stock projected to trade in the mid-30s.

Reacting to Pickens, Hartley revised the Unocal tender offer. The new terms provided that Unocal would unconditionally buy 29 percent of its shares. In addition, Unocal would consider placing 45 percent of its oil and gas reserves in a limited partnership, with the ownership interests in the partnership to be distributed to shareholders. Something like a royalty trust, this would direct the cash flow from the reserves directly to the shareholders.

Yet the terms of the revised Unocal tender still excluded Mesa. If the Unocal plan was carried out, Mesa's Unocal stock would suffer a dramatic loss in value. Pickens attacked the selective exclusion as a dangerous departure from the legal principle that all shareholders must be treated equally. Many legal experts agreed.

In line with expectations, Delaware judge Carolyn Berger held that Unocal would have to include Mesa in the tender offer if it wished to go forward. Unocal appealed Judge Berger's ruling to the Delaware Supreme Court within hours. Each side filed a 100-page document and the case was argued within three days. The court handed down its decision Friday, May 17. It was a shocker. Unocal's selective tender offer was "reasonable in relation to the threat that the board rationally and reasonably believed was posed by Mesa's inadequate and coercive two-tier tender offer." The decision was final and could not be appealed. Pickens could, therefore, be excluded.

Knowing he had been beaten, Pickens reached out to Unocal within hours, seeking a settlement. Hartley, savoring victory, was not in the mood to negotiate. However, Pickens was still Unocal's largest shareholder, and he could make a lot of trouble. Over the weekend, the two sides struggled through tough negotiations.

A deal was announced on Monday morning. Pickens would have shares included in the $72 Unocal tender, though a lower percentage of his total holdings than other shareholders. He agreed to a twenty-five-year standstill under which he could not buy more Unocal stock. As part of his agreement with Unocal, Pickens promised to hold his shares for at least a year. The press roundly described the settlement as Pickens' first major defeat, although Mesa would actually make close to $100 million.

The *Unocal* case revolved around whether the Business Judgment Rule applied to the Unocal directors' decision to institute a discriminatory self-tender. The basic idea of the Business Judgment Rule is that the Delaware courts will generally defer to the business judgment of a board of directors as long as there is no self-dealing or lack of care.

According to the *Unocal* court, a board may enact takeover defenses that thwart a bid, but those defenses will be subject to enhanced judicial scrutiny. Under this enhanced review, a court will look at the board's decision process and the substantive decision and determine whether both are reasonable in relation to the threat involved. In the case of Mesa's takeover attempt, the court held that the Unocal board had acted reasonably. Essentially, the Delaware court used a "smell" test and decided that it didn't like Pickens.

The SEC eventually overruled the Delaware court on the narrow point of whether a selective tender should be allowed. Reacting to the *Unocal* case, the commission enacted a rule banning discriminatory self-tenders. However, in a broader sense, *Unocal* created a key standard of takeover law, a rule which instantly became a focus of future takeover litigation—were the board's actions proportional to the threat? A variant of the Unocal discrimination technique is incorporated in the more sophisticated defense device, the poison pill.

Self-Restructuring

Unocal marked the final major hostile fight in the Oil Wars, but the underlying economic currents continued to favor change. A number of major oil companies restructured themselves during the late 1980s and early 1990s. ARCO chairman Robert O. Anderson, with a view of the Unocal building from his fifty-first-floor office, made his move even as the fight for Unocal was underway.

The plan—"a sort of self-acquisition"—was announced on April 29, ironically the day when Unocal had originally scheduled its annual meeting. Under the restructuring, money would be borrowed and used to repurchase $4 billion of ARCO stock. In addition, the company's exploration budget was slashed and write-offs were taken on its mining division, a previous diversification that would be divested. The overall package included a total of $1.5 billion in writedowns. Most dramatically, ARCO would shed its downstream gasoline business east of the Mississippi.

As one analyst put it, ARCO was "doing exactly what Wall Street's been telling it to do for three years." The stock price responded. It had been lingering in the mid-40s. Two weeks after the announcement, it was above 60. With this new trading price and extra debt on the balance sheet, ARCO effectively immunized itself from the Pickenses of the world.

During this period many of the other majors also felt impelled to act. Royal Dutch/Shell spent $5.5 billion to acquire the 30 percent of Shell Oil U.S.A. it did not already own. British Petroleum bought the 45 percent of Standard Oil of Ohio it did not already own for $7.8 billion. And Exxon spent $16 billion on a stock repurchase program between 1983 and mid-1990. At the same time, the company pursued smaller asset acquisitions and slashed its overhead.

The 1985 collapse in oil prices put added pressures on Big Oil. Profits plummeted; shareholders began to revolt. It was at this point that the diversification efforts of most oil companies were unwound.

Exxon wrote off Office Systems. Mobil faced agitation in favor of selling Montgomery Ward and eventually did so in a 1988 management-led LBO. Montgomery Ward limped along for almost ten years, but ultimately filed for bankruptcy in 1997.

Texaco was a special case. Marred by the overhanging Pennzoil judgment, the company declared bankruptcy in 1987. Carl Icahn sensed an opportunity. He began accumulating Texaco shares in the market at a steep discount to prior trading levels. With a large stake in place, he pushed the company to settle the Pennzoil case. In Icahn's view, any settlement would be good for the stock price. The company finally came to terms when forced to do so in bankruptcy court.

As Icahn had predicted, Texaco's stock got a boost. However, Icahn kept hounding the company. He wanted Texaco to sell off assets and pay a large dividend to shareholders. After Icahn waged an unsuccessful proxy fight, company management finally agreed to pay a special dividend. Satisfied with the outcome, Icahn sold his shares for a reported $500 million profit.

The Skirmishing Spreads

Big Oil was not the only sector of the energy business rocked by change in the 1980s. The natural gas business, a close cousin to the oil business, experienced similar volatility. The resulting hostile takeover fights matched the billion-dollar oil mergers of the day in the blaze of their intensity.

Two factors made the natural gas business a particularly fruitful field for takeover activity. First, in the late 1970s and early 1980s, many companies had agreed to "take or pay" contracts as a way to ensure supply in a tight market. The contracts obligated the companies to pay for a fixed amount of product at a set price, whether they needed the product or not. When the market price plummeted, these contracts hammered profits. Many of the companies eventually renegotiated and paid pennies on the dollar, but for a time they looked particularly vulnerable.

The impact of price volatility was magnified by deregulation. Up until the early 1980s, the natural gas business was a sleepy industry that earned stable returns. Pipeline companies transported the product to customers, primarily large industrial concerns and utilities. Rates were regulated. Then, in the early 1980s, gas prices at the wellhead were deregulated. Producers were allowed to charge whatever the market would bear. In 1985, regulators went a step further, allowing utilities and industrial customers freedom to shop around for gas. Third parties other than pipeline companies also were allowed into the business of selling gas. A host of independent natural gas marketing companies sprang up. As a result, pipeline companies, which previously had lived in a world of muted pricing and marketing pressures, were thrown into the competitive world.

Companies had varying success dealing with the new environment. Some floundered around for a few years until they found their stroke. Others took advantage of the uncertainty to build strong competitive positions. A spate of deals resulted, and the industry consolidated.

Coastal Corporation's Man on Horseback   Coastal Corporation's Oscar Wyatt saw his pipeline competitors' troubles as an opportunity. In particular, Wyatt hoped to jump-start Coastal's expansion effort by acquiring a company with existing capacity instead of spending the years required to build new pipelines.

Wyatt launched his first major takeover attempt in 1983, a $550 million hostile bid for Texas Gas Resources. However, Texas Gas eluded him when white knight CSX Corporation stepped forward. The next year, Wyatt offered $1.3 billion for Houston Natural Gas, which we represented. This bid was beaten back by incumbent management, which bought out Coastal's stake after threatening a Cities Service–type Pac-Man bid for Coastal.

For Wyatt, the strategic imperative for a major acquisition remained. The two failed attempts had only whetted his appetite. He took two steps to improve his chances for the next battle. First, Wyatt restructured the charter of Coastal so that it was immune to takeover itself, a "Death Star" not subject to the Pac-Man defense. In a creative proxy, Wyatt asked his shareholders to approve the Death Star vehicle so that he could attack other companies without being vulnerable. They overwhelmingly supported him. Second, he raised a $600 million blind pool of equity through a Drexel Burnham Lambert junk bond offering. Investors only knew the money would be used for acquisitions, not the identity of the targets.

Wyatt launched his next fight early in 1985. Rumors of an impending bid had been swirling in the market for weeks; the target was unclear. During the first week in March the answer became apparent. Coastal launched a $2.27 billion hostile tender offer for American Natural Resources. Initially, management at the Detroit pipeline and natural gas production company resisted. But Wyatt was desperate to win. ANR finally agreed to be acquired by Coastal after Wyatt bumped his offer to $2.5 billion.

After two failed attempts, Wyatt had a major victory. The price looked steep at the time. Yet Wyatt's vision was vindicated. From an operational perspective, the addition of ANR's Midwest pipelines gave Coastal a strong position in that market. From a financial perspective, ANR's strong and growing cash flow proved more than sufficient to service the debt incurred in the transaction. Coastal was able to pay down roughly $1 billion of debt by 1989. The additional cash flow also gave Wyatt the ability to pursue further expansion.

By 1989, Coastal had digested ANR but still lacked a major connection to the Northeast. Wyatt was ready for another acquisition. He quickly settled on a target—Texas Eastern Corp. The company possessed a coveted link to the Northeast. It also owned valuable North Sea oil reserves and a portfolio of Houston real estate which could be sold off to fund an acquisition.

Ultimately, Panhandle Eastern Corp. snatched Texas Eastern from Wyatt, topping Wyatt's $2.5 billion offer with a rival $3.2 billion bid. Itself a beleaguered company, Panhandle was willing to gamble that the combination of its Midwestern pipes and Texas Eastern's Northeastern pipes would create a powerful nationwide distributor. Panhandle had more miles of pipe, but Texas Eastern had three times the revenue. Initially, Panhandle's debt would increase more than fourfold. Even after planned asset sales, the burden was steep. Still, the troubled company, facing a buy-or-be-bought situation, decided the potential reward was worth the risk.

As for Wyatt, after losing the Texas Eastern fight, he decided natural gas properties had become overpriced in the market. He turned to investing money in building new pipes and expanding Coastal's network internally.

PROFILE

Oscar Wyatt

Born in Beaumont, Texas, during the 1920s, Wyatt kicked around the shipyards and oil fields in the summertime. He served as a bomber pilot in World War II. After the war, he earned an engineering degree, then started a small oil business that would grow into $9 billion a year Coastal Petroleum. Along the way, Wyatt earned a reputation as a tough customer.

During the early 1970s, Wyatt became a pariah in his home state. His companies had supply contracts with hundreds of Texas towns. When the Oil Shock jacked up the price of natural gas, Wyatt's companies didn't have enough reserves to fill the contracts. Caught between producers and customers, he shut off gas supplies to San Antonio and Austin in the middle of winter. He fought customer lawsuits for years.

Name calling didn't seem to bother him. "My job isn't to win a popularity contest," he would say. "My job is to win a profitability contest." In the early 1980s, Wyatt's maxim led him to become involved in hostile takeover attempts. In fact, Wyatt did have an advantage over other bidders. He was willing to be much more aggressive in the valuation of disputed supply contracts, figuring rightly that he could settle disputes on a more favorable basis than existing management could.

The Consolidation Widens   Oscar Wyatt was not the only player going after natural gas companies in the mid-1980s. Other strategic purchasers, as well as financial buyers, saw the consolidation potential in the industry. Rocked by price fluctuations and facing an uncertain deregulated future, many natural gas companies had traded down in the market. The nation's roughly twenty pipeline companies—some with relatively stable cash flows—were appealing targets.

One big consolidation move came in May 1985 at the instigation of investor Irwin Jacobs. Smelling vulnerability, Jacobs built a stake in InterNorth, an energy transmission and production company with access to low-priced reserves and little debt. Sam Segnar, chairman of InterNorth, preferred to act rather than react. He contacted his counterpart at Houston Natural Gas and suggested a merger. Two weeks later, the pair announced a $2.3 billion deal. InterNorth would acquire Houston Natural Gas, but HNG's CEO Kenneth Lay would take over the top spot as of January 1, 1987. Board representation would be split relatively evenly.

The combination of HNG and InterNorth made compelling strategic sense. Together, the two companies possessed a 37,000-mile pipeline system spanning coast to coast. This wide network gave the new company—renamed Enron in 1986—access to almost every major market and a wide range of supply sources. Enron therefore had the ability to provide customers and suppliers with efficient, effective service.

Once in the CEO job, Lay set about consolidating Enron's operations. He sold off noncore businesses to pay down debt, pared Enron's workforce and reorganized operations. Very shortly, the strategic vision that brought HNG and InterNorth together was vindicated. Enron was on the way to becoming a model for the competitive new superpipeline companies that have come to dominate the business.

The 1990s and Beyond

The self-restructurings of Big Oil and the preceding hostile takeover fights left a leaner, more efficient oil industry in their wake.

In recent years, oil companies have focused on reorganizing their downstream refining and marketing operations. Plagued by razor-thin downstream margins, the large integrated oil companies have moved to revive these units. For example, in 1997, Texaco and Royal Dutch/Shell agreed to merge their U.S. refining and marketing businesses into a joint venture. A similar deal between Phillips and Conoco fell apart. The moves followed Unocal's announcement that it intended to spin off its refining and retail business. Clearly, cost reduction is the main driving force behind these deals.

Meanwhile, the smaller independents have been getting together in a search for competitive bulk. Our client Diamond Shamrock's 1996 merger-of-equals with Ultramar is a good example. By combining, the companies strengthened their retailing presence. Furthermore, with strong operations in California and Texas, the new company is positioned to take advantage of the growing Southwestern market.

However, the major action of the 1990s has been among oil services, utilities and natural gas pipeline companies. Across the board, the secular trend in each of these sectors is toward consolidation.

The major drivers for activity have been fluctuations in commodity prices and regulatory changes.

The Strategic Landscape   The oil services industry is populated with drilling equipment and service companies which make it their business to serve and supply production companies. Over the past fifteen years, the business has gone through a feast-or-famine cycle closely tied to oil price gyrations. Naturally, as oil prices rise, exploration and the demand for oil services increase. Given this dynamic, the early 1980s was a boom time. Companies invested heavily in oil rigs and other production capacity, which then was leased out to producers. The 1985 crash in prices ushered in a long lean period. Excess capacity drove prices and margins down. Many weaker competitors closed down.

The tough times were a hothouse for deal activity. In one high-profile combination, Baker International and Hughes Tool merged in a $1.2 billion stock swap, creating the industry's third largest company. The merger brought together Hughes' drill bits and Baker's drilling equipment, and allowed for the parties to ride out the downturn by slashing costs.

With respect to both utility and natural gas companies, the recent deal frenzy was sparked by the continuing move to deregulation. The final plank in pipeline deregulation came in 1992, when federal authorities opened the sale, distribution and storage of natural gas to all comers. Margins in gas production narrowed further as commodity pricing took over. This gave a final shove to the natural gas companies, which accelerated their drive into the still-profitable marketing and distribution side of the business. Another wave of consolidation swept the industry.

The experience of Panhandle Eastern, the company which saved Texas Eastern from the clutches of Oscar Wyatt, is indicative. For Panhandle, the early 1990s was a rocky period. The price of natural gas went into free fall and margins collapsed. Its problems were exacerbated by the debt burden from the Texas Eastern deal. The transaction had jacked Panhandle's debt load up over $2.8 billion. While the associated interest expense looked manageable in 1989, it became burdensome when competition ate into profit margins.

Meanwhile, a number of land mines buried in Texas Eastern's operations—primarily environmental problems—surfaced shortly after the deal closed. Panhandle was forced to slash its dividend by 60 percent and its stock lost over 60 percent of its value in the immediate aftermath. The company's CEO left under pressure.

Over the next few years, Dennis Hendrix, the former chief executive of Texas Eastern, who returned to be the CEO, concentrated on reshaping Panhandle. He settled several disputes with customers, negotiated his way out of uneconomical take-or-pay contracts and wrote off impaired assets. Then, he shifted Panhandle's focus. Production was downplayed and distribution became key. Panhandle would make money moving other people's gas. Rather than spend money on finding new gas, Panhandle built new distribution capacity in the lucrative Northeast market.

A major acquisition also played a crucial role in Panhandle's overhaul. In 1994, the company acquired Associated Natural Gas, a marketing outfit, paying $591 million in stock and assuming $239 million of Associated's debt.

The desire to gain further exposure to marketing and distribution capabilities was not unique to Panhandle. Enron Corp., Coastal and other natural gas players also were busily buying up marketing capacity during the early 1990s.

Deregulation is just beginning to take shape in the utilities business. The utilities story begins in the nineteenth century, when Thomas Edison and others pioneered the commercial generation of electricity. One initial barrier they faced was the necessity for large capital outlays to develop an extensive infrastructure for the generation and distribution of power. To induce investment, a patchwork of local monopolies, each separately chartered, was developed. These companies accepted local regulation in exchange for a guaranteed market. With the chance for a payoff thus improved, investors poured millions of dollars into the construction of power plants and transmission systems, and the local power company was born.

Eventually, through mergers and acquisitions, thousands of local power companies were consolidated and became the stable, modern-day utilities of the post–World War II era. The monopoly system remained in place. Utilities were guaranteed a stable return on investment in the form of cost-plus pricing. Regulators allowed the companies to charge whatever rate was necessary to earn a "reasonable" return on money invested. Added profits would flow each time a company invested more capital to build a new power plant or purchase a new transformer. Theoretically, regulators policed the companies to avoid unnecessary spending.

The monopoly system may have been effective and appropriate in the power industry's developmental era, but its rigidity caused the industry to become inefficient as it matured. Under cost-plus pricing, when a company made a bad decision regarding an expenditure, government regulators nonetheless usually added the expenditure to the company's rate base. In effect, then, bad decisions by utility company executives and investors, as well as lax regulatory oversight, were paid for by utility customers.

The impact of this system is apparent today in the dramatic variations in the cost of energy provided by different utilities. Northern California's Pacific Gas & Electric, for example, charges its customers about 10 cents per kilowatt-hour for electricity. Oregon's Portland General Corporation, on the other hand, runs the meter at an average of something like 5½ cents per kilowatt-hour. On the eastern tip of New York's Long Island, customers dole out roughly 16 cents per kilowatt-hour.

Many factors have contributed to the high cost of electricity in particular markets. Cost overruns and ill-fated expenditures certainly play a part. Nuclear power facilities are the classic example.

When oil prices skyrocketed in the 1970s, utilities began planning for nuclear reactors. In many cases, by the time construction began, oil prices had settled back to more reasonable levels. Still, nuclear facilities were built at great cost; the final price tag often was considerably more than originally projected, partly because state and federal regulations shifted in the interim between planning and completion.

As a result, the electricity generated in the facilities ended up costing far more than power generated through conventional means and many nuclear plants proved to be extremely bad investments. Still, cost-plus pricing largely allowed utility companies to transfer the consequences to their customers.

Today, the technology and infrastructure is now in place to transfer power generated in Wisconsin to customers in California. States like California and New York have begun to relax monopoly protection, and other states promise to follow. Without monopoly protection, a low-cost producer can enter the market of a high-cost producer. The high-cost producer will then be forced to adapt or go out of business. The result is that we are on the edge of a revolution in the structure of the utility business. In particular, three overlapping trends can be discerned amid the growing flood of utilities deals: globalization, integration and diversification.

Facing the prospect of growing competition, utility companies have been looking abroad for high-growth markets. One manifestation of this trend has been the race to invest in projects in the emerging markets of South America and China. Another has been a rush by U.S. utilities into the U.K. market. For example, in 1996, Wasserstein Perella represented Virginia-based Dominion Resources in a $2.2 billion acquisition of the U.K.'s East Midlands Electricity. Other major U.K. acquisitions include Entergy Corporation's $2.1 billion deal for London Electricity and CalEnergy's $1.3 billion hostile buyout of Northern Electric.

Great Britain represents a particularly attractive market for U.S.

companies because deregulation has proceeded more quickly there. The U.K. companies have already begun offering telecommunications and other services, and are a laboratory for what will happen in the U.S. market. Moreover, U.K. companies have outpaced their U.S. counterparts in terms of growth.

Integration has been another strategic response to coming deregulation. Here, the model has been the merger of natural gas companies and utilities. Some have come at the instigation of the gas companies—Enron's $3.2 billion purchase of the Portland General Corporation, for example. More commonly, though, utilities have reached out to buy the experience and marketing savvy of the natural gas concerns. Houston Industries spent $2.4 billion for NorAm Energy. Similarly, Duke Power of North Carolina recently nabbed Panenergy—the renamed Panhandle Eastern—for $7.7 billion.

LEADING THE WAY

Kenneth Lay and Enron

Enron CEO Kenneth Lay has stitched HNG and InterNorth together into the leading gas pipeline and marketing company. Now, the purchase of Portland General signals the next phase in Enron's growth. The goal is to bring skill developed in the deregulated gas market to the deregulating electricity market.

Lay saw that the fragmented gas industry was bound to consolidate under the force of deregulation. Moreover, he understood that marketing would become the key to future success. Enron capitalized on these visions of the future by pioneering the practice of trading natural gas. Very quickly, Enron's trading operation became a de facto market maker for natural gas contracts and developed into the nation's leading wholesaler of natural gas.

Part of the Enron success has been transforming a staid utility company into an entrepreneurial, driving competitor. Lay has accomplished the shift by bringing in new people—many trained in business disciplines like marketing and finance—to recharge the Enron culture.

As deregulation proceeds in the electricity market, Lay hopes to repeat the earlier success. The acquisition of Portland General gives Enron a captive supply source. Meanwhile, Enron's traders have begun to swap electricity and already are a leading provider, behind the Bonneville Power Administration and the Tennessee Valley Authority.

Of course, a great deal of competition exists in the electricity business as hundreds of companies scramble to get a piece of this $320 billion market. California is scheduled to open its market in January 1998 and other states will follow shortly thereafter. Lay already has a staff of over 600 working on retailing strategies and has initiated a nationwide advertising program.

Whether these initiatives will pay off is an open question. However, for now, Lay and Enron are leading the way toward a future integrated energy market.

From a strategic perspective, the thread tying these deals together is the utilities' search for marketing expertise. The natural gas companies have been through deregulation once before and know how to compete in a free market. Furthermore, the eventual hope is to provide bundled services—gas, electricity, and so forth—to customers on a nationwide basis once deregulation has run full course. One company, Topeka-based Western Resources, has even decided a natural extension of its business is the home security industry.

Diversification also meshes with the vision of bundled services. Utilities possess extremely valuable customer recognition, access and information. The hope is that the envelope from the power company, which arrives at homes each month, ultimately can be used as an entrée to provide all manner of other services.

The Future The oil, natural gas and utilities industries are expected to generate continuing deal activity. Clearly, the shake-up in utilities has just begun. In the oil industry, the kickoff deal of the consolidation of the late 1990s was Union Pacific Resources' unsuccessful $4 billion hostile bid for Pennzoil. The bruising, acrimonious fight—with the opposing sides trading barbs in the press and in court—was reminiscent of the 1980s Oil Wars. However, Pennzoil's effective defense also highlighted the evolution of defensive tactics that has occurred since the 1980s.

Union Pacific Resources (UPR) first approached Pennzoil in April 1997 with a friendly $80 a share offer. Pennzoil had underperformed the market over the prior five years, but management had a turnaround plan in place, which appeared to be taking hold. Confident that this plan would deliver greater value to shareholders than UPR's bid, Pennzoil management rejected attempts to negotiate a deal.

UPR went public on June 23, 1997, with an $84 a share preemptive hostile bid. The price represented a 56 percent premium to Pennzoil's trading price thirty days prior to the announcement. UPR structured a classic two-tier offer—cash for just over 50 percent of Pennzoil's stock and UPR stock for the remainder. UPR management was trying to pressure the Pennzoil board to turn friendly.

Pennzoil shareholders embraced the UPR acquisition. More than 60 percent tendered into the front end of UPR's offer. Yet, Pennzoil's board remained steadfast in its defense. The board rejected UPR's offer as inadequate and ordered a full defense. Essentially, Pennzoil decided to just say no.

Two key defensive innovations of the 1980s gave the Pennzoil board a strong defensive position. First, the company had a strong poison pill in place, effectively precluding a hostile deal unless the Pennzoil board pulled the pill. Second, Pennzoil had a reinforced board that addressed the key weakness of a just say no defense. In particular, the board could not be removed by the consent of shareholders. Because the terms of directors were staggered, UPR would need at least two annual meetings to capture the board and force the removal of the pill.

With this strong defensive perimeter, Pennzoil effectively punched holes in the UPR bid. The first focus was on the stock offered by UPR in the back-end merger. Questions regarding the value of the stock ultimately caused UPR to shift to an all-cash offer. Even so, the Pennzoil board continued to insist that its strategic plan would provide superior returns to shareholders. Eventually, UPR concluded it would not be able to capture Pennzoil without a long and costly battle. UPR withdrew its offer, announcing it would focus on other growth opportunities.

Though UPR's bid was unsuccessful, the stirrings are in the air. Most oil company executives are reviewing acquisition opportunities and polishing off defensive strategies. The only real question is when, not whether, consolidation will again sweep the industry.

Metamorphosis: 9
Conglomerates
Transformed

> *"As Gregor Samsa awoke from unsettling dreams one morning, he found himself transformed in his bed into a monstrous vermin. . . . 'What has happened to me?' he thought. It was no dream."*
>
> Franz Kafka, "The Metamorphosis"

A corporate treasure hunt was sparked by the Oil Wars. As the oil industry restructured through the early 1980s, Wall Street buzzed with talk of "breakup value." Assuming that undervalued assets were not unique to the oil business, investors began to prowl for companies whose parts were worth more than the whole. The search was on for hidden assets buried within American businesses.

After faltering at the end of the 1960s, many large, diversified companies limped through the 1970s. In the 1980s these conglomerates became punching bags for critics. Diversification was widely held to be a failed experiment. Centralized management alone could not create a unified, efficient whole out of unrelated pieces. This was the new orthodoxy. Companies that failed to conform were punished in the marketplace.

As a result, ITT, Gulf + Western, Tenneco, City Investing, Westinghouse, Wickes, Teledyne, IC Industries, Allied, Litton, Rockwell and Textron were all torn apart. The 1980s and 1990s fed off the undoing of the deals of the 1960s.

The Brave New World

The early 1980s were a caustic business environment. Interest rates topped out above 20 percent. The Dow Jones Industrial Average fell to the low 700s, where it had been in 1963 and again in 1970. Stockholders in the conglomerates suffered particularly. LTV's stock closed as high as $136 in 1968 and below $12 in 1980. ITT's stock traded as high as $63 in 1968 and as low as $25 in 1980. Investors were irate. The centrifugal force cracked the conglomerate shell.

A number of key factors shaped the pace and scope of this trend:

Financial   Financial forces encouraged the conglomerates to consider selling assets. High interest rates in particular created a powerful inducement in favor of converting assets into cash. After the buying sprees of the 1960s and early 1970s, many of the conglomerates were left with a significant debt burden. In many cases, rising rates in the 1980s made this burden more difficult to bear.

ITT, for example, carried nearly $5 billion of debt in 1980. The resulting interest expense was manageable while interest rates were relatively low. When the prime rate hit 20 percent, ITT began to feel the squeeze. In 1981, the company was forced to pay out almost $800 million in interest, a tremendous drag on its reported earnings. Rand Araskog, Harold Geneen's successor, set debt reduction as a major goal and divestitures were obviously necessary.

Shifting Market Orthodoxy   Market forces coalesced in favor of more divestitures. The values inherent in conglomerates became the center of attention. Research analysts began to look at the pieces of a company to determine breakup value. The attention given to breakup value in the market also made companies receptive to suggested divestiture programs.

The success of the Gibson Greeting Cards buyout sparked a sequence of similar deals. Leveraged entrepreneurs snatched assets away for a fraction of their true value. Yet the conglomerates were unable or unwilling to unlock the same values on their own. The buyers took the risk and seemed more sophisticated than the lumbering companies of the 1980s. There were sufficient examples of success to lead to the boom in the leveraged buyout business and the demise of the conglomerate.

Increased Sophistication   The early conglomerates were built on a premise of ever increasing earnings through acquisition, the primacy of financial management skills, and an adoring analytical and money management community. All of these ideas were anachronistic by the early 1980s. Analysts tended to focus on core industries and operational performance became primal. Money managers could create risk diversification among industries by themselves.

A Passing of the Guard   Personality is an indispensable key to understanding the transformation of the conglomerates. Many of the companies—Textron, LTV, Gulf + Western—were built up by founding entrepreneurs. Other companies that blossomed in the 1960s featured strong leaders such as ITT's Harold Geneen.

Starting in the late 1970s, the leaders of the conglomerate era began to pass into retirement, some more gracefully than others. These men had spent their professional careers building up major diversified companies and had earned a reputation for genius in the process. Naturally, they resisted the notion that their companies needed to adjust with the times. The idea that the companies should be broken apart was anathema.

Eventually, these companies, which originally reveled in their image of having the best of "modern" management, were perceived to be the most antiquated. Indeed, one reason the LBO buyers of conglomerate divestitures did so well is that the companies were so poorly managed.

The successors who took over in top management were not tied as directly to the acquisition era and were not as emotionally invested in the idea of retaining the pieces as a combined whole. The switch in philosophy was sometimes dramatic.

Turmoil at ITT

ITT is perhaps the classic example. The company suffered through a difficult period in the early 1970s. ITT's stock, which traded as high as $67 per share in 1971, hit $12 in 1974. Earnings also suffered. ITT's string of fifty-eight straight quarterly earnings increases came to an end in 1974. Earnings for the year as a whole came in 13 percent below the previous year's record and the downward trend continued into 1975.

The economic problems at ITT were magnified by political controversies—the company's involvement in Chile, alleged improprieties surrounding the San Diego Republican party convention, the Hartford Insurance antitrust and tax cases. The bad news at times threatened to bury Harold Geneen.

Still, despite the tumult, Geneen survived. A somewhat reluctant board granted him a two-year contract extension in August 1974, ignoring ITT's mandatory retirement age of sixty-five. When that contract expired at the end of 1977, Geneen gave up one title—chief executive officer—but remained chairman. Lyman Hamilton became the new CEO.

Notwithstanding the formal transfer of day-to-day authority, Geneen was not ready to release the reins of power. Within months, he began openly sniping at Hamilton. The main source of friction was the new CEO's decision to redirect ITT's strategic focus. Geneen favored the long-standing emphasis on revenue growth, the foundation of ITT's 1960s buying frenzy. Hamilton was more concerned with the bottom line and return on equity. His strategy dictated that under-performing businesses be sold off.

Things came to a head in June of 1979. Hamilton had been at the helm for eighteen months and was ready to make a bold move—the sale of ITT's European consumer goods business. Geneen was irate when he heard the news. He leapt into action while Hamilton was away on a three-week business trip in Asia. Geneen furiously lobbied his fellow board members. Two weeks later, Hamilton was out as CEO and Rand Araskog, Geneen's new pick as successor, was in.

Araskog inherited an incredibly complex, troubled company. During the Geneen years, ITT had bought out or merged with more than 250 companies. Revenues had climbed from $765 million to over $22 billion. With the exception of the early 1970s, earnings had been strong. The first few Araskog years were not as positive. Earnings and revenues were down, the stock price continued to languish. The debt burden left over from Geneen's acquisition program was at least partly to blame.

Araskog set about reversing the downward slide. His intermediate goal was to reduce the company's debt load, which hovered near 50 percent of total capital. Like Hamilton, he saw a divestiture program as the means to this end. However, unlike Hamilton, Araskog first cleared a major impediment out of the way—Geneen. Araskog gave ITT's board members an ultimatum, and they pressed Geneen into resigning his chairmanship.

Free to act, Araskog went on a selling spree. Between 1979 and 1983, ITT sold roughly $200 million of assets each year. However, the stock price failed to respond. ITT continued to trade significantly below the range established in the early 1970s. A number of takeover threats began to circle, including those by Jay Pritzker, a Chicago real estate developer and investor, and financier Irwin Jacobs. In response, Araskog picked up the pace. By the end of 1984, ITT had divested sixty-nine companies for close to $2 billion.

Insurgent ITT shareholders nonetheless kept pounding away at Araskog. In November 1984, the company received a number of requests to put the liquidation of the entire company to a shareholder vote. ITT ultimately kept the request from going to a vote, but it spurred Araskog and the ITT board to adopt an even more aggressive divestiture program. On January 16, 1985, the company announced a plan to sell additional companies.

Araskog followed through on the plan. By 1986, the tally of divested businesses reached ninety-five, with total proceeds of $4 billion. Debt as a share of total capital slipped below 30 percent in 1988. Still, the selling of low-margin, underperforming businesses continued. Finally, in a particularly dramatic move, ITT moved away from its roots as an international telephone company. In 1992, the company sold its telephone subsidiary to a French company for $3.6 billion, keeping an international telephone directories business as its only link to the phone business.

This left ITT with operations in forest products, financial services, manufacturing and leisure. At this point, Araskog stunned his shareholders by making the strategic decision to create and expand a core leisure and gaming business. The forest products company Rayonier was spun off to shareholders. Then the company paid $3 billion to acquire casino operator Caesars World and partial ownership of Madison Square Garden, the owner of the New York Knicks and Rangers, claiming they fit with ITT's Sheraton Hotels.

The culmination of the gaming and leisure strategy came in 1995, when Araskog embraced the new market orthodoxy. In line with persistent market pressure, he announced plans to split ITT into three separate companies. The division occurred in December of that year. As a result, three companies carried the ITT name. ITT Industries operated a manufacturing and defense business, ITT Hartford Group a financial services business and ITT Corporation the hotel, gaming and sports properties, with Araskog as CEO.

The Strategic Merits of the Spin-Off

The spin-off—a kind of corporate chisel used to break a company into smaller pieces—has become a common feature on the business landscape. The roster of recent spin-off participants includes not only ITT, but also General Motors, AT&T, Viacom, Sprint, Pepsi and U S West. Although each situation is unique, the desire to appease Wall Street by becoming more focused is a common theme.

Stepping into Araskog's shoes, the attractions of the 1995 spin-off become apparent. First and foremost, the spin-off can transform a diversified large company into a number of smaller, more focused companies. The resulting pure-play companies would no longer be tagged with ITT's conglomerate discount.

Another great attraction of a spin-off is that the transaction is tax-free to the company and its shareholders if properly structured. A sale of ITT's industrial and financial services businesses, on the other hand, would likely trigger a significant tax liability. The company would be taxed on any gain realized on the sale, and if the money were then paid out to the shareholders, they also would be taxed on the dividend payment.

A spin-off also allows shareholders to benefit from future improvements in a business. Some empirical evidence suggests that both spun-off companies and their former parents tend to outperform the market in the years following a spin-off. One explanation for this is that a spin-off can unleash entrepreneurial potential. As part of a larger business, a smaller subsidiary often succumbs to the "rich uncle syndrome." The parent company protects the subsidiary in lean times and may not force the subsidiary to live up to its potential. At the same time, being part of a larger organization can stifle employees of the subsidiary.

Viewed through the lens of ITT's strategic decision, then, a spin-off was a tax-efficient way to simplify a business while still allowing shareholders to capture the benefits associated with the ownership of divested assets. Of course, this begs the question of whether the spin-off is a radical enough solution.

For ITT, this issue crystallized in 1996. Although ITT's stock ran up on the concept of the three-way split, Araskog came under intense pressure once ITT Corporation began to trade independently. Many investors believed he had "gone Vegas" during his recent acquisition spree and that the disparate parts of the new enterprise made little sense together. Criticism mounted further when Araskog launched an expensive plan to build several Planet Hollywood hotel and casino complexes. ITT's stock was pummeled in response and gave up much of the price gains from the spin-off, which set up one of the most contentious takeover fights of the 1990s.

Unlocking the Hidden Value

Throughout the 1980s, conglomerate leaders battled to close the perceived gap between the stock market and breakup values of their companies. For most conglomerates, operational adjustments were an important part of the equation. Costs were trimmed, marketing refocused, divisions reorganized. The efforts to rejuvenate internal performance were as complicated and far-reaching as the operations housed within the major conglomerates.

Rarely, however, were internal operational adjustments sufficient to close the value gap. As a result, many conglomerates also carried out financial and structural changes. Standard strategic options developed over time. A company might follow ITT's approach and sell or spin off assets not vital to its core business. Alternatively, the company might issue letter stock in a subsidiary. The common thread was that these strategies were designed to appeal to the new market orthodoxy.

The Alchemy of Divestiture

Gulf + Western followed a similar trajectory as ITT. Within seven months of Charles Bluhdorn's sudden death, his successor, Martin

Davis, announced a divestiture program. Davis' house cleaning involved the sale of over fifty units. Six years after taking the helm, he had winnowed Charlie Bluhdorn's cats and dogs into a relatively debt-free media and financial services company.

The strategic end-game came in 1989 with the $2.6 billion sale of Gulf + Western's commercial finance business, The Associates. Davis renamed the company Paramount Communications and began looking for a major media property that would supplement his new pure-play company—and use up the cash hoard that his many divestitures had generated. In 1989, he attempted to bust up the Time-Warner merger and purchase Time Inc. When that effort failed, he continued on the prowl, until the Viacom deal.

Asset sales were a popular strategic choice for two reasons. First, an outright sale generates cash proceeds, a critical resource for a company with significant debt or expansion plans. Second, a sale, particularly of a stand-alone subsidiary, can be executed quickly.

Westinghouse: The Strategic Transformation

The many strategic lives of Westinghouse over the years—from focused industrial company to conglomerate, back to a focused media company—dramatically illustrate the fluidity of corporate existence.

Westinghouse Electric Corporation began life as a single-line company. Founded in 1886 by engineer George Westinghouse, the company flourished on the basis of its alternating current distribution system for electricity. Over time, however, Westinghouse grew into a diversified conglomerate. The Westinghouse of 1981 owned a 7-Up bottler, a financial services company, radio stations and cable television systems. The company manufactured kitchen ranges, fighter jets, nuclear power plants, office furniture and light bulbs.

Like many other conglomerates, Westinghouse started the 1980s in too many businesses and with too much debt. Corporate raiders circled and investors criticized the company's poor performance. In response, a string of chief executives slashed costs and pruned operations. More than seventy businesses were sold between 1985 and 1990, netting $3.5 billion.

Westinghouse was still, however, a laggard. The company's managers desperately sought a vehicle for growth and bet on financial services, hoping to match the success of rival General Electric. On paper, Westinghouse Credit Corporation boomed, generating as much as 16 percent of the parent company's profits in peak years.

As the nation went into the recession of 1991, however, it became clear that Westinghouse was no General Electric. The Credit Corporation's loan portfolio was in shambles. Clearly, the finance subsidiary had adopted a risky strategy in search of faster growth in revenues and profits. Its roster of real estate loans and junk bonds was underwater to the tune of at least $5 billion. In 1991, Westinghouse was forced to take two charges against profits, the first for $975 million and the second for $1.7 billion. Another $2.7 billion charge was taken in 1992.

The problems were not limited to Westinghouse's finance subsidiary. Fundamentally, even after the asset sales of the 1980s, the company remained a diversified conglomerate with roughly seventy-five business lines arranged in seven groups. Included in the mix were electrical equipment, nuclear power plants, turbines, defense materials, commercial electrical supply stores, financial services, television and radio stations, and real estate development.

Westinghouse's balance sheet was in no better shape, weighed down with more than $7 billion of debt. The picture grew worse if the debt of nonconsolidated subsidiaries was included. With this adjustment, total debt reached $9 billion—roughly 80 percent of capital.

Outsiders pegged Westinghouse's problems of the 1990s on managerial failure. Finally, a 1993 boardroom revolt forced incumbent management to resign. Michael H. Jordan, a PepsiCo executive, was hired in his place. The new CEO made an early commitment to re-shape Westinghouse.

Westinghouse was not without bright spots. Both the Group W broadcasting operation and the Thermo King refrigerated-transport unit were performing well. Though Jordan professed a desire to fix rather than jettison lagging businesses, with Westinghouse's mammoth debt, asset sales were critical to recovery. In his first two years as CEO, Jordan sold five major businesses: office furniture, defense electronics, electric distribution, electrical supply stores and real estate development. More than $5 billion was raised in the process. As a result, Jordan was able to prune away at debt.

A slimmed-down balance sheet gave Jordan freedom to execute the next step in his strategy. The goal was to strengthen Westinghouse's high-margin, high-growth broadcasting operations. His first move, the $5.4 billion acquisition of CBS, came in August 1995. The next year, Westinghouse spent another $4.9 billion to acquire Infinity Broadcasting, which owned a major syndicate of radio stations, and then followed up with the purchase of the Gaylord country music cable channels.

These acquisitions left Westinghouse something of an ungainly Siamese twin, a single company with one foot in the glamorous media business and the other in the staid industrial world. In a market that values pure-play companies highly, this combination made little apparent sense. The new Westinghouse was a classic case of re-verse synergy—the parts were widely held to be more valuable than the whole. Effectively, the media division was being tarnished by its association with the industrial side of the business.

At this point, Jordan faced a number of strategic options. Westinghouse could rely on operational improvements to drive its stock price higher. Choosing the status quo would not, however, address the "conglomerate discount" plaguing Westinghouse's stock. The basic alternatives were examined: more asset sales, a spin-off or letter stock. Initially, Westinghouse selected a spin-off in which the company would be divided into two separate publicly traded pieces. The first, Westinghouse Electric Corporation, would harbor the industrial and power generation businesses. The second would hold the television and radio broadcasting businesses, building around the CBS franchise.

However, the Street was skeptical that a spin-off would work. Many of Westinghouse's industrial businesses—power generation and nuclear power, for example—had not performed strongly in recent years, though the prospects for future growth had improved. In addition, perceived litigation and environmental risk weighed down operations like nuclear power. Thermo King, the company's successful refrigeration equipment business, was the only real sizzle on the industrial side. When that business was sold to Ingersoll-Rand for $2.6 billion in September 1997, the consensus was that a spin-off of the remaining industrial businesses would trade poorly.

Perhaps because of this market skepticism, Westinghouse instead opted to sell off the major remaining pieces of its industrial empire, while continuing to build its media business. The proceeds from the Thermo King sale were used to pay down debt and to fund the acquisition of ninety-eight additional radio stations from American Radio. Then, in November 1997, Westinghouse announced an agreement to sell its conventional power generation business to Siemens for $1.5 billion. After these transactions, Westinghouse's significant industrial assets were its troubled nuclear power business and a small government contracting unit. At the time of the Siemens deal, the company announced the intention to sell these remaining businesses by the middle of 1998.

Westinghouse has now come full circle. The company was a pioneer in the early days of radio. Its KDKA station produced the first U.S. commercial radio broadcast in 1920. More than seventy years later, as of December 1, 1997, Westinghouse returned to those roots. The company changed its name to CBS, completing the long transformation from conglomerate to pure-play media company.

Letter Stock: The New Frontier?

Letter stock is designed to provide the benefits of a spin-off without the burdens. The idea is for a diversified company to issue stock that trades based on the operating performance of a specific division or subsidiary but not give up ownership of the underlying assets or control of the cash flow they generate. The entity involved is a "virtual" corporation. For example, in 1995, U S West took a diverse portfolio of media investments and strung them together in a letter stock, an arrangement which the company has now decided to unwind through a spin-off.

A letter stock can be sold for cash or distributed to existing shareholders without triggering a tax. In addition, letter stock or letter stock options can be granted to employees of the underlying business as an incentive mechanism. Though the specific features of the stock vary, the issuer generally pledges to pay out as dividends a certain percentage of the operating profits from the business.

At first glance, an issuer of letter stock looks very similar to a company that has spun off the underlying business. Separate securities trade in the market, each representing a different business. Letter stock, also known as targeted stock, tracking stock or alphabet stock, is designed to behave as if the subsidiary business were independent, but it is not. For tax purposes, the letter stock must be structured as stock in the parent company. This requirement generally means the parent company board has the discretion to reduce the dividends on the tracking stock and the tracking stock shareholders have no claim on specific business assets.

Because the businesses are not actually separated, the parent company retains the benefits of size. Health and pension plans can remain unified; marketing can be coordinated; capital can be raised efficiently. Taxes, legal flexibility and access to cash are the benefits of letter stocks. Structural confusion and the transaction costs of maintaining their complex structure are the negatives. General Motors' history with letter stocks provides one interesting case study of the approach.

General Motors Tries Alphabet Soup

Unlike ITT, Westinghouse and the other conglomerates, General Motors was a fairly focused company during the 1970s. A relatively small percentage of its earnings came from defense contracting, financial services and other nonautomotive activities. Above all else, GM manufactured cars, trucks and buses.

Generally speaking, GM's operational performance was strong during the 1970s. A quick response to the first Oil Shock in 1973 gave the company a competitive advantage over Ford and Chrysler. By 1978, GM was turning out smaller, more fuel-efficient cars. Customers loved the product. The statistics are stunning—sales of $63 billion, earnings peaking at a record $3.5 billion, market share approaching 50 percent.

Buoyed by this strong performance, GM formulated an ambitious plan to stay on top. A dramatic bet on new technology lay at the heart of the program. The company would spend some $40 billion over seven years. Every car line would be radically redesigned; every factory would be retooled. By the mid-1980s, GM would be turning out smaller, high-quality, fuel-efficient cars.

Of course, history did not progress as GM planned. Oil prices crashed. As a result, customer interest in larger cars was renewed. GM, with its focus on new, fuel-efficient models, was hamstrung by dated models. Foreign competition, especially from Japanese manufacturers, grew intense. The benefits of the capital spending program proved more elusive than hoped for.

By the mid-1980s, the wear and tear definitely was beginning to show. GM's U.S. market share, which had hovered at 48 percent in 1979, eroded to 41 percent in 1986. Profits were lower than in 1978, though revenues were significantly higher. Moreover, the new models rolling out of GM's factories were the butt of jokes. Regardless of the nameplate, all the cars looked alike. Competitors hammered the point home in effective advertisements.

GM chairman Roger B. Smith responded to these circumstances with a number of initiatives, both operational and financial. As part of this program, Smith made the decision to look outside GM for technological expertise. Within two years, between 1984 and 1986, GM spent $2.5 billion to acquire Ross Perot's Electronic Data Systems (EDS) and $5.2 billion to acquire Hughes Aircraft Corporation.

From a strategic perspective, the EDS transaction was intended to bring high-tech thinking into GM and to rationalize and update GM's computer and communications systems. Hughes Aircraft brought additional technical expertise to the table. GM hoped to transfer Hughes electronics technology to the car-making business. In addition, both EDS and Hughes were extremely profitable, high-growth businesses. The acquisitions represented an attempt to find new vehicles for future expansion outside the mature, cyclical auto business. Letter stock was used to differentiate between the mundane prospects of GM's base business and the exciting growth opportunities of the new businesses.

Specifically, in the EDS transaction, GM introduced a letter stock to fund part of the acquisition. Roughly $500 million of the $2.5 billion GM paid for EDS came in the form of so-called Class E stock. Though not legally bound to do so, GM pledged to pay an annual dividend on the Class E shares equal to roughly 25 percent of EDS's annual operating profits.

The Class E shares originally were intended to provide low-cost acquisition financing and a means to motivate EDS employees, who were accustomed to being compensated partly in stock. A majority of the original 13.6 million shares of the Class E stock were in fact held by EDS employees. Another 15.4 million shares eventually were distributed as a dividend to GM's existing shareholders and 3.1 million shares were sold to the public, raising $190 million for GM.

The Class E stock traded extremely well. Originally valued at around $44 a share, it zoomed up roughly 150 percent in the first eighteen months. Pleased with the reception, GM relied even more heavily on letter stock to fund the 1985 Hughes acquisition. Newly issued Class H shares represented roughly half of the $5.2 billion purchase price. GM pledged to pay a dividend on the shares based on the earnings of Hughes and to distribute additional shares to the public within three years of the acquisition.

In a sense, GM's foray into letter stock was a success. These special issues allowed the company to tap the glamour associated with its new subsidiaries, glamour which otherwise would have paled by virtue of being buried within a large diversified company.

Critics argued, however, that the letter stocks only papered over GM's conglomerate discount. When compared to the price/earnings multiple associated with GM's regular common stock, the high trading multiples earned by the Class E and Class H stocks emphasized the fact that EDS and Hughes were worth far more as stand-alone companies than as GM subsidiaries. By some accounts, GM would have been worth as much as 45 percent more than its market capitalization if divided into parts.

The acquisitions of Hughes and EDS also proved troubling from a more fundamental perspective. Difficult integration issues, particularly with EDS, kept GM from realizing many of the hoped-for strategic benefits. Even though EDS and Hughes prospered, the transactions diverted management's focus. GM suffered through a difficult patch in the recession of the early 1990s. CEO Jack Smith, who is not related to his predecessor Roger Smith, took over GM in 1992 after a boardroom revolt. After four tough years of restructuring, the new leader placed some of the blame on the Hughes and EDS deals: "We had a couple of great acquisitions. But what we needed to do—and we were late getting going on it—was fix our core business. And that has been our focus over the last four years."

Likewise, EDS and Hughes suffered negative side effects from being owned by GM. GM's direct competitors constitute a large part of the potential market available to EDS and to the automotive electronics arm of Hughes. These competitors hesitated to provide confidential business information, internal access and cash flow to GM.

For these various reasons, some related to the letter stock, some related to strategic fit, Jack Smith and the GM board ultimately decided to reverse the EDS and Hughes acquisitions. In 1996, GM contributed its block of Class E shares to its pension plan. After paying the parent company a $500 million dividend, EDS was then spun off from GM. The Hughes defense electronics business, on the other hand, was sold outright to Raytheon for $9.5 billion.

Financially speaking, both acquisitions and subsequent divestitures worked out well. The $2.5 billion investment in EDS was converted into the $190 million raised in 1984 through the letter stock offering, the $500 million dividend, and the satisfaction of roughly $8.5 billion in obligations to the GM pension fund. In the Raytheon deal GM's original $5.2 billion Hughes investment was converted into approximately $3.9 billion of cash and $6.2 billion of Raytheon stock. In addition, GM shared in the cash flow from and benefited from the services of EDS and Hughes over a period of years. GM also retained the Delco Electronics automotive-electronics business and the space-and-telecommunications units of Hughes.

GE: Against the Pure-Play Trend

Despite the urge to simplify, General Electric, led by Chairman Jack Welch, has successfully bucked the trend.

In fact, GE is widely hailed as one of America's best companies of the 1990s and Jack Welch as one of America's top corporate leaders. These accolades have been reflected in the performance of the company's stock, which traded on a split-adjusted basis in the $15 range in 1990 and ended 1997 at $73 per share. Over this period, GE's stock price grew at a compound annual rate above 25 percent, even before taking dividends into account. Given this performance, one might expect GE to be a tightly focused company. Quite the opposite is the case. The company is, in other words, something of an anomaly—a successful conglomerate of the 1990s.

GE's strong record raises an obvious question: What sets GE apart from other, less successful diversified companies? Jack Welch is the easy answer, and perhaps the most insightful.

During the Welch years three overlapping strategic initiatives become apparent—a drive to reduce operating costs through various restructuring programs, a drive to expand revenues through major acquisitions, and a drive to shift the company onto a post-industrial footing.

Welch was passed the leadership baton in April 1981. Already, GE was a company with a long and proud history, a history against which his performance would be measured. GE had begun life as the Edison Electric Light Company, founded in 1878 by Thomas Edison. Edison's patents for the electric light bulb and other inventions were the crown jewels of the enterprise.

For all his technical genius, Edison made an early blunder. He favored a direct current distribution system over the alternating current system advanced by George Westinghouse and others. Edison ultimately lost this "war of the currents." Edison's company suffered because of his refusal to adopt the new technology. Finally, in 1892, Edison Electric was merged with another company that held alternating current patents, forming General Electric.

Up until World War II, GE, like Westinghouse, focused mostly on its core business of supplying electrical and electronic equipment. On the industrial side, this meant equipment for the generation and distribution of electricity. For consumers, GE made fans, irons, toasters, refrigerators, washing machines, air conditioners—with the common thread being the use of an electrical power source.

The electricity and electrical goods business began to mature after the war. In keeping with the times, GE diversified far afield during the 1960s. Computers, commercial jet engines, nuclear energy, plastics, financial services, medical systems, chemicals, defense contracting—the laundry list of businesses grew from one year to the next. After the first Oil Shock, a major natural resources company was added.

For all its diversity, GE weathered the 1970s better than most conglomerates. GE earned $1.5 billion in 1980 on revenues of just under $25 billion, had over 400,000 employees and a strong balance sheet. The company was the world's number one manufacturer of electrical equipment and had strong positions in nuclear power, commercial aviation and consumer goods.

An Early Commitment to Restructuring   Welch's main concern when he became chairman and CEO in April 1981 was improving the bottom line by cutting costs. As the process began, Welch enunciated a yardstick against which each of GE's 350 businesses would be measured. A business would be retained only if it was or could become number one or number two in its market. Welch and his team took a hard look at every business in this light. "Fix, close or sell" was the general rule.

A new generation of management was in control and nothing was sacred. Utah International, the natural resources business acquired in the 1970s, was sold in 1983 for $2.4 billion. Just seven years before, GE management had identified the company as an engine of future growth.

In 1984, Welch made the even more wrenching decision to sell GE's housewares business to Black & Decker for $300 million. Housewares were part of GE's long history. The waffle irons, fans and toasters turned out by this division had made GE into a household name. Welch saw a different reality. These products had largely become commodities. GE could never hope to outsell competitors in Asia and Europe that churned out irons and blow dryers far more cheaply.

However, Welch was not indiscriminate in the businesses he sold. Some units which were not number one or number two were worth saving. The turbines business, for example, was retained even though it was in a slump. Power generation had been the cornerstone business at GE for a century, and was historically quite profitable. Fundamentally, the business was cyclical and would bounce back.

Welch's early commitment to restructuring served GE well. By 1985, much had been accomplished. More than $5.6 billion worth of businesses had been divested. Payroll was reduced by 130,000 employees through layoffs and divestitures. And the results could be seen on GE's income statement. Between 1981 and 1984, revenues were fairly stagnant, but earnings rose almost 15 percent per year.

Twice since the early 1980s, Welch has renewed cost-cutting efforts at GE. The first initiative, introduced in 1989, became known as "Work-Outs" and involved an attempt to empower employees. Town meetings were held at factories and offices. An open dialogue was encouraged. The goal was to push decision making down the chain of command. The second effort, a push for greater quality, was introduced in 1996 and is ongoing.

GE Revisits the Go-Go Years   Welch's first few years as CEO were spent focusing on cost cutting. Then, confident with the state of GE's existing businesses, Welch began to look for ways to expand revenues. Internal growth was part of the story, and Welch invested billions in capital expenditures. However, acquisitions were also a major focus. Though GE had been acquiring companies in the market fairly consistently, the major marker of GE's new acquisitive phase came in 1985. On December 12, Welch stepped to a podium and announced that GE had agreed to purchase RCA, the owner of the NBC television network, for $6.3 billion in cash.

For RCA, the friendly deal with GE represented the culmination

of its own restructuring effort. Thornton Bradshaw, a former oil executive, had taken over as chairman of RCA in the same year Welch
became chairman of GE. Bradshaw's mission was to stabilize the faltering company. He promptly divested businesses. Hertz, CIT, Gibson Greetings, Banquet Foods, Random House—all were sold to
outsiders who did much better with them than RCA. Welch bought
the remaining company, including the jewel of its defense business,
at a bargain price.

The RCA purchase, and GE's acquisition program in general,
helped to fuel dramatic growth at GE. Between 1985 and 1995, revenues increased from $28.3 billion to $70.0 billion. However, this
road to growth was not without bumps along the way.

The integration of NBC proved difficult. With the support of Jack
Welch, GE executive Robert Wright took over day-to-day management of the network. His first order of business was to reduce expenses. This proved politically difficult. NBC employees had grown
up in a creative culture and in a world where the three broadcast
networks had an assured future. They initially balked at budget cuts.
Late-night television host David Letterman was the most vocal
critic, openly razzing the folks from GE. In time, GE silenced the
critics, both internal and external. Wright built a creative team that
led the network to new ratings dominance in the 1980s and expanded
NBC into a global media company with interests in cable networks
and online entertainment.

The outcome of GE's entrance into the securities business, with
its $600 million purchase of Kidder, Peabody, was a cautionary expe-
rience. Problems emerged almost from the moment GE took control
of the struggling investment bank. First, Kidder's former M&A superstar Marty Siegel was implicated in the insider trading scandal of
the late 1980s. Then, the stock market crash of 1987 drained profits
and morale. GE's industrially trained Kidder management team became the focus of Wall Street jokes. And finally, in the early 1990s, a
government bond trader at Kidder named Joseph Jett allegedly en-

gaged in a string of fictitious trades that were designed to inflate the profits of his unit.

The Jett scandal, together with the collapse of the mortgage-backed securities market, brought Kidder to its knees. GE—which invested a total of $1.4 billion in Kidder over the years—sold part of the operation to PaineWebber and liquidated the remainder. As a result, GE reported $1.2 billion in losses and charges related to Kidder in 1994, although GE later covered much of these losses with gains on the PaineWebber stock it received.

However, notwithstanding the problems with Kidder, Welch remained committed to growth through acquisition, particularly in the financial services area. Over the course of three years in the early 1990s, GE spent more than $6 billion acquiring insurance companies, which were folded into the highly profitable GE Capital subsidiary.

A Post-Industrial GE   Third on the list of strategic initiatives at GE is a drive to create a post-industrial company. From the time he took over as CEO, Jack Welch recognized the need for this transition. The world manufacturing economy is maturing. Margins in GE's old-line industrial businesses are being squeezed; growth percolates along at 1 or 2 percent a year—and cost cutting can only go so far. Given the situation, GE needed to evolve into new markets and find new ways to make money.

In concrete terms, GE's transition to a post-industrial company means an increasing emphasis on services as a revenue source. This emphasis can be seen in the commitment to GE Capital and the purchase of NBC. By 1996, services generated about 60 percent of GE's income, as compared to 16 percent in 1980. Welch is intent on accelerating the upward trend. He recently launched a new initiative focusing on GE's industrial units. The idea is to leverage existing expertise and equipment in place as a source of service revenues. Assignments might range from the servicing of equipment to general operations and business consulting.

The Conglomerators' Legacy

With the right management and strategy, a diversified company can thrive. Assets must be shuffled to match the existing economic circumstances, and leadership must be willing to work hard at renewing mature businesses. However, history teaches that reaching beyond core competencies is very difficult, and the market will mistrust it. Few managers can be Jack Welch.

Financial Services in the Digital Age | 10

"Future shock . . . the shattering stress and disorientation that we induce in individuals by subjecting them to too much change in too short a time."

Alvin Toffler, *Future Shock*

Change is sweeping the financial services industry. Old business models are crumbling under the battering rams of regulatory, financial and technological developments. Industry players now face an entirely different competitive landscape, one that is both unsettling in its risks and exhilarating in its opportunities.

Mergers and acquisitions have been the main evolutionary instrument driving this process. Making sense of the jumbled movements can be elusive, but the following three themes crystallize:

- A blurring of the boundaries between commercial banking, insurance, investment banking and other sectors of the giant financial services market;

- A massive consolidation within sectors, particularly commercial banking and insurance; and

- The increasing importance of access to individual investors.

As a result of these developments, we are witnessing an industry-wide quantum leap in size, scope and product capabilities. The new reality is that only companies that operate on a global stage, with stock market capitalizations of $50–$100 billion, will have the strength to thrive in this environment as dominant players. Other companies must seek out protective niches and apply distinctive competencies to survive and prosper.

Augury of the Future

The February 1997 marriage of Dean Witter, Discover & Co. and Morgan Stanley stunned Wall Street and shattered the world order of investment banking. In many ways, the merger was an augury of the financial services future. The blurring of boundaries, the rise of the retail investor and the need for global size pulsed through the deal.

A Morgan Stanley–Dean Witter merger had been percolating behind the scenes for some time. Phil Purcell, chairman and chief executive of Dean Witter, and John Mack, president of Morgan Stanley, actually had been talking about the possibility of a joint venture going back several years. The discussions were facilitated by the fact that Purcell shared a long relationship with both Mack and Dick Fisher, Morgan Stanley's chairman and chief executive.

By the fall of 1996, Purcell was ready to talk more seriously. We were brought in to advise Dean Witter. Purcell and his team had conducted a strategic review and decided that Dean Witter needed a broader base to compete in the consolidating global financial services business. Morgan Stanley was the right partner. Fundamentally, the merger would be a cross-fertilization of retail and institutional powers—"Class Meets Mass," as *Business Week* trumpeted.

Until recently, the institutional and retail worlds were thought of as distinct. Institutional investment banks like Morgan Stanley underwrote stocks and bonds and provided strategic advice for corporations. Retail brokerage operations like Dean Witter sold financial products—primarily stocks, bonds and mutual funds—to individuals. Historically, the Morgan Stanleys of the world were known as the brains, the Dean Witters the brawn.

Investment banks generally viewed retail investors as not worth the trouble. They looked down on the brokerage houses as unsophisticated mass merchandising operations. Rather than compete in this realm, the investment banks concentrated on their highly profitable niche business of serving corporations. The ability to sell stocks and bonds for these clients was of course key to the process, but relationships with individual investors were not necessary. Investment banks instead relied on relatively small sales forces that focused almost exclusively on selling to pension funds, insurance companies and other large institutional investors.

The situation had changed by the late 1980s. A number of trends intersected and the investment banking business became quite crowded. Regulatory barriers between commercial and investment banks began to come down and foreign banks wanted their slice of the pie. As a result, competition became fierce.

Meanwhile, the retail side of the industry boomed. Individual investors flooded into the stock market on a record scale, partly on the strength of a long bull market, and partly due to an erosion of corporate paternalism.

Many employers no longer guarantee fixed pensions. Rather, they support investment programs, primarily 401(k) retirement plans, which allow employees to direct their own retirement savings and require employees to take responsibility for the consequences. Low interest rates have eroded the appeal of money market funds. This shift has pushed individual investors into the stock market and fueled the growth of the mutual fund and brokerage businesses. Investors have poured billions into funds. Managing that money provides growing profits for powerhouses like Charles Schwab & Co. and Fidelity.

Essentially, the emergence of the money management product and the performance of Merrill Lynch demolished the view that institutional and retail banking should not mix. Diversification into retail services is now widely viewed as the future for investment banks. Merrill Lynch provided the compelling model. Starting from a retail brokerage base, the company has built itself into a financial services giant cutting across functional boundaries.

The great appeal of the Merrill model is that the firm has successfully leveraged retail relationships into institutional mandates. The firm's 1996 annual report gives an idea of its breadth: Merrill earned more than $1.6 billion in net income from over $25 billion in revenue, had custody of more than $830 billion of client assets and over $230 billion under management.

On the institutional side, in 1996, Merrill was the world's leading underwriter of both debt and equity securities, assisted with corporate financial planning, advised companies on mergers and acquisitions and managed cash and retirement money. Individual services included investment brokerage, life insurance, financial planning, IRA accounts, mutual funds and home mortgage origination. Merrill originated more than 8,200 first mortgages, generated $1.4 billion in annuity premiums and exceeded $100 billion in IRA assets managed (more IRA assets than in the top 163 U.S. commercial banks). Quite literally, Merrill Lynch provides mass-market one-stop shopping for both businesses and individuals.

Investors recognized the difference in outlook for the institutional and retail businesses. In early 1997, Merrill Lynch was trading at 12 times earnings, Dean Witter at 11 times and Morgan at 9 times. Wall Street's estimates of potential and risk were implicit in these ratings. The blue-chip Morgan Stanley was an institutional brand—not a household one. Its business base was narrow and volatile. Dean Witter had a strong distribution system and a money-management machine. A merger would instantaneously boost Morgan's effectiveness as a banker with muscle and create critical mass in money management.

It was against this backdrop that Purcell, Fisher and Mack considered the possibility of a merger. Purcell saw Morgan Stanley as a source of additional products for his brokers to sell. Fisher and Mack looked on Dean Witter as a rich trove of relatively stable earnings. Both asset management and the Discover Card had been extremely profitable businesses for Dean Witter.

Fisher and Mack already had committed themselves to expanding more stable, fee-generating business even before serious discussions opened with Purcell. For example, in 1996, they moved Morgan more heavily into the mutual fund business with the purchase of Van Kampen. Yet growing the asset management business was expensive, and Van Kampen lacked both critical mass and a distribution system for further customer-base expansions.

The talks between Purcell, Fisher and Mack progressed very quickly. Morgan Stanley's own bankers were to be kept in the dark until late in the deal. Fisher could ably represent Morgan's interests himself. Furthermore, to keep word from leaking out, meetings were held in conference rooms at the law firm Cravath, Swaine & Moore, over their rather infamous soggy sandwiches. Somehow, the kitchens at Cravath have never reached the culinary standards of competitor Wachtell, Lipton.

As the negotiations came to a climax, the tension grew. What would be the role for senior managers from each company? How would the two companies be put together? The firms had far different cultures, and meshing financial services companies is notoriously difficult. Yet, Purcell and Mack decided the strength of a good relationship at the top would prevail. Meanwhile, rumors swirled of Morgan Stanley bidding for PaineWebber.

Purcell, Fisher and Mack made their announcement on February 6 in a crowded auditorium. The three men flashed their Discover Cards, and the audience cheered. The $21 billion deal was structured as a merger of equals. Each company would have the same number of nominees on the new board. Purcell would become chairman and chief executive of the new company, Fisher chairman of the executive committee of the board, and Mack president and chief operating officer. Morgan Stanley shareholders received a slight premium to their stock price—roughly 10 percent above the recent trading range. The other marriage provisions were carefully crafted so that legally there was no "sale" of either company. This reflected the reality and insulated both from attack.

The market response to the deal was a standing ovation. Within weeks, the market price of both stocks increased 25 percent. The two companies were experiencing multiple expansion—the market value of the combination was greater than the average market value of the pieces. Purcell, the strategist, had picked the right deal. Of course, only time will tell whether the risks inherent in combining two complicated services companies can be managed and the promising future realized.

PROFILE

Philip Purcell

Philip Purcell is not the typical securities industry executive. Unlike John Mack, a former trader who rose through the ranks at Morgan Stanley, Purcell began his career as a consultant at McKinsey & Co. A project for Sears exposed him to Edward Telling, the company's chairman. Telling hired Purcell to serve as an in-house strategic planner for Sears.

Purcell advised Sears on its move into financial services and, when Sears acquired Dean Witter, Purcell shifted to the brokerage operation. At Dean Witter, he was an early advocate of the Discover Card. Sears pumped $1 billion into the start-up, which proved extremely successful. In 1986, Purcell became the head of Dean Witter, Discover.

Reflecting his consulting background, Purcell kept Dean Witter firmly focused on its strengths as a retail brokerage firm. Dean Witter more or less stayed out of proprietary trading and the institutional side of investment banking because he perceived no comparative advantage. Purcell instead concentrated on growing the Discover Card and Dean Witter's network of brokers, using them as leverage to build Dean Witter's mutual fund operation.

A strategic shift in the 1990s led Sears to divest itself of financial services. First, a minority interest in Dean Witter was sold to the public in a 1993 stock offering. The remaining interest was spun off to Sears shareholders later the same year. As a result of Purcell's leadership, Dean Witter had the strength to survive as a stand-alone entity. Freed from Sears just as a major bull market took off, Dean Witter continued to thrive. The firm's growth outpaced the traditional Wall Street houses, putting Purcell in a position to bargain on equal terms with the venerable Morgan Stanley.

Blurring the Boundaries

The Morgan Stanley–Dean Witter deal was the opening gavel for a feverish auction of securities firms. Much of the action involved commercial banks on the prowl. Shortly after the Dean Witter deal, Bankers Trust bought Alex Brown. SBC Warburg, a unit of Swiss Bank, then acquired Dillon, Read; Bank of America teamed with Robertson Stephenson; NationsBank inked a deal with Montgomery Securities; Canada's CIBC bought Oppenheimer; Holland's ING Group acquired Furman Selz; and U.S. Bancorp teamed with Piper Jaffray. All seven acquirers have commercial banking operations. As a result of the deals, there has been a significant blurring of the boundary between commercial and investment banking.

INVESTMENT BANKS ON THE BLOCK

Date Announced	Acquirer	Target	Price Paid (Billions)
February 1997	Dean Witter, Discover & Co.	Morgan Stanley Group Inc.	$10.0
April 1997	Bankers Trust New York Corp.	Alex Brown & Sons Inc.	$1.7
May 1997	SBC Warburg	Dillon, Read & Co.	$0.6
June 1997	BankAmerica Corp.	Robertson, Stephens & Co.	$0.5
June 1997	NationsBank Corp.	Montgomery Securities Inc.	$1.2
July 1997	CIBC	Oppenheimer & Co.	$0.5
August 1997	ING Group	Furman Selz LLC	$0.6
December 1997	U.S. Bancorp	Piper Jaffray Cos.	$0.7

Regulatory revisions were the trigger for this activity, specifically the liberalization of the so-called Glass-Steagall wall between commercial and investment banking. However, the deeper impetus is that the world has changed dramatically for commercial banks over the last two decades. They have seen a continuing erosion of their traditional customer base. The ability to provide new services is necessary to survival, and the new holes in the Glass-Steagall wall make investment banking a realistic possibility. In other words, the nature of what it means to be a "bank" has been rewritten by competitive forces and ratified by regulators.

For validation of their push into investment banking, the commercial banks looked to the original full-service banking model which prevailed up until the 1930s. In those days, merchant banks straddled the division between commercial and investment banking. This model appeals to modern commercial banks as a means to extract more revenue out of their existing corporate and individual client bases by offering a broader range of services.

Regulatory boundaries had been the major impediment to realizing that vision. Following the 1929 stock market crash, a banking scandal led Congress to pass the Glass-Steagall Act of 1933 and the

Banking Act of 1935, which up until very recently defined crisp boundaries between commercial and investment banking. Among other things, Glass-Steagall limited banks to their core function—the taking and safekeeping of customer deposits and the making of consumer and commercial loans. This business became known as commercial banking. The underwriting and brokering of securities were no longer permissible for commercial banks. A new industry, investment banking, was created; an artificial "Glass-Steagall wall" separated the two worlds.

These and other regulatory reforms created a defined, segmented financial services industry in the United States. Commercial banks dominated the loan and credit business. Savings and loans collected savings deposits in passbook accounts and made mortgage loans. Investment banks underwrote and distributed securities. Insurance companies managed risks. Participants in each sector enjoyed a protected oligopoly and looked to Washington as a Big Daddy. The federal government not only defined the roles; it bailed companies out when they screwed up.

Commercial banks prospered from the long postwar economic expansion, but the enduring good times also caused them to become complacent. The commercial banking business was fairly straightforward and chiefly involved credit analysis. Described as "public utilities" or "white-collar factories," banks offered a fairly stable group of products. Institutions were hierarchical and tasks standardized. Stability and safety were emphasized. As *Time* magazine put it, "American bankers for decades operated by the 3-6-3 rule: pay depositors 3 percent interest, lend money at 6 percent, and tee off at the golf course by 3 P.M."

Of course, this world of easy prosperity could not last. More entrepreneurial, aggressive competitors emerged. These creative companies found ways to work within—and to stretch—the existing framework. Their activities eroded the artificial boundaries created by Glass-Steagall and other federal regulations. Attacked from all

sides, the commercial banks got the worst of the struggle. By offering new services like the money market account, Merrill Lynch,
Charles Schwab, Fidelity and similar companies nabbed depositors.
No longer guaranteed an easy source of funds, banks had to utilize
riskier methods to raise capital.

These developments pressured bank executives to replace the
funds now flowing to competitors. Banks were forced to pay higher
rates. This process trimmed bank profit margins. Hemmed in by
regulations, the banks looked for new revenue sources and ended
up granting riskier loans. As a result, the 1980s were a seesaw
decade during which banks repeatedly went from boom to bust. Oil,
real estate, Latin American and LBO loans all soured at different
times.

The commercial banking industry's cyclical performance has
highlighted the industry's deteriorating position, with taxpayers often
picking up the tab for failures. Driven by unrelenting competition in
their traditional businesses, commercial banks continue to push for
ways to expand and grow. The desire to get into investment banking
is part of this evolution.

Today, a consensus has developed that banks do need the freedom to offer a wider range of services if they are to survive. However,
politicians and lobbyists for the various financial services constituencies have been unable to agree on a legislative blueprint for
change. Finally, in the last year, regulators at the Federal Reserve
have taken the lead in liberalizing existing rules, triggering the wave
of recent deals.

The key event came in December 1996. Under new Federal Reserve rules a bank's securities subsidiary may earn up to 25 percent
of the total holding company's revenues. There has been a similar
hole in the Glass-Steagall wall since 1988, but the previous threshold was 10 percent. The acquisition of any significant investment
bank would have tipped the revenue mix of most commercial banks
above the 10 percent threshold. As a result, few major deals hap-

pened. By contrast, the 25 percent level gives a lot more flexibility. For instance, Bankers Trust projected that 20 percent of its revenues would come from "tainted" investment banking sources after the Alex Brown deal.

Commercial banking was not the only business defined by the existence of the Glass-Steagall wall. The investment banks also benefited from the regulatory framework. Surprisingly, they have been relatively open about uniting across the former boundary, mainly as targets rather than acquirers.

High prices certainly have lubricated the process. However, a number of other considerations are behind the willingness to forsake independence. Having a commercial bank as a parent is finding a harbor from the storm. The hope is that size and diversification will bring stability as volatile investment banking earnings are mixed with the larger, more stable flow from a commercial bank's asset management and commercial and consumer lending businesses.

Another key concern is the increasing globalization of the capital markets. Clients have become multinational in scale and interest. There is a perception that investment banks must follow their clients abroad or risk losing them to more global institutions. Moreover, much of the world's future growth will come from emerging markets in Asia, South America and elsewhere. The U.S. investment banks see these regions as fields of opportunity.

Yet going global is quite expensive. Even the largest investment banking institutions are relatively small when compared to commercial banks or insurance companies. Meanwhile, smaller investment banks simply lack the resources for major international pushes and have been forced to pick their spots. Many investment banks consequently look favorably on the possibility of a partnership with a capital-rich acquirer.

In the final analysis, post-deal implementation will determine whether the reconstruction of the old merchant banking model works. Some past experiments have foundered. Melding the Wall

Street and Main Street cultures of different institutions can be difficult. However, the commercial banks seem ready to commit the resources necessary to handle the transition.

The Financial Services Supermarket Reborn

The line between commercial and investment banking is not the only blurring boundary of the financial services world. There has been a general push toward the diversification of product offerings, a dramatic rebirth of the financial supermarket as a strategic vision. This trend was underscored in September 1997 when the Travelers Group announced its $9 billion acquisition of investment bank Salomon Brothers.

The notion of a financial supermarket is not new—several prototypes were cobbled together in the early 1980s. Enthusiasm for the idea was not limited to any single sector. Insurance companies, retailers, a credit card company and brokerage firms embraced the model. The strategic blueprint was to provide one-stop shopping for all sorts of customers. Various players rushed to translate this vision into reality. Unfortunately, implementation of the concept was more difficult than the theory might suggest.

For example, insurance companies got into the retail brokerage business. The acquisitions seemed sensible. The brokerage operations would provide new distribution channels for the insurance companies' mutual funds and other products. In return, the insurance companies would provide capital for expansion and technological improvements.

Prudential Insurance pioneered the combination. In 1981, after one week of negotiations, Prudential agreed to pay $385 million cash to buy the Bache Group. We and the other advisers working for Bache were thrilled to find a distinguished buyer willing to purchase a troubled brokerage company under fire from hostile raiders. Others followed Prudential into the securities business. Most prominently, between 1982 and 1984, Kemper swallowed five regional brokerage operations, folding them into its Kemper Securities unit.

Main-line American companies with existing financial services subsidiaries also latched on to the financial supermarket model. GE bought investment bank Kidder, Peabody and brought in an industrial manager to run it. Sears, Roebuck made an even more dramatic move. In the early 1980s, the retailer set out to build on its strong brand name and marketing prowess to create a financial services unit focused on middle-class Americans. Sears already had Allstate Insurance, which would be the core of the effort. In 1981, Dean Witter was added for $610 million. Real estate broker Coldwell Banker rounded out the group in the same year.

Sears forthrightly attempted to meld these three units into a single retail force. Kiosks were opened in Sears stores. More than $1 billion was spent to create the Discover Card. Everything was designed around the vision of Sears as a cradle-to-grave financial services provider.

Of course, existing financial services companies were not content to cede the future to Sears and other newcomers. Merrill Lynch stepped up its own diversification efforts. Building on the 1978 acquisition of investment bank White Weld, Merrill expanded to become a major investment bank serving institutional clients. At the same time, Merrill added insurance and real estate finance into its brokerage operations. Like Sears, Merrill saw itself as the broad-based financial powerhouse of the future.

However, when it came to embracing the diversification trend, American Express was perhaps the most enthusiastic participant. Chief executive James Robinson III took over the credit card, traveler's check and insurance company in 1977. An aggressive acquisition program began not long thereafter. In 1981, American Express acquired brokerage firm Shearson Loeb Rhoades for $930 million. Two years later, Robinson added the Trade Development Bank—a

Swiss private bank—for $550 million and Investors Diversified Services (IDS) for $790 million.

The IDS acquisition underscored the breadth of Robinson's vision. As a mass-market investment advisory firm, IDS was somewhat at odds with American Express' tony image, reinforced by its blue logo. Yet the purchase fit with Robinson's goal. He wanted to build a "blue box" of diverse financial services. Investment bank Lehman Brothers was folded into Shearson in 1984. Then, after the 1987 stock market crash, Robinson paid $962 million to pick up E.F. Hutton, a retail brokerage house.

Almost without exception, the financial services conglomerations of the 1980s were failed experiments. The various units simply did not mesh together into coherent, enduring institutions. For example, at American Express, the notion of bundled services was more myth than reality. Credit card executives balked at the idea of joint American Express–Shearson statements, fearing investment setbacks might tarnish the American Express brand. For similar reasons, Shearson brokers were never given full access to the valuable American Express customer list.

American Express also had trouble managing the risks associated with its far-flung empire. Losses at the Fireman's Fund and the Trade Development Bank ran to the hundreds of millions of dollars. Shearson made a series of bad commercial real estate and bridge loans, and Robinson was forced to inject new capital into the firm.

Under tremendous pressure, Robinson cleaned the troubled units up and, reversing course, put them on the block. American Express realized roughly $1 billion on the sale of the Trade Development Bank and $2 billion for the insurance company. He then stabilized the bleeding at Shearson. But this was too little, too late. Outside directors forced Robinson to resign in early 1993. Within weeks, Harvey Golub, Robinson's successor as chief executive, sold off Shearson's brokerage operations. The next year, American Express spun off the remaining Lehman Brothers investment bank and the financial supermarket was unwound. American Express' stock price zoomed.

Ironically, Robinson's vision was confirmed by subsequent events. The Dean Witter–Morgan Stanley deal, which the market reacted to with rare enthusiasm, had definite parallels to Robinson's concept. His problem was the execution, not the vision. Or Robinson simply may have been ahead of his time.

James Robinson III

At his peak, James Robinson III, a polished, patrician Southerner, had a sterling reputation as one of America's best chief executives. He jetted around the world, overseeing the far-reaching American Express empire. His counsel to world leaders on political matters earned him the title "Corporate America's secretary of state." In the late 1980s, he championed a well-received plan to solve the Third World debt crisis.

Robinson was born in Atlanta and educated at the Harvard Business School. His father and grandfather each had served as chairman of First National Bank of Atlanta. He followed the family banking tradition upon graduation, starting his fast-track career in 1961 at Morgan Guaranty Trust. Within six years, he had risen to be special assistant to the bank's chairman. He joined American Express in 1970 and became chief executive in 1977, at the age of forty.

In the late 1980s, troubles began to mount for Robinson. American Express' Lehman subsidiary was involved in advising Robinson's friend F. Ross Johnson on the failed RJR Nabisco management buyout. Some of Johnson's bad press rubbed off on Robinson. Then, in 1989, American Express revealed that another subsidiary's earnings had been overstated. Robinson also was forced to apologize publicly to Edmund Safra, the former head of the Trade Development Bank, after it became apparent American Express had targeted Safra in a smear campaign.

The succession of problems at American Express initially did little to dim Robinson's reputation. In fact, he became known as the "Teflon executive," with high praise given to his attractive wife, Linda, a public relations powerhouse, for keeping her husband's image intact. Curiously, it was during this period that Robinson seemed to broaden himself in thinking about the future strategy of financial services.

Eventually, though, the operating problems at Shearson became too great, and the stock price too low. Robinson publicly accepted responsibility and for a time enjoyed the continued support of his board. But investors wanted a scapegoat. Finally, the board bowed to pressure, and Robinson was allowed to lead the search for his own replacement. Robinson stepped aside, leaving American Express to Golub, his handpicked successor.

Resurgence

American Express was not the only company that stumbled in attempting to transform itself into a financial services supermarket. Sears faced similar problems merging its units into a coherent whole. The retailer shed Dean Witter, Discover and Coldwell Banker in 1993, Allstate Insurance in 1994. Even the legendary GE had enormous problems with Kidder, Peabody, and its hand-selected manager from an industrial background was mocked as a "tool-and-die" man. Kemper eventually would sell its securities business, renamed Everen Securities, to the brokerage firm's employees. Prudential's securities business would prove a costly, scandal-ridden liability.

In the early 1990s, then, conventional wisdom held that diversified financial services companies were short-lived dinosaurs rapidly headed for extinction. However, the pessimism was overdone. A number of successes have given renewed luster to the diversification idea. As a result, the long-term vitality of the financial supermarket model remains an open question.

Merrill Lynch, for one, appears to be firing on all pistons. The pace of its growth accelerated in November 1997 with the $5.2 billion acquisition of the U.K.'s Mercury Asset Management Group. One of the largest fund managers in the United Kingdom, Mercury added more than $160 billion to Merrill's assets under management.

Furthermore, Dean Witter and Morgan Stanley, Bankers Trust, Bank of America and NationsBank are poised to create new financial services emporiums. In the case of Dean Witter and Morgan Stanley, the merger brings together institutional and retail investment banking, asset management and credit card operations. Based on the two companies' 1996 performance, the combined firm will be the number one underwriter of U.S. equities, have 3.2 million retail customers, and manage $249 billion in assets and $37 billion in credit card loans.

The forces driving the renewed emphasis on diversified financial services are clear. As boundaries fall between sectors, competition has accelerated. Companies see diversification as both defensive and offensive—defensive because the ability to provide more services to existing clients will reduce the likelihood that competitors can find an opening to develop a relationship, and offensive because many of the untapped markets are seen as lucrative opportunities for growth.

Nor is the return of the financial supermarket all hope and promise. Others besides Merrill Lynch have managed to create functioning financial services combines. Entrepreneur Sandy Weill has cobbled together the Travelers Group, his own supermarket, by snapping up troubled companies over the last decade. Weill's story is ironic. He built Shearson through a series of acquisitions in the 1960s and 1970s, then sold the firm to American Express. Afterward, he served as president of American Express for a time. He left in the mid-1980s, an early veteran of the rocky American Express super-market. Not soured by the experience, Weill took over a small com-mercial and retail finance company and, from this platform, fashioned his own, more successful supermarket.

The first step came in 1988 with the $1.5 billion Primerica acquisition. This transaction brought an insurance company and brokerage firm Smith Barney under Weill's control. At the time, Smith Barney was bleeding, losing $100 million a year. Weill turned it around, boosting return on equity to 30 percent by 1992.

Weill's next move was a homecoming. He recaptured Shearson in 1993 and folded his former creation into Smith Barney. In the same year, Primerica acquired Travelers Insurance—which was weighed down by bad real estate investments—in a $4 billion stock merger. Weill's company took the Travelers name. Aetna's property and casualty portfolio, similarly troubled, was added in 1995 for another $4 billion.

There have been two keys to Weill's success. First, he is a disciplined acquirer with a sense for unfolding strategic developments. He bought Shearson before brokerage firms were hot properties; he took on Aetna Property & Casualty, by consensus a toxic property. In both cases, Weill saw a different future than the crowd. He timed the market, bought the businesses cheap and turned them around.

A relentless focus on post-deal implementation and management detail also has been key to Weill's success. By paying attention to relatively minor expenses, Weill's management team has had a large collective impact. Bloated insurance operations have been trimmed and made more efficient. Yet costs are not the only concern. Decades of working in the financial services industry have given Weill a deft touch when it comes to managing people. The bankers and brokers at Smith Barney have been given enough rope to operate effectively. Travelers Group has been rewarded with strong profits.

Even after spending $8 billion for Travelers and Aetna's property and casualty portfolio, Weill remained openly interested in further acquisitions. As he told a reporter, "The insurance industry is consolidating, the money management business is consolidating, the securities industry is consolidating and the lending business is consolidating. We are in all of them and we would be interested in the right thing in any of them." Weill's unabashed goal was to build a global financial services company, both through internal growth of Travelers' existing businesses and with additional disciplined acquisitions.

This global ambition hit the front pages on September 25, 1997, with the announcement of the $9 billion Salomon Brothers acquisition. Weill planned to fold Salomon Brothers into his Smith Barney unit, creating a financial services powerhouse to rival Merrill Lynch. The new firm would be the number two underwriter of corporate debt and equities and the fourth most active merger adviser, and would field the third largest number of retail brokers in the United States.

Much like the Morgan Stanley–Dean Witter deal, the marriage of Salomon Brothers and Smith Barney brought together an institutional power and a retail power. Salomon Brothers would enhance Smith Barney's global presence and add real strength in the underwriting of corporate debt and proprietary trading. Smith Barney, on the other hand, had strong retail distribution and equity underwriting.

In taking on Salomon Brothers, Weill yet again demonstrated his willingness to accept challenges others found too daunting. Salomon Brothers had a reputation on the Street for volatile earnings as a result of its heavy reliance on proprietary trading operations, and its traders were criticized as "gunslingers." The firm's bond traders routinely make large bets on market movements, some of which pay off, and some of which generate losses. This volatility, and the attendant need for sophisticated risk management, kept many potential Salomon Brothers acquirers from pursuing a deal.

Weill, on the other hand, was sanguine about the challenge posed by Salomon Brothers. He has decades of experience managing investment firms and is comfortable with the personal issues involved in handling Wall Street stars. In addition, the new Salomon Smith Barney unit would be managed jointly by Weill's longtime lieutenant James Dimon and Deryck Maughan, chief executive of Salomon Brothers. Weill realized that he could dampen the volatility and acquire a world-class franchise at a favorable price.

With the acquisition of Salomon Brothers, Weill realized his global dream. The new Travelers has a diverse range of financial services under its trademark umbrella—from property and casualty insurance to credit cards, from investment banking to retail brokerage, from asset management to commercial finance. If Salomon Brothers and Smith Barney can be integrated as smoothly as Travelers' other acquisitions, Weill will have created a functioning financial supermarket.

A Bank-Eat-Bank World

The blurring of boundaries is only one part of the financial services story. Many of the same forces driving cross-functional acquisitions have also sparked consolidation within particular financial services categories. The commercial banking sector, for one, has seen a dramatic consolidation, a bank-eat-bank world.

By the mid-1980s, the banking industry was ripe for restructuring and consolidation. Alternative revenue sources (the Latin American, LBO and real estate loans of the 1980s, for example) could not paper over the fundamental competitive realities. Too many banks had built too many branches; the bureaucracy was stultifying and the customers not there.

But precisely because they were weighed down by so much bureaucracy, many banks were slow to change. As a result, the task fell to a cadre of industry consolidators. Two strategies in particular have played out over the past decade—a super-regional approach and an in-market, cost-savings-driven strategy. In either case, mergers and acquisitions were the chisel used to effect change.

NationsBank, Voracious Super-Regional

In March 1989, Hugh McColl, chairman of what would become NationsBank, called his counterpart at Atlanta's Citizens & Southern Bank and offered to buy Citizens. The courtly Bennett Brown, chairman of Citizens, asked for time to consider the offer. "You have three hours to answer, or I will launch my missiles," McColl reportedly responded.

When Brown didn't cave, McColl kept his promise. Late in the evening of March 30, McColl had personal letters hand-delivered to each Citizens board member. The letters detailed a hostile $2.4 billion bear hug offer. News of the offer went out over the wire services at 9:57 P.M. Not surprisingly, Citizens did not take well to the no-holds-barred approach. Brown told McColl to "go the hell back to North Carolina." Within days, the Citizens board declared the offer inadequate.

Three weeks of jousting in the press followed. But even in the spirited 1980s, a hostile bank takeover would be prohibitively difficult. The regulatory barriers were just too great and Citizens easily could blow the favorable accounting treatment McColl wanted. On April 25, NCNB—as McColl's bank was then called—withdrew the offer for Citizens. Shortly thereafter, Citizens merged with Washington, D.C.–based Sovran bank.

Spurned by Citizens & Southern in 1989, the fifty-three-year-old McColl was hardly chastened. The very next day, NCNB announced its intention to bid for MCorp, a failed Texas bank being auctioned by the FDIC. McColl would not be held back from realizing his super-regional vision.

Though McColl was one of the most voracious acquirers of commercial banks, his strategy was not unique. The tumultuous financial services environment of the 1980s was the spawning ground for vast super-regional commercial banks with multistate branch networks. Taking advantage of the gradual liberalization of regulatory boundaries within specific regions, a handful of visionaries shaped these institutions.

Besides NCNB, other super-regionals include California's BankAmerica Corp., Ohio's Banc One Corporation, and fellow North Carolinian First Union. In the 1980s, the heads of these and other regional banks looked out at the competitive landscape and saw a world in which scale was the key to survival.

The super-regional approach promised a number of benefits. In part, the banking industry's bloat and sluggishness created a classic consolidation opportunity—buy up competitors, slash unnecessary overlap and boost shareholders' return on equity. Scaled-back overhead expenses could be spread across a larger operation. Where there were duplicative branch networks, savings could be even more significant.

Size also provided a technology-oriented advantage. With larger operations, the super-regionals gained the wherewithal to support an expanded technology effort. NCNB, for example, was able to launch a $100 million plan to build an integrated computer system designed to automate nearly every retail banking task. Smaller, regional banks simply didn't have the technology budget to sustain that kind of investment.

The cross-border, super-regional strategy was given a real boost by regulatory changes. Under the McFadden Act of 1927, banks were prohibited from building branch networks which extended across state lines. For a time, banks got around this rule by creating bank holding companies. A New York holding company might, for example, own formally separate New York and New Jersey bank subsidiaries.

Such arrangements made considerable economic sense, allowing the combined entities to spread marketing and other costs across a larger population, but the holding company structures were of limited utility. Each bank subsidiary was required to maintain a separate corporate charter and was subject to state regulation in its home state.

However, even this limited form of consolidation raised concerns in Congress. Mistrust of large financial institutions remained strong. Politicians favored community control of banks and local responsiveness. The result was the Bank Holding Company Act of 1956, which further reinforced the decentralized, community-based banking model.

The act prohibited a nonbank from owning a bank. Furthermore, an acquisition could only go forward with the approval of the Federal Reserve Board, which was directed to consider anticompetitive effects, financial and managerial resources and community needs. A provision known as the Douglas Amendment forbade approval of any cross-border acquisition unless "specifically authorized by the statute laws of the State in which such bank is located, by language to that effect and not merely by implication."

Until 1972, no state had enacted such an authorization. However, in that year, a few states began to relax the rules for certain kinds of transactions. The real break came in 1982, when Massachusetts adopted a law that lifted the interstate ban on a reciprocal basis for banks in New England. Connecticut followed suit by adopting a similar statute, so that Connecticut and Massachusetts banks could acquire each other. This selective regional approach, largely designed to exclude the New York money-center banks, was challenged in the courts, but was ultimately upheld by the U.S. Supreme Court in *Northeast Bancorp*. With this blessing from the Court, a number of other states passed similar legislation.

Losses related to bad real estate and oil loans also triggered a further opening to build super-regional empires. In 1982, federal legislation was passed that allowed bank holding companies to acquire failing banks in any region. The law gave healthy banks access into a few key markets, Texas in particular, and served the federal government's interest in increasing the number of bidders for failing banks.

Hugh McColl

Dubbed the "George Patton of banking" by *Forbes* magazine, Hugh McColl is a South Carolina native with an aggressive spirit. Though a fourth-generation banker, McColl doesn't fit the mold of courtly Southern banker. He has a fondness for phrases like "crush the SOBs and have a nice day," and prides himself on loyal support of subordinates.

NCNB's buying spree had started in 1982, when the bank's lawyers found a regulatory loophole that allowed the North Carolina bank to get into the Florida market. Because NCNB had operated a trust company in the state before 1973, it was free to buy Florida banks. McColl led the charge. In 1982, NCNB acquired Gulfstream Banks of Boca Raton. Exchange Bancorp of Tampa was swallowed shortly thereafter.

In 1983, McColl became chairman of NCNB and the acquisitions tear continued. He wanted to reshape NCNB into the leading bank on the Southeast coast, from Baltimore to Miami. In pursuing that goal, NCNB would acquire dozens of banks over the course of the 1980s, ballooning from a sleepy Southern bank into a powerhouse with more than $17.5 billion of revenues in 1996, making it the nation's fourth largest commercial bank by this measure.

Much of McColl's tough image can be attributed to his unforgiving standards. He once called Florida bankers lazy, and showed he meant it when integrating NCNB's early Florida acquisitions into the larger bank. He sent in platoons of fired-up young staffers to overhaul the operations. Within a short time, most of the senior staff at the bank were pushed out the door, replaced with McColl-trained people.

McColl's reputation as a tough taskmaster can sometimes hurt. His unsuccessful offer for Citizens & Southern was not the first. In 1985, he had been turned away by First Atlanta Corp. Rather than merge with McColl's army, the Atlanta institution opted to accept a lower offer from the kinder and gentler Wachovia bank.

Even with the setbacks, McColl managed to translate his vision of a regional powerhouse into reality during the 1980s. He accomplished this while avoiding most of the serious problems that plagued banks over the course of the decade. Today, McColl can claim credit for personally leading NCNB into the promised land—it has become one of the leading banks in the country.

Hugh McColl's particular super-regional vision became more than just a pipe dream in 1985, when a group of Southeastern states picked up on the *Northeast Bancorp* decision and enacted a regional banking compact. Effective in July of that year, banks in North Carolina, Florida, Georgia, Tennessee and Virginia could merge together or acquire each other. South Carolina joined the group in 1986.

Very shortly after federal and state laws provided an opening, Hugh McColl spread his acquisition net to acquire banks in Tennessee, Virginia and Georgia. He made his unsuccessful run at First Atlanta bank and moved into Maryland. However, despite the regulatory openings, the McFadden Act still prohibited cross-state branching. As a result, NCNB was forced to maintain each state's operations as a stand-alone subsidiary.

Still, this limited liberalization was enough to encourage McColl and others. BankAmerica built a stronghold in the West with acquisitions in Oregon and Washington. After surviving its own period of troubles, the bank pushed into Nevada with the 1989 purchase of

Nevada First Bank, then added operations in New Mexico and Arizona. Security Pacific—a power in Southern California that was weighed down by bad real estate loans—was acquired for $4.2 billion in 1992. Two years later, BankAmerica crossed the Mississippi for the first time, acquiring Continental Bank of Illinois for $1.9 billion.

Other banks matched BankAmerica and NationsBank. First Union built its own network of banks along the Eastern seaboard. The company's operations were primarily in the Southeast until 1995, when it acquired First Fidelity Bancorp for $5.4 billion. The deal transformed First Union by adding a strong Northeastern network of banks and branches. First Chicago NBD focused its efforts in the Midwest; Keycorp spread from an upstate New York base into the Northeast and to the west; Fleet Bank acquired Bank of New England and Shawmut to become the largest New England bank.

By developing wide branch networks, these super-regionals hoped to position themselves to become national banks. They essentially were gambling that federal bank regulations would be revised to allow cross-border branching. In that event, the super-regionals would be able to leverage their existing retail and wholesale operations across a far larger group of potential customers.

Acquirers had to be opportunistic to realize this vision. After spending a few years digesting the 1985 acquisitions, McColl made a particularly shrewd move. He took advantage of the new law allowing cross-border acquisitions of troubled banks and got into the large Texas market. Specifically, in 1988, NCNB paid a rock-bottom $210 million for a 20 percent interest in First RepublicBank Corp., a failed Texas bank that had been taken over by the FDIC. The government agreed to pick up all the costs from a $5 billion pool of bad loans and to inject $960 million of fresh capital. In addition, NCNB was granted an option to purchase the remaining 80 percent of the bank.

The media questioned McColl's move into Texas: Had he overpaid? The answer came quickly. NCNB—like Ronald Perelman in his 1988 purchase of a failed Texas S&L—was allowed to keep First Republic's tax losses. These past losses could be used to shelter future income. Within months, it became clear that both McColl and Perelman had gotten the better of the government. In NCNB's case, its new Texas operations churned out profits and NCNB's stock soared 50 percent. McColl exercised the option to buy the rest of the Texas bank less than a year later.

With First Republic integrated into its operations, NCNB renewed its acquisition streak and has been an active participant in the bank merger boom of the past several years. McColl's first deal of the decade was particularly sweet. In 1991, Citizens & Southern/Sovran was having deep problems with bad commercial real estate loans. Bennett Brown swallowed his pride and reopened negotiations with McColl. Within a matter of weeks, the parties agreed to a $4.2 billion merger. The combined entity became NationsBank, at the time the country's third largest bank with more than $100 billion in assets.

Buying Citizens was part in-market merger. The branch networks of NCNB and C&S overlapped in South Carolina and Florida, providing an opportunity for an estimated $130 million in annual cost savings. Yet the deal was more about extending McColl's super-regional vision into Georgia and Virginia, C&S/Sovran strongholds.

Perhaps the most surprising aspect of the NationsBank deal was the apparent ease with which McColl and Brown overcame the acrimony of their earlier tussle. The key, reportedly, was McColl's understated approach. Preferring one-on-one meetings with Brown to large negotiations, McColl made a strong pitch for the benefits of the merger. On several occasions, he got together with Brown in the casual environment of a South Carolina beach house. McColl promised that the senior Brown would be chairman of the combined banks. McColl would be president and chief executive. Clearly, he was willing to compromise in order to get the deal done. C&S/Sovran gave NCNB the bulk to be a truly national player.

By year-end 1995, NationsBank was a super-regional with more than $180 billion of assets. Yet McColl was not done growing. The market imperative for consolidation remained strong. A core group of large banks had quickly coalesced. These large players possessed the capital and scale to become global institutions. Their increased investments in technology and marketing were transforming the business of banking. An international race for market share was developing.

McColl sought to position NationsBank for this new global competition. In August 1996, helped along by regulatory developments, he expanded his reach yet further. NationsBank moved into the Midwest with a $9.6 billion acquisition of Boatmen's Bancshares. The combined entity had branches in sixteen states and the District of Columbia, from Maryland to Texas, from Florida to the Mexican border.

Within a matter of months, McColl followed with a different kind of deal. NationsBank had for some time been developing its own investment banking unit, with only limited success. NationsBanc Capital lacked the scale and market presence to capture significant market share. McColl faced a decision point when, following the Dean Witter–Morgan Stanley deal, the remaining independent mid-sized investment banks began to be swallowed up. The issue was, buy or build?

Apparently, McColl decided NationsBank needed to make a quick jump in its securities business. He courted Montgomery Securities, one of three San Francisco investment houses that had flourished as a result of the Silicon Valley boom. In the spring of 1997, NationsBank agreed to pay $1.2 billion to acquire the operation, dramatically upgrading its securities business. In addition, NationsBank gained an entrée into the important California market.

McColl followed the Montgomery deal with a $14.8 billion blockbuster—the September 1997 acquisition of Florida's Barnett Banks Inc. In capturing the deal after a quick friendly auction run by Barnett's CEO Charles Rice, McColl again showed his decisive streak. He topped the other bidders by several dollars a share to win Barnett, the undeniable jewel of Florida.

With the closing of the Barnett deal, NationsBank became the second largest commercial bank in the United States measured by market capitalization. Its operations span both investment and commercial banking, including stock and bond underwriting, asset management and commercial lending. The question, of course, is whether McColl can integrate Boatmen's, Montgomery and Barnett into a cohesive NationsBank culture.

Buying the Bank Across the Street

McColl and others consolidated banks throughout the 1980s, but considerable room for further restructuring remained. Overcapacity, combined with the hard times of the early 1990s, induced a new wave of bank mergers. All of the ten largest bank mergers in American history have occurred since 1990. Super-regional deals have been a significant part of this story, but in-market mergers—buying the bank across the street—also have been an important driver, reducing branch overlap and wringing costs out of the system.

The largest of these in-market deals came on August 28, 1995, when Chase Manhattan Corp. and Chemical Banking Corporation announced the intention to combine into a single banking behemoth. Just over seven months later, the corporate formalities were done and the two bank holding companies joined together. The new Chase—the older name survived, though Chemical executives control matters—has roughly $300 billion in assets, $160 billion in deposits, 4 million consumer accounts and the dominant retail banking network in the New York metropolitan area. In 1996, Chase was the third most profitable bank in the country.

MAKING HISTORY: THE TEN LARGEST U.S. COMMERCIAL BANK DEALS			
Acquirer	Target	Approximate Equity Price (Billions)	Year Announced
First Union Corp.	*CoreStates	$17.1	1997
NationsBank Corp.	Barnett Banks	$14.8	1997
Wells Fargo & Co.	First Interstate Bancorp.	$10.9	1995
Chemical Banking Corp.	Chase Manhattan Corp.	$10.4	1995
NationsBank Corp.	Boatmen's Bancshares Inc.	$9.6	1996
First Bank System Inc.	U.S. Bancorp	$8.9	1997
First Union	First Fidelity	$5.4	1995
NBD Bancorp Inc.	First Chicago Corp.	$5.4	1995
NCNB Corp.	C&S/Sovran Corp.	$4.2	1991
BankAmerica Corp.	Security Pacific Corp.	$4.2	1991

*Deal was pending as of January 15, 1998. Source: Securities Data Corporation

Cost savings were clearly one imperative in the $10.4 billion merger of Chase and Chemical. In announcing the deal, Walter Shipley, chairman of Chemical, and Thomas Labrecque, chairman of Chase, projected a reduction in workforce of 12,000 employees and the closure of more than 100 branches. These and other moves eventually would excise $1.5 billion in annual expenses from the combined company's income statement.

The deal—billed as a merger of equals—was a bittersweet moment for Labrecque and others at Chase. Though the stronger Chase name would be on the door of the new bank, in other respects, the once-proud Chase would be folded into Chemical. Chase had been founded in 1877 and later merged with Equitable Trust, growing to become the world's largest bank by the 1930s. The merger with Equitable also had brought cachet to Chase. John D. Rockefeller Jr. was the Equitable's biggest shareholder and Chase became intertwined with the Rockefeller legend. In fact, David

Rockefeller eventually took over the leadership of the bank, serving as chairman until 1981.

However, when he became chairman of Chase in 1990, Labrecque, a Rockefeller protégé, assumed the top job at a faded institution. Chase had been stung by a series of miscues, including bad Latin American loans. A few years later, Chase's large portfolio of risky real estate loans crashed.

Labrecque worked hard to turn the bank around. He cut costs and got out of unprofitable businesses. The stock price failed to respond. By 1995, Labrecque was under pressure from investors. Aggressive fund manager Michael Price had taken a large stake and was agitating for more revolutionary steps. Labrecque announced a $400 million cost cutting plan, but the stock price still didn't pop.

For Chase, then, the Chemical merger was partly defensive, a way to go from number three to number one in the New York market. To make the leap, Labrecque agreed to give Chemical Bank's Shipley the top job, with no guarantee of eventual succession. The gamble would pay off in December 1997, when Labrecque was given an expanded role at the combined bank.

Shipley's decision to merge Chemical with Chase, on the other hand, reflected satisfaction with the earlier $2.0 billion merger between Chemical and Manufacturers Hanover. The vision behind the 1991 deal was clear—bring together two New York money-center banks with high debt loads and fairly steep cost structures, and slash $650 million in annual expenses. By keeping the best of each company, Shipley had hoped to create a single, market-leading bank.

The Manufacturers Hanover deal is widely regarded as one of the more successful recent corporate marriages. While implementation took longer than some on Wall Street had hoped, the two banks melded to form a leader in corporate lending with a strong retail franchise. Annual cost reductions actually outpaced expectations, reaching $750 million.

Shipley clearly hoped to repeat the magic with an encore deal, but there would be some important differences in the Chase merger. Chemical and Manufacturers Hanover had been more equally matched. Shipley had been the leader willing to take a back seat to get the deal done. John McGillicuddy, chairman of Manufacturers Hanover, was given the top spot with the agreement that Shipley would take over January 1, 1994. Down the ranks, executive appointments were balanced to reflect the even match between the two companies. When McGillicuddy stepped aside according to plan, Edward Miller, a former Manufacturers Hanover executive, was appointed to be the new number two.

The balanced marriage and attention to sensibilities may have helped smooth the 1991 merger. Yet the format also slowed integration and cost reduction. Decisions were sometimes made for political, not economic, reasons. Former Chemical managers by contrast initially controlled the top of the new Chase. However, Labrecque's 1997 elevation to "co-equal" with Shipley puts him squarely in the running to take over for Shipley, though Labrecque is only one of several candidates.

Despite the differences, the Chemical–Manufacturers Hanover and the Chase-Chemical mergers are indicative of a wider trend toward cost-driven deals. Generally, the early 1990s were not happy times for commercial banks. The commercial banking industry had painfully struggled to the close of the previous decade like a marathon runner who has hit the wall.

Blow after blow left many banks tired and weak. Investors, weary of the episodic bad news, hammered bank share prices. The large New York money-center banks were hit particularly hard. Chase and Citicorp lost 50 percent of their respective market values in 1990, while the money centers as a whole declined by roughly 35 percent.

The industry responded to this latest bad news with a wave of cost cutting and restructuring. Announcements of multithousand job cuts were commonplace in 1990 and 1991. At the same time, credit standards were dramatically tightened. Loans became extremely hard to come by for all but the highest-rated borrowers. Commentators wondered whether the industry might slip into a widespread collapse.

Too much capacity was a big part of the problem. The United States had more bankers per capita than any other nation, outmatched only by the United Kingdom's unionized banking system. This excess labor capacity in the United States was matched by excess functional capacity. According to one recent study, banks had between 27 and 43 percent excess technological capacity. Banks had the ability to process about 220 million transaction accounts, 370 million credit card transactions, 4.4 million mutual fund transactions and 750 million fund transfers annually. However, actual usage for 1995 was far below those levels.

In-market mergers have proven a powerful tool for the reduction of capacity. Potential cost savings have been a strong motivator for deals. Of course, not all of these cost-driven mergers have gone smoothly. The $10.9 billion Wells Fargo–First Interstate deal, launched in 1995 and completed in 1996, is a recent example. In many ways, the deal was a typical in-market merger. Wells Fargo, which sparked the deal with a hostile tender offer, had 974 branches in California at the close of 1995. First Interstate, the larger organization, had a total of roughly 1,150 locations in thirteen Western states, with 450 offices in California. The overlap in California provided the main opportunity for cost savings and was the key to the deal.

As outlined by Wells Fargo, the large majority of branch closings (projected at around 350) and employee layoffs (projected at around 7,200) would come from First Interstate's California operations. Moreover, redundant headquarters staff and marketing efforts could be trimmed. These changes would generate the lion's share of the projected $800 million in post-takeover savings.

The economic logic behind the deal was strong, but Wells Fargo initially had trouble integrating First Interstate. Computer glitches embarrassed the bank shortly after the combination, while many of

First Interstate's top managers left. Customers—wooed by aggressive competitors—followed suit.

Still, by 1997, Wells Fargo was on its way to meeting its $800 million annual cost-savings goal. Market studies, which indicate that in-market mergers generate an average reduction in noninterest expenses of between 30 and 50 percent of the acquired company's expenses, suggest the full savings will materialize. If this data holds true, Wells Fargo management may be able to recover and return the company to its extremely strong 2 percent return on assets.

Whether Wells Fargo achieves the turnaround, the potential for cost savings will continue to induce further consolidation. The two Chemical Bank mergers and the Wells Fargo deal together generated over 25,000 job cuts, the shuttering of more than 500 branches, and in excess of $3 billion a year in annual cost savings. Other in-market mergers have had a similar effect. These savings are understandably appealing to bank executives, many of whom are struggling to boost profitability in the face of bruising competition.

THE NONBANK BANKS

Much of the competition faced by commercial banks comes from a rapidly proliferating animal—the nonbank bank. This group is populated by "monoline" credit card companies such as Advanta, home mortgage companies such as Countrywide Credit, and auto finance companies such as Olympic Financial.

Nimble and extremely aggressive, these companies stepped into the breach created by the credit crunch of the early 1990s. They gobbled market share by serving customers temporarily ignored by troubled banks and thrifts. For example, four monoline credit card companies—First USA, Capital One, Advanta and MBNA—pushed their share of the credit card market from 7.6 percent in 1991 to 17.6 percent by 1995. The companies feature credit cards as their sole product line, hence the name monoline. First USA's loan portfolio jumped 473 percent over the same period, compared to a 73 percent increase for all cards. Auto and home mortgage companies experienced similar growth.

There is some question as to whether this growth came at the expense of prudence. Many of these new competitors pioneered the practice of loaning money to "subprime" borrowers. Lately, investors and politicians alike have begun to question whether these loans will be paid off at the rates projected by the issuing finance companies. However, many banks appear to have embraced the consumer finance business plan. In 1997, Banc One agreed to spend a steep $7.3 billion to buy First USA.

Looking to the Top Line

A strong economy powered commercial banks to returned profitability and improved asset quality by 1994. Cost savings helped improve the bottom line considerably. However, cost savings can only go so far. Top-line revenue growth has also been key. In this vein, two specific strategies deserve mention given the prominence of the banks involved: the global supermarket approach of Citibank, and the merchant banking strategies of Bankers Trust and J.P. Morgan.

Citicorp's explicit strategic focus over the past decade has been to build a universal bank, international in scope, with a worldwide retail and consumer banking franchise, and a strong corporate client base. At the core of this strategy are Citicorp's crown jewels—international relationships that the bank has maintained for decades. Citicorp has leveraged this base into a strong international branch network covering more than forty-one countries. In all, the company operates in nearly 100 countries. Furthermore, the bank has worked to create standardized, branded products that can be marketed worldwide. Its blue-faced credit card, for example, is now available in more than thirty countries.

Following so expansive a strategy has not been without difficult challenges. In the early part of the decade, Citicorp teetered under the weight of bad loans. The bank's equity/assets ratio was barely over the threshold required by regulators. Trouble was not localized, but rather came from a diverse range of business lines: bad commercial real estate loans, rising consumer mortgage and credit card delinquencies and nonperforming LBO loans were just a few of the problem areas. A number of poorly integrated acquisitions also dragged on earnings. The net effect of all these problems was substantial red ink—in 1991, Citicorp lost $457 million.

At one point, the problems got so bad that Citicorp's preferred stock was downgraded to junk status by credit rating agencies. The bank faced a catch-22—it badly needed more equity to boost its credit rating, but the poor rating made new capital incredibly expensive.

Fortunately, the economy turned around and the Federal Reserve maintained a favorable interest rate environment in the years after 1991. Citicorp chairman John Reed slashed costs where he could without slicing away muscle. He also found a patient investor who believed in his global vision. Saudi Prince Alwaleed bin Talal bin Adulaziz Alsaud injected $800 million in exchange for preferred stock. Citicorp rebounded nicely.

The global approach now has translated into healthy growth. Emerging markets, in particular, have been a source of strength— return on assets in Latin America and Asia was 2.5 percent in 1996, compared to just 1.24 percent for mature markets, although the recent volatility of those markets poses a new challenge.

Reflecting the continuing strong performance and future potential of the international markets that Citicorp favors, the bank's stock price has climbed from a low of $8.50 in 1991 to over $120 in 1997. Now with a healthy bank to manage, Reed has begun to think about extending Citicorp's reach. His goal is to grow Citicorp's earnings between 10 and 12 percent a year and to transform the bank into a global growth company.

Acquisitions in emerging markets, or of credit card or asset management companies, would play to Citicorp's existing strengths. In keeping with this focus, Reed held widely reported talks with American Express, which features both asset management and credit cards, about a possible merger. The deal would have folded the smaller American Express into Citicorp, a possible return to the financial supermarket for American Express. Talks fell apart at the end of 1996, but periodic rumors reignite speculation. Regardless, Reed is focused on translating Citicorp's global brand name and presence into sustainable revenue growth.

Bankers Trust has adopted a much different niche strategy in its search for growth—to become a transaction-driven merchant bank positioned for expansion into investment banking. Yet, like Citicorp, Bankers Trust ran into problems with the execution of its growth strategy in the early 1990s. Overly aggressive sales practices in its derivatives operations came to light when a series of major clients sued the firm for alleged misrepresentations. The bank's image was tarnished and revenues tanked. Frank Newman, a highly regarded former BankAmerica executive and Treasury Department official, was brought in to clean house.

Under Newman, Bankers Trust revisited its strategic focus. Newman's team determined that the bank was too dependent on volatile trading and derivatives revenues. Investment banking and asset management were the keys to restoring balance.

Acquisitions were the key implementation tool. In the spring of 1996, Bankers Trust acquired Wolfensohn & Co., a niche mergers and acquisitions advisory shop. The next move was more dramatic. The purchase of Alex Brown, with its regional brokerage business and equity underwriting strengths, rounded out the Bankers Trust investment banking operation. Alex Brown gave Bankers Trust instant credibility as an adviser on initial public offerings.

J.P. Morgan has followed a similar strategy, seeking to build into a global merchant bank, with several notable differences in approach. The blue-chip bank has retained its core commercial lending franchise, while adding to its investment banking unit through internal growth rather than by acquisition. In this way, J.P. Morgan evolved a significant underwriting and advisory business. Observers initially credited Morgan as a pioneer. However, as other market participants have accelerated their development, J.P. Morgan no longer is leading the field. There is little question that there will be a further evolution of Morgan's effort in response.

TOP 10 U.S. BANKS (IN BILLIONS OF DOLLARS)	
Company	Stock Mkt. Capitalization*
Citicorp	$57.8
NationsBank Corp.	57.2
BankAmerica Corp.	50.6
First Union Corp.	48.3
Chase Manhattan Corp.	46.1
Banc One Corp.	31.9
Wells Fargo	29.4
Norwest Corp.	29.3
US Bancorp	27.5
First Chicago NBD	24.3

*As of December 31, 1997. Source: Fact Set Data Systems. Pro forma for NationsBank's acquisition of Barnett Banks and First Union's pending acquisitions of Signet Banking and CoreStates Financial.

Consolidation Spreads

The insurance business is another rapidly consolidating area of the financial services world. Every few months, it seems, another big insurer gets bought: in December 1997, American Bankers Insur-

ance Group was the target of a $2.2 billion acquisition; the follow-
ing month, St. Paul Gas bought USF&G for $2.8 billion. The indus-
try is bubbling with change, affected by many of the same forces at
work elsewhere in financial services.

Much of the deal activity has been taking place in two main insurance categories—property and casualty, and life. In both cases,
the acquisition activity is driven by four factors. First, operating
difficulties have weakened some companies, making them receptive to takeover. Second, new competitive dynamics leave even
healthy companies unable to meet their growth targets with internal, organic growth. Third, the restructuring of the big multiline insurers has provided both supply and demand in the acquisitions
market. Finally, consolidators and financial buyers have entered
the market, in the latter case hoping to arbitrage rising prices as
deal activity picks up.

Particular operating difficulties have varied by industry subline.
For property and casualty insurers, the problem has been under-
reserving for losses. The failure to set up adequate reserves can leave
a company pinched when liabilities materialize. Precisely this eventuality occurred at many companies in the late 1980s and early 1990s
as environmental, asbestos and litigation losses piled up. Huge environmental liabilities for pollution of land and water, for example,
badly dented many companies' balance sheets.

For life insurers, the main problems have been asset troubles,
which also have plagued some property and casualty companies. The
most common bad asset of late has been real estate investments.
Many insurers saw the value of their portfolios plummet when the
exuberant commercial real estate market of the 1980s collapsed.
Junk bonds also were a problem to a lesser extent. When the junk
market crashed in the early 1990s, some regulators pressed insurers
to unload their holdings at a loss. In hindsight, this response was an
overreaction. The market soon came back up and investors who
bought the paper made huge profits.

From an M&A perspective, operational difficulties are deal cata-lysts. Troubles have had the effect of pushing some companies to seek a white knight acquirer with a healthy balance sheet, or to sell businesses or parts of businesses. For instance, Continental Corp. sold out to CNA, the insurance subsidiary of Loews, in 1995. Lead-ing up to the deal, mounting property and casualty claims, chiefly for environmental cleanup, were hammering the underreserved Conti-nental. The company was forced to stop paying a dividend. As a re-sult, Continental's stock was off 60 percent from its August 1993 high.

Healthier companies face a less life-threatening but troubling problem of their own. As competition has heated up across the board, insurers have found it more difficult to grow revenues and earnings. For example, life insurance became a tough sell in the world of easy access to mutual funds. Of course, people still pur-chase pure life insurance policies that provide death benefits, but the real money in life insurance has always been in selling "cash-value" insurance, a life insurance policy wrapped around an invest-ment vehicle. The customer pays a higher premium than would otherwise be the case, and the extra money builds up in value over time. As Americans became more sophisticated about their invest-ment strategies, many became convinced mutual funds provide a better investment opportunity.

Similarly, the property and casualty business also faced increas-ing competition. Starting in the 1980s, large corporations began to self-insure. Margins on individual property and casualty business de-clined in the face of tough competition from cut-rate telemarketers and others.

Even with the new competition, many insurance companies still are quite profitable and successful. However, on the horizon, growth has become a concern. Getting the incremental dollar of sales or earnings is becoming more difficult. As a result, many companies are turning to acquisitions as a growth strategy.

Another major dimension of insurance M&A has been the restructuring of the large multiline insurers—MetLife, Travelers, Prudential and others. The multilines prospered for decades by serving all segments of the insurance market. Yet, like many large diversified companies, their very diversity proved a hindrance. In many cases, top management was insulated from the front-line business units and failed to recognize impending problems. When the problems became abundantly clear, the large organizations were difficult to maneuver.

Eventually, many industry executives came to the conclusion that the companies they led needed to slim down and focus on a shorter list of markets. Prudential sold off a reinsurance business. Metropolitan and Travelers sold their health insurance units. Aetna sold its property and casualty operations.

Consolidators and financial buyers are the final force driving insurance company acquisitions. As in other sectors of the financial services industry, changes in the insurance business have been treated as an opportunity by some. The consolidators' business plan is to combine ailing operations, slash overlapping staff and impose rigid cost control.

Sandy Weill built Travelers by following this plan. KKR also bought into insurance. However, Stephen Hilbert of Conseco Insurance and Gary Wendt of GE Capital have been the most prominent insurance company consolidators.

Hilbert has wholeheartedly followed an acquisition-driven growth plan, and been quite successful. Starting as early as 1979, Hilbert saw the vitality of the consolidation model. The former encyclopedia salesman and college dropout began snapping up insurance companies. His early deals mainly were cash acquisitions financed with debt. Lately, under pressure from rating agencies, he has switched to stock deals. The shift hasn't slowed him down. Over the last three years, Conseco has bought six different companies for a total purchase price of $3 billion.

Some have questioned Hilbert's tactics and accounting methods, but the market has been enthusiastic. Conseco's stock price increased at a compound annual rate of roughly 44 percent between the company's 1985 IPO and the end of 1997. Investors seem convinced that Conseco's growth prospects are real, both as a result of Hilbert's acquisitions and his ability to manage targets after the deals close.

Wendt's strong interest in insurance is of more recent vintage than Hilbert's. GE Capital began its insurance company acquisition spree in 1993 with the $525 million purchase of Great Northern Annuity. Over the next three years, Wendt spent more than $4.5 billion to buy another six U.S. insurance and reinsurance companies. In addition, he made a failed $2.4 billion hostile bid for Kemper and spent $1 billion on two German reinsurers.

The overall industry consolidation does not yet appear to have run its course. Hilbert has professed interest in further acquisitions. Wendt has publicly stated GE Capital's insurance operations lack "critical mass." And, of course, many other buyers are in the market.

The Golden Era of Asset Management

While the rise of the individual investor put pressure on insurance companies in the 1990s, it also has made the decade the golden era of the asset management business. Phenomenal growth years have created a well-populated universe of mutual funds, insurance companies, commercial and investment banks, all competing for assets. Virtually every proprietor of a modern-day financial supermarket sees asset management as a critical revenue source. Recently, many companies have concluded that critical mass is necessary to compete in the sector and that acquisitions are the best route to gaining critical mass.

Demographic trends have a lot to do with the rise of mutual funds and other asset managers. With the promise of living considerably longer than their parents, baby boomers have demonstrated a penchant for saving as they near retirement age. At the same time, the incredible bull market, more or less running from 1982 without much letup, has stimulated strong, though perhaps misguided, faith in the stock market as an investment vehicle. The increasing flow of information has made investors arguably more sophisticated and discerning about their investment decisions.

There has as a result been a flood of cash into the stock market via mutual fund investments. Each of the last few years has set a record—$119 billion in 1994, $129 billion in 1995, $222 billion in 1996 and $232 billion in 1997. The number of mutual fund companies has proliferated in line with the increasing flow of funds. From 1990 to 1995, the number of mutual funds in America increased from 2,362 to 5,761. To put these numbers in perspective, there are now more mutual funds to invest in than stocks on the New York Stock Exchange.

The value of asset management companies has soared along with their popularity. Despite the rich valuations, an anticipated consolidation of the fragmented industry is underway. The deals are just beginning to flow. Franklin Resources bought Michael Price's Heine Securities for $800 million. The Benham fund family was sold to Twentieth Century, which changed its name to American Century. Zurich Insurance, the big Swiss insurer, also has been an active buyer, first of Kemper Corp. for $2 billion, then Scudder Stevens & Clark for roughly $860 million.

Some of the recent asset management acquisitions have involved commercial banks purchasing mutual fund management companies to augment their asset management operations. For example, in 1993 Pittsburgh's Mellon Bank spent $1.45 billion to acquire Boston Company, a trust and investment management business, from American Express. Less than a year later, Mellon shelled out another $1.8 billion for Dreyfus, a major mutual fund company. In 1997, J.P. Morgan bought a minority interest in the new American Century fund family.

Institutional investment banks also have been buying asset management capabilities. Morgan Stanley, with its purchase of Van Kampen, is not alone in this regard. Both Merrill Lynch and Goldman, Sachs recently have expanded their asset management efforts through acquisitions.

As a business, asset management has three virtues. Lately it has been a high-growth business for established players. The likes of Charles Schwab, T. Rowe Price and Oppenheimer Capital have seen their assets under management zoom. Asset management also can be an incredibly high-margin business. Once a fund reaches a certain size, costs rise far more slowly than assets under management and revenues. Multibillion-dollar funds in particular, like Fidelity's Magellan Fund, throw off phenomenal cash flows.

Finally, asset management revenues are thought to be more stable than investment banking revenues. The notion is that there is a certain viscosity to assets under management, especially assets invested through IRAs and other tax-preferred retirement accounts. Investors may be less likely to move these assets in a market downturn. Of course, with the long bull market, this theory has not received a sharp test.

Global Shockwaves

On Friday, December 5, 1997, two thirds of the most distinguished industrialists in Switzerland secretly gathered in Basel and Zurich to consider a groundbreaking deal—the merger of Swiss Bank and Union Bank of Switzerland to form the United Bank of Switzerland, with a market capitalization of roughly $60 billion. The third not present were board members of arch-rival Credit Suisse. Security for the two companies' board meetings was tight—board members and our team arrived at the Swiss Bank meeting via subterranean tunnels.

Early Monday morning, Marcel Ospel of Swiss Bank, the new chief executive, shattered European precedent by announcing that the banks would merge. The market reaction was a standing ovation as both stocks soared. When the new UBS emerged, it would be the world's second largest bank, the world's largest money manager and the leading European investment bank.

Two strategic visions sparked the deal, consolidation and globalization. As late as 1996, consolidation in the financial services industry was principally a U.S. phenomenon. Europe's financial services market was balkanized along both functional and geographic lines. Individual countries and sectors were dramatically overpopulated with small to mid-size players.

Pressure for change had begun to build in the middle 1990s as the shockwaves from the U.S. consolidation radiated into Europe. Even on their home turf, European institutions faced the increasingly sharp elbows of companies like Merrill Lynch, Morgan Stanley, J.P. Morgan, Citicorp and others. In addition, regulatory and political developments shook the system. European Union countries were moving toward a single financial services market and a single currency.

These forces jolted European companies out of complacency. Major deals were announced with unheard of regularity—nine multibillion-dollar deals within the space of ten months.

The potential for cost savings in the European financial services sector became apparent in the Swiss Bank–UBS deal. As a result of the deal, the two banks eliminated overlapping branches and personnel. Annual costs were slashed by over $500 million.

Globalization was the second driver behind the Swiss Bank–UBS deal. The financial services market was rapidly evolving toward the creation of a handful of institutions with the scale to support a global integrated platform. Both investment banking and asset management were becoming businesses of global distribution and branding, and this deal made UBS a leader. In addition, by combining their embryonic U.S. efforts, Swiss Bank, the owner of Warburg Dillon

Read, and UBS hoped to create a platform for developing their vital American presence.

THE QUICKENING

Date Announced	Acquirer	Target	Price Paid (Billions)
March 1997	Prudential Corp. PLC	Scottish Amicable Life	$3
July 1997	Munich Re	Victoria Holding	$4
August 1997	Credit Suisse	Winterthur	$10
August 1997	Vereinsbank	Hypobank	$8
October 1997	Zurich Insurance	BAT Industries (financial services subsidiary)	$17
November 1997	ING	Banque Bruxelles Lambert	$5
November 1997	Allianz	Assurances Generales	$10
November 1997	Merrill Lynch	Mercury Asset Mgmt.	$5
December 1997	Swiss Bank	UBS	$25*

*Based on Swiss Bank value. Source: Securities Data Company and public information

Yet, the real import of the merger was not so much what it said about the present, as what it said about the likely course of future events. Just as the Morgan Stanley–Dean Witter deal had foreshadowed developments in the U.S. market, the Swiss Bank and UBS combination crystallized the inevitability of a global consolidation. The leapfrog to $100 billion in market capitalization had started.

The Financial Services Future

The financial services future is certain to reflect the acceleration of past trends: more competition, more blurring of boundaries, and more need for leadership.

For the commercial banks, the fundamental trend will be toward increased size and scale. The super-regionals' gamble has been vindicated in Congress, in the form of the Riegle-Neal Interstate Banking and Branching Efficiency Act of 1994. This law has two main effects. First, as of October 1995, a bank holding company was allowed to buy operations in any other state. Second, after July 1, 1997, banks were allowed to convert their out-of-state activities from separate, stand-alone bank subsidiaries into branch operations.

The ability to expand without restriction across state boundaries promises to have a profound impact. This unleashes the money-center banks, previously restrained by the regional state compacts. Though the super-regionals have somewhat of a head start, New York banks now may expand nationwide.

In addition, the act lowers two preexisting barriers to interstate banking: cost and convenience. With regard to cost, the conversion will allow bank holding companies to shed duplicative structure— executives, boards, regulatory filings—previously required in each state of operation. NationsBank puts such costs at $50 million a year, while BankAmerica figures the added costs at $75 million a year. Estimates for the banking industry as a whole place the aggregate savings somewhere between $2 and $5 billion over the next five years.

The result of these changes will be a further quantum leap of bank consolidation. In the process, half of the existing regional banks will disappear, swallowed by larger competitors. Others will adopt unique strategies in an effort to carve out a defensible position, as Mellon Bank has done with its focus on asset management.

Meanwhile, insurance industry consolidation will continue as companies fight to squeeze costs. Asset managers will continue to be sought after. A downturn in the stock market may accelerate the acquisition pace. The investment banks face continuing competition and globalization, as well as rising capital needs. Commercial banks and insurance companies likely will buy up the last few attractive targets.

Faced with turmoil and an uncertain future, financial services providers will continue to search for the best business mix. The action will play out across the spectrum of subsectors and on an international scale. Eventually, a handful of global players will dominate the scene while profitable niches will remain for the smart and nimble.

The Telco
Revolution

11

LOUIS XVI:
"Is it a revolt?"
DUC DE LA ROCHEFOUCAULD:
"No, Sire, it is a revolution."

Upon hearing news of the Bastille's fall

Over the past twenty years, a single telecommunications industry, served by one dominant company, has been fractured and
transformed. New industries have been spawned, based on technologies only recently conceived by man. This revolution is so shattering in its scope, its global impact of such intensity and magnitude,
that it has changed dramatically our economy and lives. The constituent pieces of the former American Telephone & Telegraph have
become independent companies and are on the threshold of competing directly against each other. New long-distance companies
have entered the scene. Cellular communications has become a viable and profitable technology.

The forces for change have been numerous and intertwined. Regulatory and political changes have had a dramatic impact, starting
with the forced breakup of AT&T and running through to the recent
enactment of the Telecommunications Act of 1996. Technological
advances have been equally significant.

More broadly, in the early 1990s, a series of related developments

288

coalesced into a conception that the telecommunications and media distribution channels would soon converge. Cable and phone companies scrambled to prepare for the coming competition. The uncertainty sparked a number of blockbuster deals. Then the bloom faded. Several of the deals fell apart, and skepticism spread. Today, however, it's clear that not only is convergence coming, but it is more important and much more complicated than imagined.

Convergence has become more complicated in part because companies must now operate on an increasingly global stage. The barriers that once protected domestic markets from outside competitors are coming down, bringing new risks and new opportunities.

The accelerating pace of all these changes has muddied the waters. Predictions about what the industry will look like in two years, let alone five or ten, vary wildly. As a result, a certain amount of grasping in the dark is taking place. All Five Pistons are firing on overdrive. The mix of regulatory, technological, and financial change, visionary leadership, and the scale versus simplicity dilemma has created an unparalleled M&A maelstrom.

The Breakup of Ma Bell

At 8:00 A.M. on January 8, 1982, representatives of the U.S. government and a major industrial empire gathered in a Washington, D.C., office. A certain amount of hostility pervaded the room, which is understandable given the years of battling that had preceded the moment. Yet more than anything, there was a sense of disbelief. With little fanfare, the U.S. Justice Department and AT&T agreed to settle *United States v. AT&T*—an antitrust case which had limped through the courts since 1974. AT&T as the world knew it would be no more.

On January 1, 1984, America's largest private employer was split into eight separate pieces. What had been the twenty-two local telephone companies in the Bell system—reconstituted as seven independently traded regional Bell operating companies (RBOCs)—were spun off to AT&T's shareholders. The parent company kept the long-distance business, known as Long Lines, equipment maker Western Electric, an installed base of millions of phones, which were leased to customers, and the world-famous Bell Laboratories.

Day One, as the breakup was known within AT&T, was not a sudden event. The process of dividing the Bell empire into separate fiefdoms had been underway ever since the 1982 settlement, and to some extent even before the settlement. Yet dividing the interconnected wires and switches of the labyrinthine telephone system into separate operating units was a technological and logistical nightmare. Dire predictions of mass failure preceded the final split. One newly anointed RBOC president picked up the phone that morning, just to check for a dial tone. To his relief, he heard the familiar buzz. However, little else of the old Bell system remained unaltered.

The drama of the moment was heightened by the long history of a unified AT&T. The Bell system could trace its roots back to March 10, 1876, when, in a Boston attic, Alexander Graham Bell articulated the first complete sentence over a telephone. By the start of the twentieth century, AT&T—affectionately dubbed Ma Bell—had already established itself as an embryonic monopoly, condemned by some for employing ruthless business practices. The company achieved monopolistic status by spurning the attempts of rival companies to gain access to the AT&T network. In the process, AT&T indirectly coerced competitors to sell out on favorable terms.

The phone company's actions did not go unnoticed by the Department of Justice, which ultimately sued AT&T on antitrust grounds. In 1919, however, an agreement was reached between Theodore Vail, then AT&T's chairman, and President Woodrow Wilson. The settlement allowed the company to go about business without government intervention. AT&T agreed to moderate its tooth-and-nails approach in exchange for the government's informal approval of the AT&T monopoly. For the next three decades, peace reigned between the phone company and the Justice Department.

AT&T's antitrust problems resurfaced in 1949, when the government focused on the fact that Western Electric, the company's man-ufacturing subsidiary, served as the sole supplier of phone equip-ment to the company's operating units. As *Fortune* later stated, AT&T "existed in a state possibly best described in terms of Zen: it was its own supplier and its own market to a degree almost unique." The company used this muscle to keep competitors out of the un-regulated equipment business. To rectify the situation, the Justice Department again sued the phone company, hoping to break up this captive monopoly.

The second antitrust case endured until 1956, when AT&T took advantage of political connections to gain a settlement. AT&T signed another consent decree which allowed it to keep Western Electric in exchange for a promise to confine new business development to reg-ulated markets. The main effect of the agreement was to foreclose AT&T from competing in the nascent computer business.

AT&T's critics, not realizing the full potential of computers, slammed the decree as a mere "slap on the wrist" that didn't go nearly far enough. These critics were outraged that the Bell System had remained intact. However, with the fullness of time, it would be-come clear that the company inadvertently had made a significant concession. Ma Bell eventually would chafe under the restriction and would strive to reverse the 1956 decree.

Notwithstanding these developments, the circumstances of the 1956 settlement chagrined the career lawyers in the Antitrust Divi-sion of the Justice Department. They quietly amassed information about AT&T's activities and waited for the right time to launch an-other attack. Their time came in the early 1970s, when new AT&T competitors, primarily MCI, complained that AT&T was restraining their growth.

In particular, competitors cited difficulty in obtaining from Ma Bell the connections necessary to attach customers to the embryonic interstate systems designed to provide an alternative to AT&T long-distance service. Under something called the "essential facilities"

antitrust doctrine, a company that owned unique facilities was required to allow other companies access to those facilities if the
facilities were essential to the other companies' competitive liveli-
hoods. Relying on this doctrine, the scrappy MCI, headed by
William McGowan, filed a private suit against AT&T in 1973 seeking
to force the company to provide MCI and other common carriers
with the same service given to Bell System companies.

Competitors in the phone equipment market similarly complained that AT&T was behaving anticompetitively by insisting that
a Bell-provided interface device be connected between its lines and
any non-Bell equipment. In December 1973, the Justice Department
responded by subpoenaing volumes of records from Ma Bell.

Almost a year later, in November 1974, the Justice Department
filed an antitrust suit against AT&T, in part to refurbish a reputation
for independence recently tarnished by the resignation of top Justice
Department officials over Watergate. The government charged that
the phone company had monopolized the market for telecommunications services and related equipment. Following President Ford's
promise that his administration would "zero in on more effective enforcement" of the antitrust laws, the suit sought to force AT&T to divest itself of Western Electric and to require the company to either
retire from the long-distance telephone business or else keep the
long-distance business but spin off some or all of its twenty-two local
telephone companies. By proposing a spin-off of the "telcos," as they
were called, the Justice Department hoped to reduce the likelihood
that Ma Bell would use its monopolistic position to gain advantages
in competitive markets.

While the suit was a boon for MCI, which continued to press its
own antitrust case against the phone company, it was a nightmare for
AT&T, as it sparked seven years of costly court battles. On January
8, 1982, a settlement was reached whereby AT&T agreed to submit
to the Justice Department within six months a plan for spinning off
its twenty-two local operating companies, from Pacific Telephone to

New Jersey Bell. The benefit for AT&T was that, after the spin, it would be free to enter practically any market it desired, including the computer data processing business. As well, divesting itself of those companies freed AT&T from contending with the public utility commissions that had regulated its operations in fifty-four jurisdictions.

New Competition

Even before the breakup of AT&T, new competitors had been struggling to hammer open the telecommunications market. The main action took place on the regulatory front. Up until the 1960s, a dual system of regulatory oversight protected AT&T's monopoly. Local phone service was regulated at the state level by public utility commissions and state officials. The Federal Communications Commission, an agency established under the Communications Act of 1934, regulated interstate long distance.

Before the breakup, AT&T had a virtual lock on the long-distance business. The local market was considerably more fragmented. AT&T's twenty-two Bell operating companies monopolized local service in less than half of the United States. More than 1,000 independents controlled the remaining markets. Major players included GTE and United Telecommunications. However, these independents had arrived on the scene late and AT&T operated in the most attractive, populated markets. Moreover, the local independents also had a cozy relationship with AT&T. All local companies shared a piece of the long-distance revenues generated over their lines, and for this reason disfavored the idea of opening the long-distance market to new competitors.

Local regulators also opposed moves that might disrupt the existing structure of the telecommunications market. The reason was simple. Individual consumers tended to value cheap local service. On the other hand, businesses tended to be heavier users of long distance than individuals. As former House speaker Tip O'Neill was fond of saying, "All politics are local," and, in the nature of things, state politicians therefore placed emphasis on holding local rates down.

The problem was that maintaining the extensive networks necessary to provide universal local service was an extremely capital-intensive proposition. Miles of copper wire and thousands of switching stations were needed. Local rates would have had to be raised considerably if the true costs of the service were to be borne solely by local phone customers. However, the AT&T long-distance monopoly allowed a solution to this dilemma. By charging long-distance users monopoly prices, AT&T was able to subsidize cheap local service. Hence, state politicians and the public utility commissioners they appointed generally supported the status quo.

The FCC also had been a friend of AT&T: the agency barred competitors from the telephone equipment and long-distance-services markets in order to protect the quality and efficiency of the phone system. However, in 1968, with some prodding from the courts, that view began to change. An entrepreneur named Thomas Carter patented a device to link phones and radio-dispatched vehicles. AT&T reacted against this new "CarterFone," threatening to shut off service to users of the device. Carter took his complaint to court and eventually the FCC sided with him.

The landmark CarterFone decision forced open the telecommunications equipment market for the first time in decades. AT&T made dire predictions that low-quality phone equipment would trigger widespread glitches in the phone system. The company forced competitors to connect their equipment through an AT&T-manufactured interface designed to protect the system. However, the concerns quickly proved ungrounded, and AT&T's foot-dragging would later be a centerpiece of the government's antitrust suit.

CarterFone represented a profound shift. Customers would be allowed to plug equipment manufactured by AT&T's competitors into the AT&T phone system. The decision accelerated the pace of new technologies, from answering machines to cellular phones. More importantly, the advent of competition set off the chain of events that ultimately led to the breakup of AT&T.

A second blow to the AT&T system came in 1969, when the FCC approved the application of a fledgling company called Microwave Communications Incorporated, which wanted to build a new phone link between Chicago and St. Louis. The company's plan had been developed by John Goeken, an entrepreneur who saw the potential of the new microwave technology. In 1968, Goeken had been joined by William McGowan, who provided capital for the start-up and became its CEO.

The basic notion behind the early MCI application was both simple and limited. MCI proposed to set up a system of microwave towers that would connect Chicago and St. Louis. The company then would sell "private line" service to business customers. The private line service was limited to connecting a single customer's branch offices. Moreover, MCI proposed only to provide the "long-distance" element of the connection. A call placed by an MCI customer would still travel locally over AT&T wires and through AT&T switching stations. Once the call reached a central AT&T switching station, it would be transmitted to MCI's system. MCI would transmit the call from St. Louis to Chicago, or vice versa, where it would be returned to the AT&T local network. MCI would pay AT&T a fee for these interconnection services.

In granting the MCI application, the FCC made clear its intention to limit MCI's scope of services to the private line variety. The commission agreed with AT&T that full-scale competition would harm the nation's phone system. MCI therefore would not be allowed to enter the basic long-distance market. However, this position ignored an inevitable reality. Once the markets were partially opened, competitors like MCI and others would do all they could to expand the boundaries of their operations. An almost inevitable progression of piecemeal deregulation ensued.

By 1973, MCI had a plan in place to build a nationwide system of microwave towers. The company had successfully used its original license as a wedge to gain approval for a broader service. Under a new ruling, gained only after contentious fights with AT&T, the company was allowed to offer connections between a single office and any caller from a specific city. So, for example, a company might establish a "local" customer service line in Los Angeles. Customers would dial the local number, but be connected to a call center in Utah or Illinois.

Other competitors also entered the market in the 1970s. The Southern Pacific Company, which operated the Southern Pacific Railroad, followed MCI's lead in establishing its own Sprint operation, which would become the number three long-distance company. In addition, dozens of other entrepreneurs set up operations, hoping to profit from the newly relaxed regulatory barriers.

As AT&T had predicted, the piecemeal deregulation of the telecommunications market put a great deal of pressure on the existing structure of the phone system. The flight of long-distance customers to competitors forced AT&T to reduce those rates. However, as long-distance rates were lowered, the local Bell operating companies no longer had a source of subsidies for local service. As a result, local rates needed to rise. Ultimately, this was the effect of the breakup. In the years leading up to 1984 and thereafter, state regulators were forced to allow local phone companies to raise rates.

In a sense, the AT&T breakup invigorated MCI, Sprint and various other relative newcomers, who over the previous decade had developed both the technical ability and the marketing skill necessary to win over former AT&T customers. Specifically, in the business market, MCI and Sprint offered cost savings as well as improved products and services. In a race to sign up individual consumers, the two companies launched telemarketing and media campaigns, lobbying customers to switch long-distance providers.

The AT&T breakup also contained the seeds of trouble for new competitors. Part of the promise of the AT&T divestiture was for "equal access." Previously, customers of MCI, Sprint and other independents were forced to dial as many as twelve digits before a phone number to gain access to cut-rate services. In exchange, the FCC awarded the companies steep discounts on charges for access to the AT&T system. With the divestiture, the RBOCs (regional Bells) would be forced to provide equal "dial 1" access to all phone companies. The discounts would be phased out. MCI, Sprint and the others would face a roughly similar cost structure to that of AT&T.

These regulatory changes represented a major strategic inflection point and led to a shakeout of competitors. Around the time of the breakup, more than 100 companies entered the long-distance market, including major companies like IBM, ITT and others. However, with new higher access charges, only those with a large enough customer base to sustain continued investment and guarantee sufficient return on investment had the strength to survive. Shaky operators began to look around for partners and a consolidation occurred. Mergers and acquisitions were a significant part of the story.

Sprint and MCI both were involved in major transactions during this period. On the way to becoming profitable, Sprint cycled through a number of corporate owners. In 1983, even before the AT&T breakup, Southern Pacific sold Sprint to the GTE Corporation for $750 million in cash. GTE proceeded to pump $1 billion into Sprint during 1984, only to see its market share remain at a relatively paltry 4 percent. Another $1 billion investment was planned for 1985, all in an effort to build an independent fiber-optic network.

The tremendous capital drain related to Sprint eventually proved too much for GTE to bear on its own. In early 1986, GTE took a $1.3 billion after-tax write-off on its Sprint investment and agreed to merge Sprint with the long-distance operations of United Telecommunications. At the time, United Telecommunications was number four to Sprint's number three. As part of the transaction, United

Telecommunications paid GTE $230 million. The new company, re-
named U.S. Sprint, was jointly owned by the two parent companies.

While U.S. Sprint enjoyed rapid growth in its first several years—
its customer base ballooned from 2.7 million to 6 million—problems
also plagued the unit. Customer service snafus and a continuing
need for capital left Sprint with significant losses.

Finally, in 1988, GTE tired of the drag on its performance. The
company put its Sprint interest on the block. United Telecommunications exercised its right of first refusal, buying 30.1 percent
of GTE's interest immediately and an option on the remainder.
To raise cash for the purchase, United Telecommunications sold
off its cellular subsidiary for $772 million. Two years later, the
decision to stick with Sprint looked shrewd. The operation had
begun to throw off strong cash flow and was solidly profitable in
1989, so much so that United Telecomm paid GTE roughly $500
million to exercise its option on the remaining 19.9 percent of
Sprint owned by GTE. United Telecomm, which also had local
phone service operations in seventeen states, changed its name to
Sprint Corp.

Like Sprint, MCI had its share of problems adjusting to the
post-breakup world. The ramp-up in access charges—which accounted for as much as 50 percent of the company's operating
cost—dragged MCI's operating profit margin down from above 30
percent in 1982 to as little as 5 percent in 1984. Cost cutting and
revenue growth brought the margins back up over the next several
years, but for a time the company's survival was not a foregone conclusion.

McGowan responded to his company's troubles by looking for a
strategic partner to provide stability and a capital infusion. He put a
call in to Paul Rizzo, IBM's vice chairman. Would IBM be interested
in merging its budding telecommunications business with MCI? Initially, Rizzo was unreceptive. However, six months later, by June
1985, the two parties had agreed to a complex transaction. The deal

gave MCI all the assets of IBM's phone subsidiary in exchange for roughly $420 million in MCI stock plus warrants to buy more stock for $15 a share. In addition, IBM agreed to invest up to $400 million over three years in exchange for further equity.

With IBM's backing and McGowan's strong leadership, MCI bounced back. Three years later, the company reported a strong profit and operating cash flow. The pace of capital investment briefly slowed to the point where MCI could afford to buy back IBM's stake in the company.

MCI's strong profitability also gave McGowan further room to expand. In 1987, MCI purchased RCA Global Communications, a telex company, from GE for $160 million. Three years later, MCI made another purchase. The company bought Advanced Transmission Systems from Western Union, getting 700 miles of installed fiber-optic cable in the deal.

McGowan continued to believe that critical mass was necessary to compete against AT&T and Sprint. In 1990, the year of the Western Union deal, McGowan launched a signature deal in his consolidation and growth strategy. MCI agreed to purchase Telecom USA, the number four player in the market, for $1.25 billion. The deal brought MCI about 1.5 percent of additional share in the $60 billion telecommunications market and 3,000 additional miles of fiber optics. Telecom USA, itself the product of a 1988 merger between SoutherNet and Teleconnect, served roughly 500,000 customers in thirty-one states.

After the Telecom USA deal, the long-distance market settled into a dogfight between the three major competitors—AT&T, Sprint and MCI. The recession of the early 1990s ushered in a few rocky years, but the market continued to grow even as the three majors carried out an unrelenting marketing war.

William McGowan

The ebullient William McGowan will always be remembered as the man who broke apart Ma Bell. A chain-smoker known for guzzling two dozen cups of coffee a day, McGowan breathed energy and life into his company for over twenty years.

McGowan grew up in the industrial belt of Pennsylvania, the son of a railroad worker and union organizer. After a stint in the Army, he worked his way through college and then attended Harvard Business School. He graduated in 1954 and eventually struck out on his own, setting up a New York City consulting business. He also tinkered with a number of somewhat successful start-ups. By 1968, he had the cash and the experience to buy a controlling stake in MCI, which needed the capital to turn founder John Goeken's dream into a much larger reality. The kernels of McGowan's success were a keen understanding of the regulatory and legal process, as well as the ability to finance MCI's ambitious expansion program.

In the early years, McGowan kept MCI going more by force of will than anything else. Regulatory issues were paramount. To grow into a profitable and viable entity, MCI needed access to a broader market than the private line business envisioned by Goeken. With cash from an initial public offering and a bank credit facility, McGowan launched a strategy of confrontation and lobbying. MCI kept a bevy of lawyers busy prosecuting antitrust suits against AT&T and other competitors, as well as lobbying the FCC and Congress, so much so that MCI was jokingly referred to as "a law firm with an antenna on the roof."

McGowan eventually succeeded in breaking his way into the full telecommunications market. Though he accumulated a pack of enemies at AT&T and was viewed as conniving by some in the

FCC and Congress, he was a folk hero to many in the telecommunications industry.

Even so, gaining entrée to the market was just one part of
the battle. Putting together the financing to build a major
telecommunications network was another major hurdle. Mc-
Gowan was prepared to make a major bet on the new fiber-optic
technology at a time when AT&T remained wedded to copper
wire. He raised more than $3 billion in junk bonds to finance the
revolutionary MCI network. By 1990, MCI was on the road to a
100 percent digital system, as was Sprint. When McGowan died
at the age of sixty-four in 1992, he left the legacy of a strong
company and an entirely revolutionized telecommunications
market.

The RBOCs Find Their Way

The January 1, 1984, breakup of AT&T left the twenty-two local
operating companies largely intact and with their individual names,
but reorganized into seven regional holding companies, each of
which was endowed with approximately $17 billion in assets. Specif-
ically, the seven RBOCs were NYNEX, Bell Atlantic, BellSouth,
U S West, Ameritech, Pacific Telesis and Southwestern Bell. Their
territories ranged from two to fourteen states. Each was expected to
provide local phone service but was forbidden to manufacture tele-
phones, switchboards and other such equipment.

According to the settlement, the regional companies would receive all of the assets and liabilities related to local telephone service
and long-distance service within certain zones. As for the new AT&T,
it was left with all of the remaining assets and liabilities related to
the development, manufacture, sale and leasing of telecommunications equipment, and to the provision of long-distance service in
zones not assigned to the regionals.

In an effort to breed healthy competition in the new communications market, Judge Harold Greene, the federal judge overseeing the AT&T breakup, also granted the regionals the right to sell (but not manufacture) telephone equipment to residential and business customers and gave them the right to publish and sell advertising for the Yellow Pages.

Even though the Baby Bells were well endowed with assets, the consensus at the time of the divestiture was that they got short shrift. AT&T kept the long-distance and computers businesses, which were projected to be high growth. The Baby Bells, on the other hand, were left primarily with POTS, or plain old telephone service. They were expected to be sleepy utilities in the business of selling dial tones.

Ironically, the Baby Bells were extremely profitable and successful. The companies together earned $8.4 billion on revenues of $69.8 billion in 1987. Meanwhile, AT&T managed to earn a relatively paltry $2 billion on $35.6 billion in revenue. The Baby Bells improved on their performance in 1988, when they earned $8.9 billion as a group, up 6.5 percent over the previous year. More fundamentally, they threw off a prodigious free cash flow.

The Baby Bells' success did not come without criticism. In part, the growth could be explained by the fact that almost every state had allowed substantial rate increases in preparation for the divestiture. As AT&T had predicted when trying to defend its earlier monopoly status, without the cross-subsidy from the long-distance business, local phone users were forced to carry the full burden of maintaining the local phone networks. Consumer advocates decried the effect on phone customers.

However, rising rates only explained part of the revenue growth experienced by the Baby Bells. The digital information revolution spawned a burst in telephone usage. Fax machines, online services, discount long distance, paging and cellular all contributed to a phenomenal growth spurt. By the late 1980s, total phone usage was increasing nearly three times as fast as the population.

The early successes of the RBOCs increased the pressure on their new managers. At the stronger companies, the question was how to continue the growth. The weaker companies struggled to develop a new identity and shape a workable strategic and operational model for the future. In either case, managers who previously had been buried in the middle of the massive AT&T hierarchy found themselves suddenly facing all the strategic issues associated with running a large, independent public company. They now had to find their way in the world.

Further diversification into unregulated industries was almost uniformly the answer to this new strategic dilemma. BellSouth, Southwestern Bell and others made add-on acquisitions in the Yellow Pages business. For instance, U S West alone added some twenty smaller directory publishers to its Landmark Communications publishing division. The company also pushed into real estate investment, expanding from the base of its existing holdings. Bell Atlantic spent $175 million to buy a computer services company and then bought a computer retailer. NYNEX followed suit, spending $275 million for the professional services and software businesses of AGS Computers. NYNEX also bought IBM's struggling computer retailing chain.

These attempts at diversification turned in mixed results. Both NYNEX and Bell Atlantic ultimately shuttered their computer retailing operations. Similar operations at the other Bell operating companies also were curtailed. On the other hand, the Yellow Pages continued to be profitable for most of the seven RBOCs.

The most significant diversification effort undertaken by the Baby Bells—into cellular communications and paging—was a dramatic success. From the beginnings of cellular, each of the Bells had its own license covering its geographic market. Soon after the breakup, the RBOCs raced to buy up even more licenses outside these markets.

Pacific Telesis got things started in 1985 with the announcement of its $431 million purchase of Communications Industries. The purchase was challenged in front of Judge Greene, but ultimately the courts ruled that the Baby Bells could purchase unregulated businesses outside their markets without judicial approval.

Once the legal issue was resolved, Bell Atlantic followed with its purchase of A Beeper Corp., at the time the third largest nationwide cellular and paging company. BellSouth spent another $710 million to acquire Mobile Communications, a cellular operator with licenses in Houston and Los Angeles. The other Baby Bells also were active.

As a result of this string of deals, the Baby Bells soon were competing against each other in the relatively unregulated cellular business. However, the Bells' decision to move into cellular was not an isolated occurrence. It was part of a larger consolidation of this new, high-growth telecommunications sector.

The Cellular Juggernaut

By 1980, the technology for cellular telephony had been around for over a decade. Developed by the Bell Laboratories in the 1960s, cellular involved the application of computer technology to radiophones, which had been in use since the 1940s. The first-generation radiophones required a powerful, centrally located transmitter. Only a handful of frequencies were available for radiophone use in each locale. Because only one conversation could be carried on a given frequency, only a small number of people could use the system. For example, in New York City, no more than twenty-four conversations could take place at any one time.

The new cellular technology vastly expanded the number of potential users to several hundred thousand in a city like New York. Cellular accomplishes this by using more frequencies and, more importantly, by reusing each frequency several times in a given area. To accommodate this sharing, cellular replaces the old, single high-power transmitter with dozens of low-power transmission stations. The frequencies involved don't carry far, so that a single station covers an area—or "cell"—two to ten miles wide.

With this cellular distribution of transmitters, a call is picked up by the nearest transmitter and relayed to a switching station, which then ties the caller into the local landline network. When the caller moves from one cell to another, a central computer recognizes that the connection to the original transmitter has weakened, and in a fraction of a second switches the call to a new transmitter. By hopscotching a call from transmitter to transmitter, a single frequency becomes available for multiple use, once in each cell.

Seeking to guarantee itself a cellular license in the markets it served, AT&T filed an application with the FCC in the late 1960s. The phone giant justified its right to the licenses partly based on its role in developing the technology, but also repeated many of the same arguments used in the ensuing antitrust fights. Cellular technology represented a potential end run around the existing local phone networks. Eventually not only voice but data might be transmitted over the new systems. If AT&T were excluded from this new market, competitors would be able to siphon revenues away from its local operating companies, further reducing the base of customers available to fund the local phone network.

Of course, AT&T's arguments carried little weight with McGowan's MCI and other potential competitors. The long-distance companies, as well as existing radiophone and radio paging companies, recognized the revolutionary nature of cellular technology. Here was the Dick Tracy fantasy of a phone in a briefcase becoming reality. These companies naturally wanted access to the new market.

The contentious environment surrounding AT&T in general spilled over into the cellular area. For years, the FCC sat on the phone company's application, uncertain how to distribute licenses to the new technology. Finally, just months before the AT&T antitrust settlement was announced, the FCC arrived at a compromise. Two licenses would be granted in each cellular market. One would go to a local wireline company, with AT&T presumably getting the majority of these licenses. The other license would be granted to a nonwireline competitor.

Many of the potential bidders for this second category of licenses were incensed by the decision. By guaranteeing the wireline companies access to the market, they were granted a precious head start in setting up systems. AT&T and GTE soon announced an alliance whereby they divvied up the licenses to the top thirty urban markets, with AT&T to receive twenty-three licenses and GTE seven. Given the powerful advantage presumed to go to the first mover in any market, it was not surprising that a host of players challenged the FCC ruling. However, roughly a month prior to the antitrust settlement, the FCC confirmed its decision. Any first-mover advantage, argued the commission, would be mitigated by a fast review process in granting the second licenses in the top thirty markets. Each of AT&T's competitors would have a fair shot at being a close second in the twenty-three markets it would compete in, if not first.

All that was left for the FCC was to distribute the second license in each market. As it turned out, though, this proved to be a time-consuming and contentious process. Still, AT&T did not get much of a head start with its first licenses. The AT&T licenses were to go to the Baby Bells, and state regulatory approval along with the administrative difficulties surrounding the breakup delayed the introduction of service.

The winner of each second license in the top thirty markets was decided by a lengthy FCC review. Applicants filed detailed, comprehensive plans for service. Competitors had a chance to respond with counterfilings. Then, after hearings, the commission decided and the winner was given its license free of charge.

Many parties saw the potential for cellular. The existing radio common carriers—paging and radiophone companies—had a head start in understanding the business, but they were predominantly small organizations and lacked the capital needed to build out cellular systems. Other entrepreneurs set up new companies to bid on licenses. As word of the new opportunity became more widely known, financial players became involved. The result was a race to assemble the cartons of documents—feasibility studies, financial and operational plans—necessary for an application.

The regulatory game of musical chairs induced by the application process also spawned a minor acquisition wave. Existing undercapitalized radio companies got together to pool resources. Financiers and large companies bought into other radio companies as a way to bet on cellular. The most active acquirer was John Kluge of Metromedia Inc., a company which owned radio and television stations. In April 1982, a friend told Kluge the cellular story. Kluge investigated and decided Metromedia had to get involved. Yet with the application deadline just two months away, there was little time to start pulling together documents. Kluge instead opted to buy into companies already well along in the process.

Over a short period, Metromedia spent $112 million buying three paging companies in Boston, Chicago and New York. The next year, Kluge added seven more companies for $169 million. Metromedia soon had a strong position in Dallas, Philadelphia, Washington and Los Angeles.

By February 1984, the FCC had granted second licenses in ten cities. Systems were hooked up in most of the top thirty markets by the end of the year. In the beginning, though, service was expensive and handsets cost roughly $3,000. The investment necessary to build out systems gobbled up revenues and required further capital infusions. As with fiber optics, the ability to finance the new technology was a crucial element of success.

Entrepreneurs continued to believe in the great promise of cellular. In fact, the FCC got so many applications for the second round of licensing—related to smaller markets—that it was forced to abandon the full-blown review process. The agency instead planned to screen out applicants unqualified to hold a license, then hold an auction among the remaining applicants. However, before this could happen, many of the applicants teamed up and split interests in most of the markets. This left a fragmented cellular industry with many licenses jointly owned by several parties.

As had happened in countless new industries over time, a consolidation wave followed. The Baby Bells played a major role, buying up licenses in markets they did not already own. Yet the early action was dominated by individual players. Kluge of Metromedia and Craig McCaw of McCaw Cellular were the new Vanderbilt and Rockefeller. They foresaw a nationwide cellular network, pieced together through acquisitions and coordinated marketing, and acted on the intuition.

John Kluge's ability to spot a new technology parallels Cornelius Vanderbilt's nineteenth-century move from steamboats to railroads. Like Vanderbilt, Kluge was in his late sixties when he made the transition, in his case from television and radio to cellular. By 1985, Metromedia owned large interests in key markets: 100 percent of a Chicago license, 52 percent in Washington-Baltimore, 45 percent in New York. These and other interests positioned Metromedia as the leading provider in the country's ten largest markets.

In 1986, Kluge's consolidation strategy was dramatically vindicated. Like its fellow Baby Bells, Southwestern Bell keenly wanted to build a cellular network outside its region. Metromedia's cellular and paging interests proved an irresistible target. Southwestern Bell agreed to pay Metromedia $1.7 billion for the properties, roughly $50 per potential customer, or "per pop" as industry insiders would say. The purchase price was roughly double the going rate of six months earlier.

Sumner Redstone, tenacious and tough, has built a multibillion-dollar media empire through acquisitions. He triumphed in 1993, when he fought off Barry Diller's QVC to win the $10 billion takeover battle for Paramount Communications.

(Ron Galella Ltd.)

Barry Diller with fashion designer Diane
von Furstenberg. Diller said of his
unsuccessful fight for Paramount:
"They won. We lost. Next." Today, Diller
is transforming his HSN into a
major media vehicle.

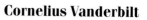

Cornelius Vanderbilt fought one of the first hostile takeover attempts with his unsuccessful 1868 assault on the Erie railroad.

(AP/Wide World Photos)

J. P. Morgan stood at the crossroads of American finance during the nineteenth century. One of the nation's first merger advisers, Morgan engineered a string of blockbuster deals—including the creation of U.S. Steel in 1900.

(AP/Wide World Photos)

Henry Kravis, with journalist Barbara Walters and *Washington Post* owner Katherine Graham, became a household name in the 1980s as the embodiment of billion-dollar leveraged buyouts. In the 1990s, he and cousin George Roberts continue to run KKR, the best-known LBO firm.

(Ron Galella Ltd.)

Carl Icahn, Elizabeth Dole and fiancée Gail Golden. As a high profile takeover entrepreneur, Icahn earned a reputation during the 1980s for an aggressive negotiating style. In the 1990s, he wrested control of Marvel Comics from financier Ronald Perelman.

(Ron Galella Ltd.)

Ivan Boesky, pictured outside the New York City federal court where he pled guilty to insider trading.

(Ron Galella Ltd.)

Michael Milken and his wife, Lori. Milken built Drexel Burnham Lambert into a leading investment bank on the strength of its junk bond franchise, only to see the firm collapse after his indictment for federal securities law violations.

(Ron Galella Ltd.)

Boone Pickens hunted the elephants of Big Oil during the takeover wars of the 1980s, launching a series of unsuccessful tender offers. Ironically, he was pushed out of his own company by insurgents in 1996.

(AP/Wide World Photos)

Rand Araskog, chairman of ITT Corp., enjoying a light moment at a 1997 Super Bowl party. The next day, Hilton Hotels launched a $55 a share hostile bear hug offer for ITT, and Araskog was locked in 1997's corporate equivalent of the Super Bowl.

(Ron Galella Ltd.)

Richard Fisher and **John Mack** of Morgan Stanley and **Philip Purcell** of Dean Witter Discover flashed their Discover cards at the press conference announcing their companies' 1997 merger.
(Archive Photos)

Bernard Ebbers remained a relatively unknown entrepreneur until his company, WorldCom, announced a $30 billion offer for MCI. Ebbers snatched MCI from British Telecom, scoring a major strategic coup.
(AP/Wide World Photos)

Joe Flom and **Marty Lipton** have frequently faced off as legal advisers on the biggest deals of the past three decades. Flom is known for his scrappy and creative style, Lipton for his role as the dean of takeover defense.

(Photos provided by Joe Flom and Wachtell, Lipton, Rosen & Katz)

John Kluge

John Kluge's 1982 jump into the cellular business was only the latest in a long line of entrepreneurial successes. At a time in his life when most contemporaries had retired, Kluge, age sixty-seven, made yet another major gamble on a business he viewed as a cheap investment.

Born in 1914, the son of a poor German immigrant, Kluge grew up in Detroit. By the time he was thirty-two, Kluge bought into the media business. However, rather than invest in the sexy new television medium, Kluge chose the relatively disfavored radio sector. Many investors thought radio was a dinosaur that would be slayed by television, but Kluge prized the cash flow. Soon Kluge had a string of radio stations to fund further ventures. He used the cash to purchase an undervalued billboard company on the cheap.

Finally, in 1959, Kluge acquired a television business. He began with Metropolitan Broadcasting and added seven major-market independent stations. Here again, Kluge selected his investments based on his view of relative value. Many thought the independents would be driven out of business by the booming networks. With his experience in radio, Kluge disagreed. He strung together seven independents. By 1980, Metromedia was the largest independent radio and television broadcaster in the United States.

In 1982, he bought his way into the cellular market by snapping up paging companies with pending cellular applications. Within a few years, he was able to sell for $750 million the companies he had acquired for $300 million, keeping the cellular licenses. Through this gambit, he got the cellular licenses for free.

Around the same time, Kluge spotted another major value— Metromedia's own stock. Kluge already owned roughly 25 percent of the company. When a series of major television flops caused Metromedia's stock to fall from the mid-50s to the low 20s in late 1983, Kluge decided to buy the remainder. Together with his management team, he took Metromedia private in a $1 billion transaction.

At the time of the LBO, the highly leveraged transaction looked like a shaky gamble. Yet, very shortly, the move paid off. Kluge sold Metromedia's television stations to Rupert Murdoch, who wanted them to start his Fox Network. Murdoch's price was a steep $2 billion, which allowed Kluge to pay off most of Metromedia's debt and still have several hundred million dollars to invest in his fledgling cellular operation. A few short years later, Kluge sold the cellular business to Southwestern Bell for $1.7 billion. The remaining Metromedia businesses were liquidated for a substantial profit, leaving Kluge with a net worth measured in billions of dollars.

Kluge, now in his eighties, vowed there would be no "deck chair" for him at the time of the cellular sale and launched a new venture, Metromedia International, to hold an amalgam of Eastern European and Asian cellular licenses.

In the aftermath of the Metromedia cellular deal, market watchers criticized Southwestern Bell as overexuberant and lauded Kluge for driving a hard bargain. Soon, though, Southwestern looked to have gotten the better deal. As the number of attractive properties on the market declined, prices continued to be bid higher. Kluge had not been the only buyer to identify consolidation as an appropriate strategy. The Baby Bells continued to build their portfolios. Others also were in the market. The price of properties went higher and higher, from the $80 per pop McCaw Cellular paid for the Washington Post Company's Florida cellular licenses to the $135 per pop Philadelphia's Comcast Corporation paid for American Cellular Network, both in early 1988. At these prices, Kluge arguably sold out early.

McCaw's Florida purchase was part of a larger effort to build a seamless nationwide cellular network. McCaw's cellular experience began with the 1982 FCC licensing process. At the time, he was the head of a growing cable television company that he and his brothers inherited from his father. Craig McCaw initially saw cellular as a logical add-on to the company's small paging business. However, after conducting some market research, McCaw understood the huge potential of the new technology and set out to build his nationwide network.

McCaw began by buying interests in individual cellular licenses. However, as the consolidation wave hit, McCaw began snapping up entire competitors. In 1986, McCaw nabbed a rough-hewn gem—the cellular operations of a cash-starved MCI—for a rock-bottom $122 million. McCaw sold the attached paging business for $74 million and in the process gained 7 million pops for a little over $6 each. Like Kluge, McCaw then sold off other operations to concentrate on the campaign. The 1987 sale of the McCaw cable business raised $755 million, much needed fuel to help build out cellular systems and make acquisitions.

McCaw followed with a series of blockbuster moves in 1989. Toward the end of 1988, the company began accumulating stock in LIN Broadcasting, which controlled licenses in New York, Dallas, Houston and Philadelphia. McCaw bought up 9 percent of the company's stock, just to "test its resolve" according to insiders. Hungry for additional capital to fund a run at LIN, McCaw next sold a 22 percent stake to British Telecommunications for $1.5 billion, or a record-breaking $140 per pop.

Five months later, on June 6, 1989, McCaw launched a hostile tender offer for LIN. McCaw's attempt at a preemptive bid of $5.9 billion came to $275 to $300 per pop and was designed to keep the Baby Bells from bidding. In part the high price could be explained by LIN's presence in premium markets like Los Angeles and New York. Yet, in one fell swoop, Craig McCaw had doubled the market price for cellular properties.

LIN's board of directors brought Wasserstein Perella in to examine the takeover offer. The situation was particularly delicate since LIN's chief executive, Don Pels, felt strongly about his responsibility to seek shareholder value. As a major shareholder, the genial Pels was thrilled by the level of McCaw's starting bid but, after studying the terms of McCaw's offer, the board rejected it as inadequate. Despite the high level of the bid, LIN felt it could do better. The company announced it would proceed to spin off its seven television stations, as previously planned, and would explore other options.

A CLOSER LOOK

Valuing Cellular

Valuing high-growth businesses like cellular companies is necessarily an imprecise, subjective process. Early cellular companies almost uniformly carried large debt burdens to finance the building of systems and the purchase of competitors. As a consequence, few earned a positive net income. Still, both in the stock market and in private acquisitions, these companies were highly valued.

McCaw Cellular provides a good example. Even before the LIN transaction, McCaw carried $1.8 billion of debt on its books. In 1988, the company lost $297 million on revenue of $311 million. Still, the stock market placed a value of $3.5 billion on the company, and equity analysts estimated its breakup value at around $4.5 billion.

Even setting aside the cost of debt, McCaw showed negative operating cash flow of $7 million. Clearly, the $3.5 billion market capitalization of its equity didn't come from the current cash flows. Rather, investors were interested in future cash flows that might be generated as McCaw increased its market penetration.

The practice of valuing cellular companies in terms of pops was an attempt to capture a picture of this future value. The number of pops, or potential customers, in a company's market was a measure of its future potential. This measure is calculated by multiplying the population covered by the licenses involved times the percent of the licenses owned by the company. The company's market capitalization then could be expressed in terms of so many dollars per pop.

Of course, using such a rough yardstick of value poses potential problems. For example, valuing different companies based on pops assumes that customers in New York or Los Angeles will generate as much future cash flow as customers in St. Louis or Minneapolis. In fact, capital costs, market penetration, rate flexibility, customer usage and future growth vary dramatically from market to market, and a more sophisticated model is necessary for a nuanced analysis.

When the LIN board rejected the McCaw Cellular offer, McCaw responded by hinting it might raise its bid if a friendly merger agreement could be negotiated. Talks began but soon fell apart. LIN then upped the stakes. Management announced the company would agree to be acquired if McCaw came up with a firm offer to buy the company for $6.1 billion.

McCaw, strapped for cash, couldn't come up with a workable $6.1 billion bid. The LIN deadline expired on July 31 without a new offer. At this point, BellSouth entered the picture. The Baby Bell was extremely reluctant to do a deal that would dilute its earnings growth. A cash bid was out of the question. In such a transaction, BellSouth would have been required to swallow the bitter pill of a huge slug of "goodwill." Under the so-called purchase accounting rules, this metaphysical accounting asset would be treated as wasting away over a number of years, reducing BellSouth's earnings by a significant amount each year. McCaw had counted on this threshold to keep the Baby Bells out of the bidding for LIN.

However, LIN and BellSouth came up with a complicated recapitalization and merger that would avoid the dilution problem. Essentially, LIN would pay a $20 a share dividend and then LIN and BellSouth would merge their cellular operations, creating a nationwide network with only slightly fewer pops than McCaw's. LIN shareholders would own 50 percent of the combined entity, as would BellSouth. The Bell could then consolidate part of LIN's earnings on its balance sheet without consolidating its large debt burden.

Over the next month, McCaw made a strong countermove. The company agreed to buy Metromedia's share of the second New York license for $1.9 billion (the first being held by the local RBOC, NYNEX). LIN, which owned the remainder of the license, had a right of first refusal to buy it from Metromedia. However, if LIN did so, the effect would be to dilute BellSouth's earnings.

McCaw then announced a new LIN offer. McCaw scaled back its earlier offer. The company would buy just enough stock to give it a controlling majority, rather than 100 percent ownership. At the same time, it bumped the offer price to $125 a share, valuing LIN at $6.4 billion. McCaw also proposed an auction process to take place in 1994. The auction was designed so that McCaw would buy the remainder of LIN's stock at that time, at a price per share roughly equal to what a third party would pay in an acquisition of the entire company. This innovative approach was designed to allow institutional investors to retain an interest in the cellular business and to conserve McCaw's cash.

In the face of McCaw's new bid, BellSouth swallowed hard and agreed to a sweetened merger plan. The special cash dividend was raised to $42 a share. LIN also would exercise its right to buy the

Metromedia share of the New York license. Finally, BellSouth agreed to a provision similar to the McCaw auction procedure.

McCaw shot back another raise, this time to $150 a share. As negotiations progressed with LIN, McCaw finally upped its bid above $154 a share. McCaw also agreed to a tax structure favorable to LIN shareholders. The deal valued LIN at a stunning $350 per pop, and Don Pels opened the champagne. BellSouth was priced out of the deal, but won a $66.5 million breakup fee.

After the LIN deal, McCaw Cellular emerged as the clear dominant force in the cellular market with over 60 million pops. For the next several years, Craig McCaw turned his efforts to capitalizing on the investment. A large part of the process involved reducing McCaw's debt by selling off unattractive licenses. At the time of the BellSouth deal, McCaw already had agreed to sell 6 million pops to Contel Corp. for $1.3 billion. McCaw also focused on its Cellular One concept. This brand brought together licenses across the country into a single national network with unified billing and marketing.

McCaw's effective withdrawal from the acquisition market, together with the recession that began in 1990, eventually hit the cellular companies hard. McCaw's market value dropped from $6.5 billion to $2 billion at the end of 1990. Other independents traded similarly. In the private market, acquisition prices ranged as low as $165 a pop in Southwestern Bell's purchase of Illinois properties from Crowley Cellular.

However, from an operational standpoint, cellular companies continued to thrive. The national subscriber base grew to 3.5 million in 1989, up 75 percent. Fifty percent more subscribers signed up in 1990. Growth continued at a healthy pace throughout the recession. Though per-customer monthly bills trended down, revenues grew on the strength of the greater market penetration. By 1993, there were more than 10 million cellular subscribers nationwide. Many cellular companies had turned the corner and begun generating significant positive cash flows and earnings. Cellular looked to be on the way to delivering on its promise.

Craig McCaw

Betting on cellular paid off in a big way for Craig McCaw. By 1994, he would be a billionaire and each of his three brothers a centimillionaire.

The story of the McCaw family fortune begins with John Elroy McCaw, the patriarch of the family. A freewheeling entrepreneur, the elder McCaw started as a partner in the first radio station in the logging town of Centralia, Washington. From this base, he built up a small media empire. He converted New York station WINS into the country's first rock station in the mid-1950s, and within nine years flipped the station for twenty times more than he had paid. At his height, Elroy McCaw owned interests in dozens of radio, television and cable television companies.

However, the early McCaw empire was flawed. Elroy kept terrible records of the interlocking ownership structures linking all his properties. When he died in 1969, his son Craig was a nineteen-year-old sophomore at Stanford University. Craig's mother spent the next eight years putting the McCaw house in order. Just about every asset was sold off to pay creditors and the tax man. The only business left was a 7,000-subscriber cable system in Centralia. Craig's father fortunately had put the business into a trust for his sons' benefit.

Upon graduation, Craig took over the family business. The next ten years were spent building a small cable empire. Craig bought up "junk-pile" systems and refurbished operations. Two of his brothers, John and Keith, joined him in the business.

In the early 1980s, McCaw came across the potential of cellular. He read a set of AT&T projections that estimated there would be 900,000 cellular customers nationwide by the year 2000. At that level, which proved to be remarkably conservative, cellular would be a profitable business. McCaw applied for licenses from the FCC, and gained the right to operate in six of the top thirty markets in the United States.

McCaw's next hurdle was to convince bankers to finance this new technology. The AT&T projections proved invaluable in this regard. Though McCaw didn't profess to know exactly what cellular licenses were worth, the AT&T projections made clear that they were worth far more than the going rate of $4 a pop. As a McCaw Cellular insider would later say, "The AT&T projections made it a no-brainer to go to 80 bucks a pop." The bankers bought the sales pitch and provided early financing.

From the outside, McCaw's fast-paced buying might have looked risky, but Craig McCaw always was thinking a step ahead and had an exit strategy prepared. The private acquisition market remained as a safety net. Whenever McCaw needed to raise cash, he could sell off less desirable licenses or interests in licenses.

The process of purchase and sale also was the central evolutionary mechanism used by McCaw to shape his national network. Economies of scale were crucial to the process, which meant clustered pops in major markets were more valuable than dispersed pops. McCaw acted on this fact by effectively swapping less desirable properties for properties near his existing major markets. He also moved to fill the major market holes in his network. By 1993, McCaw was the acknowledged master of cellular.

AT&T's Fits and Starts

AT&T's 1984 divestiture of the low-growth, capital-intensive Baby Bells originally looked like a master stroke. The parent company kept long distance and the communications equipment business, two steady cash generators, and gained the right to move into the hot computer sector. With its experience building computerized telephone switches and the technological wizardry of Bell Labs, AT&T was projected to be a major player in the field. Conventional wisdom at the time held that the computer and communications markets were converging. Clients soon would want single networks linking both computers and telecommunications. AT&T seemed just the company to provide one-stop shopping.

However, very shortly, AT&T began a long string of belly flops, both operational and strategic. The company continued to lose market share in the long-distance business. At the same time, the new computer effort racked up large losses, more than $750 million over the first two years after divestiture, more than $2 billion by the end of 1990. Meanwhile, one reorganization effort followed another, many with major accounting charges. The company wrote off $6 billion in assets at divestiture, $3.2 billion in a 1986 reorganization and $6.7 billion related to the switch to new digital technology in 1988.

Many of AT&T's difficulties were related to converting a somewhat sleepy monopoly into a market-driven competitive company. Continuing regulation also contributed to AT&T's problems. The company was forced to conduct its deregulated businesses in a separate subsidiary. As a result, the long-distance division and the computer and communications equipment division each had its own sales force. Customers faced the annoyance and confusion of separate sales calls.

Regulation further hampered AT&T's ability to match competitors in the long-distance market. The FCC refused to rescind AT&T's designation as a "dominant" carrier. Under the Communications Act of 1934, AT&T therefore was required to file each proposed service and rate package with the FCC. A proposed initiative could only take effect after a minimum forty-five-day waiting period elapsed, allowing competitors a full chance to challenge the proposal. This requirement severely hampered AT&T's ability to respond to competitors' marketing initiatives.

However, AT&T's string of major stumbles cannot be entirely laid off on continuing regulation. In retrospect, the company placed almost single-minded faith in its view that computers and communications equipment could be bundled together and marketed as a unit. While this strategy may have been sound, the execution was abysmal.

AT&T jumped into computers in 1984 with a $254 million purchase of a 25 percent stake in Italy's Olivetti. The companies launched a joint venture in which AT&T sold Olivetti computers in the United States and Olivetti sold AT&T minicomputers in Europe. The agreement flopped badly. Olivetti's systems were a tough sell. Moreover, AT&T bet on its own UNIX operating system—a software package designed to provide the basic operating architecture for computers—which never took off. The scrappy, competitive Microsoft, with its DOS precursor to Windows, badly outmarketed AT&T. These problems were exacerbated by the fact that AT&T assigned computer sales to the same people who pushed telecommunications equipment. While this move was in line with the bundling strategy, the sales force favored the telecommunications equipment, which was easier to sell.

After taking its lumps for five and a half years, AT&T finally ended the Olivetti partnership in the summer of 1989. Still, AT&T stuck to its bundled "computers and communication" strategy. The company initially looked for new partners, taking a 19.1 percent stake in Sun Microsystems over a period of months, which it then later sold. In June 1989, AT&T bought into another aspect of the computer market with its $250 million purchase of Paradyne, a modem maker.

AT&T made its largest bet on the computer sector in late 1990. The company announced an unsolicited $6 billion hostile bid for NCR Corp. AT&T chairman Robert Allen—who had been suddenly elevated to the top job after the unexpected death of former CEO James Olson in 1988—still believed computers to be critical to the company's future. AT&T's own effort was in a shambles. Allen hoped to buy a fresh start.

From the beginning of the AT&T-NCR relationship, success proved elusive. Allen approached NCR's chairman, Charles Exley, in November 1990. After two weeks of harried negotiations, NCR's board rejected an $85 a share bid from AT&T. Allen opted for a hostile bear hug. In a publicly released letter, AT&T stated its willingness to buy NCR for $90 a share, all in cash. The offer would only remain open for a few days.

Allen's approach was groundbreaking. Here was a staid member of the corporate establishment making use of the hostile takeover techniques so often decried by the Business Roundtable during the 1980s.

Exley was not happy with Allen's bareknuckle approach. In a reply letter, Exley slammed Allen's plan to put AT&T's flagging computer operations under NCR's control. Effectively, Exley wrote, AT&T was looking for someone to clean up its mess. Moreover, computer company mergers had a history of working out terribly. Not surprisingly, the NCR board rejected the AT&T offer. Exley stated his company wouldn't go for less than $125 a share.

Within days, AT&T demanded a special meeting of shareholders to vote on removing the NCR board. The white gloves of corporate civility had come off.

A shareholder vote was set for March 28, 1991. In the months running up to the meeting, the two sides attempted to weaken each other's position. NCR had fairly strong defenses. Under Maryland law, where NCR was incorporated, AT&T only needed the backing of 20 percent of NCR's shareholders to call a special meeting but needed an 80 percent vote at the meeting to oust the full NCR board immediately. Without that margin of support, AT&T could only elect one third of the NCR board each year and therefore would need two years to gain a majority. In an effort to ensure that AT&T would not get an 80 percent vote, the NCR board put a block of shares into the hands of an employee retirement trust.

With the battle lines drawn, each side lobbied shareholders for support. Exley talked up NCR's growth prospects and continued to demand a minimum of $125 a share. He insisted NCR could live with a divided board for a year while the company continued to execute its strategic plan. In response, AT&T pressed the point that its offer was almost a 90 percent premium to NCR's previous trading value.

The tactical background for the proxy fight shifted in March 1991 when AT&T successfully sued to have the NCR employee trust overturned. It became clear AT&T would win at least four seats on the twelve-member NCR board, and Exley softened his stance. The NCR board authorized him to discuss a merger at above $100 a share. Finally, an agreement was reached, made easier by the fact that AT&T's stock price had appreciated since its original offer. AT&T switched its offer from cash to stock and upped the value. Each NCR share would be exchanged for AT&T stock worth $110 at the time of the agreement, or $7.5 billion.

Almost immediately, the NCR purchase proved another disaster for AT&T. Over the next five years, NCR would lose $4 billion. Trying to salvage its purchase, AT&T poured another $2.8 billion into the business. The computer mainframe, a mainstay for NCR, was in the process of becoming a technological dinosaur. NCR failed to hit the numbers predicted by Exley and the combined computer businesses lost hundreds of millions of dollars annually.

Part of the NCR problem was management. The unit went through five top managers in five years. AT&T had promised to let NCR management run the unit with no intervention. For two years, Allen kept to this promise and let Exley's former number two executive manage the unit. After this arrangement didn't work out, AT&T put its own people in charge, even though the very idea behind the purchase had been to bring new management to its struggling computer business.

Meanwhile, as it became apparent that computers would not be a growth engine for AT&T, Allen placed less and less emphasis on the notion of bundled computers and communications. Instead, he shifted focus to a different variation of bundling. He embraced a new concept that had been receiving much attention in the market—bundled communications services.

The idea was that as deregulation progressed further, AT&T and the Baby Bells would be permitted into each other's market. Growth could then come from bundling local with long-distance service—very literally putting the old unified Ma Bell system back together. Market participants and observers alike were projecting that customers would sign up in droves for the convenient package. In addition, new communications services like cellular and Internet access could be added. This new future would make the promise of "anytime, anywhere" communications a reality.

The problem, of course, was that AT&T had little experience or presence in communications service sectors other than long distance. Strangely, the company that invented cellular technology had passed up the opportunity to take part in the rollout of the technology. AT&T had instead concentrated on selling the equipment needed to build systems. Likewise, NCR and AT&T's computer businesses placed little emphasis on the Internet.

Consistent with the strategic thrust of the NCR purchase, Allen again decided that AT&T needed to make a quick leap in critical mass. He began looking for an attractive acquisition target. Allen very quickly became interested in a potential alliance with McCaw Cellular. Such a partnership represented the opportunity to become, in a single step, a major national player in mobile communications.

Negotiations between McCaw and AT&T were an on-again, off-again proposition between 1990 and 1992. Finally, in the fall of 1992, AT&T announced a joint venture with McCaw under which AT&T

would gain a 33 percent ownership position in McCaw. The announcement of the AT&T-McCaw linkup rocked the telecommunications world. For the first time since the breakup, AT&T would be competing against the Baby Bells on their home turf. The Bells offered apocalyptic visions of what might happen. "AT&T is going to roll over everybody on the highway," predicted one of the Bells' Washington lobbyists. Immediately, the RBOCs clamored for the right to get into the long-distance business.

However, the tentative AT&T-McCaw deal was far from a certainty. The parties quibbled over how their joint venture would work. Tough issues included how to share revenues on bundled long-distance and cellular packages, which businesses would be part of the venture, and which technologies to develop jointly. By June 1993, the AT&T negotiating team had decided that full AT&T control was the only workable alternative. Over the course of trying to negotiate the joint venture, Craig McCaw also had come to believe the potential of an AT&T-McCaw link would only be realized with full cooperation.

On August 16, 1993, AT&T and McCaw again shocked the telecommunications world with the announcement of a more expansive deal. AT&T would buy McCaw Cellular for $12.6 billion in stock. AT&T's price represented approximately $280 a pop, less than McCaw had paid for LIN, but still a full valuation. A revolution had occurred in the structure of the communications industry. AT&T was going local.

However, there was little time for celebration at AT&T. The continuing problems at NCR weighed down performance to the tune of $102 million of operating losses in 1994 and another $2.4 billion in 1995. The equipment business also faced increasing difficulties as many customers—the Baby Bells and independent cellular companies—were reluctant to buy sophisticated switching gear from the same company they competed against on a daily basis. AT&T found itself toning down its attacks on competitors for fear they might cancel big orders.

Furthermore, though AT&T still controlled roughly 60 percent of the long-distance market, tough competition was severely eroding margins. AT&T faced a strategic dilemma—its core product was becoming a commodity, with customers willing to switch regularly for the promise of slight savings.

In this tough environment, CEO Allen decided it was time to jettison completely the bundled communications and computer strategy. At the same time, the equipment business would be freed from the competitive stigma associated with the AT&T name. On September 20, 1995, almost exactly one year after the McCaw deal closed, Robert Allen announced a second major AT&T breakup. Of its own accord, the company would be split into three pieces—communications, computers and equipment.

The split-up, completed by the end of 1996, represented a dramatic repudiation of much of the AT&T strategy in the twelve years since the original divestiture. After years of painful experience, the company had come to the conclusion that only smaller, more focused units could compete in the new competitive marketplace. In the spring of 1996, AT&T offered 17.6 percent of the stock in the equipment business, renamed Lucent, to the public. This initial public offering—the largest in American history—raised more than $3 billion. In June 1996, AT&T agreed to sell its leasing unit to management and a group of investors for $2.2 billion. The remaining Lucent stock and the stock in NCR were distributed to AT&T shareholders in the fall of 1996.

With the performance of AT&T's communications business now completely transparent, the problems facing the company could not be ignored. Increased focus on telecommunications services turned out to be no simple panacea. Long-distance market share dropped precipitously in 1996 and earnings fell short of expectations in the second half of the year. Observers raised loud questions as to whether AT&T could hold on to its core long-distance franchise. A number of key executives, including Allen's assumed successor, jumped ship.

The bad news for AT&T was not just internal. After years of stagnation and bickering, Congress finally looked to be close to passing a telecommunications reform bill in the fall of 1995. Revised rules would mean more competition and further commodification of long-distance service. Meanwhile, the FCC was in the process of auctioning off new wireless communications licenses. Shortly after being put together, the AT&T-McCaw network faced the loss of its cozy two-per-market competitive structure.

The performance of Lucent has been the major bright spot since the spin-off. Even more so than projected, unleashing the equipment business from the services business gave Lucent new flexibility to go after the Baby Bells, other long-distance companies and independent cellular providers for business. Sales to the Baby Bells ramped up 18 percent in the first nine months of 1996. Furthermore, the rash of new competition in the telecommunications market only helped Lucent. More competitors meant more systems, more switches and more transmitters. As a free agent, Lucent profited from the cutthroat competition. Its stock prices responded accordingly, almost doubling in the first year of trading.

PROFILE

Robert Allen

Robert Allen is a member of a vanishing breed. A true "Bell Head," Allen started his working life at AT&T in 1957 right out of college. Over the years, he rose up through the ranks to become CEO.

Allen began his career as CEO of AT&T amid crisis, and enjoyed precious little respite until his forced early retirement in 1997. His elevation to the leadership role at the age of fifty-three was not a time of triumph. On the contrary, the circumstances of his promotion were downright grim. Allen's friend and mentor, Chairman James Olson, had just died after a brief fight with cancer. Two weeks earlier, in a call with directors, Olson had identified Allen as his choice to get the top job "should anything happen to me." The board promoted Allen in keeping with Olson's wishes.

From that day, Robert Allen's tenure was undeniably rocky, despite the fact that Allen has on several occasions been lionized in the business press for his bold strategic vision. Within a short time after taking the helm, he ended the failed Olivetti computer partnership. He launched the assault on NCR. He negotiated the purchase of McCaw Cellular. In his last major strategic initiative, he broke AT&T into even smaller pieces. However, in each case, early enthusiasm waned as the promise of rejuvenation failed to materialize. Inspiration was not enough.

The final painful episode came in 1997. After his number two executive, Alex Mandl, left the prior year to run a wireless start-up, Allen agreed to retire early in order to recruit a viable successor. He then hired John Walter, a former printing company CEO, to fill the role. The choice was panned by the market and soon proved a disaster for everyone involved.

A consummate salesman, Walter threw himself into the business of rebuilding AT&T. However, in 1997, rumors of a possible merger between AT&T and SBC—the parent company for the recently combined operations of RBOCs Southwestern Bell and Pacific Telesis—hit the papers. Subsequent stories that Walter was being shut out of the talks badly eroded his position.

SBC eventually called off the merger talks when Allen initiated a public defense of the deal that wasn't. After the negotiations collapsed, the board pushed Walter out, claiming he lacked the "intellectual leadership" to take over for Allen. Walter said he certainly did.

The fallout from the turmoil further bruised both Allen's and AT&T's image in the market. It came to light that Allen had kept the candidacy of popular Hughes CEO C. Michael Armstrong—considered by many to be a stronger candidate to run a technology company than Walter—from the AT&T board in the original search.

As the severity of AT&T's problems worsened, pressure intensified for the board to bring in a strong outsider. However, Armstrong and other candidates demanded immediate control of AT&T, not the one-year transition favored by Allen, who had planned to retire in 1998. Ultimately the board forced Allen to resign almost immediately and gave the top job to Armstrong. Wall Street reacted with relief, bidding AT&T's stock up more than 5 percent.

Cellular, Part Two

In 1993, even as AT&T was spending $12.6 billion to buy McCaw Cellular, the world of wireless communications was changing dramatically. A new wireless technology, dubbed "personal communications services," or PCS, was on the brink of commercial application. Though PCS transmits on a higher frequency than conventional cellular and uses more closely spaced radio towers, the service capabilities differed little from conventional digital cellular.

Yet the advent of PCS represented a revolution. By the fall of 1993, the FCC was preparing to auction up to five new PCS licenses for each market. The cellular companies had previously operated in easygoing duopolies. Now, they faced the prospect of cutthroat competition. Furthermore, the coming unification of AT&T with McCaw promised to create a thousand-pound bully in the conventional cellular market.

These developments had a profound effect. Investors became less sure of the gravity-defying valuations placed on cellular properties. Meanwhile, the cellular companies generally raced to bulk up for the new competitive era. The development of a national network became the new Shangri-la. Financial capacity was one critical piece to the puzzle as companies prepared to bid in the PCS auctions, which offered an easy way to fill out holes in existing networks.

Though bulk was the general goal after the advent of AT&T-McCaw, some companies found unique strategic approaches. Rules promulgated by the FCC restricted the ability of a company with a cellular license in a market to own a PCS license in the same market. Pacific Telesis decided to split its cellular business away from its local phone companies. The expressed logic was to free the unregulated cellular company from the constraints of regulation and to allow Pacific Telesis to bid for PCS licenses in markets already served by its cellular subsidiary AirTouch.

Like Pacific Telesis, Sprint butted up against the FCC bidding restriction as it developed its PCS strategy. The Sprint PCS alliance—which included three cable companies, TCI, Comcast and Cox—intended to build a national communications network, providing local, long-distance and wireless service. To comply with the FCC's regulatory mandate, the company spun off its cellular business—with licenses mostly in smaller cities—under the name 360° Communications.

MCI—another major player in the telecommunications war—had been content to remain on the wireless sidelines after it sold its original cellular business to McCaw. However, the AT&T-McCaw deal put MCI under increasing pressure to find an effective response. For a time, it pursued a PCS bidding alliance, then settled on a partnership with a company called Nextel. In February 1994, MCI announced a plan to invest $1.4 billion in the company. Nextel had pieced together a national patchwork of radio-dispatch systems and hoped to convert the capacity into a wireless network. However, after MCI tested the technology, it got cold feet and attempted to lower the price on its investment. The deal collapsed.

Other partnerships were more successful. In the summer of 1994, two major cellular alliances were formed within the space of a single month. Bell Atlantic and NYNEX were the first to get together. The two companies merged their cellular operations into a single, jointly held company with roughly 1.8 million subscribers. The new company—ranked as one of the top three U.S. cellular companies—planned to bid for PCS licenses.

Three weeks later, AirTouch—the spun-off cellular business of Pacific Telesis—and U S West announced a similar deal. The two companies agreed to operate their cellular properties and any potential PCS systems jointly. AirTouch would acquire the U S West properties in three stages over a period of years.

The whirl of activity surrounding the PCS auctions continued as the process unfolded. The Bell Atlantic–NYNEX combination teamed up with the AirTouch–U S West combination to bid jointly under the name PCS Primeco. Sprint found its cable partners. MCI, on the other hand, grew cautious after the Nextel experience and ended up sitting out the auction, betting it would be able to buy excess PCS capacity at wholesale from other providers.

When the dust settled, the winning bidders in the auction had made breathtaking bets on the new wireless technology. The ninety-nine PCS licenses sold in the first wave of auctions brought a total of $7.7 billion. Sprint and its partners won the most licenses, paying $2.6 billion to gain nationwide coverage. AT&T spent $2 billion and the PCS Primeco alliance $1.1 billion. However, these numbers paled in comparison to the $4.7 billion in winning bids lodged by newcomer NextWave Telecomm, this from a company taking part in the "entrepreneurs" auction limited to "small" companies. With favorable financing from the government, NextWave and other bidders spent an average of $40 per pop, some three times more than buyers in the earlier auctions.

These high prices have left many of the winning bidders struggling to survive long enough to build their systems. Two companies have already filed for bankruptcy. NextWave also has had serious difficulties raising capital. The company was forced to delay its IPO and a planned junk bond offering, and teetered on the verge of bankruptcy. Faced with the prospect of losing the billions in licensing fees generated by the auctions, the government has been forced to give more favorable terms to some winning bidders and has taken back some licenses from companies unable to make initial payments. The FCC approved a broad program of relaxed terms in September 1997, with more favorable payment plans and partial resales of some licenses.

Although wireless companies argued the new payment plan did not go far enough, PCS has already been rolled out in some major markets. The additional wireless capacity has brought prices down. If the price differential between wireless and wireline calls continues to erode, wireless may become a viable alternative to standard local service.

Convergence: New Age Gibberish or Coming Revolution?

The promise inherent in the rise of wireless technologies has been compounded by a second technological spark—the marriage of digital technology and fiber optics. These technological developments began to reach the stage of commercial application by the early 1990s. Techno-gurus promised a future in which voice, video and data would be transmitted over both copper telephone wire and coaxial cable. Phone companies—both local and long-distance—and cable companies would compete against each other, and against new service providers taking advantage of alternative transmission systems. Convergence was imminent. There was a sense of being on the edge of a new age.

The possibilities of digital technology—which converts voice, video and data into a computer-generated series of ones and zeros—were indeed groundbreaking. Transmissions could be compressed and, as a result, estimates of the amount of material that could be transmitted over a system increased by an order of magnitude. Meanwhile, the unwanted "noise" in a system would be reduced through laser transmission over fiber-optic lines.

In the fall of 1992, two rulings from the FCC gave an added boost to the convergence movement. First, the commission ruled that phone companies would be permitted to carry television programming. The decision was a partial victory for the Baby Bells, which still were not permitted to buy cable systems in their service areas under the 1982 antitrust settlement. However, the ability to transmit video signals provided by other companies, as well as to buy nonoverlapping cable systems, opened the way for convergence.

The second ruling from the FCC cleared the way for cable companies to get into the telephony business. In a decision allowing two cable companies to buy an independent local phone company, the commission indicated that cable companies were free to provide phone service in their markets. Of course, the antitrust restrictions on the Baby Bells worked two ways. A cable company was not permitted to purchase or ally with the Baby Bell that provided service in the cable company's market.

With the regulatory groundwork laid, market participants were free to act. Initially, the hope was that existing systems would be quickly upgraded to provide added services. A war between cable and phone companies—in a sense natural competitors in the markets they served—was predicted. They did begin a number of ambitious pilot programs around this time. However, a string of interdisciplinary acquisitions turned out to be the most visible first sign of convergence.

Participants were understandably eager to enter new markets as quickly as possible. Local phone companies saw the $20 billion cable television market as an opportunity well matched to their strengths. Though the most attractive alternative—acquisitions of overlapping local cable companies—was foreclosed by regulation, local providers hoped one day to crack that market. To prepare for that day, they began to consider entering other cable markets. For the cable companies, the potential gain was even greater. In their view, a large piece of the $90-billion-a-year local calling market was theirs for the taking.

Southwestern Bell's 1993 leap into the cable business kicked off the trend. The $650 million acquisition of Hauser Communications, with two cable systems in suburban Washington, D.C., raised the interest of the other Baby Bells. A few months later, U S West made a far bigger bet. The company agreed to invest $2.5 billion in Time Warner's vast cable operations. Together, Time Warner and U S West hoped to build a modern cable network capable of delivering voice, video and data. Time Warner brought its existing cable systems to the partnership, U S West cash for capital expenditures and technological expertise.

The frenzy continued throughout the fall of 1993. In December, Southwestern Bell followed up on the U S West announcement with its own major cable partnership, a $4.9 billion deal with Cox Enterprises of Atlanta. BellSouth agreed to invest in Prime Cable. Other Baby Bells looked for partners.

However, Bell Atlantic cinched the major phone-cable alliance in October 1993, when it announced an agreement to acquire both Tele-Communications Inc. and Liberty Media in a giant stock merger. The $21 billion deal promised to bring together the nation's largest cable system operator, a major television programmer and one of the most aggressive Baby Bells. Together, the companies hoped to provide voice, video and data services on a nationwide scale. Convergence was reality.

Indeed, the breadth of the convergence vision was not limited to building new distribution capacity. Bell Atlantic and the other Baby Bells also wanted to control the media content that would be pumped over the sophisticated systems they were planning to build. This new interest sparked a number of alliances and investments designed to ensure preferred access to content. The most dramatic indication of this broader interest came in the 1993 battle for Paramount Communications, in which NYNEX backed Viacom and BellSouth sided with QVC.

However, the miniboom of 1993 fast gave way to retrenchment in 1994. The FCC played a major role in the sudden reversal. Congress re-regulated cable companies in 1992 under pressure from consumers, who had seen cable rates spike roughly 60 percent since the 1984 deregulation of cable companies. The Cable Act of 1992 granted the FCC authority to regulate rates on "basic" service. In the fall of 1993, the FCC mandated a 10 percent rate reduction. The following year, the commission added another 7 percent reduction.

The steep rate cuts put a crimp in the cash flows of cable companies like TCI. Most cable companies were already highly leveraged at this point. The burden of paying interest on that debt limited flexibility. Now, with less cash coming in under the new rate structure, the companies would face a tougher time making the major capital expenditures necessary to provide new services. Cable's future became more cloudy. The RBOCs were focused on moving away from regulated businesses into high-growth, unregulated areas. They were hesitant to dive into a business that looked to be due for more regulation.

As a result, the enthusiasm for partnering with cable companies waned considerably. The most dramatic sign of the shift came in February 1994, right after the second FCC rate reduction. Bell Atlantic and TCI called off their blockbuster deal in the wake of the projected 15 percent drop in TCI's cash flow. The visions of convergence faded, and cable stocks plummeted.

Southwestern Bell then also pulled back from its cable plans. The partnership with Cox fell apart in April over cash flow concerns. Southwestern had been counting on the huge projected cash flows from cable to fund major technology investments. Without the cash, the deal made less sense. In September 1997, Southwestern Bell, by then renamed SBC, sold the former Hauser properties for a reported $606 million.

U S West was alone among the Baby Bells in remaining committed to a high-profile cable strategy, primarily because the company was burdened with a weak geographic footprint from which to originate long-distance business, the key opportunity pursued by the other RBOCs. The company's alliance with Time Warner already had some conflicts over issues of control. Still, even in the face of the FCC actions, the company continued to purchase properties. Just five months after the Bell Atlantic–TCI deal fell apart, U S West spent another $1.2 billion to acquire two Atlanta cable companies.

The other Baby Bells did not give up entirely on video services. Rather, they launched a number of more limited ventures designed to pave the way for future expansion. In one alliance, Bell Atlantic, NYNEX and Pacific Telesis joined with Hollywood agent Michael Ovitz to create Tele-TV, a plan which has since been drastically scaled back. The joint venturers originally hoped to create a powerful interactive television network, providing video on demand to the three Bells' 30 million customers. This effort faced off against a similar programming alliance between Ameritech, BellSouth, SBC, GTE and the Walt Disney Co.

Other companies stepped into the breach. In one of the most ambitious plans, Sprint pulled together its multibillion-dollar alliance with three cable companies—TCI, Cox Enterprises and Comcast. The venture planned to build a national wireless network and provide local phone service over the cable systems' lines. Service would be marketed under the recognized Sprint brand name. The result would be one company providing voice, video and data, both locally and over long distances.

Plain Old Telephone Service

The enthusiasm for convergence waned even further in 1995 and 1996, as another major development unfolded in Washington. The

Telecommunications Act of 1996, the first comprehensive revision of federal communications law since 1934, radically redrew the competitive boundaries of the entire telecommunications industry. As a result, the phone companies retrenched. Plain old telephone service, local and long-distance, was seen as the best opportunity for future growth.

The new law was the spark for this shift. Under the Telecommunications Act, the local phone companies are now required to open their markets to new entrants, whether long-distance providers, cable companies or otherwise. To speed the process, local companies must sell competitors access to their systems at wholesale rates. Once the local phone monopolies can demonstrate that they face competition in their home markets, they will be allowed into the long-distance business.

The Telecommunications Act represents the ultimate endorsement of the bundled services model. By attempting to break down the barriers between various niches in the marketplace, Congress meant to make it easier for a single company to offer a broad package of services. However, because of the high capital costs associated with the digital revolution, the spiral of war between cable and phone companies deescalated. Cable companies lacked the money to pursue telephony and phone companies were without the resources to build out digital voice and video networks. Instead, companies chose to focus primarily on relatively familiar ground—upgraded video service for the cable companies, long-distance telephony for the local phone companies, and local telephony for the long-distance companies.

Two massive RBOC mergers announced in 1996 were the earliest signs of this shift in strategic emphasis. The one-two punch began April 1, 1996, with the announcement of SBC's $16.7 billion acquisition of Pacific Telesis. PacTel had been searching for a well-heeled partner for some time, partly to rescue it from the mounting woes that began with the AirTouch spin-off, and partly in anticipation of the coming telecommunications deregulation. SBC had strong management with an excellent operating track record. Edward Whitacre, the chairman of SBC, was confident his team could turn around Pacific Telesis and make the investment pay off.

After running a lengthy regulatory gauntlet, SBC finally closed the deal April 1, 1997. Phone service is clearly the core of the company's operating plan. A few months after the deal was finalized, the company announced a charge of more than $2 billion in costs related to the merger. Included in these expected integration expenses were the costs of shutting down the Pacific Telesis interactive video effort. As the payoff for the move, SBC projected more than $1 billion in annual cost savings from reduced overhead.

If the SBC-PacTel merger hinted at the RBOCs' renewed focus on phone service, the subsequent Bell Atlantic–NYNEX merger underlined the point. This second, larger transaction hit the headlines just three weeks after the first deal was announced, also in April 1996, and was completed on August 15, 1997.

The NYNEX deal was widely regarded as a triumph for Ray Smith, chairman of Bell Atlantic, who had led his company from the shoals of the collapsed TCI deal to the promise of a combination with NYNEX. The cable company had struggled with huge capital needs and growing competition ever since the FCC re-regulated rates. By passing on the TCI merger during re-regulation, Smith preserved Bell Atlantic's flexibility.

NYNEX had long been one of the weakest RBOCs. Burdened with relatively older systems and an abysmal customer service record, the company was particularly vulnerable to competitors that might come into the Northeast market. In short, NYNEX was not well positioned to go it alone in the rapidly changing telecommunications industry.

Large cost savings were another key factor. The savings were particularly significant because the two companies operate in neighboring regions. Today, new Bell Atlantic has emerged, astride twelve states from Maine to Virginia. With wires running up and down the lucrative Northeast corridor, the new company eventually will be able to service a significant percentage of its customers, long-distance calls entirely on its own network. The fees currently paid to long-distance providers to connect interregional calls will be eliminated. Analysts estimate savings from this change, plus other efficiencies from excising duplicative overhead, might amount to between $600 million and $800 million per year. For a business with $3.4 billion in 1996 profits, those savings will have a large impact.

In addition, the Bell Atlantic–NYNEX combination was propelled by the desire to grow revenues, not just control costs. Again, long distance was the key opportunity. Once the local phone companies are allowed into the long-distance business, customers will most often select either AT&T or the local phone company as a long-distance provider. With two populous regions to serve, the new Bell Atlantic has a strong position from which to capture significant long-distance market share once the company is freed from regulation. The potential repercussions are considerable. Roughly $20 billion in annual long-distance traffic begins or ends in Bell Atlantic's enlarged region, giving it a shot at a significant share of the long-distance market.

There was also a human element to the match between Bell Atlantic and NYNEX. Smith, fifty-eight years old at the time, had not yet designated a successor to take over when he retired. Ivan Seidenberg, chairman of NYNEX, was only forty-nine. So, a merger of equals offered benefits to both executives and their respective companies. Merging NYNEX and Bell Atlantic created a combined company with a market capitalization of over $60 billion, nearly $27 billion in annual revenue and 134,000 employees. Under the terms of the deal, Smith will run the new Bell Atlantic for the first two years, then retire. At that point, Seidenberg will take over a much larger, stronger company. Bell Atlantic thus settled the succession issue.

Up until the fall of 1997, U S West continued to be the most significant strategic outlier among the RBOCs. Rather than focus solely on telephony, the company continued with its dual-track cable and telephony strategy. The company retained its interest in Time Warner's cable systems and programming operations. Then, in 1996, U S West went a step further. The company laid out another $5.3 billion to buy Continental Cablevision. In early 1997, U S West agreed to sell its cellular assets to AirTouch in a $4.5 billion deal. U S West looked to be placing its growth bet squarely on cable and long-distance telephony.

However, the AirTouch transaction was designed around the favorable "Morris Trust" tax structure that would have allowed U S West to avoid capital gains taxes. When the Morris Trust structure was subsequently revoked by Congress on a retroactive basis, the deal collapsed. Then, in a surprising turn of events, U S West announced a plan to spin off its cable assets, which had been held in a separately traded tracking stock vehicle called U S West Media Group. The company estimated that the formal breakup of the two units would occur in the middle of 1998.

MORRIS TRUST

Closing the Loophole

Morris Trust is one of the buzzwords heard often in the deal business. However, this slang for a tax-free mechanism to sell a business slipped into obsolescence after Congress passed a proposal to curb the practice.

Slammed by some as "corporate welfare," the Morris Trust transaction is another variation on the basic spin-off. The name derives from *Commissioner v. Morris Trust*, a 1966 court case in which the mechanism was upheld as tax-free.

Basically, the Morris Trust mechanism allowed one company to split itself apart so that it could sell a particular part of the business on a tax-efficient basis. The first step was to spin off to shareholders the businesses which the buyer did not want. Then, in a prearranged transaction, the acquirer merged with the remaining business in a tax-free stock deal. Immediately after the transaction, the shareholders in the original company owned shares both in the acquirer and in the business which the acquirer did not want.

A selling company also could generate a cash return through a Morris Trust transaction. For example, the selling company sometimes borrowed money prior to the spin-off, as in GM's planned sale of the Hughes defense business, which was agreed to prior to the Morris Trust repeal. The cash stayed with GM while the liability for the new debt went to the buyer, Raytheon. In other words, the seller kept the cash and the buyer paid the loan.

Reflecting perceived abuses of the Morris Trust structure, Congress passed tax law amendments in 1997 that limited the structure. A spin-off and subsequent sale still might be tax-free under some circumstances. But a preplanned sale no longer qualifies for favorable treatment. The talk of legislative changes to *Morris Trust* prompted a major rush to get deals done under the wire, but AirTouch and U S West were too late.

The Globalization of Telecommunications

Deregulation of telecommunications markets is no longer a uniquely U.S. experiment. The bug already has spread to the United Kingdom; most European Union members opened their telecom markets to competition from foreign companies on January 1, 1998; and sixty-nine countries recently signed a deregulation treaty under the auspices of the World Trade Organization. These developments have accelerated the globalization of telecommunications. Cross-border consolidation is already underway and will continue, as large entities form to serve multinational business clients and capture a larger piece of the $600 billion global telecom market.

An undercurrent of globalization has existed since 1993, when British Telecommunications agreed to buy a 20 percent stake in MCI for $4.3 billion. The investment provided much needed cash for MCI's expansion into local service and the upgrade of its systems. For BT, the MCI stake offered a window on the growing U.S. telecom market. The company had been struggling to get into the United States for years, first with a failed attempt in 1988 to buy MFS Communications, then with its short-lived stake in McCaw Cellular, which was cashed out when AT&T bought McCaw.

The BT-MCI alliance also developed into an early effort at global marketing. The partners split the world geographically and developed bundled international telecommunications packages for large international clients.

BT and MCI were not alone in pursuing a global strategy. AT&T opted to form nonequity alliances with a number of international phone companies in its own effort at global packaging. Sprint, on the other hand, followed the MCI model. Starting in 1994, Sprint began negotiations with Deutsche Telekom and France Telecom. The strategic imperatives for a deal were apparent. The two local monopolies faced the prospect of growing competition in their home markets and sought both marketing savvy and global scale. Sprint needed cash to build its national wireless network. An alliance was struck in June 1995. Mirroring the MCI deal, the European companies would invest $4.2 billion in Sprint for a 20 percent stake. A number of regulatory roadblocks delayed the deal, but it was finally launched in January 1996.

These early steps are just precursors to the coming global telecommunications consolidation. The true scope of the coming revolution became clear in November 1996. BT and MCI announced they were giving up their alliance in favor of an outright merger. Under the original terms of the deal, BT was to acquire the 80 percent of MCI it did not already own for $21 billion in stock and cash. The surviving company—to be renamed Concert PLC—would have been an instant global heavyweight, with a market capitalization of roughly $50 billion. In the United States, MCI would have gained expertise and capital for its expansion effort. Concert also would have been positioned to snatch a share of the European market when national barriers come down.

However, Concert, like AT&T, also faced the daunting challenges stemming from its lack of local origination capabilities in the United States. The risks became apparent in the summer of 1997, when MCI announced that its losses from trying to get into local phone service would be $800 million for the year, twice previous estimates.

Fallout from the announcement rocked both BT's and MCI's stock prices. BT's shareholders began to pressure the company to renegotiate the terms of the transaction. Ultimately, MCI needed a partner. The company reluctantly agreed to reduce the purchase price by $3 billion. This development left the deal vulnerable to a competing bid from WorldCom, a more aggressive player willing to look past MCI's immediate troubles. Within a matter of weeks, the BT-MCI deal, and BT's latest attempt at geographic expansion, would be a tattered, unrealized memory.

WorldCom Crashes the Party

On October 1, 1997, WorldCom and its brash leader Bernard Ebbers became household names with a dramatic $30 billion bid to crash the BT-MCI party. In a single stroke, Ebbers reshaped the competitive landscape. If WorldCom were able to capture MCI, the combined company would offer both local and long-distance services across the United States, beating the RBOCs and AT&T to the punch. This strategic vision was bold. Ebbers would have to navigate a number of major tactical and regulatory issues to make it happen. Furthermore, the bid was even more audacious given the relative size of WorldCom, with just $8 billion of estimated 1997 revenue, when compared to MCI, with nearly $20 billion in estimated 1997 revenue.

The WorldCom story underscores just how fluid the telecom world has become. In 1983, Ebbers and three friends gathered at a coffee shop in Hattiesburg, Mississippi, and founded a start-up company later dubbed Long-Distance Discount Service (LDDS). Ebbers was originally a relatively passive investor in the operation, which planned to buy long-distance capacity wholesale from AT&T and re-sell the service to business customers.

The company struggled for several years. Eventually, in April 1985, Ebbers took over as president of the company. Under his stewardship, LDDS continued to focus on aggressive marketing to small businesses, a segment often ignored by larger providers. Ebbers also developed a passion for deals and a core acquisition strategy that would transform LDDS into WorldCom.

LDDS initially concentrated on acquisitions of smaller long-distance providers. However, in December 1992, Ebbers made a leap with a $560 million deal to buy Advanced Telecommunications. The combined company became the fourth largest long-distance carrier in the United States. A number of smaller deals followed, including the acquisition of IDB WorldCom, which gave LDDS a new name and reselling agreements with companies in sixty-five countries. However, WorldCom was still just a "gnat on steroids," as *Fortune* dubbed the company, until its $2.5 billion cash purchase of WilTel Network Services.

Ebbers was methodically piecing together the elements of a global telecommunications provider. WilTel gave WorldCom one of only four national fiber-optic networks. The Telecommunications Act of 1996 accelerated the pace. WorldCom agreed to provide long-distance services for GTE and Ameritech, and was granted permission to enter the local telephone service business in California, Illinois and Texas.

WorldCom began to receive national attention with its $12 billion stock acquisition of MFS Communications in December 1996. MFS provided local service over its own fiber-optic network. Like World-

Com, MFS focused primarily on business customers. These high-volume accounts provided the cash flow to justify the construction of local network capacity in major cities. As a result, MFS offered WorldCom considerable additional local capacity. In addition, MFS only recently had acquired UUNet—a leading Internet service provider—for $2 billion in stock.

After the MFS deal, WorldCom boasted a strong local, long-distance and data presence, but still was a relatively small player in those respective markets. The MCI deal would change all that.

Ebbers' unsolicited bid for MCI shocked many in the telecommunications industry. How could WorldCom afford to pay $12 billion more for MCI than British Telecommunications? many wondered. Analysts offered two answers to this question. First, WorldCom had considerably more operational overlap with MCI than did BT. WorldCom possessed an embryonic local network and would therefore not need to make the heavy capital investments that MCI had projected as necessary to break into local service. WorldCom and MCI also could significantly reduce overlapping overhead. While BT expected an estimated $2.5 billion of cost savings over five years, Ebbers projected at least $2.1 billion of cost savings in the first year alone.

Second, WorldCom benefited from a high market valuation. The company's stock was trading at something like 90 times forward earnings estimates. As a result, WorldCom could play the old 1960s merger game. By merging with MCI, which traded at a far lower multiple, WorldCom would see its earnings per share increase approximately 20 percent. This positive impact was helped by the fact that the deal as proposed would be structured as a pooling of interests for accounting purposes. There would be no goodwill recognized from the deal on WorldCom's balance sheet, and no annual amortization.

However, despite the steep price Ebbers was able to offer, WorldCom faced a number of roadblocks in its pursuit of MCI. BT not only had a definitive agreement to acquire MCI, the company also was MCI's largest single shareholder with a 20 percent stake. Notwithstanding BT's posturing, the company needed to break into the U.S. market and MCI was one of the last premier properties available.

Regulatory problems also threatened to scuttle a WorldCom-MCI combination. The company would have a dominant position among backbone Internet service providers and a strong long-distance market share. Consumer advocates had been expressing concern about the rash of mergers as a result of the Telecommunications Act, which seemed to be reducing rather than increasing the number of competitors in the local market. WorldCom countered that it needed the size to compete with the RBOCs and AT&T, and that consumers would benefit from having a strong counterweight to those companies.

These problems were relatively small when compared to a third impediment—GTE. Like WorldCom, GTE needed a strong long-distance brand to go with its local telephone presence. However, unlike WorldCom, GTE lacked a high-multiple stock. So, on October 15, 1997, GTE launched a surprise $28 billion counteroffer for MCI, all in cash. GTE planned to fund the deal by taking on something like $30 billion of additional debt. Though the bid was approximately 7 percent lower than WorldCom's all-stock offer, analysts speculated that MCI shareholders might prefer cash rather than potentially volatile WorldCom stock.

With two high bids on the table and a nervous shareholder base, British Telecommunications was hemmed in. The company decided against raising its offer and instead assumed the role of kingmaker. An auction developed between WorldCom and GTE. MCI's management and board agreed to meet with all three parties to discuss the merits of the two bids.

In less than a month, with a deft tactical hand, Ebbers captured his prize. MCI agreed to be acquired by WorldCom for a sweetened bid of $36.5 billion in cash and stock. The new deal offered by Ebbers had something in it for both BT and MCI. In negotiations to gain BT's blessing, WorldCom agreed to buy out the British company's MCI stake for about $7 billion in cash. The other MCI stockholders would still get WorldCom stock, but the cash payment to BT would blow pooling of interests. Ebbers was willing to take on the goodwill created under purchase accounting to win the deal.

Ebbers courted MCI management with agreements to keep them involved in the leadership of a combined company. MCI chairman Bert Roberts would become chairman of WorldCom and a number of his lieutenants would get top jobs. Ebbers was willing to concede some of the social issues so that Roberts and his team would be behind the deal. Yet, there was no doubt who would be running WorldCom after the deal. Ebbers would be chief executive and WorldCom would have a majority of the board.

Finally, for MCI shareholders, Ebbers agreed to up his $41.50 a share offer to $51 a share in WorldCom stock. Ebbers made the stunning bid to preempt the auction process established by the MCI board. The steep premium and GTE's unwillingness to budge off its offer left the board little choice but to accept. Even with the increase in price and annual goodwill amortization, Ebbers still projected that the deal would be accretive to WorldCom's earnings per share. The added costs were counterbalanced by additional cost savings identified by the WorldCom team once it got a look inside MCI.

Having outmaneuvered GTE, Ebbers was left with regulatory barriers as the main impediment to closing the WorldCom-MCI deal, which is expected to come to a resolution sometime in 1998. The combined company would be the second largest U.S. telecommunications provider in the United States, and would be the leading Internet service provider.

GTE left its cash offer on the table on the chance that WorldCom's high-flying stock might deflate somewhat before closing, in which case MCI shareholders might look favorably on a guaranteed cash return. However, GTE was left basically where it had started, with a strong local presence but little long-distance capability.

The result was more mixed for British Telecommunications. If the WorldCom deal closes, BT will receive approximately $7 billion in cash, earning a $2.2 billion pretax profit. Yet, as the telecommunications market opens to international competition, BT has repurchased MCI's share of the Concert joint venture and is without a significant presence in the key U.S. market. The company has indicated it will continue to look for a U.S. partner, perhaps GTE or one of the RBOCs. Only time will tell if the decision not to pursue an MCI deal was a strategic blunder or an opportune decision.

The Future

Globalization is just one of the intersecting trends that will carry into the future. Technological change will continue to roll forward. We are already seeing the build-out of PCS and other new wireless services. Craig McCaw and Motorola plan to develop global satellite communications networks. The cable television industry is under assault from wireless cable television and digital satellite video service.

In this unsettled environment, it is difficult to predict what telecommunications service will look like, even in the near future. Yet a number of market competitors are betting that bundled telecommunications services will be the winning business model. AT&T already provides long-distance service, Internet access, wireless and—through an alliance with DirectTV—satellite television. Rounding out the package, the company is slowly beginning to develop local service in certain markets. Other companies—the World-Com-MFS combination and GTE in particular—already are providing packaged local and long distance.

Competition in local markets has been slow to develop. However, once court challenges to the FCC's local access rules subside, pandemonium will be unleashed in local markets. The long-distance companies are not the only factor here. As the number of wireless players in each market increases, costs for local calls likely will come down and wireless may become a complete substitute for conventional wireline service. New technology also will push the process. For example, AT&T recently unveiled a new fixed wireless technology which may be a cost-effective means to build its own local networks. Apparently, the promise of this new technology was behind the company's spending spree in the PCS auctions.

Of course, more local competition will also bring more long-distance competition. Over the next few years, the Baby Bells will be allowed into the long-distance business. The dogfight for long-distance customers will become even more fierce. Likewise, wireless companies will slug it out for subscriber growth as the number of options expands over time.

If historical patterns prevail, the proliferation of new competitors and new technologies will drive a continued shuffling of assets as winners buy losers. Even established, successful players like AT&T are reeling. C. Michael Armstrong, the company's new leader, has the assets and brand name to rebound but the company's strategic dilemmas are fundamental and illustrate the pace of change. Shortly after joining AT&T in late 1997, Armstrong reached out to acquire Teleport Communications, a local phone service provider, for $11.3 billion in stock. Ma Bell was back. While size and a diversity of products provide no guarantee of success, they may be necessary ingredients.

Ultimately, these parallel developments will bring the convergence promised in the early 1990s. Economic evolution does not, however, occur in a Hegelian progression, all forces driving toward a greater truth. There is a cycle and a chaos to events.

Racing Toward Cyberspace: The Media and the Message

12

"Cyberspace . . . Unthinkable complexity. Lines of light in the non-space of the mind, clusters and constellations of data. Like city lights, receding."

William Ford Gibson, *Neuromancer*

The revolution that transformed telecommunications has spilled over to the media industries. A race toward cyberspace has commenced, and what a confused, halting, fumbling spectacle it is. All participants are one-legged men because there is no blueprint, no clarity, and a lot of motion. These are decisions under uncertainty, with high stakes, immature data, and a cyclicality of the views of informed opinion. But we are on our way.

Coming into the 1980s, each type of media content was piped through a single dominant distribution channel. For example, TV shows were broadcast by the networks, movies were shown in theaters, books were sold in stores. The limited capacity of the pipes—the infrastructure of the distribution system—defined how much content could be pushed through to customers. Ownership of those pipes was in most cases regulated and fairly static.

This situation changed in the 1980s with the full commercialization of new distribution channels and the relaxation of regulatory ownership limitations. The opportunities were enormous. Cable franchises, TV stations, videocassette and compact disc distribution, all were up for grabs. Companies battled to control the media distribution channels. Some of the players were old hands at the media business—the television networks, the big movie studios, the large media companies. However, entrepreneurs have been key architects of the converging media and telecommunications universe.

A group of some thirty individuals have been driving forces: Sumner Redstone of Viacom, William McGowan of MCI, John Kluge of Metromedia, Ted Turner of Turner Broadcasting, Don Pels of LIN, John Malone of TCI, Craig McCaw of McCaw Cellular, Amos Hostetter of Continental Cablevision, Bill Gates of Microsoft and a handful of others. Collectively, this group and the people who supported them reshaped the media and telecommunications paradigms and set a model and precedent for the hotbed of Silicon Valley.

According to my partner Fred Seegal, who has worked with many of the thirty over the years, these entrepreneurs "galvanized the transition by their sheer energy. They created industries out of science fiction—by persistence."

The Great Cable Consolidation

More than $26 billion of cable assets changed hands during the 1980s. This great cable consolidation transformed a once highly fragmented industry. Major players like Tele-Communications Inc. (TCI) and Time Warner pulled together extensive networks with millions of subscribers.

Cable television had been a land rush waiting to happen for several decades. The technology to transmit video signals over coaxial cable was developed during World War II. After the war, a number of visionary entrepreneurs promoted the new technology as the future of the television industry. Some began stringing together systems as far back as the late 1950s and already there was talk of "movies at home."

Short on capital to develop the necessary infrastructure, cable entrepreneurs picked up on the pattern followed by the electric utilities at the turn of the century, submitting to local regulation of rates and services in exchange for monopoly rights to given areas. The monopoly agreements, or franchises, typically had a term of fifteen or twenty years, with the possibility for renewal.

But in the early days a large gap existed between commercial promise and practical profitability. For a time, basic five-channel systems were the state of the art, then twelve-channel systems. Consumers viewed the services, which provided mostly just the same channels already available free over the airwaves, as a high-tech antenna. Consequently, cable sold best where existing reception was poor.

Finally in the late 1960s, cable began to become more attractive through the efforts of a handful of pioneering franchise owners. The key was developing distinctive programming alternatives. Charles Dolan, now chairman of Cablevision Systems, for example, innovated the first all-sports channel featuring New York Knicks and Rangers games, as well as Home Box Office. Dolan conceived of HBO as a channel that would show unedited, commercial-free movies, for which customers would pay an added fee.

PROFILE

Charles Dolan

Charles Dolan is one of the mavericks of cable television. He got into cable early, winning the franchise for lower Manhattan in 1965. The early years were hard. Customers were receptive to the improved reception Dolan could offer, but his underfunded

Manhattan Cable Television struggled to wire the city for service.

Strapped for cash in the late 1960s, Dolan sold stock in Manhattan Cable to the public. This move kept his system going and gave him the capital to develop the unique programming concepts that eventually would provide the model for cable programming. But Dolan also eventually ceded control over his valuable franchise and bright ideas to the public. Time Inc. saw the promise of Dolan's model and bought up control of Manhattan Cable. In the early 1970s, Time elected to buy out Dolan.

However, Dolan was an entrepreneur at heart and was not prepared to be folded into the growing Time cable empire. He instead swapped his remaining 20 percent of Manhattan Cable for a handful of Long Island cable systems which Time was willing to off-load.

Over the next twenty-five years, Dolan built his minor beachhead in the lucrative New York suburbs into the nation's sixth largest cable company, with more than 2.5 million subscribers. Dolan built his empire through a three-pronged approach. First, during the late 1970s and early 1980s, he plunged headfirst into the heated bidding wars that developed for potentially lucrative urban and suburban cable franchises. Cablevision eventually won a number of spots such as Boston, but only after committing to provide state-of-the-art services at rock-bottom prices.

Second, Dolan's creative flair for programming was critical. Though he lost control of HBO to Time when Time bought 100 percent of the network, Dolan developed a number of regional sports and news channels, as well as the Bravo arts channel and the American Movie Classics channel.

Third, Dolan recognized the consolidation trend in the industry and matched the acquisition campaigns of major competitors. Between 1980 and 1990, Cablevision spent more than $1 billion acquiring new systems. The company focused its efforts in Long

Island, where it built one of the largest contiguous networks of cable systems in the country. By clustering franchises, Dolan gained marketing clout and efficiency.

In 1994, Dolan made another major move, joining with ITT Corporation to buy Madison Square Garden—which owns the MSG Sports Channel, the NBA Knicks and the NHL Rangers—for just over $1 billion. Two years later, Dolan agreed to acquire full ownership of the Garden from ITT, which came under pressure to sell assets as a result of Hilton Hotels' hostile bid.

In recent years, Dolan himself has come under some pressure. Cablevision—along with other cable companies—has been punished in the market for its steep debt burden, continuing losses and large capital needs. In an effort to appease outsiders, the company is in the process of pruning about 400,000 noncore subscribers to reduce debt. However, beyond that, Dolan responds that he is doing what he always has—building a valuable asset base on the foundation of strong programming, and, in fact, lately cable has bounced back.

This stubbornness has many positives, but may have cost shareholders a short-term financial opportunity. At the height of the 1994 frenzy brought on by the Bell Atlantic–TCI deal, Dolan opened talks with a number of potential acquirers. However, Dolan decided against going forward and was rumored to have turned down a bid of $120 per share. Subsequently, Cablevision traded as low as $27 per share before bouncing back.

Dolan can afford to take the long view. His experience with Time taught him the value of retaining voting control over his company. Though he took Cablevision Systems public in the 1980s, Dolan retained a slug of supervoting stock entitled to ten votes per share and today controls more than 80 percent of the Cablevision votes. This firm grip effectively shields Cablevision from hostile takeover. His son Jim Dolan recently was appointed CEO of the company.

Even with the promise of HBO, cable continued to limp along for a number of years. Then, in 1975, the world changed. RCA launched its SatCom I satellite into orbit. By leasing satellite time from RCA, HBO gained an instant nationwide distribution system. Cable operators could pick the HBO signal out of the sky with satellite dishes and pipe the channel to customers. Suddenly, cable was more than just an expensive antenna.

As cable became more attractive, the competitive landscape shifted. The value of franchises increased and cable entrepreneurs found themselves competing against larger, more established companies. First, a number of aggressive companies raced to lock up rights to the remaining unfranchised territories. The areas involved were potentially quite lucrative—including all of New York City other than Manhattan, Boston, Washington, Chicago and other major cities. In the rush to grab territory, companies promised municipalities cutting-edge service at bargain prices.

These wild promises would later come to haunt many companies after they won the franchise. Competition from free broadcasters was strong and capital costs steep, particularly where operators pledged to provide two-way interactive systems and other new technologies. For example, Warner Amex Cable, a joint venture between Warner Communications and American Express, found tough going in many of the markets it entered. The partners sunk more than $100 million into building its interactive system only to face low subscriber interest.

A consolidation wave followed as stronger competitors bought up the weak. Of course, the pattern is not unique to cable. Sparked by a gold-in-the-streets mentality, the ranks of cable companies boomed in the late 1970s. When the actual building—as opposed to bidding— process began, it became apparent that success was less a sure thing than had been expected. Rather than struggle with the losses and headaches of building systems, some companies sold out entirely. Others simply narrowed their focus. For example, Warner Amex Cable brought in new management, sold off a number of systems and raised cash by selling part of its interest in MTV: Music Television.

Meanwhile, several stronger cable companies thrived on the opportunities presented by this first-generation Darwinian shakeout. Time Inc., Cox and Continental Cablevision all continued to be acquirers of systems, and John Malone and TCI evolved into the most aggressive buyers.

By the early 1980s, TCI was already an established player in the cable business. The company had grown to become the nation's third largest cable provider based on subscribers. However, Malone and TCI operated mostly below the radar in those early years. Perhaps because the company had been through a near-death experience in the early 1970s, Malone steered clear of the top-dollar bidding wars for new urban systems. Instead, he bought up older, established rural systems. Malone ran these mostly twelve-channel systems on a shoestring and resisted putting the cash flow into new technology.

At the time, skeptics questioned Malone's approach. Multi-channel, interactive systems were seen as the wave of the future, and TCI arguably risked alienating municipalities with its cash-harvesting tactic. Yet TCI's strong cash flow left it in a position to pick up the pieces when other operators stumbled. The cash funded more system purchases and, following this strategy, TCI grew from just over 700,00 subscribers in 1978 to more than 2.7 million in 1983, and became the nation's largest cable system operator.

John Malone—The Early Years

John Malone has been called the King of Cable, Darth Vader and the Godfather of the Cable Cosa Nostra. An engineering Ph.D., Malone began his career as a consultant for McKinsey & Co. After a few years, he moved to a subsidiary of General Instrument, a supplier of electronics to cable systems. In those days, most cable entrepreneurs were building systems on shoestring budgets. Malone stuck by them and earned their loyalty.

One operator in particular was quite taken with the young Malone. In 1973, Bob Magness, a former Texas rancher and the head of TCI, hired Malone to run the company. Magness had founded TCI in 1956. By legend, he sold some of his cattle to build his first cable system. Over the next decade, Magness had strung together operations in small towns across the West.

Magness' decision to hire Malone was a near-desperation move. TCI had raised some capital by going public in 1970, but the bulk of its financing came from borrowed money. Magness had hoped to pay down some of the debt with another stock offering, but the market for cable stocks crashed in 1972. When the thirty-two-year-old Malone joined TCI, the company was on the brink, in danger of defaulting on millions of dollars in loans.

Malone earned his reputation as a tough negotiator in those early days. Not long after joining TCI, Malone called the company's creditors to a meeting and issued an ultimatum. Either the creditors would back off or they could have the company. The brinkmanship paid off as TCI gained a measure of breathing room. Still, over the next several years, Malone continually fought a rearguard action against TCI's creditors.

At the same time, Malone struggled against local officials in a number of the communities served by TCI. For example, the city council of Vail, Colorado, wanted TCI to upgrade its service but was unwilling to let TCI boost rates to pay for the upgrade. Malone's tough competitive streak showed again. Over a weekend, he cut all cable service to the town and instead ran the mayor's phone number on the blank screen. The city capitulated.

By 1977, Malone had turned matters around to the point where TCI was showing a positive cash flow. A group of institutions loaned the company $77 million, and Malone was turned loose to build TCI. Like Magness, Malone had little concern for positive earnings, which translated into a positive income tax liability. He instead focused on growing the asset base, capturing new franchises and adding market share.

Malone avoided the franchise bidding wars of the late 1970s, in which competitors promised to plant thousands of trees or provide ultra-high-tech service. He continued to build TCI's cash flow and waited for the shakeout.

When values came down, Malone and TCI were waiting to pick up the pieces. In 1984, Malone jumped into the high-density urban and suburban franchises with a $93 million purchase of the Pittsburgh system from the ailing Warner Amex partnership. However, Malone did not relax his disciplined operating philosophy. Before taking over in Pittsburgh, TCI extracted concessions from the city. TCI would not be held to Warner Amex's promises of interactive service and would instead provide a basic system.

Though Malone had not made it onto the front pages, by the mid-1980s, he was the recognized industry trendsetter. For his part, Magness gave Malone freedom to manage TCI and acquired a significant chunk of equity in the business. Further, with supervoting stock in the hands of Magness and Malone, the two men were free to set TCI's agenda with little concern for potential raiders.

Malone's shift to a high-density, urban acquisition strategy came at an opportune time. The cable landscape changed dramatically for the better again in 1984. When the expensive realities of building systems became apparent, cable companies began lobbying Congress for help. In October 1984, the politicians responded with a federal cable law. The legislation deregulated cable rates and restricted the ability of municipalities to revoke systems. Cable systems were allowed to raise rates for basic cable by 5 percent in each of 1985 and

1986, and, in areas covered by at least three broadcast channels, could charge whatever the market would bear starting in 1987. Local television stations and telephone companies were barred from franchise ownership. However, after intense lobbying, newspapers managed to have removed from the bill a provision barring their ownership of cable assets.

The 1984 Cable Act represented nothing less than a tectonic shift in the strategic landscape for cable. Higher basic cable rates meant more cash flow, and more cash flow meant increased cable values. Overnight, systems that had been trading at between $800 and $900 per subscriber now brought an additional $100 to $150 per subscriber. At the same time, the capital needs of cable companies tailed off as they completed their initial build-outs. Between 1985 and 1988, cable systems prices zoomed from $1,600 per subscriber to $2,700.

Yet the higher prices did not dampen interest in cable. In fact, the 1984 Cable Act only accelerated the consolidation trend as the future of cable began to look somewhat brighter. The established cable companies captured most of the large deals. Other players also elbowed for position—mainly newspapers and financial buyers.

For the newspaper companies, the writing had been on the wall for a number of years. Their industry was in a long, slow decline. Even before the 1984 Cable Act, several newspaper companies had moved into cable television looking for growth. The Times Mirror Company and the Tribune Company each had significant cable assets already. With the passage of the Cable Act, the question of the legality of overlapping cable and newspaper ownership was resolved in the papers' favor.

The Washington Post Company promptly bought into cable, paying $350 million for Capital Cities' cable assets. Other papers added systems to their portfolios. However, as prices escalated, not all papers remained committed to cable. For example, the Tribune Company sold off its systems in 1985 for $238 million to fund the expansion of its television station portfolio.

Cable's strong and growing cash flows also attracted the interest of financial buyers. The appeal was not immediately apparent. Cable and broadcasting companies lacked the features of a prototypical LBO candidate. They were far afield from steady manufacturing companies or conglomerates with little debt. Most cable companies already had significant debt and were trading at healthy multiples to existing cash flows.

With cable, as in other areas, KKR was a pioneer. Kravis and Roberts were convinced the growing cable cash flows could support the additional debt necessary to fund a purchase. Further, cable depended on subscriber payments instead of advertising revenues for cash flow, and therefore seemed less susceptible to a downturn in a recession.

The buyout shop got its first taste of the cable business in 1984, with the purchase of a midsized conglomerate called Wometco Enterprises. Hidden among its Japanese wax museum, the Miami aquatic park, vending machines and food service operations were a pair of crown jewels—television stations and cable systems primarily in the Southeast. KKR bought the whole package for just over $1 billion and sold off everything but these two pieces. Two years later, tempted by soaring cable values, KKR put Wometco's franchises on the market. The Robert M. Bass Group, another financial buyer, bought the properties for $620 million, a stunning $1,800 per subscriber.

The Wometco experience only whetted KKR's appetite for cable assets. Already by 1985, the firm had confirmation of its cable strategy and was ready to make a larger purchase. The opportunity came in March of that year. A company called Storer Communications, which owned TV stations and cable systems, was under pressure from a group of insurgent shareholders. The company's management was looking for a white knight. KKR—in alliance with management—stepped forward with a winning $2.5 billion LBO bid.

Over the next several years, the value of cable distribution capacity continued to escalate. Other buyers followed KKR into the cable business. In 1987, Sumner Redstone made his $3.4 billion acquisition of Viacom. The purchase gave Redstone control of the nation's tenth largest cable system, as well as cable channels Showtime and MTV, five TV and eight radio stations. The same year Canadian entrepreneur Jack Kent Cooke, owner of the Washington Redskins and real estate interests, and an early cable investor, returned to the business with his $790 million purchase of Craig McCaw's cable assets.

Facing new competition for properties, the large cable buyers stepped up their activities. Time Inc., Cox, Comcast, Continental Cablevision and others continued to build their networks of systems. For most of these players, the focus was on clustering systems to form contiguous service areas, which allowed for marketing and other efficiencies.

Even with the continuing industry consolidation, there was no shortage of systems on the market. A number of operators continued to struggle with the high debt burdens and low earnings associated with cable systems. Struggling to remake itself from a lumbering conglomerate, Westinghouse put its Group W cable business on the market in 1985. Heritage Communications, a midsized independent operator, raced to find a white knight in 1987 as hostile raiders circled.

Some of these cable deals also had an underlying regulatory impetus. Both Westinghouse and the Tribune Company sold cable to fund the acquisition of more television stations. The move was necessary under FCC regulations which barred cross ownership of cable, newspaper and broadcast properties in the same area.

Other properties on the market came from financial buyers looking for an exit. KKR put Storer's cable systems on the market in late 1987. Robert Bass hired bankers to sell Wometco in early 1988. Jack

Kent Cooke followed suit a few months later. Further, the high valuations accorded to cable assets motivated some cable owners to put systems on the market as a source of funding for other investments.

The problem for buyers was not availability of properties, but the escalating cost of acquisitions. As the industry consolidated, the host of midsized players grew. These operators lacked the financial capacity or the desire to build a large-scale subscriber base. Still, they were large enough that it was difficult for a single acquirer to digest them whole. Moreover, a target often owned a dispersed group of systems that did not fit with a single acquirer's existing clusters.

As a natural outgrowth of these concerns, a pattern of bidding consortiums developed. Two or more of the majors would band together and purchase another operator. The unit then could be operated jointly or more likely split into pieces. Consortiums captured almost all the major properties on the market. Time, TCI and Comcast won the Group W systems in 1985 for $1.6 billion. TCI and Comcast worked together again in their 1988 purchase of Storer's cable operations for another $1.6 billion. InterMedia Partners, TCI and several regional operators eventually convinced Cooke to sell, but only after Cooke broke off an earlier agreement as prices continued to escalate. Again, the combined purchase price was roughly $1.6 billion.

Each of these major deals involved a bidding war between rival consortiums. However, not all the big deals went to multiple parties. The larger operators also acted alone to buy up choice systems. For example, Alan Gerry's Cablevision Industries snapped up part of Wometco cable in 1988, giving Robert Bass a healthy profit on the former KKR properties.

Without question, TCI remained the most aggressive purchaser in the market. Throughout the second half of the 1980s, Malone consistently stuck to his urban and suburban acquisition strategy. In addition to its participation in the Group W, Storer and Cooke acquisitions, TCI also made a number of independent purchases.

After three years as a suitor, TCI bought control of United Artists Communications in 1985. The company—unrelated to the movie studio of the same name—owned the nation's largest theater chain of 2,000 screens and cable systems with 750,000 subscribers. Then, in 1987, Malone agreed to the $1.3 billion acquisition of Heritage.

FEEDING THE ALLIGATOR

Building a cable empire in the 1980s was like feeding a cash alligator. Franchises had to be won, systems built, acquisitions funded. Slow growth was not an option in the world of cable consolidation. Plum franchises were being snatched off the market month by month. The big players had leverage to negotiate with content providers and hammer down marketing costs. Companies that failed to act feared they would be left without the scale to survive and prosper. Cash was the oxygen that kept the whole process going.

The high-yield market raised roughly $8 billion for TCI, Viacom and Cablevision Systems. Stock issuances provided the other leg on which the cable networks were supported. Weighed down by massive interest payments and huge capital expenditures that generated noncash depreciation expense, cable companies like TCI and Cablevision reported accounting losses for years.

However, the salesmanship and hustle of the cable entrepreneurs convinced investors to value cable companies not on the prevailing earnings-per-share model, but based on earnings before interest, taxes, depreciation and amortization (EBITDA). The argument was twofold. First, using EBITDA as a yardstick was appropriate because the figure looked past a company's debt burden. The EBITDA construct allowed investors to focus on the fundamental issue of operating performance, leaving high-debt operators the flexibility to grow. Second, an EBITDA approach strips away depreciation expenses to get at the core of a company's ability to survive as an operating business. The concept was that, for cable companies, with their large capital needs, annual depreciation charges obscured a prodigious cash-generating potential. Eventually, these two arguments stuck, and cable investors became accustomed to looking at companies on what was considered to be a cash flow basis.

The high-debt financing model prevalent among cable companies involved a debt-to-equity ratio in the range of seven or eight to one. In other words, roughly 15 to 20 percent of the value of a company belonged to stockholders and the remainder to creditors. This leverage ratio left little margin for error. Consequently, cable company stock prices were quite volatile and fluctuated widely with changes in perceptions regarding cable's future.

The high-debt, low-earnings financing model also caused valuation problems for large diversified public companies with interests in cable, such as Time Inc., Westinghouse and American Express.

The hot market for cable properties came to a screeching halt in 1989. For the next several years, virtually no deals of significance took place. Continuing cable rate increases generated a groundswell of consumer discontent. There was talk in Washington of re-regulating cable rates. In this environment, cable providers were unable to raise the funding necessary to buy new properties. Companies saw a steep decline in cable values. Properties that might have fetched 15 to 18 times cash flow were priced in the 7 to 12 times range.

The great cable consolidation of the 1980s left a handful of multiple-system operators in control of a large chunk of the market. TCI's continuing acquisition frenzy sealed its status as the nation's largest cable operator. As of June 1991, TCI controlled more than 10 million subscribers. The next four largest operators were Time Warner with 6.6 million, Continental Cablevision with 2.8 million, Comcast with 1.7 million, and Cox with 1.6 million. Together, the top five operators controlled 44 percent of the nation's 51.6 million subscribers. These and other operators presided over a relatively mature, developed national cable system.

Still on the Air

The ownership of traditional distribution capacity—mainly television and radio stations—was also very much up for grabs in the fluid media world of the 1980s. The explanation for the deal boom is part regulatory and part financial.

On the regulatory front, with respect to radio and TV stations, the government rolled back ownership restrictions. For radio, in 1981, the FCC bumped the maximum number of stations a single company could own from seven AM and seven FM stations to twelve each. The FCC similarly revised the television ownership rules in 1984. Under the new rules, a single company was allowed to own twelve stations, up from the previous seven, so long as their signals reached 25 percent or less of U.S. homes. In addition, the commission indicated it would not use the requirement that it approve changes in station ownership to stand in the way of takeovers.

On the financial side, the rush of radio and TV deals coincided with the rise in financial buyers and the new appreciation of the importance of cash flow versus earnings. Broadcasting had for years been an extremely cash-generative business capable of supporting significant leverage. Public-market investors generally overlooked this quality because of their focus on earnings. However, private investors who understood the importance of cash flow began accumulating broadcasting assets in the 1970s. Then, in the late 1970s and early 1980s, financial buyers became interested in broadcasting. KKR's Wometco and Storer deals, which had both broadcasting and cable aspects, did a great deal to uncover the values hidden in broadcasting assets. As the strength of the station business became apparent, banks and other lenders reversed their longtime aversion to loaning money against broadcast assets.

Driven by these factors, separate but related waves of radio and television deals swept the markets. Each wave hit full stride a few years after the FCC acted. In radio, 1,558 stations changed hands in 1985 for a total consideration of $1.4 billion. The prior year, 782 properties were sold for $977 million. This deal flow compared to annual volume in the low $100 millions during the 1970s. New technologies contributed to the booming prices and volume of deals. The most dramatic gains came from the miniaturization of radios. Sony—with its Walkman—and other electronics companies effectively expanded the radio audience.

With new freedom to operate, a new generation of radio operators emerged. Mel Karmazin of Infinity Broadcasting was one of the more successful players. In 1981, after eleven years working for John Kluge at Metromedia, Karmazin jumped ship to Infinity. The company had been founded by two former Metromedia executives and then owned just three stations. Karmazin was given the top spot, along with a slug of stock options.

Over the next five years, Infinity bought up stations. Karmazin's strategic thesis was to buy only top stations in major cities. He wasn't shy about paying top dollar, either: $70 million for New York's all-sports WFAN AM station and $116 million for a Los Angeles oldies station. Once Infinity acquired the stations, Karmazin emphasized distinctive programming. He bought exclusive rights to air sporting events and backed popular shock jocks like Howard Stern and Don Imus.

The Karmazin strategy played well in the market. Following his mentor's pattern, Karmazin took Infinity public in 1986, then led a leveraged buyout in 1988, and finally a second public stock offering in 1992. Shareholders prospered immensely along the way, as did Karmazin and his management team.

Television deals necessarily had a higher profile than radio deals. More money was involved and the properties were more visible. KKR closed an early big deal in 1983 with its $280 million purchase of Golden West Television. Just two years later, in a dramatic turn of events, it sold Golden West's single station—KTLA in Los Angeles—to the Tribune Company for $510 million. In all, $1 billion of station deals were closed in 1984, $12.8 billion in 1985 and another $3.5 billion in 1986.

Many of the deals in the 1980s involved independent stations. These stations—unaffiliated with a network and often with lower-power UHF signals—had been relatively cheap before the age of strong cable systems. Cable brought these stations to a wider audience and made them far more attractive. Major examples include the KTLA sale and Westinghouse's $313 million purchase of another independent Los Angeles station from RKO.

Without a doubt, though, Rupert Murdoch pulled off the blockbuster television station deal of the 1980s with his $2 billion purchase of John Kluge's seven independent Metromedia stations. Murdoch immediately resold the Boston station to Hearst Corp. for $450 million. The press harped at the deal, fixing on the price of 16 times cash flow as a sign of market mania. Yet Murdoch's move was backed by a strong strategic vision. His six new stations were to be the foundation for a fourth television network. With the help of Barry Diller, Murdoch hoped to build his newly acquired Twentieth Century Fox film studio into a television powerhouse as well.

Though Karmazin's and Murdoch's moves worked out for their respective companies, prices eventually reached an unsustainable level. A number of station deals—both radio and television—fell apart. Storer Television was one of the more prominent failures. In 1987, KKR sold the Storer stations to an entity controlled by investor George Gillett Jr. for $1.3 billion. At roughly 15 times 1988 cash flow, the deal was fully priced. KKR—which received $1 billion in cash from the deal—kept a 45 percent ownership interest in the stations.

Very quickly, it became clear that Gillett had assumed more debt than the stations could bear. The company eventually collapsed into bankruptcy only to be bought by Ronald Perelman, who in turn sold the Storer stations to Murdoch. Yet even with the loss on Storer Television's bankruptcy, KKR's fund showed a roughly 60 percent annual gain on its original Storer acquisition, taking into account the sale of the company's cable properties and the $1 billion from the 1987 station transaction. Moreover, strong, well-managed companies like Infinity and Murdoch's News Corporation weathered the recession with little difficulty. They emerged in the 1990s healthy and ready to continue growing.

Networks on the Block

Inevitably, the advent of strong cable systems also changed the world for the three big networks. Hemmed in by federal regulations, the networks were primarily in the business of distributing entertainment content. The FCC's financial/syndication rules—referred to in the business as "fin/syn"—prohibited the networks from owning most prime-time programming and from profiting on the syndication of reruns. These extremely profitable businesses were more or less left to the movie studios. Still, for years, the networks dominated the television distribution business almost effortlessly.

Matters changed for the worse starting in the late 1970s. Cable systems began to offer alternative programming. The networks faced tough competition where there had been none. Viewership plummeted. Just 75 percent of American homes tuned into one of the three networks in 1984, down from 92 percent in 1976. Network advertising revenues declined in 1985 for the first time since 1971. Moreover, the free fall looked likely to continue as more cable systems with more channel capacity were built each year.

At the same time, the networks possessed an incredible portfolio of assets. The brand names of NBC, CBS and ABC were priceless, as were the existing relationships with network affiliates around the country. Each also owned a stable of television and radio stations, some valuable real estate and programming capabilities—primarily in sports and news.

However, given the bleak perceptions regarding the future of network television, the asset values were not reflected in the companies' stock prices. Starting in 1984, rumors of impending hostile takeovers began to circulate. Many discounted the likelihood that a transaction would go through. There was some history to back up the skeptics. Texas oilman H.L. Hunt had made an unsuccessful run at CBS in 1965. In 1968, ITT's agreement to acquire ABC fell apart under pressure from government antitrust authorities. Then, recluse Howard Hughes made an unsolicited offer for ABC, only to be turned away when he refused to testify in person before the FCC.

In the fall of 1984, the primary takeover speculation surrounded CBS and ABC because RCA—which owned NBC—was seen as too big to swallow. The word on the Street was fairly clear regarding CBS. Ted Turner supposedly was planning a takeover attempt. On the other hand, with ABC, the rumor mill generated a host of possible names.

Behind the scenes, ABC was talking to Capital Cities about a possible merger. Tom Murphy, chairman and chief executive of Capital Cities, approached Leonard Goldenson, the seventy-nine-year-old head of ABC, about merging the two companies. In fact, Goldenson had already been studying the merits of such a deal.

Goldenson initially hesitated at the idea of selling ABC. One of the fathers of network television, in 1953 Goldenson had gambled the then-huge sum of $25 million on his vision of a third network. Goldenson ran the United Paramount Theaters movie chain at the time. ABC—which began as one of two NBC radio networks—was owned by Life Savers founder Ed Noble. The network had only fourteen affiliates and was losing money. Goldenson convinced his board to make a calculated leap and acquire the network. Over the next thirty years he built it into an equal to CBS and NBC.

Naturally, then, Goldenson had a strong sentimental inclination to keep ABC independent. However, he prided himself on being a practical businessman with a commonsense focus. For some time he had been nervous about leaving ABC in the hands of its current executive team. The ABC ratings successes of the late 1970s had given way to an eroding viewership and declining numbers. Goldenson wanted to pass ABC to a strong hand with the vision to turn things around. Furthermore, there was also the looming possibility of a hostile takeover. Goldenson was not sure he could repeat his performance fending off Howard Hughes.

Goldenson brought us and takeover lawyer Joe Flom in to consider his strategic options. After deliberation, Goldenson concluded that he preferred Murphy as the man to continue his legacy. Murphy, however, was afraid of the size of the deal relative to his borrowing capability and was also concerned that if there were some bumps in the performance of the two companies, Capital Cities might itself become a target. He therefore brought in Warren Buffett as a major Capital Cities shareholder.

Though Goldenson and Murphy both wanted to do a deal, there was a spread in price expectations. A package of warrants was used to bridge the gap. The warrants would give the holder the right to buy Capital Cities stock at $250 a share at any time within two and a half years of closing and would also be convertible into cash for a short period at $3 per share.

On March 18, 1985, the news of the Capital Cities–ABC deal was announced to cheers from the Street. Tom Murphy had bitten off a lot—the $3.5 billion price tag made Capital Cities' acquisition the largest nonoil deal up to that point in U.S. history. Most of the purchase price was cash. Still, despite the hard bargaining, Capital Cities was perceived to have gotten a good deal.

Capital Cities had little trouble raising the cash. Even under the more liberal FCC ownership rules, the combined company was forced to sell some cable properties, as well as a handful of radio and

TV stations. These sales were expected to raise around $800 million. Buffett provided $500 million. The remaining money was raised through bank financing.

Capital Cities stock zoomed in the aftermath of the announcement. Investors appeared to believe there was indeed hidden value in the network stocks. These collections of assets were classic "beachfront property," in limited supply. The distribution oligopoly of the networks was under siege, but they still got product into 60 percent of American homes.

Thomas Murphy

When Capital Cities acquired ABC, Tom Murphy had already grown his company into a diversified media power. By reputation the nation's best-managed media company, Capital Cities owned television and radio stations, magazines and newspapers, and cable systems.

Murphy's early days as a television executive were far from glamorous. In 1954, at the age of twenty-nine, he took over a bankrupt UHF station in Albany, New York. A graduate of Harvard Business School, Murphy had been working at Lever Brothers. He knew nothing about managing a TV station but was anxious to run his own business.

Murphy spent his early days in Albany counting every penny, and carried that strong cost focus with him throughout his career. Once the Albany station was stabilized, Murphy began thinking about adding more properties. He brought in Daniel Burke—a fellow Harvard graduate—as a strong number two. They set off on a string of classic bootstrap acquisitions.

There was a rhythm to the process. Capital Cities would acquire a new property, using debt to fund the large portion of the purchase price. The partners watched every dime in the till and used the money from cost savings to pay down debt. At the same time, they would invest to grow the businesses where prudent.

Capital Cities achieved remarkable results following this business model. With a tight control over costs, its stations showed operating margins over 50 percent. This compared to 33 percent margins at ABC's stations, which were the most profitable network-owned stations. Yet the Capital Cities stations were not myopic in their cost cutting. Murphy learned early that a strong local news program would translate into strong entertainment ratings. He committed the capital necessary to build first-rate operations. However, here as elsewhere, Capital Cities accomplished more with less, achieving top ratings with fewer staffers.

Murphy's only real problem was regulatory. Capital Cities soon ran up against the station ownership limits both for radio and television. Not to be held back, Murphy shifted into other advertising-supported media. Piece by piece Capital Cities acquired a group of newspapers and trade publications, including the *Kansas City Star* and *Institutional Investor*.

As Capital Cities became larger, the imperative to find bigger add-on acquisitions increased. Capital Cities had the financial strength—little debt and strong cash flow—to manage a major purchase. The regulatory relaxation of 1984 gave Murphy the room to make this quantum leap in size and scope.

Despite his professionalism, Murphy exuded the warmth of the friendliest man in town. Always with a twinkle in his eye, Murphy had a special touch with people. This combination of ability and charm made Murphy an attractive partner for Goldenson.

The ABC deal instantly put the other two networks in play. CBS was next on the block. A conservative group associated with Jesse

Helms already had announced an effort to take over the network, though the plan wasn't given much credibility. More menacing was Ivan Boesky, who bought 2.6 million CBS shares on the open market—nearly 9 percent of the outstanding shares. The company began to appear as a regular subject of rumors in the business press. Trading turnover in the stock was phenomenal.

Meanwhile, CBS began lining up its defensive strategy. As the top-rated network and a successful record producer, the company was in a fairly strong position. Yet a number of cracks were beginning to appear in the edifice. Earnings in records, broadcasting and toys were falling off. To bolster its defenses, CBS sought political support by emphasizing the importance of an independent CBS News. CBS chairman Tom Wyman called around to a number of investment banks to discourage them from helping with a hostile bid.

The other shoe dropped within a month. Cable mogul Ted Turner launched a much-anticipated takeover bid on April 18, 1985. However, unlike Capital Cities, Turner Broadcasting lacked the financial wherewithal for a cash offer. Turner instead offered a complicated package of stock and junk bonds which Turner's bankers valued at $5.4 billion.

CBS parried Turner's thrust by contending his offer amounted to a hostile leveraged buyout and threatened an FCC battle. Ironically, though, in winning the battle for independence, Chairman Wyman ultimately lost his position running the company. Under the stress of attack from Turner, CBS looked favorably on putting a block of stock in friendly hands, as Tom Murphy had done with Warren Buffett. Laurence Tisch, who with his brother Robert controlled Loews Corporation, agreed to take on the role for CBS. Loews announced it would build a 25 percent stake in the network through gradual purchases.

Other raiders still persisted. Financier Marvin Davis made a $3.1 billion all-cash offer for the network only to be rebuffed by Wyman. Eventually, however, the pressure of constantly being in play together with a steep erosion in operating performance left Wyman vulnerable. In September 1986, he proposed that CBS be sold to Coca-Cola. Both Tisch and legendary CBS founder William Paley refused. Wyman was forced out, and Tisch took over as CEO of the company. Tisch's investment in CBS suddenly began to look shrewd. He had gained control of CBS by buying only a quarter of the company at market prices.

Most people assumed RCA—with its collection of industrial assets and size—was relatively untouchable. Of course, GE changed that perception with its $6.3 billion acquisition of RCA, including NBC. The deal rounded out the network bidding wars. After the deals, there was pain and dislocation as the networks adjusted to the new competitive world. Costs were cut, jobs lost, but the pace of change kept accelerating.

The Videocassette Boom and the Death of the LP

The development and commercialization of the videocassette—which actually first appeared in the 1970s—opened another new distribution channel and changed the economics of the movie business.

When the Supreme Court ruled in 1984 that the taping of programs off television for personal use was not a copyright violation, the studios shifted the timing of movie releases. Previously, movies were released to television before being put on the video market. The pattern was soon reversed to maximize rentals. This new market was a huge shot in the arm for movie producers—in 1987, over $3 billion of the roughly $8 billion in studio revenues were attributed to cassettes.

The videocassette boom also created a whole new retail channel. When Wayne Huizenga and his partners bought Blockbuster in 1987 for $19 million, the company had nineteen stores in a highly fragmented industry. Three years later, Blockbuster had more than 1,000 units nationwide. The chain's signature was large, well-lit stores with 7,000 titles, many more than the mom-and-pop competition. Customers loved the format, but Huizenga did not just rely on organic growth. He went on an acquisition spree, picking up ten separate video chains and Blockbuster's largest franchisee.

Huizenga eventually sold Blockbuster to Sumner Redstone's Viacom in the midst of the Paramount battle. The price tag on the merger was $8.4 billion. After the sale, it became clear that video stores were approaching maturity and slower growth as a distribution channel.

Similar developments swept the music business in the mid-1980s. The new digital compact disc players flew off the shelves and baby boomers rushed to replace old LPs and cassettes with the state-of-the-art medium.

The new passion for compact discs was manna for the music business. The Big Six music companies converted large parts of their music libraries to CD and began releasing new albums on this platform. With a higher retail price and fatter margins than records or cassettes, the companies enjoyed rising revenues and profits. A near-euphoria set in.

Content Becomes the Scarce Commodity

The distribution side of the media business churned throughout the 1980s, altering the balance between the supply and demand of media content. New distribution channels had to be fed with product. Where a regimented marketplace had once existed, chaos now prevailed. Opportunities developed over a short period, and the rewards went to companies able to bring inventive creative product to market. Meanwhile, the value of proven content providers skyrocketed and a decade-long bidding war for control began.

Early Asset Plays   The studio wars started with the carving up of the old Twentieth Century Fox, the maker of *Star Wars*. Oilman Marvin Davis was intrigued by the turmoil at Fox, as its top executives publicly feuded with each other, and rumors circulated of an attempted bid by Saul Steinberg's Reliance Group. Davis liked the studio's collection of assets—a Coca-Cola bottler, prime Los Angeles, Pebble Beach and Aspen real estate, television stations and the movie studio. He and his partners bought the studio for $724 million, funding the acquisition largely with debt.

Over the next several years, Davis sold off television stations to reduce Twentieth Century Fox's debt and spun off some of its real estate. He recovered most of his equity investment in Fox through these asset sales. However, the studio had failed to release a major blockbuster in some time and was struggling under its still significant debt burden. Hoping to turn things around, Davis lured Barry Diller from Paramount. Meanwhile, Saul Steinberg, spurned by Fox, focused on Disney.

By 1984, Disney had been in decline for years. Yet even with its problems, the Walt Disney Company possessed a fabulous group of assets. In addition to its theme parks and movie studios, the company owned large blocks of California and Florida real estate.

Steinberg saw his opportunity when Roy Disney, son of the company's co-founder, resigned from the board in a protest over the strategic deemphasis of animation and films. A group of investors led by Steinberg amassed an 11 percent stake in the company and launched a hostile tender offer. Disney greenmailed the group, paying $325 million for the block of stock. Steinberg netted around $60 million on the investment, though he later returned a portion of that to settle a lawsuit filed by Disney shareholders.

Steinberg's withdrawal had predictable consequences. Disney's stock price deflated, falling as low as $45 a share. Institutional investors and arbitrageurs carped. A month later, Disney management found another insurgent at its doorstep. Investor Irwin Jacobs acquired his own block of stock and began a takeover campaign. Jacobs pledged not to sell his stock back to Disney.

The Disney board responded by firing Disney's president and chief executive. Michael Eisner, who worked under Diller at Paramount, was recruited for the top job. He brought with him a Hollywood dream team including Frank Wells and Jeffrey Katzenberg. Eisner's team gave Disney a refurbished credibility, and the Bass brothers of Texas, who already held a big chunk of Disney stock, agreed to increase their stake to 25 percent on a friendly basis. As part of the plan, they bought out Jacobs at a profit and agreed not to increase their stake any further. With the Basses supporting Eisner and a newly announced stock buyback plan, Disney had defended the Magic Kingdom.

Strategic Buyers Nibble   Strategic buyers also began to shop for content in the early 1980s. One of the earliest high-profile deals came in 1982, when Coke acquired Columbia Pictures. The $692 million friendly deal was greeted with jeers on Wall Street. Coke was bucking the growing pure-play trend in favor of diversification. Yet Chairman Roberto Goizueta did a great deal to silence his critics. He set the bar for Coke's new entertainment sector high, targeting 20 percent annual growth, and Columbia delivered. The studio spent $750 million to acquire Norman Lear's Embassy Communications and Merv Griffin Enterprises. Despite weak creative output on the movie side, these strong television operations and the videocassette boom propelled Columbia to returns above 30 percent in Coke's first three years of ownership.

Australian Rupert Murdoch, whose News Corporation controlled publishing assets in Australia and Great Britain, then made his first attempt at expanding into the electronic media in 1983. At the time, Warner Communications was reeling from losses at its acquired Atari division. The problems ultimately would cost Warner nearly $1 billion in losses. The company's other interests—a studio, a record label, a publishing company and the cable television joint venture with American Express—were more attractive. Murdoch made an offer to buy the company, but Warner chairman Steve Ross refused to sell.

Ross was a survivor. He had built Warner's collection of world-

class media assets up over twenty-five years from a collection of funeral parlors and parking lots. Though he owned less than 1 percent
of Warner, Ross was unwilling to capitulate. Like Disney, he brought
in a friend as his protector—Herbert Siegel's Chris-Craft Industries.
The two companies swapped assets, and Siegel ended up with more
than 25 percent of Warner's stock. Murdoch gave up the battle, his
dream of building an integrated international media empire deferred. Ironically, Ross would spend the next five years bickering
with Siegel over how to manage Warner.

Cable Gets Creative   The dynamic growth of cable also had
repercussions for the content side of the entertainment industry.
Cable fed off of, and encouraged growth in, new programming.

Throughout the 1980s, cable companies faced an imperative to
grow more content as channel capacity expanded, and consumers
demonstrated a thirst for fresh programming. The studios were one
obvious source for additional content. However, most smaller cable
operators lacked the time, money and sophistication to acquire
movie rights from the studios directly. By 1975, Time Inc. had acquired complete ownership of Charles Dolan's HBO service. Over
the next ten years, Jerry Levin—today chairman of Time Warner—
and others at Time grew the channel into the dominant force in pay
television. In the process, Jerry became the prophet of cable.

The seminal event for HBO was the launching of communications satellites, which permitted the company to beam the service to
cable operators nationwide. The rest was shrewd marketing and operations. Time decided early on not to charge by the movie. This allowed HBO to avoid the complicated technical and other problems
associated with pay-per-view. Time also put together a unique mix of
nonmovie programming, including stand-up comedy and coverage of
Wimbledon. Finally, as a pioneer of the format, HBO had the leverage to negotiate favorable contracts with the studios. Notwithstanding the studios' protestations about the prices they received for

broadcast rights, they had to be on HBO if they wanted to leverage their content over this additional distribution channel.

The runaway success of HBO prompted a flurry of channel start-ups. Warner Amex threw its weight behind MTV and Showtime. Getty Oil branched into programming with ESPN. Dolan's Cablevision started American Movie Classics and Bravo. Others followed suit.

Ted Turner's Turner Broadcasting was one of the most stunning cable programming successes of this period. Turner began in business at the age of twenty-four, when he took over the family billboard company after his father committed suicide. Turner got into television in 1970. He bought a low-power Atlanta station with few prospects. Following HBO's lead, he transformed the station into WTBS and bounced its signal off satellites to local cable operators. This new "superstation" featured movies, reruns and sports—primarily the games of Turner's Atlanta Braves and Hawks.

WTBS became extremely profitable, and its cash flow funded Turner's next bright idea—a twenty-four-hour news channel. CNN began operations in 1980. After five years of losses, the station turned the corner. By 1985, Turner's two stations were the backbone of many cable systems' basic service.

Thirst for Content Grows   The global thirst for media content grew significantly over the course of the 1980s. In 1985, the escalating value of content became abundantly clear with Ted Turner's acquisition of MGM/UA. Turner agreed to buy the two combined studios for $1.5 billion from investor Kirk Kerkorian and public shareholders. As part of the deal, Turner Broadcasting would assume $600 million of MGM debt. Turner would then sell United Artists back to Kerkorian for over $400 million. Initially, Turner hoped to keep both the MGM film library and the studio itself. However, troubles with financing led Turner to sell all but the film library back to Kerkorian and another group. So, in the end, Turner paid more than $1 billion for a library of over 3,000 films.

Kirk Kerkorian

Kirk Kerkorian is a folksy, charming man with a commonsense investment approach. Working with a small group of trusted advisers, he controls a $3-billion-plus portfolio of investments from his Las Vegas headquarters. The soft-spoken Kerkorian keeps a remarkably low profile but is incredibly focused. He was in the news most recently as a result of his activist investment in Chrysler, but remains more interested in the bottom line than in headlines.

Kerkorian has a long history of involvement with the movie business. However, he made his first fortune from an airline. Kerkorian started a charter business after World War II and astutely cashed in on the Las Vegas gambling boom. Kerkorian sold the tiny airline—which flew gamblers to Vegas in DC-3s—in 1968 for $107 million.

The next year, Kerkorian invested a piece of the money in Western Airlines and began a turnaround effort, but soon became more interested in the hotel and movie business. He announced a tender offer for 17 percent of MGM in July 1969 and took control of the board. One of his first steps was to reduce the studio's production schedule to four films a year.

Over the next twenty years, Kerkorian repeatedly shuffled the assets of MGM in an effort to maximize the studio's value, profiting along the way. He spun off the hotel group in 1978 as MGM Grand Hotels. In 1981, he acquired United Artists and raised his MGM/UA stake to 50 percent. The Turner transaction looked at first like a major withdrawal from Hollywood for Kerkorian. But the withdrawal was short-lived and Kerkorian kept the studio. Finally, in 1990, Kerkorian sold the studio to Italian Giancarlo Parretti.

Parretti's company turned out to be built on a quicksand of bribe-induced loans and bad management. Within a few months of his taking over, MGM was in bankruptcy. Parretti's French bank forced him out and eventually installed Frank Mancuso to turn things around.

Then, in an ironic twist, Kerkorian, Mancuso and Australia's Seven Network bought MGM from the French for the same $1.3 billion price Kerkorian had received in 1990. Though Mancuso has considerable independence in running the studio, the 1996 deal once again put Kerkorian at the heart of the market for creative content. In 1997, he and his partners completed a $600 million add-on acquisition, buying a 2,200-film library from John Kluge's Metromedia International, and then took MGM public.

The vision behind Turner's MGM deal was purely content-driven. He wanted the studio's old movies, and originally hoped to have its new product as well, to feed his WTBS and other cable channels. Analysts were skeptical. The Street consensus was that Turner—smarting from the CBS brush-off—had overpaid. It was a long road, but Turner proved his critics wrong.

Meanwhile, in the cable business, established brand-name channels were hot commodities. When one came on the market, buyers lined up. Texaco's acquisition of Getty Oil triggered the first opportunity. Texaco put ESPN on the block to help fund the deal. Turner Broadcasting made a bid. However, ABC had a leg up on Turner. The network already had exercised an option to acquire 15 percent of the channel and had a right of first refusal to buy the remainder. ABC eventually paid $202 million for full ownership.

Financial distress was the motivating factor in many content sales. Steve Ross of Warner Communications prized Warner's interest in Showtime and MTV, held through the Warner Amex cable joint venture. Unfortunately, American Express wanted out of cable. In June 1985, American Express agreed to sell Warner Amex to a joint venture of Time and TCI. The only way Ross could keep his prized cable assets was to exercise Warner's right of first refusal to buy American Express out. However, Ross was hemmed in as a result of the defensive measures he had taken in response to Murdoch's earlier bid. Herb Siegel of Chris-Craft didn't like the idea of purchasing more cable. Ross eventually agreed to sell off Showtime and MTV as a way to get the cable deal through. Viacom picked up control of these hot properties for roughly $700 million.

Vertical Integration   The steep values being placed on MGM, cable channels and other properties gave a jolt to the media business. A market consensus began to coalesce in favor of an old business model—the vertically integrated media company.

Initially, the trend in favor of vertical integration was obscured in the haze and upheaval of rapid-fire media deal flow. Rupert Murdoch changed that in 1985 with two blockbuster transactions. First, for $250 million, News Corporation finally succeeded in breaking into Hollywood. Though Barry Diller had begun to turn things around at Twentieth Century Fox, the studio was still on the ropes. Rather than put more of his money into the studio, Marvin Davis agreed to sell a half interest to Murdoch. A significant chunk of the purchase price—$132 million—would go into the studio's coffers.

Murdoch soon topped the Twentieth Century Fox deal with his $2 billion agreement to purchase John Kluge's seven television stations. In a single transaction, Murdoch had stations reaching 18 percent of the United States and began talking about building a fourth television network. Within six months, he committed another $225 million to the vision, buying Marvin Davis out completely.

The wisdom of Murdoch's huge bet was not immediately apparent. For almost $3 billion, he had a sputtering studio with promising talent and a group of independent stations. Stitching this all together would take time. Diller was the key. His content machine would need to turn out movies to survive and television programs to feed the station network. However, Murdoch's faith in Diller was well placed. Within a year, the studio began to rack up box-office successes.

Despite early doubts about Murdoch's success, the core logic of the vertical integration model propelled others to unite content and distribution under the same roof. For example, a number of movie studios bought into theater chains—MCA acquired 50 percent of Cineplex Odeon, Columbia bought Walter Reade, Tri-Star snagged Loews and made an abortive deal for the United Artists theaters. The growing value of successful movie content was the imperative driving these deals. Favorable placement and promotion of new releases was viewed as critical to building product which could then be exploited in the videocassette, cable and television distribution channels.

In the cable world, content became even more important with the deregulation of rates. Cable providers needed more channels to justify higher basic rates. At the same time, cable channels represented a major cost to cable companies, which typically paid for channels on a per-subscriber basis. Thus, distributors were motivated to buy interests in established and developing channels.

John Malone, for example, made a major move to embrace the vertical integration model in 1987. Turner Broadcasting was having difficulty handling the debt from the MGM purchase. Ted Turner began shopping for an investor to provide much-needed equity. Rumors abounded that Turner would sell out to NBC or one of the other two networks. Alarmed at the prospect of having a crucial content provider in the hands of the competition, Malone, Time and a coalition of cable providers stepped up with $563 million for a 35 percent interest in Turner Broadcasting.

The Turner investment was just a beginning for Malone and TCI. Over the next several years, TCI expanded its programming interests.

Malone eventually amassed stakes in the Discovery Channel, Black Entertainment Television, Court TV, QVC, the Family Channel and American Movie Classics. In fact, TCI's channel portfolio grew to the point where it became a source of criticism. New channels needed access to TCI's large subscriber base. Competitors argued that the company used this leverage to buy interests in channels at below-market prices. Reacting to the criticism, Malone spun off TCI's programming assets as a separate company called Liberty Media in 1991. However, he remained at the head of both companies.

PROFILE

Laurence Tisch

In his role as CEO of CBS, Laurence Tisch bucked every trend.

Larry Tisch and his brother Robert have a long history of contrarian investments which have paid off extremely well. The two inherited a small hotel in the Catskills in the 1950s. They picked up the Loews theater chain from MGM in 1959 when government antitrust authorities forced the studio to sell. From this base, the Tisch brothers built a small hotel and entertainment empire. Part of their genius was building hotels in Manhattan and elsewhere when others were unwilling. During the Go-Go 1960s, the Tisches diversified Loews into insurance and tobacco through CNA Financial and Lorillard. These investments earned Larry Tisch a reputation as a sharp investor who made money bottom fishing.

In a way, the 1986 investment in CBS was another contrarian bet. The consensus was that the networks would underperform for a number of years. Yet buying into CBS was also a dramatic shift. Controlling such a high-profile media property brought Tisch an unaccustomed level of attention.

On taking control of CBS, Tisch moved to reposition the network. He slashed costs in the news division and sold off assets.

Then Tisch took a page from Ted Turner's takeover plan. In December 1986, he sold the CBS music publishing business for $125 million. The magazine division went six months later in a $650 million management buyout. Sony purchased CBS Records the following year for $2.2 billion. In a short time, Tisch had transformed CBS into a pure-play broadcasting company. He used the proceeds from asset sales to fund a whopping $2 billion stock buyback in 1990.

At the time of each asset sale, Tisch was widely considered to have gotten beyond top dollar. The $125 million price for music publishing was a record at the time, as was the $650 million for the magazine business. But, in perfect hindsight, he sold cheap. The new owners of the music publishing business resold it after three years for $337 million, management sold off the magazine business for about $1 billion within a year, and CBS Records turned in an exceptionally strong performance for Sony.

Furthermore, Tisch was subjected to unending public scrutiny of his management of CBS. Fired employees complained about being "Tisched." Current staffers squealed when their expense accounts were cut. Self-anointed visionaries felt that Bill Paley's temple of media excellence was being ransacked, neglecting the fact that Paley encouraged Tisch to invest and that Tisch boosted CBS' profile by bringing in the able programmer Les Moonves. Tisch supporters would argue that he made the tough decisions necessary to groom CBS for a comeback.

In fact, the CBS investment worked out quite well for Loews, despite weak ratings at the network. After a 1994 deal to merge the network with Barry Diller's QVC home shopping company fell apart, CBS bought back another $1 billion of its stock. At this point, Loews already had recouped its investment and still owned 18 percent of the network. A year later, Westinghouse made its $5 billion deal to acquire CBS. Investors who bought CBS shares in 1986 for about $125 each ended up with proceeds of $405 if they held until 1995. Given the boom in media properties, they might have made even more if Tisch had expanded rather than contracted CBS.

Meanwhile, Larry Tisch has returned to managing the large Loews empire, though a second generation of Tisches is taking a more active role. The family continues its disciplined investment philosophy, buying up disfavored assets and companies.

Time Warner   The capstone of the 1980s vertical integration movement came in 1989 when Time and Warner Communications merged to form a $15.2 billion media company with interests in cable, movie and television production, book and magazine publishing, and the record business.

Time's executive board began to consider an expansion into the entertainment business as early as 1983. By the fall of 1987, a consensus in favor of expanding into entertainment was reached by the committee. Gerald Levin, then Time's vice chairman and chief strategist, and now chairman and CEO of Time Warner, wrote a memo to J. Richard Munro, who was then chairman and CEO of Time. In the memo, Levin recommended a consolidation with Warner.

Levin's proposal rested on three considerations: first, Time wanted to better control the content provided over its cable channels, which included HBO and Cinemax; second, Time wanted to use Warner's assets as a stepping-stone to position itself for the increasing globalization of the media business; and third, Warner's key assets were simply growing faster than Time's.

We were hired as strategic advisers in Time's search for an entertainment deal. Warner became the leading candidate and negotiations began, but eventually fell apart. The sticking point was who would run the combined entity. Time's board was very concerned that any acquisition be structured to preserve Time's commitment to journalistic integrity. At a practical level, this meant that Time wanted to control CEO succession in the combined entity. Warner Brothers chairman Steve Ross took this as a slight and would not agree.

This temporary impasse blocked a Warner deal, so Time started to look elsewhere. However, none of these other companies were as attractive as Warner. In early 1989, Ross decided to accept Time's proposed merger, perhaps motivated by a recent illness. He shared the vision of a vertically integrated media power. Time owned strong distribution assets—cable systems, HBO, book and magazine distribution. Warner also had interests in cable systems, but its primary strength was in content. If Time and Warner were brought together, content from the Warner studios, record label and publishing house could be leveraged across Time's distribution channels.

The deal gathered momentum once the key governance issues were resolved with a compromise. Formally, Time and Warner would have equal board representation and the combined company would have co-CEOs. Ross and Munro initially would split duties, then Ross and Nick Nicholas, Time's CEO-designate. When Ross retired after a defined period, Nicholas would become the sole CEO. In the interim, a subcommittee of the board would be designated to govern editorial matters at Time's publications. Representatives of Time would hold a majority of the seats on this committee. This compromise opened the door, and the parties eventually agreed to a stock-for-stock merger.

Although critics subsequently charged that Steve Ross was taking over Time, in fact, Ross was fearful of dying from his recent illness and wanted to assure his legacy in the absence of an obvious successor at Warner. This was a marriage, but the clear long-term intention was for the Time team to take over for Ross, while Warner's gifted movie division leaders, Bob Daley and Terry Semel, would continue to wield power.

To protect their deal, Time and Warner put several defensive measures in place, including an automatic share exchange that could be triggered by either company and a "no-shop" clause. Under the share exchange, Time would receive 9.4 percent of Warner's outstanding common stock and Warner would receive 11.1 percent of Time's outstanding common stock. The agreement incorporating these terms was signed. Proxies were mailed to Time shareholders, who needed to approve the merger, but that approval was expected and the deal looked to be done.

However, Martin Davis of Paramount was not an easily spurned suitor. On June 7, 1989, just before the Time shareholders were scheduled to vote to approve the deal, Paramount announced a cash offer to purchase all Time shares for $175 per share, well above the pre-announcement price of $126.

After recovering from shock, the Time board shifted into high gear to consider the Paramount offer. The directors met on several occasions, often without management present. Reflecting the new circumstances, Wasserstein Perella's fee arrangement with Time was shifted to a flat fee structure, removing the financial incentive to favor a Time-Warner merger. We then made a detailed presentation on Paramount and its offer. We advised the board that Time shareholders would receive materially more than $175 per share if a full auction of the company were held. After deliberating, the board rejected Paramount's offer as inadequate and turned it down.

The board next acted to preserve the Warner deal, which board members thought more attractive. Paramount responded by upping its offer for Time to $200 per share. The Time board rejected this bid too, partly because Paramount was viewed as a threat to the Time journalistic culture.

Exasperated with the actions of the Time board, Paramount and a group of Time shareholders filed suit in Delaware court. A few intense weeks of legal sparring followed. Lawyers on either side worked around the clock to build documentary evidence. The trial was quick, and the judge ruled in favor of Time on both counts. An expedited appeal then went up to the Delaware Supreme Court, which affirmed the lower court ruling, and the Time-Warner deal went forward. The gist of the ruling was that a company need not abandon a strategic merger and sell itself to the highest bidder so long as the planned merger does not constitute a change in control.

The Time-Warner deal has generated considerable criticism. Time Warner's stock price has not performed as hoped. Adjusting for a subsequent split, Paramount's $200 a share offer amounts to $50 per current Time Warner share, somewhat below recent highs. However, in the interim, the S&P 500 has climbed significantly. In hindsight, critics argue shareholders would have been better off taking the Paramount offer and investing the proceeds elsewhere.

Of course, however, today's trading price doesn't represent a comparable acquisition value. On an acquisition basis, Time clearly could have gotten more than $200 per share at the time. The key issue is whether a company has a duty to sell when its trading value is below its sales price. Secondly, the capital structure of the company has changed and the asset mix altered. For example, Time Warner has issued new shares many times over in the past eight years, including the 1991 issuance of 140 million shares through a rights offering to existing shareholders. The shares were offered at a deep discount to the then-current stock price, heavily diluting the value of outstanding shares. This dilution was compounded by other stock deals, including the company's 1996 acquisition of Turner Broadcasting System Inc. Finally, it is true that the values of cable assets have not appreciated at the anticipated pace because of federal rate regulation, although lately they have been perceived to have increased value.

Even so, as evidenced by the QVC and Viacom bids for Paramount, in fact the assets of the old Time have appreciated with the market. The problem is that the recapitalized Time Warner is a very different and more complex company. It has assembled a premier group of assets, which are only now beginning to be recognized.

The Global Pipeline

The ascendancy of content over the past decade was not merely a domestic matter. New distribution technologies—cable, satellite, videocassettes—blossomed overseas as well. A new global thirst for "software" developed. Movies, compact discs, books and television shows were sought-after commodities on the global market. As this global pipeline mushroomed, the companies involved began to look across borders for opportunities. For American content companies, the goal was to develop foreign distribution platforms. However, the more dramatic development was a growing international interest in owning American content providers.

Nowhere have the contours of change been more evident than in the record business. International interest in American music boomed starting in the mid-1980s. With strong distribution networks outside the United States, a number of international media companies saw an opportunity to expand to become global powers. A position in the United States was the critical missing link. The companies began to shop for U.S. record companies, sparking a consolidation of the record business.

Germany's Bertelsmann was the first to strike. The company—which already owned an interest in RCA/Arista records—bought the remaining 75 percent from RCA in 1986. RCA Records was a down-and-out label, a money-loser at the time. The $330 million purchase price prompted speculation that the Germans had been duped by their American counterparts. Within two years, the Germans proved the contrary. They refurbished the label, brought out a number of big hits, and used their international marketing experience to score international sales.

As the record boom accelerated, so too did foreign acquisitions of U.S. record companies. Sony moved next, with the 1987 purchase of CBS Records. Again, the purchase price seemed steep at the time, but proved cheap. In 1989, PolyGram—a subsidiary of the Dutch-based Philips Industries—followed suit with the $500 million acquisition of A&M Records. The flurry of international acquisitions left David Geffen's Geffen Records the only remaining significant independent U.S. record company.

A year later, the consolidation was completed. Geffen sold out to MCA in a $545 million stock deal. This left just six multinationals largely in control of the music business—two U.S., one German, one Japanese, one British and one Dutch. These Big Six were Time Warner, MCA, Bertelsmann, Sony, Thorn-EMI and Philips.

The global balance shifted again in 1992 when Matsushita of Japan bought all of MCA—Geffen Records included—for $7.4 billion (with assumed debt). This followed Sony's $4.8 billion purchase of Columbia Pictures from Coke. Both deals were brokered by Hollywood agent Michael Ovitz before he joined Disney.

In movies as in music, international players were looking for content. Sony and Matsushita hoped to profit from the growing international market for American entertainment. As equipment manufacturers, they also saw strategic benefits from owning the content that consumers played on their hardware.

The idea of linking software and hardware was not new. Indeed, RCA had sold radios by setting up its NBC radio network and color televisions with NBC programs like *Bonanza*. More recently, content had been critical to the videocassette recorder's earlier success. Sony's higher-quality, higher-priced Betamax format had been an expensive flop because Sony failed to recognize the importance of the video rental business in promoting the product. When video rental stores decided to stock the cheaper VHS tapes, Sony lost the market share war. Now, Sony and Matsushita planned to use content as a source of additional marketing leverage for the introduction of new electronics.

Unfortunately, the promise of this "Japanese invasion" into Hollywood has yet to be realized. Shortly after the MCA deal, Matsushita and Sony were rocked by a stock market crash that wiped out more than $2.6 trillion in value on the Tokyo Stock Exchange, along with a major recession and real estate crash. Legendary studio chairman Lew Wasserman had agreed to sell to Matsushita partly in the hope it would provide the capital for growth and acquisitions. The new economic realities in Japan made this difficult.

Matsushita's failure to back Wasserman's growth plans caused considerable friction between the parent company and MCA. Wasserman and MCA president Sidney Sheinberg pressed to buy a record company or part of a television network. Essentially, Matsushita neither trusted Wasserman and Sheinberg to chart a strategy, nor was the company willing to take over management directly. The feud broke into the public in 1994, deeply embarrassing Matsushita.

Sony's troubles were even more serious. Columbia was a troubled property from the outset. Sony hired what it saw as an expert Hollywood management team—Peter Guber, a lawyer, and Jon Peters, Barbra Streisand's former hairdresser. Guber and Peters had produced box office hits like *Batman* and *Rain Man*, but had never run a studio. Sony bought their independent film company for $250 million and put them in charge of Columbia. Their tenure was rocky from the start. Warner Brothers sued to enforce a contract it had with the duo, and Sony was forced to settle in a deal valued by Warner at several hundred million dollars.

Guber and Peters then allegedly took advantage of their Japanese employer. They decorated lavishly, and hired layers of high-priced managers. Each had a corporate jet; $175 million was spent on refurbishing the studio's Culver City lot. Most damaging, Guber and Peters made a string of expensive box-office bombs like *Last Action Hero* and *Hudson Hawk*.

In November 1994, Sony accepted its black eye, then renewed its commitment to succeed with Columbia. The parent company took a $3.2 billion write-off of its Columbia investment. Guber, Peters and their protégés were jettisoned. The next year, Nobuyuki Idei was named the new president of Sony. In an assertion of leadership, he took vigorous reins over Columbia. Idei hired the able and well-respected Howard Stringer, a former CBS executive, to head Sony's U.S. operations, but also inserted Japanese managers to play a role. John Calley became the new studio chief at Columbia.

Though Sony's Columbia investment experience was difficult, the new management team appears to have matters back on track. Columbia has done well at the box office recently, releasing *Men in Black, My Best Friend's Wedding* and *Air Force One* in quick succession. Costs are coming under control, and Sony professes to remain committed to the strategic marriage of software and hardware.

Matsushita, on the other hand, chose to exit Hollywood entirely. In a way, the company was more spooked by Sony's troubles than Sony. Shortly after the Columbia write-off became public, Matsushita management decided to sell MCA to Seagram CEO Edgar Bronfman Jr., who had taken over day-to-day management of the Canadian spirits company from his father. In the spring of 1995, Seagram announced it would sell most of its highly profitable stake in DuPont, which it had received as a result of the Conoco fight. Bronfman then used roughly $5.7 billion of the $7.7 billion after-tax proceeds to buy 80 percent of MCA. The deal valued all of MCA at over $7 billion. However, because the Japanese yen had appreciated nearly 60 percent since Matsushita's purchase, the sale triggered a significant currency loss.

Bronfman's swap of an interest in DuPont for control of MCA was a bold strategic shift, trading a large interest in chemicals and oil, the source of as much as 70 percent of Seagram's earnings, for the entertainment business. Of course, the merit of the move is not yet entirely clear. However, Bronfman has taken steps to ratchet up growth at MCA.

Wasserman and Sheinberg left MCA as part of the ownership shift. Bronfman installed Frank Biondi, brother of my partner Mike Biondi and a highly regarded professional manager who had recently parted ways with former boss Sumner Redstone, as chairman and chief executive. Under Frank Biondi's leadership, the movie and television operations have been restructured across the board. So far, the market has reacted favorably. Seagram's stock price is up and the implied value of its MCA stake significantly higher than the $5.7 billion invested, but lower than the implied value if it had held on to DuPont.

Convergence Revisited

As in most industries, the recession of the early 1990s slowed the media merger wave. However, the slowdown was only temporary. On the cusp of the digital age, technological change was in the air. Digital compression promised to expand vastly the capacity of coaxial cable. This so-called fat pipe would be able to carry voice, video and data transmissions into the home. John Malone hailed the coming digital revolution in a famous 1992 speech in which he predicted the arrival of a 500-channel world.

The height of the first convergence wave came with the $21 billion Bell Atlantic–TCI merger. Of course, the bubble burst when the FCC—implementing the congressional re-regulation of cable—slashed cable rates and the deal came unglued. Still, the strategic imperatives inherent in the convergence vision did not evaporate. The question was not whether convergence eventually would come to pass, but when. A cable industry peopled with dispersed single-city operations no longer made sense. Clustering of franchises into large contiguous operations continued to be the consensus business plan of the future, new digital services the perceived growth engine.

The failed TCI deal did not slow the pace of cable consolidation. TCI itself spent $1.6 billion in 1994 to acquire 741,000 subscribers from Tele-Cable and joined with others to buy Viacom's cable systems. Between September 1994 and February 1995, Time Warner also participated in the acquisitions of four cable companies for more than $8 billion.

Integration Accelerates

The 1993 no-holds-barred fight for Paramount Communications ushered in a new period of large-scale media deals. By combining Viacom, Blockbuster and Paramount, Sumner Redstone put cable channels, television and movie production, video distribution and publishing all under one roof—a vertically integrated media power to rival Rupert Murdoch's News Corporation. Spurned by Paramount, Diller's QVC agreed to a merger with CBS, only to have the $1.9 billion deal falter when TCI and Comcast acquired the roughly 65 percent of QVC they didn't already own. On the distribution side, a new burst of radio station consolidation took off.

To a certain extent, the 1990s deal flow was sparked by the same imperatives that had prevailed in the previous decade. Yet new regulatory and technological developments defined the specific scope and dynamic of the merger market.

The geography of the content business was changed dramatically in 1995 when the FCC scrapped its fin/syn rules, which dated back to 1970. In those days, the networks controlled access to 95 percent of American homes and used that power to extract favorable deals from content providers. Starting in the early 1980s, the networks fought a running battle with the studios, trying to remove the rules. The studios were not willing to give up their near-monopoly on the production of TV shows without a fight. Most disinterested observers agreed the rules made little sense in a world of cable and videocassettes, but the studios had a powerful Washington lobby. The rules came close to dying once in the 1980s until President Reagan—as a former actor, an obvious friend of Hollywood—killed the plan.

Finally in 1991, the FCC voted to relax the rules somewhat. Not pleased with the partial repeal, the networks sued in court and won. The rules were again revised in 1993, this time to repeal the fin/syn barriers completely within two years.

The removal of fin/syn, which became official in September 1995, amounted to a revolution. For decades, the rules had effectively barred networks from owning studios. Such a merger could have taken place under the old rules only if the studio then divested all interests in television production, a profitable business segment. Now, no such barrier remained. The networks were free to enter the $6-billion-a-year syndication market. Talk of big network-studio mergers permeated the market.

The approaching footsteps of change energized the studios. Two of the big players—Time Warner's Warner Brothers and Viacom's Paramount—responded by starting their own fledgling networks. These were defensive moves designed to guarantee the studios distribution for their television product. Warner and Paramount hoped to duplicate Barry Diller's feat and create a captive distribution channel from the ground up.

In addition, the broadcast networks were again a major focus of activity. With NBC on a roll, Jack Welch and GE were not likely sellers. The other two networks were attractive targets. Capital Cities/ABC was the first to go in a blockbuster merger with Disney. The $19 billion stock-and-cash deal—announced August 1, 1995—married one of the strongest creative talents in the media business with the number one broadcaster.

Like Rupert Murdoch's deals of 1985, the Disney-ABC merger crystallized the vertical integration strategy. Disney's move was made possible by the new regulatory environment and Disney's strength. The company was again a dominant entertainment power, widely hailed for its creative and marketing prowess. Michael Eisner had rejuvenated the Disney legacy. Now, Eisner was ready to launch a new stage of growth.

In joining content and distribution, Eisner embraced Murdoch's model, but arguably with stronger constituent parts. When the deal was announced, ABC was the number-one-rated network. Its emphasis on family-oriented programs meshed well with Disney's focus. Disney, on the other hand, had become a programming juggernaut. Preferred access to Disney's strong slate of animated and live-action movies and television programs would give ABC an edge over the competition. Further, Disney could apply its legendary marketing tie-in abilities to generate new viewers for the network. On the distribution side, Capital Cities also owned ten local TV stations, twenty-one radio stations and ESPN. Disney would benefit from a guaranteed channel to distribute new television programs and other content. The network also would provide yet another outlet to promote Disney movies.

Since closing of the Capital Cities/ABC deal in February 1996, press accounts of the merger have gone from glowing to skeptical. Clearly, Disney has hit some roadblocks. Ratings for ABC have dropped off considerably, and the network is fighting CBS to maintain its position.

Disney also has lost a number of top managers—the extremely capable Frank Wells, who died in a helicopter crash, Jeffrey Katzenberg, who feuded with his mentor, Eisner, and Michael Ovitz, who never integrated into the Disney system. However, the initial notion that Disney-ABC would be an overnight success was unrealistic. The broadcasting business is by nature cyclical and ABC was bound to come down from its ratings highs. More importantly, the integration of two major media concerns just takes time. Buying ABC was the fulfillment of a dream for Eisner, but owning it has had aspects of a nightmare. Eisner remains committed to the process, and his past successes at ABC, Paramount and Disney suggest he will realize the strategic vision.

PROFILE

Michael Eisner

When Michael Eisner joined Disney in 1984, the company was under pressure from raiders and had a $1.9 billion market capitalization. Today, the fifty-five-year-old Eisner heads a company with a $64 billion market capitalization. The dramatic turnaround has not been without bumps along the way, but Eisner is widely regarded as one of the media business's strongest CEOs.

Eisner, like Barry Diller, stands out among Hollywood executives because he combines an acute sense for business with an ability to manage the creative side as well. He grew up on Manhattan's East Side. By the time he graduated from college, he had become interested in the entertainment business. A job as an NBC usher gave him a start. After spending a few years rising through the ranks at the network, Eisner sent out dozens of résumés. He ended up landing a job working for Barry Diller at ABC.

Eisner spent ten years at ABC. He and Diller drove the perennial also-ran to the top rating spot. When Diller jumped to Paramount, Eisner followed to become president of the studio. Again, the Eisner-Diller duo worked media magic. They pushed Paramount to become one of Hollywood's top performers with movies such as *Raiders of the Lost Ark* and *Saturday Night Fever.*

Diller and Eisner parted ways on leaving Paramount. Eisner wanted the freedom to run a company on his own, and the opportunity presented itself. Originally, Eisner was recruited for the number two spot at Disney, but he held out for the CEO job. The company desperately needed help and gave him the offer he wanted.

In his first decade as CEO of the Magic Kingdom, Eisner avoided major acquisitions. Instead, he focused internally. One of the first tasks was to rebuild the filmed entertainment unit, which had been lagging badly. Prior management had considered closing down the business, but Eisner and his creative team revived the operation and built it into the envy of the industry. Strong creative content was part of the story. Animated features like *The Lion King* appealed to children and families, while Touchstone and Miramax turned out more adult fare.

> The content was just a first step, the raw material which pro-
> pelled Disney to record earnings. Marketing was also key. Eisner's
> team refined the concept of marketing tie-ins to a science. For ex-
> ample, *The Lion King* topped the box office in 1994. However, that
> was just part of the success. The movie also generated the num-
> ber one album for the year and the best-selling video of all time.
> Clearly, the promise of these kinds of profitable combinations
> contributed to the appeal of a Disney-ABC merger.

The vertically integrated media company became the industry prototype as the 1994–96 burst of consolidation continued. After drawn-out negotiations, Time Warner moved even further toward this ideal with its $7.5 billion acquisition of Turner Broadcasting. The deal grew out of Ted Turner's frustration with the continuing role TCI and Time Warner played in his company. The two companies together owned about 40 percent of Turner Broadcasting as a legacy of the cable operators' earlier bailout. At the time, Turner had ceded veto powers to his new shareholders, who could block any major Turner Broadcasting deal. With their blessing, Ted Turner had managed to move TBS toward vertical integration with the purchase of two independent Hollywood studios, New Line Cinema and Castle Rock. But Turner still yearned to own a broadcast network and chafed at Time Warner's continued opposition. Starting in early 1995, he searched for a way to have Time Warner bought out.

The negotiations repeatedly hit snags. Time Warner was reluctant to sell its stock interest for cash, which would generate a large tax bite, and, in fact, hankered for controlling all of TBS, particularly CNN, the news network. The August 1995 announcement by Westinghouse that it would acquire CBS reenergized Turner. A Time Warner–TBS deal offered many of the same strategic benefits. Turner and Jerry Levin shared a similar vision, and the deal was announced in September 1995.

Over the next year, tough negotiations with John Malone and federal antitrust regulators threatened to break up the combination. Eventually, though, the perseverance of Jerry Levin and Ted Turner paid off. The deal finally closed in early October 1996.

Meanwhile, new business models continue to be developed for the changing structure of the industry. Barry Diller is one prominent example. Diller left QVC shortly after Comcast and TCI acquired the company in 1994. Diller's relatively short stint at the company left him considerably richer, but without a platform for his talents. In 1996, he created his own. Diller merged three companies—Silver King, Home Shopping Network and Savoy Pictures—to form a single company with the flagship home shopping channel, a string of independent UHF television stations and interests in four Fox stations.

Diller planned to fashion the independent stations into a new network. The so-called must carry rules—which require cable operators to carry local broadcast stations including small UHF stations like Diller's—were one key element to the strategy. These rules were challenged in court but upheld by the U.S. Supreme Court in March 1997.

Once this regulatory issue was settled, Diller applied his unique programming talent to the assets he had collected. Diller announced a plan to create high-end local programming for each station. The idea was to fill a niche not served by existing channels, with programs that appealed to local community interests.

On October 21, 1997, Diller added a national element to his programming stable in a complicated deal with Seagram's Universal Studios. Diller's HSN essentially acquired control of Seagram's USA and Sci-Fi cable channels and most of Universal's television production assets. Seagram had just acquired full control of the USA Network from its former partner Viacom for $1.7 billion.

Diller's HSN agreed to pay Universal $1.2 billion in cash and a 45 percent stock interest in HSN, to be renamed USA Networks. In addition, Universal retained an option to purchase, at an undisclosed price, up to 80 percent of the new entity in four years or if Diller left. Diller gained control of a larger platform with the capacity to provide national programming for his fledgling network, while Universal effectively hired the talents of Diller to rebuild its troubled television operation.

Diller, Murdoch and others have bet on a content plus captive distribution business model. As always, however, the market is not without contrarians. While other content providers were buying up distribution, Sumner Redstone sold Viacom's cable systems to TCI in a tax-free transaction. In defending the move, Redstone contended that in a 500-channel world, content providers with hot product will always have leverage and that Viacom's relatively small cable system just wasn't at critical mass.

Rupert Murdoch

Rupert Murdoch has continued to build his empire even as others embrace his strategic vision. Triangle Publications—which owned a portfolio of magazines, including *TV Guide*—was added for $2.8 billion in 1988. Then, in another successful pioneering effort, Murdoch launched an early direct satellite service in the United Kingdom. By getting to market first and tying up broadcast rights to sought-after content, News Corporation's British Sky Broadcasting grabbed market share from existing cable operations.

Like many other leveraged companies, News Corporation had some trouble in the late 1980s. Murdoch's aggressive building—satellites, publishing, broadcasting—sucked up cash. However, by selling some publishing assets and managing operations closely, Murdoch weathered the storm and kept his company largely intact.

The 1990s have been a new phase for Murdoch. The driving goal remains—the creation of a unified global media company. But as the supply of attractive media properties has dwindled, Murdoch too has focused on building new distribution and content. He launched a $2 billion U.S. satellite joint venture with MCI in 1995 and started up a Fox twenty-four-hour news channel in 1997. Both of these efforts have since run into some difficulty. The proposed WorldCom-MCI merger changed the dynamic of the satellite venture and a subsequent deal with satellite company EchoStar Communications fell apart. Meanwhile, News Corporation had difficulty finding cable operators willing to carry the Fox news channel.

Murdoch nonetheless continues to express optimism about the prospects for News Corporation, as he did during the costly start-up phase of the Fox network. The company again has the balance sheet to weather these difficulties. Murdoch also continues to jump at new opportunities as they arise. The central strategic move came in late 1996, when Fox spent $2.5 billion to acquire New World Communications—with its ten Fox-affiliated stations—from Ron Perelman. Murdoch wanted the added stations to expand the network's group of owned stations, which reached 40 percent of all homes in the United States after the deal. The enlarged station group gave Murdoch an unrivaled platform from which to promote his programming.

Today, Murdoch ignores the familiar refrain of complaints that he overpaid and instead focuses on integrating these latest pieces.

The Digital Future

We are on the cusp of a new digital age. Of course, the evolution has been a sputtering one. Five years ago, the future was one of converging voice, video and data. Phone and cable wires were the main focus of the race to shape the new dominant business platform. Hence, the Bell Atlantic–TCI vision was of a single company providing bundled services.

Today, the Internet boom has shifted the focus of the convergence story. Just in the space of a few years, the use of the World Wide Web has exploded. Commerce is now finding a home online: book retailers like Amazon.com and Barnes & Noble have created virtual stores and are doing a brisk business; home shopping is transitioning to a Web-based format; and C/net—the producer of a cable television show and Web page focusing on the computer and digital revolution—has built the most successful advertiser-supported site on the Internet. Seizing on the trend, Barry Diller's HSN (now USA Networks) acquired a controlling stake in Ticketmaster. The ticket retailer operates a fledgling Web site and gives further bulk to USA Networks' Internet efforts.

The new model is a bundling of distribution, technology and content. Software and interactive media are important elements of the mix. For instance, digital television promises to bring together the Web and traditional broadcast television in a new interactive model. The obvious question is, who will control this new medium—the content creators, the cable companies or the computer software providers?

Early hints of the emerging digital future were seen in Microsoft's abortive deal with Intuit. The strategic concept behind the deal—online banking, interactive home-based financial services, bundled software—has broad application beyond the financial services arena. Though the deal crashed when the Justice Department balked over antitrust concerns, the imperative remains.

The true harbingers of the digital age came starting in 1995. Again, Microsoft was the messenger. The software giant initially had underestimated the popularity and strategic import of the Internet. However, in typical Bill Gates fashion, Microsoft has made up for the oversight with an aggressive development and acquisition campaign. In one high-profile investment, Microsoft contributed $220 million to a joint venture with NBC, forming the MSNBC cable and Internet news channel.

Microsoft followed up the MSNBC deal with a number of other internal content creation efforts. The company created *Slate*, an online magazine headed by journalist Michael Kinsley, and a series of online commerce sites focused on cars, travel and real estate.

Notwithstanding these efforts, the real battle has centered on who will define the architecture of the new digital future. Microsoft has been an active participant in this area, with a series of major investments designed to capture the initiative. In April 1997, Microsoft spent $425 million to acquire Web-TV, a Silicon Valley start-up with a promising software and hardware Internet interface for television sets.

Then, in June 1997, Microsoft agreed to invest $1 billion for an 11.5 percent interest in Comcast. From Comcast's perspective, the money helped the cable company with its debt load, allowing a faster rollout of upgraded digital services. More broadly, the investment triggered a broad shift in market perceptions. Gates essentially was endorsing the notion that the cable infrastructure was the best hope for wider distribution of digital products.

Gates' reputation as a technology visionary caused investors to take another look at the disfavored cable sector. There was a realization that the strategic doubts about cable had been overdone. Satellite television was not gaining converts as quickly as feared. Meanwhile, cable television companies possessed an installed base of cable that runs past 95 percent of all homes in the United States. This cable in the ground is a fast, high-volume pipeline, and has the virtue of already being in place. As investors began to focus on the potential, the cable companies experienced a rebound in their stock prices that coincided with the Microsoft investment.

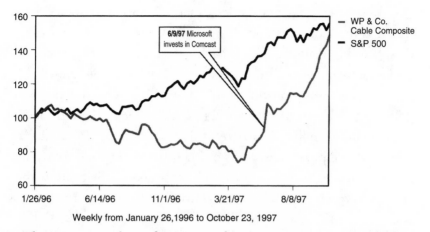

Weekly from January 26,1996 to October 23, 1997

The strategic subtext for Microsoft's investment was an unfolding battle to define the standards for mass Internet access over this cable infrastructure. Gates wanted to position Microsoft to bridge the gap between programming and consumers, whether on the Internet, on television, or through some other medium. He advocated making a version of Microsoft's core Windows software product the engine for digital cable boxes. These hardware units, known in the industry as set-top boxes because they generally sit on the top of a consumer's television, already were being developed by a number of manufacturers. The expectation was that new digital set-top boxes would replace the older versions and provide high-speed Internet access and interactive television.

In pushing the new Windows CE operating system, Microsoft was attempting to replicate its market position in the computer industry. The conventional Windows product—the dominant operating system for desktop computers—represented a kind of annuity for Microsoft. The company's revenues grew in line with the penetration of computers. Furthermore, Windows was a powerful platform to introduce new products and services. Microsoft controlled the gateway and could gain market share for add-ons by folding them into Windows, a practice that attracted renewed antitrust scrutiny from the Justice Department in 1997.

Gates initially floated the idea that Windows CE should be selected as the industry standard software driver for set-top boxes. Microsoft would collect a fee for each unit, plus a fraction of the fees cable companies would charge for new services. The math behind this approach was straightforward. While roughly 20 million households in the United States have a personal computer and modem, more than 64 million have televisions connected to cable. The growth in computer sales was slowing. Microsoft would have a hard time continuing to increase earnings at a double-digit rate without additional revenue sources. Interactive digital television is one possible new market for Microsoft.

Web-TV's second-generation product, introduced in September 1997, provides a window on the future potential of this business. The set-top box allows a television viewer to gain high-speed Internet access and pay-per-use video, music or games. In addition, the technology allows the Internet to be accessed while viewing television, in a picture-in-picture format. The promise is clear: television programming linked to Internet-based marketing tie-ins. For example, a program might be linked to a site with related products. Microsoft eventually hopes to get a small fee each time a consumer orders a movie or buys a book using its software.

However, John Malone and other cable executives balked at Bill Gates' vision. They had witnessed Microsoft's rise to dominance, as well as the evolution of the VHS versus Betamax war, and understood the importance of controlling technological standards. Cable companies would be at the mercy of Microsoft if the company were allowed to define industry standards.

Nor was Microsoft the only company that saw the potential of the interactive television market. Microsoft's competitors, chiefly Oracle Corporation and Sun Microsystems, launched their own efforts. Oracle owns a majority interest in Network Computer, which is developing a television-Internet interface. Other recent start-ups such as Worldgate are also racing to develop competing systems.

A group of cable companies also have their own effort underway, under the auspices of At Home, a start-up founded by Silicon Valley venture capitalists in 1995. At Home is now controlled by five cable companies including TCI and Comcast.

At Home is working to build the hardware and software needed for an Internet access capability over the cable infrastructure. The core of the system is a private network of computers designed to parallel the Internet, only at higher speed. Initially, the focus is access for personal computers, but the service is expected to expand into interactive television. In exchange for developing the technology, At Home receives 35 percent of the fees generated by affiliated cable companies.

At Home's exclusive relationships with large cable operators represent the most direct challenge to Microsoft's role in the digital future. Though Time Warner and U S West, two large cable providers, are not aligned with At Home, the company has pacts with cable companies that serve over 44 million households. These agreements place At Home at the center of the debate over future technological standards.

Microsoft's Comcast investment was in part an attack on the At Home consortium. Under the terms of the deal, Microsoft was given the right to force Comcast to end its exclusive relationship with At Home in June 1999. Microsoft has since pursued the other major cable providers in the At Home group, as well as Time Warner and U S West.

The cable companies have not relied exclusively on the efforts of At Home. Precisely because the development of set-top boxes is so critical to the cable industry, a consortium of cable companies including TCI established CableLabs. CableLabs is a research and development center charged with the responsibility for choosing set-top box industry standards to be used by the participant companies.

The consortium considered over twenty proposals from various companies, including Microsoft. In November 1997, CableLabs declined to select a single industry operating system and instead endorsed an open-architecture approach. The idea is to mirror the Internet, which allows the use of various operating systems.

As a result, the fight to design the digital future rages on. Microsoft and its competitors have now switched to marketing their systems to individual cable operators. The stakes in the continuing struggle are high and Microsoft's investment in Comcast has created a sense of urgency, just as competitors were jolted into action by the Bell Atlantic–TCI merger announcement. In early 1998, TCI split the difference, giving a piece of its set-top box business to Microsoft and a piece to Sun.

The geometric pace of technological change means that cable, phone, media, software entertainment and computer companies face a complex, exciting, but daunting and tough, future.

Over the past fifteen years, the shifting sands of technology and regulation have shaped an entirely new, unstable competitive landscape. Further changes—technological, regulatory and financial—continue to unfold rapidly. Business models that were cutting-edge a year ago have been repudiated, and the deals continue as companies rush to catch up with developments. Secondary shock waves are sweeping the hardware business, as indicated by Compaq Computer's agreement to acquire Digital Equipment for $9.6 billion.

The burst of deal activity between 1980 and 1998 can be traced to two particular developments. First, the media business has been swept along in a whirl of technological and regulatory change which caused an expansion of distribution possibilities. Second, an inexorable globalization has multiplied the size of the potential market for media products.

Regulatory shifts have an ongoing impact. For example, the Telecommunications Act of 1996 rewrote the ownership restrictions covering television and radio stations. Predictably, a new round of consolidation followed. More than $15 billion of radio deals were announced in 1996 and the race to own broadcast frequency is unabated.

Westinghouse's $4.9 billion purchase of Karmazin's Infinity

Broadcasting was one prominent deal of 1996, part of Michael H. Jordan's strategy to build Westinghouse into a media power centered on the CBS radio and television network. Deals continued into 1997, most prominently with the $570 million merger of Evergreen Media and Chancellor Broadcasting, which then acquired Viacom's radio stations for $1.1 billion. The resulting corporation, renamed Chancellor Media Corp., is for the moment the owner of the nation's second largest radio chain behind Westinghouse. In September 1997, Westinghouse added to its leading position with the $1.6 billion acquisition of American Radio Systems, a ninety-eight-station group.

The internationalization of the U.S. media business also will continue. Of course, the process is not without volatility—Matsushita recently pulled back with its sale of MCA. However, the sale replaced one international owner with another, specifically Seagram of Canada. Other multinationals remain committed to the U.S. market as an important source of creative content for global distribution.

Despite skepticism about their staying power, old-line businesses remain extremely profitable. Radio has been a huge success for Westinghouse. For Viacom, Simon & Schuster turned into one of the gems of the Paramount deal. These data points suggest a continuing vitality for "old" media formats as the market for content continues to expand.

The future nonetheless clearly lies with the digital technologies. Across the spectrum of the media and telecommunications industry, companies are at the dawn of a new post-industrial age. On the edge of this frontier, the participants share a palpable sense of tremendous implications but there is no clear crystal ball.

The digital world is here, but we are not quite ready.

The Tumultuous World | 13
of Health Care

"Who shall decide when doctors disagree?"

Alexander Pope, *Moral Essays*

Ten years ago, the world of health care looked remarkably different than it does today. Large insurance companies provided most health coverage, and hospitals and doctors worked as independent providers of health services. The pharmaceutical industry was fragmented, populated by extremely profitable companies not accustomed to competing based on price.

This has been a defining decade for health care. From insurance companies to health care providers to pharmaceutical companies, tumultuous upheaval has reshaped the landscape. The fundamental dilemma is how to find more efficient means of production and delivery for health care. Around the world, technological advances have created wonderful new opportunities in pharmaceuticals, biotechnology and medical instruments. However, an aging population makes it difficult to maintain the delivery of care even at current levels, given the existing health care cost structure. This stark reality can be seen in the rapid escalation of health care expenditures as a percentage of America's gross domestic product.

Health Care Expenditures as a Percent of GDP

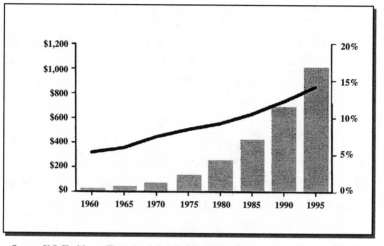

Source: U.S. Healthcare Financing Administration

The policy tensions inherent in the system relate to the balance between three themes: social equity, economy and quality of care. An ideal system would maximize the breadth and equity of patient care, as well as the quality of care. However, these two goals in combination conflict with the need for relative economy. President Clinton's 1993 health care plan represented an attempt to mediate these concerns, but the plan was impractical and political backlash made the proposal untenable. After resistance grew, it was withdrawn.

Many mergers in the health care industry are part of the struggle to reduce the effective cost of maintaining health care for consumers. Bulk brings opportunities for straightforward cost reductions such as the elimination of overhead and the consolidation of overlapping sales forces. However, mergers have also been sparked by a broader imperative. For companies in the sector, pricing issues have become a major concern and growth is constrained. Companies need to expand creative capabilities and product offerings to grow market share in this environment.

On the other hand, controversies regarding quality of HMO care and allegedly fraudulent practices at some health care companies raise the question whether economy is being accomplished at the expense of social equity or prudence. Moreover, the emphasis on efficiency may reduce investment in new technologies and erode the incentive to innovate. As a result of these crosscurrents, the health care industry continues to bubble with change.

Aetna Busts Out

Aetna's $8.9 billion acquisition of U.S. Healthcare hit the news wires on April 1, 1996. The transaction was a major signpost marking the company's attempt to transform itself into a high-growth health care company: Aetna was busting out of its Rosen's Cube. However, the deal also had a broader significance as a dramatic extension of other recent mergers, a pointer to future consolidation and an indication of the inevitable bumps along the road.

From the perspective of Ronald Compton, at the time chairman of Aetna, the U.S. Healthcare deal was the realization of a four-year strategic makeover. Compton took over an ailing company when he was promoted from president to CEO in the spring of 1992. The company's $23 billion portfolio of real estate investments was heavily peppered with bad loans, the property and casualty business was troubled and Aetna's structure bureaucratic.

Compton and Richard Huber, then Aetna's vice chairman for strategy and finance, were determined to remake Aetna into a high-growth company focused on core businesses. Health care was the Aetna management team's number one priority. Already in 1990, Aetna had reorganized its health care businesses around a new managed care focus. Compton knew the transition would not be easy, but hoped to extend this focus and add breadth of product offerings.

First, though, Compton moved to lighten Aetna's load in other areas. A few months after becoming chairman, he sold American Reinsurance for $1.4 billion to KKR. The deal—which turned into a major success for KKR—was a necessity for Aetna, which needed cash to reinforce its real estate portfolio. Weeks after clinching the sale, Aetna announced plans to lay off 10 percent of its workforce in an effort to boost profitability. Another major round of layoffs came in 1994.

With Aetna's operations stabilized, Compton turned to health care in earnest. The next stage began in early 1995 with a comprehensive strategic overview of Aetna's business portfolio. We were brought in to assist in the process. Eventually, a dramatic decision was made: Aetna would exit the property and casualty insurance business.

From an economic perspective, the decision was relatively straightforward. The business property and casualty had earned just $60 million in 1994 on revenues of $5.3 billion and would generate a $1 billion charge related to environmental cleanup liabilities in 1995. On the other hand, Aetna had been in the property and casualty business for over 100 years. Selling the operation would be a wrenching experience, but Compton eventually decided sentiment was not enough. Action was necessary if Aetna was to thrive into the next 100 years. Consequently, in December 1995, the company divested the property and casualty business to Sandy Weill's Travelers Group for $4 billion.

The Travelers deal positioned Aetna for a major health care acquisition. However, purchasing a health maintenance organization, or HMO, would be a revolutionary step, the first deal of its kind involving a major insurance company as acquirer. The risks were palpable. Compton was determined to act deliberately. The threshold issue was whether the long-term strategic merit of a health care acquisition would be sufficient to outweigh the obvious short-term costs.

After considerable detailed analysis, Compton and the Aetna board decided that investors would see past the near-term costs of an acquisition to the underlying growth prospects of a stronger health care business.

The bedrock for this decision was an understanding of industry dynamics. By 1995, the health care sector was entering a second phase in its evolution toward managed care. Cost had been the driver of the first phase, which had stretched roughly from the mid-1980s to the 1994 failure of President Clinton's health care reform proposals. The Clinton focus on rising health care costs had been the peak for traditional HMOs. Now, Aetna faced a different reality—choice was the hot-button issue.

PHASE ONE

The Early Evolution of Managed Care

During the early evolution of managed care, traditional HMOs boomed in membership and revenues. The growth was fueled largely by simple economics. Traditional HMOs had been around for years. However, starting in the mid-1980s, rising health care costs pressured employers to seek out cheaper alternatives and HMOs were able to provide coverage at a steep discount to what insurance companies were charging.

Basically, the traditional HMO unified the financing and delivery of patient care. One central feature was the requirement that patients stay within a tight network of doctors and hospitals, each of whom contracted with the HMO to provide services according to the HMO's treatment regimen. The HMO received a set premium per patient and forced health care providers to accept some of the financial risk associated with patient care. As a result, providers had an incentive to balance the cost of care against the likely benefits.

The HMO product was a reaction against the inefficiencies inherent in the health care indemnity model. Under the indemnity approach, employees were given coverage for medical expenses above a certain annual deductible. Employers sometimes took the risk of paying the future bills. Otherwise, insurance compa-

nies bore the risk in exchange for annual premiums from employers. In either case, the insurance companies were fundamentally
just traffic cops in the health care system. They processed claims
and paid doctors and hospitals.

The indemnity model was structurally biased in favor of rising
costs. Insurers were relatively invisible claims processors. Under
this arrangement, quality and levels of care were determined by
patients and doctors. Neither party to the doctor-patient relationship had an incentive to favor efficiency because employers
footed the bill. Any review of health care costs was principally ret-
rospective. There was little opportunity to be proactive about cost
reductions.

These inefficiencies in the indemnity insurance model created
an opening for HMOs. At the height of phase one, the cost differential between traditional insurers and HMOs was around 30 percent. Employers started giving employees economic incentives to
enter managed care in the form of lower out-of-pocket expenses.
Many employees were willing to accept a limited choice of doctors and restricted care alternatives in order to save money.

Initially, HMOs had little trouble getting costs significantly
below the norm for indemnity policies. By restricting their patients to a list of approved doctors, hospitals and other providers,
the HMOs interposed themselves as active intermediaries in the
market. This allowed them to aggregate patients into large pools
and demand volume pricing.

For example, an HMO could go to a local hospital and require
a large discount over the costs being billed to individual patients
under indemnity policies. The hospital often agreed because the
HMO was able to promise greater patient flow. By way of contrast, an insurance company had little control over where the patients it covered would seek care. Insurers therefore lacked the
negotiating leverage of the HMOs.

The opportunity for larger organizations to capture efficiencies drove many phase one deals. Companies got together to increase their patient population for greater negotiating leverage with providers and to spread overhead across a larger business.

Volume purchasing squeezed much of the easy juice out of the health care cost structure. The HMOs then deepened their relative cost advantage through the application of technology and sophisticated demographic analysis. In the indemnity model, doctors made care decisions on an independent basis. They generally worked with fairly few information resources and lacked the capacity to track outcomes. There was little awareness of whether treatments were cost-effective. HMOs changed that. They studied each element of the health care cost structure, eliminated unnecessary tests and searched for other efficiencies.

As a result of these and other measures, HMOs for a time operated under a big price umbrella. They were able to offer employers the option of covering employees at a much lower cost than under indemnity insurance. These simple economics drove the first phase of HMO growth, and, at the peak of phase one, the conventional wisdom was that everyone would end up in a traditional HMO.

The new emphasis on choice working its way into the market in the early 1990s was a watershed event. For Aetna, there were two practical implications—the rise of an alternative managed care model, known as "point of service," and the consequent segmentation of the health care benefits market.

Point of service essentially is a hybrid product that grafts choice onto the traditional HMO model. Under the new arrangement, members have the option of staying within a company's provider network. If that option is selected, care is delivered on the traditional HMO basis with patients paying only small co-payments for visits. However, if a patient chooses, he can go outside the provider network under a discounted "preferred provider organization" network or a traditional indemnity relationship. The patient pays a relatively large deductible and the managed care company picks up the majority of the remaining costs.

Even as point of service developed, the indemnity model also showed continuing vitality. Defections began to level off in markets with a mature managed care presence. A certain percentage of the population proved willing to pay more for more flexibility and control. Earlier notions about the eventual extinction of indemnity programs turned out to be overstated. Rather, the future health care benefits market would be segmented with various product offerings.

The new business model—analogous to bundled local, long-distance, cable and wireless telecommunications services—was for a single company to provide large employers a package of different products. Scale is an important element. Large employers with multiple sites in different states preferred to deal with a single benefits company for administrative convenience and cost efficiency. Yet they also wanted the ability to provide employees a range of alternatives. As a result, in phase two, breadth of product offerings became as important as sheer size.

This shift reinforced Aetna CEO Ronald Compton's view that a health care acquisition was a critical element in his company's transformation. Aetna had a strong foundation to face the new health care environment. The company had a successful indemnity and account-servicing track record, and a large customer base. However, Aetna had limited experience with point of service and other managed care products, which require different capabilities than the indemnity product. Managing point-of-service plans requires sophisticated modeling of patient care costs and effective cost containment programs. Extending into this new field independently would have been costly and risky.

After developing a picture of the market, Compton and the Aetna board made the judgment that a combination of Aetna and an able managed care company was necessary if Aetna was to bust out of its constraints. The acquisition analysis therefore entered a second stage, with the focus on potential targets.

U.S. Healthcare was an obvious acquisition candidate for Aetna. The company had a strong presence in its home markets, primarily in the Northeast, and a reputation for efficiency, with the highest operating margins of any major player in the managed care industry. A combination would bring Aetna the added capabilities it wanted.

After an initial approach was favorably received, negotiations opened in early 1996. As it turned out, Leslie Abramson, chairman of U.S. Healthcare, had his own reasons to favor a merger with a company like Aetna. As early as a year before the Aetna deal, Abramson saw a shifting market. Numerous competitors were crowding into U.S. Healthcare's lucrative Northeast markets. The company needed bulk to gain negotiating leverage over employers and providers, in order to defend its leadership role.

Moreover, the migration toward bundled managed care and indemnity products was already taking shape in the marketplace. Travelers Insurance and Metropolitan Life Insurance had joined their sluggish health operations in 1994 to form MetraHealth. Just a year later United HealthCare—a Minneapolis-based HMO with national aspirations—bought MetraHealth for $2 billion. This joining of a managed care company and an indemnity insurance expert was a seminal phase-two deal.

Abramson foresaw a market eventually dominated by five or six national players with broad product offerings. He wanted U.S. Healthcare to be one of the six, but his company lacked the resources for the fast nationwide rollout required to capture position. Nor was U.S. Healthcare experienced at managing indemnity products or multisite client relationships. Aetna, with its twenty-one-state network, offered a quick inroad to a national presence.

So, the strategic vision for an Aetna–U.S. Healthcare deal was apparent. Aetna would bring its size, national presence and multisite capabilities. U.S. Healthcare would bring its managed care expertise and technology. Together, the companies would have a formidable market presence and be in position to build a functional nationwide managed care network.

Selling a company also has a human side. Abramson had founded U.S. Healthcare in 1976 and had led it through two decades, from the early days to a 1983 IPO, on to a $7 billion market capitalization. He would be a major shareholder, a board member and a key adviser to the surviving company. Still, Abramson necessarily would have to give up considerable control as a result of an acquisition. After some initial misgivings, he eventually decided a combination with Aetna was too promising to pass up.

Under the terms of the deal, U.S. Healthcare shareholders would receive $34.20 in cash, 0.2246 of a share of Aetna Inc. common stock and 0.0749 of a share of a mandatory convertible preferred stock for each U.S. Healthcare share. The package was worth roughly $57 a share. This represented a premium to U.S. Healthcare's trading value—the company's stock closed at just under $46 the day before the deal was announced. The price represented roughly 20 times U.S. Healthcare's projected earnings for the next twelve months, on the low end compared to other recent HMO acquisitions. Further, most other HMO deals were basically acquisitions of additional membership. The Aetna–U.S. Healthcare deal brought Aetna both new members and management capabilities, making the price even more attractive.

However, this deal structure butted up against several of Aetna's Rosen's Cube constraints. For example, Aetna's cash needs posed a challenge with regard to the $5.3 billion cash payment to U.S. Healthcare shareholders. The cash made available by the sale of the property and casualty business would fund roughly $4 billion of that amount. Aetna's balance sheet was relatively strong and could support considerable additional leverage. From a theoretical standpoint, then, the company could fund the remaining $1.3 billion through borrowing.

However, there was a problem with this approach. Aetna planned to remain in the insurance business. Maintaining a favorable credit rating was therefore important. The interest payments from the acquisition and the capital needs of an expanded health care operation would likely consume a large portion of Aetna's cash flow. As a result, the Aetna board essentially faced a choice between reducing the company's dividend or borrowing the money. This raised a question. Would a dividend cut cause Aetna's shareholder base, accustomed to a relatively high dividend yield, to flee the stock?

One alternative, of course, would be to increase the $3.6 billion stock portion of the deal. However, Aetna's price/earnings ratio was considerably lower than U.S. Healthcare's ratio. A stock deal therefore would be substantially dilutive to Aetna's earnings per share. In essence, Aetna would be playing the old earnings-per-share game of the 1960s—high P/E buys low P/E—but in reverse.

The part-cash, part-stock deal that Aetna chose amplified this negative earnings effect with annual goodwill expense. To an extent, this goodwill expense is an accounting fiction. No cash drain is involved. Still, as a consequence, Aetna would not meet its earnings-per-share targets in the immediate future. Sophisticated investors would normalize Aetna's earnings per share for the effect of goodwill, but health care services companies trade based on earnings per share. The question for Aetna was whether investors would penalize its stock price as a result of earnings dilution.

Of course, all Aetna could do was make an educated projection of how the market would respond to a lower dividend and lower earnings per share. After exhaustive analysis, the judgment was that if the deal were properly presented, Aetna would experience a transformation in the eyes of investors from a low-growth value investment to a high-growth hot stock. If that happened, the company's price/earnings multiple would expand, making up for any fall in earnings per share. In other words, the pattern had to be broken to define a new vision.

These expectations were realized. Aetna benefited from some multiple expansion as a result of its shift toward health care. In September 1995, just before the company confirmed rumors of a planned sale of its property and casualty business, Aetna traded at 9.7 times estimated 1996 earnings and 8.9 times estimated 1997 earnings. A few days after the U.S. Healthcare deal was announced, the comparable figures had risen to 13.2 times and 11.6 times.

As a reward for his vision, Aetna's vice chairman Richard Huber was selected to succeed Compton as chief executive officer. Huber took over at the end of July 1997, just as integration problems with U.S. Healthcare became apparent. Smoothing the transition to a unified health care operation naturally became the first order of business, though Huber continued to be interested in expanding the scope of Aetna's health care business.

CONVERTS

A Creative Financing Tool

Creative financing reduced somewhat the negative earnings-per-share impact of the Aetna–U.S. Healthcare deal and was crucial in allowing Aetna to maintain its credit rating. In particular, as part of the stock consideration in the deal, Aetna opted to use a convertible preferred stock—an acquisition financing tool first popularized during the 1960s merger wave, refined to include a mandatory conversion feature.

As is often the case, the creative application of an existing idea sparked new interest. In fact, almost simultaneously, another of Wasserstein Perella's clients was involved in a major transaction funded with a similar mechanism. The particular

deal involved two cellular companies—AirTouch and CCI. We
represented CCI, which was already partly owned by AirTouch.
In the deal, AirTouch acquired complete control of CCI in exchange for a package of 28 percent cash and 72 percent convertible securities. These two deals put convertible stock back
on the acquisition radar screen. Over the course of 1996, some
$4 billion of mandatorily convertible securities were issued as
merger consideration.

Mandatorily convertible preferred stock is a hybrid of conventional preferred stock. The idea behind the conventional convert
is to raise capital more cheaply than would be possible with regular preferred stock. A regular preferred stock accrues an annual
dividend. Payment of the dividend can be delayed in a given year
but must be made before any dividend can be paid on common
stock.

By comparison, a convertible preferred accrues a lower dividend. To compensate investors for this loss, the instrument has
an option feature whereby the preferred stock can be converted
into common. The conversion ratio is typically set so that the effective price for the common is 20 to 25 percent above its trading
price on the day the convert is issued. Of course, a holder has no
incentive to convert at that price unless the underlying common
stock has appreciated above that level.

Mandatorily convertible preferred incorporates somewhat different terms than the conventional model. The Aetna instrument
is indicative. It pays a 6.25 percent annual dividend and is
mandatorily convertible after four years at $76.125 per share—
the issue price—plus accrued and unpaid dividends. Boiled
down, this and other terms created three possibilities. On the
conversion date, if the common stock price were less than the
convert's original issue price, the holder would bear the loss, offset by the past dividends received. The investor would not benefit
if the stock price varied in a defined band from the issue price to

22 percent higher, and would only receive the dividend. Finally, if the stock appreciated more than 22 percent, the investor would keep roughly 80 percent of the upside.

This kind of arrangement has benefits to an issuer if the underlying common stock price appreciates. Effectively, the mandatorily convertible preferred is a common stock, except the issuing company keeps part of the upside. If the stock declines, the holder bears the brunt. As a result, a company effectively raises cheaper equity capital, though the benefit is offset by the higher dividend on the instrument relative to regular common stock.

From Aetna's perspective, the mandatorily convertible stock had two specific benefits. First, both claims ratings agencies and credit ratings agencies, responsible for rating Aetna's ability to pay insurance claims and debt obligations respectively, usually treat a mandatorily convertible stock as common stock, not debt. As a result, Aetna's debt-to-equity ratios would be more favorable than if additional cash were raised through a debt offering.

Second, on the assumption that Aetna's stock price would remain flat or go higher over the next four years, the converts also reduced the earnings dilution that would otherwise have occurred if the same number of common shares were issued. In those scenarios, the convertible would be exchanged for fewer common shares after four years. The effective earnings per share therefore would be higher.

The Second Phase Continues

The second phase of managed care evolution, exemplified by the Aetna deal, continued into 1997 as companies partnered to compete in a world of choice. Shortly after the Aetna deal, PacifiCare Health

Systems acquired FHP and Foundation Health Corp. merged with Health Systems International, both in multibillion-dollar deals. Size and scope were the imperatives behind these combinations. Pacifi-Care became the country's fifth largest HMO serving nearly 4 million members across fifteen states. Foundation Health Systems, the product of the marriage of Foundation and Health Systems International, topped that with nearly 5 million members, vaulting it into position as the fourth largest HMO.

In March 1997, insurer Cigna bought Healthsource, a troubled managed care company whose stock dropped over 60 percent in 1996. The $1.5 billion cash deal was announced eleven months after the U.S. Healthcare acquisition and endorsed the trend toward cross-capability mergers.

Like Aetna's acquisition of U.S. Healthcare, these deals—and the promise of further consolidation—were favorably received in the market. Opportunities for continued revenue growth were viewed as limited and potential cost savings as a possible counterweight.

However, in the second half of 1997, the promise waned somewhat as a series of acquirers experienced integration problems. Not only Aetna, but also Cigna, PacifiCare and United HealthCare suffered disappointing results.

Part of the problem was endemic to the health care business—costs continued to increase at a faster rate than premiums. Problems of standardization also were significant for some acquirers. Different operating procedures, provider contracts and computer systems all needed to be lined up. The health care business, balkanized for decades, proved more difficult to integrate than expected.

However, the economic realities that had driven companies together still prevailed in the marketplace. Even at companies suffering through post-closing indigestion, executives continued to identify the acquisition of broader capabilities and wider geographic scope as critical to survival. Only the strongest plans would have the leverage to negotiate the shoals. Large companies have the power to demand concessions from doctors and hospitals, and the efficiencies to provide geographically diversified employers with low-cost, one-stop shopping. In addition, larger companies have the critical mass to sustain the necessary investment in technology that is required to manage the broad range of products.

Even as difficulties emerged in the marketplace, the deal imperative was underscored when rumors circulated in October 1997 that Prudential would be the next big insurer to reach out for a solution to its health care dilemma. Prudential reportedly placed its health care operations, a mixture of HMOs and indemnity operations in forty states, on the block. Like Travelers and MetLife, Prudential apparently decided to exit the health care business if a suitable acquirer could be found. Many of the very companies having difficulty with past acquisitions were mentioned as potential buyers, a striking testament to the perceived need for further strategic consolidation among health care benefit companies.

The Lone Wolf on Life Support

The same cost pressures that triggered the rise of managed care also changed the world for health care providers, whether doctors, hospitals or otherwise. In fact, for providers, the managed care companies have been the intermediate source of these pressures.

As a result of the rise and expansion of assertive managed care companies, the lone-wolf medical practitioner is on life support. Doctors have seen their presumptive authority over patient care wither. With much recrimination, they have joined managed care physician networks which regiment the kind of procedures and care they can dispense. In addition, many doctors are now paid a fixed cost per patient under a so-called capitation model. This has pushed some of the risk of providing care off on doctors. For a solo practitioner, the potential downside is substantial: a slightly higher rate of costly illnesses can significantly reduce a year's income.

One upshot of these market developments is that the size imperative has worked its way into the physician's world. The market has responded with a new model of health care practice, the "physician practice management" company, or PPM. These companies are consolidators. Initially, concerted acquisition programs allowed the industry leaders to expand rapidly. More recently, though, investors have begun to question whether growth has come too quickly and the stocks have fallen somewhat out of favor.

PhyCor was an early pioneer of the PPM model. The company was formed in 1988 by four former hospital executives and proceeded to acquire more than forty-seven large multispecialty practice groups, thirteen in 1996 alone. By the end of 1996, PhyCor had cobbled together more than 12,000 doctors into a single network with revenues of $770 million.

The specifics of PPM acquisition structures vary from deal to deal, but general characteristics do emerge. A company like PhyCor typically buys the assets of an existing group practice. The building, the computers and medical equipment become property of a new subsidiary of the acquiring PPM. However, the doctors remain independent contractors working for their practice group, which signs a long-term contract to provide services to the purchasing PPM.

This arrangement has several attractive features for doctors. A new holding company is set up to run an acquired practice, typically governed by a board with even representation for the PPM and the selling doctors. Representatives of the PPM have final say on budget issues, but the doctors control care regimens within the cost guidelines established by employers, managed care companies and other clients of the clinic.

With the size to spread costs over a wide network, a PPM also brings professional management and cutting-edge technology to the table. These are increasingly important in the world of capitation. Structuring effective contracts with managed care companies and employers requires a deep understanding of where costs come from, demographics and how to economize. Before the advent of PPMs, most practice groups lacked the size and sophistication to handle these issues independently.

Size also brings economies of scale, the ability to handle risk, and the leverage to negotiate with ever larger health care benefits companies. The economies of scale come from the bulk purchasing of everything from malpractice insurance to paper cups. Risk spreading is also more effective with a larger patient population; idiosyncratic developments with one or two patients have a less significant bottom-line impact. Finally, size brings negotiation leverage, which allows the PPMs to pull some of the money flowing to the managed care companies back into doctors' pockets.

For the PPMs, when stock prices were high, the attraction of acquisitions was clear. Terms varied, but an acquiring company typically was entitled to a percentage of the acquired group's future pretax earnings, ranging from 10 to 20 percent for a primary care practice and from 20 to 40 percent for a specialty practice. Inefficiencies in the market made this cash flow extremely valuable. Privately held group practices could be purchased for 6 to 8 times pretax cash flow. Meanwhile, though PPMs no longer traded at the sky-high 60-plus multiples to earnings they once enjoyed, they still traded in the market at around 20 to 25 times projected earnings.

This gap created an arbitrage opportunity. A company like Phy-Cor—which was trading at around 40 times projected earnings for 1997—could afford to pay a premium for a group practice in a stock deal. If PhyCor paid, say, 10 times earnings for a practice, and the future earnings were then valued in the market at even 20 times earnings, the company instantly added $10 of market capitalization for every $1 of earnings purchased.

Of course, success bred imitation. As more PPM companies entered the market and the prime practice groups disappeared, the spread between public and private market valuations declined. Earnings-per-share growth as a result became more difficult.

PhyCor is not the only player in the PPM market. FPA Medical Management and MedPartners have been particularly aggressive competitors. For instance, MedPartners, led by CEO Larry House, was founded in just 1993 and grew at a breathtaking pace. Again, acquisitions were the strategic tool. MedPartners acquired a number of other PPM companies, as well as smaller independent practice groups. The company took a leap in 1996, acquiring competitor Caremark International for $1.9 billion.

Many on the Street expected House to take some time in integrating Caremark into MedPartners, but he showed no sign of slowing. In 1997, MedPartners followed up on the Caremark deal with a $490 million acquisition of InPhyNet Medical Management, a Florida-based PPM. House made no apologies for his strategy. As he said at the time of the Caremark announcement, "We want to be superconsolidators."

MedPartners' aggressive acquisition campaign appeared to pay off in October 1997, when PhyCor agreed to acquire the larger company for nearly $7 billion in stock. The deal would have created by far the largest PPM in the United States. However, initial reaction to the deal was negative. Investors worried the price was too high and the integration too difficult. MedPartners' stock fell 17 percent, while PhyCor's stock was off 19 percent. Two months later, the deal collapsed.

Though the parties blamed cultural differences, it soon became apparent that MedPartners would not hit its numbers for 1997. The Street assumed PhyCor had gotten cold feet once it got an inside view of MedPartners. Investors pummeled MedPartners' stock down 45 percent. Nor was PhyCor immune to the downdraft. The company's stock fell 15 percent on news of a significant restructuring. In the space of a week, the consensus view regarding PPMs had shifted entirely.

The gloom regarding PPMs likely was overdone. While the failed merger certainly demonstrated the potential pitfalls in the deal business, the underlying impetus for physician consolidation remained.

More than half of all doctors still are self-employed and roughly two thirds practice in groups of less than three. These doctors face tremendous pressures in the new health care market. Yet only 7 percent of all physicians are affiliated with a public PPM.

From the PPMs' perspective, capturing the hearts and minds of doctors is the key to future profitability. Doctors control the allocation of as much as 75 percent of all health care spending, a $1 trillion industry. For these reasons, the trends certainly favor more acquisitions.

Hospital Empires

Doctors are not the only health care providers feeling the pinch as a result of the unfolding health care revolution. Hospitals likewise have seen costs rise and revenues decline as managed care companies and the government reduce reimbursement levels. Overcapacity plagues the system—even successful hospitals have trouble keeping more than 40 percent of their beds filled, the national average. As with doctors, the pressures have resulted in a profound consolidation, the creation of vast hospital empires from what once were proudly independent, locally run institutions.

Most of the 5,200 hospitals in the United States are not-for-profit organizations. Yet, these institutions are not immune to cost pressures, as can be seen in the trend toward mergers of hospitals affiliated with medical schools. Prominent examples include the completed merger of Stanford University Medical Center with UCSF and proposed merger of NYU with Mt. Sinai. Possessed of sterling reputations and state-of-the-art facilities, university hospitals nonetheless have a tough time filling beds in a managed care world. With a declining revenue base, the cost savings available from consolidation are necessary to survival.

However, the main driving force behind hospital consolidation has been for-profit, public corporations. Humana and Hospital Corporation of America were early pioneers. Columbia/HCA, which swallowed the hospitals of both of its competitors, then became the major force in the sector. Columbia now controls roughly half of the nation's 700 for-profit hospitals. Recently, though, the company has been racked by charges of impropriety and a federal investigation that is still running its course. The resulting turmoil has highlighted the significant public policy issues involved with introducing the pressures of Wall Street into the world of health care.

Richard Scott founded Columbia in 1987 with the backing of financier Richard Rainwater. Scott drove Columbia to $20 billion in revenues with a tough management style and aggressive acquisitions. At its height, the chain controlled roughly 350 hospitals, 550 home-health-care offices and many other managed care businesses.

Columbia made its first acquisition in 1988—two struggling hospitals in El Paso. More deals pushed Columbia to a portfolio of twenty-five hospitals by 1993. Then, over the next two years, Scott made the leap to national player. Two deals were key. In 1993, Columbia scooped up Galen Health Care, the spun-off hospitals business of Humana. The following year, Columbia bought Hospital Corporation of America. These two transactions grew Columbia to more than 180 hospitals.

A single-minded focus on costs and overcapacity propelled Columbia's growth. These two gravitational forces began to rip apart both for-profit and not-for-profit hospitals in the late 1980s. Like doctors, hospitals had become accustomed to a world where price was not an issue. Employers and the government footed the bill for health care and were relatively price-insensitive. America's health care system often adopted a "damn the torpedoes" approach to medical practice with high utilization of costly procedures, bloated hospital staffs and a hospital in every neighborhood. Incredible overcapacity was built into the system.

Hospitals experienced a rude awakening when employers, health care benefits companies and the government all began to cut reimbursement rates for care. Suddenly, competition for patients became a new reality. With too much capacity, price cuts became a necessary fact of life. Many hospitals began to bleed red ink.

Columbia's strategy, and the strategy of other publicly traded hospital companies, was partly a consolidation play. The companies would buy up a number of hospitals in a city or region, shut down some and reduce staff at others. Many not-for-profit hospitals also lacked the managerial capacity and experience necessary to survive in the world of health care competition. The trustees of such institutions, typically owned by local governments, churches or schools, sought out the expertise of Columbia and its competitors.

When it took over operations at a hospital, Columbia brought a bottom-line approach. Scott organized the company into regions. Regional heads were given ambitious monetary targets for cost reductions and revenue growth. Managers who hit the targets were rewarded with handsome bonuses; managers who missed the targets came under intense pressure. Bareknuckle marketing was introduced to a field unaccustomed to such things.

From a financial perspective, the formula seemed to work. Earnings skyrocketed, and Columbia's stock price quadrupled. Yet the approach also generated considerable negative publicity. Local politicians slammed the company for practicing "Wall Street" medicine, more concerned about profits than providing care to the poor or having a positive community impact. Medical professionals complained Columbia slashed costs to the bone, and then some. Instances of understaffing were highlighted as indicative.

Recently, government investigators have begun to focus on alleged fraudulent billing practices at Columbia hospitals and particularly in Columbia's home-health-care business. Critics argued these practices resulted from the pressure on financial results. Federal agents in Texas served search warrants against the company in March 1997. A number of Columbia executives were indicted and the company was sued after its stock price dropped in response to the charges. Columbia's board forced Scott and several subordinates to resign. Dr. Thomas Frist Jr., co-founder of HCA and former vice chairman of Columbia, was selected to replace Scott as CEO.

Frist pledged cooperation with the federal investigation and initiated an overall shift in strategy. Rather than be the largest, most acquisitive hospital company in the country, Frist planned to remake Columbia into a smaller operation focused on its core markets, perhaps by spinning off as many as a third of the company's hospitals. Of course, the federal and state investigations will have to run their course before it becomes clear whether this strategic shift will allow Columbia to survive and prosper once again.

Even before the Columbia scandal broke into the open, there generally was an increasing resistance to the sale of nonprofit hospitals to for-profit companies. When a nonprofit is sold, the proceeds typically go to the creation of a new charitable foundation. Columbia and other profit-making hospital companies argue that this benefit, plus future tax revenues generated by a switch to for-profit status, more than outweigh any social costs of converting a local hospital. Critics disagree. The main concern has been the commitment to providing care to uninsured patients and support to the community.

Yet the logic for consolidation of hospitals remains considerable. Too many beds, too much brick and mortar remains in place. Not-for-profit hospitals can only afford to run at a loss for so long before they must begin to look for alternatives.

Other for-profit consolidators besides Columbia remain in the market. Tenet Healthcare is one of the largest challengers. The company, formerly named National Medical Enterprises, went through its own near-death experience in 1993. Six hundred federal agents descended on the company's Santa Fe headquarters, the culmination of an investigation into the billing practices of National Medical's psychiatric division. Board member Jeffrey Barbakow stepped in to take over operations. He paid out more than $500 million in fines and settlements, then refocused the business on its core hospital operations.

A series of acquisitions have rejuvenated Tenet. The company purchased National Medical Holdings for more than $3 billion in 1995, doubling its hospital portfolio to near seventy-five. In 1997, Tenet acquired OrNda, the nation's third largest hospital company. Though Tenet now has over 125 hospitals, it remains a distant number two compared to Columbia.

In the aftermath of the Columbia scandal, it looked as if that would change. Tenet and Columbia were rumored to be in merger talks. Reflecting Columbia's troubles, Tenet management was expected to take over if a deal occurred. However, when Dr. Frist assumed the CEO job at Columbia, he put the merger negotiations on hold. A deal still may happen, but probably not until the financial impact of the Columbia investigation becomes more certain.

Regardless, hospital ownership will continue to concentrate in the future. Regulatory and political developments may shape the pace and scope of consolidation. Eventually, though, the cost savings possible with consolidation will push the trend forward.

Big Pharma

By almost any measure—aggregate dollar volume, global scope or otherwise—the pharmaceutical deals have been the most significant aspect of the unfolding health care evolution. Over the past ten years, the big pharmaceutical companies have taken part in a mammoth merger wave with two major peaks, first in the late 1980s and then in the mid-1990s. These deals have had a major economic impact, driving the combined market share of the top ten companies from 25 percent in 1988 to 34 percent in 1996. The social impact has also been widespread. Layoffs, research cutbacks and cost eliminations have altered the face of the industry. The implications for ongoing drug development are as yet unclear.

The merger bug bit the pharmaceuticals industry fairly late in the 1980s. In 1988, an attempted hostile takeover by Roche, a Swiss company, of Sterling Drug ended when Sterling fell into the arms of white knight Eastman Kodak for $5.1 billion. Similarly, a bidding war erupted the same year for A.H. Robbins Company. American Home Products ended up the winning suitor, leaving Sanofi of France disappointed.

This consolidation was triggered by an industry-wide drive to fill out sales and marketing capacity. The pharmaceutical industry was going global, and companies were doing deals to catch up. Even in the purely domestic deals, the desire was to gain more capacity to build market share.

TOP TEN PHARMACEUTICALS COMPANIES
(RANKED BY 1996 U.S. SALES, IN MILLIONS OF DOLLARS)

Company	Equity Market Value*
Merck & Co., Inc.	$134.1
Novartis	112.2
Pfizer Inc.	100.8
Bristol-Myers Squibb Co.	94.9
Glaxo Wellcome PLC	94.9
Johnson & Johnson	92.8
Roche Holding Ltd.	92.7
Eli Lilly and Company	76.2
SmithKline Beecham PLC	67.1
Abbott Laboratories	54.4

*As of January 1998.

The first merger wave crested in 1989 with two big deals—the $16 billion merger of SmithKline Beckman and Beecham, followed shortly by the $12 billion merger of Bristol-Myers and Squibb. In many ways, the SmithKline-Beecham deal was indicative of industry trends.

By and large, the 1980s were boom years for the pharmaceuticals business. Companies were able to raise the cost per prescription at rates faster than inflation and a number of breakthrough drugs inflated into billion-dollar-a-year revenue machines. As a consequence, even though the industry remained highly fragmented, the pharmaceuticals business was the most profitable sector of the American economy. Returns on equity outpaced the median for Fortune 500 companies by roughly 50 percent. Success motivated entrepreneurs to enter the industry with new start-up companies.

However, as the decade came to a close, things had begun to deteriorate somewhat. Patent protection was about to expire on many of the blockbuster drugs that had propelled earnings growth and stock market appreciation over the prior decade. In addition, escalating competition had shortened the profitable life of new drugs. Companies piggybacked on each other by turning out modifications of existing drugs. So, for example, ulcer medication Tagamet became a billion-dollar-a-year drug for SmithKline Beckman. Glaxo countered with its Zantac formulation, which claimed fewer unfavorable interactions with other drugs. Strong marketing pushed Zantac also above the billion-dollar mark in annual revenues.

The shorter life cycle of these and other drugs caused experts to predict diminishing returns from this kind of incremental innovation. Drug companies needed to develop entirely new blockbuster drugs, but few such innovations were in the lengthy approval pipeline.

This was precisely the pressure faced by SmithKline. Rumors that the company was a takeover target began to circulate toward the end of 1988, largely because of uncertainties surrounding the future of Tagamet. The company had risen to star status on the strength of the product. Yet despite spending hundred of millions of dollars annually on research, no successor had been developed. Sales of Tagamet were already declining and patent protection would expire in much of Europe by 1992. The American patent would last just a few more years, until 1994.

Beecham, on the other hand, owned a portfolio of strong over-the-counter brands like Tums, and had several promising new drugs in the pipeline, including a heart attack medicine and an arthritis remedy. However, the U.K. company wanted to beef up its U.S. marketing presence.

SmithKline's stock price shot up on continuing merger speculation, and the pressure grew. Within two weeks, matters came to a head and the Beecham deal was announced. The two companies would join in a stock-for-stock merger of equals. SmithKline's chairman, Henry Wendt, would become chairman of the combined entity; Beecham's chairman, Robert Bauman, would be the chief executive.

Bauman—the first American to run the British Beecham—saw increased size and breadth as critical to Beecham's future success. Increased research and development were necessary to fuel drug discovery. Drug companies already spent a much higher percentage of revenues on R&D than other kinds of companies. The expectation was that a major drug company would need to spend more than $500 million a year on research to be successful. Moreover, that amount would need to grow 10 to 15 percent higher each year. There would be dry spells where no significant developments emerged. Few companies in the industry could afford that level of expenditure on their own. Beecham and others faced an unattractive choice. Either gamble on a few seemingly promising areas, or work more slowly on the broad range of projects.

Many companies found neither alternative attractive. Growing larger through mergers, on the other hand, would allow the surviving company to support a larger combined research effort. The best projects from each company could be backed fully and discovery time slashed. This appeared to be the price of survival.

However, research costs were just part of the SmithKline

Beecham deal. The merger also had a broader strategic resonance. Many of the largest companies in the industry were European players—Glaxo, Roche, Sandoz, Beecham. While these companies were successful, they lacked a strong U.S. presence. The U.S. market accounts for roughly 30 percent of worldwide pharmaceutical sales. Building a beachhead in this market was particularly important because drug prices were unregulated in the United States, unlike the situation in other markets. As a result, U.S. sales of a drug effectively subsidized non-U.S. sales.

Hence, the international players had a donut hole to fill. They needed to crack the U.S. market, and acquisitions were one way in the door. Financial fluctuations—particularly the dollar's decline to postwar lows and the U.S. stock market swoon of 1987—lubricated the process.

The trend in favor of European suitors for U.S. companies first became apparent in the Sterling Drug bidding war. Roche made a play for the U.S. maker of Bayer aspirin and various prescription medications. However, Sterling Drug found white knight Eastman Kodak, a company interested in diversifying away from reliance on the photographic business. Sanofi had a similar experience with its failed bid for A.H. Robins. Beecham was the first company to succeed in jumping into the U.S. market, perhaps because it was led by an American.

From a U.S. perspective, Eastman Kodak's struggles with Sterling demonstrated the importance of having a global presence. The company lacked the global drug distribution network to boost international sales. As a result, Sanofi eventually gained a measure of vindication. In 1991, Kodak fashioned a global alliance with the French company. Then, in 1994, Kodak got out of the drug business entirely. The prescription pharmaceuticals operations were sold to Sanofi for $1.7 billion, the over-the-counter lines to SmithKline Beecham for $2.9 billion, and the diagnostic businesses to Johnson & Johnson for $1.0 billion.

As the 1980s came to a close, the cross-border imperative remained strong. In 1990, Rhône-Poulenc, a French chemicals and pharmaceuticals company, paid over $2 billion to acquire the Rorer Group, a U.S. drug company that owned over-the-counter brand Maalox and various prescription businesses. Glaxo, Sanofi, Sandoz, Roche and others continued to shop for merger partners. While the downturn of the early 1990s slowed the process, in time the European invasion would accelerate again during the second merger wave of the 1990s.

On the domestic front, the SmithKline Beecham deal opened the consolidation floodgates. Shortly thereafter, Dow Chemical announced a multibillion-dollar deal for Marion Laboratories. Dow would acquire control of Marion in stages over several years, with the first 39 percent acquired immediately for cash. Bristol-Myers and Squibb followed with their marriage. Each successive deal increased the pressure on competitors. Even companies like industry-leader Merck, which avoided major acquisitions, looked for strategic partners in the consolidating industry. Merck agreed to a joint venture with DuPont, which had spent more than $2 billion on pharmaceuticals research over the previous few years, and others.

However, the deals of the 1980s were just a first step in the consolidation of the global pharmaceuticals business. Even with all the billion-dollar matches, each of the top five companies in the industry had less than 5 percent of the total market. The pharmaceuticals business remained highly fragmented and ripe for further consolidation.

The Biotech Future

Intersecting with the consolidation among main-line drug companies, biotech companies—long the hot stocks of the previous decade—came under pressure when revenues and earnings failed to meet expectations for fast growth. One by one, the crippled companies were swallowed by healthier acquirers. The large pharmaceutical deals slowed to a trickle while companies focused instead on biotechnology. However, these deals were relatively small compared to the multibillion-dollar pharmaceutical mergers, and only obscured the larger undercurrents in the market. Biotechnology was essentially a sideshow, though an interesting one.

The pressure on biotech companies built up as a result of long years of predictions regarding a coming revolution. Biotech companies were routinely vaunted as the heirs to the future; their ability to identify and map genes, and engineer new drugs from plant, animal and human proteins, promised to unlock cures for cancer, heart disease and other ailments. Biotech also had potential applications to agriculture and livestock breeding.

By 1990, the promise of biotech remained, but developments were taking longer than hoped. Time and again throughout the early part of the decade, the approval of a biotech company's hot new drug would get held up by the FDA and its stock would plummet.

Biotech companies also faced an escalating cost for research, but lacked the stable cash flows of the big pharmaceutical companies. When the biotech start-ups stumbled, they began to look for partners to help bridge the gap between current cash needs and eventual revenues from technologies under development.

A smattering of such deals began to appear in 1986. Targets included Connaught Biosciences, Hybritech and Genetic Systems. However, none of these deals was large enough to generate much attention, and the deal flow really accelerated in 1990 with the landmark alliance between Genentech and Roche.

Genentech's situation was a classic example of the pressures imposed when financing an early-stage venture on Wall Street. Genentech founder Robert Swanson had turned to the public markets as a means to finance the realization of his vision—an integrated, independent pharmaceutical company built on the strength of biotechnology. He was not shy about advertising his ambitious goals for the company. Genentech, he projected, would generate $1 billion in annual revenues by 1990.

Setbacks contributed to Genentech's need for capital. The FDA approval process for the company's heart drug TPA had taken longer than originally expected. Moreover, initial sales of the drug, which came in at about $200 million in 1989, fell well short of expectations. The company had projected more like $400 million in annual sales for 1988, with annual increases thereafter.

By 1989, Genentech was looking for an escape valve, hoping to bleed off some of the pressures that had built up. The company also had identified more promising research opportunities than it could afford to fund. Basically, Genentech needed a stable, patient source of capital. Wasserstein Perella was hired in the summer of 1989 to help look for candidates.

Roche, on the other hand, was still hoping to realize its U.S. ambitions. The highly creative, entrepreneurial Genentech was an attractive partner. Negotiations began in the fall and a deal was announced in February 1990. Under the agreement, Roche would pay $2.1 billion for 60 percent of Genentech. The purchase would take place in two parts—Roche would buy 50 percent of the 84 million outstanding Genentech shares from shareholders and then another 22 million new shares from the company. The issuance of new shares to Roche would provide roughly $500 million in fresh capital to Genentech. Roche also would have an option to acquire the remaining 40 percent of the company in the future. The option, originally set to expire in 1995, was later extended to 1999.

The Genentech deal was viewed in the market as an endorsement of the industry's future at a time when investor sentiment had soured. Large pharmaceutical companies became interested in finding biotech partners. There was a fear that the few prime properties would be swallowed.

About a year after the Genentech deal was announced, American Home Products followed suit with its own acquisition of Genetics

Institute. Seeking to bolster its pharmaceuticals operations, AHP paid a steep premium in the $666 million deal. Again, the acquirer bought part of its initial stake from the public and part from the company itself. AHP, like Roche, would end up with an initial 60 percent stake and an option to buy the remainder of its target. Unlike Roche, though, American Home Products exercised its option in 1996, buying the remaining 40 percent of Genetics Institute for another $1.25 billion.

The Genentech and Genetics Institute deals set intriguing strategic precedents: the operational marriage of biochemical and biological research promised access to a fuller range of new products. Other deals followed. Many kept to the earlier pattern, that is, large pharmaceutical buys struggling biotech company. For instance, drug and chemical company American Cyanamid bought a controlling stake in Immunex.

However, not all deals involved an established pharmaceutical company as acquirer. Strong biotech companies also sought out partnerships as a way to consolidate their position. Chiron's acquisition of Cetus Corp. is the primary example. Financial distress again triggered the seller's interest in a deal.

Cetus owned a gene mapping technology known as PCR, but otherwise had been unable to convert promising technologies into marketable products. The company hit a wall in 1990 when the FDA delayed approval of its interleukin-2 cancer treatment. Shortly thereafter, with our help, Cetus began looking for a partner. Chiron eventually emerged as the winning suitor. Because it lacked the cash for a stock purchase, the deal was structured as a stock swap. Capital would be raised through the sale of the PCR technology to Roche.

This deal bought some time for Chiron and Cetus, but in 1994 the combined companies turned to much larger Ciba-Geigy for a cash infusion. The Swiss company bought slightly less than 50 percent of Chiron at an almost 100 percent premium to the prior trading price of Chiron stock. In addition, Ciba-Geigy committed to provide financial backing for future research.

A few fortunate biotech companies were able to survive and thrive as independents. Amgen was the most successful, effectively stepping into Genentech's shoes as the standard bearer for the publicly traded biotech companies. The company had what others lacked—two approved drugs, Epogen and Neupogen, generating significant revenues. In fact, the company was sufficiently flush with cash so that it could acquire a smaller rival, Synergen, for $262 million in a 1994 deal. The following year, the company weathered rumors of an impending takeover by Bristol-Myers Squibb.

By 1996, Amgen, along with the broader biotech industry, was back in favor. Amgen in particular generated $2.2 billion of sales, primarily on the strength of its two approved blood therapeutics. As a result of the strong performance, the company was rewarded on Wall Street with an overall stock market capitalization in excess of $15 billion.

Notwithstanding Amgen's relative success, the shakeout in biotech was to be expected. The frenzy to snap up the next big thing had led to a large number of publicly traded companies with little more than an idea and start-up capital. A number of these companies were bound to stumble. Some failed. Others still had strong science and just needed a boost.

The consolidation wave of 1990 to 1994 was indicative of a broad market realization that few companies could afford to go it alone. By and large, the new model has become a semi-independent entity within a larger company. The core of this model is the continuing expectation that biotechnology is the best hope to produce the next generation of blockbuster drugs. However, the equity market capitalization of the top fifty-one biotech companies, at roughly $56 billion, is just a fraction of the $1.2 trillion value of the top thirty-four pharmaceutical companies. Biotech may be the future, but its promise is not yet fully developed.

Recapturing the Distribution Channel

In the early 1990s, conventional pharmaceutical companies were much healthier than the biotech companies and had the capacity to act as "rich-uncle" strategic acquirers. However, in the same period, the big drug companies were having their own troubles. The sources of concern were both economic and political.

On the economic side, managed care companies were pushing for price containment, meaning the drug companies could no longer count on revenue growth from price increases. At the same time, President Clinton and other politicians were focusing unfavorable attention on the pharmaceutical companies. There was a real concern that legal limitations would be imposed on the companies' ability to price their products, as is already the case in many other countries.

Pressures associated with managed care had come to bear on the pharmaceutical industry. While companies struggled to fend off what they saw as a political threat, they also began to look for new was to compete in the managed care world. One answer emerged with three major deals between drug companies and pharmacy benefits management companies (PBMs).

Merck was the first mover. In 1993, the company agreed to pay $6.6 billion for distributor Medco Containment. The next year SmithKline Beecham announced a similar $2.3 billion deal to pick up Diversified Pharmaceuticals Services, and Eli Lilly bought PCS Health Systems, the benefits division of McKesson Corp., for $4.1 billion. Three other drug companies—Pfizer, Rhône-Poulenc Rorer and Bristol-Myers Squibb—formed a strategic alliance with managed care company Caremark International.

The rationale behind this rash of deals was simple: drug companies saw their control of the distribution channel for pharmaceuticals slipping away, along with their favorable margins. By acquiring the big pharmacy benefits companies, the drug companies hoped to recapture the initiative.

Only a few years old, the acquired drug distributors basically acted as middlemen. They catered to employers and managed care companies, with the idea of reducing the cost of providing prescription drug benefits. Costs were kept down in two ways. First, the pharmacy benefits managers bought drugs in bulk, so they were able to negotiate favorable discounts. Second, the PBMs maintained lists of preferred drugs for given conditions. Cost was a significant factor in making the list. Doctors in a managed care plan were then encouraged to select drugs from the list. If they instead selected a more expensive drug, the PBM might have its employees call in an effort to encourage a switch to equally effective but cheaper drugs.

During the 1980s, it was sophisticated marketing that transformed the $200 million drugs of the previous decade into $1 billion blockbusters. The key was the ability to market directly to doctors. If a company won over doctors to its products, it won market share. Once the doctor prescribed a particular drug, patients were unlikely to switch. For chronic conditions, a single prescription could mean a long-term revenue stream.

Companies consequently developed doctor-focused marketing systems. Salespeople were hired and trained to push product in one-on-one sales calls. Studies were commissioned to highlight the benefits of a particular product and presentations made at medical conferences. Many busy physicians lacked the time or inclination to do their own research regarding the latest developments in drug research. As a result, the drug companies themselves were often the source for information.

A doctor would wade through the competing claims of drug companies and select what seemed the best medicine. Though decisions generally were made aboveboard, abuses did occur. For example, one drug company designed a controversial, and ultimately withdrawn, program under which doctors could receive frequent flyer miles for prescribing a particular drug.

Of course, all this activity became increasingly less relevant with the rise of managed care. Many prescription decisions were taken away from doctors and put in the hands of the pharmacy benefits managers. By buying control of the PBMs, the drug companies hoped to recapture the ability to encourage doctors to favor their drugs.

Unfortunately for the acquiring drug companies, antitrust issues limited their ability to benefit from having captive PBMs. The first two deals—Merck-Medco and SmithKline-Diversified—gained government antitrust approval fairly easily. However, by the time of the third deal, political pressure had mounted. Lilly was forced to consent in advance to maintain an "open formulary," or a relatively liberal list of favored drugs. Competitors' drugs could not be excluded from the list. Moreover, Lilly was required to set up a "fire wall" between it and its new subsidiary so that it would not receive information regarding what other pharmaceutical companies charged for their drugs.

The Lilly restrictions eventually whipsawed Merck and SmithKline. Government antitrust officials reviewed their deals a second time, after the fact, as is permissible under antitrust regulations. Merck and SmithKline ended up accepting the same restrictions as Lilly.

Partly because of these limitations, the PBM deals have turned in mixed results. Lilly has fared the worst. In June 1997, the company cut the original $4.1 billion book value of PCS by $2.4 billion, taking a large one-time charge in the process. The charge was a tacit admission that Lilly had overpaid for PCS. Merck, on the other hand, has had good success with Medco. The company has gained market share and roughly $400 million of annual profitability, not even counting the separate profits of Medco. Analysts attribute the recent growth in part to Medco's influence. SmithKline Beecham also professes to be happy with its Diversified Services purchase.

As things turned out, though, recapturing the distribution channel was not as important as it once seemed. Political winds shifted, and the pharmaceutical industry was not regulated. In addition, the rise of managed care actually has turned into something of a boon for pharmaceuticals companies. Significant pressure on unit costs remains, but the new emphasis on preventive care has boosted unit sales, hiking revenues overall.

Jan Leschly

Since taking over as chief executive of SmithKline Beecham in April 1994, Jan Leschly has shaped the company into a global power.

Leschly has spent ten years at the epicenter of the pharmaceutical consolidation wave. A courtly Dane, he began his professional life not in the executive suites, but on the tennis courts, where he rose to be the tenth-ranked player in the world. When his tennis career came to an end, Leschly joined Danish pharmaceutical company Novo and began a fast-track rise to the top of the pharmaceutical industry.

Leschly moved across the Atlantic in 1979 to take a job at Squibb. He quickly stood out as a marketing and management expert. At Squibb, he oversaw the introduction of Capoten, a hugely successful heart drug which eventually grew into the second biggest selling prescription medication in the world.

By 1988, Leschly was president and chief operating officer of Squibb and was often mentioned as a likely successor to CEO Richard Furlaud. However, at that point, Furlaud decided to sell

Squibb to Bristol-Myers. Leschly was given the opportunity to stay on, but felt the odd man out. He resigned and spent a year at Princeton University studying philosophy and religion. Eventually, though, Leschly missed the action and excitement of running a business. In 1990, he joined SmithKline Beecham to run its pharmaceuticals division.

Having been through an acquisition in which one party predominated over the other, Leschly was determined to integrate the SmithKline and Beecham operations on an even basis. He spent the next several years putting the pieces together. Remarkably, sales and profit growth remained strong through the 1990s recession and transition of Tagamet to over-the-counter status.

The payoff for Leschly came in 1994, when he took over as CEO of the parent company. In keeping with his determined, aggressive style, he moved quickly to act on his strategic vision. He looked across the spectrum of the pharmaceuticals industry and saw a clear trend. Size and global scope were becoming critical. Only five or ten truly international players would emerge with the assets and capability to discover innovative new products.

SmithKline's acquisitions and divestitures of 1994 were the first steps toward preparing the company for this future. The acquisitions of Diversified Pharmaceuticals and the over-the-counter businesses of Sterling Winthrop dramatically expanded SmithKline's global distribution network. As a PBM, Diversified Pharmaceuticals provided a managed care distribution channel. Sterling Winthrop meanwhile offered strong international over-the-counter brands and, more importantly, an experienced international sales force to supplement SmithKline's overseas efforts.

Leschly followed the two acquisitions of 1994 with two major divestitures. Part of the Sterling Winthrop business, mainly U.S. OTC products including the rights to the Bayer name, were sold to Bayer AG of Germany for $1 billion. Bayer had long been after the American rights to its flagship brand, which it lost after World

War I. The Bayer deal was followed by the $1.5 billion sale of SmithKline's animal health division.

With the balance sheet reinforced from the proceeds of these sales, Leschly has focused on building an even broader research and distribution capacity. The main strategy since 1995 has been to build through a number of joint ventures. However, as the international consolidation continues, Leschly clearly has an eye on further potential acquisitions or marriages with other large pharmaceutical companies such as Glaxo Wellcome.

Cost and Capabilities

The biotech and PBM deals obscured the impact of cost pressures and shifting competitive landscape for a few years. Yet, even with higher unit volumes, slower revenue growth than in the past is a fact of life for drug companies. Mergers were necessary, both to build broader product lines with opportunities for cross-selling and to reduce the cost of drug development and delivery. As a consequence, a second major pharmaceuticals merger wave—a sprint of multibillion-dollar deals—kicked off in 1994.

The ability to reduce costs was one overriding concern behind many of the second-wave mergers. In general, the pharmaceuticals industry had significant embedded costs. Dozens of fairly large companies competed for pharmacy shelf space. Even the largest had single-digit prescription drug market shares. Each of the companies maintained an expensive sales and marketing operation, typically spending upward of 30 percent of revenues in this area. Hundreds of "detailers," expert salespeople, many of them doctors or pharmacists, visited doctors across the country pushing a particular company's offerings. Trimming these costs would be a major boost to profitability.

Broadening the product mix was also seen as an important goal. Managed care companies and other providers of health care benefits were themselves increasingly focused on efficiency and cost savings. Drug companies with wide product lines possessed a marketing advantage because they could offer one-stop shopping. Higher volume with single customers could translate into volume pricing for the customer and more efficient distribution for the manufacturer.

The twin gods of cost and capability were widely recognized across the spectrum of pharmaceutical companies. As a consequence, competition for merger partners intensified. Success came to companies willing to be creative, to break through the boundaries of conventional industry norms.

American Home Products, under the leadership of Chairman Jack Stafford, demonstrated such a willingness in its pursuit of American Cyanamid. Stafford defied convention on two accounts: in the normally clubby pharmaceuticals business, he launched a $9.2 billion hostile bear hug offer for Cyanamid, and he put a slug of goodwill on the combined company's books as a result of the all-cash deal structure.

AHP made its offer in August 1994. Stafford had been considering a deal with Cyanamid for some time. In fact, he and Cyanamid chairman Albert Costello had scheduled a meeting for the end of the month. However, Stafford was pushed to act more aggressively when word leaked of negotiations between SmithKline Beecham and Cyanamid. The two companies reportedly were considering a multi-billion-dollar swap of SmithKline's vaccine and animal health business for Cyanamid's prescription drug and consumer products businesses.

Of course, it was precisely Cyanamid's prescription and consumer products brands that Stafford wanted. Cyanamid, which had divested most of its chemical business in 1993, was an attractive fit for AHP. The company's generic business would fill out AHP's prescription lines and give it better position with managed care providers. In addition, Cyanamid's over-the-counter and consumer brands had received relatively little marketing and promotion attention. Stafford calculated that his company's sales force could pump up sales of these products.

The tactical situation required AHP to make a strong bid or no bid at all. Consequently, AHP's initial offer was $95 a share, all in cash, or a 50 percent premium to the previous closing price of Cyanamid's stock. Normalizing for the run-up in Cyanamid's stock price as a result of deal rumors, the premium was even higher. Yet the Street endorsed Stafford's strategy, bidding AHP's stock higher on news of the offer.

AHP's bid was widely viewed as an attempt to preempt other potential acquirers. The approach worked. Cyanamid's board pursued talks with SmithKline and others, but no other company was willing to top the bid. The price was full and few American companies were willing to consider taking on the amount of goodwill that would be created.

Still, Cyanamid's takeover defenses gave it some negotiating leverage. By continuing to stall and look for potential white knights, Cyanamid eventually teased an additional $6 a share out of AHP. Two weeks after the AHP bear hug, the parties agreed to a $9.7 billion friendly deal.

Clearly, the potential for cost savings was a critical foundation for Stafford's willingness to bid at that level for Cyanamid. Within the year, AHP announced plans to lay off 4,300 of the combined company's 74,000 total employees. Annual cost savings from the deal were estimated at $650 million, or 11 percent of combined overhead.

The benefits of these cost savings, and strong merger implementation, have powered American Home Products in the stock market. Adjusted for a subsequent split, American Home Products' stock was trading around $28 before the bear hug letter was made public in August 1994. In August 1997, the stock traded at approximately $75 a share. Over the three-year period, then, AHP has appreciated 39 percent a year, significantly outpacing the broader market.

AHP's sterling performance came despite the fact that the goodwill created by the Cyanamid deal initially reduced AHP's earnings per share. Fundamentally, the market saw the underlying economic sense of the deal, as Jack Stafford had predicted. The dollars-and-cents benefits of consolidation were underscored, only increasing the competition for merger partners.

Globalization Accelerates

Much of the pharmaceutical mating dance of the early 1990s took place on an international scale. From a strategic perspective, the result has been a dramatic extension of the existing evolution toward a global business model.

The cross-border consolidation picked up pace in 1994 and became highly visible. Many of the deals were sparked by the continuing focus among international drug companies on getting into the U.S. market. Roche followed its Genentech investment with another big deal. In 1994, the Swiss company bought Syntex, a troubled California drugmaker, in a $5.3 billion deal. The next year, Germany's Hoechst ended Dow Chemical's unsuccessful foray into the pharmaceuticals business by acquiring Marion Merrell Dow for $7.1 billion. Pharmacia cracked the U.S. market in a merger of equals with Upjohn.

International differences in accounting rules also have something to do with the fact that many U.S. targets have ended up with foreign acquirers. Despite AHP's pioneering willingness to take on goodwill, most U.S. drug companies resist the resulting earnings dilution. European companies, on the other hand, are governed by more favorable accounting rules. Goodwill is written off immediately and does not flow through the income statement. There is therefore no earnings impact, giving European acquirers a bidding edge.

However, the biggest drug company mergers and acquisitions of the past five years have been purely European affairs. Starting in 1995, each successive year brought another multibillion-dollar European pharmaceuticals deal. In 1995, Glaxo launched a successful $14 billion hostile takeover of fellow British company Wellcome. The deal created the world's leading pharmaceutical company in terms of market share. Ciba-Geigy and Sandoz followed in 1996 with a friendly $36 billion merger creating a new company named Novartis. Roche kept pace with its own $11 billion acquisition of Germany's Boehringer Mannheim, announced in May 1997.

The Novartis deal in particular underlined the tremendous changes taking place in the global pharmaceuticals business, and in the European view of corporate mergers and acquisitions. Valuing the deal based on Sandoz's roughly $36 billion market capitalization at the time the deal was announced, the merger with Ciba-Geigy was the largest in history.

Cost savings were central to the deal. This represents a dramatic shift. Until recently, European executives have resisted mergers as a mechanism for corporate restructuring. The pressure has been on maintaining full employment rather than boosting profitability. Over the last few years, the emphasis has changed. European companies, like their American counterparts, have started to feel growth concerns and cost pressures. The merit of mergers has become apparent.

Mergers have had a powerful catalyzing effect in the European pharmaceuticals industry, creating the opportunity for huge savings. The Novartis deal is the most dramatic example. As part of the deal, Ciba-Geigy and Sandoz projected $1.5 billion in annual cost savings as a result of reduced overlap. The news almost immediately added $12 billion to the combined company's market capitalization, which rose to $76 billion. Between March 1996, before the deal was announced, and October 1997, the combined market capitalization appreciated by nearly 100 percent.

Novartis was not the only case of major cost savings driving a European cross-border merger. Similarly, Glaxo and Wellcome promised over $1 billion of annual cost savings by 1998.

Research capacity is also an issue. Glaxo Wellcome plans a $1.8 billion R&D budget; Novartis will spend $1.6 billion a year. Clearly, the stakes in the global race for new drugs have been raised. Smaller

European companies see a more concerted assault on their existing products as the giants churn out better refinements. At the same time, the leading companies have a much greater ability to cover the research horizon, diversifying their research portfolio.

The focus on cost savings and greater geographic coverage continues to propel deals. In 1997, Novartis picked up an insecticide and fungicide business from Merck for $910 million. Rivals will join to challenge Merck and Novartis. The race is on to be one of the four or five companies that define the industry. As a result, more major marriages of middle-tier players are inevitable.

The Future

Across the health care spectrum, the need to consolidate will not go away. The entire industry has been reshaped by cost-driven mergers and acquisitions. Yet in the last several years, health care costs have continued to escalate at rates in excess of general inflation. The tension between equity, quality of care and technology is unresolved. Managed care companies, doctors and hospitals will face an ongoing struggle to react. Change is coming, but it will be imperfect and painful.

Part Three | # Doing the Deal

"*Nothing astonishes men so much as common sense and plain dealing.*"

Ralph Waldo Emerson, *Essays*

A Guide to the Players | 14

*"It is better to be making the news than taking it;
to be an actor rather than a critic."*

Sir Winston Churchill,
The Story of the Malakand Field Force

The process of translating a strategic concept into a successfully executed deal can be incredibly arcane and difficult. Even the best concepts can founder on the rocks of poor execution. Spurred on by a combination of high stakes and complexity, an industry of takeover advisers has developed over the last thirty years.

The intensity of big-deal M&A draws particular individuals who thrive under the pressure. Otherwise highly capable people find they have no taste for the roller-coaster binges of intellectual effort. It is also true that the best people at this business are very good and the dedication and professionalism are high.

Unfortunately, the process also attracts its share of hustlers and swaggering mediocrities who think that aggressive posturing is a substitute for talent. Moreover, the bundled services offered by large financial institutions don't necessarily promote excellence.

If you hang around the deal business long enough, you become accustomed to the cycle of boom and bust. A flush of adrenaline is generated when a deal is fresh. If you lose the sense of excitement and curiosity, it's time to leave the business.

Lawyers and investment bankers are the highest profile outside merger advisers, but many other professionals play important roles. Included in the mix are accountants, proxy solicitors, public relations professionals and even private investigators. In addition, institutional investors, arbitrageurs and business journalists are key players in determining which strategy appeals to "the market."

The Lawyers

Lawyers have been midwifing corporate combinations as far back as the nineteenth century. In 1891, for example, John R. Dos Passos, the author's father, reportedly earned a $500,000 legal fee for setting up a sugar trust.

Today, the legal team working on a large friendly merger or acquisition may have as many as fifteen or twenty lawyers, including corporate or M&A lawyers and specialists such as tax, environmental, employee benefits, real estate and intellectual property lawyers.

The split between M&A lawyers and specialists reflects the nature of mergers and acquisitions. Specialists advise with respect to the regulatory frameworks involved in a deal. M&A lawyers, on the other hand, have a more general expertise. They help to negotiate the contractual agreement between the buyer and seller and act as an interface with the regulatory world.

If a deal becomes hostile, the legal team involved necessarily gets larger. The use of litigation as a takeover tactic drives this expansion. A target company may file various lawsuits in an effort to stave off a hostile acquirer. Or a hostile bidder may use litigation as a tool to force the target to relax antitakeover defenses. Common grounds for litigation include antitrust, securities law, state antitakeover statutes and general state corporate laws regarding the fiduciary duties of board members. In the most actively contested deals, it is not uncommon for a single takeover contest to generate several lawsuits in various locations.

With the high level of mergers and acquisitions activity, corporate lawyers have prospered. In 1996, for example, the top ten law firms in the United States, ranked by gross revenues, brought in more than $4.2 billion of revenue according to a survey by *The American Lawyer* magazine. The same survey shows that partners in each of the top ten firms, this time ranked by profits per partner, on average earned more than $900,000 in 1996.

In a large merger or acquisition, speed is critical. For this reason, a handful of firms, primarily located in New York, have developed into leading players in the M&A advisory business. According to *Corporate Control Alert*, the top ten M&A firms, ranked for 1996 by frequency of involvement in M&A transactions, were:

TOP TEN M&A FIRMS

Firm M&A Volume Rank	1996 Revenues*	Profits Per Partner*	# of Lawyers*
1. Skadden, Arps, Slate, Meagher & Flom	$710,000,000	$990,000	1,032
2. Dewey Ballantine	201,500,000	650,000	380
3. Sullivan & Cromwell	346,000,000	1,330,000	395
4. Shearman & Sterling	324,000,000	815,000	560
5. Simpson Thacher & Bartlett	279,500,000	1,155,000	411
6. Wachtell, Lipton, Rosen & Katz	133,500,000	1,390,000	126
7. Cravath, Swaine & Moore	240,000,000	1,515,000	323
8. Fried, Frank, Harris, Shriver & Jacobson	184,000,000	615,000	361
9. Jones, Day, Reavis & Pogue	450,000,000	480,000	1,093
10. Weil, Gotshal & Manges	322,000,000	735,000	585

*Source: *The American Lawyer*

However, these statistics are misleading because they don't differentiate between the roles firms performed in the deals and the individual lawyers within the firms. Also, many other firms, including regional powerhouses, play important roles. Each of these major firms has a different culture and history.

Perhaps the most has been written about Skadden, Arps, Slate, Meagher & Flom. The firm was founded by Marshall Skadden, Leslie Arps and John Slate. The date on which the firm was founded—April Fools' Day, 1948—reflects something of the firm's early character: irreverent, unconventional, ambitious, yet a bit unsure of itself. From the start, Skadden had something to prove. Each of its founding members had been passed over for partnership at an old-line Wall Street law firm. When the three recruited Joseph Flom, fresh out of Harvard Law School, as their first associate, they described their joint venture as a "flier."

Notwithstanding the principals' enthusiasm, the early years at Skadden, Arps & Slate were lean. With only ten lawyers, the firm took on proxy contest work spurned by the more established partnerships. During this period, Flom emerged as the driving force at Skadden and worked on a series of high-profile contests that put the firm on the map, such as the successful defense of American Hardware Corporation against an insurgent stockholder who owned one third of the company's stock.

The proxy contests of the 1960s foreshadowed the hostile tender offers of the 1970s and 1980s. From a lawyer's perspective, a critical moment in the rise of the tender offer came in 1968 when the Williams Act was passed. The act amended the Securities Exchange Act of 1934 and was designed to regulate tender offers. Yet providing federal rules and regulations had the unintended side effect of legitimizing tender offer tactics, creating an entirely new field for takeover lawyers, who now had a set of rules to interpret.

Lawyers with proxy contest experience were well positioned to take advantage of this potential market. Flom and Skadden jumped into the budding M&A market without reservation in the 1970s, while other more established law firms hesitated. Flom in particular was sought out by investment bankers at Morgan Stanley, who felt their regular lawyers didn't have enough experience in the area. He was hired by Morgan Stanley to advise Inco on the 1974 takeover of

ESB. The success of that takeover led to a series of engagements, which in turn propelled Flom and Skadden to the forefront of the takeover movement.

The results were dramatic. Largely on the back of its M&A expertise, Skadden grew from ten lawyers in 1960 to over 1,000 lawyers in 1996. Along the way, Flom and his partners advised one side or the other in the large majority of blockbuster deals during the 1980s and 1990s.

As the firm grew, it branched out into other practice areas outside the field of takeover work. Flom used the leverage of the retainers Skadden received from takeover clients to do legal work in other fields. He then persuaded stars in these nontakeover fields to join the firm because of the breadth of its client network. Flom thus created his vision of the multioffice, multipractice firm of the future.

The early 1980s were heady times for Skadden. Takeover litigation was the legal frontier. Skadden was one of the more aggressive practitioners of scattershot lawsuits as a tactical maneuver and earned a reputation as a firm willing to take the gloves off for its clients.

In one of Flom's more famous episodes, he advised oil company Conoco on its 1981 defense against Seagram. Conoco eventually agreed to be acquired by DuPont, but not before Flom had fought a colorful rearguard action against Seagram. Under his guidance, Conoco sued to enjoin the liquor company's bid in North Carolina and Florida. Those states' laws arguably barred a liquor company from owning gas stations where the company's products were sold. Conoco managed to get several local judges to delay Seagram's bid. The effort was ultimately futile—Seagram had the injunctions overturned. Still, the tactic added to Skadden's reputation for creative advocacy.

The latest upswing in deal activity has demonstrated once again the immensely profitable nature of Skadden's core M&A franchise. According to *The American Lawyer*, in 1996 the firm earned gross revenues of $710 million and had average profits per partner of $990,000. Reflecting this success, the culture of Skadden is hard-charging. Lawyers and support staff routinely work through the night. When Friday rolls around, associates joke about being happy that only two more days remain in the workweek. On top of this, the firm has a low ratio of partners to associates. As a result, each partner benefits from the revenues of several other lawyers.

Yet there is a sense of camaraderie at Skadden of people who have been through the wars together. Flom's leadership and personality, the mix of ambition and creativity, ooze through the pores of the firm. They have beaten much of the white-shoe Wall Street legal world and are proud of it.

Today, Flom is in semiretirement, but his four key disciples control the bulk of the M&A deal flow: Peter Atkins, Roger Aaron, Morris Kramer and Finn Fogg. Each has a different personality. Aaron and Fogg are the consummate client counselors and handholders, Atkins a smooth, immaculately groomed adviser to boards, and Kramer a buzzsaw of creativity and energy. Skadden retains its reputation as a tenacious, powerful M&A presence. Or, as Flom puts it, "We're very strong. We're permanent. We're an institution." Flom is more than a distinguished lawyer; he has been a business prophet.

Fried, Frank, led by Arthur Fleischer Jr., is similar in structure to Skadden but lower-key. Fleischer, known for his combination of professional erudition and biting humor, sports three-piece suits and colorful patterned English shirts. The firm seems to recognize that being less intense has its attractions, and they take pride in their client relations. The M&A legal business' version of *Crossfire* is Skadden's Morris Kramer negotiating with Arthur Fleischer. The opening gambit is that Fleischer lectures precedent while Kramer attacks. They beat each other to a pulp, seeming to enjoy the sport, then their partners do the deal.

Skadden's main competition for the title of premier takeover law firm has come from Wachtell, Lipton, Rosen & Katz. Wachtell was founded a generation after Skadden, in 1965, by Herbert Wachtell, Martin Lipton, Leonard Rosen and George Katz, four law-school classmates from NYU Law School. The firm's founders made an effort to ensure a collegial environment. Only the best young lawyers were hired, and, unlike other firms, the expectation and hope was that every associate who remained committed to the firm would make partner. In exchange, lawyers were expected to work very hard and treat the firm as family, the center of life.

Indeed, the intensity at Wachtell may be even higher than at Skadden because of the sense of community, but the anxiety about making partner is less. Wachtell, Lipton chose to remain small and focus almost exclusively on takeover and bankruptcy-related legal work. As a result, Wachtell's staff of approximately 120 lawyers is a far cry from Skadden's 1,000, and Wachtell limits itself to a single outpost, a one-lawyer office set up in Chicago.

Beyond sheer size, however, Wachtell distinguished itself from Skadden in other more substantive ways. Throughout the 1980s, Wachtell refused to represent hostile acquirers. The firm's anti-takeover position proved an excellent marketing tool. The firm's lawyers inveighed against the "hostile two-tier, leveraged, bust-up" acquisitions of the time, lobbying in Congress, writing articles and giving press interviews to advance their views. The effort positioned Wachtell well with corporate CEOs worried about losing their companies to a takeover, and contributed to making Wachtell the pre-eminent hostile defense firm.

Along with Herb Wachtell the litigator, Marty Lipton is the star of the firm. He was born in 1931 to a middle-class family and was raised in Jersey City, New Jersey. After graduating from law school, Lipton spent a year working for a judge, then joined Selig & Morris as a junior associate, where he worked on his first takeover.

By the mid-1960s, Lipton had already developed a reputation in proxy contests. In the same year that he founded the Wachtell, Lipton firm with his three friends, Lipton worked on the contest for Illinois Central Industries. Later, the Tisch brothers hired Lipton for a series of high-profile deals in the 1970s, including the essentially hostile fight for CNA Financial Corporation, a financial services company. The network of friendships built from the contacts made in the early deals created a wide web of clients.

Lipton's prominence derives from his role as the first-call takeover defense lawyer for many CEOs. His masterstroke came in 1982, when he developed the poison pill defense. Essentially, the first-generation poison pill was a mechanism to make hostile takeovers too expensive. Existing shareholders were given special securities. If a raider then bought up shares and tried to merge with the target, the special securities held by everyone other than the raider would convert into a high number of target company shares. As a result, the raider would own a significantly lower percentage of the target. Over the next several years, Lipton evolved the strategy, and when the Delaware Supreme Court blessed the approach in 1985, Lipton and the pill were in great demand.

Wachtell, Lipton proved itself incredibly adept in takeover contests again and again throughout the 1980s. Though relatively small, as a takeover specialist, the firm was able to throw a dozen or more lawyers on a hot deal. Its comparative advantage was the combination of Lipton with an all-star litigation team headed by Wachtell. The heavy emphasis on defense work fed on itself: business came in, Wachtell lawyers demonstrated a penchant for coming up with creative strategies, and more business came in. The Wachtell lawyers also emphasized their willingness to cooperate with local firms, whereas Skadden, with its network of offices, was in competition with them.

As a further testament to the quality of Wachtell, Lipton's work, the firm often takes on clients for fees based on the size of a transaction, rather than hours billed. Wachtell lawyers argue they are integral to the successful resolution of the matters on which they work and should earn fees commensurate with the intense, complicated nature of the transactions.

The deal flow flooding through Wachtell's doors and its billing practices have made the firm among the most profitable in America on a per capita basis. Though the latest *American Lawyer* survey puts Wachtell at number 61 in terms of gross revenue—generating roughly $133 million in 1996—the firm brought in more than $1 million in revenue per lawyer and profits per partner averaged almost $1.4 million.

Lately, Wachtell has relaxed somewhat its stricture against representing hostile acquirers, mainly for large corporate clients. In 1991, for example, the firm took on AT&T as a client, advising the phone giant in the fight to acquire NCR, the computer company. However, Marty Lipton's phone still routinely rings with calls from CEOs under fire.

As compared to Skadden and Wachtell, Cravath, Swaine & Moore embodies a more traditional approach. Cravath—which can trace its roots back to 1819—has a premier reputation attributable to two characteristics. First, the firm has perhaps one of the most blue-chip client lists in America. Longtime Cravath clients include IBM, Chemical Bank (now Chase Manhattan), CBS, Time Warner and Bristol-Myers Squibb. Second, the firm has been able to develop legal stars who excel on high-profile matters, such as litigator Bob Joffe and dealmakers Alan Stephenson and Allen Finkelson.

The Cravath System was first declared by Paul Cravath in the early 1900s. By legend, his notion was to institutionalize the practice of law. In fact, he grabbed the bulk of the profits and had a supporting bureaucracy. Under his system, lawyers were to be selected based on merit rather than bloodline. Senior lawyers were to mentor and guide junior lawyers. Steady, capable advice was the goal. Partners would be added only through internal promotion, and lawyers passed over would be asked to leave.

Cravath now has roughly 375 lawyers, seventy-two of which are partners. The firm eschewed frenetic growth in the 1980s, though to a lesser extent than Wachtell. Partnership status is still revered. Unlike most other firms, where new associates basically are assigned work out of a pool, new Cravath associates spend the first several years working directly for a series of partners, each for an extended period. This Cravath System survives today, more or less as handed down, and has served the firm well. In the 1997 *American Lawyer* survey, Cravath topped the profits per partner list at over $1.5 million.

During the 1970s and early 1980s, Cravath played a relatively small role in the rough-and-tumble world of hostile deals. While many other old-time firms resisted becoming involved in such deals for fear of alienating clients, Cravath rarely faced the issue. The firm simply lacked the necessary staffing to handle takeover litigation because Cravath was heavily involved defending IBM against a government antitrust case. However, when the IBM case settled in 1982, Cravath came charging back. Today, the firm routinely is involved in major M&A transactions such as the 1995 Disney–Capital Cities/ABC merger and the 1997 Dean Witter–Morgan Stanley merger.

Sullivan & Cromwell, whose most famous leader was John Foster Dulles, is the quintessential Wall Street law firm. S&C often represents investment bankers such as Goldman, Sachs on deals. Regarded historically as somewhat stuffy, S&C has worked hard to modernize its practice by building up a specialized M&A team. Yet the conservatism of S&C has its advantages. For example, protecting directors of outside committees is one of the firm's strong points.

Simpson Thacher, led in recent years by former Secretary of State Cyrus Vance, has grown in visibility and prestige in the past decade. Presiding partner Dick Beattie, a former Marine Corps carrier pilot known for plain talk and sharp insight, has played a major role in the evolution. Beattie's early focus was on LBOs. During the 1980s, he often served as counsel of choice to KKR, most famously on the RJR takeover. Beattie has used this experience with KKR as a wedge to tout his firm as a dealmaker, and the effort has translated into a growing M&A practice.

Shearman & Sterling used to be dominated by its relationship with Citibank. Today, however, the firm is a major player in the mergers business on the strength of relationships with bankers such as Merrill Lynch and Morgan Stanley, their very strong international client base, and the deal savvy and mature judgment of presiding partner Steve Volk. Clients have been receptive. Volk represented Morgan Stanley in the Dean Witter deal and his firm has been involved in many other major deals of the 1990s—Bell Atlantic–NYNEX, Sandoz–Ciba-Geigy, and the fight for MCI, for example.

Recently, New York firm Paul, Weiss, Rifkind, Wharton & Garrison has become another major contender for merger work. The firm's corporate practice was built on business relationships developed by the firm's legendary senior litigation partner Arthur Liman, who recently passed away. His disciple Toby Myerson currently leads the firm's growing corporate practice, which is known for its international expertise and long-term client focus.

The New York takeover bar captured a commanding share of the M&A advisory business in the 1970s and 1980s. Proximity to the capital markets and investment professionals was partly responsible. Morgan Stanley fed business to Flom and then to Steve Volk. Henry Kravis came to depend on Beattie. Investment bank Lazard Frères became closer to Marty Lipton. A perception that the New York law firms had unique capabilities in the takeover field also contributed to their dominance.

Yet regional strongholds like Vinson & Elkins of Houston and Jones, Day of Cleveland crop up in major deals on a regular basis. These firms used long-standing relationships with the major corporations on their home turf to break into the deal business.

Vinson & Elkins, for example, has long enjoyed a national presence. The firm was founded in 1917 by James Elkins Sr., a Texas native known as "The Judge," and William Vinson. The pair built a thriving practice representing local oilmen. Swept along in the Texas oil boom, Vinson & Elkins bloomed into the nation's third largest firm in the late 1970s. When the Oil Wars flared, the firm naturally became a frequent M&A adviser. Though Vinson & Elkins' relative size has declined when compared to other large firms, it retains a strong position in Texas and is poised to take advantage of the next oil patch merger boom.

Jones, Day is no longer a regional firm. With more than 1,000 lawyers, the firm is a global institution, the second largest law firm in the United States. Still, Jones, Day's foundation is its status as a fixture in Cleveland and the greater Midwest. The firm has strong relationships with major industrial companies in the region and has levered these relationships to build a strong position.

Investment Bankers

As far back as J.P. Morgan's U.S. Steel deal of 1901, bankers have been involved in an advisory capacity in major corporate transactions. Morgan worked before the creation of the Glass-Steagall wall between investment and commercial banking. Consequently, he could wear several hats. He could loan money directly to clients—what we now think of as the commercial lender's role. He could raise capital in the markets, mostly debt and some equity, by arranging the syndication of securities, which is the corporate finance function of modern investment banking. He could also provide strategic advice to deal participants. All of which his successors at J.P. Morgan are able to do again today as a result of regulatory change.

However, the bank regulatory framework created in the 1930s for a time divorced commercial and investment banking. During the Great Depression and World War II, Wall Street was a relatively quiet place. In the immediate postwar years, investment bankers were kept busy raising the capital to fund the great American industrial expansion then underway.

The American M&A advisory business was limited during the 1950s and early 1960s. Acquisitions and mergers boomed, however, in the frothy stock market of the late 1960s, and continued to be strong into the early 1970s. In the process, the first M&A powerhouse was born—Lazard Frères & Co.

Lazard New York is one of three independent but affiliated Lazard Houses (the others being in London and Paris). The story of the Lazard Houses stretches back to the middle of the nineteenth century, when three brothers emigrated from France to America. They settled in New Orleans, where they founded a clothing store. When the store was gutted by a fire that swept the city, the brothers picked up and moved to the boomtown of San Francisco. They established themselves first in the dry goods business, but soon shifted to the more lucrative area of trading gold and currency. Eventually, they founded the three merchant banks with the same name.

None of the three Lazard brothers had a son. Control of the firm passed to David David-Weill, the son of Lazard cousin Alexandre Weill, who had joined the brothers early on in San Francisco. Under the guidance of David-Weill and others, the Paris bank grew into a major force. The New York bank, however, was not as successful. Into the twentieth century, Lazard New York was known chiefly for bond underwriting. Everything changed, however, in the 1940s. Among those fleeing Hitler's approaching shadow were André Meyer, a brilliant young partner from the Paris bank, and Felix Rohatyn, whose family came from Austria to New York via Casablanca and Rio de Janeiro.

In 1943, Pierre David-Weill—David's son—asked Meyer to take over management of the New York bank. Meyer, who had known Rohatyn's stepfather in Paris, later gave the young man a summer job; Rohatyn stayed on to become Meyer's chief protégé.

Perhaps before anyone else, Meyer saw that an investment bank could earn high margins by focusing on the M&A business—which required little committed capital. As one of Meyer's first directives, he shuttered the firm's retail operations; bond salesmen and the like were fired. Then, with an iron fist, the autocratic Meyer set about implementing his vision. By the mid-1960s, the transformation was complete. Lazard had earned a reputation as the "merger house" and, in 1968, Meyer was called "the most important investment banker in the Western World" by *Fortune* magazine.

Felix Rohatyn

The conglomerate wave of the late 1960s launched the rise of Felix Rohatyn. Rohatyn was born in Vienna in 1928, the son of prosperous brewery operator Alexander Rohatyn. Of Jewish heritage, the Rohatyns grew increasingly fearful of the Nazi presence in Europe in the early 1940s. The family fled to America in 1942.

Upon arriving in the United States, Rohatyn enrolled in high school. From there he went to Middlebury College and earned an undergraduate degree in physics. Rohatyn described his college experience as undistinguished: "The physics faculty and I both reached the conclusion that I did not have a future in the sciences."

Fortunately, Rohatyn had been working for investment bank Lazard Frères during the summer. The young clerk caught the eye of André Meyer one evening and was offered full-time employment. After a number of years as an apprentice, Rohatyn developed a reputation for technical financial skill and negotiating prowess. More importantly, he learned to deal with Meyer's explosive temperament. The two men—both expatriates—developed a strong working relationship.

While Meyer gave his young disciple an entrée into the world of finance, Harold Geneen would make Rohatyn into a superstar. Geneen started sending ITT's work to Lazard in the early 1960s. Then, in 1965, ITT bought Avis from Lazard. In the course of the transaction, Geneen was greatly impressed with Rohatyn, who from then on became ITT's investment banker. At the height of the relationship, Rohatyn worked side by side with Geneen—he would visit ITT's offices almost every day, and attended Geneen's brainstorming sessions at the Waldorf Hotel. Rohatyn advised on almost every major deal ITT did in the 1960s and 1970s—Bobbs-Merrill Publishers, Sheraton Hotels, Levitt & Co., Hartford Insurance.

Like Geneen, Rohatyn was attacked over the Hartford Insurance affair. Ultimately, though, after a lot of mudslinging by critics, he was exonerated. Rohatyn's reputation was further enhanced in the mid-1970s, when he teamed up with attorney Marty Lipton on the pro bono committee that saved New York City from insolvency. At the time, New York faced a budget shortfall of hundreds of millions of dollars—the culmination of years of spending more money than it was taking in. Banks refused to honor the city's bonds, and New York was on the verge of declaring bankruptcy. The situation continued in a progression from bad to worse. The governor brought Rohatyn and others onto the scene. Under their guidance, New York City slowly got back on its feet.

Meanwhile, Rohatyn's long relationships served him well. When takeovers surged again in the 1980s and 1990s, he emerged as the elder statesman of the profession. Although he publicly questioned the advisability of the leveraged transactions that were taking place, he was fully immersed in the new wave of activity. In the 1990s, he has retained a unique position as a distinguished public figure. He retired from investment banking in 1997 to become the U.S. Ambassador to France.

While Rohatyn and Lazard profited heavily from advising M&A clients, the major investment banks generally shied away from the business in the 1960s. Each had perhaps a few professionals assigned to the field, but the firms rarely charged clients for advice. The M&A practice was viewed as a tool to maintain underwriting relationships, a loss leader to bring in more corporate finance business.

However, by the early 1970s, M&A bankers at several of Lazard's competitors began to see the fee-generating potential of the advisory business and fought, both within their organizations and in the marketplace, to develop the business. For example, Morgan Stanley's M&A unit wanted to outdo Lazard. Their opportunity came in 1974 when Morgan Stanley was approached by Inco, a client of the firm seeking advice on its planned hostile bid for ESB. Morgan Stanley, like many investment banks at the time, had a policy of not handling hostile acquisitions. The fear was that to do so would alienate the firm's roster of blue-chip underwriting clients.

For a time, debate raged within Morgan Stanley. The M&A camp made three main arguments. First, Inco had come to Morgan Stanley for help. Offering advice was a matter of client service. Second, the underwriting business was suffering from declining margins. Fixed brokerage commissions, long a staple of New York's big investment houses, were on the way out. Third, and perhaps most importantly, hostile takeovers were an inevitable trend. If Morgan Stanley refused to assist clients in this area, its competitors would take up the slack. These arguments carried the day, and Morgan Stanley became a major player in the M&A business and built up an aggressive team.

In a symbiotic way, Goldman, Sachs, led by Steve Friedman, who eventually became the firm's chairman, benefited from Morgan's inroads. Goldman used its wide web of corporate relationships as the foundation for the leading takeover defense group. Friedman, combining intellect with a gracious manner, made Goldman an attractive safe choice for corporate executives.

When the M&A effort at First Boston seriously began in the late 1970s, the problem was how to crack the Lazard-Goldman-Morgan oligopoly. The solution was simple: first find the holes in the market, and then raise the stakes by outprofessionalizing the competition.

Specifically, Goldman focused more on company sales and the defense side. We went after the buy side for their clients. Meanwhile, fair or not, a good number of Morgan's clients were mad at the firm, mainly because of conflicts, or because they had lost a bid, or Morgan's aggressive manner chafed them. These companies were natural prospects.

The second stage was to professionalize the business. We expanded our M&A group, added industry specialties such as energy and insurance, formed an idea-creation unit and focused on products such as divestitures. Eventually, the old First Boston became one of the three M&A leaders. Our competitors then also built up. As a result, the industry was transformed.

Among the large leading firms today are Morgan Stanley, Goldman, Sachs, First Boston and Merrill Lynch & Co., and among the smaller banks Lazard and Wasserstein Perella.

M&A bankers provide a number of services, including:

- general strategic advice
- presentation of acquisition ideas
- tactical know-how
- negotiation support
- valuation and fairness opinions
- technical execution and coordination, and
- the structured sale of a business.

There is a significant difference in the quality of service offered by firms; even at the same firm, especially the larger ones, different bankers have varying merit. The small firms argue that they can provide excellence and focus, while the large firms sell market power and breadth of product. Quality does matter, as does attention. Some advisers go through the mechanical motions and others make a contribution.

Do bankers really make a difference? Often not. The role can be prophylactic, to insulate a board, or routine. However, sometimes bankers are the creative generators of the concept of a deal, a nerve ending in an informational web, or the catalyst in the implementation of a transaction. The best bankers have a large databank of comparative experience and can draw on it to ask the right questions, helping executives make their decisions.

An interesting recent phenomenon is the development of industry-specific M&A bankers. These professionals have many advantages in their in-depth knowledge of a business, but there are important limitations. Tactical considerations know no industry bounds, and it may, in fact, be useful to have a broader experience. Secondly, even the strategic issues can cut across business lines.

THE GESTATION OF THE BIG DEAL

Big corporate transactions have many fathers. First of all, one must distinguish between financial and strategic buyers, which go about the process in a different manner. Financial buyers, by definition in the business of buying and selling companies, are constantly on the lookout for potential targets. They are peppered with suggestions daily and tend to look opportunistically for the valuable "special situation."

Corporate acquirers, on the other hand, go through a more idiosyncratic process. A corporation may have been thinking about an industry for a while, but may finally act when a deal comes up. The DuPont-Conoco deal is a case in point. DuPont had been considering vertically integrating into oil for some time.

However, Conoco was not a specific target until the Seagram imbroglio triggered an interest.

Philip Morris' move into the food business followed a different pattern. They began by broadly studying the food business with us. Eventually, the analysis focused on specific targets. Dozens of candidates were screened based on both fundamental and financial factors. The process culminated first with the acquisition of General Foods in 1985 and then of Kraft in 1988.

Some deals are generated by a ricochet effect. An initial deal in an industry ripe for change will trigger shock waves. Competitors reassess strategy and a rush of deals results. For example, the Dean Witter–Morgan Stanley deal focused attention on the new structure of financial services. As a result, a sequence of deals followed, including the Salomon–Travelers Group transaction.

Finally, some deals are promoted by investment bankers. The better bankers realize their long-term interest lies in presenting deals with a strategic logic. Of course, some push deals for the sake of deals but few are effective. Ultimately, the investment banking business is about building a long-term trusting relationship with clients. In the end, management makes the decision; an investment banker only provides advice and offers options.

Accountants

Accountants provide three main services in the mergers and acquisitions area: tax structuring advice, financial structuring advice and due diligence assistance. The Big Six accounting firms are Price Waterhouse, Andersen, Coopers & Lybrand, Deloitte & Touche, Ernst & Young and KPMG Peat Marwick. Each firm has M&A SWAT teams, with members able to handle issues in all three substantive areas who are experienced with the rapid-fire timing of a major transaction. However, the Big Six may become the Big Four if the pending mergers of Coopers with Price Waterhouse and KPMG with Ernst & Young go through.

In the area of tax structuring, accountants, or alternatively tax lawyers, can be vital. The formal structure of a deal determines how it will be treated for tax purposes. The same substantive economic result often can be accomplished in many different ways, with dramatically different tax results.

The structure of a transaction also impacts the reported earnings of the combined company. Accountants attempt to navigate the complicated rules so as to preserve pooling accounting treatment where possible.

Finally, accountants can be helpful in performing due diligence review, which is closely analogous to the audit function. This review is performed prior to the closing of a friendly merger or acquisition and examines a potential merger partner's operations and finances. Site visits, management and employee interviews, and document reviews are typical. Lawyers and investment banks play a role, as do accountants, who typically review financial documents.

Very little, if any, due diligence can be performed in a hostile acquisition. Rather, the acquirer must rely on publicly available documentation.

Proxy Solicitors

Before the hostile takeover became an accepted part of the corporate arsenal, the proxy contest was the only way to wrest control of a company from incumbent management. Today, the proxy contest remains an important tactical option, sometimes used as a cheaper alternative to a full-scale bid and sometimes used to clear the way for a hostile bid. As part of the process, both an insurgent shareholder and incumbent management often hire one of the handful of firms, known as proxy solicitors, that specialize in lobbying shareholders.

In a proxy contest, an insurgent shareholder nominates a slate of directors and sends out an alternate proxy solicitation. The shareholders must then decide which slate to favor, the insurgent's or management's. The candidates who receive the most votes, whether cast in person at the company's annual meeting or by proxy, will be elected to the board. If the insurgents win a majority of the board, the new board in turn can replace incumbent management.

A proxy contest is a political campaign, with the attendant questions of "spin" and expenses of mailings and advertisements. The process is made somewhat easier when a takeover is involved because the bulk of shares generally will be held by a relatively small number of institutional investors and arbitrageurs. Still, at large companies, a significant chunk of shares may be held in small lots by individual investors. Communicating with shareholders, getting the message out, can be difficult.

A relatively small number of firms operate in this specialized field; D.F. King & Company and Georgeson & Company are the major proxy solicitors. These firms have the established infrastructure to conduct mass mailings to shareholders and concerted calling efforts. The machinery is used to collect votes in the regular, uncontested annual shareholder votes at most large companies, but really comes into play during proxy contests, when "fight letters" are mailed to shareholders.

One of a proxy solicitor's additional tasks is information gathering, generally known as a "stock watch" program. The identity of a company's beneficial owners can be critical in a contest because they have the right to vote a share.

It is not easy to uncover shareholders' identities, as many shareholders' stock is held in agent's names, typically by various brokerage houses. Major investors want their identities concealed while they accumulate a stock position to keep others from mirroring their actions, driving up the company's stock price. The process of gathering information about these shareholders is a sensitive issue for the proxy solicitor, as financial firms are expected to keep their clients' trading positions secret and are usually unwilling to supply the information.

Private Investigators

Potential takeover targets as well as some corporate raiders use private investigators as a tool for extracting comprehensive financial data, detailed biographies of executives and information about any possible wrongdoing on the part of their opposition. Investigators who handle this kind of work are not, however, the Sam Spade, rumpled-trench-coat type. Rather, a number of discreet, professional firms, staffed largely by former prosecutors, FBI agents and investigative journalists, have sprung up to serve corporate clients. Kroll Associates and Investigative Group Inc. are two of the largest.

New York–based Kroll Associates, founded by Jules Kroll in 1972 and acquired by O'Gara Co. in 1997 for $101 million, earned a reputation in the 1980s as Wall Street's private detective. In the early days, Kroll worked mostly for financial printers, ferreting out improper conduct by employees. When the takeover boom hit in the 1980s, however, Kroll recognized the value of information to takeover targets. Capitalizing on this profitable business, Kroll Associates has grown to have several hundred employees in thirteen countries, not counting hundreds of regular subcontractors. The company has more than $50 million in revenues.

Though the firm prides itself on discretion, involvement in a number of high-profile takeover contests during the 1980s generated considerable publicity for Kroll. In the 1984 contest for Phillips Petroleum, for example, a court ruling—later reversed—temporarily barred Kroll from gathering information on Boone Pickens. Pickens later complained that Kroll Associates had amassed a thick file on him, a copy of which the firm reportedly would sell to any Pickens target for $500,000.

Kroll had a major triumph in the United Kingdom when it contributed to the successful defense of ICI from Hanson PLC, a major conglomerate. Kroll uncovered allegations that Lord White of Hanson had bought a string of racehorses with company money. The embarrassing revelation took some of the wind out of Hanson's bid, which the company eventually withdrew.

Several years later, in 1989, Kroll Associates reportedly helped Avon Products defend against Amway Corp. and financier Irwin Jacobs. Six days after filing its original bid, Amway did a dramatic about-face, withdrawing its offer. According to newspaper accounts at the time, Kroll had uncovered a number of pending lawsuits against Amway and possible insider trading by two of the company's executives.

Kroll Associates uses two basic investigative techniques in the takeover field. First, the firm's computer analysts, largely recent college graduates with strong technical training, delve into public and proprietary databases of information. The goal is to build a complete picture of a subject, which can be used to assess the ability to raise capital for a bid and to anticipate tactical maneuvers. A survey also might turn up information regarding a raider's past bankruptcy, criminal conviction or other embarrassing misdeed.

Second, Kroll employs former FBI and CIA agents, investigative journalists and the like for field investigations. This can involve calling former employees or acquaintances, various forms of surveillance and locating assets. Of course, the abuse of any detective system can easily misfire. Overall, detective firms are best used for "due diligence."

The Market

The parties to a deal and their advisers attempt to structure the most advantageous, appealing transaction possible. For the buyer, or for merger partners, the goal is a transaction that will be applauded by shareholders and the market. More specifically, the hope is that current shareholders will grant any approvals that are necessary to execute the deal. Second, the market price of the surviving company hopefully will rise, both in the near term and the long term, the ultimate blessing.

For most large companies engaged in a merger or acquisition, the base of shareholders is made up of two key groups: institutions and arbitrageurs. The perceptions of these and other shareholders are shaped in part by the business press.

Institutional Investors   Institutional investors control a major portion, often a majority, of the stock in America's Fortune 500 companies. For example, institutions own roughly 57 percent of GE's outstanding common stock and 54 percent of IBM's. In the aggregate, institutional shareholders own more than 40 percent of the publicly traded corporate equity in the United States. These large stakes, combined with a number of developments over the past fifteen years, give institutions a major say in the future of most corporations.

The world of institutional investors is well populated and diverse. However, the players can be arranged into four main groups: the public-employee pension funds, the private pension funds, mutual funds and insurance companies. Public-employee pension funds were the most visibly active in the 1980s. For example, the giant California Public Employees' Retirement System, known as CalPERS, developed a reputation as a tough and independent shareholder. Not content to act alone, CalPERS and similar funds were instrumental in forming the Council of Institutional Investors to advance their interests.

With a fiduciary duty to serve the interests of pension holders and few loyalties or ties to corporate America, the public pension fund managers tend to focus on short-term performance. They push companies to maximize shareholder value and often pressure management to accept merger proposals if a concrete better alternative is not on the near-term horizon.

The Council of Institutional Investors

The Council of Institutional Investors has been a driving force behind the effort to hold managers' feet to the fire over poor performance. The group was formed in 1984 at the behest of California State Treasurer Jesse Unruh and other leaders with responsibility for large public pension funds. Now with 103 pension funds as members, the group speaks for institutional investors with the responsibility for investing more than $1 trillion.

During the 1980s the council actively battled against greenmail and other defensive tactics. The feeling among pension funds was that these measures unduly entrenched poor management. For example, the council flexed its muscle in the battle over the Phillips recapitalization. Pickens, company representatives, Icahn, Boesky and others were grilled in advance of the shareholder vote. The sessions contributed to the feeling among pension funds that the plan was unfair and led to the defeat of the original recapitalization proposal.

In the 1990s the council has targeted companies on its annual list of underperforming companies. The council's main weapons in its struggle have been publicity and the combined voting power of its members in proxy contests. No CEO wants his or her company to appear on the council's list of target companies. Newspapers generally run stories on the list and CEOs who appear more than once rarely last long. The council also takes a more active role in specific situations. In the past, it has coordinated attempts to oust managers or reform corporate governance provisions.

Because the council sometimes opposes incumbent management, its membership tends to be heavily weighted toward public-employee pension funds and university endowments.

Corporate pension plan managers tend to be more supportive of incumbent management than their public-employee and union counterparts. Observers generally attribute the trend to the relationship between the funds and their corporate parents. A corporate fund manager often faces direct or indirect pressure from senior management not to vote with outsiders or sell stock into a hostile tender offer. CEOs, frustrated by the market's short-term view, have directed their captive pension plans to take a more long-term approach. Recently, the Labor Department has put pressure on corporations to take a more active role in managing their pension funds. However, corporate pension plans still lean toward management on controversial questions.

Mutual funds and other asset managers hold a growing share of America's financial assets. In terms of relative activism, these institutions tend to fall somewhere between the public and private pension funds. Mutual fund families that serve individual investors tend to be more focused on near-term performance than corporate pension funds. However, with the rise of 401(k) retirement plans, corporations often have the ability to favor particular fund families by designating them as providers for the plans. Other asset managers often depend on corporate pension plans for direct investments. These groups consequently have reason to avoid alienating corporate America, and their activism is tempered.

The constant inflow of capital to institutional investors in the 1990s has increased the pressure on them. With fresh billions to manage each year, it becomes more challenging to deliver strong investment returns. Beating the market is difficult when investing on the scale required of managers at CalPERS and other groups.

Rather than actively trading stocks, many investment groups now focus on trying to improve company performance through active shareholding. The institutions are, in other words, attempting to reunite ownership and control, repairing the divide observed sixty years ago by academics Berle and Means.

Of course, like a single individual shareholder, a single institution rarely carries enough weight to impact a large corporation. A handful of institutions, on the other hand, may have the combined voting power to be decisive. However, until recently, institutions were hampered in their ability to act together. Under federal securities regulations, an institutional shareholder was required to file a proxy statement with the government and mail it to all fellow shareholders before seeking support from other institutions.

These rules were changed in 1992. The new proxy rules allow shareholders to talk without filing any proxy materials. Only a shareholder who is seeking actual proxies or who holds a large percentage of a company's stock must file proxy materials. Shareholders also may announce how they intend to vote on a matter and advertise their position without first mailing materials.

The impact of the new rules became apparent soon after they were implemented. A series of boardroom coups in 1993 and 1994 were widely attributed to increased pressure from activist shareholders. CEOs were forced out at Westinghouse, Sears and IBM.

With their new power, institutional shareholders play a major role in corporate strategy. They are lobbied in proxy battles. Advisers and executives focus on their response to a proposed merger or acquisition. In a hostile deal, institutions often sell their stock after the initial run-up in price, happy to take the sure gains. However, increasingly, institutional investors hang in until the end and decide outcomes, particularly in the case of large deals.

Arbitrageurs The practice of risk arbitrage involves buying the stock of a takeover target after a deal is announced. Unless the market expects a higher bid, stock in a company with a deal pending often trades at some discount to the offering price, reflecting the risk that the deal may collapse or not all tendered shares will be accepted. Arbs buy the stock. If the deal goes through, they make a profit off the spread. Even with narrow spreads, the profits can be significant under the right circumstances. First, the faster a deal closes, the higher the returns. Second, returns can be enhanced further with leverage. Third, if another bidder comes along with a higher price, the arbs make even more money.

By the end of a successful offer, a large portion of the trading float is in the hands of the arbitrageurs, in a medium-size deal, as much as 50 percent of the shares. Thus any offer must be structured to contemplate their needs. In addition, if a competing bid is made, the arbitrageurs often play a decisive role in determining its success.

Arbs are the ultimate short-term investors. They focus on maximizing the value of their investment over the briefest period possible. Each day a deal is open, interest accrues on their margin loans and returns fall. As a result, when a company's stock is concentrated in the hands of arbs, they begin to put pressure on management to deliver fast results. The arbs barrage managers and advisers with phone calls, work the press and do everything they can to advance their narrow self-interest. The key, from management's perspective, is to understand the goals of the arbs and keep in mind that much of what they say often is nothing more than bluff and posturing. On the other hand, in some situations, the arbs do carry the deciding vote. Therefore, it can be dangerous to ignore their presence.

From an arbs' perspective, success depends in part on the ability to judge how quickly a deal will go through and whether a new bidder will come along. Information gathering and analysis are critical elements of the process. Arbs provide liquidity for institutional shareholders and others who would rather have a guaranteed return than a chance at a slightly higher return. The more arbs in the market, the narrower the spreads become.

During the 1980s, few deals fell apart and bidding wars often erupted. Risk arbitrage was extremely profitable. The market became crowded with arbitrage funds, set up as investment partnerships, and most investment banks rushed into the arbitrage game. Estimates put the total money invested in deals as high as $18 billion.

Risk arbitrage received bad press after Ivan Boesky's arrest. A tough period of low deal flow followed in the early 1990s. Then, in the latest merger wave, the prevalence of stock deals has made the business more complicated. As a result, arbitrage is once again a profitable but relatively quiet corner of the market. Total arbitrage money in the market has been put somewhere between $6 and $10 billion.

PROFILE

Robert Rubin

While Ivan Boesky chose a flashy style, most successful arbs operated below the public radar. Their names rarely appeared in the press and they almost never granted interviews. Rather, they were content to ply their trade out of the public eye. Before moving to Washington, D.C., Robert Rubin, now treasury secretary under President Clinton, was the classic arb.

Rubin was born into a New York City family with long Democratic Party traditions. He graduated near the top of his class from Harvard University. He then studied at the London School of Economics for two years. On his return, he attended Yale Law School, graduating in 1964.

After two years as a Wall Street lawyer, Rubin definitively decided the law was not his calling. He landed a job at Goldman, Sachs in the equity arbitrage department. There he worked under the tutelage of legendary Goldman chairman Gus Levy, the man who professionalized arbitrage.

Rubin proved to be a gifted arbitrageur. Highly analytical, Rubin would pore painstakingly over deal documents. A yellow pad was a constant companion. There were always questions. What was the chance the bidder would raise the cash needed? Would the government block the deal on antitrust grounds? Rubin would constantly question his co-workers and search through the documents for answers.

By 1974, Rubin was Goldman's chief arb. He ran a desk that took positions in as many as 250 deals a year and was recognized as one of the most professional. Most deals worked well, but some did not. In one month in 1979, his traders reportedly ran up losses that exceeded the firm's entire profits in its best year. On balance, though, the small arb operation was tremendously profitable. The unit was regularly the second most profitable at the firm, behind the M&A department. Therefore, the arrest of Rubin's partner, Robert Freeman, for securities law violations was a shocking event. Throughout, however, Rubin's personal reputation remained untarnished.

In 1984, Rubin moved from the arbitrage desk to oversee Goldman's foreign exchange and options trading operation. He promptly turned the business around, winning respect within the firm.

Outside Goldman, I served with Rubin on the takeover legislation panel advising Congress. He'd always be promoting reasoned dialogue, though an undercurrent of firmness was evident.

These skills as a consensus builder eventually led his partners to elevate him to co-chairman of the firm. He served in that position for two years before joining the Clinton administration, where he has been the most effective treasury secretary in recent years.

Public Relations

Public relations experts are having an increasing impact on M&A transactions. In the world of M&A, maintaining a strong, consistent story serves several purposes. First, it can help convince investors and research analysts that a prospective friendly deal will be beneficial. Perception can be as important as reality, and getting the story out early may allow the participants to define the terms of debate.

Second, in a contested situation, image can have an impact. From a target's perspective, all the public relations in the world will rarely deter a well-funded, determined bidder willing to pay cash. However, the perception of a bidder can be important, especially in stock deals or ones subject to regulatory approval or litigation. Shareholders naturally are concerned to know the character and history of the people whose performance will determine the future value of the stock.

Morale is also crucial to a takeover fight. As in any contest, a defense team functions best when the members believe in the worth of their struggle. Furthermore, regulatory bodies and courts do, as a practical matter, keep an eye on the media, and the "rapacious villain" role is not desirable. Image is important, especially on issues of how long a court should extend a pill.

In an effort to get favorable coverage, public relations professionals sometimes selectively "leak" information to the media or grant "exclusives" to a journalist the night before a breaking event. Although often attractive to the PR adviser, who gets points with the reporter who is given the story, there are serious issues with this approach. First, of course, are the legal and ethical issues. Second, other reporters may be alienated.

Overall, a number of potential pitfalls exist in implementing a public relations program. Consistency of message is sometimes a problem. Company executives may have views different from those of public relations people. The key is to ensure that the public relations professionals' agendas match with the company's. Tone is also a matter of concern. Like all advocates, public relations people can lapse into the hyperbolic in defense of their clients' interest. The approach can backfire.

Ideally, a communications program should be ongoing. Institutional investors and other major shareholders hold critical votes in a takeover contest. Developing a trusting, strong relationship with this constituency can provide powerful defensive leverage.

From a bidder's perspective, public relations can serve to defuse potential roadblocks. Political opposition and perception can make it harder to close a deal. If not careful, a bidder can be cast as a carpetbagger, a liquidator of businesses or a threat to local communities. On the other hand, these images can be countered with an effective communication plan.

Grand Metropolitan's 1988 hostile bid for Pillsbury provides a classic example. Under the tutelage of Linda Robinson, Grand Met—a British company—launched its bid from Minneapolis, home base to Pillsbury, rather than from New York or London. The announcement was followed by a round of meetings with local reporters and politicians. Designed to convey Grand Met's commitment to maintaining a strong presence in Minneapolis, the strategy played well. Local newspapers ran favorable stories under banner headlines. Pillsbury, the hometown team, felt outmaneuvered.

Robinson received positive reviews for her work with Grand Met, but was faulted for her handling of Ross Johnson's RJR bid. She took an extremely active role in the deal. Failure taints all participants. Robinson was, therefore, attacked for the terrible press Johnson received, particularly a *Time* magazine cover story that cast his bid as "a game of greed." Unfortunately, visibility is a two-edged sword. Limited publicity is sometimes the best policy.

Kekst & Company, founded in 1971 by Gershon Kekst, is often cited as the leader in the field of financial PR firms, which includes Hill & Knowlton, Robinson Lerer & Montgomery, hotshot newcomer Sard Verbinnen & Company, and crisis intervenor Clark and Weinstock.

Today's stock deals depend on market reaction even more than cash takeovers. Beyond any direct effect, image also affects a board's will to fight in a contested deal. Since an essential part of offense tactics is to crack the willpower of a board, Kekst and his competitors are experiencing a boom.

PROFILE

Gershon Kekst

Gershon Kekst—the dean of the financial public relations community—is an anomaly in his business. With an understated approach and discernible aversion to press clippings, Kekst is far from gregarious. He speaks in hushed, barely audible tones and describes himself as shy. Yet he has had a role in many of the major deals of the last twenty years. Memorable clients have included Henry Kravis in the RJR Nabisco takeover, Martin Davis in Paramount's defense against Viacom, and Jim Manzi in Lotus Development's defense against IBM.

Born to Hebrew school teachers, Kekst retains an intellectual, professorial air. He happened into the field of financial PR by something of a coincidence. The firm's first office was in the same Manhattan office building as Skadden's offices, and Kekst managed to get a number of early referrals from Joe Flom.

The first such referral involved a company called Sterndent, a maker of dental equipment. A group of investors—including the heirs of a well-known Jewish philanthropist and some Arab partners—made a takeover offer for the company. Flom was hired to defend the company. He brought in Kekst. Together, the two came up with a strategy that became known as "the Jewish dentist defense." They reasoned that many dentists, Sterndent's customers, would not want to be involved with a company partially owned by Arab investors. They conceived an advertisement that played up the investors' ethnicity. Sure enough, complaints poured in. The approach also drew some criticism as xenophobic, but is credited with helping to turn back the bidders.

Kekst keeps his edge by offering broad strategic advice and maintaining a bond with corporate chief executives. To be iconoclastic, when he competes for business his advice is often "Do nothing" as his competitors frantically scramble for nonviable creative ideas.

Corporations keep Kekst on retainer. As with Flom and Wachtell, the money bought a kind of double insurance policy. Kekst would be available if something happened, and would be neutralized as a resource for raiders. If a big deal is in the news, Kekst is quite likely at the center of the action.

The Press

The business press acts as an increasingly ubiquitous interface between companies and investors. As in politics, the first story about a deal often defines the terms of debate and can have a significant impact on how institutional investors and arbs view the transaction. To an even greater extent, the business press shapes the view of individual investors who often lack the time or inclination to dig below the surface.

The rising tide of mergers in the 1980s and a long bull market have brought an increased interest in business news. More competition crowded into the field and television became a factor with the advent of CNBC. Meanwhile, the mainstays—*The Wall Street Journal, The New York Times, Business Week, Forbes* and *Fortune*—upgraded their coverage of mergers and acquisitions.

Today, even more news outlets exist. CNN and others have added channels to compete with CNBC. Online business news reaches more homes each month. For strength of impact, though, *The New York Times* and *Wall Street Journal* still predominate.

Of the two papers, *The Wall Street Journal* has the strongest combination of professional reporting and in-depth, sophisticated business news. The *Times*, with more limited space for business news, tends to cover stories on a more focused basis. Both receive their share of criticism. People in the investment community have been treated differently and have their individual complaints. Friction is understandable. Being the subject of press scrutiny is a rather remarkable experience, even for someone sympathetic to journalists.

Much of the criticism is attributable to misunderstandings on the part of interview subjects. For this reason, very clear ground rules are extremely helpful. Terms of art like "for background" or "not for attribution" mean different things to different people. An interview subject should understand their meaning in context before proceeding. Another practice which causes confusion is that reporters sometimes will conduct an interview, then use quotes months or years later.

To a certain extent, though, friction cannot be avoided. Journalists and those they cover simply have different agendas and perspectives. In the nature of things, a series of positive stories is likely to cause some reporter to gun for a negative story as a contrarian "scoop." Trading favors such as access or information for favorable coverage may not be the answer. A company's competitors of course will lobby reporters just as hard as the company. A strong relationship with reporters therefore is never bulletproof. Moreover, reporters don't necessarily control their final product. Editors can change the meaning or slant of a story with a headline or new opening paragraph.

Norman Pearlstine

Norm Pearlstine, currently the editor-in-chief of Time Inc., is the father of modern business journalism. Before joining *Time* in 1995, Pearlstine spent twenty-three years at *The Wall Street Journal*, first as a reporter, then as managing editor and executive editor. He guided the paper's editorial staff during the heyday of the 1980s merger boom and was responsible for reshaping coverage of the M&A business.

Pearlstine cut his teeth as a reporter working out of the *Journal*'s Dallas office. He then spent a number of years living the itinerant life of a rising star reporter—first in Detroit, then Los Angeles, then Tokyo. Pearlstine was appointed the Tokyo bureau chief in 1973. From that platform, he helped found *The Asian Wall Street Journal* as the paper's first managing editor. After a two-year intermission as an executive editor of *Forbes* magazine, Pearlstine was lured back to become the *Journal*'s national news editor. He rapidly rose to become managing editor, a job he held from 1983 until 1991.

Pearlstine left a considerable mark on the *Journal*'s pages. He organized the paper into its current three-section format in 1988 and expanded news coverage. But, most of all, he professionalized the paper. Page-one special reports became a regular feature. Beat reporters were encouraged to develop the expertise necessary to cover complicated economic and business issues. The best of the *Journal* was second to none. Jim Stewart's reporting, for example, on mergers and the insider trading scandal was recognized as the best in the business.

As the *Journal* rejuvenated, a star system developed, with the key reporters becoming celebrities and the lesser reporters resentful, creating internal friction. Critics contended that this desire for fame at times eroded some of the paper's objectivity, as reporters looked for notches in their belts rather than a balanced story. Pearlstine, however, deserves considerable credit for pushing the paper to a new level of excellence and excitement.

Pearlstine left the *Journal* in 1992 to try his hand at media ventures. In 1995, he was lured back to journalism by Time Inc., where he has editorial responsibility over a powerful magazine portfolio, including *Time, Money, Fortune, People* and *Sports Illustrated*. Under Pearlstine's tutelage, the magazine group was shaken up, many of the editors replaced, and the business is thriving.

The goal from the perspective of company management and their advisers is to maximize the chance that a company's story will receive a fair hearing in the press. Here, it is important to keep in mind the constraints faced by journalists. Print journalists have deadlines. They are under constant pressure to turn out material. Television journalists face an even shorter time frame. In this environment, there is little time for research. Sometimes goodwill can be generated by providing background material to journalists, but this approach is sure to backfire if the material is biased or hackneyed. Journalists are by nature skeptical and are likely to uncover the other side. Full disclosure or no disclosure usually is the best policy.

The first story on a subject can have a large impact, and news cycles can take a day or longer to turn. It is important, therefore, for a company to have its position reflected in the early story. Reporters generally are good about giving the affected parties a chance to respond for the record. However, the nature of most print deadlines is such that journalists are likely to call during hours when most businesses are closed. Making a contact available after hours therefore can be critical. In fact, the more negative the story, the more likely a call will come in around 6:00. If there are errors in the story, editors almost always fiercely defend their reporters.

Like all professions, journalism has its mixture of dedicated professionals, superficial sensation seekers and people who miss the point. As always, the thrill of a scoop is exhilarating, and the dream of being the next best-selling author an objective. Therefore, treating reporters with respect but caution is most professionals' advice.

The Price | 15

"What is a cynic? A man who knows the price of everything, and the value of nothing."

Oscar Wilde, *Lady Windermere's Fan*

The ultimate judgment in mergers is whether to pay the price. To rationalize that decision, buyers go through a bevy of pyrotechnics, with reams of paper consumed in obscure calculations. All the analysis is directed at answering a simple question: Should the bidder offer a higher price? The pressure becomes particularly intense in a competitive process with more than one bidder.

Buying companies is like participating in an art auction. At the end of the day, the losers think the winner overpaid and, if there are ten potential buyers, the bidder in fifth place seems the most reasonable. Of course, he hasn't bought anything. Meanwhile, the losers often spend time denigrating the wisdom of the buyer.

Truth, here, is not only elusive, but intensely subjective. It may well be the price paid by the buyer makes perfect sense for it and none for the fifth-place finisher. For example, Shell Oil could pay more than its competitors for the Belridge Oil properties because Shell had superior recovery technology.

To further confuse the calculus, it usually takes a long time to figure out whether a buyer overpaid. A large part of determining success comes not only from the price at which an asset is bought, but how it is run in the future and how well the subsequent opportunities the deal provides are exploited. No one can foretell the future and every business is different. The best a bidder can do is to collect the data and make a judgment as to the appropriate price. To maximize the chance for a positive outcome, a buyer tries to understand the dynamics of a company, analyze its characteristics and then finally look at future value.

Fundamentals

A common mistake buyers make is to leap into the morass of evaluation without first thinking about context. The first three rules of merger valuation are: fundamentals, fundamentals, fundamentals. First, the overall timing of a potential investment needs to be thought through. Are we at the peak of a bull market or the bottom of a bear cycle? Even if the target were a great company, a purchase in September of 1929 may not have been wise. Second, a review of industry fundamentals is important. A good company in a bad industry is likely to be dragged down to the level of its peers. Finally, a thoughtful analysis of each key market and product in which a company participates goes a long way. What really drives the business? Particular issues worth considering include:

- the business environment and applicable government regulations
- the impact of the business cycle on the business and a recognition of the current stage
- geographical spread and country risk
- cost structure, including materials and labor
- the ease of financing the business and the permanence of capital availability
- the state of facilities and capital investment status and requirements

- competitors and potential entrants, with an eye on comparative strengths
- channels of distribution and outlook for change
- characteristics and needs of key customers
- price flexibility, inflationary expectations and margins
- strength of management, ages, experience and depth
- technological position and record of research and innovation
- brand support, advertising and promotion
- legal risks and potential liabilities
- opportunities for expansion

The process of fundamental analysis deserves more than lip service. Quantification without a clear articulation of premises is absurd, merely a garbage-in, garbage-out exercise in eighth-grade math.

Quaker Oats is a good example of the role of these fundamental drivers. In 1984, the company purchased Stokely–Van Camp for $220 million. Some analysts called the price too generous, but by 1990 the deal would be hailed in a *Business Week* article as one of the "standout acquisitions" of the 1980s. Gatorade was the hidden gem in the deal. Stokely had sold the sports beverage line mostly in the Southeast and lacked a coherent marketing strategy. Looking at the fundamentals, Quaker saw an opportunity.

Ticking down the list, CEO William Smithburg saw a strong but underutilized brand, room for geographic expansion and channels of distribution similar to Quaker's other lines. Gatorade was a brand he could grow.

On this basis, Quaker bought Stokely, then sold everything but Stokely's pork-and-beans line and the Gatorade brand, reducing Quaker's net purchase price to $95 million. Distribution and marketing were the focus for the next five years. Quaker bumped ad spending, and in particular targeted sports promotions and athletic endorsements as key opportunities. The acquisition paid off phenomenally well. Sales grew at a 30 percent annual rate through 1989. In that year, Gatorade's operating profit of $125 million accounted for roughly one fifth of Quaker's total. Competition from Coke and Pepsi emerged in the 1990s, but Gatorade remained a billion-dollar global brand.

The Gatorade deal stands in stark contrast to Quaker's more recent Snapple acquisition, which may go down as one of the worst deals of the 1990s. Quaker bought the business in 1994 for $1.7 billion and sold it two years later for just $300 million. In the interim, Quaker absorbed $100 million of losses from Snapple, and Smithburg quit as CEO.

Of course, hindsight is perfect, but a number of fundamental problems with the Snapple business made it an unlikely target for a repeat of the Gatorade success. Snapple's juice and tea beverage concept had exploded in popularity over the previous several years. However, around the time Quaker bought the business, sales growth was slowing and competition growing. In fact, Quaker bought Snapple on a downward blip in its stock price following a horrible third-quarter earnings report.

Further, the plan to integrate distribution of Snapple and Gatorade presented tough challenges. Snapple was distributed mainly by a network of small independents. This reflected a major difference in Snapple's and Quaker's primary distribution channels. Quaker focused on grocery stores and other large outlets, Snapple on convenience stores and gas stations. Mastering each channel required different skills.

Comparing Gatorade to Snapple underscores the extent to which fundamental operating issues define the success or failure of a transaction. Clearly, price cannot be understood in isolation. Problems cannot always be foreseen, but a fundamental analysis can go a long way.

Warren Buffett

The investment record of Warren Buffett—the "Sage of Omaha"—is a testament to the value of fundamental analysis. Stock in his investment company, Berkshire Hathaway, has appreciated a phenomenal 27 percent a year over a period of thirty years, far outstripping the performance of broad market averages. Berkshire Hathaway is now one of America's twenty largest companies.

Buffett owes this success not to skill as an operating manager but to investing skill. He credits much of that skill to his years under the tutelage of Benjamin Graham, the co-author with David Dodd of the seminal 1934 tome *Security Analysis*. Published in the midst of the Depression, Graham and Dodd's book faced an extremely skeptical audience. Few investors were interested in putting money into stocks. Yet, over time, the work became recognized as the foundation text of fundamental analysis.

Buffett's exposure to Graham began in college, when he read Graham's *The Intelligent Investor*. Buffett was taken with Graham's analytical approach and enrolled in Columbia Business School in 1950. At Columbia, Buffett soon distinguished himself and came to be Graham's star pupil. He learned how to analyze a company's financial statements, how to sniff out fraud, how to measure a company's "intrinsic value."

The secret, according to Graham, was to remain objective. His portfolio had been badly scarred by the Crash of 1929 and the ensuing market slide. Having survived that experience, Graham emphasized the importance of a long view. Historical performance over a number of years, investigated through financial ratio analysis, was the arbiter of value. Current trading prices were not.

In 1956, Buffett returned to Omaha and began his career as an independent money manager. He raised money from friends and family, and on the strength of recommendations from Graham. Buffett proved incredibly adept at managing money. Following Graham's precepts, he would buy up major stakes in companies that were trading below their intrinsic value. He racked up a decade and a half of superior returns. Then, in 1971, he liquidated his investment partnerships. On the winding up of the partnership, Buffett received $25 million and a controlling interest in Berkshire Hathaway. He turned to running the company on a full-time basis.

When Buffett acquired control of Berkshire Hathaway, it was a failing New England textile company. However, Buffett looked past the warts and saw the cash-generating capability of the business. He installed professional management, then used the Berkshire cash flow to fund investments in other businesses. In this fashion, he built up a major portfolio of diversified businesses.

Buffett has had stunning successes. He tripled his investment in General Foods when it was bought out by Philip Morris in 1985. He helped fund Capital Cities' successful purchase of ABC. Major stakes in Coca-Cola, Gillette and the Washington Post Company have paid off handsomely. Of course, Buffett has had his share of troubling setbacks. An investment in USAir fared poorly, and an investment in Salomon Brothers earned only a modest return when Travelers acquired the company in 1997. On balance, though, Buffett's returns have been staggering.

The essence of Buffett's approach—a refined Graham and Dodd analysis—is deceptively simple. His concern for fundamental financial analysis remains. However, numbers must be understood in a context. Buffett invests only if he sees a strong business behind the financials.

This analysis takes place on two levels. From a strategic perspective, Buffett looks for companies with a "great franchise." In the 1970s these were newspaper and broadcasting companies.

Not only did they meet the threshold condition of being cheap in the market, they also had strong market positions with little competition. In the 1980s and 1990s, Buffett shifted to consumer products companies with strong brands and market share. Coca-Cola and Gillette are examples.

In addition to a strong strategic position, Buffett looks for able managers he likes and admires. When he finds a company that meets all these criteria, he buys stock and holds.

Picking good companies is not the only key to Buffett's success. He brings considerable insight, and his reputation also contributes to his success. Managers and board members are flattered to have him as an investor. Even people sitting across the table from Buffett in a negotiation get a charge from dealing with him. This aura—and an understated, but tenacious style—work in Buffett's favor.

Buffett also knows when to sacrifice a pawn. When we negotiated the sale of ABC to Capital Cities, Buffett realized that the television network was a prize and was willing to be flexible on the issuance of warrants to clinch the deal, even though he philosophically disliked issuing warrants.

The Body Count

Within a context, financial numbers do sing a song to the sensitive listener. They are certainly an important tool in conducting a fundamental analysis. Yet accounting is limited and flawed, notwithstanding its central role in business. The accounting rules are part good-faith best effort to describe economic reality and part counterintuitive arcana, full of vagaries and inconsistencies. The challenge is to filter the bad information from the good, to uncover the buried bodies: Why are the numbers presented in this form? What was the objective of the management? How do these numbers relate to the fundamental analysis of the company? Then the numbers and ratios need to be cross-compared to those of competitors.

To begin to understand a company, the first step is assembling a databank—information provided by the company, all public filings, including exhibits, all news articles for five years, and all recent security analysts' reports about the company and its competitors. For financial information, a buyer should start by reading the footnotes, where the interesting information is buried. It is in the notes that a company will explain its policy regarding revenue recognition and depreciation and amortization. The notes often will contain a company's explanation of restructuring and other one-time charges, debt repurchases and the like.

Once a buyer develops a preliminary feel for the numbers, the question becomes whether any buried bodies remain hidden. The three deceits of buried-body accounting are overstated earnings, managed earnings, and hidden assets and liabilities. Recognizing these patterns, accounting figures can be massaged into useful data.

Pumping Up the Bottom Line   Because so much attention is paid to reported earnings, pumping up the so-called bottom line is common. A company can use one of three basic techniques to accomplish this goal. Revenues can be boosted; expenses can be pushed off into the future; one-time gains can be triggered.

BOOSTING REVENUES   If expenses are held constant, higher revenues trickle down to the bottom line on a dollar-for-dollar basis. Current revenues can be boosted either by shifting future revenue to the current period or by fabricating additional revenues.

Under U.S. generally accepted accounting principles, or GAAP, revenues can be recognized only when they have been both earned and realized. Revenues are earned when a company provides goods or services to its customer. Revenues are realized when the customer in return provides cash or another asset, such as a binding promise to pay that is likely to be fulfilled. Fuzzy areas abound, for example, when refunds are available or when the obligation to pay doesn't have much bite.

This revenue recognition test is highly subjective. As a result, a continuum exists. Some companies take a conservative stance, understating their revenues. Other companies take an aggressive approach, overstating their revenues. The most common blowup is when shipments to customers who distribute a product are pumped up so that the pipeline is filled to overflowing. Eventually, there will be excess returns, but the company will already be sold.

PUMPING SALES

The MiniScribe Fiasco

The now-defunct MiniScribe Corporation is a classic example of a company that got too aggressive with the recognition of sales. MiniScribe was a high-flying technology company of the late 1980s, run by "Dr. Fix-It," as Mr. Q.T. Wiles was known. Wiles, who also served as chairman of high-tech investment bank Hambrecht & Quist, had come to MiniScribe in 1986. At that time, the company was deep in crisis. It had just lost IBM's business and was suffering through a major industry slump. As a result, the company was hemorrhaging cash and losing customers.

Notwithstanding the difficulties, Wiles parachuted in and quickly turned MiniScribe around, at least as far as the outside world was concerned. In October 1988, MiniScribe announced its thirteenth consecutive quarter of record-breaking sales.

However, problems lurked not far below the surface. Seven months later, the company jolted the financial community by announcing that its record sales growth was pure fiction. The books had been cooked. It wasn't just that the company had inflated inventory figures or aggressively booked sales. Not satisfied with such manipulations, company employees actually shipped ordinary bricks to distributors and booked the shipments as disk drive sales. They also tried to convince outside accountants to book as sales the cargo on a freighter that supposedly had set sail in late December 1986. The accountants refused, and the cargo and the freighter, apparently a fiction, weren't mentioned again.

Other employees were unwilling to accept no as an answer from the accountants. When the auditors uncovered discrepancies, these employees broke into locked trunks to change the auditors' work papers. Despite all these irregularities, Coopers & Lybrand, the company's accounting firm, issued clean audit reports to the company and reportedly overlooked questionable practices such as the back-dating of sales. What's more, Coopers approved a decrease in MiniScribe's bad-debt reserve even as accounts receivables ballooned.

Ultimately, the accounting shenanigans led to MiniScribe's bankruptcy, liability payments for Hambrecht & Quist and Coopers & Lybrand, and a criminal conviction for Wiles.

UNDERREPORTING EXPENSES   The underreporting of expenses is most often accomplished by moving expenses from the current period into the future.

The GAAP rules regarding depreciation and amortization afford the most straightforward opportunity to shift costs. GAAP generally requires that the depreciable value of a long-lived asset—measured as the difference between acquisition cost and predicted salvage value—be expensed over its useful life. The portion of the total that is written off each year will depend on the depreciation method selected. Under the straight-line method, the depreciable value is written off ratably over the asset's useful life. Other accelerated depreciation methods front-load the process, with more expense recognized in the early years.

GAAP depreciation standards leave open three possible cost-shifting strategies. First, a company can inflate an asset's predicted terminal value, which reduces its depreciable value. Second, a company can inflate the useful life of an asset. A longer useful life results in a reduced annual depreciation expense. Third, a company can select straight-line rather than accelerated depreciation.

For example, prior to a 1993 accounting change, Delta Air Lines depreciated its Boeing 727s on a straight-line basis over a fifteen-year period. TWA, on the other hand, depreciated its 727s over a twenty-year period. As a result of the different depreciation periods chosen by Delta and TWA, Delta's 1992 earnings were understated by approximately $35 million when compared to TWA's. If the same valuation multiple were applied to both companies, Delta's value as a company would be understated. Perhaps for this reason, Delta lengthened its depreciation period in 1993 to the now-industry-standard twenty years.

This phenomenon of differential depreciation is by no means uncommon. General Motors provides another example. A *Forbes* magazine article points out the impact of GM altering its depreciation policy. Prior to 1987, the automaker depreciated tools and dies much more quickly than other car companies. Then, in 1987, GM stretched the period out, more in line with that of Ford and Chrysler. The impact was significant, increasing earnings over 33 percent.

The classic cautionary tale is that of Leasco Data Processing Equipment Corp. Based on his Wharton thesis, the creative Saul Steinberg set up a company in the early 1960s which leased IBM computers. IBM took the conservative position that its computers would become obsolete fairly quickly. Accordingly, Big Blue offered customers short-term leases at high rates and depreciated machines over a short time frame. Steinberg, on the other hand, bought machines on credit and offered longer, noncancelable leases at lower rates. Leasco effectively was betting the machines would be useful over the longer period.

For a time, the assumption held, and Steinberg cleaned up. The initial lease rates covered most of the cost of buying equipment. As customers signed on, Leasco's earnings popped because of the significant spread between the rental terms and the stated depreciation on the machines. Results were great and Steinberg was a hero. IBM then came out with a new line. Leasco's machines were obsolete even though not fully depreciated and the earnings overstated. The company's stock price crashed. Steinberg had, of course, the tenacity to bounce back and prosper with what eventually became Reliance Insurance.

The decision whether to capitalize costs in the first place affords a more fundamental opportunity for cost shifting. A guiding premise is that a cost should be capitalized only if it will provide future benefit. If not, the cost should be fully expensed in the current period. Examples of borderline expenses that are sometimes capitalized include advertising, research and development, and start-up costs.

Shoe and apparel manufacturer L.A. Gear is a good example. The company, initially a hot growth prospect, began to falter in the late 1980s. Then, in 1988, L.A. Gear capitalized a portion of its advertising expenditures. The gimmick contributed to a record year for reported earnings, which increased 377 percent over the prior year. The company continued the practice into the first quarter of the new year, capitalizing $3.9 million of $7.2 million in total ad spending. Soon, however, the reality regarding L.A. Gear's boosted earnings became widely recognized, and the company's stock price deflated.

Ultimately, the capitalization question comes down to basic common sense. Will the claimed asset really provide future benefits?

Retirement and health care costs are also sometimes shifted to future periods. Theoretically, a company should expense such costs over the working lives of covered employees. Complicated actuarial formulas are used to estimate the cost that should be attributed to a given year. The predictive nature of this process gives a company some leeway to shift costs by taking an aggressive stance with respect to projected liabilities, the projected return on invested cash, and so on.

Even with all the accounting gimmicks in the world, though, bad news cannot be put off forever. The cumulative effect of expense shifting is to reduce future reported net income. Some companies attempt to mitigate this reality by periodically cleansing their financial statements. Expenses are piled together into one period in the form of a restructuring or other one-time charges. These charges often are justified as costs associated with a strategic shift. At some companies, however, there is a tendency toward "big-bath" accounting. The approach is to include as many expenses as possible in the one-time charge. This gets all the pain over with at once, so that future earnings will not be handicapped.

In an article, *The New York Times* used AT&T as an example of a company that has used big-bath accounting. The telephone company recorded four "one-time" restructuring charges during the decade ending with 1996. These charges totaled $14.2 billion, an amount almost 50 percent greater than the company's entire reported earnings over the same period.

NONRECURRING GAINS   The selective triggering of nonrecurring gains provides another opportunity to manage earnings. Such gains theoretically should be ignored from a valuation perspective because they are unrelated to the company's operational performance. The problem, however, is that one-time income items act as a kind of white noise, obscuring basic performance, and they are commonly built into corporate performance. In fact, nonrecurring gains are sometimes recurring.

A nonrecurring gain often comes when a company sells off an asset with a low book value. Real estate, inventory and debt are common sources of one-time gains. In the case of real estate, the incipient gain generally results from the simple passage of time. The real estate appreciates in value, while the book value remains fixed at historical cost. The difference can be recognized as revenue if the property is sold.

Harold Geneen and ITT's Earnings

ITT chairman Harold Geneen was an accounting Svengali. In 1971, the burgeoning conglomerate acquired Hartford Insurance. At the time, Geneen reportedly crowed that the Hartford acquisition gave ITT an "opportunity to have programmed earnings."

The key was Hartford's large portfolio of stocks, bonds, mortgages and other investment reserves. These reserves had a certain amount of built-in gain—that is, there was a positive difference between the market value of the investments and their historical cost. So, whenever ITT needed a boost to make an earnings target, it could simply sell some of these assets.

In 1974, for example, Hartford's entire portfolio was $241 million underwater. Nonetheless, through judicious asset sales, Geneen was able to generate $22 million in after-tax gains. This careful management prompted one former ITT executive to remark that "the Hartford portfolio was played like a violin."

A company that sells inventory in the ordinary course of business generates operating profit. It is possible, however, to manipulate one-time inventory sales, and gains from this type of transaction should be segregated as nonrecurring. The last-in, first-out (LIFO) inventory valuation method is the source of this opportunity to manage earnings. The LIFO method, sanctioned by GAAP, is widely used in calculating gross profit. The idea is that the most recent costs should be charged against current sales. As a result, a company's inventory on hand may have a book value per unit that is much lower than the current unit cost. The aggregate difference between book value and current cost—called the LIFO reserve—represents a built-in gain. This gain can be recognized by liquidating the inventory.

The flip side of the inventory income generation maneuver is the failure to recognize the real value of the inventory in write-downs. Stale inventory of finished goods is quite common.

A company also may be able to generate one-time gains by repurchasing its outstanding debt at a discount. Debt will trade at a discount when market interest rates exceed the applicable interest rate. Depending on the terms of a particular debt instrument, the issuing company may have the right to repurchase the debt at market value. According to GAAP, the difference between this market value and the principal amount of the debt is booked as a one-time gain even if the debt is replaced by new instruments carrying the higher rate.

Income Smoothing   Like efforts to boost the bottom line, income smoothing is symptomatic of the emphasis placed on reported earnings. However, income smoothing has more to do with trends than with the absolute amount of earnings.

Income smoothing involves the creation of reserves for future expenses as a way to shift "excess" earnings into the future. These earnings are banked for a rainy day, and can be released in a tough year. *Forbes* has singled out oil companies in particular as "champions of income smoothing," implying they manage earnings by selectively booking environmental cleanup expenses. For example, in 1990, Amoco had an extraordinary gain of $471 million from settling claims related to asset seizures during the Iranian revolution. In the same quarter, Amoco added $477 million to its reserves for environmental damage, thereby giving itself future earnings flexibility.

Hidden Assets and Liabilities   A company's book value is defined as the difference between the value of assets and liabilities as shown on the company's balance sheet. Generally speaking, however, book value is a notoriously flawed measure of value.

ASSETS   Balance sheet asset values rarely match current market values. The divergence comes because GAAP values certainty over accuracy. This ethos dictates that assets generally should be recorded on a company's books at historic cost. There are exceptions, of course, such as marketable securities, the book values of which are marked up or down to current market value. But the historic-cost convention otherwise holds, with sometimes dramatic results.

For example, in the fall of 1988, Northwest's stock was trading in the low 50s, giving an equity value of roughly $1.5 billion. The company then disclosed that it had rejected a Japanese investor's offer to buy Northwest's Tokyo residential compound for $200 million. The news came as a pleasant surprise to investors, who subsequently discovered that Northwest held this and several other pieces of extremely valuable Japanese real estate. None of these properties, which together were worth roughly $500 million, had been separately disclosed in the company's financial statements. When we worked on the takeover bid for Northwest, the Japanese real estate was a key factor in the valuation.

Real estate is the most commonly undervalued asset on company books. Other hard assets, such as plants or production facilities, may also be similarly undervalued. Unfortunately, though, undervalued assets may be buried in such a way that their true value is not apparent.

LIABILITIES   With liabilities, problems arise because claims are not recognized on a company's books at all, or have been shifted off the books.

There are a number of circumstances in which companies sometimes fail to record a liability when they arguably should. Companies that receive payment up front for goods or services that will be provided over time sometimes record the entire payment as current revenue. The more appropriate treatment is to record the amount related to future goods or services as a liability. Naturally, this situation arises most often in industries where up-front payment is common, like franchising, magazine publishing or prepaid vacation sales.

Companies also sometimes fail to report contingent liabilities. These might be the result of litigation or other disputes. According to GAAP, a company should record a liability when a loss is more than likely and the amount can be calculated with reasonable certainty. With litigation, there is a lot of room for discretion.

The practice of shifting liabilities off the balance sheet is even more widespread. In recent years, companies have developed sophisticated financial engineering tools for this purpose. Asset securitizations have been the main technique. For example, a common securitization strategy involves the pooling of receivables, which are then sold to third parties. The selling company will in some cases go so far as to guarantee that the receivables will be paid. This basically amounts to a secured loan. Though the fact of the guarantee typically is disclosed in financial statements, companies have some flexibility to account for the transaction as an outright sale. In that case, it can come as quite a surprise if the company is forced to make good on its guarantee.

Uncovering the Bodies

Buried-body accounting eventually catches up with a company. The fiction of artificial earnings can only hold up for so long before the underlying reality becomes apparent. Of course, the key is to uncover problems before they are disclosed. Only then is the knowledge valuable.

Outright fraud unfortunately is difficult to detect. However, in other cases, financial ratio analysis can act as an early warning system. Attention to three key ratios—inventory turnover, accounts receivable turnover and the cash ratio—will tell a great deal about the quality of a company's earnings.

A company's inventory turnover ratio equals its cost of goods sold for a period divided by its inventory (including the so-called LIFO reserve if any). A declining inventory turnover means a company is building inventory faster than sales. Rather than address the fact that sales are declining by scaling back production, the company simply ignores reality and continues production at an unrealistic pace. Eventually, some of that added inventory will need to be written off, meaning that current earnings are overstated, as are assets.

A company's accounts receivable turnover equals its sales divided by its accounts receivable. A declining turnover means a company is taking longer to convert sales into cash and perhaps is loosening credit standards to boost sales. The sales may never be converted to cash, again causing earnings and assets to be overstated.

Finally, a company's cash ratio equals its cash items divided by current liabilities. A declining cash ratio indicates an impending liquidity crunch. In essence, this ratio provides another window into the accounts receivable problem mentioned above, but also captures other cash management problems. If a company's revenues are increasing but cash is decreasing, that may indicate an overly aggressive accounting posture. The company may be booking shipments as sales or may not be writing off an appropriate percentage of accounts receivables.

These three ratios provide a good start for an analysis. However, ratio analysis should be supplemented with a careful reading of the footnotes to a company's financial statements. A real-world sanity check also is helpful. In other words, do a company's reported numbers match with market realities? If not, what explains the variation?

Buyers place considerable weight on variations from the norm precisely because accounting is such a flexible tool. There is no such thing as "true" earnings, but financial statements prepared based on consistent principles provide one means of comparative valuation.

Spotting the Value

Of course, a set of data points on a business is just a starting point—all the data then has to be filtered and analyzed. Success in the merger business comes from spotting the underlying value. Henry Kravis and George Roberts are masters of the art, as evidenced by their highly successful purchase and sale of Duracell.

KKR's involvement with Duracell began in late 1987, when Kraft Inc. decided to sell the business. The battery operation, which Kraft had picked up as part of its earlier merger with Dart Industries, was not really core to Kraft's other food businesses. Stockholders had been pressuring John Richman, Kraft's chairman, to divest the business. Moreover, Richman had begun to hear market rumors of an impending Kraft takeover. A Duracell sale might stave off the hostile attack.

When bidding opened, Richman expected the sale would bring a bit more than $1 billion. He was pleasantly surprised when a bidding war erupted among a handful of financial buyers. Ted Forstmann eventually tried to preempt the action by offering a $1.5 billion exploding bid. The bid would be withdrawn if not accepted almost immediately.

Kravis responded to Forstmann's move by approaching Richman. KKR was prepared to go higher, but had to know the next round of bidding would be the last. Richman agreed. KKR bettered its first-round bid of $1.2 billion by $600 million. Expecting another round of bidding, Forstmann, Clayton & Dubilier, and Gibbons, Green all came in lower. At $1.7 billion, Forstmann was the next highest bidder. He demanded a chance to top KKR, but Richman kept his word to Kravis.

Kravis and Roberts had become interested almost as soon as they saw the Duracell offering book describing the business. What did they see in Duracell that made it worth $1.8 billion, almost $800 million more than Richman had expected? The fundamentals of the business were strong. Duracell was second to Ralston Purina's Eveready in the battery market, and led the booming alkaline battery segment. The inexorable miniaturization of electronics equipment continued to drive demand higher. Duracell had few competitors and operating income margins over 10 percent.

In addition, Duracell's president Robert Kidder and the company's other managers chafed under Richman's leadership. They were primed to lead a buyout. As the bidding process unfolded, Kidder identified a number of areas where costs could be reduced. He also made a strong case that the business could be expanded.

With the fundamentals and management looking good, KKR turned to the numbers. Kidder's projections for Duracell showed strong and growing cash flow. KKR liked the fundamentals and the numbers so much, it agreed to fund the Duracell acquisition with just over $350 million in equity for a debt-to-equity ratio of four to one.

Skeptics regarded the $1.8 billion price put on Duracell as a stretch. Some reports chalked it up as another case of LBO guys needing to spend the money they controlled. The price represented roughly 14 times Duracell's 1987 earnings before interest and taxes (EBIT) and 11 times EBITDA (EBIT plus depreciation and amortization, a measure of operating cash flow). This at a time when Gillette—a somewhat comparable consumer products company—traded in the market at 10 times 1987 EBIT and 8 times 1987 EBITDA.

The key was seeing the future value in Duracell. KKR liked Kidder's enthusiasm and believed his projections. Crunching Kidder's numbers into an LBO consequences model, KKR saw that Duracell could carry the $1.45 billion in debt that would be used in the deal. Cash flow would be sufficient to pay down debt without any major asset sales. If Duracell hit its projections, KKR, its investors and Duracell management would earn a solid return on the equity in the deal.

As it turned out, Duracell soared. Kidder and his team trimmed sales and administrative costs, increased R&D spending and grabbed market share from Eveready. Innovations like a disposable battery tester and strong international sales drove cash flow above the original projections. Duracell was able to repay $224 million of senior debt ahead of schedule.

By 1991, things were going so well at Duracell that KKR took the company public. In one of the year's hottest IPOs, Duracell issued $450 million of stock. The stock—priced initially at $15 a share— was bid above $20 within the first few days of trading. The company used the proceeds from the offering to reduce debt even further. Meanwhile, the KKR group, which didn't sell any stock in the offering, retained a 73 percent stake in Duracell. KKR's Duracell stock, purchased at $5, was now trading in the market for four times that amount. Over the next several years, KKR would capitalize on this run-up through a series of stock sales which reduced its stake to 34 percent.

The ultimate takeout came in 1996, when Gillette purchased Duracell in a stock-for-stock deal. Under the deal, each Duracell share was exchanged for .904 of a share of Gillette stock. The merger of Gillette, a strong international marketer, and Duracell, with limited international presence outside Europe, wowed investors. In the two days after the deal was announced, Duracell's stock rose 27 percent in the market and Gillette's 8 percent.

The Gillette deal was finalized in December 1996, closing out an extremely successful investment for KKR. Taking into account Gillette's stock price at that time and KKR's earlier stock sales, the firm's original $350 million investment had grown to approximately $3.7 billion. As can only be seen in hindsight, the Duracell purchase price had been a bargain.

The Valuation Framework

The Duracell story is indicative of the valuation process. Having analyzed the fundamentals of a company and its financial history, it is possible to build a model of its future performance and come to a point of view regarding its worth to a bidder.

All valuation methods have their flaws, but they are very useful as cross-checks. The new science, with quantitatively derived answers, is almost laughable in its simplicity despite the ostensible precision. Sophisticated companies don't pay the same attention to theoretical financial models as newly minted MBAs.

Essentially, every five years a bright business school professor or economist comes up with a new twist on corporate finance theory and publishes it in the *Journal of Finance* or some other academic periodical. It filters down, often through consultants and bankers, to corporations, who adapt variant forms of the theories. But it's all theoretical as hell, so naturally the theories get adapted and tangled. As long as a sense of humor is kept, the exercises are worthwhile.

There are three generic types of valuation methods: discounted future projections of cash, comparable companies analysis and consequences models.

The Discounted Cash Flow Model

According to the discounted cash flow model, or DCF, the value of a company should equal the present value of its future cash flows. The model is formulaic. Cash flows are projected for some number of years into the future. Each year's cash flow is then "discounted back" to determine its present value. Finally, a terminal value—the value at the end of the last year for which projections are developed—is determined. This terminal value also is discounted to the present. The company's aggregate value is the sum of these present values.

Two main concepts underlie the DCF model. The first is that

projected cash flows, not earnings, are the appropriate stream for discounting. The presumption here is that cash flows better reflect economic reality. Earnings are more of a metaphysical construct, calculated according to flexible accounting principles. Cash flows therefore are the tool of choice, although, in fact, the stock market is still sensitive to earnings.

The second foundation is the time value of money. The basic principle is that a dollar of future cash flow is worth less than a dollar of current cash flow. This observation rests on the fact that a dollar of current cash flow can be invested at some rate of return. With 5 percent growth using simple interest, for example, a dollar invested today becomes $1.05 a year from now.

From a mechanical standpoint, there are four steps involved in building a DCF model. First, cash flow projections for the company must be developed. Unlevered free cash flows—which back out the effect of any debt—are used. Second, the company's terminal value at the end of the projection period must be calculated. Third, the appropriate discount rate must be estimated. Fourth, the present value must be calculated using the discount rate.

Though different methodologies can be used, this four-step approach is the most common. The resulting present-value number reflects the operating value of the entire firm, independent of its capital structure. This facilitates comparison of operating businesses. The value of a company's common equity then can be determined by backing out the value of debt and other non-common-equity claims.

However, because DCF analysis is more theoretical than the other valuation models, a dose of common sense is critical to its use.

Cash Flow Projections The "cash flow" in DCF projections does not mean the number reported at the bottom of a company's cash flow statement. This number takes into account money from financing and investment activities, which can vary dramatically from company to company. The DCF model instead uses a different cash flow concept, known as "unlevered free cash flow." This is the amount of cash thrown off by the operating business in a given year.

Net income can be used as a starting point to calculate free cash flow. Depreciation and amortization are added back to net income because they are noncash expenses. This also eliminates issues as to differential depreciation practices. Increases in working capital and capital expenditures—which consume cash but are not incorporated as expenses in the net income figure—are subtracted. On the flip side, any noncash income or a decrease in working capital should be added to the net income figure.

The final step is to unlever the cash flow. This is accomplished by backing out any interest expense on a tax-adjusted basis, which involves two steps. First, interest expense must be added back to the adjusted net income figure. Second, the tax shield provided by the tax-deductible interest payments must be subtracted from the figure.

Once interest is backed out, the remainder is free cash flow to the unlevered firm, the basic building block of DCF analysis.

The Projections   The DCF model requires unlevered free cash flow to be projected for some number of years into the future. There are two basic sources for the necessary accounting data: management and research analysts.

Aside from issues of inaccuracy, management projections or analyst reports are limited in providing data for projections. Analysts seldom project performance more than two years into the future. Management may project five years of data but the outer years are often mechanically executed. The DCF forecast horizon generally is longer. The rule of thumb is that a company's unlevered free cash flow should be projected out until the company reaches a "steady state." In theory, projections should extend until the company achieves stable growth and a stable capital structure.

Though generalizations are difficult, the typical time horizon for projections is five to ten years. For cyclical industries, the forecast period should capture at least one full cycle, which may be longer than ten years. DCF projections in the outer years are very subjective, and capital expenditures are often underestimated. The easiest way to jigger a DCF analysis is to defer or underestimate new capital expenditures or research and development expenses or, for a consumer company, marketing expenses. But it is precisely those outer-year numbers that are capitalized to create the all-important terminal values. Therefore, particularly for growth companies that do not have early cash flow, DCF can become mere gut feel cloaked in science.

To counteract this problem, the base case needs to be tested. Margins and growth rates should be scrutinized. Does the picture presented comport with the industry's strategic dynamic? Any divergence from industry norms deserves particular attention. For example, expanding margins in a competitive industry must be justified. Likewise, continued growth in a stagnant industry needs to be explained.

THE WORST CASE

Novell Buys WordPerfect

Consideration of the worst-case scenario—and its impact on value—should also be part of a DCF analysis. Of course, the worst case sometimes happens, as was demonstrated by Novell's experience after it bought WordPerfect in 1994. The stock deal initially was valued at $1.4 billion. At the same time, Novell bought the Quattro spreadsheet program from Borland International for $125 million.

The WordPerfect deal ran into trouble from the start. Investors dumped Novell stock when the diversification was announced. The price plunged from $24 to $15.25 by the time the deal closed, driving Novell's effective acquisition price down to $855 million.

The problem was Microsoft. The world changed for other software companies with the 1990 introduction of a vastly upgraded Microsoft Windows operating system. With an approachable format, this new package became a marketing sensation. Microsoft began to bundle various applications in a single unit. The asking price for the package was not much more than the price for a single application.

By the time of the 1994 Novell purchase, the privately held WordPerfect was being routed. Marketing blunders compounded by the slow introduction of a Windows-based product drove sales down. The company's two owners were ready to sell.

Novell faced competing visions of WordPerfect's future. In one, sales would continue to decline, margins erode and profits evaporate. In the other, with new stronger management, WordPerfect would rebound and become a strong number two to Microsoft. With its purchase, Novell clearly endorsed this latter vision.

Unfortunately, the worst case happened, probably to an even greater extent than Novell might have imagined. Novell bundled WordPerfect with Quattro in its own package. But Microsoft continued to out-innovate and out-market the WordPerfect business. Novell's sales force—accustomed to selling networking software—proved incapable of pushing the new products. Margins vaporized and more than 4,000 of WordPerfect's employees had to be laid off. Finally, in 1996, Novell sold both WordPerfect and Quattro to Corel, a Canadian company, for about $125 million—incurring an $875 million loss in less than two years.

Novell clearly bet on the wrong technology. In business, companies necessarily take risks. The trick is to take calculated risks and avoid gambles.

Terminal Value Once projections have been made, the next step in a DCF analysis is to calculate the value of cash flows generated in the years beyond the projection period—the gross terminal value. One common method is to derive a valuation multiple for comparable companies and apply it to the free cash flow in the year after the projection period. So, for example, comparable companies might trade at 10 times EBIT. This multiple could be applied to a company's projected EBIT to determine the terminal value.

In calculating terminal values, some buyers prefer to multiply by the ratios at which comparable companies trade in the stock market and some use higher private-market acquisition prices. Obviously, the scope of discretion allowed, and the sensibility of applying today's ratios to tomorrow's projections, are somewhat questionable.

The other methodology for calculating terminal values, which superficially looks more scientific, is to capitalize the final projections based on some perpetual growth rate. Because nothing grows forever, it is rare that a high growth factor is used at the terminal point.

The Discount Rate In theory, a company's weighted average cost of capital (WACC) is the appropriate discount rate to use in the DCF analysis. The WACC is the weighted average of a company's equity and debt costs. An estimate of a company's cost of debt generally is calculated based on the implicit rates at which its outstanding debt is trading. The cost of equity capital is based on the reward above an average market return investors require in a stock.

As a practical matter, for mature businesses, companies today discount cash flows at between 10 and 15 percent, centering around the 12 to 13 percent level depending on the riskiness of the target's business, although in today's relatively more stable economic environment some theorists are arguing that a 9 to 11 percent rate is more realistic.

CALCULATING THE WACC

Over time, a fairly standard method for calculating a company's WACC has evolved.

THE CAPITAL STRUCTURE   Despite its potential flaws as an indicator, a company's existing capital structure is the starting point for analysis. However, a company's capital structure often shifts with time. The WACC calculation does not contemplate a shifting capital structure. For this reason, the market-value weights should not necessarily be calculated based on a company's current structure, which may be anomalous. Theoretically, a target capital structure instead should be developed and used in the model. As a practical matter, either the subject company's existing capital structure or an industry composite is often selected.

THE COST OF COMMON EQUITY   The next step is to calculate the cost of common equity capital. Here, the common approach is to use the capital asset pricing model (CAPM), a theoretical model designed to measure the cost of equity. The premise is that the cost of equity equals the "risk-free return" plus a risk premium, which compensates investors for market risk, and any adjustment to it necessitated by the systematic risk associated with the target company's equity. This risk in a target's stock, as compared to market risk, is the company's "beta."

Mechanically, then, a company's cost of equity equals the risk-free return plus the risk premium times the company's beta. The risk-free rate is a theoretical construct, the return on a security with no default risk. A ten-year U.S. Treasury security generally is used as a proxy.

The market-risk premium represents the difference between the return on a diversified market portfolio and the risk-free rate, roughly between 5 and 7 percent. Historical data is used to calculate this difference.

A company's beta, like the market-risk premium, most often is drawn from a third-party database. A company called BARRA compiles predicted betas for over 6,000 publicly traded companies. The betas are predicted using a multivariate analysis of thirteen factors that change over time. A company's beta reflects the riskiness of its existing capital structure. If a different capital structure is used to calculate WACC, the beta must be adjusted.

From a theoretical perspective, this approach holds together. However, real-world evidence challenges the predictive power of market betas. Based on empirical research, various academics have argued that other factors—such as company size, degree of leverage and equity book-to-market ratios—provide more accurate measures of the risk premium. The results of CAPM therefore should be judged with a critical eye. Still, CAPM remains the most functional measure of the cost of equity.

Potential Pitfalls DCF analysis, with its complex calculations and forecasts, has the appearance of precision to it. Yet the DCF model is something like a sausage factory. A number of different ingredients—the assumed capital structure, projected cash flows, the cost of capital—come together in the final result. When the casing is peeled away, it becomes clear that each of these ingredients can be of varying quality. A testing of each critical assumption is helpful, but there is little question this is an imprecise tool. It is certainly helpful when a mature company with a predictable capital structure buys a similar target. On the other hand, three situations are particularly difficult to analyze with the DCF technique.

One is a company with so-called hockey stick projections, in which a firm with a mediocre historical performance is projected to have a dramatic turnaround. Though rebounds do happen, the timing, scope, cash impact and long-term stability of this kind of turnaround play havoc with the DCF technique.

Similarly, a company in a cyclical industry doesn't neatly fit conventional patterns. If the company is in the middle of a downturn, the projections may show declining or stagnant cash flow for the early years. If the company is on the upswing, the projection may show ramping-up cash flows. The danger is that the impact of a part of the cycle is exaggerated by the technique.

DCF valuations of high-growth or start-up companies are also difficult. Such a company often has negative cash flow in the early years. Assuming the company will be a success, projecting performance over a number of years can be extremely dicey. In addition, the cost of capital generally must be calculated based on industry comparables.

Ultimately, the question of an appropriate valuation still resolves into a question of judgment.

DCF Becomes EVA®   Though DCF valuation is an imprecise tool, a variant recently has gained popularity as a management tool. Rechristened "economic value added" by consulting firm Stern Stewart, which holds a trademark on the acronym EVA, this theoretical approach is designed to help management and investors assess corporate performance. The basic notion is inherent in the DCF framework—a company that does not earn its cost of capital is shortchanging capital providers.

A company's economic value added for a given year equals its operating cash flow minus its dollar cost of capital. In this context, operating cash flow means net income plus certain adjustments such as the addition of goodwill amortization. The dollar cost of capital is calculated by multiplying a company's WACC times its capital base. In essence, then, the WACC is treated as a hurdle rate. Economic value added is positive when a company earns more than its cost of capital.

Arithmetically, given a set of projections, the economic value added approach derives precisely the same value for a business as DCF. The theoretical foundations of the two models are the same. Still, economic value added has become a popular tool. Companies have begun to use economic value added as a benchmark for incentive compensation programs and as a tool to judge internal investment decisions. Research analysts are beginning to report economic value added as another measure of company performance. Even some investors are following the calculation.

The chief difference between DCF and economic value added is one of presentation and focus. By highlighting the fact that capital has a cost, economic value added spotlights the importance of capital budgeting decisions. Economic value added also provides a transparent year-by-year tally of company performance. DCF, on the other hand, obscures the underlying economic value trend by treating a dollar of free cash flow the same whether it merely covers the cost of prior capital investments or actually provides a return above the cost of capital.

Of course, economic value added faces some of the same challenges as DCF. First, the cost of capital is difficult to measure with precision. Second, projections of future performance are inherently uncertain. However, this latest version of management science is helpful because it highlights the tendency in DCF models to deemphasize the need for future capital expenditures and reap the benefits created from old ones.

Comparable Companies Valuation

Given the difficulties with DCF, buyers often revert to a simple comparable company valuation. This approach has a strong intuitive appeal. From real estate to cars to consumer goods, it is natural to value things in terms of what similar products might cost. This practice translates easily into the valuation of companies. The United States has an active public market and strong disclosure laws. As a result, a significant amount of quantifiable data exists. Because comparable companies analysis relies on publicly available information, the method is fairly easy to use.

The basic concept of multiple-driven analysis is to develop a database of companies that are comparable to the company being valued. Various trading multiples are then calculated for the comparable companies. Multiples, by definition, indicate that some measure of a company's value is so many times greater than some operating or other statistic. For example, a group of consumer products companies might have an average EBITDA multiple of "13 times." The value of a comparable company might then be estimated at 13 times its EBITDA. Such multiples can be calculated both based on the subject company's historical accounting data and off consensus projections of results.

Multiples of net income, EBITA (earnings before interest, taxes and amortization) and EBITDA are the standard drivers of comparable companies analysis. These alternatives can be thought of as the points along a spectrum, with operating cash flow (EBITDA) on one end, profit on the other (net income), and EBITA in between. Though all three measures are often explicitly reported in a particular model, one of the three generally is considered most relevant. As a rule of thumb, EBITDA multiples are preferred for companies in more capital-intensive industries, in which depreciation is a more significant factor, because such multiples correct for the impact of differential depreciation, or in industries where there have been extensive acquisitions and the amortization of goodwill distorts the picture. Net income multiples are used for less capital-intensive industries.

Each of these methods may hide a problem. For example, companies that focus too much on EBITDA have found that, as a measure, it tends to favor intensive capital spending because the resulting increased depreciation is not included.

Net income multiples and EBITA and EBITDA multiples also differ from an important computational standpoint. The theoretical basis for the difference is that a multiple calculation should compare apples to apples. Payments on debt are deducted from operating profits to arrive at a company's net income, which represents the profits to the common shareholders. Therefore, for consistency, net income multiples are calculated on the basis of the company's stock market capitalization. The measure of value is matched to the stream of earnings—the value of a company's common equity is compared to the profits attributable to the common.

EBITDA and EBITA multiples are broader operational measures. Interest on debt has not been deducted from these operating statistics. Both creditors and stockholders have a claim on these earnings streams. As a result, the multiples are calculated based on adjusted market value, the value of both equity and debt.

As an added measure, book value multiples are often reported in a comparable companies analysis, but are generally only given weight when applied to specific industries. Financial services companies—banks, insurance companies, finance companies—are the classic examples. The same concept of matching applies to the calculation of a book value multiple. Book value is a measure of common stockholders' equity in a company. Hence, market capitalization is the appropriate measure to use in calculating a book value multiple.

In certain industries, these standard four multiples have been supplemented with industry-specific rules of thumb. Cable companies, for example, are valued in terms of subscribers, cellular companies in terms of the population in the region covered by their licenses, and soft drink bottlers in terms of cases shipped.

Practical Issues The discretion inherent in the comparable companies analysis again underscores the important role common sense plays in the merger process, both in constructing the analysis and in using the results. Obviously, the result of the analysis depends on which companies are selected as comparable. Take one top performer off the valuation list, and a particular multiple might drop by a point.

Comparable companies analysis also depends on "trading" multiples. These multiples are tied directly to, and fluctuate with, stock prices. Timing issues therefore can have a major impact, especially in industries with volatile trading. Multiples might drop significantly over the course of a single week if the relevant sector is trading poorly. A company's "true" value arguably should not change so drastically from day to day. Moreover, the multiples of companies in a cyclical industry will vary over the course of the cycle. Attention to these timing issues is necessary to ensure that comparable companies analysis is not misused.

In addition, comparable companies analysis does not incorporate the control premium that is typically paid in private-market acquisitions. Usually, a control premium of 30 to 50 percent is added to trading value to determine acquisition value, another exercise in discretion.

Comparable Acquisitions Valuation

In the comparable acquisitions model, the database of comparable companies is restricted to those that have taken part in a recent merger or acquisition. Both the equity market value and adjusted market value of comparables are calculated based on the purchase price paid in the relevant transaction. This use of market transactions for pricing information results in transaction multiples that already incorporate a control premium. Then, as with the comparable companies analysis, various multiples are calculated and applied in some fashion to the company that is being valued.

The problems are obvious. How comparable are the precedents in terms of the companies involved, the prevailing market conditions and the transaction structure? Nevertheless, this technique is a necessity because everyone wants to understand the terms of the other deals in the industry. Sometimes, this model also is used as the basis for a "breakup" valuation of the pieces of a company. A breakup model is always necessary as a double check because any of the cash or earnings models can be highly misleading if a low-earning asset such as real estate is buried in a company.

Consequences Model

Finally, a company thinking about a deal also wants to know the pro forma impact of doing the deal. Will earnings be diluted? What will happen to the stock price? Will management get jeers or applause? Modeling the impact on earnings, cash flow and the balance sheet under alternative transaction structures is a necessity.

The process of building a merger consequences model is similar to building projections for a DCF valuation. The starting point is the income statement for the first year after the transaction. An assumption about how the transaction will be funded—with debt or equity, or some combination of both—is made. Other key variables are the cost of funding the debt and the appropriate tax rate. With this information, a year-one income statement is built. The year-one earnings provided by the target business is the output of the model. This number can be added to the acquirer's projected earnings to determine a pro forma earnings per share. Of course, the hope is that a transaction will be accretive to earnings per share.

However, for sophisticated acquirers, the immediate earnings impact is not the critical focus. Rather, they want to know the impact over, say, a three-year period because often the patterns reverse. A transaction that is dilutive in the first year may nonetheless be viewed as a positive development. The markets now generally give companies a year of grace. The long-term earnings and cash flow impact are more determinative of how a deal will be perceived.

In modeling the impact of a deal beyond the first year, it is imperative to normalize the capital structure. If a transaction is financed with debt, what will be the impact of future debt reduction on earnings per share? Alternatively, if a stock-for-stock merger is contemplated, the resulting company may be overcapitalized. A merger consequences model should account for any planned share repurchases, although care must be taken not to violate pooling eligibility guidelines.

These variations are incorporated in a merger consequences model by tying a cash flow statement and balance sheet into the income statement. On the modified cash flow statement, noncash charges are added back to the year-one earnings. The cash needs of the business that were not reflected on the income statement—chiefly for additional working capital and capital expenditures—are subtracted. The result is a free cash flow number. This amount then can be fed into the balance sheet as debt paydown or share repurchase. On the year-two income statement, a new debt balance may result in lower interest expense, increasing earnings per share. A lower number of shares outstanding also may increase earnings per share.

There is further complexity involved in building a merger consequences model, but the basic iterative feedback among income statement, balance sheet and cash flow statement is the fundamental mechanism. Like any model of the future, assumptions need to be tested and the final result should be viewed with some skepticism. Various interest rates, projected growth rates, capital needs and so on are fed into the model to determine the impact. An awareness of the sensitivity of outcomes is the raw material for the exercise of an informed judgment regarding a proposed transaction.

Of course, even if there is earnings dilution, the deal may make sense. First, it is also important to consider the impact before the amortization of goodwill. Free cash flow could be increasing even if earnings are diluted. Second, the impact on a company's price/earnings multiple must be considered. If a cement company buys a biotech venture, short-term earnings may well be diluted, but future prospects nonetheless may be brighter. Earnings dilution does not necessarily mean a lower stock price.

Forstmann Little Scores with Topps

Strip away all the fancy mechanics, and the valuation process crystallizes back to the fundamentals. What one thinks of the multiples, the projections, the DCF model—it all resolves into a question of basic business judgment. Is this a strong business that can thrive with the planned capital structure? The answer to that question can only be investigated in the present and is determined in the future.

An acquisition or merger essentially is a calculated gamble that a particular vision of the future can be made to come true. Forstmann Little's 1983 acquisition of Topps Company is a case in point.

The trading card company, controlled by the Shorin family, had a long history. Founded by four Shorin brothers in 1938, the Topps Gum Company got into baseball cards in 1952. The Brooklyn-based Topps had a monopoly on the Major League Baseball card business until 1980, when Fleer broke Topps' hold on the market through litigation.

By 1983, Chairman Arthur Shorin—a son of one of the founders—was interested in selling the business. He put a value of $100 million on Topps and wanted us to find a buyer who would fall in love with the idea of owning the baseball card company.

Topps proved to be a tough sell. We pitched the business to a number of corporate strategic buyers, but they all balked. Topps lacked the identifiable, stable growth and defined cash flow that could be easily fed into a model. No good comparables for the business existed, making it tough to value.

Still, having watched the trading card business cycle over a number of years, Shorin knew a new fad would come along and

Topps would capitalize on it. He didn't know what it would be, but he knew it would happen. In addition, Shorin saw great potential in the baseball card business, which eventually would bounce back to popularity.

Topps simply was the kind of business that required an imaginative, entrepreneurial buyer. Forstmann Little eventually agreed to pay $95 million—just short of Shorin's original asking price—financed with $10 million of equity and $85 million of debt.

Over the next decade, Shorin's instincts—and Forstmann Little's inclination to trust those instincts—proved remarkably on target. The next big thing for Topps turned out to be its phenomenally successful Garbage Pail Kids line. Baseball card sales also surged dramatically. Overall sales more than doubled and debt was paid down early.

Forstmann Little took Topps public in 1987, selling a small stake. Success continued. With a significantly reduced debt load, Topps was able to borrow $140 million a few years later. The money funded a special dividend to shareholders. Forstmann Little continued to reduce its stake with stock sales, then, in 1991, distributed its remaining 53 percent interest to the original investors who funded the deal.

The trading card boom eventually flattened, taking Topps' stock price down—along with the value of Ron Perelman's Marvel. However, by that time Forstmann Little and its investors had been vastly rewarded for their willingness to think outside the formal valuation box. All told, the firm grew the original $10 million of equity in the deal more than 70 times over.

Models and Muddles

With computer time cheap, there is a tendency to provide valuation wisdom by the pound. A thick book of backup materials is presented to justify a particular number or range. The level of detail can be overwhelming; valuation can devolve into a mechanistic averaging of the outputs from various seemingly sophisticated models.

A better approach is to view valuation as a triangulation process. The outputs of various models are assessed with an understanding of the limitations of each technique and what assumptions were used as inputs. Even if the models are perfect, the room for fundamental error is huge because models assume a projection of future value based on the world of today. In addition, the terminal value in the DCF model, and the comparable companies in that analysis, reflect today's market value.

Obviously, many of the deals of the 1980s and 1990s have turned out well simply because of the dramatic rise in the market. Of course, during some periods, markets go down as well. In the end, the question of price is one of judgment.

Structuring | 16
the Deal

*"Architecture begins when you place
two bricks carefully together."*

Mies van der Rohe

The architecture of a deal is defined by a complex mosaic of corporate law, the tax code and accounting rules. Their impact ripples through the process and defines the tactical possibilities. The challenge is to integrate these considerations with corporate objectives. Selecting a particular structure is seizing the ramparts of a transaction. Each possibility has its tactical, legal and financial benefits as well as defects which need to be carefully weighed. All of the considerations are interrelated, somewhat complex and, yet, vital to any understanding of the deal process.

Corporate Mechanics

In mergers, form does have a function. This point was underlined recently by developments in the merger of Bell Atlantic and NYNEX. The deal, billed as a "merger of equals," was originally cast in the form of a combination. A new holding company was to be created. This holding company then would issue shares in exchange for the outstanding stock of both NYNEX and Bell Atlantic.

This structure served the objective of preserving the "merger of equals" format. However, as it turned out, the structure also created roadblocks to completing the deal. Because the ownership of both NYNEX and Bell Atlantic would shift under the plan, regulatory authorities in each of the thirteen states served by the two companies would need to approve the deal. The parties quickly decided the marginal benefit of a transaction structure enshrining the merger of equals concept was less important than a smooth review process.

For this reason, the merger agreement was revised so that Bell Atlantic was the acquirer. The companies then took the position that the ownership of Bell Atlantic would not shift under the plan. This conclusion rested on the fact that the resulting entity would be more than 50 percent controlled by former Bell Atlantic shareholders. By avoiding a separate approval process in each of the seven Bell Atlantic states plus the District of Columbia, potential pitfalls were minimized.

Getting a big deal like the NYNEX–Bell Atlantic merger done, therefore, necessarily involves a certain amount of mechanics. Skillful navigation can be critical to success. As a starting point, large M&A deals break down into two primary transaction types—the merger and the stock purchase. Each has unique attributes. The specific steps vary from state to state, but Delaware law governs the majority of major U.S. corporations and is in many ways indicative.

The Merger

A merger essentially melds two corporate organizations into one. The terms of a deal are specified in the merger agreement. In particular, the agreement typically outlines the mix of consideration to be paid on the merger (cash, securities or otherwise), the conditions for the transaction becoming effective, any representations made by the parties and the effective date. On the effective date, the acquirer issues cash or securities in the appropriate ratios to the target's former security holders. The target's assets, contract rights and liabilities, disclosed or not, pass automatically to the surviving company unless otherwise specified in the merger documents.

The merger mechanism has a number of advantages. First, the procedure is flexible. The parties can define the consideration involved however they like. Target shareholders can be given stock, debt securities, cash or any other form of payment for their shares. The automatic transfer of assets and liabilities from the target to the acquirer without complicated documentation is another benefit.

Finally, once a merger has the necessary approvals, there is a "cram-down" effect. Target stockholders who voted against the merger must either accept whatever payment is offered or seek their remedy in court, through appraisal rights. The old target corporate entity no longer exists. Thus a key advantage of the merger is that no minority stockholders remain; they have been forced out in exchange for cash or an interest in the acquirer. This effect allows the acquirer to run the target free of the legal and operational complications that sometimes crop up with minority shareholders.

However, the merger process can have unwanted side effects. The flexibility of payment sometimes leads to shareholder discontent. Most state statutes provide appraisal rights for shareholders not satisfied with the payment to be received. Appraisal is a formal procedure in which a shareholder can contest the amount being paid in a merger, but there are limitations. Under the Delaware statute, for example, there are no appraisal rights for a stockholder in a public company if the stockholder is receiving stock in another public company.

Appraisal procedures must be handled quite gingerly. First, the methods of evaluation used by courts can differ considerably from market value. For example, in Delaware, market value, book or liquidation value, and dividend yield are all weighed as factors in the valuation analysis.

The automatic transfer of assets and liabilities in a merger also can be troublesome. This process poses the danger that the acquirer will be subject to the undisclosed liabilities of the target. Furthermore, some contracts—leases and rights to use intellectual property, for example—specifically provide that they do not pass to a successor, and this provision can raise serious obstacles to a merger.

Even in the best of circumstances, the merger procedure is somewhat unwieldy. Under Delaware law, for example, a merger generally must be approved by the directors of each company and then be submitted to the target company's stockholders. So, if the target's directors are recalcitrant, the merger route obviously doesn't work. Mergers therefore rarely work as the first step in the hostile takeover context.

Most big mergers also require the approval of the acquirer's shareholders. Technically, no vote is required if any stock to be issued in the transaction has already been authorized by shareholders. However, for this exception to hold, the stock to be issued must constitute less than 20 percent of the outstanding stock of the acquirer. In any event, the New York and American Stock Exchanges both require a vote by the stockholders of the acquiring company if the stock being given in connection with an acquisition equals more than about 20 percent of the acquirer's outstanding voting stock (18.5 percent is technically used as the demarcation line).

Where the approval of shareholders is required, state law typically provides that the approval be in the form of a majority vote. However, a company's bylaws or certificate sometimes requires a higher margin for merger approvals.

One way to smooth the merger process is to structure a deal as a triangular merger. Here, the approach is for the acquirer to create a special merger subsidiary, setting up the triangle between the acquirer, its new subsidiary and the target. The subsidiary is funded with the consideration to be given in the merger. The subsidiary and the target then merge. Either company can be the survivor.

The main advantage of the triangular merger technique is that it may eliminate the need for the acquirer to hold a shareholder vote.

Because the acquirer is the sole shareholder of the new special-purpose subsidiary, the approval process may involve just the subsidiary's board of directors, which can be the same as the parent company board. The acquirer also acts as sole shareholder. However, the 20 percent rule of the Stock Exchanges still may force a vote of the acquirer's shareholders.

Holding the target as a separate subsidiary also may insulate the parent from the liabilities of the target. This can be a significant advantage where the target is in a business with high litigation or environmental exposure, although in certain cases the parent may be held liable despite the separate corporate formalities.

Regardless, all the structuring sophistication in the world can't avoid a simple truth: potential booby traps abound in the merger process. A Clausewitzian view of deal tactics would stipulate that delay is an enemy to a deal, and mergers take a lot of time. For instance, holding a stockholder vote can be a source of delay. If it isn't time for the annual meeting, the expenses of calling a special meeting for a public company are high. The public stockholders must be provided with a proxy statement describing the transaction and a prospectus outlining the terms of the securities that they are going to receive.

So, a merger involving a publicly held company inevitably requires a substantial waiting time between the conception of a deal and its implementation. Five months is a realistic estimate. Aside from giving stockholders adequate notice of a stockholder meeting (usually about thirty days in advance), both the proxy statement, which asks shareholders to vote in favor of the deal, and any registration statement, which is required if securities are to be issued in the deal, must be cleared through the SEC before these documents can even be sent.

Mechanically, the proxy statement is filed with the SEC for review like any other registration of securities. The SEC sometimes has comments and changes must be made. But the biggest delay is in the preparation of the document itself, especially if the combined financial statements, or pro formas, are complicated. During this lengthy delay process, a deal is very vulnerable.

The Mechanics of Time Warner

The importance of corporate mechanics to the deal process was played out across the front pages in the merger of Time and Warner. Paramount pounced at the last minute and the parties defended their deal only by shifting its structure.

Initially, a merger was the implementation structure for the combination of Time and Warner. This transaction format was an attractive alternative for accounting reasons and because the consideration was originally meant to be all common stock. Under the accounting rules, a stock-for-stock merger would allow Time Warner to avoid goodwill charges, which otherwise would reduce future accounting earnings. Time also wanted to avoid taking on debt. Funding the deal with stock satisfied this goal.

Days before the shareholder vote to approve the deal, Paramount came in with its higher cash offer for Time. The Time board preferred to stick with Warner but, as structured, the deal would have required a Time shareholder vote to go forward. Several Time directors felt shareholders might not see the long-term strategic value in the Warner deal. If a vote were held, the Warner merger probably would be rejected in favor of the immediate cash payoff offered by Paramount.

Time and Warner went back to the drawing board. The decision was made to restructure the deal as a cash tender offer by Time for Warner stock. This format would not require a vote of Time's shareholders until after Time had control of Warner. The parties agreed that Time would acquire Warner for cash and securities. In the first step, Time would buy 51 percent of Warner's stock for $70 cash per share, a relatively low premium. Time would borrow between $7 and $10 billion to fund this purchase. Later, in a back-end merger, the remaining Warner stockholders would receive securities worth roughly $70 a share.

With this relatively simple change, Time shifted the entire tactical landscape. Paramount's only recourse was to sue Time and Warner in an attempt to block the deal. When the suit failed, Time's deal for Warner went through before Paramount could procedurally buy Time.

The Stock Purchase

As demonstrated by the Time-Warner deal, an alternative to a merger is for control to be assumed through a stock purchase, usually followed later by a merger. Payment for target company stock can come in the form of cash, stock, debt or other property. The main advantage of this approach from a corporate law perspective is the lack of required formalities. This is why Time turned to a stock purchase of Warner when its merger was attacked.

Neither the target company board of directors nor shareholders must formally approve a stock sale. Of course, target company shareholders have de facto approval rights in the sense that they can decide whether or not to sell their shares. The acquirer's board usually approves any major purchase, but a vote of shareholders is generally unnecessary if the acquisition is funded with cash or debt securities, significantly reducing the time between offer and purchase. For this reason, hostile takeovers most often involve a stock purchase through a tender offer.

Another advantage of a stock purchase is that it allows the acquirer to maintain the corporate existence of the target, thereby retaining in the acquired company any valuable contract rights, such as franchises that cannot be assigned. However, sometimes there are "change of control" provisions in instruments that void this advantage.

The preservation of the corporate shell does not result in the squeezing out of minority shareholders, a disadvantage relative to a merger. One method of eliminating minority shareholders is to have a cleanup merger sometime after an initial stock purchase. If the acquirer purchases majority control in the front end of the deal, the back-end merger vote becomes a formality. Recognition of this fact obviously impacts the position of target company shareholders when faced with a decision whether to sell their shares in an offer. Taking the up-front money may be far more attractive than waiting to see what happens on the back end.

In fact, for the back-end merger, an acquirer may be able to use a "short form" procedure that does not require a stockholder vote. For example, in Delaware, once an acquirer owns 90 percent of the outstanding shares of target company stock, the acquirer's board of directors may approve a short-form merger of the target into the acquirer. No vote of the minority holders is required. However, the minority stockholders may be entitled to appraisal rights.

Issuing Stock or Securities as Consideration

The federal securities laws regulate the issuance of stock or securities as consideration in a corporate merger or acquisition. In particular, two Depression-era statutes govern the issuance of securities: the Securities Act of 1933 and the Trust Indenture Act of 1939.

The Securities Act   In the context of a business combination, the 1933 act requires that, absent an exemption, any shares or other securities offered to target company shareholders must be registered, a process which takes months.

The SEC has created a special form to be used for securities issued as part of a business combination or exchange offer. For large public companies, this Form S-4 has the advantage of allowing an abbreviated presentation. Rather than detail all the financial information required in the longer Form S-1, a company can incorporate such information by reference to previous company filings.

Alternatively, in a case where the target company's shareholders must vote to approve the transaction, the proxy statement also can serve, with modification, as a registration statement for any securities offered. The Form S-4 in essence wraps around the required proxy statement, which is then also used as a prospectus.

For greater flexibility, corporations frequently involved in acquisitions sometimes use a technique called "shelf registration," which limits the need to file a new registration statement with every merger or acquisition. Generally, securities can be registered only if they will be distributed in the near future. However, SEC regulations permit a large company engaged in a continuing program of acquisitions to register a reasonable number of securities for future offerings. Those registered but unissued securities then can be "put on the shelf," with the registration statement being periodically amended after its filing to keep it current.

The appeal of a shelf registration is that, if an acquisition opportunity arises, the already registered securities can be used without the delays of first commencing a registration process. Absent the shelf, stock and securities generally will not be available in time for use in the front end of a two-tiered offer. Of course, even with an active shelf, if a stockholder vote is required, a proxy statement is still necessary.

Trust Indenture Act   When debt is being issued in a deal, it will become subject to the Trust Indenture Act. The act requires that publicly held debt be issued pursuant to a contract, called an indenture, containing specific provisions to protect the public. For each debt issue, there must be a trustee whose obligation in the event of a default on the debt is to protect the public debt holders as if the trustee were a "prudent man" acting on his own behalf.

The 1939 act also specifies the wording of certain provisions of indentures, particularly those dealing with events of default and the responsibilities of the trustee. Essentially, the way most indentures are structured, the trustee must notify the holders within ninety days if there is a known event of default.

Once there has been a default, the trustee must act prudently. The holders of a majority of the securities may take control from the trustee if the trustee's costs are covered. However, without the consent of each individual holder, no right to principal repayment may be waived, and most indentures do not allow any waiver of interest.

A natural question arises as to why a trustee is required for debt instruments and not for equity securities. As a general proposition, debt securities are more complicated than stock. First, there is the payment of principal and interest, which is due rather than discretionary as with stock dividends, and the presence of various prepayment rights, which are, however, also often used in preferred stocks. Second, there are the various restrictions on the issuer to police. Third, there are generally no default provisions in equity securities, although sometimes preferred stockholders are entitled to additional directors based upon the occurrence of certain events.

THE ASSET DEAL

Large corporate transactions rarely deviate from the merger or stock purchase alternatives. However, in some cases, an acquirer opts to pursue an asset deal. This approach involves the purchase—for cash, stock or other payment—of certain specified assets.

Under Delaware law, a majority shareholder vote is required for the sale of all or substantially all the assets of the company. That means that, under the right circumstances, it may be possible to sell 35 percent of the company without shareholder approval. Unlike a merger, stockholders objecting to the asset transfer have no appraisal rights under Delaware law.

The ability to select carefully the liabilities being assumed is one key advantage to the acquisition of assets. For example, if the target company previously sold defective products or broke its contracts with impunity, the acquiring company has the option of not assuming the contingent liabilities. In contrast, when stock is purchased, the acquiring company owns the target with both its assets and its liabilities. So an assets-for-stock deal has much to recommend it if there is concern about the assumption of liabilities.

However, not assuming the old corporate shell can be a weakness in the acquisition of assets. Every asset has to be specifically assigned, including every contract. There can be literally thousands of documents. Many contracts have clauses which state that they may not be assigned without the consent of the other party. These formalities can create enormous burdens, and quite often the problems are not merely administrative. For example, a key supplier with a no-assignment clause may well see the assets deal as a perfect opportunity to renegotiate the contract. This is the reason large, fast-paced acquisitions rarely take the form of an asset deal, as well as the enormous tax problems created if there are gains on the assets being sold.

Tax Issues

The tax law adds another layer of complexity to a transaction. A merger or acquisition may be structured as either a tax-free or a taxable transaction, with dramatically different consequences for sellers and purchasers. In this fashion, the tax law can have a substantial economic effect on a transaction and may represent a decisive element in considering a deal.

The Tax-Free Merger

A stock-for-stock merger is eligible for tax-free treatment, so that target shareholders receive the acquirer's shares tax-free. Although the Internal Revenue Code provisions regarding mergers are relatively simple, in tax law, simplicity seems to be a metaphysical impossibility. The courts have interpreted these provisions, and the Internal Revenue Service has added gloss of its own.

Most big mergers are structured using the triangular merger format. The approach—also favored by acquirers for corporate law reasons—has been enshrined in the tax law. First, the acquiring company sets up a wholly owned subsidiary, creating the triangle between the acquirer, the subsidiary and the target. The target then is either merged into the subsidiary, or the subsidiary into the target. In either event, the target ends up as a wholly controlled subsidiary of the acquirer. Under the applicable tax rules, shareholders of the acquired company may receive stock or debt of the parent company, but not of the subsidiary.

For mergers, tax-free status is in theory possible whether target company shareholders receive payment in the form of cash, stock or debt. This flexibility is one key advantage of a merger and is in sharp contrast to other tax-free vehicles for corporate combination. However, the IRS and the courts have limited the scope of this freedom by requiring that selling stockholders must maintain a "continuity of interest" in the surviving corporation.

The continuity test is satisfied if the selling stockholders get stock in the surviving entity equal in value to roughly 40 percent or more of the value of the stock surrendered.

Furthermore, target company shareholders must maintain ownership of the stock that was used to satisfy the 40 percent threshold for at least two years or show that any earlier disposition was not part of a plan that existed when the transaction was consummated.

A continuing interest includes any form of stock—including non-voting preferred. Long-term debt, however, is not considered to be a continuing interest even though the interests of a long-term debt holder are very similar to those of a holder of nonvoting preferred stock.

In addition to the continuity test, courts also tend to integrate a series of transactions and consider them as one deal. This "step-transaction doctrine" lets courts look beyond the form of a transaction and examine its substance. So, if stockholders receive cash to redeem their stock immediately before or after a merger, a court may deem the payment to be part of the merger terms and count the cash against the stockholder in applying the continuity-of-interest tests.

LEARNING THE ABCs

Learning the ABCs of the takeover game is critical to sounding like an initiated player. Lawyers and accountants use shorthand references to describe the standard tax-free deal structures. The terms are derived from the relevant subsections of the Internal Revenue Code.

The straight stock-for-stock merger is an "A reorganization" or "A reorg," named after Code Section 368(a)(1)(A). The triangular merger is either a "forward" or "reverse triangular reorganization" depending on which corporate shell survives. A tax-free stock swap without a merger is a "B reorg," the rare tax-free asset deal is a "C reorg" and a spin-off is a "D reorg."

Implications   When analyzing the tax implications of a deal, the constituencies to consider are target company shareholders, the target company and the purchasing company.

The broad implications of a tax-free merger are fairly straightforward. Target company shareholders who exchange their shares generally will not recognize a tax gain or loss to the extent they accept acquirer stock as payment. Instead, the shareholders' original investment is transferred to the acquiring company stock. When the new stock is eventually sold, the gain or loss on that transaction equals the difference between the price received and the seller's original investment in the target company stock.

However, even in a tax-free transaction, target shareholders are taxed on any "boot" received. Boot is anything other than acquiring company stock. Meanwhile, neither a target company nor the acquirer recognizes gain or loss in a tax-free merger.

The acquirer also faces a crucial second question: What will be the tax basis of the purchased assets? The answer to this question can have a substantial impact on the cash flow from the deal. Tangible assets with limited lives generally are depreciable for tax purposes. This means that, each year, a portion of an asset's purchase price, or "tax basis," is treated as an expense that may be used to offset otherwise taxable income. The higher an asset's basis, the more depreciation generated.

As an asset is depreciated for tax purposes, its tax basis is reduced a like amount. Because the tax law applies depreciation rules different from those used in financial accounting, an asset's tax basis rarely equals its net book value. Furthermore, accelerated tax depreciation rules often leave a target company owning assets worth considerably more than their current tax basis. If an acquirer purchased these assets for cash at fair market value, the acquirer would have a new, higher tax basis equal to the purchase price, In other words, the acquirer would enjoy a "basis step-up." However, in a tax-free merger, the acquiring company takes a carryover basis in the assets acquired. The acquirer therefore does not benefit from the income shield of the higher depreciation that would result if assets were purchased for cash in a taxable transaction.

Viewing this summary of tax implications, it is easy to see why sellers generally prefer tax-free transactions. If a stock has run up in price—as most stocks have over the past fifteen years—the tax-free transaction allows the owner to defer taxes on the transfer of the old stock. However, notwithstanding this benefit, some sellers prefer a taxable transaction for one of two reasons. First, there sometimes is a loss rather than a gain on the security being sold; therefore, stockholders often want a recognition event so that the tax loss can be used to shelter other income. Second, the seller may be a tax-exempt investor, such as a pension fund, that would rather have immediate cash liquidity than the ongoing investment required in stock-for-stock tax-free deals. Even for taxable investors, cash is often more highly regarded than a security, which may or may not be worth its estimated value.

From the purchaser's perspective, the chief drawback of structuring a deal as a tax-free transaction is that the purchaser must forgo a basis step-up. On the other hand, structuring for a tax-free reorganization may be a necessity because the sellers may otherwise be unwilling to sell. The seller also may accept a lower price given the obvious tax savings.

Tax-Free Stock Purchase

Like a merger, a stock purchase can be tax-free, but only where one firm acquires at least 80 percent of another in a stock swap, measured by vote. So, for example, Company A buys 80 percent of the shares of Company B, paying for the purchase with new Company A shares.

From the tax point of view, a stock swap, the "B" reorganization, is a fragile animal. For example, boot—consideration other than voting stock—is absolutely forbidden in a tax-free stock deal. The continuity of interest tests also apply.

In terms of mechanics, a tax-free stock deal often is accomplished through a triangular merger—the acquiring company forms a subsidiary into which the target is merged. The end result is that the target company becomes a wholly owned subsidiary of the acquirer.

A hostile exchange offer, in which the acquirer publicly offers to exchange its stock for target company shares, also is sometimes used to effect a stock purchase. Without the 80 percent control, the tax-free nature of the transaction will be jeopardized. Therefore, a condition is sometimes put into the offer stipulating that it will not be consummated unless the requisite 80 percent control is attained.

Implications In a tax-free stock swap, target company shareholders take a carryover basis in the stock they receive as part of the transaction. Because absolutely no boot is allowed, there is no possibility for gain recognition. The acquiring company takes a carryover basis in the target company stock it purchases. No capital gains tax is triggered for the target company, which retains the same basis in its assets.

NET OPERATING LOSSES

From the perspective of an acquirer, a target company's accumulated losses from prior years may be an asset. Judging the value of net operating losses, or NOLs, is an important aspect of the deal analysis.

Generally, a corporation may use NOLs generated in the previous fifteen years as a deduction against current profits, thus lowering taxes.

In theory, each $1 of carryover should have a net after-tax value of 35 cents—the amount of taxes saved by a corporation in the usual 35 percent bracket if the carryover can be used. But the particular facts of a situation may make a dollar of carryover worth anything from 35 cents to nothing for an acquiring corporation.

Under the current tax rules, a target company's NOLs generally remain in place following a stock purchase or tax-free merger. However, if the acquirer buys more than 50 percent of the target company, the ability to use the NOLs may be limited. Specifically, the company may only be allowed to use an amount of NOLs each year equal to the fair market value of the target company stock at the time of acquisition multiplied by a government-determined interest rate, roughly 7 to 8 percent.

Taxable Stock Purchase

The taxable purchase of stock is straightforward. The buyer pays selling shareholders with cash or nonvoting securities, or some combination of the two. The selling shareholders recognize a capital gain or loss equal to the difference between their respective tax bases in the shares and the value of the property received in exchange. The seller takes a basis in the target company shares equal to the purchase price paid.

Post-Acquisition Tax Basis   Absent a special election, the tax basis of target company assets will not be stepped up following a stock purchase. The target company remains intact and is treated as a black box from the acquirer's perspective. After all, General Motors doesn't shift its asset basis each time someone sells a hundred shares of stock. A taxable stock purchase is just a large-scale stock sale.

However, there is an exception. An acquirer can elect to have a taxable stock purchase treated as an asset purchase and take a stepped-up basis. This increased basis in turn may generate higher depreciation and amortization, as well as other deductible benefits, reducing the target company's post-acquisition taxable income.

The tax law provides two kinds of election—each with different requirements and different consequences. The "regular" election is available without regard to the identity of the selling shareholders. If this election is made, the target company is treated as selling its assets at fair market value to a new corporation. This deemed sale triggers a corporate-level tax on any gain inherent in the assets. The acquirer then owns a "new" target company with a stepped-up asset basis.

On a present-value basis, the tax imposed under this regular election usually will outweigh the future benefit from the step-up. The step-up may be a net benefit, on the other hand, if the target company has incurred past losses which can be used to shield the tax. In that case, the parties must decide how to share the net benefit.

The second, more limited election only applies when an acquirer purchases a subsidiary of another company, and is designed to avoid two levels of taxation. In order to qualify, the seller must own 80 percent of the subsidiary, by vote and value, prior to the sale.

This limited election also applies to the selling shareholder. In other words, the stock sale is ignored entirely and the selling shareholder is treated as if the target company had sold its assets and then liquidated. The asset sale is deemed to take place while the target company is owned by the selling shareholder. Thus, the selling shareholder is responsible for the target company's tax on any gain from the deemed asset sale, but is not taxed a second time on the liquidation of its stock position.

The net effect is to impose a single layer of tax on the associated-basis step-up. In most cases, the combination of the single tax and any available step-up will make the parties financially better off as a whole. Again, the parties decide how to divide the net benefit.

Tax Rulings and Opinions

A company planning a merger, acquisition or spin-off that is meant to be tax-free sometimes will seek an advance ruling from the IRS regarding the tax-free status of a deal. The alternative is to rely instead on an opinion from tax lawyers. A private letter ruling provides greater certainty regarding the tax treatment of a transaction but several countervailing concerns exist.

A private letter ruling is a formal document provided by the IRS to a taxpayer. The taxpayer to whom the ruling is addressed can rely on the document as binding. This certainty has value, particularly in a large transaction where the potential tax liability might be quite significant.

Yet certainty is elusive. Private letter rulings generally are based on a factual description of the contemplated transaction provided by the relevant taxpayer, as well as a number of assumptions. If any of these assumptions or facts change, the ruling is no longer binding.

Another problem with seeking a ruling is the cost, time and energy required to secure the document. First, a written ruling request is filed with the IRS, perhaps preceded by a preliminary conference. The issue then is assigned to someone in the IRS's Chief Counsel office who calls with a preliminary response roughly three weeks after assignment. There are opportunities for further submissions to address concerns. If the IRS lawyer indicates an inability to grant the ruling, the taxpayer is entitled to a conference with a supervisor. Assuming a decision is made to issue the ruling, a letter is drafted and sent to the taxpayer.

The entire ruling process generally drags out over five or six months, and can take longer. Some lawyers specialize in the rarefied practice of shepherding clients through the gauntlet. At times, it seems as if the IRS is looking for magic words from some prior ruling or case. If a ruling request fits the mold, approval is granted. If not, the review is much more painstaking and the IRS's ruling guidelines in certain areas are more strict than the law would seem to require.

Furthermore, politics plays a role in the process. The mood of the moment might favor tightening up to reduce merger flow or loosening to allow a more free merger market. A transaction that does not pass muster with the IRS might be ruled tax-free in the courts if it were contested, which is unlikely given the associated time delays and negative public exposure.

The alternative is to rely on a tax opinion, which can be obtained quite quickly. Moreover, expert tax counsel can reflect on the full scope of the law.

A tax opinion is a letter from private tax counsel, usually from a major corporate law firm. In the context of a merger or spin-off, a tax opinion might state that the contemplated transaction "will" be treated as tax-free. However, there are a number of gradations to opinion standards. The issuing law firm might only state that the transaction "should" be tax-free, or that it is "more likely than not" that the transaction will be tax-free. These are terms of art intended to capture varying levels of certainty.

A tax opinion provides comfort on two levels. First, top-notch firms guard their reputations closely. A strong opinion therefore is a good indication that a sound position in favor of tax-free status exists. Second, an incorrect opinion may provide grounds for malpractice litigation. However, any eventual malpractice liability payments are likely to pale in comparison to the resulting tax liability. Clients nonetheless joust with counsel attempting to force a stronger opinion, mainly to ensure that lawyers are willing to stand up for the advice they are giving.

Of course, even the strongest opinion is just an opinion. This is the reason why the large majority of public companies contemplating a spin-off—a particularly complicated and subjective area of the law—condition the transaction on the receipt of a favorable ruling.

Accounting Treatment

Accounting treatment, like tax law, is at the heart of the merger business. How a deal will be priced, the consideration involved, and how the market will react are often driven by accounting. When one company acquires another or when two companies merge, the corporate combination can be accounted for as either a pooling of interests or as a purchase. The choice of purchase versus pooling has absolutely no impact on a company's underlying health or performance. However, from a financial accounting perspective, the survivor's earnings can differ dramatically depending on which approach is taken. This accounting impact is the focus of the merger consequences model and, with many investors focused on earnings, companies often hesitate to take on dilutive transactions.

Purchase Accounting

If a firm buys a piece of equipment for cash, the cost of the asset is reflected on the company's books at its purchase price. Similarly, when a company purchases another company's stock for cash, the total price paid is reflected under the "purchase" method of accounting. However, the price paid often is above the fair market value of the target company's tangible assets. The difference between the purchase price and the tangible asset value is considered goodwill.

In order to reflect the full cost of the transaction, the buyer enters both the value of the acquired firm's tangible assets and the related goodwill on its balance sheet. Thus, for example, if a company has tangible assets worth $10 and it is purchased for $15, $5 would be goodwill. Goodwill is almost universal in acquisitions because earning power usually makes a firm worth more than the value of its tangible assets.

The critical question then is how the frequently arising goodwill should be treated. As a general default rule, U.S. companies must amortize goodwill over not more than forty years (tangibles such as plant and equipment are depreciated, intangibles such as patents and goodwill are amortized), with an important effect on earnings. Accountants now often require amortization over a shorter period. For example, if a firm with a tangible worth of $40 million and earnings of $10 million a year before taxes were purchased for $80 million, the amortization of the $40 million in goodwill could well have a dramatic impact. If the goodwill were amortized over, for example, twenty years, annual earnings would be lower by $2 million.

As the result of a 1993 tax law revision, goodwill generated in an asset purchase may be tax deductible in some instances. In that case, the net bottom-line impact of the goodwill is reduced by the amount of tax savings generated from the resulting deductions. The tax law requires deductible goodwill to be amortized over a fifteen-year period.

Naturally, executives actively involved in either selling or buying companies have historically opposed the amortization of goodwill for financial reporting purposes. The theoretical basis for this position is that goodwill is not a wasting asset—it lasts as long as the company. For added support, executives pointed to Great Britain, which until recently allowed companies to write off acquired goodwill directly against shareholder equity. The cost did not, therefore, flow through the income statement, and reported earnings were higher than would otherwise be the case. This arguably gave U.K. companies an edge over U.S. companies when attempting an acquisition. Under new rules implemented in 1998, U.K. companies will be required to carry goodwill on their balance sheets and amortize it over time unless they can show the goodwill has not declined in value.

ON THE BATTLEFIELD

Wells Fargo Busts Pooling

Wells Fargo Bank's 1995 hostile takeover of First Interstate was a rare exception to the rule in the banking world. Wells Fargo chairman Paul Hazen, in the top spot just a year, made the decision to go hostile.

Hazen's predecessor had long pined over First Interstate, and had made several unsuccessful approaches to First Interstate management. So, when Hazen took over, he knew private talks were not the answer. With a reputation as "the king of the hardball bankers," Hazen considered the idea of taking a tougher stance. Winning First Interstate was not the problem. Hazen was confident that could be managed. The accounting rules for mergers were the main stumbling block.

Bank mergers almost uniformly are accounted for as poolings of interests. The consensus before Wells Fargo launched its bid was that the market would punish a bank with goodwill on its books. In addition, if Wells Fargo wanted to try for pooling, it would have to suspend its share repurchase program, a critical part of Hazen's strategy to boost Wells Fargo's share price.

After consideration, Hazen decided there was much to gain from playing the maverick. He was confident he could convince the equity analysts who followed Wells Fargo to look past the artificial impact of the resulting goodwill. Plus, a hostile takeover was the only way to nab First Interstate. On October 18, 1995, Hazen announced his tender offer for First Interstate. Under the plan, Wells Fargo would pay $10.9 billion in stock for its target.

Hoping to avoid being swallowed by its crosstown rival, First Interstate rushed into the arms of a white knight. First Bank System, a Minneapolis bank with far fewer overlapping operations, agreed to merge with First Interstate in a stock deal valued at $10.1 billion. Unlike Wells Fargo, First Bank was depending on accounting for the deal as a pooling of interests.

Over a period of three months, Hazen traded barbs and lawsuits with his two counterparts. Ultimately, though, the market decided the contest. Because both deals on the table involved stock as consideration, the relative values of the two bids fluctuated with the banks' stock prices.

Hazen and his team traveled to New York and wowed the Wall Street analysts. At the time, Wells Fargo was turning in a strong performance. Hazen promised to turn his bank's tough cost cutters loose on First Interstate. The market responded by bidding up Wells Fargo's stock price.

As a result, First Bank's friendly deal was hanging by a thread. Then, the SEC ruled that First Bank would be barred from buying back any shares for two years if its merger with First Interstate were to go through. Like Wells Fargo, First Bank viewed share repurchases as critical to its effort to make its stock more valuable.

Rather than continue the fight, First Bank took its $200 million breakup fee and Wells Fargo emerged the winner.

However, First Interstate's former management enjoyed a measure of vindication in the months after declaring defeat. First Interstate's top managers almost uniformly took their golden parachutes and moved on. Meanwhile, Wells Fargo had great difficulty integrating the two banks. A host of customer service problems, sparked by the post-deal brain drain and difficulties in meshing computer systems, plagued Wells Fargo. Depositors pulled their money from branches and Wells Fargo's stock price fell 20 percent, while other banks enjoyed a boom.

Hazen responded to the integration problems with an aggressive turnaround effort, which began to take hold in the fall of 1997. The First Interstate deal may yet be a triumph.

Pooling

Accountants have felt that the purchase method is not appropriate for all merger transactions, especially stock-for-stock transactions. Pooling is an alternative accounting concept under which the purchase of a company is essentially ignored for accounting purposes in certain limited circumstances; rather, the two independent concerns involved are treated as though they had always been together. The purchase price is not reflected on the acquirer's balance sheet because the assets of the companies are pooled.

For example, if a company with assets of $30 million book value purchases a company with assets worth $20 million for $30 million in voting stock, conventional "purchase accounting" would state that goodwill of $10 million was present in a combined company with $60 million in assets. Under pooling, however, the goodwill would be ignored, and the total assets on the surviving company's books would be valued at $50 million (assuming the target's book value is $20 million). Hence, pooling—which avoids the creation of goodwill—can make an important difference in earnings results.

The original theoretical foundation for the pooling approach was that two companies of roughly comparable size involved in a stock-for-stock purchase should be treated as though they joined one another. Over the years, however, because of the favorable earnings impact, companies of grossly disproportionate size used the pooling method, and the stock-for-stock standard was diluted. The American Institute of Certified Public Accountants (AICPA) came out with study after study over a period of twenty years that suggested criteria for limiting the use of pooling, including rough comparability of size among companies.

At the height of the 1960s merger wave, critics, including the Federal Trade Commission, argued that pooling increased the incentive to merge by jacking up earnings. The SEC finally brought pressure on the AICPA to reform. In a first draft opinion, the AICPA did, indeed, state a comparability-of-size test for pooling. The howl from the nation's leading companies and their accountants was, however, overwhelming. As a result, a rough compromise was fashioned in the final AICPA opinions. These governing rules are vital to any merger analysis.

In order to be eligible for pooling treatment, a merger must meet a number of somewhat arbitrary rules. For example, each of the combining companies must be independent and cannot have been a division or subsidiary of another company in the last two years, the deal must be completed within one year in one transaction, and the consideration involved must be voting common stock for substantially all of the target company's voting stock. The surviving company also generally must have refrained from share repurchases for the two years before the transaction and may not agree to repurchase the shares issued in the transaction.

Recently, the SEC has stated that stock buybacks within six months after a transaction will blow pooling. In addition, the SEC will disallow pooling where the agency believes a share repurchase completed within two years after a transaction was contemplated at the time of the transaction.

THE BATTLE OVER GOODWILL

Fundamentally, whether a merger is accounted for as a purchase or pooling shouldn't matter. The annual goodwill expense consumes no cash and is unrelated to the underlying operating performance of a business. A sensible approach would be to add back goodwill amortization to the earnings of all companies with goodwill on their books, normalizing the presentation for comparison purposes, unless the value of the assets was impaired.

As a practical matter, though, investors do follow earnings per share and the presence of goodwill may have at least a psychological impact on perceptions of performance. As a result, companies in the past have been reluctant to do deals that generate considerable goodwill.

However, lately, investors are becoming more sophisticated about discounting the real-world impact of goodwill charges. Moreover, there is growing recognition that the avoidance of goodwill has a cost, the issuance of more stock than optimal by acquirers to fund deals. From an economic perspective, with low interest rates and the tax-deductibility of interest expense, financing with debt may be otherwise more beneficial. Of course, eventually shares can be repurchased but only after the passage of time because of the pooling requirement.

Wells Fargo and several other high-profile companies have seized on this fact and have demonstrated a willingness to do deals under purchase accounting, despite the large slugs of goodwill involved. Bell Atlantic's short-lived deal with TCI, for example, would have generated roughly $20 billion of goodwill, for $2 billion a year of goodwill amortization over ten years. This amount would have wiped out TCI's earnings, making the deal highly dilutive for Bell Atlantic. However, Bell Atlantic chairman Ray Smith was focused on cash flow, not earnings. Before the FCC acted to lower cable rates, TCI was projected to have a strong and growing cash flow. This money could be used to pay down debt or upgrade TCI's systems to digital technology. Furthermore, like Smith, investors were willing to look past the goodwill to see the logic of the deal. Bell Atlantic's stock climbed almost eight points on the announcement of the deal.

The Bell Atlantic–TCI deal ultimately fell apart, but others have picked up the banner for purchase accounting deals. Disney's acquisition of ABC was accounted for as a purchase and created more than $18 billion of goodwill. Aetna's purchase of U.S. Healthcare created $8 billion of goodwill. Both deals were favorably received on Wall Street.

Notwithstanding these exceptions, the general rule still is that companies like to avoid goodwill. However, there are inklings of a wider shift percolating through the system.

The Financial Accounting Standards Board (FASB), the private-sector entity that governs the GAAP rules, has said it is considering the purchase versus pooling dichotomy. Originally, there was some talk of limiting or doing away with pooling, but the FASB's flexibility is limited, given the political pressure to retain the more favorable treatment.

More recently, the FASB has indicated it may opt for an intermediate approach more akin to the British practice. Right now, American companies are disadvantaged in doing deals because of the difference in accounting for goodwill. Under the proposal, a company would carry goodwill on its balance sheet. There would be no annual goodwill charges. Instead, the goodwill would be tested annually for "impairment," and, if the value of the goodwill were lower than book value, the company would be required to take an immediate write-off of the difference. Of course, the problem with this approach is that goodwill is notoriously difficult to value.

These issues will be the subject of debate for some time. Given the contentious issues involved, the precise contours of any eventual reform in this area remain unclear. However, if the FASB indeed eliminates annual goodwill charges, a flood of cash deals may be unleashed.

The Leveraged Recapitalization

In the days of the classic LBO, financial buyers cared little about the intricacies of purchase versus pooling. Goodwill amortization was an accounting fiction with an Alice in Wonderland quality, something they simply ignored. Cash flow was the focus and private-market sales to like-minded acquirers the anticipated exit strategy.

In recent years, financial buyers have been capitalizing on the hot IPO market by taking portfolio companies public. Indeed, acquisitions are now made with the intention of taking the resulting company public as quickly as possible. High prices are justified as a variant of momentum investing. Financial buyers have as a result begun to focus on strong earnings as an important marketing tool.

Purchase accounting is one critical barrier for strong reported earnings. The leveraged roll-up is one strategy to get around the problem of inordinate goodwill amortization. In this format, an initial public company is purchased and then used as a vehicle for stock mergers. However, in most cases, financial buyers need to invest cash.

Facing the dilemma of how to invest cash without creating goodwill, financial buyers developed the leveraged recapitalization structure. The typical transaction has two steps. First, the target company borrows enough money to create a leveraged capital structure, say with a four-to-one debt-to-equity ratio. This cash is paid to existing shareholders as a dividend or in a stock redemption.

Second, the financial buyer or other acquirer buys shares in the target, either from the target or from its shareholders. The end result is a leveraged company, up to 80 percent of which is owned by the acquirer and 20 percent owned by original target company shareholders.

Curiously, with careful structuring, the accounting rules treat this transaction as a recapitalization of the target. No goodwill is created at the target level, with the desired preservation of favorable earnings.

The magic to this process is avoiding so-called push-down accounting. Under GAAP, an acquirer must record goodwill in reflecting the target company investment on its books. Financial buyers use dummy companies as acquisition vehicles and couldn't care less about the goodwill at this level. The problem is that the SEC may under certain circumstances require this goodwill to be "pushed down" to the target company's books, reducing earnings. Generally, the key to avoiding this result is for the buyer to keep its ownership under 80 percent. If the continuing shareholders own 5 percent or less of the company, push-down accounting is absolutely required.

Implementing the Deal | 17

". . . But were you effective?"

Brian D. Young, LBO specialist

Implementing a deal is a blend of psychology, business judgment and technical dexterity. While taxes, accounting, and corporate law provide the skeletal frame of transactions, optimizing position is the purpose of direct negotiation. Aside from skill and effort, an in-depth knowledge of the inherent pitfalls in the deal structure is essential. Conceptualizing a deal is quite different from executing it.

Negotiation Tactics

Successful negotiation tactics are partly instinctual, but also rely on accumulated insight and interpersonal skills. Unlike litigation—where one side wins and the other loses—negotiated deals necessarily involve working with the other party to a mutually satisfactory resolution of the issues. Experts on the strategy of negotiations stress the need for a cooperative approach. In a truly successful bargaining session, everybody can feel some satisfaction. This is not a zero sum game.

In complicated deals, the ability of the negotiator is fundamental in two respects: First, the terms negotiated can substantially alter the economics of a transaction. Second, and more importantly, the negotiator may be the determining factor in whether the deal survives. Unless skillfully handled, a myriad of small issues sometimes builds into mutual antagonisms. Unfortunately, out of this accumulation of irritation, the building up of lethargy, disorganization and lack of creative problem solving, many a deal that should have lived has died.

Objectives

Before entering into any bargaining session, well-advised parties engage in some preliminary reflection. The first, and perhaps the hardest, task is determining objectives. One reason for the difficulty is that the differing representatives of a party often will not share the same perspective or, even worse, will not have thought in depth about the main issues. A key challenge is, therefore, dealing with one's own side and helping to focus their energies. To consider techniques independent of a clear set of objectives makes little sense.

For instance, the relative negotiating positions of Quaker Oats and Triarc, as implied from Triarc's 1997 Snapple purchase, were defined by different objectives. Going into talks, Quaker clearly wanted out of the Snapple debacle and had been shopping the company. Quaker's write-down of Snapple on its books only underscored that fact for potential bidders. Yet Quaker needed a credible purchaser and as much of a face-saving price as was possible.

Triarc, on the other hand, sought critical mass for its noncola beverage business. However, Triarc was a disciplined buyer, only willing to pay so much for Snapple. An attractive return on investment was the goal.

As it turned out, Triarc and Quaker had different but complementary goals. Quaker was willing to lower its price threshold—closure on the failed Snapple investment was more important than price. Triarc refused to raise beyond $300 million because price was the key issue. Yet, with a presence in the beverage business and a history of successful turnarounds, Triarc was a credible buyer. In selling to Triarc, Quaker would clearly be admitting a failure, but would also be able to say the Snapple business would continue. The parties ultimately agreed to terms because their objectives intersected.

Preparation

Extensive preparation gives an edge to a negotiator. Not only is it desirable to research the issues, but knowing as much as possible about the other side's representatives and its current position and techniques is invaluable. Determining the needs of the other side, both in personal and economic terms, is fundamental to successful negotiation.

Financial modeling can be helpful. If a party is likely to focus on the earnings-per-share impact of a deal, understanding the impact at various transaction values and with different structures can give a sense of the negotiating range. What is the projected earnings per share for the first couple of years after a deal? What is a likely trading price? How much can the other side afford to give?

Likewise, modeling the cash flow impact of a deal at various prices and with different capital structures gives insight to the perspective of a financial buyer. Of course, if the party on the other side of the table is using different assumptions in modeling the transaction, the results will vary.

Just as important to the flow of a negotiation is an understanding of the mannerisms, personalities, and reactions of each side's representatives. Sometimes, there is a clear mismatch of styles or personalities. Skillful negotiators step in and smooth the irritation to keep the deal on track.

Despite conventional wisdom, it is often helpful if the other party is being represented by a sophisticated advocate. When the other side at the bargaining table does not have a knowledgeable team, an atmosphere of suspicion and delay often arises. Knowledge gives the confidence to be flexible, as when Warren Buffett agreed to the warrants in the Capital Cities acquisition of ABC. He had the credibility and the sophistication to understand that the strategic imperative of the deal was worth the trade-off. When it makes sense, the strong can afford to be weak.

On the other hand, the natural reaction of someone in over his head is to be recalcitrant. To take a typical situation, if a buyout of a small company has complicated tax implications, it is extremely difficult to persuade someone who does not understand the tax laws to devise a structure that uses those laws to maximum advantage.

Techniques

Techniques are mechanisms to obtain objectives. Obviously, the appropriate technique depends on the particular objective. There are, however, some universal guides.

Control   A key element in negotiation is retaining control. For example, the basic maxim is to keep the master document and do the drafting. When parties are making comments around the table, the copy that will be sent to the typist is the one the negotiator controls. Naturally, this position of control gives the negotiator a good bit of added leverage. First, the negotiator usually has the choice of redrafting a comment later or inserting language now. Second, if the negotiator feels the debate on any point should continue, the issue can be kept open simply by not writing anything down or bracketing conflicting language.

Pace is a related point. Good negotiators never let a deal get away from them; if substantive issues are being discussed too rapidly without careful thought, haste may haunt the negotiator later. One ideal way in which to control pace is to be the host for the meeting. The negotiator controls when the documents are distributed, when breaks are taken, and often what the time pressures are. It is very important, however, to be cordial and accommodating so that the adversaries will want to return. For example, Wachtel, Lipton works hard at being a gracious host by offering extensive support services and lavish lunches and dinners. Just as in sports, where the home team usually performs better in its own stadium, a negotiator often obtains improved results by bargaining in friendly territory.

On the other hand, it is also the responsibility of the negotiator to make sure the pace of issue resolution is such that the deal survives. Long hours, lists of key issues and constant prodding may be necessary, but a deal is like a soufflé; timing is of the essence.

PROFILE

Sam Butler—Mr. Friendly Deal

Lawyer Sam Butler, presiding partner at Cravath, looks like a former Harvard football player, which he was, crossed with a fraternity president, which he also was. Always smiling, always gracious, Butler is a nice man whose avid hobby is theater. Yet Butler was also an editor of the *Harvard Law Review* and a U.S. Supreme Court clerk, and has a crack legal mind with a unique instinct for compromise. Behind the amiable facade, Butler knows how to move deals along. He is a maestro of the deal process who will cut fools to ribbons if they bluff, but remain gracious to those who go along. If Marty Lipton is Mr. Defense, Sam Butler is Mr. Friendly Deal.

Butler's natural ability is supplemented by an ingrained sense of the power of small incremental advantages. When negotiating a document, he lives by his rule "control the master." However, Butler goes beyond this truism, always having agendas and lists of open points in a negotiation. Controlling these administrative details provides the opportunity to shape the process. Butler's focus and discipline shine throughout the process. The Butler legend is that when he was an associate up for partnership, he finished the bound volumes of documents on a big deal—which usually memorialize a transaction six months after the event—at the time of the closing, an astonishing feat.

Skill and the wisdom of experience put Butler in high demand. Though his press profile may be lower than that of Marty Lipton or Joe Flom, Butler has led numerous high-profile deals to closing. For example, he handled the corporate law side of the 1989 Time-Warner deal for Cravath client Time Inc., and in 1995 advised GEICO when Warren Buffett bought out the minority stake he didn't already control. Also in 1995, Butler simultaneously represented both Capital Cities/ABC and CBS in their respective sales. Butler meanwhile guided Cravath to retain its status as one of America's leading corporate law firms.

Credibility   It is very important to establish credibility early in a negotiation. Credibility is accorded some negotiators because of their reputation, and unless they demonstrate otherwise, they have no need to establish that stature. For example, a senior partner in a major law firm or investment bank is assumed to be skilled. However, a young colleague may not be assumed to have that credibility. Here is where preparation comes in handy. An awesome familiarity with the documents and a few obviously salient points earn respect and credibility.

A related problem is that of firmness. Although negotiating is a cooperative process, most parties are prepared to pick the other's pockets if the opportunity presents itself. If one side thinks that the other is an easy mark, the negotiations will inevitably degenerate. Usually, the tendency of inexperienced negotiators is to be too belligerent and inflexible. When these negotiators realize that the goal is to close on reasonable terms rather than to bulldoze the other side, this overindulgence is soon toned down. But the art of not being too pliant is a more delicate one, depending in large part on the situation.

One way to handle overbearing advocates is to take one issue as a test case and spend extra time resolving it. Hopefully, the other side will realize that, if necessary, bullying will be firmly resisted and will desist. Sometimes, the other side will be represented by an adviser who is obstinate for obstinacy's sake. If all else fails, experienced negotiators try to make sure that the clients on both sides watch a performance in person. Often a rebuke will follow, and behavior will change with surprising swiftness.

Then, of course, there is the occasional pathological bully. Some people just can't help themselves and rant and rave with red-faced demonstrations of temper. My favorite response is to speak softly and say, "Everybody else in the room can scream. We can resume business when you're done." The bully craves sensible limits.

Sensitivity Because negotiation is necessarily a cooperative process, both sides have to be reasonably happy for the deal to work. It is therefore important to be reasonable, although not obsequious, and, ideally, to give the other side enough so that its advocates do not feel resentful. A little psychology is required. All those involved in a deal like to feel that they made a positive contribution and that they obtained some concessions. After all, otherwise their presence wasn't required.

It's not that all parties need to be equally happy with the results of a deal; it's just that everyone should have some limited solace. Courtesies, such as specifically marking changes, providing extra copies of documents and giving personal assistance, may also bear important dividends, especially if the parties are to have an ongoing relationship, such as in a joint venture. When a side has bargaining strength, it sometimes becomes giddy with power. Retention of perspective is important; one day, the tables may turn, and a loss of dignity is seldom forgotten or forgiven.

In addition to these universal techniques, other strategies are very much dependent on the situation.

Confusion Versus Clarity   Generally, it is advisable to articulate a clear, concise position. Sometimes, however, there is great advantage to confusion, especially if time is running against the other side. For example, in buying a company with a tax-loss carry-forward, the excuse can be used that operating managers have difficulty understanding or caring about after-tax impacts, since incentive compensation is based on pretax results. Such an excuse is frustrating but much less bothersome than stating that those rights are valuable and then refusing to pay for them.

Similarly, confusion often simplifies bargaining by limiting flexibility. For example, an advocate may assert that though there is great merit in the twenty modifications sought by the other side, the client is a large organization with standard policies and it would require months of delay and myriad committee decisions to alter the documents as suggested. Confusion, whether just apparent or real, gives the other side a rational reason for accepting proposals which are irrationally unfair. Even if one does not care to use this confusion gambit, it should be recognized in the techniques of others.

Emotions   The Russians historically have developed a reputation as negotiators who kick and scream over every comma. Pretty soon, the other side becomes immune to the dramatic effect. But there are negotiators who can skillfully turn on righteous indignation at precisely the right point and be extremely effective. Certainly, control over feelings is useful and histrionics are seldom persuasive, but all anger need not be repressed. Especially if one has been co-operative and reasonable, a show of anger may well be justified by the situation, particularly if you feel the other side has begun to try to take advantage of your flexibility.

Support   As a general rule, experienced merger negotiators like to have some balance between the number of representatives on their side and the other side at a meeting. Otherwise, there is an element of feeling overpowered, especially to the inexperienced negotiator. There are, however, some caveats. First, if you overwhelm the other side with numbers, the reaction may well be obstinacy instead of willingness to make reasonable concessions. Second, the lack of full representation gives a negotiator more personal control and more chance to ferret out information from the other side without a quid pro quo.

The more people from the negotiator's side present, the more likely that negotiation planning will be upset. For example, in a large conference, it is common for two businesspeople to begin talking directly to each other instead of going through the negotiators about issues that one negotiator would rather have brought up later. What usually makes sense is the development of a small team with the negotiator as the authorized spokesperson who can turn to the others on the team as appropriate. Some coordination is required, or the team will act as a jumble of individuals with contradictory ideas and techniques, which cannot help but weaken a side's bargaining position.

Agents Versus Principals   For sessions to be productive, the negotiators must have the bargaining authority, subject to their principals' comments, to compromise the less-material issues. A more fundamental question is whether a principal should always be present to make the major decisions. Without doubt, proceedings are expedited if disputes can be immediately resolved, but there are serious drawbacks—most important, the loss of time for reflection and an opportunity to keep the various outstanding points in balance. Furthermore, principals often get impatient with discussions of details which may be cumulatively important. It frequently helps to have the principals present at early meetings to discuss fundamental terms and then let their staffs attempt to implement the agreed-upon principles. If, as usual, there is a list of major items that cannot be agreed upon by the staffs, the principals can meet again to resolve them.

One common tactic is for the negotiator to try to elicit concessions from the other side and then refuse to make corresponding compromises because of a lack of authority. If this technique is allowed to succeed, the result is a one-way give-up. Either insist on principals being present or agree that both sides can in good faith revise their positions, but that the concessions are points the negotiators will, respectively, recommend.

PROFILE

Carl Icahn

Carl Icahn is a tough negotiator. Whether he ultimately buys a company, motivates a white knight to buy the company or sells his stock back to the target or in the market, one thing remains constant. Icahn is never content to split the difference—he wants to win on every point.

One of Icahn's tactics in the 1980s was to get a full night's sleep the day before a negotiation, perhaps even take a nap in the afternoon of the negotiating day, and then show up late to the meeting. He would stubbornly drag the debate into the early morning hours. Since he was well rested and his adversaries presumably were not, Icahn figured he would have the advantage.

In his early days, opponents underestimated Carl. He speaks in a circular, rambling style with no attempt to get to the point, sometimes affecting a thick New York accent. When clients found out that he was a Princeton graduate and extraordinarily sharp, they used to be shocked. Now the corporate community knows Carl is a serious player who doesn't scare easily. U.S. Steel, Texaco and RJR have all felt Carl's bite.

The most effective opponent to Icahn we represented was the chairman of U.S. Steel, David Roderick. Icahn bought an interest in Roderick's company in late 1989 and began to agitate for a breakup of the company's oil and steel businesses. The two men eventually sat down to try and work something out. Roderick, who was used to labor negotiations, liked to spin a yarn as much as Icahn. He kept talking and talking. Finally, a reasonable settlement was achieved. Each party had tired the other out.

Contract Issues

Legendary Hollywood producer Sam Goldwyn reputedly once said, "A verbal contract isn't worth the paper it's written on." This may be hyperbolic, but in the context of a merger or acquisition, documentation is important. A detailed negotiation regarding the terms of a deal reduces the likelihood of future disagreement. Though every eventuality cannot be anticipated, comprehensive documentation focuses attention on the major issues.

A contract can allocate the risk of economic loss from undisclosed defects in the target company and provide protection in the case of a later disagreement. These protections have limits, of course, but can provide significant and sometimes decisive leverage in any dispute. A contract might even specify dispute resolution procedures.

Many executives understandably get bored with the legal byplay on drafting provisions. In the end, however, the wisdom of the conference room discussions is unimportant; it is the wording and clarity of the contract that counts. The slip between verbiage and paper is a recurring problem in deals.

The Five Pillars of Contract

The variety and number of issues that arise in big-deal negotiations are virtually limitless, but a certain amount of order can be introduced to the process. A typical merger or acquisition agreement covers five basic areas, each of which raises issues for negotiation. These five pillars are: pricing terms, representations, covenants, conditions and indemnities.

Pricing   Pricing, which on its face should be one of the most obvious parts of a deal, is often the most elusive. The form and terms of consideration (cash or stock), their tax impact, the assumed liabilities (present and contingent), the assumption of costs, and the post-closing adjustments are all big items that get less attention than deserved. Lawyers all too often are fuzzy on these subjects because they are technical business matters that are specific to each deal.

For example, just the closing adjustments related to noncash working capital can be a multimillion-dollar item. Noncash working capital consists of current assets other than cash, chiefly accounts receivable and inventory, less current liabilities such as accounts payable. The danger in an acquisition is that a seller will convert current assets to cash and slow down payment of current liabilities. If the cash generated is drained from the business between the time a deal is signed and when it closes, the buyer can end up with a crippled company.

One approach to protect against this eventuality is to prohibit cash dividends out of a business between signing and closing. Another approach is to take cash off the books at closing, but to adjust the purchase price based on working capital fluctuations. In this case, a "peg" balance sheet is established at signing. If working capital is higher at closing, then the buyer pays the difference, but if working capital declines, the buyer reduces its purchase price by that amount. The seller then has no incentive to convert working capital to cash. Of course, for a business like retail, some provision also may need to be made for seasonal fluctuations.

Even with a no-dividends provision, a buyer often argues for a purchase price adjustment mechanism. A deal can take months to close. Buyers generally make the purchase decision based on some projection of operating performance and cash generation in the interim. However, projections are by nature uncertain. A question of who bears the business risk between signing and closing often arises. The buyer will argue that the seller should bear the risk, since it will control operations until closing. Conversely, the seller will argue the buyer should take the business as is. A purchase price adjustment typically is the mechanism for risk sharing.

Representations Representations are contractual assertions as to the state of affairs at the time a contract is signed. While buyer and seller typically both make representations, the seller's representations regarding the target company and its operations are key.

The main representations are that the information contained in the financial statements and other informational materials provided by the sellers is correct and without material omissions. These two provisions often are supplemented by a representation that no "material adverse change" has affected the business since the date of the last financial statements. This so-called MAC clause is often resisted by sellers on the ground that a buyer should make its decision based on the existing facts and other terms of the agreement. A MAC clause nonetheless is often included, though the parameters may be narrowly defined in an effort to screen out changes related to wider economic shifts.

Other common representations include detailed provisions regarding environmental matters, copyrights or patents licensed or owned by the company, major real estate and equipment, key leases and contracts, pending litigation, tax liabilities and so on. Theoretically, all representations other than those about the informational documents and the financials should be irrelevant because if they are about material facts, they should be reflected in the documents. However, it is generally preferable from a purchaser's point of view to go through the litany of more detailed representations for two reasons.

First, the detailed representations, in effect, define what the concept of materiality means for the agreement. For example, if the company represents that all employee contracts for salaries over $100,000 a year are listed in Exhibit X, presumably that is the cutoff level of materiality for employee compensation. Defined representations also have the ancillary benefit of providing a number of triggers which can be used as closing conditions. The result is that more representations gives the buyer more leverage in adjusting the price at the closing.

Second, and as important, there is solace in detail for the buyer. Specificity increases the probability of effective due diligence by the company in ferreting out material facts. Generalizations are easier to ignore than specifics; if, for example, a company has to list all loans to officers, it may well stumble over some which should have been described in the draft of documents provided to the purchaser but weren't. Specific lists give the purchasers a comprehensive idea of the documents they or their representatives should examine before investing. Of course, for the seller, an anal buyer who insists on a lot of representations is a nightmare.

Representations can be more or less favorable to a buyer depending on how they are drafted. One common method of watering down a representation is to add a reference to knowledge or materiality. A seller's representation that the target company has filed all tax returns, for example, might be altered by limiting the coverage to "material" tax returns or conditioning the representation on the seller's knowledge regarding any failure to file. If knowledge is used as the qualifier, a contract typically will state whose knowledge counts—anyone at the selling company or only its directors or officers, and so on. In either case, adding knowledge and material qualifiers gives the seller wiggle room in any future dispute. The seller, of course, will argue that any problems were not material and that it had no knowledge of the condition.

The strength of representations ultimately depends on the extent to which they survive the closing. At one end of the spectrum, a pro-buyer agreement might provide that representations survive indefinitely. A pro-seller approach would be to have the representations evaporate at closing. At stake in the difference is the buyer's ability to recover for a breach of the representations under any indemnity provision or otherwise. Tactically, a seller may be willing to represent everything under the sun as long as it doesn't survive. The seller is really saying, look at everything, but once you buy it, it's yours. A common middle-ground solution is to have the representations survive, but only for a short period, perhaps six months. Certain representations, specifically those regarding taxes and environmental matters which involve third-party claims, often are carved out and given a longer life.

Naturally, the public-company deal is documented somewhat differently than a private-company deal. Unless there is a large controlling stake, it is unusual to have representations survive the closing. In this context, the representations are essentially a lever to walk before closing or to lower the purchase price.

Covenants Covenants (or promises) of the sellers can be divided into preclosing and post-closing covenants. Common preclosing covenants include the seller's ensuring that the target continues operating according to its ordinary course of business and provides access to the purchaser. The target also often agrees to maintain life insurance policies on the key executives, facilitate the transition and comply, at the option of the investors, with the information requirements of the federal securities laws. Common post-closing covenants include the seller's covenants not to compete with the target after the sale, to preserve the confidentiality of information and to provide transition assistance.

Conditions   Conditions—or prerequisites to closing—protect the parties to an agreement. When a condition is breached, the aggrieved party typically has the power to cancel a transaction. A loosely drafted condition that runs in favor of the buyer, for example, effectively transforms a "binding contract" into an option agreement; if the buyer does not like the target company's prospects at the time of closing, the loose condition can provide a justification for termination. Alternatively, tight conditions enhance the likelihood that a buyer will follow through on its commitment to purchase. Conditions are, therefore, an important pressure point.

One powerful condition found in many agreements stipulates that the representations are true as of the closing date, and the seller is in compliance with the covenants. From the buyer's perspective, this "bring-down" provision serves several purposes. First, where a document will be signed far in advance of closing, the bring-down motivates the seller to put time and effort into operating the target company. Otherwise, the target may breach a condition, and the buyer will be off the hook.

Second, with favorable representations, particularly a MAC clause, and a bring-down in place, the buyer maximizes the chance it will have an out should it find substantial problems through later preclosing due diligence. Even if the buyer doesn't terminate the deal, a MAC clause provides leverage for renegotiation of price.

Sellers often receive the same protection in a stock-for-stock merger. The seller is not required to close if there has been a material adverse change in the buyer's business. This reciprocal commitment essentially reinforces the protection target company shareholders have from the shareholder vote requirement in a stock-for-stock merger. If changes in the buyer's business subsequently make the deal unattractive, the shareholders simply can vote against the transaction. However, if controlling shareholders made an agreement to support the deal, the MAC is an important added protection. Again, it can be used as a tool for renegotiation.

An "antitrust out" is another common condition. Such a provision might give the buyer the right to kill a transaction that is challenged by the government or a third party on antitrust grounds. Here, as elsewhere, an agreement can be drafted to favor buyer or seller. A pro-buyer version of the condition has a hair-trigger—for example, the condition might require that no lawsuit or other proceeding be pending which might lead to an unfavorable antitrust ruling. A more limited condition might be triggered only if an actual ruling has been rendered that blocks the consummation of the contemplated transaction on antitrust grounds.

In either case, a buyer usually is also protected by a condition triggered if the government's antitrust review process remains open as of the closing date. Whether the antitrust out was used in good faith was the cornerstone of the suit by Cities Service against Gulf over the 1982 cancellation of their merger.

The buyer's securing of financing is one of the most sensitive conditions. A financing condition obviously favors the buyer, and is often excluded from contracts. Sometimes it is left in with a good faith representation to get the money. In an auction of a division or a company, it has become increasingly common not to accept a financing condition. To cover themselves, buyers sometimes get financing sources to bridge the deal. Sellers have to beware, of course, that the buying entity isn't an unfunded shell.

A consents condition typically requires a seller to secure all third-party consents that are necessary to allow the transfer of assets and contracts. Valuable leases, for example, may require the lessor's consent if they are to be transferred from seller to buyer. This is often an opportunity for a holdup. The lessor who thinks its consent is valuable often asks for a renegotiation of terms and sometimes may impact the economics of the whole deal.

Finally, both sides to a transaction often will require a legal opinion from the other side's outside lawyers as a condition to closing. Such opinions state the lawyers' conclusions as to the valid and binding effect of the pertinent agreements and their enforceability, that the federal securities laws were not violated and that the lawyers' clients have the power and authority to carry out the contemplated transaction.

The opinion of the counsel to the company can be expanded to be more comprehensive. Counsel will resist any expansion fiercely— after all, lawyers sensibly don't want added risks if they can avoid it. But as with all legal opinions, the intent is not to sue the lawyers in case they are in error; rather, it is hoped that the responsibility of an opinion will goad the lawyers into doing a more thorough job of diligence.

The concept is that investors should be aware of the problems before they go into the deal. In addition to requiring a paragraph stating that no agreement of the company known to them is violated by the deal, buyers should also get a statement that, to their knowledge, company's counsel is not aware of any material misstatements or omissions in the relevant deal documents. This sort of assurance should be required despite the howls of learned counsel who insist that they give opinions only on law rather than on fact.

Conditions carry weight because they give the parties the ability to cancel an otherwise binding contract. The existence of such an extreme remedy is, however, not the only possible outcome in the case of a breached condition. Under most contracts, an aggrieved party has the power to waive a breached condition in writing. This power allows the party to decide whether the deal still makes sense in light of the new developments.

Alternatively, a contract may give a breaching party the power to cure. In this case, an aggrieved party is required to give notice to the party in breach, who has a specified period of time to remedy the breach. Only if the breach remains unresolved does the aggrieved party have the power to terminate the agreement. The danger of allowing cure is that it may give a party the ability to drag out the time before closing by repeating the process of breach and cure. A drop-dead date solves this problem: either party is allowed to cancel the contract if the deal has not been closed by a specified date sometime after the original planned closing.

Indemnities Indemnities specify the circumstances and the manner in which an injured party to a contract will be reimbursed or seek damages.

Sellers typically moan and groan quite a bit before indemnifying a buyer. Nonetheless, an indemnity is sometimes forthcoming, usually in the context of an asset deal or the sale of a subsidiary. Every dollar of undisclosed liabilities paid by a buyer constitutes additional purchase price. So, a cautious buyer who must bear such costs will assume a certain amount of undisclosed liabilities in its valuation analysis. This assumption will result in a lower up-front purchase price.

With an indemnity in hand, a buyer can value the target on the basis of zero undisclosed liabilities. If no such liabilities materialize, granting the indemnity costs nothing, in theory. However, it does provide another source of contention, and experience teaches that the fewer of them, the less the risk for a seller.

The time period during which an indemnity claim can be raised is determined by the extent to which the representations survive the closing. A seller will often refuse to indemnify the buyer, and the contract usually states the transaction is on an "as-is" basis.

Likewise, the seller will want to be notified if the buyer becomes involved in court proceedings or some other controversy that may give rise to an indemnity claim against the seller. The seller often will also demand the right to appear in and control the proceedings. Of course, the argument in favor of this demand is that, in the typical indemnity, the seller must pay for all reasonable expenses related to a claim, including attorneys' fees. If the seller is on the hook for the expense, it will argue, it should be able to dictate how the claim is litigated and when it is compromised.

The buyer, on the other hand, may fear that the seller will take undue risks in litigation, risks that might have a secondary impact on its reputation or operations. A possible middle ground is to allow the buyer to take back control if it is willing to give up any indemnification claim. Alternatively, the buyer might retain basic control, with approval rights on any settlement going to the seller.

Often, an indemnity with a "basket" is used to bridge the gap between buyer and seller. The notion of a basket is that it must fill up to a specified amount before the buyer can recover anything under an indemnity. A basket is a compromise in the sense that it immunizes a seller from the bother of relatively minor damages, while protecting the buyer from major problems.

An indemnity provides little protection unless the indemnifying party has the ability to pay a claim. Indemnified parties therefore often seek to backstop the indemnity with an escrow or a setoff against any deferred payments due.

The Documents

In structuring a deal, the fundamental principles are first informally circled and, perhaps, itemized in an incomplete term sheet. However, if the deal is significant for either party, an actual agreement, even a handshake, may trigger required disclosure before the parties are prepared for publicity. The issue becomes whether a letter of understanding or a term sheet should be drawn up to highlight these major points or whether the parties should begin working on the definitive papers.

A term sheet summarizes the key points of a deal. Usually, letters of intent are not legally binding—they are generally subject to the approval of the respective boards of directors and the drafting of an acceptable definitive contract. However, these letters do have the advantage of limiting the scope of debate in the negotiations, morally if not legally. After all, if a term sheet says a debt instrument will have a stated sinking fund, it's rather difficult to raise the point as a fresh issue in negotiations.

The problem is that as a letter of intent becomes more detailed, it consumes energy and time which could better have been spent working on the definitive contract. If it is not detailed enough, allegations may be made that some point was waived. The risk is worthwhile, however, if there is a desire to pin down the other side on the fundamentals before extensive bargaining begins. Because letters of intent have no implementation teeth, spending too much time on details can become a dangerous delusion. There is a sense of progress, but there is no impediment to keep a competing bidder from scooping up the prize.

When it comes to the actual binding contract, different documents are used for the various forms of negotiated transactions.

The Stock Purchase Agreement   A stock purchase agreement— whether payment is made in stock or cash—is only practical where the selling company is owned by a limited group of shareholders or they have a significant ownership stake so that it is advantageous to have them explicitly committed to a deal. Otherwise, a tender offer is used.

A stock purchase agreement generally covers the five pillars— price, representations, covenants, conditions and indemnifications. Essentially, in the stock purchase agreement, the buyer agrees to buy and the seller agrees to sell a defined package of stock for a specified price. The key question associated with a stock purchase agreement is under what circumstances the selling shareholder has an out. For example, if the sellers own 30 percent of a company and agree to sell and another company bids, who keeps the profit?

Our experience with the sale of Maybelline provides an example of one approach. Our partners owned roughly 30 percent of the company, which had originally been a leveraged buyout and then went public. We were very pleased when L'Oréal, the French cosmetics company, after weeks of intensive private negotiations, agreed to pay $35 per share for Maybelline. Then we got to negotiating the contract.

L'Oréal wanted us to sell our shares pursuant to a stock purchase agreement at $35, regardless of whether there was a higher offer. We had not, however, shopped the company to other potential buyers and were, therefore, reluctant to make that commitment. After much wrangling, we split the difference. L'Oréal offered to pay $36.50 for the company in return for their receiving half our profit above $36.50 if there were another bid. If L'Oréal itself raised its price, the increase was ours.

L'Oréal's archrival, German cosmetics giant Benckiser, eventually came in to top L'Oréal's bid. After a series of bids, L'Oréal finally won at $44, and luckily our partners got to keep the increase.

The Merger Agreement　Where a target company is a division with a single corporate shareholder or a privately held company with few shareholders, a merger agreement can be very similar to a stock purchase agreement with the addition of the mechanics of the merger. If the target company is publicly traded or has many shareholders, however, the nature of the merger agreement necessarily changes.

A public-company merger agreement typically has only limited representations which do not survive the closing and no indemnity is provided. Two factors account for this arrangement. First, considerable information regarding the past performance of a public target company is available in SEC filings. This information theoretically reduces the need for aggressive due diligence. The representations therefore lose bite as a disclosure mechanism. Second, upon consummation of the merger, the consideration paid by the buyer will be dispersed broadly to the target's shareholders. The logistical problems associated with an indemnity are considerable in this context and, though an escrow might be used to protect the buyer, this approach is rarely adopted. As a result, a large public-company merger is often simpler legally and takes much less time than an acquisition of a division or a private company.

The Asset Purchase Agreement The asset purchase agreement mirrors the stock purchase agreement with a few important exceptions. First, where the target company is selling the majority of its assets and intends to liquidate shortly thereafter, the same indemnity problem found in a merger may arise. If the target is closely held, a purchaser might demand an indemnity from the target's shareholders, or an escrow arrangement might be decided upon. Oddly, there seems to be less resistance to the use of an escrow when a public company sells its assets than when a merger is involved.

Second, the assets that will pass at closing must be identified. This task can be far more difficult than it sounds. A large business may have multiple operations, various legal and other intangible property rights, and numerous fixed and mobile assets. As has been discussed, the list of items requiring individual transfers may be extensive and could result in thousands of individual documents. When consents are needed for certain transfers, a key question in the document is whether the closing will occur if permission hasn't been obtained. Unless all these assets are being sold in a bulk transfer, the parties must specify with particularity what goes and what stays behind, especially which related liabilities are being assumed.

Defending the Deal

Depending on the circumstances, both a buyer and a seller may have good reason to worry that a third party will bust up an existing deal. Paramount's attempt at breaking apart the Time-Warner deal and QVC's later run at Paramount illustrate the reality of the fears.

From the buyer's perspective, a great deal of time, effort and expense may have been invested to develop a particular transaction, and the buyer also may have secured a particularly attractive deal. On the seller's side, defensive measures may represent nothing more than a negotiating carrot used to induce a buyer to offer full value or make other concessions. Or there may be a genuine strategic interest in preserving the original deal.

The parties to acquisition and merger agreements, acting on the desire to defend their transactions, have implemented a number of defensive mechanisms. Prominent examples include stock and asset options, bust-up fees, and no-shop and window shop agreements. These mechanisms can be implemented together or on a stand-alone basis, but are often weakened by the inclusion of a fiduciary out for the seller, which allows the seller to pursue other deals if doing so is necessary for the seller's board to fulfill its fiduciary duty to shareholders.

REVLON AND LOCKUPS

Lockups—contractual provisions designed to protect a deal from outside bidders—are an obvious pressure point for a hostile bidder attempting to bust apart a friendly deal. They often sue to block these provisions in cases where an entire company is being sold, arguing the favorable terms are designed to protect the interests of incumbent managers rather than shareholders. There is no bright-line rule regarding the propriety of the various available mechanisms. The courts generally look at an arrangement based on the particular circumstances.

Revlon is the seminal sale-of-control case involving a lockup arrangement, decided by the Delaware Supreme Court in 1985. The case centered on Ronald Perelman's bid to take over Revlon. Because Perelman was persistent in his pursuit, Revlon concluded it should seek out a white knight. Forstmann Little was selected, and an agreement was negotiated. In its final form, the agreement provided Forstmann with a crown jewel lockup option to buy certain Revlon assets at an attractive price, as well as a breakup fee and other concessions designed to preclude an acquisition by Perelman.

Perelman challenged the agreement between Revlon and Forstmann Little. Revlon's directors, he argued, had breached their duties to shareholders. The Delaware Supreme Court agreed and invalidated the lockup and breakup provisions of the contract. In the process, it created what has come to be known as the "*Revlon* duties" applicable to a sale of control.

The *Revlon* duties are triggered when a sale of control or breakup of a company becomes "inevitable." This became apparent in the *Revlon* case, according to the court, when Perelman raised his bid to match and exceed Forstmann Little's bid. The board's approval to negotiate with potential white knights was the final "recognition that the company was for sale." Once the sale-of-control threshold is crossed, the duty of a board "change[s] from the preservation of Revlon as a corporate entity to the maximization of the company's value at a sale for the stockholders' benefit." In other words, the directors became "auctioneers" rather than defenders of the corporation and its policies.

The implication of *Revlon* is that a board involved in a sale of control may favor one bidder over another as a means to encourage an active bidding process. Defenses that preclude another bidder from offering a higher bid are, however, inappropriate and invalid under *Revlon*. In other words, the courts have developed a smell test of reasonableness. However, the courts have subsequently limited the circumstances where a *Revlon* duty is triggered, especially in stock deals.

While most states analyze lockups under a *Revlon*-type analysis, some do not. Pennsylvania, for example, has a state statute that allows the board more latitude to protect nonshareholder constituencies.

Stock Options

As a defensive tactic, a target company sometimes gives a buyer a lockup stock option to purchase authorized but unissued shares. The Time Warner merger agreement, for example, included cross stock options through which each party could purchase roughly 10 percent of the other's common equity. Typically, the exercise price for such defensive options is set at the share price to be paid in a stock purchase or at the market price in a merger.

The lockup stock option serves two purposes. First, it gives the buyer an opportunity to influence the outcome of any target company shareholder vote. This can be accomplished by exercising the option and voting the shares. Second, an option allows a prospective buyer to profit should a higher bidder come along. The option thus provides a kind of compensation for the original bidder's efforts, which arguably induced the new bidder to materialize.

Lockup stock options have received mixed reviews from courts. As a general rule, options are permissible if granted to induce a favorable transaction. Options may not be used, however, to cut off bidding. A corollary of this rule is that an option is viewed more favorably when demanded by a buyer than when suggested by a seller. Moreover, the longer the period between the signing of a definitive agreement and a planned closing, the more receptive a court will be to a significant lockup. The rationale is that a buyer faces greater risk and cost in this circumstance, and should receive reasonable compensation for taking on that risk.

Asset Options

An asset option is an alternative to a stock option. The asset option, or "crown jewel lockup," gives the prospective buyer the option to buy an attractive asset—frequently a key subsidiary or division that is less than approximately one third of a company's value. The option price generally is an approximation of fair market value, though often toward the low end, and is triggered by a specified event. Underlying the concept is that the asset is strategic to the buyer. Even though the price may be fair, the buyer is happy walking away with its prize. Common triggers include another bidder's accumulation of a certain percentage of target company stock or the target's failure to consummate the planned transaction by a given date.

An asset option is another means of compensating a bidder for taking the risks associated with negotiating a transaction. The option also may discourage other bidders who were interested in acquiring the assets covered by the option. Taxes can compound the defensive nature of an asset lockup. In theory, a bidder may be willing to pursue an acquisition absent these assets. The reality, however, is that the target may have to pay taxes on any capital gain from the asset sale. While the price may be a fair one, the leakage from these taxes may leave the target significantly worse off on a net basis.

This defensive potential makes courts skeptical of crown jewel options. Courts often will disallow options with a price that is less than full value or if the agreement seems to preclude other bids. *Revlon* is one of the most well-known examples of a court overturning a crown jewel lockup. In that case, Revlon CEO Michel Bergerac and the Revlon board granted Forstmann Little a $525 million lockup on the company's National Health Laboratories and Vision Care businesses. Under the agreement, Forstmann Little could buy the two businesses if another bidder ended up with 40 percent of Revlon's shares.

The option terms were the focus of some bargaining: Ted Forstmann insisted on the lockup as part of his firm's agreement to raise its outstanding white knight bid. However, the Delaware courts focused on the fact that the purchase price was some $100 to $175 million lower than the value placed on the businesses by Revlon's bankers at Lazard. This flunked the court's smell test, and it tossed out the option as part of its larger ruling in favor of Perelman.

The *Revlon* case presented unique facts. In the typical situation, the precise measure of full value can be difficult to determine. Courts will make relative judgments based on expert testimony, the parties' own valuation and the extent of arm's-length negotiations involved. However, even in the face of tough arm's-length negotiations over price, courts remain skeptical.

For example, in the 1982 takeover fight for Marathon Oil, a federal district court judge, applying Ohio law, upheld a crown jewel option granted to white knight U.S. Steel, only to be overturned on appeal. The agreement in question granted U.S. Steel the right to buy Marathon's half interest in the valuable Yates oil fields of West Texas for $2.8 billion. This right would be triggered if an acquirer other than U.S. Steel were to acquire more than 50 percent of Marathon's common stock.

U.S. Steel's lockup right had considerable defensive teeth. The Yates field, which produced 100,000 barrels of oil daily, was the key Marathon asset sought by both U.S. Steel and other bidders. Mobil argued that the Yates interest was worth roughly $1 billion more than U.S. Steel was to pay under the option agreement.

The district court rejected the argument and upheld the option, largely because Marathon was able to show that the price had been the subject of tough haggling. U.S. Steel initially wanted the option price to be set at $2 billion. Marathon had held out for the $2.8 billion "even if it was a deal breaker." This stance, and U.S. Steel's original unwillingness to pay $2.8 billion, supported the price as fair. The Marathon board also had considered detailed valuation reports on the Yates field before approving the option.

Despite these facts, a federal circuit court overturned the lower court's ruling on appeal. The court found that the Yates field option constituted an impermissible "manipulative" practice under the federal securities law. Fundamentally, the court was worried that the option circumvented the "natural forces of market demand" for Marathon stock.

So, even with extensive negotiations and good facts, a crown jewel lockup necessarily opens a board to criticism over price. Stock options raise some of the same issues, but are more favored as a defensive mechanism because publicly traded stock is much easier to value. A premium to the stock's recent trading value is easier to support than a crown jewel agreement.

Bust-Up Fees

Bust-up fees provide a somewhat more direct, and consequently more obvious, defensive mechanism. The notion is that the target agrees to make a payment to a prospective buyer if the parties' transaction is not consummated. A variation is to trigger the payment at some earlier point, perhaps even when another bidder appears on the scene with a higher offer.

Generally, a bust-up fee is designed to cover a buyer's expenses and to provide some additional return. For a large transaction, the typical fee is in the range of 1 to 2 percent of the transaction value. Bust-up fees in smaller deals ($50 to $500 million) tend toward the higher end of the range.

Like other defensive mechanisms, a bust-up fee is subject to judicial review. A fee that by itself exceeds 2 percent of transaction value is particularly suspect in a large deal. A fee under that threshold generally will be allowed. The standards are somewhat more flexible in smaller deals.

No-Shop Clause

While lockup options and bust-up fees usually are implemented as part of a definitive and binding agreement, a no-shop clause is sometimes agreed to earlier as part of a letter of intent.

Under the typical no-shop clause, a target company may not seek or encourage a third-party offer, nor may it provide information to or negotiate with other bidders. This prohibition is subject in most cases to a fiduciary out. The window-shop provision is a variation on the same theme. It gives the target company the freedom to provide confidential information to and negotiate with *unsolicited* bidders. The art form is in limiting the size of the window to real new bidders, not browsers.

Like other defensive mechanisms, a no-shop or window-shop clause must be reasonable or it will not be sustained under a court challenge. Courts have found no-shop clauses particularly troublesome where they operate to bar the target company from discovering the value and terms of a prospective offer.

The modern innovation is to tighten no-shop clauses without running afoul of court oversight. A common approach is to include a five-day-notice provision that requires a selling company to notify the acquirer in advance of accepting any offer from a third party. The no-shop clause thus effectively becomes a right of first refusal, which reduces third parties' willingness to bid. In addition, no-shop clauses now commonly require any third-party offer to be fully financed before the selling company can accept. The financing requirement further limits the number of potential bidders without precluding other offers.

Fiduciary Outs

The fiduciary out is designed to protect the directors of a target company from having to choose between violating their fiduciary obligation to shareholders and violating a purchase agreement. Under a fiduciary out, the directors need not take some action if they determine that doing so would constitute a violation of their fiduciary duty. So, for example, a board might be able to negotiate with a third party notwithstanding the existence of a no-shop clause. Other obligations that are often waived include the requirement that a board recommend a merger to shareholders prior to their vote on the matter. As a check on the invocation of the fiduciary out clause, an agreement often requires the target to receive an opinion of outside counsel stating that the required action or the prohibition involved in fact would constitute a fiduciary violation.

Raising the Cash

Of course, a deal won't get done unless the acquirer can finance the purchase. Issuing stock or other securities is an option for corporate acquirers, in which case the registration process is the main hurdle. However, a deal that involves all or partial cash consideration raises a different set of issues.

Cash on hand is one obvious source of funding. A large corporate acquirer may have accumulated cash flows from operations, sold a division or raised capital in the markets. Financial buyers generally have equity capital under management. In most cases, though, cash on hand is insufficient to fund an entire deal. Financial buyers also target the higher returns on equity associated with a leveraged deal. Therefore, both corporate and financial buyers might look to finance a deal with some debt.

Leveraged acquirers, whether financial buyers or less established corporations, tend to use three types of debt: bridge loans, bank loans and high-yield bonds.

Bridging to the Deal

In the context of takeover bidding wars, or even in heated friendly auctions of companies or divisions, the ability to provide assurance of financial capacity can be critical to winning the target. Shareholders will discount an offer made contingent on financing. Fully funded bidders are more likely to prevail. The problem is that raising money from banks or through a high-yield offering takes time. Bridge loans have evolved as a way to gain the advantage of a fully funded offer on short notice.

For an acquirer, a bridge loan is expensive short-term financing meant to fill the gap until other, cheaper debt can be raised. Lenders—investment banks, commercial banks or other financial intermediaries—tend to look at bridge loans as a necessary tool to win more lucrative bank and high-yield finance business. The risk of the bridge financing is reduced by arranging for third parties to provide part of the loan in exchange for a share of the fees involved. In fact, a number of investment banks have raised bridge loan funds from third parties in order to guarantee fast response time on potential bridge loan situations.

The terms of a bridge loan are designed to reinforce the loan's short-term nature. Economic incentives encourage the borrower to repay the loan with the proceeds from other borrowings. The lender commits to provide bridge financing in exchange for an up-front fee, roughly 1.5 percent of the amount committed. Another funding fee, also around 1.5 percent, must be paid if the money is actually drawn down.

Bridge loan interest rates are expensive. Furthermore, if the loan is outstanding for longer than a few months, the rates begin to ratchet up. This gives a strong incentive to find other financing.

Fundamentally, a bridge loan is uneconomic to draw down and acquirers try to avoid using the money. The time between an offer and a closing, which must be at least twenty business days in the tender offer context but can be longer, is used to negotiate bank loans or raise high-yield, convertible or equity capital. Even if the bridge loan is drawn down at the closing, having long-term financing commitments ensures that the bridge will be taken out in short order.

Bank Loans

As compared to bridge loans, bank loans are a cheaper and longer-term source of financing. Most bank loans have variable rates. The rate is defined in terms of some base rate, most commonly the London Interbank Offered Rate or LIBOR, plus a certain amount. As the base rate varies, the rate on the bank loan also varies. The spread over the base rate depends on the acquirer's credit history and asset quality, and market conditions at the time the loan is negotiated.

The usual acquisition bank loan comes in the form of a credit facility with both a term loan component and a "revolver." A term loan is used to fund the acquisition and must be repaid after a fixed period, typically ranging from five to seven years. The revolver, on the other hand, is meant to fund the working capital needs of the acquired business. For example, seasonal working capital buildups can be funded with the revolver, which then is paid down once the working capital is reduced.

Both the term loan and the revolver are senior to other borrowings, so that the bank will be paid before other lenders in an insolvency. If the loan is also secured, the bank has a right to look to specific assets for repayment.

Today, banks syndicate most credit facilities. The lead bank arranges for other banks to provide part of the capital in exchange for a share of the fees and interest. Of course, the lead bank grabs the biggest share of the fees in exchange for organizing the process.

There are four main pitfalls with bank financing. First, banks require an acquirer to agree to tight covenants. Essentially, these are rules about how the business can be run, how much additional debt can be borrowed and when dividends can be paid. Bank loans also include maintenance tests that require the borrower to have a certain amount of cash flow to cover its interest payments. Attention to the covenants is crucial—a violation of a covenant may put the borrower into default, in which case the loan may automatically become due.

A second potential pitfall has to do with amortization schedules. Depending on the circumstances, a bank may require the borrower to begin paying off a loan before the end of its term. These cash payments can be a drain on the underlying business, making the amortization schedule a common sticking point in bank loan negotiations.

The variable nature of bank loan interest rates also can pose problems. If rates rise in the market, a company can get pinched. Some companies use derivative contracts as a way to manage this risk. However, these agreements can be quite complex and expensive.

Finally, because bank loans must be repaid in fairly short order, some thought must be given to how the loan will be taken out. If the acquired company will be held for the long term, it may be more prudent to find a longer-term funding source. Of course, if the plan is to sell off assets quickly, a bank loan may be the appropriate funding vehicle.

James Lee Jr.

Despite the traditional feel of its paneled offices, Chase Manhattan Bank has emerged as the most aggressive bank lender to leveraged borrowers in the 1990s. Jimmy Lee is Chase's point man in leveraged lending and, as a Chase vice chairman, is leading the charge to convert Chase into an investment bank.

Known for his silver-dollar suspenders and blue shirt with white cuffs, Lee is a gregarious banker who joined Chemical Bank out of college and rose through the ranks. Though charming, Lee thrives on competition. He headed Chemical's loan syndication unit at the time of the credit crunch of the early 1990s. Because Chemical continued to lead syndicates and make loans when others would not, the bank gained the loyalty of borrowers. In particular, Lee forged strong relationships with the leading leveraged buyers. The bank emerged in 1996, after the Chase merger, with 20 percent of the lead manager position in the $888 billion syndicated loan market.

Today, Lee is looking to build from this foundation. Chase has capitalized on its leadership in the senior bank debt business to gain a share of the junk bond market. Lee's troops have even begun to dabble in the corporate finance and merger advisory business. The ability to provide one-stop shopping is the goal.

Competition in each of the markets Lee has targeted is fierce, but he has made some headway. In one high-profile example, Chemical scored a clean sweep of business in the financing of the 1996 Riverwood International buyout. Chemical led a syndicate of banks in funding LBO firm Clayton, Dubilier & Rice's $2.8 billion purchase and advised the firm as well. Chemical also led a $650 million junk bond offering and made an equity investment in the deal.

Lee appears committed to gaining more of this kind of lucrative assignment. His investment banking unit continues to build staff, hiring bankers away from the competition at double the salary for multiyear contracts. Lee's challenge is to knit the pieces together into a coherent whole. Wall Street is skeptical, knocks Lee's team, and expects Chase to hedge its greenfields approach and attempt to buy a securities firm. Meanwhile competitors are running to catch up with Jimmy.

High Yield

High-yield bonds, popularly known as junk bonds, provide the final layer of financing. Approximately $400 billion of high-yield bonds currently are traded in the market, with some $120 billion issued in 1997. These instruments generally have a fixed rate and a seven-to-ten-year term. With respect to repayment priority, they generally are subordinated to bank loans. This feature accounts for the fact that junk bond rates are higher than the rates on bank debt of an equivalent term from the same borrower. From a bank's perspective, the junk is a cushion protecting its loan.

For the issuer, the main advantages of high-yield debt are that it has a long term, fixed rates and less onerous restrictions than bank debt. In particular, high-yield instruments generally do not have maintenance covenants—which require the borrower to maintain a certain cash flow to interest payment ratio—or principal amortization requirements, giving the borrower somewhat more flexibility on the downside.

Attention must nonetheless be paid to the remaining covenants to make sure they do not unduly restrict the issuer's flexibility. In addition, call provisions can be important. The call provisions in an instrument give the issuer the right to repay the bonds early. This can be attractive if rates fall in the market or if the issuer's financial circumstances change. From the issuer's perspective, call provisions are designed to provide the maximum flexibility at the minimum cost. Of course, lenders discipline the process and require some compensation on a conversion.

The high-yield issuance process varies depending on how quickly capital is needed. If an acquirer has sufficient time, the bonds are registered with the SEC in the same way stock is registered prior to a public offering. An offering document is filed for review. Once it is completed, the bonds are issued to investors and publicly traded.

In more urgent situations, high-yield bonds can be privately placed with sophisticated investors. Under an exception to the federal securities law known as Rule 144A, the initial bonds need not be registered. However, they also cannot be publicly traded. As a result, the purchasers typically demand that the issuer conduct a follow-up registration of bonds, which are then exchanged for the original bonds. Investors end up with a publicly traded instrument. Issuers prefer this process because the follow-up registration can take place after the acquisition is closed. In fact, during the recent bull market in high-yield securities, the 144A route has become increasingly popular, with little or no penalty to the issuer.

Even with a Rule 144A offering, raising high-yield money takes some time. An extremely accelerated process involving public companies with information already available might only take a few days. If the target company is not public, the process might take eight to twelve weeks.

In the interim, an acquirer sometimes gets a "highly confident" letter from the investment bank that will act as underwriter. Essentially, a highly confident letter from a reputable investment bank indicates that an experienced underwriter has concluded the deal can be financed, giving sellers some assurance the funding will come through. However, while highly confident letters are viewed by most investment bankers as a credible indication of the ability to finance a deal, such letters are not nearly as valuable as a commitment letter or bridge loan. On the other hand, highly confident letters are much less expensive than commitment letters.

The Takeout

The common theme in financing a deal is that an acquirer should match its book—long-term cash needs should be met with long-term financing sources, short-term needs with short-term sources. Otherwise, an acquirer builds a house of cards that can be easily blown over when the refunding date comes.

The Morning After

The real challenge of the buyout business begins the morning after the deal closes. Successful acquisitions are defined by the way the acquired business is managed after the purchase. The challenges are as varied as the nature of the businesses that are acquired. Sometimes the initial transition is smooth and the follow-through clear. However, surprises do crop up, as the Union Pacific Railroad discovered in its $3.9 billion acquisition of the Southern Pacific Rail Corporation.

In 1997, trouble integrating the two railroads' computer systems and other operational snafus slowed traffic on Union Pacific's tracks to a crawl. Railcars destined for Kentucky ended up in Mexico. The company, the nation's largest railroad, could not locate other cars for weeks on end. Eventually, the government stepped in and opened part of Union Pacific's system to competitors. The company meanwhile struggled to clear up the difficulties.

Different categories of acquirers also have different goals when it comes to managing purchased companies. Financial buyers focus on financial performance and the broad strategic sweep of the business. Day-to-day management is left to operating executives. Strategic acquirers tend to take a more hands-on approach. These acquirers may have premised their purchase price on the realization of synergies. Post-closing integration therefore is crucial to success.

Ted Forstmann Flies Gulfstream

When a buyout hits bumps, financial buyers necessarily must take a more active role. Forstmann Little's investment in Gulfstream illustrates the advantage of stamina and vision.

Forstmann Little bought Gulfstream, a maker of corporate jets, in 1990. The $850 million transaction was structured as a conventional management buyout led by Gulfstream CEO Allen Paulson. Forstmann Little and management invested $100 million of equity, while Gulfstream took on $750 million of debt, much of it provided by Forstmann Little's mezzanine debt fund.

The early years of the buyout were rocky. Almost immediately after the deal closed, the economy slumped, and the bottom fell out of the corporate jet market. Gulfstream hit a wall in 1993 with a $275 million loss. Ted Forstmann lost confidence in Paulson, and Gulfstream touched the brink of bankruptcy, coming within a few weeks of defaulting on its bank loans.

Yet Forstmann did not turn away from Gulfstream. He took over the company chairmanship and launched into Gulfstream's daily operations. The first order of business was to stanch the bleeding. Forstmann hired new financial and operations people, who restructured operations and cut costs. At the same time, he converted the $450 million in subordinated debt held by his fund into preferred stock that would not require current cash payments.

Forstmann also renewed his commitment to Gulfstream's on-going project to develop a new long-distance business jet. Forstmann had conceived of the plan to build a Gulfstream V model. Now, he saw the project as the key to the company's survival. Competitors were working on similar prototypes and the first to market would gain valuable market share.

Today, Gulfstream has soared back to profitability. The $800 million G-V program has turned out a leading-edge plane. Forstmann's tenacity and foresight allowed the company to bring it to market at the end of 1996, well ahead of a comparable product from competitor Bombardier. Sales are up, helped along by personal calls from Forstmann and other high-profile members of the Gulfstream board he assembled.

The strong results allowed Gulfstream to raise $1 billion in a 1996 IPO. The company also paid off the preferred stock held by Forstmann's fund. Though the Forstmann Little equity fund still owns about 40 percent of the company, the firm figures its mezzanine investors earned a healthy 22 percent a year on the Gulfstream preferred and equity investors roughly 40 percent a year on the deal.

Post-Closing Implementation

Businesses are complex and unique. There is no by-the-numbers approach that will ensure successful post-deal implementation. Yet attention to four basic rules can go a long way toward avoiding major problems.

At the outside, it is important to have a good strategic concept of the deal, grounded in industry fundamentals. Post-deal management is made much easier if a clear vision is defined as part of the acquisition process. Furthermore, the vision should be fleshed out to the level of specific operating directives. Once the deal closes, a further review of the business from the inside can then be followed up with rapid implementation.

The second rule feeds off the first. Studies show that intense post-deal implementation is more successful than a slower process. Major strategic and operational changes should be made in the first six months after the deal closes. In that period, the acquirer has the traction to make changes. Managers and employees can be focused on new initiatives. After about six months, the newness wears thin, and change becomes far more difficult.

Given the importance of fast and decisive action, acquirers that provide strong leadership are the most successful. Top management can come from within the target or from the outside. In either case, the presence of a focused and able executive team with the firm backing of the acquirer is necessary to implement the strategy. Because the first few months are so critical, having executives in place at the outset is absolutely critical.

Finally, if the strategic and operational framework is indeed defined before the acquisition, operating executives should be involved early in the process. These are the individuals who know the industry and may be the same people charged with implementing the strategy. Therefore, it makes sense that they be involved in defining the future path.

Of course, these are just rules of thumb. Volumes have been written on the topic of acquisition management and scores of management consultants are in the business of providing assistance. The point is that the follow-up on a deal can be as determinative of success as the deal itself.

Offense: 18
Battlefield Tactics

"These things are rather bloody, you know."

Thomas Mellon Evans,
a veteran of corporate takeovers

The mist clears. All the analysis, calculation and frenzy comes to this. The deal is launched. Pressure builds. An avalanche of calls, rumors and demands sweeps away any semblance of tranquillity. The sputter of the crowd is incessant. In the midst of the mayhem, the distinguishing mark of the skillful bidder is an inner sense of calm. This equilibrium is achieved through preparation, preparation and more preparation.

What are the pitfalls? Where are the ruts? What can go wrong? Of course, inherently, decisions are made under conditions of uncertainty, but it is possible to anticipate the range of the risks. The most important element is to have a clear, focused sense of strategy. Then the tactics need to be consistent with the strategy and well executed.

Crafting the tactical staging of a deal has its delicacy. Aside from economic and legal considerations, this is an art, not a science. Recently, large corporate bidders seem to prefer preemptive bids. Make an offer inevitable, reduce the fuss and the controversy, stun the target board, and crack the feasibility of resistance.

On the other hand, there is much to be said for the notion of satiation, the idea that the target is so exhausted with its defenses that it is vulnerable to a raised bid. This requires patience, time and a thick skin. Either tactic may make sense. Deciding which route to travel requires a deep understanding of both the bidder's and the target's psychology.

Therefore, a potential acquirer in a major public transaction needs to think about the total sense and spirit of a deal before embarking on the journey of making a proposal. There are three basic options: attempt to negotiate a friendly transaction, use the bear hug approach, or simply launch a hostile tender offer. Each of these alternatives has both risks and rewards.

The Friendly Approach

An informal approach involves a trade-off between the possibility of a friendly solution and the loss of surprise. An attempt at negotiation tips the acquirer's hand and provides some warning as to possible hostile intent. By seeking a friendly negotiation, an acquirer may jeopardize a later aggressive deal.

If a dialogue is started, the immediate question is whether the bidder will sign a standstill. A standstill agreement prevents one signatory from pursuing a merger or acquisition with the other, except on friendly terms. From the perspective of the pursued, the agreement allows for negotiations without the coercive threat of an unwanted pursuit. The willingness to sign a standstill is also a kind of litmus test, an indication of true intentions.

On the flip side, a potential acquirer's willingness to sign a standstill agreement depends almost entirely on whether it intends to pursue a hostile transaction should a friendly deal not be forthcoming. For a company not willing to go hostile, the approach is relatively straightforward. If the target company expresses interest in a deal, the standstill is signed and negotiations begin. Otherwise, the potential acquirer respects the target's wishes and goes away.

For a determined bidder, a poorly drafted standstill agreement is not necessarily a barrier to a later offer. Ron Perelman demonstrated this reality in his 1986 and 1987 dealings with Gillette. Using Revlon as his vehicle, Perelman made a bid for Gillette. The company responded with a plan to sell a large block of convertible preferred stock to a friendly party, which would effectively foreclose a successful Revlon hostile bid. Perelman therefore agreed to sell his shares back to Gillette, making a $35 million profit. Yet Perelman soon came to feel the decision had been a mistake. Gillette's white squire never materialized, and the company remained an attractive target. The problem was that Perelman had signed a ten-year standstill when selling his Gillette shares.

Searching for a way around the standstill, Perelman publicly approached Gillette with a new $4.7 billion friendly offer conditioned on the elimination of the standstill. Perelman increased the pressure by upping his offer to $5.4 billion. All the while, he insisted Revlon would only do a friendly deal in keeping with the standstill.

Eventually, Perelman gave up the pursuit, but not before he had created a precedent for how to work around a standstill agreement. Gillette subsequently was forced to fight off another takeover attempt—this time waged by Coniston Partners—with a major leveraged recapitalization and stock buyback. Ultimately, Gillette became a high performing stock of the 1990s with the launch of its new Sensor shaving system.

The mid-1970s were the years of the lightning-fast hostile tender offer. With a slump in stock prices, American and foreign companies saw an opportunity to acquire firms with high potential in a bear market. Tender offers were quick and effective. Without warning, a chief executive could wake up in the morning and find a huge two-page ad in the paper announcing a surprise attack. These "Saturday Night Special" deals could be completed in as little as seven days.

Things have changed since then. A state and federal regulatory framework now impedes the rapid takeover. For deals of any significant size, federal antitrust laws require a minimum fifteen-day waiting period. Federal securities law requires that a tender offer be held open at least twenty days. Several key states also require shareholders to approve certain kinds of offers. In addition, management has become increasingly adept at rapid response. Many large corporations have a takeover preparedness plan in place. In fact, with the advent of corporate delaying devices such as poison pills, a hostile offer usually drags out for months.

Given the new legal environment, the slight advance notice provided by an attempt at friendly negotiations may have little import. However, where the target company's management has a known antipathy to the possibility of an acquisition or merger, as with Rand Araskog of ITT, the chances of a successful negotiation may be slim.

The key advantages of surprise relate to litigation issues and shareholder reaction. Many litigators feel it is imperative to obtain the right jurisdiction for the inevitable flood of litigation. Bidders like to offer a premium, which is easier before the trading price of the target is affected by news of a pending deal. A negotiation raises a higher risk of a leak and a spurt in prices. The slight tactical advantage gained from surprise could then weigh in favor of adopting a different approach.

The Bear Hug

A bear hug is used either if the friendly approach is deemed inappropriate or after an unsuccessful friendly approach. The idea is to make a formal acquisition proposal to the board of directors as a nudge toward a negotiated transaction. Such an offer plays on the fiduciary responsibilities that officers and directors owe to shareholders, and is particularly effective where the target company has a sizable constituency of institutional investors. The boisterous pressure from institutional shareholders and arbitrageurs is designed to sap the will of the board.

In some cases, this strategy has been adopted by an investor who has accumulated a stake in a target on the open market. His objective is to stimulate potential acquirers to buy at a premium to the investor's cost. When a bear hug becomes public, the arbitrageurs will step in and add to the pressure. The bear hug, therefore, may put a company in play.

Of course, this was a common tactic for Icahn, Pickens and other takeover investors of the 1980s. These players viewed public agitation as an integral part of their investing process. With a host of well-financed acquirers in the market and relatively undeveloped takeover defenses, the strategy often proved effective: Pickens pushed Gulf into the arms of Chevron, Icahn forced Phillips Petroleum to sweeten its recapitalization plan.

Though the advent of the poison pill has reduced the sting of the bear hug, the tactic remains part of the modern takeover arsenal. For example, in June 1997, investment partnerships associated with the Bass family made a formal offer to Fisher Scientific. Fisher is a Fortune 1000 distributor of scientific equipment. Certain Bass partnerships already owned roughly 10 percent of the company. After some discussions with Fisher management, the partnerships, including the Trinity Fund and the Texas Pacific Group, sent a letter to the Fisher board laying out a proposed leveraged recapitalization plan. At the time of the offer, Fisher stock was trading at around $37.50. The plan would have provided shareholders a suggested price in the range of $47 to $48 a share.

With the pressure of a premium offer on the table, the Fisher board rushed to find a friendly suitor. The company quickly canvassed for white knights and in August inked a $51 a share deal with buyout shop Thomas H. Lee Co. One month later, a major UPS strike negatively impacted Fisher sales and market share, and the acquisition price was revised to $48.25 a share. Nonetheless, the bear hug letter had served its purpose, sparking a deal. Although the Bass partnerships may have preferred to acquire Fisher, the Thomas Lee deal brought Fisher shareholders liquidity at an attractive price.

Within the broad category of bear hug letters, the specifics can vary considerably. Including a price in a bear hug has the advantage of increasing the pressure on a hesitant board. Directors who vote to reject such an offer must face the possibility of stockholder lawsuits. If the offer is at a significant premium to the target company's current trading price, dissatisfied stockholders can argue the rejection of a higher offer constitutes a violation of the directors' fiduciary duty.

Sometimes, as an inducement to negotiation, the bidder will state that it will offer "at least" a specified dollar amount or indicate that upon the receipt of additional information, it might consider a higher price. This was the approach in the Bass offer for Fisher. The difficulty with this concept is that the target always knows there is more money in the bidder's pocket. On the other hand, it protects the bidder from the preemptive strike of a competing friendly offeror. The white knight might bid a higher price in exchange for lock-ups before the initial bidder puts his best foot forward.

To have maximum public effect, a bear hug letter usually needs to be in a form that requires disclosure. An intermediate tactic is to make the bear hug offer conditional, so that it does not require disclosure. The target knows that the offer might be disclosed at any time, but the initial show of restraint allows for the private friendly decision without the hubbub generated by disclosure.

BAXTER CRACKS THE BOARD

The bear hug is a flexible tactical weapon. In 1985, for example, Baxter Travenol Laboratories used a bear hug to crack apart a merger between Hospital Corporation of America and American Hospital Supply.

HCA and American Hospital announced their merger—basically a takeover of American Hospital by HCA—in June 1985. As a hospital company, HCA had few obvious overlaps with American

Hospital, and thus relatively little potential for cost savings. The deal essentially was a vertical integration of customer and supplier. This posed a problem for many of American Hospital's customers, who threatened to pull business from the company because it would be part of a direct competitor. Reflecting these concerns, both HCA's and American Hospital's stocks declined in value on the announcement of the deal.

Almost immediately, Baxter became interested in pursuing an alternate deal with American Hospital. The motivation was clear. Both companies had operations in hospital supply and medical equipment. These industries were competitive and the opportunity for cost savings from a merger appealing.

The difficulty for Baxter was that HCA's $3.6 billion stock swap with American Hospital included defensive mechanisms, particularly reciprocal stock options. These options would make a hostile deal for American Hospital prohibitively expensive. Yet the agreement was nonetheless vulnerable. American Hospital had a large constituency of institutional investors, many of whom failed to see the logic of the deal. They were looking for a better alternative, a reason to vote against the HCA merger.

Still, Baxter faced the practical dilemma of how to break apart a done deal. The company had one key advantage. Its businesses offered greater potential for cost savings in an American Hospital merger, giving it room to outbid HCA. Baxter crafted a strategy to play on this strength. The company bear-hugged the American Hospital board, topping HCA's $36.50 per share offer with a $50 offer. This wide margin was critical to the success of the approach. Baxter was not ready to pursue a hostile deal, as it made clear in its letter to the American Hospital board. Baxter therefore needed a much stronger offer, which would put the American Hospital directors in a fiduciary bind.

HCA refused to up its bid for American Hospital because a higher stock bid would be too dilutive to its stock and a cash deal would kill pooling. Eventually, the board gave in to the pressure from investors and arbs, and American Hospital agreed to a slightly sweetened $51 a share offer with Baxter. Baxter meanwhile settled with HCA, paying a breakup fee but gaining a lucrative supply contract.

After the deal closed, Baxter faced a difficult task bringing its two hospital supply divisions together into an efficient whole. Integration problems proved to be a costly distraction. In 1996, the company spun a significant chunk of its hospital supply operations off as a stand-alone business, now called Allegiance Corporation. Baxter International, the renamed parent, retained American Hospital's lucrative cardiovascular equipment business.

Going Hostile

Mounting a hostile offer can be expensive. Of course, the willingness to pay a premium price is critical to success, but price is rarely enough to guarantee victory. The likelihood of a successful campaign also depends on a number of key nonfinancial factors, which potential bidders analyze with extreme care.

Stock Ownership   The identity and sentiment of a target company's stockholders is a critical issue in any hostile takeover. Their feelings about incumbent management are crucial. Generally, an acquirer begins its analysis with a determination of the ownership by management, officers and employee benefit programs whose investment decisions are controlled by management. Related, but distinct, is the block owned by all other employees. Employees may or may not have strong feelings of loyalty to present management, but officers almost always will.

Next, a breakdown is compiled of the types of other key holders: for example, what percentage are institutions versus individuals, what are their average holdings, and how long have they held the securities? The objective is to first determine the "float" in the market—the trading shares that will easily flow to the highest bidder—and then those that can be acquired with a little work.

Some companies are very hard to attack: management owns a high percentage of the stock, employees are loyal, stockholders have held the stock for years and have prospered, and the trading float is thin. Following financial reverses, however, stockholder loyalty often disappears. For this reason, tender offers are often made for companies that are underachieving; a disillusioned stockholder is usually willing to sell and a defending management merely seems protectionist.

Corporate Structure   The corporate structure of a target firm can be a key factor in determining the success of an offer. A potential acquirer must study the provisions of the target's bylaws and corporate charter (sometimes called a certificate of incorporation). Provisions for a staggered board, the inability to remove directors without cause, or high quorum requirements for approval of mergers could make life very difficult for the would-be acquirer, even if the offer itself is relatively successful. On the other hand, the lack of a staggered board or the ability of shareholders to call a special meeting can be pressure points. Provisions such as cumulative voting can be a double-edged sword. They make entry onto the board easier but make elimination of minority opposition more difficult.

Analysis of Possible Defenses   Possible defenses to a tender offer will be discussed in detail later, but obviously an acquirer should analyze all likely strategies. For example, are the executives signed to long-term contracts, is a poison pill in place, are there substantial authorized but unissued shares available for defensive mergers, will there be a competitive bid, and so on?

An acquirer also must be aware of the weaknesses in its own position: sensitive and blurry disclosure issues, antitrust and regulatory hurdles, state antitakeover laws and the company's own record. A key question is the consideration being offered. Cash is cash: it is very difficult to litigate the value of a cash deal. When securities such as common stock are being offered as part of the transaction, litigators and PR firms load up for target practice.

PROFILE

Martin Sorrell — Pushing the Envelope

On June 11, 1987, Martin Sorrell, chief executive of WPP Group, rocked Madison Avenue with a $45 a share hostile tender offer for JWT Group, the parent of ad agency J. Walter Thompson and public relations company Hill & Knowlton. Two weeks later, JWT Group's chairman, Don Johnston, capitulated, signing an agreement endorsing a sweetened $55.50 a share deal, and the first successful hostile takeover in the advertising business was sealed.

Sorrell's dramatic coup pushed the envelope on hostile deals. In the process, he shattered the conventional wisdom that a hostile attack on a services business is unworkable. Skeptics pointed out that the chief assets of an advertising or public relations agency, namely its top people, could easily walk out the door, leaving little of value behind.

Sorrell was well equipped to challenge this view. A graduate of Harvard Business School who returned to his native London after graduation, he eventually became finance director of advertising firm Saatchi & Saatchi. He served the Saatchi brothers for nine years, and was the chief financial architect of the global expansion plan that transformed their firm into the world's largest.

In 1986, Sorrell left Saatchi, looking for his own show to run.

He bought Wire & Plastic Products, an improbable little manufacturer of wire shopping carts, a company with $5 million in annual revenues. He set out to transform WPP into a marketing powerhouse.

The makeover began with acquisitions of a number of small advertising and marketing companies. A bullish London stock market allowed Sorrell to raise more equity and pursue larger deals. Finally, a strong British pound and lofty valuations in the U.K. market interested him in potential U.S. acquisitions.

WPP's 1987 J. Walter Thompson deal, a $566 million purchase, was the first result. However, this was just a start. In 1989, Sorrell approached a second major target in the rapidly consolidating U.S. advertising business—Ogilvy & Mather. WPP opened with a bear hug rather than an outright hostile bid. Sorrell hoped to pressure Ogilvy's management into a friendly deal. After an acrimonious campaign of mudslinging and two raises from WPP, Ogilvy acquiesced, again in two weeks. Sorrell had his second target in an $860 million deal.

WPP's two major acquisitions demonstrated that unfriendly approaches can work in the services context. There were some hiccups, of course. Staff members of one J. Walter Thompson subsidiary bolted and set up a rival shop. The employees ultimately paid WPP a $10 million settlement, but the defections cost the firm prospective business.

The J. Walter Thompson acquisition was a success. Sorrell adopted a hands-off approach. He installed top management with the freedom to run operations. Most creative people stayed with the firm, and relationships with key clients had deep institutional roots. Sorrell contributed financial discipline to the mix, balancing staff costs and revenues, and managing the financial side. JWT's margins increased from a dismal 4 percent of revenues to a more normal 9 or 10 percent.

Ogilvy was tougher. WPP struggled through the recession of

the early 1990s, burdened with its heavy Ogilvy debt. However, Sorrell successfully restructured the debt, issuing equity in its place. The firm emerged from the recession strong and intact, with Sorrell still at the helm. In 1996, WPP had revenues of approximately $2.9 billion and a net profit of $190 million. Sorrell had stymied the critics.

Before the Hostilities

Historically, a potential bidder often accumulated a block of stock before making an offer. Regulatory changes have since altered the tactical landscape dramatically. A meaningful accumulation above $15 million is almost impossible today without public disclosure.

The temptation to buy a preoffer block of stock is obvious. In an active merger market, a third party may make its own, more attractive offer for the target company. A potential acquirer can find itself a loser in a bidding war, with nothing but a pile of legal and other expenses to show for its efforts. Buying stock in the market at preoffer prices can reduce the sting of this situation. The losing bidder then has a gain on the stock to offset expenses and perhaps provide a net profit on the transaction.

A sizable block of target company stock can also provide valuable leverage in an eventual takeover contest. Most directly, the bidder can benefit from the voting power associated with the shares it owns. Voting power can be critical at various stages of a fight for control, which may involve a proxy fight, shareholder approval under a state takeover statute or the election of directors.

Federal antitrust law is the main barrier to a secret preannouncement accumulation. Generally, if a stock or asset purchase comes within the so-called Hart-Scott-Rodino framework, seen at work in the DuPont-Conoco deal, the purchaser must report the transaction to the federal government and must observe a waiting period before making the purchase. These rules apply to transactions between all but the smallest of public companies, with some exceptions. Under Hart-Scott, the practical limit of accumulation without disclosure is $15 million, a minimal threshold when dealing with large public companies. There is, however, an exemption from the antitrust reporting requirements and waiting rules that covers the purchase of up to 10 percent of an issuer's voting stock if the stock is held "solely for the purpose of investment." Also, in some cases, purchasing stock through partnership voids the filing requirements.

The securities law provides an additional barrier to secret accumulation. Section 13(d) of the Securities Exchange Act of 1934 requires disclosure of ownership that exceeds a 5 percent threshold. In particular, a purchaser must file a Schedule 13D with the SEC, the pertinent stock exchange and the company within ten days of acquiring indirect or direct beneficial ownership of 5 percent or more of any class of a company's stock. Beneficial ownership basically means the right to determine how securities will be voted.

An investor is not restricted from making further purchases during the ten-day lag period between crossing the 5 percent threshold and the filing date. As a result, investors can accumulate considerably more than 5 percent by the date of filing, when the actual ownership percentage on that date must be revealed. However, Hart-Scott makes this window of little use, since the buyer likely will already have disclosed its intentions in an antitrust filing.

In addition to the percentage of stock owned, the Schedule 13D discloses the purchaser's background, the manner in which the securities were acquired and the purchaser's future plans regarding the target. This last point is key. A 13D filer must state whether it intends to seek control of the relevant company. Also, if the filer increases its ownership by more than 2 percent or if there are other material changes in the information disclosed, an amendment is required. A purchaser who originally disclosed a passive investment strategy therefore must disclose a change to a more active strategy.

These requirements cannot be avoided by dividing an investment among affiliates or by acting with a group of ostensibly separate purchasers. The disclosure rules of the 1934 act are broadly worded and interpreted so that the holdings of a group of related purchasers will be aggregated. The essential point is that initial purchases, even assuming they are not integrated into any eventual tender, have to constitute less than 5 percent of the target's stock or be completed within the ten-day lapse period. Otherwise, the purchaser must make full public disclosure of its intent before a tender offer is formally announced.

Certain state laws similarly restrict the ability to accumulate shares. For example, responding to perceived takeover abuses during the 1980s, a number of states enacted control share provisions. These laws require that a purchaser receive approval from current target company shareholders before acquiring stock in excess of a specified limit. In addition, the conventional poison pill of the 1980s prevents an accumulation of more than 10 or 15 percent of a target's stock.

The combined effect of federal and state disclosure laws is to make a "creeping acquisition"—the purchase of a controlling block of stock in the open market—effectively impossible. When the purchaser's intentions become public knowledge, the target company's stock price will react upward. As a result, a bidder often times its tender offer to coincide with the first disclosure of its stock holdings and hostile intention.

Fighting by Proxy

Once the decision to pressure for a deal is made, tactics take center stage. The proxy fight—the main arrow in the 1960s insurgent quiver—has again become an important weapon as defensive mechanisms have proliferated and become more effective. High-profile examples abound: IBM's successful assault on Lotus; Kirk Kerkorian's proxy threat in his running battle with Chrysler; and Hilton

Hotels' proxy attack on ITT. Similarly, Carl Icahn's long fight to force a split-up of RJR Nabisco featured one failed proxy contest and a second threatened one.

Takeover-related proxy fights are either the main weapon or a clearing action for a tender offer. In the first instance, the insurgent seeks control of the target's board by running a slate of candidates to run against the incumbent directors who are up for reelection. The shareholders then choose which slate should govern. This approach has a decided appeal for a dissident investor. Waging a proxy fight is expensive, but a winning proxy fight can give effective control with far less capital than an outright purchase.

This was Carl Icahn's agenda with RJR Nabisco. In 1995, Icahn followed Bennett LeBow into RJR. Icahn put together a 7 percent stake buying on margin, then Icahn and LeBow launched a proxy fight in the fall of 1995 to take control of the board and break RJR into separate food and tobacco companies. Their chances initially looked good after they narrowly won a preliminary nonbinding vote in favor of splitting up RJR, though the tally went against LeBow's Brooke Group if votes submitted after its self-imposed deadline were excluded.

LeBow then made a huge tactical blunder. He controlled Liggett, a small, flailing tobacco company, tiny compared to the major market players like RJR and Philip Morris. In a stunning move, LeBow engineered a settlement of tobacco litigation against Liggett. As part of the settlement, Liggett made admissions that would be damaging to RJR and agreed to help plaintiffs' lawyers. RJR shareholders went ballistic. Icahn tried to recover by dumping LeBow's name from the slate, but it was too late. The insurgents lost.

Still, for the next ten months, Icahn continued to press RJR. He prepared for a second proxy fight, this time without LeBow, pulled together a slate, and looked ready to keep up the struggle. However, not one to get emotional over a stock position, Icahn ultimately decided the proxy contest was a losing battle. RJR's stock price was up from his average cost per share. He sold his stake in a block trade for $730 million, netting a reported $130 million gain and an annualized return in the 40 percent range.

A proxy fight also is sometimes a technique to clear the way for a tender offer. Many modern defenses can only be removed through a shareholder vote or by the corporate board. Issues might include rescinding a poison pill or waiving the application of a state anti-takeover law. Alternatively, the proxy fight might attack new defenses proposed by management.

IBM used a proxy contest when going after Lotus in 1995. The deal was groundbreaking, the first ever hostile bid from blue-chip IBM and the first hostile deal in the software industry. IBM's team—led by Chairman Louis Gerstner—saw Lotus as a critical piece in the shift toward a higher profile in the software business. Numerous friendly overtures were made, but Lotus CEO James Manzi refused to negotiate. Gerstner worried that Manzi would find another partner. Taking a calculated risk, IBM chose the hostile route.

This approach was fraught with peril. In software, as in advertising, people were the chief asset. An acrimonious takeover fight might drive them to the exits. Gerstner hoped to minimize the risks with a swift knockout punch. IBM bid a full $3.3 billion price to discourage a bidding war. IBM's public relations team fanned out in the market to explain the strong strategic fit between the two businesses. Lotus employees were lobbied to back the deal, including over the Internet.

Finally, capitalizing on a major hole in Lotus' defenses, IBM launched an accelerated proxy fight. The Lotus certificate of incorporation allowed an insurgent to solicit consents directly from shareholders rather than wait for a vote at the annual meeting. IBM filed documents with the SEC to conduct a campaign to replace the Lotus board. Within sixty days, its candidates could be in place.

Seven days after the IBM offer, Lotus crumbled under the pressure. A deal was negotiated, and Lotus became part of Big Blue.

Fundamentally, a proxy fight is defined by an issue and a meeting date. The issue is control of corporate policy. A meeting date nominally determines when shareholders will gather to vote on the various proposals. However, rather than attend the meeting in person, many shareholders vote in absentia, granting a right, or proxy, to someone else, who then votes the shares. A shareholder generally will give its proxy either to management or the insurgent, depending on which side the shareholder favors.

Soliciting proxies amounts to an election campaign governed by SEC rules. Lately, institutional investors have become much more sophisticated and proprietary about these contests, which they often decide. The sight of corporate executives deferring to them seems increasingly to be a process they enjoy. Furthermore, the efforts of institutional investors have been aided by the SEC's revision of the proxy rules, which now allow investors to confer without having to file a proxy statement.

In this new environment, even the threat of a proxy campaign can expedite a dispute over corporate policy. Kerkorian's battle with Chrysler is a case in point. A classic contrarian, Kerkorian began building a large Chrysler stake in 1990 as the company slumped along with the auto industry. By 1994, Chrysler was on the rebound and Kerkorian controlled nearly 10 percent of the company's shares. Kerkorian—who bought in at $12 and $18 a share—was sitting on a significant paper gain. But, shortly thereafter, the stock skidded and Kerkorian grew disenchanted and even offered to buy the company in a friendly deal that was promptly rejected.

After his deal fell through, Kerkorian hired Jerome York—formerly the CFO of Chrysler and then CFO at IBM—to lead the next charge and Wasserstein Perella to help present his views. Kerkorian's main problem with Chrysler was its growing cash hoard—nearing $7 billion. Minivans and light trucks provided most of the growth and cash. As an active investor, Kerkorian wanted change.

Primarily, Kerkorian wanted Chrysler chairman Robert Eaton to pay a chunk of the company's cash out to shareholders. Kerkorian also hoped to purchase a larger Chrysler stake but was blocked by a poison pill. Eaton countered that Chrysler needed its cash to ride out the next recession.

Jerry York turned up the pressure, encouraging Chrysler management to raise its dividend and increase its stock buyback program. York also wanted a number of defensive measures removed. In particular, he wanted the threshold on Chrysler's poison pill raised to 20 percent so Kerkorian could safely buy more stock.

Eaton and the Chrysler board remained adamant for a time. York indicated a proxy fight was in the works, hoping to shake things loose. Kerkorian bought added shares through a tender offer to put muscle behind the threat. The strategy worked. Eaton eventually came to the table with a favorable proposal, which gave Kerkorian a representative on the Chrysler board. Chrysler also agreed to double its 1996 share repurchase program to $2 billion and buy back another $1 billion of stock in 1997. In exchange, Kerkorian agreed not to raise his Chrysler stake for five years.

Curiously, Chrysler appears to have embraced Kerkorian's platform even more so than required by the settlement agreement. The company continued to increase its dividend and voluntarily doubled its 1997 share repurchase to $2 billion. The company thus endorsed York's original position that the company could afford $2 billion in annual buybacks.

Kerkorian now has over 90 million shares of Chrysler stock, which is trading at roughly $37 a share after a two-for-one split, amounting to a paper gain of roughly $2 billion.

The Tender Offer

The tender offer is the most direct weapon in the takeover arsenal. Rather than attack the corporate board, the battle is taken to shareholders, who are given a specific choice: keep or sell. A premium offer is a powerful inducement to action.

In the early 1980s, the tender offer was virtually unstoppable.

Selling out to a white knight bidder was one of the few defenses to a fully funded tender. Yet there is a dynamic to the development of takeover tactics. New weapons spark new defenses. With the rise of the poison pill, the force of the attack was blunted. Today, shareholders rarely can be pushed into a rapid response to a tender.

Still, the tender offer remains an important tool. In the hostile context, tactics have evolved to meet the new realities. When combined with a proxy contest, a premium tender offer can splinter a company's defenses, as in the IBM takeover of Lotus. Even without an imminent proxy contest, the premium offer pressures a board to act.

A tender also can be a powerful way to bust up an existing friendly deal. This was Paramount's plan in attacking the Time-Warner merger and QVC's plan in bidding for Paramount. Once a sale of control is initiated and the *Revlon* duties triggered, a board can no longer rely on the pill to fend off a tender offer.

Consequently, when a bidding war erupts, as in the battle for Paramount, shareholders are often presented with dueling tender offers. Each party laid out the terms of the various offers in long and complicated tender documents. With each revision to the offer, an amended document was released to shareholders. At the same time, QVC and Viacom lobbied shareholders in full-page advertisements featuring pithy headlines and bulleted key points.

Furthermore, tender offers are not always unfriendly. A firm can tender for its own shares and a friendly deal might be structured as a tender offer for timing, tax, accounting or other reasons.

What Is a Tender Offer? Offers can be for cash or for another security, in which case they are referred to as "exchange offers." The common denominator is that both cash tender offers and exchange offers are made directly to all public security holders of a company. By contrast, a merger is, in effect, carried out between the corporations themselves.

Federal securities law imposes a number of reporting, disclosure and antifraud obligations on a bidder who launches a tender offer. A bidder may not, for example, purchase any shares in a target company once a tender offer has commenced other than through the mechanism of the tender.

The Securities and Exchange Commission takes the position that the term "tender offer" covers more than the formal solicitation of offers through public announcements or mailings directed at shareholders. According to this view, privately negotiated and even open-market purchases may, under certain circumstances, constitute tender offers.

THE SEC TEST

As guidance regarding what constitutes a tender, the SEC has suggested an eight-factor test, which also has been cited with approval by several courts. The factors are:

- Active and widespread solicitation of public shareholders;
- Solicitation for a substantial percentage of the issuer's stock;
- The offer price constitutes a premium to the prevailing market price;
- The terms of the offer are firm rather than negotiated;
- The offer is contingent on the tender of a fixed number of shares;
- The offer is open for a limited time;
- Stockholders are pressured to sell stock; and
- Public announcement of a plan to purchase shares that precedes or accompanies rapid accumulation.

Not surprisingly, the tender offer definition has generated considerable litigation. Although the SEC has taken the contrary position, no court has held that open-market purchases by themselves constitute a tender offer. To the contrary, one court has held that a series of open-market purchases did not qualify as a tender offer where the total shares purchased were less than 5 percent of the outstanding shares. Another court held that an attempt to gain voting control through a series of open-market purchases did not involve a tender offer.

Even "street sweeps"—large block purchases of an issuer's stock on the open market over a short period of time—have been found not to be tender offers by several courts. Hanson Trust PLC made dramatic use of the mechanism in its 1985 attempt to take over SCM Corporation.

When SCM announced a defensive restructuring, Hanson withdrew its tender offer and bought 25 percent of SCM's outstanding shares. The stock, together with Hanson's existing holding, allowed Hanson to block SCM's restructuring. Hanson accomplished this coup with just six purchases because SCM's stock was largely in the hands of arbitrageurs.

After reviewing the purchases, a federal appeals court ruled that Hanson's maneuver did not constitute a tender offer. Factors cited by the court included the fact that the purchases took place at the market price and did not involve pressure or secrecy. Of course, today, the ability to carry out a street sweep is limited by antitrust laws unless a bidder has already received antitrust clearance.

Where open-market purchases are combined with privately negotiated transactions, courts have found the existence of a tender offer. These cases generally seem to hinge on whether the "pressure-creating characteristics of a tender offer" are present. Pressure is created, for example, where a public announcement precedes a rapid series of purchases. On the other hand, where no such announcement was made and the purchases occurred more slowly, a court ruled no tender offer had occurred.

Courts are generally divided with regard to privately negotiated transactions. Some privately negotiated transactions will qualify as tender offers, but most will not. The test seems to be one of intent: "Any privately negotiated purchase that interferes with a shareholder's 'unhurried investment decision' and 'fair treatment of . . . investors' defeats the protections of the Williams Act and is, most likely, a tender offer."

For example, in *Wellman v. Dickinson*, a bold sneak attack was planned by Sun on Becton-Dickinson, a massive distributor of medical supplies. A subsidiary of Sun made secret offers to twenty-eight of the target company's largest shareholders, who together held 35 percent of the target's stock. The parent company's identity was not disclosed. Each shareholder was given a short period of time to consider the offer—ranging from one half hour to overnight.

On these facts, a federal district court held that a tender offer had taken place, citing the eight-factor test. Even though the approach may have been conceived of masterfully as a legal matter, the actual performance of some of the overly enthusiastic solicitors fouled up the deal. Moreover, the fact that the subsidiary was called LHIW, for "Let's hope it works," couldn't have thrilled the court.

Obviously, the subject of what constitutes a tender offer is a legal tightrope since superb execution by the numbers is difficult to achieve in an open-market purchase.

THE U.K. TENDER OFFER RULES

The notion of a hostile takeover is not uniquely American, but the rules vary in other countries. In the United Kingdom, for example, the mechanics and procedures of a takeover offer are primarily determined by the nonstatutory Takeover Code, which is enforced and administered by the Takeover Panel, a nongovernmental organization with members drawn from various sectors of the U.K. financial community. The broad object of the code is to ensure that all share-holders, particularly minority shareholders, are treated equally in the takeover context. While the code does not have the force of law, it is considered binding by most market participants.

A number of rules regarding the purchase of stock are incorporated in the code, which explicitly contemplates open-market purchase programs. Important provisions include the following:

- If a bidder has purchased 10 percent or more of the target company's stock in the twelve months before the offer, the offer must be for cash or have a cash alternative at the highest price paid in that period;

- If a bidder purchases 30 percent or more of a target company, then a bid must be announced immediately which is conditional only on obtaining 50 percent of the votes and approval by antitrust authorities;

- No more than 10 percent of a company's shares can be purchased in any seven-day period;

- Once an acquirer crosses the 3 percent ownership threshold, purchases have to be disclosed to the market within forty-eight hours (or sooner under certain circumstances); and

- Defensive techniques are limited.

The tactics in hostile takeovers of British companies are determined both by these and other rules of the code and by its nonstatutory nature. British courts recognize the role of the Takeover Panel as arbiter and are seldom asked to interfere in the bid process. Rather, U.K. takeover bids are fought on the basis of economics, and skillful exploitation of the opportunities for purchasing shares in the open market often is determinative.

Crafting the Offer

A tender or exchange offer is a fast-paced, complex, highly charged and extremely dangerous situation, whether the deal will be a friendly merger or a hostile tender offer. The consequences of a mistake in judgment can be much greater than merely the failure of an offer; liability for damages and expenses in suits can be staggering. With a top quality team in place, a bidder can turn to the terms of the offer.

Cash Versus Securities   Each form of payment in an offer has its tactical advantages. Cash offers historically have been much more sudden, and a more effective surprise attack, because there was no built-in delay period before the offer could be made; in contrast, securities have to be registered with the SEC. Not only is there delay in getting the SEC to declare the registration effective, but the preparation of the registration statement itself is quite time-consuming. Furthermore, securities can be of debatable value, are a target for litigation and are easily defeated by a poison pill.

Some thought also must be given to the issue of what sellers might prefer. In a friendly deal, especially a "marriage" of companies of similar size, or even in a sanctioned bidding contest, offering shareholders a future interest in the combined company may be an advantage. Of course, risk-averse shareholders may prefer the certainty of a cash return. If the selling shareholders instead accept securities, they necessarily subject themselves to the risks of the acquirer's business.

Actually, two kinds of market risk are involved in a stock deal—preclosing risk and post-closing risk. Preclosing risk derives from the fact that a selling shareholder often must decide whether to tender its shares a considerable time before payment will be received. A company likewise must decide whether to proceed with a merger long before the deal will close. Over the period between the tender or signing of the merger agreement and the actual closing of the transaction, the promised securities may decline in value, leaving the selling shareholder with a lower return than expected.

This issue of preclosing risk came to bear in the original British Telecommunications–MCI merger. Like most major mergers, the BT-MCI pairing had to progress through a long regulatory process before it could close. The delay was compounded by the international element. By July 1997, the approvals were in process and the deal almost done. Surprising news out of MCI then blew apart the original transaction.

When MCI announced that losses from its efforts at entering local phone markets could reach $800 million for the year—double prior estimates—stock prices were hit hard. BT shareholders began to question the wisdom of joining their fate to MCI. They pressured the company to renegotiate terms, but MCI had a favorable contract that specifically excluded local phone losses from status as a "material adverse change." This language arguably gave MCI a strong negotiating position, but BT shareholders ultimately were able to push part of the preclosing risk onto MCI shareholders. The deal was renegotiated at a $3 billion lower price. Of course, the BT shareholders ultimately paid a price for the revision when WorldCom snatched MCI for itself with a $36.5 billion offer.

Post-closing risk derives from the fact that the value of the securities received may underperform in the market. This risk is particularly troublesome where the selling shareholder must commit in advance to hold its shares for an extended period of time to receive favorable tax treatment.

Reflecting the reality of preclosing and post-closing risks, buyers have come up with several approaches to minimize these concerns for sellers. The idea, of course, is to smooth the acquisition process.

Pricing Formulas and Preclosing Risk   In a contested bid, an acquirer has a strong incentive to reduce preclosing risk. A selling company also may demand such protection in a friendly deal. In these circumstances, acquirers will sometimes put a safety net underneath a securities bid. Although the variations are numerous, the primary mechanisms include the floating exchange ratio, the collar, the fixed exchange ratio within a price collar, and the walk-away.

The floating exchange ratio can be understood as a reaction against the standard fixed exchange ratio. Under the fixed exchange ratio, the number of acquirer shares to be exchanged for each target share is set at the time the offer is made or the definitive agreement is signed. The arrangement allows an acquirer to know with certainty how many shares it must issue—for example, two for one. Working from this number, the acquirer is able to judge the impact of the deal on its earnings per share. On the other hand, from the perspective of selling shareholders, a fixed exchange ratio involves the maximum preclosing risk. Any decline in the value of the acquirer's stock will translate into less value received by the seller.

In contrast, the floating ratio shifts this preclosing risk from the seller to the acquirer. A floating ratio is structured to provide a set value to the seller. The exchange ratio is allowed to float to the number that will achieve this goal. Calculations of the exact exchange ratio often are based on an average market price prior to the deal announcement. The acquirer takes the risk that its stock price will decline between the time when deal terms are established and when the deal closes. Conversely, the acquirer stands to benefit from any appreciation in the value of its stock.

A floating ratio opens an acquirer to the possibility of extreme earnings-per-share dilution—the more shares it has to issue, the less earnings per share it will have. This situation may be unacceptable to an acquirer, particularly since any stock price decline may be only temporary and may reflect broad market factors not specific to the acquirer.

An acquirer can limit the risk of a floating ratio by capping the maximum number of shares to be issued. As a trade-off, acquirers often agree to include a minimum number as well. This arrangement—an upper and lower limit on the number of shares to be exchanged—is known as a "collar." Generally, the wider the range between ceiling and floor, the less protection provided for the acquirer.

Alternatively, the standard fixed exchange ratio can be combined with a price collar. This formulation provides a fixed exchange ratio so long as the acquirer's stock trades within a given price range. For example, if the acquirer's stock is trading at $50 when an agreement is signed, the parties might agree to a one-to-one exchange if the stock remains within a 10 percent band (that is, between $45 and $55 per share). If the stock goes above or below the outer limits on the price collar, the exchange ratio is allowed to float so that the seller receives stock with a value equal to the nearest endpoint on the price collar. So, if the acquirer's stock declines to $40 per share, each target company share would be exchanged for the number of shares equivalent to $45 (that is, 1.125 shares).

Finally, a "walk-away" is an extreme mechanism to reduce pre-closing risk in a negotiated transaction. A walk-away allows either party to cancel a deal under certain circumstances. For example, a seller might negotiate for the right to walk away from a deal with a fixed exchange ratio if the acquirer's stock price declines below a certain level. Or, an acquirer might seek the ability to walk away from a floating exchange ratio if its stock price declines too much.

MARKET DYNAMICS AND THE COLLAR

In a fixed exchange ratio deal, some form of a collar is very compelling from a seller's point of view because stocks often decline during the pendency of a deal. Investors may not be convinced the deal will be good for the buyer. For example, they may be concerned that earnings will be diluted in the short term. Or there may simply be the technical concern that too many shares are being issued, which will be an overhang on the market.

This was clearly the dynamic in the Paramount battle. As the bidding climbed toward $10 billion, investors in the market began to discount the stock of whichever bidder was perceived as more likely to win. The effect was pronounced when it became increasingly apparent that Viacom would be victorious after Sumner Redstone announced the Blockbuster deal. Between January 10 and February 15, 1994, when Viacom finally won, QVC's stock price climbed from $39.25 to $50.25, an almost 30 percent increase. Over the same period, Viacom's Class B stock declined over 25 percent, from $38.25 to $28.00.

Without a collar, under a floating exchange ratio, a bidder is forced to issue more shares as its stock price declines. The real problem is the ratcheting effect. Investors know that additional shares will be issued when a stock involved in a deal declines. Hence, it will ratchet and decline more. From a tendering shareholder's perspective, this feature makes it extremely difficult to judge the relative values of competing offers.

A buyer can lose out on the other end of a fixed exchange ratio, though this is a pleasant problem to have. In particular, if the buyer's stock price rises after the announcement of a deal, the fixed exchange ratio effectively pays the selling shareholders a higher price. Gillette's stock purchase of Duracell is one example of this situation. The deal—struck at a fixed exchange ratio of 0.904 of a Gillette share for each Duracell share—was a hit on Wall Street. Gillette's shares appreciated from $65.13 on the day before the deal was announced to $77.75 on the day of closing, making the deal even more beneficial for Duracell.

Derivative Securities and Post-Closing Risk   Tactical pressures also sometimes press an acquirer to minimize post-closing risk through arrangements most commonly called "contingent value rights" (CVRs). For instance, a version of CVR was the Diller killer of the Paramount fight.

The idea behind a CVR is to provide some assurance to the selling shareholders as to the value of the acquirer stock they receive. However, unlike the fixed-value exchange, the assurance is keyed off post-closing share prices. If the acquirer's stock trades below a set price for a defined period of time, the selling shareholders will receive some additional compensation. This compensation can come in the form of cash, stock or securities, often at the acquirer's option. The acquirer also may have the right to extend the period of the CVR. Of course, the extension comes with a price—an increase in the protection offered.

In Paramount, each Diller killer CVR represented the right to receive, in cash or securities of Viacom (at the option of Viacom), the amount by which the trailing sixty-day average trading value of Viacom Class B common stock was less than $48 per share. The initial measurement date for the CVR was the first anniversary of the transaction closing, and the CVR had a floor of $36 per share if Viacom chose not to exercise its extension rights. Under the extension rights, Viacom could push the measurement date forward one or two years. For each year of extension, the target price and the floor would be increased.

The advantage of a CVR is that it gives the acquirer's stock time to recover from any decline associated with the announcement of the deal. If the acquirer's stock price increases to a point above the CVR price, the CVR costs virtually nothing. However, if the acquirer's stock does not perform as planned, a CVR effectively requires the acquirer to pay more for the related acquisition. In the Paramount deal, Viacom ended up paying $82 million to retire the CVRs.

Part Cash, Part Stock Deals   Under certain circumstances, an acquirer may prefer to sacrifice the accounting and other benefits of an all-stock deal and instead structure a blended package of cash and securities. Offering some cash to selling shareholders provides a measure of certainty both to the acquirer and to selling shareholders. In addition, the allocation of cash and securities can be structured to allow short-term shareholders to select all cash and long-term shareholders to choose all stock.

Like a fixed-value exchange ratio, a fixed cash price immunizes selling shareholders from a decline in the value of the acquirer's securities. However, given a choice between paying with a fixed-value exchange ratio or cash, an acquirer may find cash superior. When paying cash, the acquirer avoids the uncertainty of not knowing how many shares it will need to issue at closing.

A part-cash, part-stock transaction also allows an acquirer to satisfy various constituencies. Some selling shareholders may prefer the immediate liquidity provided by an all-cash payment. Other selling shareholders may wish to gain the tax deferral available in an all-stock exchange. By allowing shareholders to choose between these alternatives, an acquirer may gain support for its offer.

The pricing structure of a stock-and-cash deal is even more complex than is the case in a pure stock deal. An acquirer must determine both the manner of the exchange ratio to be used and the relationship between the cash and stock portions of the package. How these two questions are answered can have dramatic effects on the dynamic among selling shareholders.

For example, one possible approach is to combine a fixed exchange ratio per share with a fixed amount of cash per share. A certain percentage of the tendered stock would be converted into acquirer stock and a certain percentage into cash. Under this approach, given the fixed exchange ratio, the value of the stock offered by the acquirer will fluctuate. If the acquirer's stock price goes up, selling shareholders will be induced to tender for stock. If the price goes down, the cash portion becomes more attractive. This approach is therefore inappropriate where the acquirer wishes to allow selling stockholders to decide between cash and stock on the basis of their favored tax treatment.

As an alternative, a floating exchange ratio can be paired with a fixed cash price. This format holds the relative value of the cash and stock constant. Selling stockholders are therefore free to choose between cash and stock on the basis of their tax concerns.

An acquirer must also decide how to allocate the cash and stock components of its offer among tendering shareholders. Straight proration is one option. This approach dictates that each tendering shareholder receives a fixed percentage of cash and a fixed percentage of stock. The receipt of cash likely will trigger some capital gains tax for each shareholder.

If the desire is to give shareholders the ability to exchange their shares on a wholly tax-free basis, a cash election offer is more appropriate. Basically, selling shareholders are given the option of choosing either cash or stock. Investors interested in immediate liquidity would select cash; investors seeking a tax-free carryover of their investment would select stock. As mentioned above, a cash election merger works best where the components have the same value.

Minimum Requirements   A minimum requirement dictates the lowest number of shares that must be tendered for an offer to become effective. There is a danger in setting a minimum requirement below which the offeror is not obligated to buy securities.

The problem with a high minimum is that it may prevent arbitrage. If the market price moves up above its preoffer level, an arbitrageur takes a substantial risk: if the offer fails because the minimum number of shares were not tendered, the price will decline back to its old level. Therefore, arbs lack an incentive to pick up the float.

A low minimum also can be dangerous. An acquirer rarely wants to be stuck with the securities of a company in which it has less than majority control. For example, a hostile offeror with 15 percent of a target company is in a no-man's-land. There is no control; indeed, a rival bidder or insider may have a larger block. Yet the market for re-sale of such a large block may be illiquid and registration may be re-quired of the securities involved—all in all, not an enviable position. Similarly, a minimum control level may be desired to qualify a deal as tax-free, for accounting purposes or to satisfy loan covenants. Worse, a rival bidder may get 50 percent and merge the 15 percent holder out with unwanted securities.

Of course, this is what happened to Seagram in the Conoco fight. Seagram ended up with 32 percent of Conoco's stock, but was then forced out in a back-end merger. The liquor company was left with a 20 percent stake in the winning bidder, DuPont. Seagram pro-fessed to be happy with the deal. Indeed, in Seagram's case, the mi-nority investment worked out well. The DuPont stake proved quite profitable and eventually provided the capital for the purchase of movie studio MCA in 1995.

Pricing Tactics   The heart of any deal is the pricing. However, within the value constraints of a bidder, the issue of how to present a bid in its best light is perhaps the most difficult aspect of struc-turing the deal, particularly given the range of possibilities and the dollars involved. Acquisition premiums to the market price in ten-der offers vary from hardly anything to more than 100 percent. According to *MergerStat*, the average premium has ranged from a high of 50 percent in 1974 to a low of 25 percent in 1968, when the firm started keeping statistics. The average premium paid in 1996 was 37 percent. Of course, merger premiums—particularly for marriage transactions—were substantially lower than tender offer premiums.

Pricing strategy depends on the facts. A contested offer with po-tential rival bidders is likely to result in a higher premium than an uncontested deal. Pricing, then, is meant not only to placate the tendering stockholder but also to preempt a rival from entering into a bidding contest.

Pricing is complicated by the possibility of amending an offer. On the face of it, one can test a low bid and always raise it. However, an unsuccessful low bid may attract a competing bidder. On the other hand, some bidders like to take the risk and test the market, making sure they are not overpaying. The risk is "sudden death," a lockup created by another bidder. So to play the "test the market" game, a bidder needs to be particularly humble and willing to bid against himself when concerned with competitors.

In any event, some tacticians believe in the concept of satiation, that it makes sense to bid a couple of dollars low so that everyone can be a hero when a settlement comes. Lately, preemptive priced deals by large industrial companies have been the vogue, such as IBM's bid for Lotus.

One common difficulty is the prospect of a tender creating an artificially high price in a thinly traded stock. Despite all precautions, it is not uncommon, especially in friendly tenders, to have the market anticipate a tender. This may not reflect any conspiracy so much as a widely spread analysis that a company is a likely tender target or common knowledge that the target has had many visitors from other companies lately. One tactic in this sort of situation is to let the speculation die down by delaying the offer. Another is to offer at a low premium on the theory that the securities are readily available at that level because the assumed premium is already reflected in the price.

THE TACTICIAN

Hamish Maxwell

Hamish Maxwell, former chairman of Philip Morris, is a deft tactician with a natural gift for takeover maneuvers. The son of a third-generation tobacco leaf dealer in London, Maxwell came to

Philip Morris in 1954. He rose through the ranks on the strength of operating skill. Eventually, he was given responsibility for Philip Morris' international tobacco business, which he shaped into a major growth engine. He became chairman of the company in July 1984.

As chairman, Maxwell proved to be a bold strategic thinker. He was the guiding hand behind Philip Morris' diversification into the food business, launched soon after Maxwell took the lead job. First came the acquisition of General Foods in 1985, then the takeover of Kraft in 1988. Throughout these landmark deals, Maxwell was always one step ahead.

The General Foods bid germinated in the spring and summer of 1985. Maxwell had initiated a broad strategic review. Fundamentally, Philip Morris was quite strong, and its tobacco operation was a cash machine with improving margins. The real problem was what to do with the money aside from buying back stock. After a thorough review, Maxwell and his board decided to move into the food business as a diversification from tobacco, and we were hired to assist.

The food business in particular was selected for two primary reasons. First, the industry complemented Philip Morris' strength as a marketer of consumer packaged goods. The company had experience with the applicable distribution channels and marketing needs and felt it could leverage these strengths. In addition, Maxwell saw stable cash flows and room for improved performance.

The General Foods campaign opened on September 23, 1985, when the Philip Morris board authorized Maxwell to approach his counterpart at General Foods. Maxwell was authorized to bid as high as $115 a share. The stock was trading around $85.

Maxwell understood the subtleties. Institutional investors controlled General Foods' stock. As a result, the General Foods board would come under considerable pressure in the face of a premium bid. Philip Morris' strong balance sheet put it in a good position to capitalize on the sentiment of arbs and institutional investors with a cash bid. Yet the General Foods board would want to feel it had fought the good fight. Everyone needed a sense of victory for the deal to proceed quickly.

Maxwell opted for a classic bear hug. He called James Ferguson, chairman of General Foods, and offered to do a friendly deal in the $110 to $111 a share range. He told Ferguson to shop the company quickly to the most likely buyers, and Ferguson would see that Philip Morris had the strongest bid. The iron fist also glinted from beneath the velvet glove. Maxwell told Ferguson that Philip Morris was prepared to launch a hostile bid if Ferguson didn't respond positively after shopping.

Ferguson hired investment bankers, who scrambled to find a white knight. KKR looked at the business, but didn't see a bid above $110. The board also considered taking on a slug of debt to pay a special dividend, perhaps in conjunction with a defensive acquisition. Ultimately, though, Maxwell overcame the board's resolve to fight. He met with Ferguson and raised the Philip Morris bid to $115, at the same time making clear a hostile bid would be forthcoming shortly if the parties couldn't come to terms. The board decided the Philip Morris bid was the best thing for shareholders. They accepted, and Maxwell had a victory.

Philip Morris spent the next three years digesting General Foods and running its businesses. But Maxwell wanted to build further critical mass in the food business.

Maxwell launched the Kraft tender offer on October 17, 1988, just weeks before Ross Johnson would move to take RJR Nabisco private. Again, Maxwell understood the need for satiation. KKR and other potential rivals also stood in the wings, making a quick resolution important. Kraft had a poison pill and other takeover defenses in place.

Philip Morris initially bid $90 a share, a 50 percent premium to the recent $60 trading price. The offer was designed to be high enough to put pressure on the Kraft board, but still leave room to raise if necessary to get a deal done.

Kraft conducted a short defense. Management came up with a recapitalization plan which it valued at $110 a share, then told Philip Morris that $110 was the minimum price it would accept. Maxwell opened negotiations and eventually raised to $106. Eleven days after the initial offer, Philip Morris and Kraft agreed to a friendly deal. Maxwell rounded out Philip Morris' food business in July of 1990 with the $3.8 billion purchase of the Swiss company Jacobs Suchard.

From a tactical standpoint, both the Kraft and General Foods acquisitions were successes. The price paid in the end was exactly what Maxwell expected to pay. He just played his cards well.

The shift into food has also been a substantive success. Philip Morris has performed well under the tutelage of Maxwell and his successors, despite the overhang of litigation risk related to the tobacco business. In fact, adjusting for splits, the price of Philip Morris stock has climbed from around $3 in July 1984 to roughly $45 today, or more than 20 percent per year on average.

The Tender Offer Rules

In reaction to the rising tide of takeovers in the 1960s, Congress adopted the Williams Act in 1968. The act, named after Senator Harrison Williams, was later amended to expand its coverage and has been implemented by SEC rules. These rules are an integral factor in structuring a deal.

Section 13(d)—the basic protection against a creeping tender—uses its 5 percent reporting threshold to flush potential acquirers out into the open. The rule forces acquirers to show their plans earlier than they might like, but gives shareholders information material to their decision to hold or sell.

Section 14(d) covers tender offers. When the Williams Act amendments to the 1934 act were passed, it was felt that the public needed the same sort of protection on cash offers as was provided in exchange offers through the stock registration process. Any person making a tender offer that will result in the offeror owning more than 5 percent of any class of equity security must file a Schedule 14D-1 and all solicitation material with the SEC. If a position of over 5 percent has been accumulated in the last ten days and a tender offer is being announced, a combined Schedule 13D and 14D-1 is usually filed.

Having required these disclosures, the law attempts to assure their accuracy. Section 14(e) is an antifraud provision which specifically provides that the disclosures required under 14(d) may not contain an untrue statement of a material fact or omit to state a material fact. In addition Rule 10b-5, the general antifraud provision of federal securities law, is also applicable.

A series of statutory sections and regulations limit the actions of the offeror during the tender. Among the most important of these provisions are the following.

Directors   If, pursuant to any arrangement or understanding, a majority of the directors of the target company are to be elected or designated other than at a shareholder meeting, the rules require a full-fledged proxy statement. The statement must be sent to shareholders at least ten days before such persons can take office. Of course, the objective is to provide to the public full disclosure about such backdoor arrangements.

Other Purchases   Once an offer is announced, a purchaser may not buy any security subject to the offer except pursuant to its terms. This rule is intended to prevent preferential deals once the tender is underway. Thus, if there is a desire to pick up large private blocks separate from the offer, this must be done before or after the tender, but not during it.

Terms of Offers   The rules contain a number of technical provisions to protect the public as regards the fairness of the terms of the offer. A bidder must allow shareholders to withdraw tendered shares so long as the offer remains open. Offers must be kept open a minimum of twenty days. Another rule provides that if too many securities are tendered for a limited offer, the cutbacks will be pro rata. Under current law, a tendering shareholder is entitled to participate in the proration pool if shares are submitted while the tender offer is open. Any increase in the price during a tender must also be paid to shareholders who have already tendered.

In response to the *Unocal* case, in which T. Boone Pickens was defeated by Unocal's discriminatory self-tender, the SEC recently enacted the "all holders" rule, which forbids discriminatory tender offers by either an issuer or third party.

THE SCHEDULE 14D-1

The Schedule 14D-1 is the principal tender offer regulatory document. Reflecting its role as an information source for shareholders, the 14D-1 contains background information on the issuer and key business highlights. In general, the following must be disclosed:

1. Any transactions (including contracts) between the bidder and the target.

2. Any contacts, negotiations or transactions in the past three years between the bidder and the target concerning a deal.

3. The source and amounts of the funds being used for the offer.

4. The purpose of the offer, including any plans to acquire control, liquidate, sell the assets or merge the target, or to make other major changes in the business or corporate structure of the target, including any changes in dividend policy, capitalization, directors or listing of securities.

5. Any target company shares owned by the officers and directors of the offeror and their associates and any trading done within the past sixty days.

6. A description of contracts or understandings with any person regarding the securities.

7. All persons retained to make solicitations for the securities and the terms of their employment.

8. Any other material relationships between the bidder and the target and a description of any regulatory requirements, the applicability of the margin and legal issues.

The Offer to Purchase

The actual offer to holders of the target's securities is not made through the 14D-1, but rather through an Offer to Purchase, which is mailed directly to the record holders and incorporates the important information in the 14D-1. Traditionally, a summary advertisement has also been published in national newspapers.

The first part of the Offer to Purchase usually deals with the terms of the offer, including the price and, if applicable, the minimum shares required, the maximum commitment, the withdrawal dates, the date through which the proration obligation applies and the mechanics for tendering. Care is taken in this section to state explicitly whether the offer may be extended or amended.

General information is then provided about the offeror and the target. In most instances, the information about the target is quite simple. The description is usually terse, consisting of brief capsule financial information, a summary description of the business lifted from the annual report, and sometimes a quote from incumbent management about the company's prospects.

If the offeror, however, has any nonpublicly available information from the target such as projections, the situation becomes complicated. Such material, even including projections, must be disclosed to avoid liability for the failure to state a material fact, although a disclaimer is usually put in stating that the offeror cannot attest to the information's accuracy. This is one of the most interesting sections of the Offer to Purchase.

Among the most difficult sections of the Offer to Purchase are those dealing with the purpose of the offer and the future plans of the offeror. The instinct of most offerors is to be as vague as possible, but federal securities law specifically requires a detailed statement as to these items and mandates that they be included in the Offer to Purchase. Unlike the rather cursory general financial disclosures in an Offer, courts have been insistent that the description of future intent be specific, particularly in the case of offers for less than all the shares.

The judicial theory on a limited offering seems to be that there will necessarily be a continuing relationship between the stockholders who do not sell and the offeror, which requires full disclosure. However, logically even in an offer for all shares, security holders have a right to know what is the offeror's intent as to untendered shares and what will happen to the company if they remain shareholders.

The most pertinent question regarding future intent is whether there is a desire for control and whether there will be a merger in the future if control is achieved. To indicate the particularity of the courts on this question, one U.S. Supreme Court case, *Missouri Portland Cement*, actually stands for the proposition that an offeror for 50 percent of the outstanding stock should have explicitly stated that the purpose of the offer was control. Similarly, if the primary purpose of the offer is to frustrate a takeover by another party in a defensive alliance, full disclosure must be made.

Perhaps the most difficult disclosure situation occurs when the offeror's management has studied a series of alternative possibilities but has not made any definitive commitment. In the *Otis* case, a federal district court held that a plan should be disclosed if there was evidence of its adoption, explicit or implicit, by high corporate officers. For example, in *Otis*, a study was presented to the board of directors regarding a tender offer followed by a merger. The board explicitly approved the tender but did not act on the merger; however, the court held that the merger possibility should have been described. On the other hand, more recently courts have recognized that the purposes point has become a key target for dilatory litigation by target companies, and they have discounted the protestations of incumbent management accordingly.

Arrangements or understandings regarding the company's securities are often very simple to describe: usually, there are none. Sometimes, however, there are options regarding the holdings of large holders or voting-trust agreements, and these, of course, must be fully described.

If there are any particular regulatory hurdles to implementation of a possible plan, they also must be set out. Similarly, if any other governmental approvals are required, including those of foreign governments (Canadian approval has sometimes been a subject of contention), disclosure is required. In addition, the antitrust status of the transaction should be indicated: Was clearance sought; were any antitrust difficulties expected; was there notification of government antitrust authorities? The implications of the offer, if any, on the listing status of the target company's stock on the exchange on which the stock is traded should also be described.

State Regulation

An increasingly important role is currently being played by state legislation in the tender offer field. Under pressure from local businesses, state officials reacted to the large number of tenders by passing laws which, in effect, have a delaying impact on hostile tenders. Most of these state statutes are, however, by their terms inapplicable to offers recommended by the target's management. State antitakeover laws generally apply to companies that are either incorporated in the state in question or which conduct a substantial part of their business in the state. The laws generally include one or more of the following provisions: a fair price rule, a merger moratorium, a control share rule and a cash-out rule.

The purpose of a fair price rule is to curb unfriendly coercive two-tier bids. Basically, a fair price rule forbids a back-end, squeeze-out merger between a bidder and a target unless the consideration paid is the same as that paid to acquire securities on the front end. A merger moratorium similarly blocks a bidder from merging with a target for a period of time after initial stock purchases absent approval from a supermajority of stockholders or the target board of directors.

Control share rules require shareholder approval before a bidder can acquire more than a specified percentage of target company stock. Depending on the state, the rules either simply forbid further acquisitions or strip any shares acquired of voting rights.

Like the fair price rule, a cash-out rule is targeted at two-tier tender offers. The cash-out rule gives shareholders a right to sell their shares to a bidder at the same price and on the same terms as initial purchases. The rule is triggered when an acquirer buys a certain percentage of target company stock.

Two states provide interesting examples of antitakeover statutes: Delaware and Pennsylvania. The Delaware statute is particularly important given the high concentration of major companies incorporated in that state—roughly half of all NYSE-listed firms.

Under the Delaware procedure, a hostile bidder that buys 15 percent of a company's outstanding voting stock may not complete a business combination with the company for three years after the bidder acquires the 15 percent interest. This effectively bars the back-end merger. Three exceptions apply. First, a combination can take place if the board approves the transaction prior to the bidder's crossing the 15 percent threshold. Second, there is no limitation if the bidder acquires 85 percent or more of the company's voting stock in the front-end deal. Third, a business combination can go forward if approved by the company's board and a two-thirds majority of its shareholders (excluding stock held by the bidder).

The Pennsylvania law is generally considered the toughest state antitakeover law in the country. The statute limits the voting rights of a bidder that acquires 20 percent or more of a covered corporation's voting securities. Pennsylvania also has a business-combination rule and a cash-out rule. In addition, a board of directors is expressly allowed to consider constituencies other than shareholders in deciding whether to accept a takeover bid.

Most importantly, though, Pennsylvania has adopted a so-called disgorgement approach. A "controlling person or group" may be forced to return certain short-term profits to the target company. The particular profits covered are those earned on shares sold within eighteen months of the date on which the 20 percent threshold was crossed. A controlling person or group is defined to include a single investor or group of investors acting in concert who hold at least 20 percent of the company's vote. Anyone who discloses the intent to acquire control of a corporation by any means is also a controlling person. Under the law, the target company, and in certain cases shareholders, have standing to sue a controlling person or group.

States other than Pennsylvania and Delaware have similar antitakeover laws. Each state law has its own variations and complications, and multiple states might argue that a corporation does a substantial portion of its business in their jurisdiction. As a result, hostile bidders have learned to spend considerable energy studying the applicable statutes before launching a takeover attempt.

Defense: | 19
Fight or Sell?

*"Firstly, on the moment of his awakening, the
thought occurred to him: 'Why do I lie here? The
night is wearing on, and at daybreak it is likely
that the enemy will be upon us.'"*

Xenophon, *Anabasis*

The threshold question is when to fight, and when to sell. Sometimes the time has come, and the eloquence of execution is the
key issue. Disgruntled shareholders, no clear management succession, adverse business prospects, the real strategic benefits of a combination or a blow-out price may all impel a sale.

But there are sales, and there are sales. A forced sale to an unde-
sired buyer under time pressure is very different from a carefully
honed private process. Of course, some sellers purely interested in
price prefer the frenzy of a public auction. For many companies,
however, the prospect of an untimely sale is most unattractive. The
competing rights of short- and long-term shareholders, managers
and the community make up the vortex that generates the most passion about deals.

If directors decide a strategic shift is timely, they typically consider
the relative merits of three alternatives—some sort of sale or merger, a
corporate spin-off or the issuance of a targeted stock. Once the decision has been made, implementation takes center stage. Every deal has

its own life. The stakes are high, with the future of a corporation up for grabs. In this context, cookbook solutions are for bookstores.

Selling a Division

A sale of a subsidiary may be the most attractive solution. The sale process can be completed more quickly than a spin-off, and may be mandated by cash needs. Some cash can be harvested through a spin-off by having the subsidiary take on debt to pay a dividend before the transaction. However, a sale of the business also converts the equity interest in the subsidiary to cash. This cash can be used to fund operating needs or capital investment. Also the disposed operations may lack the size or critical mass to survive as a separate stand-alone business.

Tactical concerns related to a hostile bid may also weigh in favor of selling a division. An outright sale of the business sought by a bidder, much like a crown jewel lockup, is one way to reduce interest in a takeover of a multidivision company. Alternatively, the cash from a sale might be the war chest for defensive maneuvers such as a defensive acquisition or the payment of a special dividend to shareholders.

These potential benefits must be weighed against the relative costs of a sale. Some of the pitfalls are familiar. Taxes can be one significant problem, though structuring alternatives may minimize the impact. The cost of retained corporate overhead—which will be spread over a smaller business—must be factored into the equation, as in a spin-off or split-off.

Once a sale process begins, word may leak out. An unsuccessful or busted sale marks the unit involved as damaged goods and can reduce its value for the near term. A full IPO of the subsidiary is another alternative, but a failed or weak IPO undermines value.

In a cash sale transaction, the value of lost earnings is another concern. The issue arises where a parent company is trading at a higher multiple to earnings or cash flow than it receives on the sale.

For example, a parent might be trading at 20 times earnings but only receive 15 times the subsidiary's earnings in a sale. In an efficient market, this difference would not be a problem. Investors would value the parent company based on its constituent parts. If a multiple of 15 were appropriate for the subsidiary, that multiple would be embedded in the parent company's price. In other words, the 20 multiple would be the blended average of the multiples for the parent's various business units.

Yet markets are not efficient. In a world of multiple expansion, it is possible that the parent's trading value incorporates something more than a 15 multiple for the subsidiary's earnings. A sale of the subsidiary at the lower multiple then might be a value-destroying action from the parent company's perspective.

The defensive sale raises other concerns. A sale must be completed quickly to have any tactical impact. Of course, a fast sale under duress probably will not generate a full valuation. Selling too cheap opens the board to breach-of-fiduciary-duty charges, while selling too slow can be meaningless.

Marketing a Business Selling a company is like selling any other product. The fundamentals are important, but positioning and presentation play a role. Sizzle sells. A sense for the target market to a considerable extent determines the approach taken. The world of potential private-market buyers can be broken into two main categories: financial buyers and strategic buyers.

A financially oriented buyer generally is more concerned with price, financial structure and projected returns than with the intricacies of operations. For this reason, a financial buyer often retains the existing management. However, these buyers sometimes instead partner with free-agent management teams.

Financial buyers favor transactions structured as cash purchases or leveraged recapitalizations. The cash sale is straightforward. A leveraged recapitalization is really just a partial cash sale. Under this approach, a seller retains some interest, perhaps 20 or 30 percent, in the divested subsidiary. The seller gains cash but also keeps a portion of any upside from the business; the buyer gains control and runs the business. Furthermore, if push-down accounting can be avoided, no goodwill is created.

An understanding of the financial buyer's viewpoint impacts the way in which a business is pitched. Financial performance and management quality are key issues. Price and risk largely determine the sense of value.

By way of contrast, a strategic buyer looks for companies that might be combined profitably. The focus is more on operations, strategic fit and post-deal integration. Potential cost savings give a strategic buyer the opportunity to bring in higher incremental profits than a financial buyer for the same revenues. As a result, strategic buyers tend to place higher values on most companies, although companies with high cash flow and low reported earnings are common exceptions.

With stock as a possible acquisition currency, strategic acquirers also have more transaction alternatives than financial buyers. Both the cash purchase and the leveraged recapitalization are possibilities. In addition, a stock-for-stock merger with the divested company is possible. This form of transaction leaves the selling company with an interest in the combined company. The seller can either retain the interest as a passive investment or distribute the stock to shareholders in a taxable distribution.

The Importance of Good Grooming Ideally, the decision to sell a business is made a year before the business is put on the market. The intervening period allows for the all-important grooming process.

Grooming a business for sale requires a delicate balancing act. Operational improvements should be made where possible. Top management should start thinking about the trade-offs involved in the whole range of management decisions. For example, increased capital expenditures might be put off in favor of higher returns on capital. Increased marketing might be put off in favor of higher margins.

At the same time, little is to be gained from operating a business too far outside the ordinary course. Purchasers are likely to see through short-term improvements, especially in the face of wide disparities in spending. It also can be difficult to sell a business that has peaked recently. Buyers are more interested in a growth story than in a rebound story. Likewise, if all the cost savings have been wrung out of a business and every expansion option exploited, little room is left to pitch the upside.

Of course, the natural inclination for potential buyers is to be skeptical about any business the owner no longer wants. The challenge is to package an opportunity. As when marketing any product, the key is to figure out sales points. Possibilities include projected revenue growth, improving margins, potential cost savings, or a consolidating industry. Why the seller wants to dispose of the business is the first question asked. Lack of strategic fit is sometimes persuasive. Modesty is also effective. Selling the notion that somebody with a different skill set is needed to take advantage of latent opportunities works.

Another aspect of dressing a business for sale is to motivate and retain key executives throughout the sale process. Top-flight management talent can add considerable value to a business and smooth the divestiture process. Retention plans with "stay" bonuses, golden parachutes and other arrangements are commonly put in place for such individuals. Of course, such arrangements need to be disclosed to potential buyers, especially where the company may be on the hook for a material amount of additional compensation expense.

Once the actual sale process begins, even in the preliminary stages, managing the information flow is important. If news of a pending sale leaks, employee morale, customer and supplier support, and market perception can erode. To avoid these negative results, the number of people involved in deliberations should be kept to a minimum and the sale completed as swiftly as possible.

The IPO Alternative An IPO can be an attractive divestiture mechanism, particularly when the new-issues market is frothy. Three factors typically drive a company's IPO analysis—valuation, the story and implementation.

For many prospective issuers, the most important question is how much they will receive upon issuance. Comparable trading multiples are the main data source used to answer this question. Price/earnings ratios and other multiples derived by looking at comparable companies are applied to the business to be offered to the public. The only difference is that an "IPO discount" of 10 to 15 percent is subtracted from the aggregate valuation to arrive at the issue price. This discount reflects the common investment banking practice of issuing shares at a discount to their projected trading value. Basically, the bargain price greases the distribution channel, making initial investors more willing to buy up the stock.

The new-issue process is something of a black box for the uninitiated. Stock is issued at a given price, the market equilibrates and the "value" of a company is determined. This view glosses over the importance of telling a story in marketing an IPO. How the story is told, how a stock is positioned, can have a great deal of impact.

For example, we worked on a public offering for American Pad and Paper, at the time majority-owned by Bain Capital, a highly successful financial buyer. AmPad makes paper-based office products. In taking the company public, there were two stories that could be told. One would have positioned AmPad as a paper company. Instead, the approach taken was to position AmPad as a "consumer products" paper company because this sector benefited from higher multiples. By successfully telling the consumer products story, Bain floated shares in AmPad at a significantly higher price than otherwise would have been possible.

The urge to be creative is constrained by two factors. First, the market can be a skeptical, incredulous animal. The AmPad pitch only worked because it was grounded in reality. Second, federal securities law and regulations enforce honest disclosure. The IPO registration process is much like the process necessary to distribute stock in a spin-off. A lengthy registration statement and proxy must be drafted by the issuer and approved by the SEC. The "red herring"—a preliminary version of the document with only the price left blank—is distributed to potential purchasers. The final version goes out with the shares.

Whether an IPO or a private-market sale will be more favorable cannot be determined with scientific certainty. A judgment must be made based on available information. Public-market trading multiples can be compared to private-market acquisition multiples for some guidance. Yet, as with all decisions as to price, value is a metaphysical concept that can only be estimated.

It is also possible to straddle the fence between the private and public markets. The IPO process is public. A registration statement must be filed relatively far in advance of the offering. The filing sometimes triggers interest among bidders, which might preempt a planned IPO with a premium offer to purchase the entire company.

Xerox benefited from this dynamic on the sale of its Van Kampen asset management unit. As part of an ongoing effort to refocus, Xerox filed for a public offering of up to 38 percent of Van Kampen's stock in 1992. However, as the deal approached market, buyout firm Clayton, Dubilier and Rice—the successor to Clayton & Dubilier—swooped in with a $360 million offer to buy the whole company. Xerox was ecstatic with the price and accepted. Clayton, Dubilier ended up holding Van Kampen for less than four years, selling it to Morgan Stanley in 1996 for a nice gain.

Tactical Considerations   The private-market sale is a more varied process than the IPO. A spectrum of approaches exists. Nonetheless, it can be helpful to think of the range of possibilities in terms of two ideal types—the classic two-step auction and the negotiated sale. The basic demarcation between these alternatives is the scope of the marketing effort. An auction is the broader alternative. A negotiated transaction may involve just one other party besides the seller, while an auction may be opened up to dozens of bidders.

Neither approach is intrinsically superior. Each serves different objectives. A wide-ranging auction generally maximizes value, particularly since the "best buyer" on paper is not always the party that eventually pays the highest price. Having multiple bidders builds natural tension into the process and generates more energetic bidding. The absence of secrecy or speed is the main downside of an auction. Meanwhile, a negotiated sale may not wring the last dollar from a property, but generally will bring a faster result and maximize secrecy. A defensive sale therefore is more likely to be conducted as a negotiated sale.

The Classic Two-Step   The classic two-step auction starts with the drafting of an offering memorandum. This memorandum describes the business that is for sale at some length. A list of potential buyers is created along with the offering document, and the identity of the prospects influences the contents of the document.

Once the offering memorandum is prepared, prospective purchasers are contacted. Those who express an interest are asked to sign a confidentiality agreement before they receive materials. Copies of the offering document then are distributed to prospects and a follow-up program carried out.

Interested parties might be given more information at this stage based on requests. At some predetermined date, potential buyers who wish to proceed must submit nonbinding preliminary indications of interest. Such indications usually state a price range.

Based on the ranges and other factors, a number of prospects will be asked to enter a second round of bidding. Top management usually makes a presentation to these potential purchasers. A tour of facilities also might be arranged and a "data room" filled with documents regarding the company's business organized and made available. The well-run data room can make an important difference in the bid process. Not only can easy access to data help bidders, but issues on the sale can be addressed at an early point. Moreover, in a rigid two-step, buyers are expected to complete their due diligence review prior to the final bid date.

As the bidding process nears its climax, a bidding procedures letter is circulated to the final bidders along with a sample purchase agreement. The letter generally outlines the nature of an acceptable bid. On the final bid date, bids are received and a winner is declared.

Price often is the determining factor in an auction, but other issues sometimes make a critical difference. One bidder might offer a high price, an unfavorable contract and no concrete details regarding financing. Another bidder might be willing to pay less, but offer a "clean" contract and quick closure.

Once a winner is selected, the contracts are negotiated and executed. The transaction typically closes one to two months after a definitive purchase agreement is signed, though in large public-company deals, the process can take significantly longer.

The garden-variety two-step auction is also known as a sealed-bid auction. A "dripping wax" auction is a variation on the two-step in which the "final bids" are not really final. Instead, the seller goes back to the few highest bidders. The high bid is used as leverage over the others in an attempt to force a raise. If successful, the new prices can be used against the former high bidder. However, this kind of trading tactic can backfire. If the seller has a reputation as a dripping wax auctioneer, potential buyers may underbid initially as a protective mechanism.

Running an Auction   Though the two-step procedure is by now standard practice, running a successful auction is an art, like writing a suspense novel. There must be a frame to the story, a formal skeleton to the process. Spontaneity must be managed so the story is not lost in the confusion. Yet pressure must run throughout.

The auction format naturally creates tension. This is particularly true with a blind auction. Bidders are not told how many other parties they are competing against. Information on other bids is released selectively. If the auctioneer is skilled and the integrity of the process is maintained, even a single bidder can be induced to enter a full bid.

However, structural stress is not the only motivating factor in a well-run auction. If the process is managed correctly, bidders will be pulled along by the desire for more data. The offering memorandum might describe the business and industry, with some limited projections. Further detail might be made available in stages. One capsule might come after indications of interest are in, another as part of the management presentation. A subtle touch is required to maximize the effect.

THE AUCTIONEER'S RULE BOOK

1. Always have more information than the buyer.

2. Understand the buyer's focus.

3. Control pacing.

4. Sell an opportunity.

5. Provide realistic projections.

6. Have a professional data room.

7. Describe problems; have answers.

8. Radiate the integrity of the process.

9. Be flexible.

Naturally, sophisticated bidders will do their best to circumvent the auction format. For example, bidders frequently attempt to wheedle whatever additional information they can out of the auctioneer or seller. Information leaks all too easily and undermines the process. More dramatically, a prospect might make a preemptive bid that explodes if not accepted by a certain date.

Of course, this is the story of Kraft's Duracell auction—Forstmann Little came in with a preemptive bid. The reaction to such tactics depends on how steep the bid is and how critical the bidder is to maintaining the process. With many interested bidders, Kraft felt able to shop the offer. The company approached Henry Kravis, who, like Forstmann, attempted to short-circuit the process. He offered to make one more raise so long as he had a guarantee that it would be the last round. This extra knowledge proved decisive.

Sometimes a bidder will raise its bid after the final deadline despite the rules. The auctioneer is then in a quandary and sometimes invites another round of bids. Obviously, the original "winning" bidder will be furious.

The true challenge of running an auction is maintaining the integrity of the process. Rules must constantly be defended from encroachment. Prospective buyers must be motivated to continue in the process, but can't be pushed too hard or a sense of desperation will develop. Above all else, flexibility must be maintained.

The Negotiated Deal   Of course, a negotiated sale process can involve just one prospective buyer. The prospect is approached and if interested signs a confidentiality agreement. Information is exchanged; negotiations open. Neither party wants to be the first to name a price, but this can be coaxed out of an aggressive bidder. The momentum of a bidder's ambition can be used as a tool to gather information for a seller. If the parties agree to a price, a letter of intent might be signed, followed by contract negotiations and an eventual closing.

The most common mistake sellers make in negotiated transactions is granting a prospective buyer the exclusive right to negotiate a purchase for a period of time. Buyers often will request this right based on little more than a preliminary nonbinding bid. The problem is that the buyer then may perform due diligence and come back with a much lower offer, claiming problems were discovered. At that point, the buyer has leverage over the seller. If the deal falls apart, the company on the block is viewed as damaged goods by other prospective purchasers.

A seller can avoid this circumstance by refusing to grant an exclusive. Moreover, a limited auction might be conducted even though one particular prospect appears to be the likely buyer. Having just one other real bidder in the picture gives the seller negotiating leverage and can improve the outcome considerably. Of course, a unique buyer or the strong desire for a quick execution may dictate the exclusive arrangement.

After a Busted Sale   Even in a full-blown auction, there is the real possibility that no bidder willing to pay the seller's minimum price will emerge. A party also might be selected as the winning bidder and then later back out of the transaction. Contractual language can be drafted in an attempt to avoid this outcome, but the risk cannot be eliminated.

Of course, a busted sale becomes more likely as the number of bidders in the picture declines. A smart bidder who perceives itself to be the only player in negotiations may force matters by making a low ball offer or refusing to bid.

A seller can rebound from a busted sale in one of three ways. It can accept a sale on a distressed basis, taking a lower price than would come through a more patient approach in exchange for being able to move on in its corporate life. The seller can remove the property from the market with the intention of remarketing in a few months or years. Alternatively, it can remove the business from the market and commit to managing the business.

BUYING OFF A BUSTED SALE

A busted sale can be a buyer's gain. If the seller needs cash or has unalterably decided to divest the particular business, a buyer may be able to scoop up a rough-cut gem at a bargain price. Maybelline's buyout followed this pattern.

In 1989, Maybelline was owned by Schering-Plough Corporation, a large pharmaceuticals company. The cosmetics company was perceived as a dowdy brand under pressure from competition, and Schering decided to put it on the market. Despite Maybelline's problems, analysts placed its value at around $500 million.

Schering-Plough's auction did not proceed smoothly. Strategic buyers showed no interest, and Schering eventually settled on a $320 million offer from a financial buyer. Two months later, the deal stumbled as the buyer wanted to slash the price.

Through an investment buyout fund, we had been in the Maybelline bidding early on, and had researched the company. On hearing reports of the busted sale, we offered $305 million for the company with a time fuse for acceptance. Schering-Plough accepted the offer.

As things turned out, Maybelline was a bargain purchase. When the company was bought, its brands were distributed primarily in the domestic market. One of the initiatives was to expand the company's international exposure. Maybelline dabbled in a number of markets. The strategy was not to demonstrate strong profitability overseas—the company lacked the resources. Rather, the idea was that the Maybelline brands were extendable.

In 1996, L'Oréal saw the opportunity and grabbed it. They bought and melded Maybelline with their existing international personal care business. The $761 million purchase price included $158 million of assumed debt. Taking into account several prior dividends and the cash received in a prior recapitalization, this amounted to a return of $623 million on the $160 million of equity originally invested in the Maybelline buyout.

Selling the Entire Company

Selling an entire company is in many ways similar to selling a division. Grooming the business for sale can have a big impact. Keeping employees on the job and maintaining morale are just as difficult. An auction or negotiated sale are possible approaches. However, there are a number of differences between the two tasks, differences with important tactical implications.

Cash transactions are less common. Tax-free stock-for-stock mergers are often the preferred structure.

The mechanics of deal implementation are also different. A vote of shareholders in both the target and acquirer may be necessary to approve a merger, while friendly cash deals typically are accomplished by way of a tender offer. In either case, the reaction of shareholders and other constituencies is of immediate import.

Perhaps the most significant difference between a divestiture and a corporate sale is the larger role played by the board. Directors have an undeniable responsibility to affirm or reject a plan to sell their company. Decisions are more likely to be challenged with the stakes so high. Consequently, throughout the process, directors pay close attention to their legal and fiduciary obligations.

The Business Judgment Rule   Courts generally will not second-guess the business judgment of corporate directors. This deference is embodied in the business judgment rule. As articulated in the Delaware courts, the rule holds that "directors' decisions are presumed to have been made on an informed basis, in good faith and in the honest belief that the action taken was in the best interests of the company."

The normal business judgment rule applies in most cases where a company is sold. Under the rule, a decision of the board will not be overturned unless a plaintiff is able to carry a heavy burden of proof. Specifically, the plaintiff must show that the board failed to meet either its duty of care or its duty of loyalty.

To prove the duty of care was breached, a plaintiff must show that directors were grossly negligent. Yet the duty-of-care doctrine is not without teeth. In 1985, the real possibility of personal liability was underscored for corporate directors by the case *Smith v. Van Gorkom.* Most directors are protected by liability insurance, but the Delaware court's sharp rebuke of the Trans Union Corporation board in *Van Gorkom* dramatically sensitized directors to their responsibilities.

Trans Union was a company with large investment tax credits and no way to use them on its own. In 1980, Jerome Van Gorkom, the company's chairman and CEO, decided to sell the company. Having done almost no financial analysis, Van Gorkom approached the Pritzkers, the prominent Chicago investors, and suggested they buy Trans Union for $55 a share. The Pritzkers were quite interested and negotiations proceeded quickly. Van Gorkom called a board meeting on one day's notice. Trans Union's investment bankers were not invited and most of the company's directors and officers knew nothing of the deal until the meeting.

At the board meeting, Van Gorkom gave a brief verbal presentation on the deal. The directors were told by the company's CFO that the deal seemed at the low end of what would be fair. Van Gorkom assured the directors that Trans Union would be able to accept other offers for ninety days under the terms of the Pritzker deal. The actual merger agreement was not presented. After a two-hour discussion, the deal was approved.

Four years later, a Delaware court found the Trans Union directors to have been grossly negligent. The price received in the merger represented a significant premium over the company's trading price and no other bidders had emerged. Still, the court said the directors did not live up to their duty of care. As particular flaws, the court highlighted the lack of valuation data and the failure to review the merger agreement.

Van Gorkom underscores that a key aspect of the duty of care is the process involved. Directors who "inform themselves of all information reasonably available to them and relevant to their decision" are not grossly negligent. Furthermore, directors may reasonably rely on information and opinions provided by qualified third parties, such as company lawyers, executives and investment bankers, without breaching the duty of care. If the process is duly deliberative, directors are unlikely to be considered grossly negligent.

A breach of the duty of loyalty is equally tough to prove. A plaintiff must show that the board engaged in "self-dealing." Self-dealing is defined to mean a case where directors have a direct financial stake in a transaction up for board approval, such as in a management buyout, or where the directors stand to gain some improper financial benefit.

Courts use an amorphous, fact-specific analysis to decide whether the self-dealing of a single director or a small group of directors rises to a level that calls an entire board's actions into question. If the duty of loyalty is breached, the business judgment rule will no longer apply. Instead, the burden shifts and the board must prove the "entire fairness" of the deal.

FAIRNESS OPINIONS

As part of the deliberative process, a board often will hire an investment bank to give a fairness opinion regarding a planned transaction. The opinion itself is a relatively brief document which states that, in the investment bank's opinion, the transaction is fair. The narrow focus is on fairness from a financial point of view. Shareholders are the only constituency considered. Although a lot of analysis is done, the conclusion is one of art—not science—taking into account all of the data considered.

A fairness opinion helps insulate a company and its board from liability to shareholders. But an opinion is only partly designed to reduce litigation risk. The analysis and advice of an investment bank provides data to directors regarding a transaction's financial and strategic impact. With more information, directors presumably can make better decisions.

While a fairness opinion is short, considerable backup documentation is prepared as foundation. Fairness is, after all, a subjective quality. The fairness inquiry must be contextual. The question is, Fair under what circumstances, at what point in time?

In preparing a fairness opinion, a feeling for past performance and strategic situation is critical. Then, both the subject company and the consideration to be received in the transaction are valued using various methodologies.

With a database assembled, the analysis comes down to a cumulative judgment. For example, most firms require a fairness opinion committee to approve any opinion. The committee is composed of senior professionals with broad experience and perspective. A give-and-take exchange takes place regarding the merits and a consensus is reached.

The fairness opinion process at times draws fire. Some of the more heated criticism has come when an investment bank grants a fairness opinion and its client completes a deal even though another higher offer is on the table or the market price exceeds the offer. How can the lower offer be fair?

The answer lies in an understanding of what a fairness opinion signifies. Fairness does not mean the reviewed transaction matches some objective sense of intrinsic value, nor does it mean the target will receive the highest auction price attainable.

Of course, if an all-cash offer is matched with another all-cash offer, it is difficult to endorse the lower deal. However, if the terms are different, with varying degrees of risk, or if the consideration is different, the situation changes. For example, an all-stock tax-free deal with upside continuity for the shareholders may, indeed, make more sense than an all-cash deal. Sometimes the market price exceeds an offer because of frothy speculation rather than fundamentals.

Both banks and clients also have been criticized on the basis of fee arrangements. Investment bankers commonly receive a "success" fee if a deal for which they are providing strategic and financial advice goes through. If the deal collapses, the banker receives a much lower fee. This bifurcated structure gives the investment banker an interest in seeing a deal go forward. Critics argue that a banker in this position is biased in favor of granting a fairness opinion. As a result of the perceived conflict, companies sometimes negotiate for the investment bank to handle the fairness opinion for a flat fee. Regardless, bankers do take pride and care in their opinions because their reputation is on the line.

Obviously, the more extensive the analysis and unbiased the bank, the more valuable the opinion. For this reason, a company sometimes will hire a second investment bank—in addition to the bank providing broader strategic advice on the transaction—for the sole job of providing an opinion. This arrangement leaves less room for the argument that the bank giving the opinion has a stake in the deal.

The *Unocal* Standard   In certain circumstances, courts have found the traditional deference shown to the business judgment of directors to be misplaced. Company insiders who also serve as directors may tilt board decisions in favor of arrangements that ensure continued employment, no matter the consequences to shareholders. Second, directors who are ostensibly independent outsiders may act in a similar fashion out of loyalty to corporate insiders and to preserve access to the perks associated with being a director.

These concerns came to light in *Unocal v. Mesa Petroleum*, the case in which the Delaware Supreme Court reviewed Unocal's defensive response to Boone Pickens' takeover bid. As part of its defensive strategy, Unocal initiated a self-tender for its shares at a substantial premium to Mesa's hostile offer. The key to the strategy was the exclusion of Mesa from the offer. Pickens sued to have the discriminatory self-tender invalidated.

In *Unocal*, the Delaware Supreme Court recognized the "inherent conflict" facing a board when deciding whether to pursue a defensive maneuver. As a result, "there is an enhanced duty which calls for judicial examination at the threshold before the protections of the business judgment rule may be conferred."

This enhanced scrutiny involves a two-pronged analysis. A board must show that it had "reasonable grounds for believing that a danger to corporate policy and effectiveness existed." *Unocal* also requires a board to show that the defensive measures were "reasonable in relation to the threat imposed."

These two burdens can be satisfied largely by showing that a reasonable investigation was undertaken prior to the decision to adopt defensive measures. Courts have paid particular deference when decisions are approved by a majority of independent directors, especially if these directors have been counseled by outside legal and financial advisers.

However, cases subsequent to *Unocal* make clear that the purported threat must be specific and defined. Specific threats so far recognized as acceptable include the coercive nature of a two-tiered hostile tender offer, the general inadequacy of an offer in comparison to perceived intrinsic value, and timing concerns related to arranging counteroffers. Moreover, the defense of an existing, defined corporate strategy such as in *Time* qualifies as a valid defensive motivation.

"The nature of the threat associated with a particular hostile offer sets the parameters for the range of permissible defensive tactics," according to *Unocal*. Reasonableness in the context of this proportionality inquiry is defined as a range, not a single value, and defenses that are not preclusive or coercive generally will be shown some deference.

Courts in particular disfavor responses that force a transaction favored by management on shareholders. Yet the measure of what is preclusive is legal, not practical. The recent takeover fight for Wallace Computer Services makes the point. In the summer of 1995, Moore Corporation made an all-cash tender offer for the outstanding shares of Wallace. Completion of the offer was conditioned on the redemption of Wallace's poison pill. At $56 a share, the offer represented a 27 percent premium over the trading price of Wallace stock before the announcement. Moore subsequently raised its offer to $60 a share.

Notwithstanding the market premium, the Wallace board considered the offer and declined to negotiate, citing the inadequacy of the price in light of the company's improving operating performance. The board—in a decision supported by a Delaware federal court—therefore refused to redeem Wallace's pill despite the fact that 73 percent of the company's shareholders tendered into the offer. Essentially, the *Wallace* court was satisfied that the poison pill under review did not preclude the bidder from contesting a proxy contest.

From a practical standpoint, though, the Wallace pill effectively precluded a successful takeover. In addition to its poison pill, Wallace also had a staggered board. Thus, while Moore was free to fight a proxy contest, the company would need at least two years to gain control in this fashion. Moore indeed pursued a proxy contest and won a block of board seats in the first election, but gave up before the second election.

The Sale of Control   The *Unocal* standard governs if a board is determined to fight off a hostile bidder and remain independent. However, in many cases, a company responds to a hostile tender offer by seeking out a white knight to buy the company on more favorable terms. The white knight strategy raises concerns similar to those addressed in *Unocal:* directors might favor one bidder over another out of self-interest. Consequently, the courts have had to deal with the appropriate standard for director behavior during the sale of control. The starting point is the *Revlon* rule that directors must maximize shareholder value in a sale.

The problem for the Delaware court, however, was that *Revlon* could be read too broadly, preventing strategic corporate combinations because of their tactical vulnerability. If any merger were viewed as a sale of control, only the strongest of companies would initiate a transaction. Therefore, the scope of *Revlon* was nipped in the landmark *Time* case. The court held that the proposed strategic Time-Warner merger did not involve a change of control and, therefore, did not trigger the *Revlon* duties. In essence, then, *Time* is the godmother of corporate marriages.

At base, in *Time*, the court found the Time-Warner merger to be in keeping with Time's long-term strategy of creating a "vertically integrated video enterprise" while at the same time preserving the "Time culture" of journalistic integrity. This type of strategic merger does not trigger *Revlon* duties. Rather, two circumstances trigger such duties—first, when a corporation explicitly initiates an auction, and second, when a corporation "abandons its long-term strategy" in response to a hostile bid and instead pursues a white knight.

However, in *QVC*, the pendulum swung back the other direction when the Delaware court limited the scope of *Time*. The *QVC* case involved Barry Diller's hostile bid for Paramount. Viacom and Paramount responded by renegotiating their merger contract. As part of the deal, Paramount agreed to keep the stringent defensive measures in place to protect the Viacom merger, and Viacom agreed to raise its price.

Even though the Viacom-Paramount merger was styled as a strategic merger, the court held it was a change in control that triggered *Revlon*. Sumner Redstone's controlling interest in the merged Viacom-Paramount entity—he would have 40 percent of the common stock and 70 percent of the voting stock—was the key factor in this analysis. Redstone, the court found, would control the new entity and could determine its corporate strategy going forward. As a result, the merger constituted a sale of control that entitled Paramount's shareholders to receive the control premium associated with an auction. The court basically was not convinced that the Paramount board had acted "reasonably to seek the transaction offering the best value reasonably available to the stockholders."

PROFILE

Judge Andrew Moore

For twelve years, Judge Andrew G.T. Moore refereed America's corporate legal battles. As a justice of the Delaware Supreme Court, he was the author of many of the leading legal opinions that form the basis for modern takeover law, including *Revlon* and *Unocal*. He also sat on the panels that decided the *Time* and *QVC* cases. He may well have had more of an impact on modern corporate law than any other individual.

A native of New Orleans, Moore was stationed in Delaware while in the military. He returned to the state after law school to clerk for the chief justice of Delaware's Supreme Court. He then moved on to become a corporate litigator at Connolly, Bove, Lodge & Hutz, of Wilmington, Delaware. After eighteen years at the firm, he was appointed to the Supreme Court in 1982.

While on the court, Moore developed a reputation for pragmatic judgment or, to be more practical, the use of a flexible smell test. He seemed philosophically opposed to hostile takeovers by junk bond raiders. Yet he argued that the quality of corporate directors also needed to be improved, and came down hard on any lack of corporate propriety.

Much of the takeover litigation coming across Moore's desk involved the fundamental question, How much leeway should a board be allowed in moving to stave off raiders? Moore usually took a balanced view. For example, in *Unocal* he wrote an opinion upholding a controversial defensive technique. Yet in *Revlon* he held that a board's response to a hostile takeover attempt must be reasonable.

Moore came up for reappointment in 1994. Despite widespread support among both institutional investors and members of the takeover bar, he was not offered a second term. The decision generated an uproar in Delaware and was rumored to be political in nature.

Today, Moore is a senior managing director at Wasserstein Perella, where he specializes in corporate defense work and provides advice to boards. He also teaches as a visiting professor at various law schools.

Nonshareholder Constituencies   The *Revlon* case makes clear that a board's duty in Delaware lies with the shareholders it represents and not other constituencies such as bondholders, workers or the community at large. As the court put it:

> A board may have regard for various constituencies in discharging its responsibilities, provided there are rationally related benefits accruing to the stockholders. However, such concern for non-stockholder interests is inappropriate when an auction among active bidders is in progress, and the object no longer is to protect or maintain the corporate enterprise but to sell it to the highest bidder.

However, the view is different in states other than Delaware. For example, the Pennsylvania takeover statute clearly contemplates the weighing of varied interests and the 1997 litigation surrounding the hostile fight for Conrail illustrated that the Pennsylvania courts will go out of their way to protect local corporations.

The Fine Art of Corporate Marriages   Directors sometimes make the commitment to sell, and an auction is chosen as the best value-maximizing alternative. However, a company may be unwilling to sell itself to the highest bidder for valid strategic and business reasons. In this situation, as a result of the *Revlon* string of cases, not triggering an auction becomes the tactical focus. If a *Revlon* auction is triggered, the selling company loses control of the process. Price becomes the only question. Of course, for hostile bidders, the trick is to force a board into the *Revlon* mode.

Under the *Time* analysis, the strategic merger is the most effective tool for a selling company to control its own fate. An agreement to merge with a strategic partner is far more defensible against interlopers than a cash transaction. However, the deal still is somewhat vulnerable because shareholders of both companies must vote to approve a corporate marriage. This leaves an obvious point of attack for an outsider gunning for the deal.

The modern bias in favor of strategic mergers has a practical impact on the way a company is shopped. Often, a company will hire an investment banker and announce an intention to study "strategic alternatives." Potential merger candidates consider this an invitation to make an offer. At the same time, though, the company is not put up for sale and arguably avoids a *Revlon* auction.

A secret negotiated merger of equals is another common tactic to avoid *Revlon*. The greatest danger in this approach is that word of negotiations will leak out. If nothing then comes of the discussions, pressure can build to do some alternative transaction.

Recent examples of major marriage transactions include the Dean Witter–Morgan Stanley deal and the Chase-Chemical merger. Merger-of-equals deal terms vary. However, several defining characteristics can be identified. A corporate marriage involves a merger between two parties of roughly comparable size. The exchange ratio is set basically at market-to-market pricing. Executives from both companies share the management roles in the combined entity.

The three main issues in negotiating a marriage are the exchange ratio, corporate governance and post-deal integration. With regard to the exchange ratio, market-to-market is the theme. The working hypothesis at the outset is that neither company's shareholders should receive a premium. Having said that, the parties inevitably posture over the appropriate ratio. Relative trading values vary over time, so the period selected can alter the result. The impact of unusual events, leaks regarding the deal or sharp fluctuations all can be debated. A party may argue that an independent valuation would be a more appropriate measure of the exchange ratio.

For these and other reasons, the ratio announced with the terms of the deal sometimes deviates from the no-premium norm, with the smaller company more often getting a slight premium. Once the ratio is set, the parties must determine whether to use a fixed or floating exchange ratio, with or without a collar.

Agreement on the key corporate governance issues is another critical sticking point. The big questions are board makeup, executive representation, headquarters location and corporate name. Both parties generally are reluctant to cede board control. One solution is to have an evenly divided board. In other cases, board representation might be traded off against other issues.

Executive representation is a concern for top management. For a merger of equals to work, the parties have to be willing to share power. A common solution in this regard is to have the chief executive of one company become the chairman of the combined entity's board. The other chief executive retains that title. Then, after some period of years, the chairman agrees to retire, and the CEO takes over the top spot as well. A variant is for the older CEO to remain in that position and the younger to be president for a short period. The committee structure of the board also is carefully crafted to assure balance and to thwart the possibility of a coup.

Headquarters location and the corporate name can be particularly emotional issues. A large company often has a major presence in its community. Furthermore, management and other employees may be unwilling to move across the country. Compromise is often necessary. In the Ultramar–Diamond Shamrock merger, for example, Connecticut-based Ultramar agreed to move the combined corporate headquarters to San Antonio, Texas.

The name of the combined entity is held important mainly for its signaling effect. In a true merger of equals, neither party wants to appear to have sold out. For this reason, the combined entity will often carry the name of both formerly independent companies, as in the Morgan Stanley–Dean Witter deal.

Post-closing integration determines whether a transaction advertised as a merger of equals turns out to be one. Matters sometimes fail to go as smoothly as envisioned. Veterans of one corporate culture may come to dominate the surviving company. The danger, of course, is that infighting will damage the prospects of the combined company.

The Spin-Off

The notion of a spin-off is deceptively simple: a parent company distributes shares in a subsidiary to shareholders; afterward, the shareholders own interests in two stand-alone businesses. Yet the spin-off process can be complicated, due to a thicket of tax rules.

Three specific transaction structures fall under the generic spin-off rubric. In a basic spin-off, the stock in a subsidiary business is distributed pro rata to shareholders. No sale is involved. The spun-off entity becomes a completely separate company with its own board of directors, management, assets, liabilities and owners. However, immediately after the transaction, the original parent company shareholders own both the spun-off entity and the remaining company.

A second alternative is to precede a spin-off with an equity carve-out, as when Sears sold a minority interest in Dean Witter to the public prior to its 1993 spin-off. A portion of the stock in the subsidiary is sold to the public in an IPO. The remaining interest is then distributed to parent company shareholders, as in the basic spin-off. Both the IPO and the distribution can be structured as tax-free transactions. However, to qualify for tax-free status, no more than 20 percent of the subsidiary may be carved out prior to the spin-off.

Finally, there is the split-off. Like the basic spin-off, this is a non-sale transaction. However, shares in the subsidiary business are not distributed pro rata to shareholders. Instead, an exchange offer is made, giving shareholders the option to turn in all or part of their old shares for new shares in the subsidiary. The offer effectively is a share buyback, with shares in the subsidiary as the consideration. At the end of the day, some shareholders own an increased interest in the remaining company. The other shareholders own an interest in the new company.

Qualifying a Spin-Off

Once the business issues are settled, the requirements for a non-taxable spin-off must be satisfied. For example, prior to distribution, the parent must control at least 80 percent of the stock of the entity to be spun off; the parent must distribute at least 80 percent of the stock in the spin-off; and both the parent and the spun-off entity must have been engaged in an active trade or business for at least five years. Parent company shareholders also must maintain a continuity of interest going forward and the spin-off must be accomplished for a valid, corporate-level business purpose.

The IRS has issued extensive interpretive regulations and rulings on each of these requirements. The courts have added considerable precedent as well, but few cases ever reach litigation. As a result, the IRS has become more or less the final arbiter on issues of interpretation, and fulfilling its requirements is like tiptoeing through the tulips.

Much of the uncertainty surrounding the status of a proposed spin-off stems from the business purpose test. Lawyers make careers interpreting the IRS's rather idiosyncratic views. The test is amorphous and requires a fact-specific inquiry. Arbitrary distinctions and hairsplitting are par for the course. For example, increasing shareholder value is not an acceptable business purpose but achieving cost savings is.

Other business purposes recognized by the IRS as valid include: providing an equity interest to employees, facilitating a stock offering or borrowing, resolving management or other problems arising from operating two different businesses, resolving competitive conflicts with customers or suppliers, facilitating an acquisition of or by the company, and insulating one business from the risks associated with another business. Once a valid business purpose is identified, the taxpayer has the burden to show that a spin-off is the only practical and efficient way to achieve that purpose.

Advantages   A spin-off offers many potential advantages. The disaggregation of diverse businesses is applauded in the market. After a spin-off, investors and research analysts have an enhanced ability to follow the distinct businesses. The creation of formally separate companies gives the full benefit of pure-play trading values.

Another effect is to unleash entrepreneurial potential. As part of a larger business, a smaller subsidiary often succumbs to the "rich uncle syndrome." The parent company protects the subsidiary in lean times and may not force the subsidiary to live up to its potential. At the same time, being part of a larger organization can stifle employees of the subsidiary.

While many of these same benefits can be captured through a sale, a spin-off also has several special advantages. The most glaring difference involves tax treatment. A spin-off is tax-free both to the company and to recipient shareholders. A sale, on the other hand, may trigger a significant tax liability. The company would be taxed on any gain realized on the sale, and if the money were then paid out to the shareholders, they also would be taxed on the dividend payment.

A spin-off also allows shareholders to retain their interest in the business. As a result, the shareholders have the opportunity to benefit from any future growth of the business. Empirical evidence suggests that both spun-off companies and their former parents tend to outperform the market in the years following the spin-off. This analysis is especially true of companies selling at a conglomerate discount or where the market expects a takeover bid after the spin.

Although the spin-off is an invaluable tool for strategic planning, the long time fuse involved limits its value as a response to an immediate hostile threat. However, the announcement of a planned spin-off may be enough to make a company's share price pop and placate shareholders. ITT followed this route in its defense against Hilton.

Preceding a spin-off with an equity carve-out has a number of additional advantages. First, the sale of stock in the subsidiary generates cash. If stock representing less than 20 percent of the subsidiary is sold, the money can then be distributed to the parent tax-free. In addition, by floating shares in the subsidiary, a trading market is created. This can be important in the case of a large spin-off.

AT&T's 1996 spin-off of Lucent illustrates the technique. With a projected market capitalization in excess of $17 billion, Lucent would be among America's largest companies. Inevitably, the distribution of a large block of Lucent shares would temporarily depress the share price. Hoping to counteract the downdraft, AT&T chose to offer almost 18 percent of the company to the public in the largest IPO in American history. The remaining stock was distributed only after this initial chunk had been trading in the market for several months. An active trading market, research coverage and other after-market support minimized the negative impact of the sudden float following the spin-off. Of course, this advantage is counterbalanced if the shares sold in the carve-out trade at a discount in anticipation of the subsequent spin-off.

A split-off similarly reduces the pressure on a divested entity's stock price. The shareholders who exchange their stock in a split-off do so by choice. As a result, they are less likely to look for a quick sale immediately following the exchange. A split-off also may be preceded by an equity carve-out. This approach has the advantage of creating a trading value for the subsidiary which can be used to value the company and set an exchange ratio for the split-off. From the parent company's perspective, a split-off also enhances earnings per share by reducing the number of outstanding parent shares.

VIACOM SPLITS OFF CABLE

Viacom's 1996 split-off of its cable operations, which were then acquired by a TCI subsidiary, is indicative of the complexities and potential rewards of the transaction structure.

The gist of the transaction was that Viacom raised $1.7 billion in cash by borrowing against its cable business, retained the cash, and divested the business in a split-off. Specifically, Viacom shareholders were given the option to exchange a portion of their Viacom common for stock in the cable business. Once the split-off was completed, TCI injected $350 million of equity into the stand-alone cable unit in exchange for control. The cable company shares that Viacom shareholders had received in the split-off exchange were converted automatically into a preferred stock interest.

This deal structure—negotiated and agreed to before the split-off—walked a high wire in terms of the requirements for a tax-free split-off. When the transaction was completed, Viacom shareholders had no common stock interest in the former Viacom cable business. This fact did not cause a continuity-of-interest problem because, under established precedents, preferred stock qualifies as a continuing interest. Yet the shareholders also relinquished voting control over the cable business, which made the tax treatment a closer question.

The IRS nonetheless granted a favorable ruling in June 1996, after considering the prospect for almost a year. The transaction was completed shortly thereafter and the cable split-off was a coup for Sumner Redstone's Viacom. Following the Paramount and Blockbuster deals, the combined company had a heavy debt burden. The $1.7 billion cash payment in the TCI deal helped and the unique transaction structure allowed Viacom to unload non-core assets at a favorable price, enhanced by the absence of tax. The number of outstanding common shares also was reduced, beefing up Viacom's long-term earnings-per-share potential.

Disadvantages   Perhaps the chief criticism of a spin-off is that it often represents nothing more than a paper shuffling of assets. Unless management improvements go along with the change, a spin-off may not significantly enhance shareholder value. The continuing troubles at AT&T and ITT—both of which recently carried out high-profile spins—underline a fundamental truth. A spin-off can be a catalyst for change, but is not by itself the be-all and end-all of improved performance.

Another potential disadvantage of a spin-off is that any cost savings related to size are lost. The spun-off entity may need to add additional administrative layers and may face a higher cost of capital than it did as a part of the larger entity. Similarly, the distributing company may be left with unneeded overhead. Without reductions, the same administrative staff manages a smaller organization. An operational restructuring at the parent company level may be necessary to maximize the positive impact of a spin-off.

The complex tax and legal process to accomplish a spin-off or split-off is the main implementation hurdle. Where the consequences of failing to qualify for tax-free treatment are significant, a spin-off rarely goes forward without a favorable advance ruling from the IRS. The IRS ruling process can take six to nine months, involves steep legal and accounting costs, and consumes valuable management time. Other legal aspects of a spin-off add further costs and complexity.

Structuring Issues   A spin-off or split-off implicates many difficult structuring issues. If the business to be spun off has not been operated as a separate subsidiary, a decision must be made as to the appropriate segmentation. Assets and liabilities must be divvied up and new legal structures created.

Considerable thought also must be given to the corporate governance of the subsidiary to be spun off. Issues include where the company should be incorporated, what kind of takeover defenses the company should have, the makeup of its board and its management structure. If the business has been operated as a separate subsidiary, existing practice can be used as an appropriate starting point. However, a spin-off is an opportunity to revisit past practices, which may not be appropriate for a stand-alone entity.

For example, the allocation of debt is a key business issue. The subsidiary may not have its own separate debt, yet part of the parent's borrowing may be attributable to the subsidiary's cash needs. It may be appropriate to assign a portion of the parent company debt to the subsidiary, or to have the subsidiary issue debt and pay a dividend to the parent. The goal in allocating debt is to balance benefits to the parent with the viability of the subsidiary. A desire to leave the subsidiary with a strong credit rating usually acts as the practical ceiling on the amount of debt the company can bear.

Implementation   Generally, no shareholder vote is necessary to accomplish a pro rata spin-off, whether preceded by an equity carve-out or not. A company's board in most cases has the authority to distribute a dividend so long as the company will not as a result become insolvent. Therefore, a spin-off is often implemented through the relatively simple process of distributing shares to existing shareholders. Shareholder approval may, however, be needed if more than half the assets are being distributed.

Of course, just like any IPO, the shares in the subsidiary also have to be registered with the SEC prior to distribution. Once the registration is finalized, a company can simply dividend the shares out in a spin-off or proceed with a formal exchange offer to effectuate a split-off. If an exchange is pursued, the offer must be held open for a minimum of twenty business days, as with any tender offer. Furthermore, a tax-free exchange offer is made contingent on meeting the tax requirement that 80 percent control in the subsidiary be distributed.

The central issue in any split-off is the exchange ratio. An exchange offer must specify how many shares in the subsidiary a tendering shareholder will receive in exchange for each share offered. This ratio is determined by the relative values of the parent company and the subsidiary. If a preliminary carve-out has been completed, the trading value can be used as an indication of the appropriate value. In other cases, the company estimates the appropriate value and sets the exchange ratio. Calculating this exchange ratio is a high-stakes art form. If the ratio is miscalculated, the whole deal fizzles in the sunlight of the public market.

Targeted Stock

The targeted stock alternative has become increasingly popular and is likely to become even more so. Proponents argue that targeted stock is the happy medium between divesting and retaining a diverse business portfolio. Critics counter that targeted stock merely papers over the negative side effects of diversification.

Basically, a targeted stock is a separate class of stock issued by a company with multiple business units. The targeted stock, also known as letter stock and tracking stock, is designed to provide a return to investors that reflects the performance of a defined business unit. However, the targeted stock is not a stock in the separate business unit but rather stock of the parent company. It is a modern creation—in effect, "virtual" common stock.

By definition, then, a company with a targeted stock will have at least two classes of stock. One will track the targeted business, the other will track the remaining businesses. For example, U S West's media stock was targeted to its cable and cellular assets, pending the planned spin-off of the media group, while the other class of U S West stock tracked the performance of the company's conventional telecommunications assets.

Advantages   Some corporate managers and directors find targeted stock appealing because of the hybrid nature of the mechanism. Targeted stock allows a company to straddle the boundary line between pure-play and diversified companies. Targeted stock can achieve this result without triggering corporate tax, unlike most sales.

With a separate stock for each distinct major business line, a diversified company becomes a pure-play. The company thus captures some of the benefits that flow from conforming to the new market orthodoxy. Wall Street research analysts provide separate coverage for disparate units. For example, by using a targeted stock to acquire EDS, GM avoided having automotive analysts cover the technology business. Instead, automotive analysts could follow the "regular" GM stock, and technology analysts the GME stock.

The universe of potential investors interested in holding a company's stock can be expanded as a result of a targeted stock issuance. Some major investors, such as mutual funds, may limit their field to certain industries. A targeted stock—and the separate financial reports generally provided for each business—allows investors to value each target business separately. Some may be interested in owning one segment but not another.

Targeted stock may allow a company to close the gap between current trading value and the projected trading value of its businesses as stand-alone entities. Most of these stocks trade in line with comparable pure-play companies. So if a company's trading value implies a discounted value for a particular business, a targeted stock issuance should generate the same multiple expansion associated with a spin-off. The targeted stock will be free to trade at a higher multiple. In the aggregate, the company may enjoy a fuller valuation.

Another benefit of being a notional pure-play company is that management incentive programs can be refined. The pay of managers at the targeted company can be tied more directly to the performance of the business they control. Entrepreneurial incentives can be strengthened with the objective of achieving superior economic results and increased shareholder value. Of course, this was a large part of the GM-EDS story and one of the motivating factors in issuing the targeted GME stock.

At the same time, a targeted stock issuance does not involve a true corporate fission. Some of the positive aspects of operating as a single consolidated business remain. The parent company retains full ownership of and control over the targeted business. The operating businesses still can share overhead expenses. Because the businesses remain combined, borrowings may be structured so that creditors of one business can look to the earnings of the other business for payment. As a result, borrowing costs and capital availability may be improved. The bulk of the combination may enhance takeover defenses. Finally, the combined company can still file a consolidated tax return. Earnings from one business thus can be offset with losses from another, reducing the overall tax bite.

Keeping the businesses together also preserves flexibility to unwind the arrangement at a later date. For example, General Motors has revisited the structure of both its Class E and Class H stocks, as has U S West with its Media Group stock. By way of contrast, once a company is spun, it's gone.

Disadvantages   The targeted stock approach is not without disadvantages. A targeted business remains under the control of existing management and investors do not have a direct claim on the assets of the business. As a result, if the "moral" credit of the parent company is in doubt, the targeted stock may trade at some discount to what would be the stand-alone value. During the 1990s bull market, letter stocks have traded very well.

Furthermore, in some situations a targeted stock may be unworkable. There is the potential problem of liability overhang. The targeted business is not legally separated from the remaining company. A large claim against the remaining businesses may impair the assets or profitability of the targeted business. A company with perceived litigation risk or other significant contingent liabilities may have difficulty convincing investors that a targeted stock is attractive. RJR Nabisco faced this issue in 1993 when it was forced to withdraw a proposed targeted stock linked to its Nabisco food operations, partially because investors raised concerns regarding the potential legal liabilities associated with RJR's tobacco business.

Targeted stock also introduces considerable complexity into a corporate ownership structure. The typical implementation process is time-consuming and can take as long as four to six months. The parent board must deal with two classes of stock and investors, each with its own interests. Balancing these interests raises inevitable conflicts. For example, the capital allocation decision can be a zero-sum game—more money for one business means less for the other. A board bears a fiduciary responsibility to all shareholders, and the friction associated with a targeted stock may induce additional shareholder litigation.

The legal structure of the targeted stock also can hamper flexibility. A back-end exchange is sometimes necessary if the company wishes to unwind the targeted stock arrangement, often at a premium to market price. This reality can act as a barrier to a restructuring or the sale of the company. However, careful drafting of the targeted stock documents can get around most such problems, and, on balance, the targeted stock can be a helpful innovation which allows a company to arbitrage inefficiencies in the market.

Implementation Issues   Structuring a targeted stock involves a number of business, legal, tax and accounting issues.

At the threshold, an issuer must decide on a division of business units. The targeted business group need not be segregated in a distinct legal entity. Hence, there is a great deal of flexibility and room for creativity. Assets, including goodwill, and liabilities, including debt, must be allocated.

In carrying out this process, thought must be given to the profile of the new hypothetical companies. For example, the targeted business might be structured as a high-growth business that will be valued primarily on a cash-flow basis. The remaining business grouping might contain the more mature operations that will be valued on an earnings basis. To facilitate such a split, noncash expenses such as goodwill need to be thoughtfully divided.

The relative rights that will be attached to the different classes of stock must also be defined. There is a tension to this process. The more a targeted stock has separate, defined and unalterable rights, the more marketable the stock. However, for tax reasons, the targeted stock must be structured as a stock of the parent company. If the targeted stock were treated as stock in a subsidiary business for tax purposes, the parent company might be taxed on the issuance and the distribution treated as a taxable dividend. The targeted stock shareholders therefore make a number of concessions to ensure favorable tax treatment.

Dividend policy is one area of concern. Targeted stock shareholders would prefer an ironclad guarantee that they will receive a fixed payout from the targeted business, but this arrangement would make the targeted business appear too separate for tax purposes. Dividends on the targeted stock usually are set at some percentage of the targeted business's net income. However, the parent company's board retains the sole discretion to adjust the amount, as with all dividends.

Targeted stock dividends also are subject to the same legal limitations that govern the payment of stock dividends generally. In other words, if the combined company becomes insolvent, the targeted stock's holders will not receive a dividend. This effective link between targeted stock dividends and the parent company's overall earnings argues in favor of treating the targeted stock as stock in the parent.

The treatment of dividends plays an important role in defining the virtual company underlying the targeted stock. For example, in designing its Media Group targeted stock, U S West broke with tradition and included no dividend on the stock. This approach was in line with the company's objective of creating a high-growth profile for the business. Like actual cellular and cable companies, this virtual company would keep its cash flow for investment. Essentially, by forgoing the dividend payout, U S West signaled the market as to how the business should be treated.

A letter stock also specifies how future sale proceeds will be treated. Several alternatives exist. Under one common approach, if the targeted business is sold, the company is required to pay some portion of the net proceeds to the targeted stockholders. Alternatively, the company might have to convert the targeted stock to regular common stock at a premium.

Tracking stock typically has voting rights, though there is no requirement that tracking stock be voting stock. The usual approach is for the tracking stock to have a number of votes per share that floats with the relative value of the targeted stock and regular stock. A floating system has two advantages. First, it allows voting power to reflect the underlying economic reality. Second, it avoids the situation where "cheap votes" can be acquired. A fixed voting ratio, on the other hand, may cause the votes attached to one class to be cheaper than the votes attached to the other.

The relative value of votes is important because in most matters, such as the election of directors, the two classes vote together. However, where the outcome of a vote would have a special effect on the targeted business, the targeted shareholders may need to approve the action in a separate class vote.

Many of these legal issues have a financial reporting impact. The targeted business remains consolidated with the parent company business for accounting purposes. As a result, the parent still must prepare consolidated group financial statements. In addition to the consolidated group financials, a parent also prepares audited financials for the targeted business. The targeted financials often are appended to the parent company financials and sent out as a unit.

Mechanics   A shareholder vote is necessary to incorporate the terms of the letter stock in the corporate charter. At the company's option, either a special shareholder vote is called or the issue is brought up at a regular shareholder meeting.

The final implementation step is distribution. There are several possible approaches. First, the company can simply distribute the letter stock to existing shareholders in a tax-free dividend or exchange offer. Second, the company can use the letter stock as an acquisition currency, giving it to selling shareholders. Third, the company might sell the letter stock to the public in an initial public offering. The particular context and needs of the issuer determine which alternative is selected.

We are all still on a journey of exploration with letter stocks and do not have the wisdom of extensive experience. There have been a number of targeted stock issuances that were misguided at conception or bungled in execution. However, in general, the record has been exceptionally positive and, if executed thoughtfully, letter stock will become an increasingly important tool in achieving shareholder value.

Defense: Building the Battlements | 20

"Force is never more operative than when it is known to exist but is not brandished."

Admiral Alfred Mahan

When a company falters, the carrions of prey circle. A low stock price relative to underlying asset values, an aging CEO without a successor, a weak board, a cash-rich balance sheet and obvious opportunities for cost reductions all attract attention. These circumstances put a company squarely in the takeover crosshairs. A target not in motion is a sitting duck.

The key to defense is advance preparation. Few companies are immune to attack, and size is not necessarily an insurmountable barrier. Nor does a healthy balance sheet guarantee protection. The best prophylactic is a resolute management and board of directors, a high stock price and good shareholder relations. Keeping a board informed and resilient is one of the key responsibilities of a CEO. During a deal, directors get bombarded with lawsuits and pressure. Building a bond with them before it all starts is invaluable.

Most companies have a raw sense of their vulnerabilities, but a disciplined analysis crystallizes the intuitions. Working from this foundation, a company can build quite effective defensive battlements, reducing the vulnerabilities.

Early Warning Systems

Shareholder Analysis

Shareholder analysis is to a takeover contest what polling is to a political campaign. This data can be extremely helpful in crafting a defensive strategy and in opening a channel of communication with shareholders. Relevant considerations include the geographic distribution of share ownership and the breakdown of share ownership by individual investors, institutions, employees, customers and suppliers.

For example, shareholders who live where a company has significant operations may be more likely to side with management. Individuals and employees likewise are more favorably disposed toward management than institutional investors. On the other hand, shares controlled by fiduciaries such as trustees or mutual fund managers are more likely to be in favor of a hostile raider.

The frequency with which company shares trade can have significant defensive implications. A high shareholding turnover may signal a disenchanted shareholder base with a short-term investment horizon, while a more stable base of shareholders bodes well for management. On a related point, companies also attempt to estimate the tax basis of major shareholders. A low tax basis, which reflects a large built-in capital gain, may make major shareholders relatively more unwilling to sell their shares for cash, given the resulting high tax liability.

Systematic communication with major shareholders can enhance a company's chances of winning a subsequent proxy fight or of fending off a tender offer. Shareholders who are part of a dialogue are more likely to be receptive to management. A shareholder-relations operation also creates proxy fight machinery.

Stock Watch Programs

Trading activity in a company's stock sometimes spikes upward in advance of a takeover attempt. Many companies have initiated "stock watch" programs designed to uncover stock accumulations or stock price movements that reflect possible leaks regarding a deal.

Even without insider trading, rumors of impending deals often circulate. As a natural law, the larger the team, the higher the chances word will get out. Often the leaks are inadvertent—the executive who cancels his well-known plans or the adviser who, to avoid legal liability, "restricts" his research and trading divisions from being active in the stocks. A bank loan can be a prime source of rumors because the number of people in the know multiplies.

A stock watch program is designed to track trading patterns in a company's stock. The company's transfer agent, which handles the administrative details involved in transferring ownership of shares, is one key source of information. The transfer agent is admonished to prepare timely transfer sheets and report any unusual movements. Though shares often trade in the "street name" of brokers, the bunching of large block trades can indicate a potential hostile bidder is accumulating shares.

If properly cultivated, the specialist or market maker who handles trades in a company's shares can be valuable. A specialist is the member of a stock exchange who is responsible for making an orderly market in a company's stock. The specialist accomplishes this task by buying and selling stock for its own account when there is a market imbalance. Similarly, a market maker maintains a trading market for a company's stock if it is traded over the counter, such as through the NASDAQ system. Specialists and market makers often will be the first outsiders to know about large block trades.

A stock watch program includes routine surveillance of government filings. Any Schedule 13D securities filings are perused for information. However, because hostile bidders are aware of the various filing requirements, they often structure their activities so that an actual hostile bid follows quickly on the heels of any public filing. Since the revisions in the Hart-Scott-Rodino requirements, secret accumulations of more than $15 million are rare. Therefore, a stock watch program can occasionally be helpful but is rarely a silver bullet.

Defensive Overview

Large public companies conduct regular reviews of their takeover defenses. An annual presentation to the board often provides the catalyst for discussions of a company's current defensive posture. Such meetings serve a dual purpose. First, a board presentation.jogs the corporate memory and motivates a careful defensive review. Second, a presentation educates directors as to "state of the art" takeover defenses. This process is critical, given the central role played by directors in any takeover contest.

The starting point for defensive analysis is a strategic overview of corporate policy. A company's defensive position is enhanced greatly if the board of directors has a standing, conscious policy of keeping the company independent. Both the *Time* and *Wallace* cases underline that the board has the power to determine corporate policy and strategic decisions will be respected, absent unreasonable or improper behavior.

Once corporate policy is established, a thorough defensive overview involves a multilayered analysis of defensive provisions in a company's charter, bylaws and loan agreements. The terms of any poison pill are also important. In addition, the relevant state antitakeover statutes and case law should be studied for their defensive implications, as should applicable regulatory frameworks. Finally, on a more substantive level, a review of corporate structure can provide insights regarding business strategies that reduce the likelihood of an attack.

The intellectual state of the art of takeover defense is constantly evolving as hostile raiders develop mechanisms to counteract existing technology. As a result, a company should regularly update its takeover defenses. Building an insurmountable barricade is not necessarily the goal. A court will invalidate abusive defenses. Rather, the objective is to build enough friction into the system so that management and shareholders will have the time to make informed decisions about the strategic alternatives. If a sale is the right answer, shareholders will get a higher price from an orderly process.

The Approach

Bidders often approach a company informally, with a casual pass in the form of a call to a board member or executive. These discussions are the first opportunity to establish a firm defensive posture. Unfortunately, this opportunity sometimes is squandered because the recipient of the call is unprepared to respond with a forceful rejection. An ambiguous response can be misread as an indication of interest and generate an unwanted suitor. The classic example is Conoco CEO Ralph Bailey's waffling response to the Dome Petroleum offer, which spawned a takeover bid.

As part of the defensive review process, the board should authorize the CEO and other executive officers to discourage any casual overtures. For maximum effectiveness, the policy should be conveyed to managers down the line, and directors prepared to respond as well. The recipient of a takeover solicitation should be encouraged to notify the CEO. Of course, any formal offer requires a careful, thorough board review.

Companies resist disclosing casual passes out of concern that to do so will put them in play. Negotiations of a friendly deal also can be extremely sensitive, and the parties prefer to wait until a concrete agreement has been reached before making disclosure.

The disclosure question has focused on just how far negotiations must progress before an obligation arises. Both the SEC and the U.S. Supreme Court in *Basic v. Levinson* have taken the position that a company's disclosures must be accurate and complete in all material respects. The Supreme Court said that a company has an obligation to make nonmisleading statements once it has commented on a situation. However, the Court also stated that a company's reply of "no comment" would be treated as silence and, therefore, not misleading.

The practical result for most companies is never to comment on pending merger discussions until an agreement in principle is reached. Up to that point, anything other than "no comment" will only cause problems, as when former AT&T CEO Robert Allen publicly defended the embryonic AT&T-SBC merger of 1997, which proceeded to fall apart under the glare of media attention.

Preventive Defense

The state of the art in the defense field has evolved through a Darwinian process of attack and response. As attacks became more potent, an array of defense devices are developed that parry the thrusts and create a more balanced system.

Three major categories of defensive mechanisms have been developed: poison pills, structural devices generally referred to as shark repellents, and golden parachutes. The cumulative effect has been to make a hostile takeover more difficult and more costly.

Poison Pills

A kind of spring trap, the poison pill makes an unfriendly takeover prohibitively expensive. The idea is simple. A corporation issues a new class of securities to shareholders. These securities have no value unless an investor acquires a specified percentage of the company's voting stock (typically 10 to 20 percent) without prior board approval. If an investor crosses the threshold, the securities activate in a way that devalues the investor's stake in the company.

A poison pill serves two possible purposes. First, it is a vehicle to slow the attack and give directors and shareholders a reasonable period of time to consider a takeover bid and, if appropriate, develop alternatives. Certainly, the pill can counter the arguably coercive nature of two-tiered offers. Second, the pill might be used as a means to preclude takeovers altogether.

In its 1985 *Household International* decision the Delaware Supreme Court expressly confirmed the authority of a board to issue a poison pill as a preventive defensive measure. The court also held that the business judgment rule would apply to the decision to enact a pill so long as the *Unocal* reasonableness test is satisfied. This position was reaffirmed in *Revlon*, where the court approved Revlon's initial implementation of a poison pill as a reasonable means to counter Ronald Perelman's two-tiered bid. The frontier of the poison pill debate thus focuses on when, if ever, a board should be required to pull the pill.

Early Evolution   The first-generation poison pill was developed by Marty Lipton in 1982. This type of pill, which evolved out of a series of "special power" preferred stock called "blank check preferred," involved the distribution of a preferred stock as a dividend to shareholders. In a takeover of the issuer in which the issuer was merged into the acquirer, each share of preferred stock would be converted into forty shares of the acquiring company. The pill would thereby substantially dilute the ownership interest of the acquirer.

As originally conceived, preferred stock plans had several disadvantages. First, the preferred stock could only be redeemed after an extended period of time, typically ten years. This severely limited the flexibility available to an issuer if it later decided to pursue a merger. Second, the preferred stock had a negative impact on an issuer's balance sheet because credit rating agencies sometimes treat it as long-term debt when assessing a company's strength.

The second-generation pill—called a "rights plan" or "flip-over pill"—was designed to address these problems. Under a flip-over plan, a company would issue rights to its shareholders. If the company were involved in a merger or other business combination not approved by its board, the rights entitled its shareholders to purchase stock in the surviving company at a substantial discount. The targeted shareholders could thus flip over to become acquiring shareholders, diluting the acquirer in the process.

A major weakness of the flip-over pill was dramatically demonstrated by Sir James Goldsmith's 1985 takeover of Crown Zellerbach Corporation. Ironically, Goldsmith became interested in the San Francisco–based paper company when it put its pill in place. Less than six months later, Goldsmith was revealed as a major buyer of Crown Zellerbach stock when he filed a 13D with the SEC. And within another seven months Goldsmith had purchased voting control of Crown Zellerbach.

How did Goldsmith manage to overcome the Crown Zellerbach pill? Quite simply, after purchasing voting control on the open market, he stopped short of a back-end merger. Without tripping this doomsday trigger, the Crown Zellerbach rights never became active in the sense of allowing a bargain purchase of stock. The rights never flipped over.

Patience was the key to Goldsmith's strategy. He was satisfied to hold 51 percent of Crown Zellerbach's outstanding stock and hold off on a back-end merger until the rights could be redeemed. In fact, Goldsmith was able to turn the pill to his advantage. By crossing the initial ownership threshold that made the rights nonredeemable, he severely limited Crown Zellerbach's options. The board—unable to redeem the rights—found it hard to find a white knight willing to step in and buy the company. The problem was that, like Goldsmith, any such white knight would have to swallow Crown Zellerbach's pill if it wanted to gain full control.

Flip-In, Flip-Over Pill   A third-generation pill—the "flip-in, flip-over"—was developed in reaction to Goldsmith's victory. It is the most common form of poison pill currently in use. Though endless variations exist, this type of pill generally has certain standard features.

The pill is implemented through a special dividend of one stock purchase right per outstanding common share. This purchase right is dormant until a triggering event. Typical triggering events include the acquisition of 15 percent of the company's voting stock without prior board approval or a hostile tender for 30 percent or more of the company's voting stock.

When the rights activate, all holders (except the investor who triggers the rights) become entitled to purchase additional stock in the issuing company at a substantial discount. This is the flip-in.

Also, if the issuing company takes part in any business combination or asset sale after the triggering event, all rights holders other than the triggering investor may buy voting securities of the surviving corporation at a substantial discount. In certain circumstances, this right allows target shareholders to buy stock in the bidder. This is the traditional flip-over.

In most cases, the rights can be redeemed at any point prior to a triggering event for a nominal amount such as $.02 per right. The board may amend the rights at any point prior to a triggering event.

Two features make the flip-in a potent defense against a Goldsmith-type acquisition. First, the flip-in right is fully activated by a single step—the acquisition of stock in excess of a specific amount. Second, the flip-in rights are discriminatory. The acquirer who triggers the flip-in is not given the opportunity to purchase target company stock on the cheap.

Both the flip-in and the flip-over impose considerable dilution on a hostile raider. If the threshold is crossed and the rights are exercised, the value of the raider's investment will drop precipitously.

Why retain a flip-over when the flip-in protects against the circumstances covered by the flip-over? The main reason is that the legal status of the discriminatory flip-in was unsettled for a time. Hence, the flip-over was retained as a backstop to provide what protection it could. However, the flip-over has become largely unnecessary given that, since *Household*, at least twenty-four states have adopted statutes that permit corporations to put in place discriminatory flip-in, flip-over pills.

Implementation   The modern poison pill can be, and is typically, put in place by the board of directors without a shareholder vote. The rights—usually with a ten-year life—are then issued as a dividend on the common stock. These rights are effectively stapled to the common stock until a triggering event. The rights and stock trade together. However, upon the occurrence of a triggering event, the rights can be traded separately. The issuer then will mail separate certificates to shareholders.

OSCAR WYATT UNHORSED

The power of the pill was put on dramatic display in the 1989 battle for Texas Eastern, with Oscar Wyatt of Coastal Corporation pitted against his old nemesis Dennis Hendrix. Wyatt's $2.5 billion cash offer put Texas Eastern in play, but a well-designed pill gave the board the time to conduct an orderly auction. As a result, Texas Eastern shareholders instead received $3.2 billion in cash and stock in the Panhandle Eastern buyout.

Wyatt had a history with Texas Eastern and its CEO, Dennis Hendrix. As the head of Texas Gas in 1983, Hendrix had turned Wyatt away by agreeing to sell out to white knight CSX, whom we represented. Then, in 1984, Coastal had bought a block of shares in Texas Eastern. A rumored takeover attempt failed to materialize. However, Coastal retained a nearly 5 percent stake in the company.

Finally, in 1989, Wyatt decided to pursue Texas Eastern. The takeover attempt did not begin auspiciously. Coastal announced its intention to bid on Martin Luther King Day, January 16, 1989. Wyatt's team apparently forgot about the relatively new holiday.

At the last minute, Coastal discovered that the SEC was closed, so the company could not file its tender offer. Coastal was forced to wait a day to make a formal announcement. The tactical gaffe gave Hendrix an extra day to prepare Texas Eastern's legal defenses.

On January 17, Coastal made a $42 a share, $2.5 billion offer official. The market responded by dramatically bidding up Texas Eastern's stock, which closed above $46. Over the next few days, the price floated up even further, touching $48. Apparently, investors believed Wyatt had low balled the company, and that some deal would go through at a higher price.

Considering the history, Hendrix naturally was loath to have his company folded into Wyatt's empire. Hendrix quickly realized that Texas Eastern would not survive as an independent company, and investor pressure was fierce. The defense team, which included us, calculated that we needed some maneuvering room. We kept Texas Eastern's pill in place, but with a board commitment to remove it on March 15. This would allow time for an orderly auction without the risk of a court removing the pill.

Ultimately, Panhandle Eastern topped Wyatt's $42 a share cash bid with an offer of $53 in cash for 80 percent of Texas Eastern and stock worth roughly $53 in a back-end merger. The pill facilitated the month-long process of soliciting a large group of bidders, providing information in a Houston data room and gathering bids.

Effect   Considerable research has been conducted on the effect of poison pills. Some studies analyze the stock-price impact of installing a pill; other studies investigate the pill's effect on takeover premiums. The research is somewhat contradictory. However, the consensus seems to be that the implementation of a pill has a slight negative effect on a company's stock price, while the presence of a pill increases the premium a company receives in a takeover. The net effect on shareholder value is unclear, but likely positive.

Redemption By the late 1980s, the poison pill defense had evolved into an effective stopgap measure that could delay the most determined suitor. Even though a pill might not permanently thwart a raider, it halted any stampede. However, the pill is by no means insurmountable. The board's ability to redeem a pill—a common feature—opens the way to attack. A hostile bidder can take advantage of this feature by launching a tender offer that is conditioned on the redemption of the pill. If the bidder offers a substantial premium, the board is placed under pressure to vote in favor of redemption.

The so-called dead-hand pill is one approach designed to close off this vulnerability. A dead-hand pill includes a provision that vests the ability to redeem or amend the pill exclusively with continuing directors—that is, directors who were on the board prior to a bidder's attempted takeover, or who were appointed by a majority of the continuing directors. If a dead-hand provision is in place, a bidder cannot gain control of a targeted company's board through a proxy fight and then remove its pill.

Dead-hand pills are rare, mainly as a result of *Bank of New York v. Irving Bank*, a 1988 case in which a New York court invalidated a dead-hand pill under New York law. However, in 1997, a Georgia court upheld a dead-hand provision. The *Invacare v. Healthdyne Technologies* case turned on an interpretation of Georgia law, but the result may reinvigorate the use of dead-hand pills.

Regardless, the possibility of a proxy contest raises an obvious question: Why adopt a redeemable rather than a nonredeemable pill? The answer is twofold. First, in approving the poison pill as a defensive measure, the Delaware courts have placed considerable weight on the redemption feature. In *Household*, for example, the Delaware Supreme Court cited the possibility of redemption as supporting its view that the pill does not preclude a takeover. Rather, the court found, the pill simply redressed the previous power imbalance between bidder and target.

Second, the redemption feature provides necessary flexibility to an issuing board. By including a redemption feature, a board retains the ability to adopt positive transaction alternatives, as was the case in the Texas Eastern defense. Furthermore, an unredeemable pill simply may alienate institutional investors in a proxy fight.

Under Delaware law, once a bid is launched, the decision whether to retain a pill is subject to the same fiduciary test applied to other defensive measures—the *Unocal* standard. *Unocal* and *Household* require that the board show both procedural and substantive reasonableness with regard to the decision to keep a pill in place rather than accept a specific tender offer. Hence, the board must show good-faith investigation of the offer and other alternatives, and keeping the pill in place must be reasonable in relation to the threat posed by the offer.

Given the inherently fact-specific nature of the *Unocal* inquiry, it should not be surprising that the courts have yet to develop a simple consensus regarding when a pill can be retained. Rather, the courts conduct a wide-ranging analysis. Important factors include the perceived coerciveness and financial adequacy of the offer. The characteristics of the alternative advanced by the board also seem important. Courts are particularly skeptical where a board uses a pill to protect its own preferred transaction.

The most fundamental redemption issue is whether a board should be required to pull a pill in the face of an all-cash, all-shares offer. Even on this point, the law remains uncertain. Some cases have found no threat to shareholders under those circumstances and have required the pill to be pulled, for example in the 1988 battle for Pillsbury.

The Pillsbury battle began on October 4, 1988, when Grand Metropolitan, a British company, announced a surprise tender offer at $60 a share, all in cash. Pillsbury's stock had been trading at $39 the day before. Given the over 50 percent premium, the food and spirits conglomerate was widely viewed to be looking for the quick knockout. Of course, the bid was conditioned on the redemption of Pillsbury's poison pill.

From the perspective of a target's board, an all-cash, all-shares bid creates the most pressure to redeem an existing pill. The arguably coercive aspects of a two-tiered offer are missing. In this situation, the main goal becomes using what leverage the pill provides to get the highest bid possible. Shareholders then can decide whether to tender into the offer.

This was the predicament that faced Pillsbury CEO Philip Smith and the Pillsbury board. The company launched a series of litigation maneuvers to hold off Grand Met. Almost immediately, the board came to the conclusion that Pillsbury would have a tough time remaining independent. However, Grand Met had implied it might raise its bid, and the board wanted to get as much as it could for shareholders.

The problem, of course, was that Pillsbury needed a credible alternative to tease a higher bid out of Grand Met. Seeking to encourage other bidders, the Grand Met offer was rejected as inadequate. A number of potential white knights were pursued, but Grand Met's preemptive bid kept most from getting involved. Smith and the board decided to pursue a recapitalization as the next best alternative. A plan was drafted to spin off Pillsbury's Burger King, pay shareholders a special dividend and sell a number of other businesses.

All this activity was really just a prelude to the final negotiation. Matters came to a head in early December 1989. Pillsbury had won an earlier battle in Delaware court when a judge refused to force the company to redeem its pill. The court reasoned that Pillsbury should have time to pursue other options that might benefit shareholders.

In December, a second hearing was held in Delaware court. Pillsbury had already managed to get a higher bid—$63 a share—out of Grand Met, but the second round in court went to Grand Met. Using a *Unocal* analysis, the court found the only major threat to shareholders to be an economic one. The all-cash, all-shares offer was not coercive and the shareholders should be allowed to decide the issue of value. Pillsbury would have to redeem its poison pill.

Little negotiating leverage remained. Pillsbury quickly came to terms with Grand Met and a merger agreement was signed. Even so, Grand Met raised its final bid to $66 a share. Pillsbury's aggressive defense had forced a 10 percent increase in an already full-priced bid.

At the time *Pillsbury* was decided, legal experts generally read it to mean that a bidder could force a pill redemption with an all-cash, all-shares premium bid. However, the waters have since been muddied by *Time* and *Wallace*.

For example, in *Time*, the court refused to force Time to delay its tender offer for Warner so that shareholders could accept the Paramount offer. The case therefore was not directly a pill redemption case. Yet, in its opinion, the court expressly rejects the idea that the only threat from an all-cash, all-shares offer is that the price may be too low. Rather, the court implied that other concerns might reasonably keep a board from allowing shareholders to accept an offer. This aspect of the *Time* case has since been stretched to a point where *Time* arguably overturns the lower court decision in *Pillsbury*.

Wallace, in particular, makes a more direct attack on *Pillsbury*. The federal district judge in *Wallace* expressly ruled that the company need not withdraw its poison pill. Shareholders thus were barred from accepting Moore Corporation's all-cash tender offer. In justifying this outcome, the judge applied a *Unocal* reasonableness analysis and relied on *Time* for support. He determined that the Moore offer reasonably could be construed as a threat because shareholders might accept the offer without a full understanding of Wallace's future prospects.

However, notwithstanding the outcome of *Wallace*, the fact remains that an all-cash offer puts considerable pressure on a board. If the board stands behind its pill and rejects such an offer, it likely will find itself the subject of litigation and a proxy fight. In *Wallace*, the judge expressly recognized that there is a point at which a board will have a fiduciary duty to redeem a pill. Precisely when that duty arises will remain murky until the Delaware Supreme Court revisits the issue directly on a different set of facts.

THE DELAWARE PRISM

Trying to predict how the Delaware Supreme Court will resolve a particular takeover challenge is like tracking a beam of light through a prism. One can calculate the course of light as it bounces through based on the size and position of the prism's faces. Similarly, takeover decisions of the court are a pragmatic response to many different factors. By weighing the totality of the circumstances in a given case, the outcome is easier to predict.

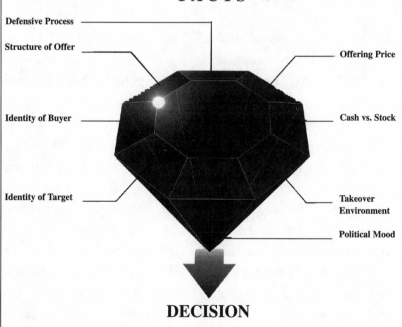

FACTS

Defensive Process

Structure of Offer

Offering Price

Identity of Buyer

Cash vs. Stock

Identity of Target

Takeover Environment

Political Mood

DECISION

A number of issues in particular seem to animate the Delaware case law. These are the facets of the Delaware prism: the premium offered, the process involved, the structure of the deal (two tiers or one), the personality and reputation of the buyer, the form of consideration (cash or securities), the personality and reputation of the target and its board, the takeover environment and the political mood regarding deals.

So, for example, *Unocal* went against Boone Pickens because, though he offered a premium price, the deal was two-tiered; he had a reputation as a raider; the back-end consideration was a package of securities of uncertain value; Fred Hartley was a member of the business establishment; and there was a growing backlash against hostile attacks.

Shark Repellents

Corporations and their advisers have identified a number of defensive mechanisms—loosely referred to as "shark repellents"—that can be embedded in either a corporate charter or bylaw. These mechanisms were developed before the poison pill came into being and share a common purpose. They were intended to make an unfriendly takeover more difficult and costly. The hope was that the mere presence of shark repellent would have a deterrent effect. This proved somewhat optimistic: the mixed success of shark repellents led to the evolution of the poison pill.

However, though the pill has developed into the centerpiece of most defensive strategies, shark repellents still have an important role to play. The pill does not, for example, prevent an insurgent from gaining board control through a proxy contest at an annual or special meeting or a consent solicitation. Shark repellents therefore supplement and contribute to the overall defensive posture created by a poison pill.

When it comes to implementation, there are basic distinctions between different types of shark repellents. Some require shareholder approval, others can be put in place by the board of directors without shareholder approval. This distinction generally parallels the split between provisions that must be enacted through charter amendment and those that can be enacted by amendment to the bylaws.

The law of the state in which a company is incorporated, along with its existing corporate charter and bylaws, determine what may be enacted as a bylaw without shareholder approval. Generally, only the more procedural rules may be accomplished through bylaws. Most forms of shark repellent require amendments to a company's corporate charter, which in turn require a shareholder vote.

The decision to implement shark repellents is not without risk. If a company is already in a precarious position, seeking shareholder approval for defensive measures may prove disastrous. An unwelcome proxy contest may result, and the shareholders may reject the shark repellent. Not only would this leave the company unprotected, it also promises to generate unwelcome attention from hostile bidders. A shareholder defeat effectively communicates the lack of shareholder support for incumbent management and may even trigger a proxy fight for control of the board.

A company considering the use of shark repellent should spend time analyzing its shareholder base and voting history. Although it can be difficult to predict the course of a shareholder election, certain general trends are apparent. Individual shareholders tend to side with management. Institutional investors, on the other hand, have a known antipathy to most forms of shark repellent. Some institutional investors actually have adopted a policy of voting against them. With the help of an experienced proxy solicitor and these general observations, a company can get a good sense for the prospect of shareholder approval.

Almost endless variations exist within the category of shark repellent. The most typical varieties include staggered board elections, restrictions on shareholder action, antigreenmail provisions, super-voting stock and various debt-based repellents.

Reinforcing the Board of Directors   Control a company's board of directors, and you control the company. It is no surprise that the board is often a hostile raider's prime target. This makes reinforcing the board an important part of any defensive package.

Common board-related defensive measures include a staggered board and limitations on cumulative voting and the removal of directors. These can frustrate a raider's attempts to take control of a company through a proxy fight. A poison pill provides no protection.

A staggered board is created by amendment to the charter. Directors are divided or classified into a number of classes, with only one class up for reelection each year. So, for example, a nine-person board might be divided into three classes. Directors in each class would serve a three-year term, with one class elected each year. The defensive virtue of this arrangement is that a raider who holds a majority of the stock theoretically still must wait for two elections to capture board control.

As a practical matter, though, a board may not be able to hold out against a major stockholder. The board instead may bow to the inevitable in the face of pressure from the stockholder, whether exerted through litigation or by other means.

Careful design can maximize the protective capacity of a staggered board. Limits must be placed, for example, on the ability to increase the size of the board. Otherwise an insurgent shareholder might simply add seats to the board, allowing it to elect a majority at a single meeting.

Under cumulative voting, a shareholder can cumulate its votes for a single candidate. So, for example, a shareholder with 100 shares would have 300 votes in an election for three open seats and could cumulate all 300 votes for a single candidate. This has the effect of maximizing the board representation of minority shareholders.

In the context of a takeover contest, cumulative voting cuts both ways. On the harmful side, cumulative voting may allow a hostile bidder who is a minority shareholder to gain board representation. A bidder can thus gain access to confidential company information. On the helpful side, if a hostile bidder becomes a major shareholder, cumulative voting, like a staggered board, can delay its assumption of control.

From a defensive standpoint, then, the ideal arrangement would be to allow cumulative voting only once a single investor or an affiliated group of investors acquires a major stake in the company. A less favorable approach would be to avoid cumulative voting altogether.

Depending on where a company is incorporated, its ability to adopt either of these alternatives may be limited. Some states permit cumulative voting, others require it. States that take the permissive approach generally set up a default rule and then require a corporation that wishes to take the opposite position to do so through a provision in the charter or bylaws. While a company that is incorporated in a permissive state theoretically can rid itself of cumulative voting once it is in place, this may prove difficult to accomplish if a supermajority vote is mandated by state law.

In addition to other board reinforcement mechanisms, a provision specifying that directors can only be removed "for cause" or under certain specified circumstances enhances the defensive posture. To give such a provision teeth, it should also be supported by a supermajority requirement for amendment or repeal.

Restricting Shareholder Action   Defense of the board becomes somewhat superfluous if shareholders have the power to bypass the board and gain direct control of their corporation. A number of companies have experienced this, much to the chagrin of insiders.

Attention to a number of details can compensate. In particular, a company can limit the ability of shareholders to call special meetings and act by consent, and can require advance notice of shareholder proposals for action. Finally, the approval of a supermajority can be required for certain transactions.

Unless a company's certificate of incorporation specifies otherwise, many states require a corporation to call a special shareholder meeting if the holders of a specified percentage of the corporation's outstanding shares so request. A special meeting poses a number of potential problems for corporate insiders on the defensive.

First, if the board is not properly reinforced, an insurgent shareholder may be able to use a special meeting to take control. This can be accomplished by expanding the number of board seats and electing new directors or by removing sitting directors if they are not protected by "for cause" language in the bylaws or charter.

Second, an insurgent shareholder can use a special meeting as a forum to contest a proxy fight. An unfavorable vote can weaken the corporation's defenses in a number of ways. A majority of shareholders might vote in favor of a nonbinding resolution to remove a poison pill. The board can then be faced with the prospect of either surrendering to the insurgent or ignoring shareholder wishes.

For these reasons, companies often restrict the ability of shareholders to call a special meeting. The relevant corporate statute in each case regulates the possibilities. At the extreme, the right to call a special meeting can be reserved solely to the board and the CEO. Or shareholders might be permitted to call a special meeting, but only if a supermajority agrees. The possible agenda items at a special meeting might also be restricted.

Consent solicitations pose another problem. Under some state statutes, a company may permit shareholders to act by written consent, without a meeting. A raider can use this power to take control of the board or enact some other change on an expedited basis, although a consent solicitation must generally abide by the disclosure requirements and procedures applicable to proxy contests. The process might be completed as soon as documents are filed with the

SEC and holders with the requisite number of shares sign the consent.

Two approaches have been used to limit shareholder consent rights. Some companies have proposed charter amendments that restrict the ability of shareholders to act by consent. However, a shareholder vote is required to enact such an amendment. Consequently, other companies have favored bylaw revisions, which can be adopted by a board without shareholder approval. While bylaw revisions have this advantage, courts have subjected restrictive bylaws to tough scrutiny, fearing that they might be used to circumvent the required shareholder approval process.

As an added defensive measure, a corporation may enact a bylaw that requires advance notice of shareholder proposals and board nominations. Provisions vary as to the length of notice required, but sixty days is not uncommon. The receipt of notice serves several defensive purposes. First, it gives a board sufficient time to consider the appropriate response or to select its own slate of candidates. Second, a long notice period tends to reduce the likelihood of challenge because an insurgent shareholder may simply overlook the deadline. By the time another meeting comes around, the challenge may have died.

Supermajority rules provide another effective barrier to a hostile takeover. The general approach has been to require a higher level of approval for a merger or other transaction involving an "interested shareholder." While different standards are used, a 5 or 10 percent ownership threshold is commonly used to measure "interest."

Various mechanisms qualify as supermajority provisions. For example, 80 percent shareholder approval might be required for a merger with an interested person. Or, the approval threshold might be set on a sliding scale—the higher the interested person's shareholding percentage, the higher the required supermajority. Another alternative is to require approval from a majority of the shares other than those held by the interested shareholder.

A supermajority rule, like other preventive defenses, should be supported by a suitable amendment provision. In other words, a similar supermajority vote should be required to amend the supermajority rule. Otherwise, a hostile raider might circumvent the requirement.

Johnson & Johnson Goes for the Heart

Two 1995 takeover contests demonstrated just how gaping a hole the consent solicitation leaves in a company's defensive structure. First there was IBM's one, two punch of a premium bid for Lotus backed by a consent solicitation. Then, later the same year, Johnson & Johnson adopted similar tactics. The defender in this second battle was Cordis Corp. of Florida, a maker of heart instruments.

Johnson & Johnson had made friendly overtures to Cordis early in the fall of 1995, but Cordis management refused the offers. In the eyes of Ralph Larsen, CEO of Johnson & Johnson, the strategic imperative for a deal was strong. Johnson & Johnson had a hot cardiac product known as a stent, an implant used to clear blocked arteries. Yet Johnson & Johnson lacked a broader line of cardiology devices. This segment of the industry was divided among a number of smaller competitors like Cordis. Larsen saw an opportunity for consolidation.

On October 19, 1995, Johnson & Johnson launched a $100 a share hostile tender offer for Cordis. The bid amounted to a fairly slim premium of 16 percent over the latest close. However, the Cordis stock price had been bid up on takeover rumors and Johnson & Johnson's bid represented a 30 percent premium to the closing price thirty trading days prior to the deal announcement. In total, Johnson & Johnson was offering $1.6 billion in cash. The company also left the door open for a friendly stock deal at $105 a share.

Like IBM, Johnson & Johnson backed up its bid with an immediate SEC filing of materials for a consent solicitation. Once the materials were approved, Johnson & Johnson could begin soliciting consents from shareholders. If 50.1 percent backed Johnson & Johnson, it could replace the Cordis board.

Cordis rejected the $100 offer and began an accelerated search for white knights. For a time, it looked as if Cordis might try to hold off Johnson & Johnson. The main source of its defensive power was a controversial "dead-hand" poison pill. Cordis had put the pill in place only a few days prior to the Johnson & Johnson bid. This variant of the pill can only be redeemed by the actual directors who voted on the original plan, or their handpicked successors. The idea was to circumvent the consent solicitation process by keeping a hostile bidder from being able to redeem the Cordis pill even if it gained control of the board.

As part of its assault, Johnson & Johnson immediately sued to have the dead-hand pill revoked. The consensus of legal observers was that Johnson & Johnson had a strong case. Cordis management apparently agreed. When no white knights stepped forward, the company capitulated, though it was able to get Johnson & Johnson to sweeten its bid to $109 in stock.

Antigreenmail Provisions   Greenmail refers to the practice of repurchasing shares from a hostile bidder at a premium to the current market price. In the mid-1980s, the perception was that the prospect of receiving greenmail was a major motivation for hostile raiders to profit immediately from a hostile bid.

On the theory that if you take away the honey, you can avoid the bees, many corporations enacted antigreenmail provisions. These typically involve charter amendments that restrict the corporation's ability to repurchase shares at a premium. Another provision might require shareholder approval before stock can be repurchased from a shareholder who holds more than a specified percentage of stock. Waivers are generally included that cover open-market purchases and purchases at the market price (which still can profit a raider, if the market price exceeds his purchase price).

The popularity of antigreenmail provisions has declined with the introduction of a federal greenmail tax. In addition, companies have come to realize that a strict antigreenmail provision might actually reduce the flexibility needed to deal with a hostile bidder.

Supervoting Stock   Placing a supervoting stock in friendly hands is quite attractive from a defensive perspective. By giving certain shareholders more voting power per share than others, an incumbent management and board can ensure that friendly shareholders will be in control. This tactic can effectively preclude the possibility of a hostile takeover and is most commonly used where a founding individual or family holds a large block of stock. Notable examples include Sumner Redstone's block of supervoting Viacom stock, John Malone's TCI stake and most newspaper companies (such as the New York Times and Dow Jones), which have two classes of stock.

However, there are limits to the use of supervoting stock as a defensive mechanism. First, implementation generally involves some form of recapitalization, with the approval of existing shareholders a necessary precursor. Shareholders in many cases may be unwilling to disenfranchise themselves. Second, supervoting stock is only useful as a defensive measure where its ownership can be concentrated in the hands of pro-management investors. Third, the creation of a new supervoting class of stock is generally forbidden under the uniform Voting Rights Policy of the NYSE, the AMEX and the National Association of Securities Dealers (NASD). Public companies listed on these exchanges consequently may be foreclosed from adopting supervoting stock.

Several exceptions to the Voting Rights Policy explain the continuing existence of supervoting stock among public companies. The exceptions arise from the history of the Voting Rights Policy, which was put in place in December 1994. Prior to that, between July 1988 and June 1990, the Securities and Exchange Commission had a so-called one share/one vote rule in place. This rule grandfathered dual-class voting structures that were in place before July 1988. Then, on June 12, 1990, a federal appellate court overturned the SEC rule as outside the scope of the agency's authority. The Voting Rights Policy was developed as a response to this ruling. The policy allows the continuation of any supervoting arrangements permitted under the prior SEC rule and also grandfathers arrangements put in place between the time of the court ruling and the enactment of the new uniform policy.

This somewhat idiosyncratic history means that a company with an existing supervoting arrangement can continue to issue supervoting shares of the same class, but most other public companies cannot adopt a defensive supervoting structure.

Debt Instruments   Shark repellent–type provisions also can be incorporated in debt instruments. After a flurry of popularity, however, they are losing their appeal because they result in a lack of flexibility for the company.

Employee Severance Arrangements

Employee severance arrangements with change-in-control provisions can supplement a company's defensive posture. The Chrysler Corporation, for example, put a so-called golden parachute plan in place in response to Kirk Kerkorian's 1995 takeover attempt.

Severance arrangements can allay concerns among covered employees and encourage them to remain with a company. This protection is important because recruiters besiege key employees with alternative job offers during the pendency of a deal.

Severance arrangements can also ally the interests of top management with shareholders. The theory is that management will not be as recalcitrant if its downside is protected.

Common change-in-control severance plans can be grouped into two categories: golden parachutes and silver or tin parachutes. The chief distinction between the two categories is the percentage of employees covered.

Golden Parachutes　Large contractual compensation payments to management triggered upon a change in control, popularized as golden parachutes, were a controversial element of the 1980s mergers boom. For example, in the 1989 RJR Nabisco takeover, CEO F. Ross Johnson lost his job and earned an estimated $53 million in the process. Executive Vice President John Martin earned roughly $18 million.

A golden parachute plan covers the few dozen key employees of a major company. Such agreements obligate the company to make a lump-sum payment to employees who are terminated after a change in control. Some golden parachutes have a fixed term, such as a year; others are "evergreen." An evergreen agreement has a one-year life but is automatically extended for a year if no change in control occurs during the year.

Compensation under a golden parachute is calculated as a multiple of recent compensation. So, for example, an agreement might provide for a payment equal to three times the compensation earned by a covered executive in the most recent year. The payments are due whether the termination is voluntary or involuntary.

A change in control is usually defined to take place when an investor accumulates more than a specified percentage of stock. The threshold is often set in the 25 to 30 percent range, but companies have adopted parachutes with a much lower threshold. Exemptions can be built in for friendly transactions, a merger or reorganization that results in substantial continuity of shareholder interest, or other particular situations. However, these exemptions may erode the ability of a golden parachute to address employee retention concerns.

Silver or Tin Parachutes   A silver or tin parachute functions like a golden parachute, but covers more employees. At the extreme, a tin parachute might cover all full-time employees. Like a golden parachute, these arrangements usually guarantee a lump-sum payment, and perhaps continued employee benefits, to a covered employee. The lump-sum payment is typically measured as a multiple of length of service.

A tin parachute in most cases is triggered by an employee's termination after a change in control, unless the termination was "for cause." The definition of cause is delineated under the terms of the plan, and is usually fairly narrow.

Implementation   Employee severance arrangements can be implemented by a board of directors without a shareholder vote. Board approval may not even be necessary for a tin parachute that excludes top management, but is certainly advisable.

The decision to implement golden parachutes, if made prior to a specific takeover threat, will generally be protected by the traditional business judgment rule. However, where a golden parachute is a response to a specific threat, courts will apply the *Unocal* test. The board therefore must show that it conducted a reasonable and good faith investigation of the perceived takeover threat and that the parachute plan represented a reasonable response.

Outside the courts, golden parachutes have sparked considerable criticism. Opponents argue that such plans represent self-dealing by managers who control the adoption process. These arguments were particularly heated in the late 1980s, when several instances of large parachute payments occurred. Reacting to these criticisms, most large companies now have established compensation committees made up of outside directors to examine these benefits.

Tax Implications   In 1984 and 1986, the federal tax law with respect to parachute payments was revised to curb the practice. The new law imposes tax penalties on certain parachute payments. In particular, an "excess parachute payment" is subject to a dual tax penalty. First, such payments are not tax-deductible to an employer. Second, a recipient must pay a 20 percent excise tax in addition to normal income tax. The definition of an excess parachute payment for this purpose is extremely complicated, but creates a penalty if the chute exceeds three times an executive's average compensation for the last five years. In deals, buyers pay "gross-up" amounts to managers to compensate them for the taxes.

Reincorporation as a Defensive Strategy

A wholesale defensive strategy is also available—reincorporating in a state with laws more favorable to takeover defense. A company might, for example, reincorporate in Pennsylvania to take advantage of its tough antitakeover statute. Historically, this happened when many major corporations incorporated in New Jersey moved to Delaware.

A particular state is attractive for a number of reasons. The takeover-related provisions of the relevant corporate statutes are, of course, important. Particular issues include the treatment of poison pills, cumulative voting, staggered boards and hostile tender offers. In addition, the attitude of the courts, particularly regarding the fiduciary duties of corporate directors in the takeover context, is critical.

Tactical issues must also be considered. Reincorporation involves the creation of a subsidiary in the new state, followed by the merger of the parent into the subsidiary. Because a merger of the parent is involved, shareholders must approve the transaction. A company therefore must analyze its shareholder base (as it is advised to do before implementing shark repellents through corporate charter amendments). Reincorporation should be pursued only if a company expects to win the necessary shareholder approval.

Reincorporation is most effective if implemented before a specific bidder has emerged. But the strategy can be used as a reaction against an offer. In 1983, Gulf Oil tried reincorporation in order to defeat Boone Pickens. When Pickens began to circle, Gulf was incorporated in Pennsylvania. The state's corporate law had several unattractive features, including required cumulative voting and a low threshold allowing 20 percent of a company's shareholders to call a special meeting. Pickens already had 9 percent and would likely be able to find another 11 percent to call a meeting.

In an effort to boost Gulf's defensive posture, the company's board of directors approved reincorporation in Delaware. Management narrowly won the contested vote. While the new rules applicable to Gulf may have slowed Pickens somewhat, the shift amounted to only a tactical victory. The company got a bare majority, an expression of relative shareholder discontent. Three months later, the Gulf board agreed to a friendly deal with Chevron.

Final Perspective

All of these defensive devices have their limits. The battlements can become their own Maginot Line, building in an undeserved complacency. Performance by a company is the substance of defense.

Defense: | 21
Battlefield Tactics

"Isn't the best defense always a good attack?"

Ovid, *Amores*

Takeover contests are fast-paced, draining affairs. A company must file its response to a hostile tender offer at the SEC within ten days. Major tactical decisions must be made and responses implemented very quickly.

The corporate boardroom is the epicenter of the action, the place where critical strategic decisions are made. How should the target respond to a hostile bid? What path should a business take? The questions can be agonizing and decisions are not reached lightly.

Adding to the pressure, directors face the specter of shareholder lawsuits. In the context of a takeover fight, directors can be sure that virtually any defensive response will draw some sort of litigation. Insurance coverage protects against personal liability, but the annoyance and potential for damage to personal reputation cannot be avoided. Almost as bothersome is the incessant criticism from shareholders and the press, the feeling of being in a glass fishbowl.

Defending Against an Unsolicited Offer

An unsolicited offer can manifest itself in several ways. The first hint of impending trouble may come in the form of an apparent stock accumulation. A company might learn of accumulation through a variety of channels: a stock watch or market surveillance program or a Hart-Scott-Rodino or Schedule 13D filing from the accumulator.

Alternatively, notice of an impending offer can come directly from the offeror in the form of an expression of interest. The expression can vary in terms of formality. An interested party might simply make an "informal pass." Or, a formal bear hug letter might be sent to the target's board. In either case, the contact may or may not contain a forthright expression of hostile intent.

A third possibility is that a full-blown tender offer might represent the first concrete indication of interest. The hostile bidder has shrouded any market accumulation in secrecy and announced the bid prior to crossing the Hart-Scott-Rodino and Schedule 13D filing thresholds.

Once a target company becomes aware of a potential takeover threat and determines to fight, the first step is to review the existing framework of preventive measures. Certain of these measures can be usefully revised even with a tender offer on the table. Beyond a review of structural defenses such as the poison pill or staggered board elections, a number of specific responses are available to a target company. These responses range from passive to active and entail varying costs and risks. Though no list can be exhaustive, the main alternatives are as follows:

- The "just say no" defense;
- Negotiating a standstill agreement;
- The payment of greenmail;
- The Pac-Man defense;
- Finding a white knight or white squire;
- A recapitalization or restructuring;

- Issuing shares to an employee pension trust;

- Going private;

- A defensive acquisition; and

- A litigation and public relations blitz.

A universal is to keep the team well rested. Terrible decisions are made by exhausted people, and after a couple of weeks of incessant meetings and belligerent pestering from arbs, even the feistiest defenders simply get tired.

Overall, there is no paint-by-the-numbers approach to takeover defense that can be applied in every case. The intent here is to describe the range of possibilities.

Just Say No   Faced with an unsolicited offer, a board may simply fortify its defensive barricades and decline the bid. Of course, both the addition of new defenses and the refusal to redeem an outstanding poison pill must pass muster under *Unocal*, the Delaware case that set a two-prong test for the conduct of boards on defense. The first *Unocal* prong, which focuses on defensive process, is fairly easy to satisfy—a well-founded board determination that the offer is inadequate and represents a threat to existing corporate strategy generally will suffice. The second prong requires proportionality between the remedy and the threat, but will not cause problems for defensive measures other than the "preclusive" and the "draconian."

So, under *Unocal*, common structural defenses such as the poison pill are generally safe if properly implemented, except perhaps in the face of an all-cash, all-shares offer. A larger question remains: Will the just say no defense work? The *Time* and *Wallace* cases, both under Delaware law, suggest it can.

However, the just say no defense is certainly not impregnable. For example, Moore had already gained three of nine Wallace board seats through the proxy machinery when it gave up its fight for Wallace. If Moore had continued, it might have gained a majority of the board, giving it the power to redeem the Wallace poison pill.

Even in the absence of a successful proxy fight, a well-financed and motivated hostile bidder can place considerable pressure on an incumbent board. An offer that represents a significant premium can create difficulty for a board under *Unocal*. The higher the premium involved, the more likely shareholders are to agitate in favor of acceptance. In addition, a board may find it hard to characterize an all-cash offer at a significant premium to market as a "threat to the corporation or its shareholders." To the contrary, the Delaware courts have expressly stated that "at some point, the failure to redeem a poison pill can constitute a fiduciary breach."

DOA

Loewen Says No to Service Corp.

A vital poison pill is not essential to a successful defense, as indicated by the Loewen Group's fending off a $2.9 billion hostile bid from Service Corp. International. The two companies—number one and number two in the "death services," or mortuary, business—battled to a draw after four months, at which point Service Corp. decided that withdrawal was the better part of valor.

The fight began in September of 1996. On the same day Loewen was switching from the NASDAQ stock listing to the New York Stock Exchange—normally an auspicious occasion for a company—Service Corp. announced a bear hug bid for its competitor. Even before the bid, the companies shared bad blood. The funeral service business had been undergoing rapid consolidation for a period of years, and Loewen and Service Corp. had grown to be the primary competitors.

Raymond Loewen, chairman, CEO and founder of Loewen, almost immediately vowed to fight Service Corp.'s initial $43 a share offer. Service Corp. sweetened the bid to $45 a share, but Loewen remained defiant.

In a certain sense, the Loewen Group was a vulnerable target. The company had been forced to settle two breach-of-contract cases in 1995, for a total liability payment of $205 million. Furthermore, while Loewen had a poison pill in place, under the applicable Canadian law, courts tend to force pill redemption after sixty to ninety days. The board could afford to just say no only for so long.

Recognizing this reality, Loewen still had a number of strong defenses. Foremost was the fact that Raymond Loewen, his family and associates controlled 20 percent of the company's stock. British Columbia law—which applied since the company was incorporated in that province—required that 75 percent of the shareholders approve any deal. With Loewen staunchly opposed, Service Corp. would need nearly all of the remaining shareholders to agree.

Loewen was not content to rely on this structural barrier to a takeover. The company also continued on its own acquisition spree, buying up over $325 million in other death services companies. Top employees were granted fairly generous golden parachutes. Finally, government antitrust officials were lobbied to oppose any combination as anticompetitive.

Ultimately, though, Service Corp.'s failed bid had more to do with price and financial structure than anything else. The $45 bid, all in stock, just didn't excite the largely institutional shareholders who owned most of Loewen. Without a stronger bid, the shareholders stuck by management.

Greenmail and the Standstill Agreement   The practice of paying a potential acquirer to go away was common in the 1980s. Texaco bought a block of stock back from the Bass brothers for $1.2 billion, or roughly 3 percent above the previous closing price; Disney bought Saul Steinberg's stake for $325 million plus a $28 million expense payment; the Belzbergs of Canada sold stock back to USG.

Greenmail is a payment to repurchase shares at a premium price in exchange for the acquirer's agreement to forgo a hostile offer. The payment is accompanied by a contractual standstill agreement. This agreement specifies the amount of stock, if any, that the acquirer can accumulate or retain; restricts the circumstances under which the acquirer can sell any retained shares, often including a right of first refusal for the target company; restricts how the acquirer can vote retained shares, such as by foreclosing the acquirer from participation in a proxy contest; and states a specified term for the agreement.

The point is to craft an agreement that effectively forecloses future agitation on the part of the potential acquirer. Naturally, a potential acquirer is unlikely to agree to such stringent terms without inducement. Hence a target sometimes will agree to pay greenmail, either in the form of a direct share repurchase or a more indirect benefit.

From the perspective of incumbent management, a greenmail payment may be viewed as a small price to pay to avoid the turmoil and expense of a prolonged takeover contest. Critics argue, however, that the payment of greenmail unfairly discriminates against other shareholders and represents a bald management-entrenchment device. In the mid-1980s, such criticisms developed into a consensus against the practice. Consequently, managers and board members must be prepared to deal with negative publicity if greenmail is paid to a potential acquirer.

Litigation is another frequent by-product of greenmail payments. Shareholders will often sue board members in a derivative capacity on behalf of the target company, asserting that the approval of such payments constitutes a breach of fiduciary duty. These kinds of claims generally have received short shrift in Delaware courts. Following a *Unocal* analysis, the courts have found greenmail to be a reasonable response to the threat posed by potentially disruptive hostile raiders. Courts in other states, California in particular, have taken a far less favorable view.

For instance, the Disney greenmail payment to Saul Steinberg and companies he controlled generated years of litigation. Shareholders sued under California law, arguing that the Disney board had breached its fiduciary duty to shareholders by granting preferential treatment to Steinberg. Two California state courts agreed. The trial judge in the case granted a preliminary injunction in favor of the shareholders. An appellate court upheld the decision.

Finally, in 1989, the Disney case was settled. Steinberg's Reliance Group agreed to pay about $21 million in damages. Disney itself was liable for $22 million in damages, though its insurers picked up most of the tab.

More troubling than the litigation threat is the prospect that the payment of greenmail may be tactically counterproductive. The presence of a potential acquirer in the market generally will push the price of target company stock higher. On news of a greenmail payment and standstill agreement, the stock price may fall back to previous levels. In that case, a new acquirer may come on the scene, hoping to take advantage of the target's apparent willingness to pay greenmail. This dynamic can result in a continuous stream of hostile investors, as St. Regis discovered in 1984. After St. Regis paid off two successive major shareholders, a third greenmailer took a stock position in the company. St. Regis saw no end in sight and agreed to be acquired by a white knight.

The receipt of greenmail payments can also have unfavorable tax consequences. Under federal tax law, a greenmail payment triggers a 50 percent tax on the gain associated with its receipt. The law, enacted in 1987, defines a greenmail payment as money or other value paid to acquire stock from a shareholder who made or threatened to make a tender offer for the payor's stock and who held the stock less than two years. The payment must also be discriminatory.

These various drawbacks have severely reduced the attraction and use of greenmail payments as a defensive tactic.

The Pac-Man Defense   A more aggressive approach is to go on the offensive. In other words, a target of a hostile bid can turn around and bid for the bidder. This tactic was used on several occasions in the early 1980s—Cities Service counteroffered for Boone Pickens' Mesa Petroleum in 1982; Houston Natural Gas did the same for Coastal Corp. in 1984; American Brands swallowed KKR's Beatrice spin-off, E-II Holdings, in 1988.

The fundamental message of a Pac-Man counterattack is that a particular combination in fact makes strategic sense, but makes more sense reversing directions. Sometimes, the issue is perceived management quality. Cities Service management could make a plausible case that it was better prepared and suited to managing a business of the size that would result from a Cities-Mesa merger.

There is also a defensive element to the counteroffer. The tactic sends a strong message that the original hostile bid will be opposed at all costs. In addition, the possibility that the bidder may itself be put in play can encourage the bidder to withdraw.

Of course, to proceed with a Pac-Man defense, a target company must have the capacity to buy the bidder. The question of capacity can revolve around borrowing capacity in the case of a cash deal or stock market valuations in the case of a stock deal.

The Pac-Man approach is a doomsday machine. If both sides proceed with their offers, shareholders of each company receive cash for their stock, squeezing the equity out of the companies. The result can be two companies with infinite debt-to-equity ratios. Insolvency is an inevitable by-product.

Timing is another critical issue. The first mover has an advantage in most takeover contests because its tender offer will expire first. This advantage allows the first mover to purchase control of its opponent before the opponent can counter. An understanding of the tender offer rules and other statutes is crucial.

However, the real question is which corporation can actually control the other first. The answer generally comes from the relevant state corporate law. Specific answers only come through a thorough review of each company's corporate governance provisions and the relevant statutes. Staggered boards, delayed shareholder meetings and the like can keep a company from capturing effective control.

If the Pac-Man threat is carried out and the initial aggressor doesn't blink, a circular ownership structure will result. One company might own a majority of the other, and vice versa. The question then arises, who controls whom? Under many state statutes, including the Delaware corporate law, a subsidiary is not permitted to vote stock it holds in its parent. These types of provisions arguably mean that neither side can control the other. By this reading, the stock essentially becomes nonvoting and any remaining stockholders attain control.

SWALLOWED BY PAC-MAN

The Bendix–Martin Marietta Fight

All these issues played out in the classic Pac-Man battle, featuring four aggressive managers and four major corporations—Bendix, Martin Marietta, United Technologies and Allied Corp. The principal protagonists were William Agee at Bendix, J. Donald Rauth at Martin Marietta, Harry Gray at United Technologies and Ed Hennessy at Allied Corp. Agee and his advisers at Salomon Brothers got the whirling corporate slugfest started on August 25, 1982, with a $43 a share bid for Martin Marietta.

The most controversial aspect to surface during the ensuing battle was Agee's relationship with Mary Cunningham. Agee was a native of Idaho and a graduate of Harvard Business School. He had risen quickly through various corporate jobs to become Bendix chairman at age thirty-eight. Cunningham—also a Harvard Business School graduate—had joined Bendix as Agee's executive assistant in 1979. Infatuated with the "science" of strategic planning, Cunningham was a business school zealot. Her relationship with Agee developed into a romantic one, and she eventually was forced to resign. She was hired into the Seagram planning department, then married Agee in 1982. Her role as Agee's most trusted adviser in the Martin Marietta bid drew considerable resentment.

Martin Marietta was advised by investment banker Marty Siegel, who plugged himself as the Minister of Defense. Siegel convinced Rauth to launch a counterbid for Bendix. Throughout the ensuing contest, Rauth stuck to his guns. Marietta strengthened its position even further when Harry Gray of United Technologies bid for Bendix as well. Matters had escalated.

The situation came as something of a shock to Agee, although members of the Bendix camp had considered and rejected the possibility of a Martin Marietta counterbid. Compromise became the focus as the parties tried to avoid the disastrous consequences of Bendix buying Marietta and vice versa.

Yet no compromise had developed by the deadline for the Bendix tender. Agee went ahead and bought up the tendered Marietta shares. This gave Bendix a timing advantage, but a feature of the Maryland law that governed Marietta threatened to upset Agee's plans. Under Maryland law, a shareholder had to wait ten days to call a special meeting. As a result, Bendix could not take control of the Marietta board. Bendix, on the other hand, was governed by Delaware law, which allowed a majority shareholder to take board control almost immediately.

Bendix neutralized the timing advantage provided by the Maryland statute to a certain degree by convincing a Delaware judge to enjoin Marietta from voting any Bendix shares it might purchase. The ruling relied on the fact that Marietta technically was a subsidiary of Bendix.

This opening gave Bendix time to find a way out of the complicated mess, though Agee lost his top spot in the process. Ed Hennessy of Allied—who had learned the acquisition business under Gray at United Technologies—had developed a competitive relationship with his former mentor. We were brought in by Agee at this late stage to persuade Hennessy to bid for Bendix as a white knight. Hennessy topped the Marietta and United Technologies bids, but Marietta went ahead and purchased shares in Bendix. The resulting ownership structure was spaghetti.

Ultimately, the cross-purchases were unwound. Bendix—now controlled by Hennessy at Allied—and Marietta swapped the shares they had purchased in each other. The Marietta stake held by Bendix was more valuable, so that Bendix ended up keeping some Marietta stock. Agee became president of Allied, but lasted only a few months in the job, until June 1983.

Eventually, Agee's black eye from the Martin Marietta fiasco healed and he landed on his feet as chairman of the struggling Morrison Knudsen. Yet he and Cunningham continued to generate a lot of controversy. The turnaround effort at Morrison Knudsen collapsed amidst recriminations in 1996, and Agee was again out of a job. Martin Marietta meanwhile prospered and eventually merged with Lockheed in 1995. Agee had the concept right, but the resentment over his image overwhelmed any appreciation for his business insights.

Finding a White Knight   A white knight transaction, in which a target company merges with or is acquired by a friendly suitor, may be the best alternative for a company faced with a well-financed and motivated bidder. Though the white knight strategy necessarily involves a loss of the target company's independence, it may nonetheless be preferable to the alternative. A white knight may pay a higher price, promise to retain target company employees and management, or support the existing corporate strategy.

With a hostile bidder banging down the door, the process of finding a white knight is necessarily urgent. An investment banker conducts the search, canvassing various alternative suitors. Many companies often hesitate when offered the opportunity to act as a white knight out of fear that a costly bidding war will develop. As a result, an interested white knight generally will demand protective provisions in any acquisition agreement with a target.

A prospective white knight might demand a stock or crown jewel lockup, as Forstmann Little did in the fight for Revlon. A stock lockup option gives the white knight the right to purchase authorized but unissued shares in the target company. From a white knight's perspective, such an option has two advantages. First, the white knight can exercise the options under certain circumstances, in which case it might vote the shares in favor of the proposed transaction between the white knight and the target. Second, the options provide a hedge against the possibility that another acquirer will pay a higher price for the target. If that happens, the white knight can exercise the options and sell the shares to the eventual acquirer for a profit.

A crown jewel or asset lockup gives a white knight the right to acquire key assets from the target under specified circumstances. The acquisition price is set at a level that is fair, but the deal is strategic for the white knight. If the assets covered by the lockup are viewed as critical or central to the target company's operations by other holders, a lockup arrangement reduces the likelihood of intervention.

Revlon may pose a problem for any defensive provisions in an agreement between a target company and a white knight, unless the auction was fully explored. Because of the risk of judicial challenge, lockups are not used as frequently as they were during the 1980s.

The White Squire   Taking a different tack, a company can issue new shares as a defensive maneuver. The principal defensive advantage of this approach stems from placing the shares into the friendly hands of a white squire.

A white squire investment can have three defensive benefits. First, the white squire presumably will vote in line with management. Often these deals are done in combination with a recapitalization and establish a solid management-friendly block. Second, a standstill agreement can be structured so that the white squire shares will not be tendered into a hostile offer. A hostile bidder therefore will be less likely to get the minimum number of shares needed to complete its offer. Finally, simply increasing the number of shares outstanding may make an acquisition more expensive.

Finding an appropriate white squire can be difficult. With a potential hostile acquirer in the wings, a squire must be willing to face the possibility of becoming a minority shareholder in an unsettled situation. In addition, from the target's perspective, a number of restrictions are necessary to ensure that the squire remains friendly. A squire therefore must be willing to make a sizable long-term investment with limited prospect for control.

Even once a squire is identified and negotiations are concluded, issues of implementation remain. The stock can be issued directly from the target only if it has sufficient authorized but unissued shares available. Otherwise, either the target company will have to amend its charter to provide for additional shares, which requires shareholder approval, or the squire will have to purchase shares in the open market.

An issuer must receive adequate consideration and must issue the securities for a proper purpose. If a white squire arrangement is initiated in response to a particular takeover threat, the board must satisfy the *Unocal* analysis.

The particular security issued to a white squire varies. However, convertible preferred stock is favored. The preferred dividend provides some measure of certainty to the white squire. Plus, many companies have so-called blank check preferred in place that can be used for this purpose. Blank check preferred—provided for in a corporation's charter—is authorized but unissued preferred stock, the terms and conditions of which can be established by the issuer's board without further shareholder approval.

Shareholder approval may be necessary even if a company has authorized but unissued shares available to sell to a white squire. The New York Stock Exchange requires such approval if shares are to be sold to officers, directors or significant shareholders, or if the shares to be issued have voting rights equal to 20 percent or more of the voting power previously outstanding. This latter rule applies to securities convertible into voting stock.

THE WHITE SQUIRE IN ACTION

Buffett and Salomon Brothers

Warren Buffett is the most renowned white squire investor of the past decade. In 1987 he kept Ron Perelman from buying a large block of stock in investment bank Salomon Brothers. The purchase ultimately would prove to be one of Buffett's less fortunate, but it illustrates how he structured these investments.

For Buffett, the Salomon Brothers drama began in the summer of 1987. Buffett had developed a relationship with John Gutfreund, head of Salomon, over the years. The two chatted fairly regularly about the prospects for Salomon Brothers.

In September, Buffett got a different kind of call from Gutfreund. Minerals and Resources Corp., known as Minorco, was a major Salomon shareholder with a 14 percent stake. Minorco was unhappy with its investment and hired Felix Rohatyn to find a buyer. Word spread and Ron Perelman became interested.

Rohatyn ratcheted up the pressure on Gutfreund by negotiating a tentative deal with Perelman, an unpleasant prospect for

Gutfreund. In fact, Perelman only wanted to do a friendly transaction and to get two board seats along with his Salomon stake.

Gutfreund was cornered. Salomon Brothers could not afford to repurchase Minorco's shares at the $38 price offered by Perelman, roughly a 20 percent premium to the market price. Gutfreund turned to Buffett. The two men met in Wachtell, Lipton's offices. Within a matter of hours, Buffett agreed that Berkshire Hathaway would purchase a $700 million block of convertible preferred from Salomon. The securities would carry a 9 percent guaranteed yield and could be converted into Salomon common stock at an effective price of $38 per common share.

In structuring his Salomon investment, Buffett intended to create an instrument that would give Berkshire Hathaway a 15 percent overall return. He estimated that the 9 percent coupon plus appreciation on the underlying common stock would accomplish that goal. From Gutfreund's perspective, the capital infusion would allow Salomon to buy out Minorco.

Salomon has had its problems since 1987. The stock market crash in that year, plus a Treasury trading scandal and management turmoil, initially contributed to an unstable performance. However, as the bull market of the 1990s heated up, Salomon prospered. The 1997 acquisition of Salomon by Sandy Weill's Travelers Group converted Berkshire Hathaway's roughly 30 percent Salomon stake into a 3 percent stake in Travelers. Buffett, a frequent home-run hitter, characterized the deal's $80 per share valuation as a "scratch single" for Berkshire Hathaway.

Recapitalizations and Restructurings   A company can initiate a wide variety of financial and operational changes in response to a potential bid. Common strategies include a leveraged recapitalization, the assumption of additional debt, the issuance of new shares, the purchase of outstanding shares and a spin-off or split-off.

In the context of takeover defense, a leveraged recapitalization involves the target company's assumption of new debt to fund a dividend payout or share repurchase. The defensive recapitalization is a variant on the model used by financial buyers in friendly deals. The company is recapitalized as equity capital is replaced with debt. As a result, the target company's debt-to-equity ratio is increased. This kind of transaction can have several defensive benefits.

First, the assumption of additional debt reduces the target company's debt capacity. If the hostile bidder planned to use the target's surplus debt capacity to fund the acquisition of control, the recapitalization can be an insurmountable barrier. Likewise, if partially funded with existing cash balances, a recapitalization can remove a source of funding for a hostile bid.

Second, the payment of a large special dividend should significantly improve the disposition of shareholders toward the target. A major share repurchase likewise offers the benefit of providing liquidity to shareholders who might otherwise have opted for a hostile tender. This can reduce the percentage of "dissatisfied shareholders" in the marketplace.

Third, the interest payments on new debt provide a tax shield for the target company's earnings that is not available from recurring dividend payments. The target company's operating income as a result may be shielded from tax. In addition, a high debt load may increase management's incentives to improve operations, providing benefits similar to those associated with a leveraged buyout.

The combined effect of a recapitalization may be to increase the value of shareholders' target company holdings. For example, the sum of money received through a special dividend and the remaining equity value of shares held after a recapitalization may be greater than the value of target company stock prior to the recapitalization. Of course, a recapitalization will be most effective as a defensive measure when it provides greater value to shareholders than a proposed hostile bid.

A target also can take on additional debt without paying a special dividend or carrying out a share repurchase. The cash generated can be used to fund operations, make acquisitions or otherwise. Whatever the use, the target company's debt capacity is reduced. Again, this may deter a raider intent on funding an acquisition with a target company's own borrowing capacity.

Debt can be added to a company's balance sheet either by issuing publicly traded bonds or by borrowing money directly from a bank or other lender in a private transaction. While publicly traded debt may be more cost-efficient due to lower interest charges, time pressures may make public debt impractical for a defensive restructuring. Publicly traded debt must be registered with the SEC, which can delay the ability to respond to a hostile bid. If a company anticipates the use of publicly traded debt in this context, it may, however, shelf-register debt securities so they can be drawn down on a moment's notice.

Cash—whether raised through a new borrowing or already on hand—also can fund a defensive share repurchase plan. The advantages of this approach include the reduction of the "float" (that is, shares held by investors who are inclined to accept a hostile tender offer), the reduction of target company resources that might be used by a hostile bidder to fund an acquisition, and the possible increase in overall shareholder value. A share repurchase plan can also have a helpful side effect from the perspective of an incumbent board. If insiders choose not to sell shares into the repurchase plan, their ownership percentage will be concentrated.

The federal securities law limits a target company's ability to purchase its own shares after a third party has made a tender offer for the company's stock. So long as a third-party tender offer is open, the target company must file a statement with the SEC before repurchasing any shares. The statement must set forth the following information: a description of the securities to be purchased, the purpose of the repurchase, the method of repurchase and the source of funds for the transaction. In addition, the issuer must send a statement containing the same information to shareholders, unless such information has already been provided within the previous six months.

The chief tactical distinction between an open-market purchase plan and a self-tender offer has to do with timing and flexibility. Once the issuer disseminates the information required by the securities regulations, open-market purchases can be initiated. If the target has funding, purchases can begin more or less immediately. Alternatively, an open-market plan can be drawn out over a period of months or even years.

A self-tender offer, on the other hand, is subject to rules that basically mirror the third-party tender offer rules. Under the self-tender rules, an issuer must file a statement with the SEC in conjunction with the commencement of an offer. A self-tender must remain open for at least twenty days from the date of commencement. If the price offered is increased or decreased, the offer must remain open for an additional ten days. Tendered shares must be accepted on a pro rata basis where the issuer will purchase less than all such shares.

In light of these requirements, the self-tender offer is a more stylized and defined alternative when compared to open-market purchases. This difference makes a self-tender offer somewhat more of a blunt instrument than open-market purchases. At the same time, the time line and mechanics of a self-tender, as well as the greater certainty involved, translate into a more dramatic effect.

Cash from operations and additional debt are not the only available sources of funding for a recapitalization. Target companies also sometimes sell assets or operations, or partially or completely liquidate as a defensive response. Alternatively, rather than pay a large cash dividend, some targets choose to spin off operations into the hands of shareholders.

The sale of divisions or assets can serve two purposes. First, the sale of a particularly attractive asset—referred to as a crown jewel sale—may discourage a potential bidder intent on acquiring the asset. Second, the proceeds from the sale can be used to fund various recapitalization alternatives. The cash can be paid to shareholders as a dividend or can be used to fund a share repurchase program.

However, the main problem with an asset sale is that it is difficult to accomplish in a short period of time. Once a hostile tender or other bid is on the table, a target company may not be able to find an acquirer and negotiate a transaction soon enough to have a defensive impact. Even if this can be accomplished, a rapid sale may not maximize the selling price. A target company board of directors must be careful in this regard. While an asset sale is generally protected by the business judgment rule, if the sale is defensively motivated, the *Unocal* test may apply. Particularly if the price received on the sale is low, the transaction may be enjoined and the directors may be charged with having violated their fiduciary duties.

A partial or total liquidation is another possible defensive strategy. A partial liquidation involves the sale of assets and payment of the proceeds to shareholders as a dividend. In a total liquidation, the company is broken up and sold piecemeal with the expectation of generating a higher return than promised by a hostile bidder.

Both alternatives implicate the same timing dilemma as an asset sale. A liquidation of all or substantially all of a target's assets must also be approved by shareholders. Thus, while a liquidation may promise a higher return to shareholders, the drawn-out process involved and the associated uncertainty may make the option unpalatable to shareholders and therefore unrealistic as a defensive alternative.

If a target is unable to find a buyer for assets, it can instead carry out a spin-off. This approach has the advantage of focusing market interest on each entity as a separate piece and can cause the combined value of the pieces to increase relative to the target's pre–spin-off value. However, like an asset sale or liquidation, a spin-off can take some time to accomplish. For instance, Pillsbury floated the idea of spinning off Burger King as part of its Grand Met defense, but, as expected, shareholders proved too impatient for this approach.

A company that is contemplating a spin-off will, therefore, often complete the transaction before a raider appears on the scene. The hope, of course, is that the spin-off will enhance shareholder value and thereby reduce the likelihood of a hostile offer.

Clearly, the range of defensive options expands if a pill and other defensive structures are in place, but there is the risk that any overt action may result in a court forcing redemption of the poison pill.

ESOPs The employee stock ownership plan, or ESOP, provides a valuable alternative to the white squire as friendly shareholder. Regulated under federal employee benefits and tax law, an ESOP is, in fact, designed to hold company stock as an undiversified retirement investment for employees. The chief defensive benefit from placing a block of shares with an ESOP derives from the presumption that employees will tend to vote against a hostile bid that might jeopardize jobs. However, this result cannot be guaranteed through a standstill agreement. Rather, the employee beneficiaries of an ESOP generally must be given the freedom to control the shares in an ESOP, with the protection of confidentiality.

Notwithstanding this drawback, an ESOP can have considerable defensive force, particularly in conjunction with state antitakeover laws. Under the Delaware statute, for example, a hostile bidder that acquires more than 15 percent of a company's stock cannot complete a back-end merger with the company unless either a two-thirds majority of shareholders other than the bidder approve or the bidder acquires at least 85 percent of the target company's stock. An ESOP that owns as little as 15 percent of a company may have the power to block a bust-up transaction that is predicated on the acquisition of 100 percent control.

Another advantage of an ESOP-based defense is the speed with which it can be implemented. A company can either issue shares directly to an ESOP or the ESOP can purchase shares on the open market. The dilutive effect of issuing new shares to the ESOP can be offset by open-market purchases if desired. Under applicable regulations, the ESOP may borrow up to 100 percent of the cost of acquiring company shares and may use the company's credit guarantee for this purpose. The company then may make tax-deductible contributions to the ESOP to fund the loan payments.

In setting up an ESOP, care must be given to the price paid by the ESOP for company securities. If the ESOP overpays for the securities, the purchase and sale will constitute a "prohibited transaction" under federal employee benefits laws. If, however, the ESOP is allowed to purchase the securities at a bargain, the company's officers and directors open themselves to a claim that they violated their fiduciary duties to other shareholders.

There is a major distinction between putting shares into an ESOP and selling shares to a white squire. While a white squire pays for its shares, an ESOP is funded by the target company. The cost of funding an ESOP therefore is part of a company's overall compensation expense structure and must be evaluated in those terms. Simply adding an ESOP without reducing other benefits provided to employees could represent a substantial increase in compensation expense. A company consequently may need to reduce other benefits in conjunction with the creation of an ESOP. Setting aside takeover-related issues, such a shift in compensation structure can have implications for employee morale.

THE ESOP IN ACTION

Ashland Creates Employment Ownership

Management at Ashland Oil learned a quick lesson when the Belzberg family of Canada bought a 9 percent stake in the company. By March 1986, when the stake came to light in an SEC filing, the Belzbergs already had a reputation as successful takeover specialists. Samuel Belzberg, chairman of First City Financial, made his first big strike in the early 1980s with an investment in Bache Group. When Prudential Insurance bought the company, Sam Belzberg pocketed a large gain.

Fearing their company would be put in play, Ashland managers at first refused to comment on the offer. However, behind the scenes, the company opened talks with the Belzbergs. An agreement was reached quite quickly. Ashland agreed to buy the Belzbergs' stock back at $51 a share, the takeover-inflated market price. The Belzbergs reportedly made just over $15 million on the transaction before taxes.

The Ashland board was glad to be rid of the Belzbergs, but understood the 1980s market dynamic. Their company was now in play. However, the board came up with a package to pull Ashland off the market. Key features of the plan were a stock buyback program covering up to 23 percent of the company's stock and possible asset sales. The central feature was a powerful new ESOP. Funded with bank loans, the Ashland ESOP would purchase shares in the market.

By September 30, 1996, the ESOP controlled 13 percent of Ashland's outstanding common stock and the continuing presence of the block helped ward off repeat attacks.

Going Private   When faced with a determined hostile bidder, target company management may conclude that, in one form or another, a sale of the company is inevitable. In this circumstance, management is not without an option. Taking the target company private in a leveraged buyout may provide an attractive solution both for shareholders and management—public shareholders can receive a premium price for their shares and management retains control of the target company.

The prospect of going private of course raises various financial structuring issues. In addition, a management-led leveraged buyout in the context of a takeover contest raises two other issues. First, with management on one side of a buyout transaction, the board necessarily must assume an even more proactive role in safeguarding the interests of shareholders. Second, management must comply with specific federal securities disclosure requirements applicable to a going-private transaction.

As reflected in Delaware case law, the heightened role for corporate directors reflects a commonsense view of shareholder rights. The worry is that the self-interest of managers will motivate them to push through a sweetheart deal. Of course, when competing bidders are already on the scene, even an entrenched management may find it difficult to structure an advantageous deal. A defensive management buyout still is fraught with potential pitfalls for a board; the slightest appearance of impropriety likely will generate shareholder lawsuits, with all the attendant unpleasantness.

In any lawsuit that does develop, the behavior of directors will not be measured under the forgiving business judgment rule. Rather, the courts will impose the far more demanding "entire fairness" review that applies to transactions that involve self-interested directors. Entire fairness review requires a far-reaching judicial inquiry. Particular emphasis is placed on both procedure and price. If a challenged management buyout is to go forward, the court must be satisfied that shareholders were treated fairly.

These concerns are often addressed by establishing a special committee of independent outside directors, not affiliated with management, to assess a going-private transaction. For instance, when Ross Johnson proposed a management buyout of RJR Nabisco, a committee of outside directors was established. The committee took charge of the process, hired its own financial and legal advisers, and solicited additional bids for the company. Of course, the special committee eventually selected KKR as the winning bidder.

If carried out properly, the special committee process can restore the protective shield of the business judgment rule to a transaction.

The possibility of triggering an "entire fairness" review is not the only hurdle in the way of a management buyout. In addition, the SEC's "going private" rules also impose significant obligations with which management must comply before a transaction can be consummated. These rules apply only if the purchase leaves the issuer with 300 or fewer shareholders or results in the issuer being delisted from a national securities exchange. The SEC takes the general position that a leveraged buyout with management involvement will be covered where managers will participate in the deal on a basis that leaves them owning 10 percent or more of the surviving company. As a result, the going private rules apply to almost every management buyout.

The substantive going-private rule has two components. First, an acquirer must satisfy certain mandatory reporting rules by filing a schedule with the SEC. The schedule includes information on the purpose of the transaction, a description of the transaction structure and a discussion of alternatives that were explored. An in-depth defense of the transaction's fairness must be included and any reports from third parties must be fully disclosed. Second, an acquirer must wait a minimum of twenty days between the time of filing and the first purchase of stock.

The going-private rules, and in particular the extensive disclosure obligations, magnify the importance of deliberate board consideration of any management buyout. In the fast-paced environment of a takeover contest, it can be easy to lose sight of this fact. However, with full disclosure required and entire fairness as the standard, even the appearance of impropriety can scuttle an otherwise well-conceived management buyout.

The Defensive Acquisition   Defensive acquisitions are another option for a company with a strong stock price or borrowing capacity. The idea is twofold. First, by increasing its debt load, a company derives many of the defensive benefits of a leveraged recapitalization. Bidders are less likely to be attracted to a company that has already utilized a significant portion of its debt capacity.

Size and scope also have a certain defensive quality. Simply by becoming a larger concern, a company raises the stakes for a bidder seeking to acquire the new, larger company. More cash must be raised, more stock issued.

The 1979 defense of Daylin is a classic case where a defensive acquisition was used to advantage. W.R. Grace bid to take over the company and knew there were no white knights in the wings. Daylin CEO Sanford Sigoloff then decided to bid for a third company, Narco Scientific, in an effort to force a higher bid out of Grace. The premium bid for Narco worked. Grace upped its offer, and Sigoloff accepted.

Of course, the kind of defensive acquisition used by Daylin now may need to pass muster under *Unocal*. A thorough analysis and reasoned approach are critical to supporting eventual acquisition decisions. While the board has the authority to set strategic policy under *Time*, the acquisition process should be above impeachment so that a court will have no reason to enjoin or overturn such moves.

Timing can also be an issue. Similar to a sale, an acquisition can take considerable time and energy from start to finish. However, for defensive purposes, it may be sufficient to sign a definitive agreement binding the company to future action. In any event, the perceived propriety and ease of execution are likely to be enhanced where an acquisition has been under consideration for some time.

Litigation and Public Relations Blitz   Litigation and public relations remain important aspects of a full defensive strategy, but rarely are decisive factors. Courts have become quite skeptical about most kinds of legal claims related to takeovers. Outright abuses will be curbed. Yet the courts are not prepared to be the arbiters of every takeover contest. As a result, rules of standing and other procedural barriers have been erected to limit overzealous litigators.

Common subjects of takeover litigation include antitrust matters, securities law violations, breach of fiduciary duty cases and breach of confidentiality cases. Antitrust law is the only area where a consistent possibility of delivering a decisive blow exists.

The public relations story is slightly different. With the preponderance of strategic stock-for-stock deals, pitching the story of a deal to the markets is increasingly more important and common. Clearly, there is a role for public relations professionals in the merger process.

The Hotel War—Hilton Versus ITT

On January 27, 1997, Hilton Hotels Corp. launched a $55 a share bear hug offer for ITT Corp. Many themes of the takeover arena—both strategic and tactical, on offense and defense—were reflected in the battle, which dragged out over eleven months and ranged from the courts of Nevada to the boardrooms of Manhattan.

On the strategic side, the roots of the ITT battle stretch back to the conglomerate days of the 1960s when Harold Geneen diversified the company away from its traditional telecommunications base. Rand Araskog—the West Point graduate most responsible for unwinding Geneen's legacy—already carried several battle scars from past defensive campaigns. After a series of spin-offs, he had focused the company down to a hotel essence, only to add a gaming business with the acquisition of Caesars. This was the sixty-six-year-old Araskog's play to build a strategic legacy, a premier "destinations" company. ITT shareholders reacted skeptically. Both the strategic design and the execution were called into question as ITT Corp.'s stock gave back the gains from the 1995 spin-off plan.

The continuing problems at ITT triggered the interest of Stephen Bollenbach, a gifted corporate dealmaker with an impressive résumé who had recently taken over as head of Hilton Hotels. Before joining the company, Bollenbach earned acclaim on Wall Street as chief financial officer for Donald Trump's real estate business, then Marriott and finally Disney. In the process, he helped Trump avoid bank-ruptcy, guided Marriott through a highly successful split into two businesses and orchestrated the financial aspects of Disney's Capital Cities/ABC acquisition.

Bollenbach came to Hilton with a mandate to turn around the conservative hotel company. He opened with a bold stroke—a $3 billion acquisition of casino company Bally Entertainment. Then, in the fall of 1996, Bollenbach became interested in ITT.

For Bollenbach, ITT looked like a company in trouble. ITT's Planet Hollywood strategy seemed misguided. ITT had agreed to put up all the cash to build Planet Hollywood casinos—more than $1 billion—but would pay Planet Hollywood 10 percent of the cash flow as a license for using the hip brand name. Bollenbach likened this to "Coca-Cola leasing A&W Root Beer." ITT had its own strong casino brand in Caesars and less costly opportunities for growth.

Bollenbach began planning a bid for ITT in October 1996. The initial question was how to approach, whether by friendly offer, bear hug or outright hostile tender. Although Araskog had repeatedly demonstrated his antipathy to being taken over, Bollenbach decided to make an attempt at a friendly deal.

Throughout the fall, Araskog rebuffed several informal offers to negotiate a deal. Finally, in January 1997, Bollenbach gave up and launched a tender offer at $55 a share, an $11.25, or 26 percent, premium over the trading price prior to the announcement of the offer.

True to history, Araskog immediately put ITT on alert for a takeover defense. This veteran of the takeover skirmishes of the 1980s—which he later described in an autobiographical book entitled *The ITT Wars*—found himself again arguing a raider was trying to snatch ITT "on the cheap." Though ITT had significantly under-performed the market during Araskog's tenure, Araskog and the ITT board rejected the offer as inadequate and launched an aggressive defense. Planned capital expenditures were slashed and an extensive asset sale program triggered. The annual shareholder meeting—normally held in May—was delayed until November.

Many on Wall Street agreed that the Hilton bid was low. Bollenbach had faced the modern dilemma of takeovers—either be preemptive with a high bid or face a grueling duel. Bollenbach appeared to be opting for a drawn-out test of wills in an attempt to keep the price down. Of course, the danger was that Araskog would have time to respond. One alternative was a higher bid which would pressure the ITT board. The board was a key constituency because Hilton's offer could not proceed unless the ITT board were to remove its poison pill. Faced with a low bid, the board credibly refused.

Essentially, Bollenbach seemed to be calculating there was a chink in ITT's defensive armor. The company lacked a staggered board, which meant all of its current directors were up for election at the next annual meeting. As part of its bid, Hilton announced its intention to nominate a slate and conduct a proxy fight. Bollenbach assumed shareholders would have an opportunity to decide the contest by November at the latest—the outside edge of how long ITT could delay its shareholder meeting. Bollenbach chose to take an option on a low-price deal rather than pursue the more likely success of a higher bid.

Araskog proceeded to take aggressive steps to forestall any shareholder vote. He unloaded the recently acquired Madison Square Garden and several other properties for a profit. In May 1997, ITT agreed to sell five hotels as part of its larger divestiture strategy. The company also began to entertain bids for some of its marquee properties. ITT was not, however, getting out of the hotel business. Rather, the company retained the contractual right to manage the hotels for a fee. Hilton wanted the hotels and likely would not purchase ITT without them.

These hotel sales had an additional defensive aspect embedded in the related management contracts. The contracts incorporated change-of-control provisions that allowed the new hotel owners to discontinue the management arrangement should the ITT hotel company get bought out. This language, while relatively common in management contracts, amounted to shark repellent in the takeover context. If Hilton were to take over ITT, it would face the risk that part of the value of the company it had purchased would simply walk away.

In what was meant to be a knockout punch, ITT next announced a two-step restructuring plan. The first step would be another breakup of ITT into three separate companies, a hotel and casino operator, a technical school company and a publisher of telephone directories. Afterward, the Yellow Pages company—the successor to the "old" ITT—would buy back $2.1 billion of its stock in a $70 a share tender offer, well above Hilton's initial $55 offer.

For a time, it looked as if Araskog's maneuvers had effectively foreclosed a Hilton takeover. The spin-off and subsequent restructuring amounted to a two-tier, front-end-loaded self-tender offer. ITT shareholders would receive some cash on the front end and a package of stock in the three new ITTs on the back end. Moreover, each of the two spin-off companies—including ITT Destinations, the hotel company that Hilton wanted—would be restructured with full takeover defenses.

Two features in particular looked to give ITT Destinations impenetrable armor. First, the terms of ITT Destinations' board members would be staggered, so that Hilton would not be able to gain control for several years. Second, the spin-off of Destinations would be tax-free to ITT shareholders. A set of complex tax rules would have to be satisfied to achieve this treatment, and a subsequent purchase of ITT Destinations by Hilton arguably would blow the tax-free status. Hilton would then be on the hook for $1.4 billion of taxes. This hidden poison pill likely would make Destinations too toxic to be taken over. But the ITT team had overdone it. They were effectively taking away the public shareholder vote and foreclosing the possibility of a takeover.

Bollenbach sensed ITT's vulnerability and, in August 1997, raised the Hilton bid to $70 a share. The terms of the new bid called for Hilton to buy a majority of the shares for cash and the remainder for Hilton stock.

At the same time, Hilton filed a challenge to ITT's restructuring plan in a Nevada federal court. The idea was for the new bid to put maximum pressure on the court. Six weeks later, on September 29, 1997, Hilton won a court order that required ITT to put its restructuring plan to a vote. Hilton had argued in court that ITT's plan, with its imposition of staggered boards where none had existed, effectively disenfranchised shareholders. The Nevada judge agreed, rejecting ITT's arguments that the plan amounted to a simple dividend of stock in ITT Destinations and the technical school company. To the contrary, the judge ruled that the ITT restructuring plan had "as its primary purpose the entrenchment of the current board."

The ruling in favor of Hilton dramatically eroded ITT's position. ITT now was required to have a shareholder vote by November 14, 1997. After months of dogged resistance, Araskog's complex defenses had crumbled. ITT suddenly faced the prospect that Hilton's slate of directors might be elected, ensuring Hilton a victory.

Both ITT and Hilton rushed to lobby shareholders for support. Each company placed a stream of full-page advertisements in *The New York Times* and *The Wall Street Journal*. A certain amount of mudslinging broke out as Araskog and Bollenbach pressed their points. In a published *Barron's* interview, Araskog called Bollenbach "a drive-by financier who has held four jobs in five years and has a lot less impressive business career than people give him credit for." Bollenbach shot back: "What Araskog has shown ever since we made our first offer in late January is that he will do anything just to try to fend us off and preserve his own job."

Bollenbach's statement proved to be only half right. Araskog was committed to defeating the Hilton bid, but he would sacrifice his job in the process. With the clock ticking toward the November ITT shareholder meeting, ITT made a dramatic late October announcement. The company had found a white knight who seemed to be willing to top Hilton by a considerable amount. Starwood Lodging, a hotel and real estate company, had agreed to acquire ITT in a friendly deal valued at $82 a share, or $9.8 billion.

The Starwood deal represented an ironic turn of events for ITT. Starwood was a high-growth, high-multiple tax REIT with relatively little earnings. Measured by stock market capitalization, Starwood was a much smaller company than ITT. Yet, Starwood's high-priced stock gave it the currency to go after the larger company. In essence, a high flyer of the 1990s would be buying the remnants of a high flyer from the 1960s. The deal would be massively accretive to Starwood's earnings thanks to Harold Geneen's old earnings-per-share game of the 1960s. If the market priced the combined company at a higher multiple than the blended average of the two stand-alone companies, as initially appeared to be the case, the merger would create value for shareholders.

In any event, Araskog again looked to have delivered a knockout punch. While Starwood was offering a 1960s-style stock deal, Hilton was offering mostly cash. Each raise would drain some of the company's borrowing capacity, make a deal less accretive and reduce post-deal operating flexibility. Starwood's $12 per share premium to Hilton's offer appeared to have priced Hilton out of the fight. Bollenbach applauded Araskog for doing "the right thing" for ITT shareholders and essentially conceded defeat. Hilton was not "going to chase the deal."

The only chance for Hilton would be if Starwood's stock price dropped considerably before the deal was approved. ITT's shareholders were partially protected against this eventuality by a price collar included in Starwood's offer. Shareholders were guaranteed to receive $82 in cash and Starwood stock so long as Starwood's stock traded in a band between $53.26 and $61.26 per share. This collar discouraged shareholders from discounting the Starwood stock in its offer.

On October 27, 1997, a single-day 554-point drop in the Dow average dramatically changed investor psychology. People began to question the value of high-flying stocks such as Starwood. Bollenbach jumped at the opportunity and again raised Hilton's bid.

Under the new bid, Hilton would pay ITT shareholders $80 per share, 55 percent in cash (up from 50 percent) and the remainder in Hilton stock. Hilton also included a contingent value right (CVR) that would pay ITT shareholders an additional amount if Hilton's stock failed to trade at an average of $40 for any twenty-day period in the following year. The $40 target price would make the two Hilton shares given to ITT shareholders on the back end of the Hilton offer worth the same $80 as the cash paid on the front end. If the stock didn't reach that level, Hilton would pay holders of the CVRs up to $12 per share. In the worst case, this guarantee would cost Hilton more than $600 million.

These terms compared favorably to Starwood's offer, which included only $15 in cash and $67 in stock. ITT's board finally budged. Exercising the fiduciary out provisions in the merger agreement with Starwood, the company announced it would auction itself off to the highest bidder and established a special board committee of outside directors to evaluate competing bids.

Meanwhile, Starwood faced pressure to raise its bid. The ITT shareholder meeting would elect a new board. If Hilton's slate of directors were elected at the meeting, the contest would be over. Starwood instead hoped ITT shareholders would back the company's incumbent board one last time. To encourage shareholders to vote for the ITT slate and keep the auction going, Starwood raised its bid to $85 per share and increased the cash portion in advance of the meeting.

ITT shareholders dramatically rewarded Starwood for its generosity. An estimated 72 percent of the shareholders backed ITT's incumbent slate of directors. Within twenty-four hours after the meeting, the ITT board had endorsed the revised Starwood offer.

Though the new merger agreement included a fiduciary out for ITT, any new offer would have to top Starwood's price and be fully funded or possible to finance. Hilton meanwhile withdrew its offer. Bollenbach conceded the price for ITT had gotten too rich: "Once it was clear the market would treat [Starwood's] stock like cash, I think it was a lost cause."

Araskog had his victory, but it was bittersweet. He would walk away with an estimated $55 million lump-sum payment. However, his efforts to keep ITT independent had failed. The Starwood deal would mark the final death of the conglomerate built up by Harold Geneen. In addition, Araskog would relinquish both his board seat and the top job to Starwood's Barry Sternlicht.

Araskog couldn't resist one last barb at Bollenbach even as the Hotel War wrapped up. In interviews after the shareholder vote, Araskog said the outcome would have been different if Hilton had bid $75 per share for ITT at the outset rather than $55. Then, Araskog asserted, the ITT board would have felt obliged to negotiate with Hilton.

Of course, it is impossible to know what would have happened, but Bollenbach rejected the idea that a preemptive bid would have overcome ITT's resistance. In his view, the board was never prepared to sell control of ITT until forced to do so. An original bid of $75— at the high end of what Hilton could afford to pay—would only have priced Hilton out of the fight from the outset, according to Bollenbach. Critics disagree with this view.

Bollenbach was philosophical: "In thirty-five years I have been through lots of deals and I usually lose. That's the deal business. This is part of what I do for a living."

The Government Intervenes

22

"The great corporations . . . are the creatures of the state, and the state not only has the right to control them, but it is in duty bound to control them whenever the need for such control is shown."

Theodore Roosevelt,
in a speech at Providence, Rhode Island,
August 1902

The government lurks in the background of the deal process. It is everywhere from creating the rules in terms of securities and tax laws, to drafting the regulations that restructure industries, to direct intervention. This all-pervasive giant influences the structure, pace and scope of transactions.

Antitrust law is the most direct interface between government and deal participants. As a practical matter, the antitrust law is a costly web that can entangle the most sophisticated acquirer. The perceived risks of an antitrust challenge can have a determinative impact in a hostile situation, such as occurred in the bidding war for Conoco. Alternatively, in the friendly-deal context, if the government decides to launch an antitrust challenge, the acquirer must either back out or subject itself to lengthy litigation. A dealmaker therefore needs to understand both the substantive and procedural rules of antitrust before entering a contest.

The Renewed Power of Antitrust

Antitrust challenges to mergers and acquisitions were relatively infrequent during the Reagan and Bush years. Of course, the major antitrust milestone of the period was the breakup of AT&T. However, most deals sailed through the antitrust review process.

Lately, the winds have shifted. Government authorities have shown a renewed interest in challenging proposed transactions, sometimes with dramatic effect. The 1997 challenge to the Staples–Office Depot merger was a particularly dramatic showstopper, a sign of the new assertive posture and of the courts' willingness to block a deal.

The government's growing interest in the antitrust limitations on mergers has been in the headlines for several years. Microsoft was one of the first companies to feel the sting. In 1994, the software giant agreed to acquire Intuit, the maker of Quicken, a popular financial software package. The Justice Department attacked the deal as anticompetitive. When the government wouldn't back down, Bill Gates pulled the plug on the deal.

Less than two years later, another major transaction suffered a similar fate. The Federal Trade Commission (FTC) challenged Rite Aid's agreement to purchase Revco for $1.8 billion. Essentially, the government argued that together the two drugstore chains would have the power to keep health care groups from negotiating lower prices for prescription medicines. Rather than fight, Rite Aid dropped the deal and instead acquired Thrifty Payless. CVS then acquired our client Revco in 1997.

While Microsoft and Rite Aid were signposts pointing to a more skeptical government review process, the Staples case had a wider impact. Not only did the government challenge a major transaction—once a rarity—but the government actually won a preliminary round in court.

The concept of a big-box retail store devoted entirely to office products was relatively unheard of as late as 1990. Staples founder and CEO Thomas Stemberg and his rivals at Office Depot pioneered the retail format. They quickly rolled out stores across the country. By the fall of 1996, the two chains together had over 1,000 stores with more than $10 billion in annual revenue.

A simple vision animated the office superstore business plan—low-cost office supplies for the small business and home office markets. Before the superstores came on the scene, these markets were served by the highly fragmented stationery industry. Stemberg prided himself on ruthless competition for business, and by constantly finding ways to lower prices, he grabbed a large market share for Staples.

In September 1997, Staples and Office Depot announced a plan to merge in an approximately $4 billion stock swap. Office Depot's shareholders would receive 1.14 Staples shares for each Office Depot share. The combined company would control the largest chain of office superstores and Office Max—with 503 stores and $3.3 billion of revenue—would be its only remaining competitor.

Of course, Stemberg and David Fuente, the chairman and CEO of Office Depot, anticipated that the merger of the number one and number two players in a three-company industry would attract some government attention. However, they believed that the relative lack of geographic overlap between the two companies' stores weighed in favor of the deal. The companies had a strong history of lowering prices for consumers. To underscore this history, the two men stood in front of a banner that read "Save Even More" when they announced the deal. The merger would bring $4 billion of projected cost savings according to the companies. These savings would be passed in part on to consumers, who could look forward to even lower prices. In the final analysis, Stemberg and Fuente expected these factors would convince government lawyers to approve the deal.

This forecast proved to be wrong. In March 1997, the FTC voted to challenge the deal in spite of the fact that the two office superstores would have less than 6 percent of the total U.S. office supply market. Nor were government lawyers swayed by the fact that the tremendous growth of the office superstore format had come as a re- sult of these chains' strategy of undercutting mom-and-pop com- petitors on price.

Critics lambasted the FTC's decision. They argued that a merger of Staples and Office Depot would pose no danger to consumers. Members of the takeover bar expected the government to settle, es- pecially after Staples agreed to divest sixty-three stores in overlap markets to Office Max.

However, the FTC was not persuaded. The commission argued that the superstore segment of the office supply business represents a market unto itself. A combination of the number one and number two competitors in that narrow niche would be anticompetitive. For support, the FTC relied on a pricing study which showed that Sta- ples charges somewhat higher prices in markets where it lacks a su- perstore competitor. The combination with Office Depot would dramatically increase the number of markets without a second store.

Unlike Rite Aid or Microsoft, Staples decided to fight the FTC. The company and its merger partner went to court to defend the deal. Commentators gave the companies a good chance of prevail- ing, primarily because the government's narrow market definition seemed to fly in the face of reality. The notion that customers would buy a particular group of widely distributed products only from a par- ticular class of stores was relatively novel.

Yet again, the predictions were wrong. On June 30, 1997, federal district judge Thomas Hogan ruled in the government's favor, grant- ing a preliminary injunction blocking the merger. Hogan was per- suaded by the government's pricing studies—largely an analysis of bar-code scanner data from checkout counters—and by evidence that the office superstore chains priced differently in markets with- out another superstore. In addition, there was evidence that Staples and Office Depot thought of each other, and Office Max, as their primary competition.

Within days of this stunning upset, Staples and Office Depot dropped their plan to merge. Arbitrageurs—who had been listening to lawyers predict a Staples victory—lost large sums on their investments. Takeover professionals were left speculating whether the case represented a new dawn of restrictive antitrust enforcement. They took some solace in the FTC's contemporaneous approval of the $14 billion merger of Boeing and McDonnell Douglas Corporation. Meanwhile, Stemberg and Fuente went back to being competitors after having spent months anticipating a deal. Antitrust enforcement was alive and kicking.

Procedural Rules

The subtlety of antitrust is that both procedural and substantive aspects play vital roles. Two branches of government administer the antitrust laws: the Antitrust Division of the Justice Department and the Bureau of Competition of the Federal Trade Commission. The agencies coordinate their activities, with one of the two designated to review each particular transaction.

This bifurcated authority on its face makes no sense, although a host of legal articles solemnly argue that nothing could be more appropriate than some competition in enforcement of antitrust laws. A more sophisticated defense advanced by supporters of antitrust enforcement is that the two existing bodies have more political clout separately than when combined. Reformers have periodically pointed out the inanity of it all—split resources, duplication, lack of coordination and so forth—with no impact, so diffuse government policy in this field probably will remain institutionalized.

Certainly, the Federal Trade Commission is the more colorful of the two branches. The FTC was established in 1914 as an independent regulatory agency to combat the abuses of businesses. Over the years, it has varied from being a vigorous and imaginative enforcement agency to, more often, a phlegmatic repository for political cronies. Every few years, another reform group springs up to salvage the FTC, but the impact of the reports of these groups has historically been fleeting. Recently, however, the FTC has been in a periodic upswing.

As an administrative agency, the FTC brings complaints which have first been recommended by the staff and approved by the commission. Each complaint is heard by one of the FTC's hearings examiners, and the commission as a whole then votes whether to accept or reject the hearing examiner's findings. The decision of the commission can then be appealed in the federal circuit courts.

In theory, by having hearing examiners and commissioners who specialize in the trade regulation field, the FTC should be able to make more sophisticated and better decisions than the courts. This was the cutting edge of economic planning theory circa 1914.

Among the problems in fact is that many of the commissioners and hearing examiners have not been of the highest caliber. In addition, as a system, there is the inherent difficulty of commissioners who decide, on the basis of staff recommendations, whether or not to bring complaints and then later judge the ultimate merits of those actions. Indeed, much of the significant byplay at the FTC occurs at the complaint issuance and settlement level. In antitrust, the art of negotiation is every bit as important as prowess in the courtroom.

Finally, there is the question of timing. Working through the process from complaint to final commission ruling historically has taken years. Recently, the FTC implemented new guidelines designed to speed the process. Under the new fast-track rules, the commission is committed to making a final decision on a complaint within thirteen months. But this new process is untested.

The Antitrust Division, by way of contrast, brings its proceedings through the federal court system. Since the days of the Franklin Roosevelt administration, when Thurman Arnold reinvigorated the division (after the Supreme Court indicated that the president's alternative program of economic regulation, the price-fixing codes of the National Recovery Act, were unconstitutional), the Antitrust Division has generally had the more professional reputation of the two enforcement branches, although at times the FTC has had more populist intent.

Robert Pitofsky

Robert Pitofsky is the man most responsible for reviving the moribund FTC and sparking the revival of antitrust law. Pitofsky took over as chairman in 1995, returning to the agency from a stint in private practice. The former dean of Georgetown University's law school and a Carter administration FTC commissioner, Pitofsky was very helpful years ago when I was part of a Ralph Nader team examining FTC merger policy.

As an academic, Pitofsky developed a reputation for a relatively tough antitrust stance, emphasizing the political importance of antitrust. To Pitofsky, large business entities posed a democratic as well as economic threat that regulators should curb. Media conglomerations were a particular concern because such combinations might put too much power to control the public debate in the hands of a few businesses.

Yet, as chairman, Pitofsky has not taken a uniform "big is bad" position. The FTC has instead adopted a more nuanced— and somewhat confusing—approach. At times, Pitofsky has taken a tough stand against mergers that pose little real anticompetitive threat, while on other occasions he has expressed a willingness to recognize potential efficiency gains as a countervailing justification for some deals.

In fact, Pitofsky is a bundled package of instincts: he is certainly bright and professional; he is a populist by inclination; he

has a romantic faith in the purpose of the FTC as a viable institution guiding America's economic future; and he is an astute politi-
cian whose agenda is pleasing the president.

Pitofsky's political grandstanding was reflected in his challenge of Time Warner's acquisition of Turner Broadcasting. Pitofsky fought hard with the Justice Department to get jurisdiction
over the deal. Having won that battle, the FTC requested box after
box of documents, more than a million pieces of paper. For almost a year, the FTC's staff sorted through all the paperwork and
hemmed and hawed about the deal.

Finally, after long negotiations, the case was settled. Time
Warner agreed to relatively light concessions, which was not surprising since the legal issues were minimal. But Pitofsky could
declare victory and go home. The agreement did cap TCI's ownership in Time Warner, drawing some blood from TCI, at the time
one of the least popular companies in Washington circles. Time
Warner also guaranteed that it would carry an independent all-
news channel on its cable systems. Curiously, though, many of
the requirements of the settlement were already part of the
Telecommunications Act of 1996.

Despite the controversy surrounding the drawn-out Turner
process and subsequent Staples challenge, Pitofsky continues to
take aggressive positions in particular cases while attempting to
find a middle road. He favors allowing U.S. companies to combine if
to do so would allow them to become more competitive in a global
marketplace. Nor has the FTC challenged large defense industry
mergers necessitated by declining government budgets. Moreover,
in 1997, Pitofsky's FTC joined with the Justice Department in endors-
ing new antitrust guidelines that recognize potential efficiencies as
a factor to be considered in reviewing deals, although the substance
of these initiatives is not yet clear.

While Pitofsky has succeeded in raising professional standards at the FTC, the conflicting signals coming from the agency

have made the merger review process a bit of a crapshoot. Even antitrust experts have trouble predicting where the FTC will come down on a particular deal. Of course, that might be precisely the result Pitofsky wants. Uncertainty is a powerful regulatory hurdle for a practical populist.

Reporting Requirements In late 1976, Congress passed the Hart-Scott-Rodino Antitrust Improvements Act. Before the law was passed, two companies could merge without giving the government an opportunity to review the transaction in advance. Rather, the government could analyze and challenge a transaction only after the fact. Because a completed transaction is more difficult to unwind than a proposed transaction, the government was put under considerable pressure to overlook marginally anticompetitive deals. The idea behind the statute was to give the government enough time to review and challenge a proposed deal before it becomes unduly difficult to reverse.

To implement this plan, Hart-Scott-Rodino and the associated regulations require firms involved in substantial acquisitions to file notification forms with both the Federal Trade Commission and the Antitrust Division of the Justice Department. Generally, the parties to an acquisition must file if acquiring $15 million or more in voting stock or assets. The parties must also provide substantial information about the transaction to the government. Substantial penalties—as much as $10,000 per day—may accrue if a company fails to file.

There are four principal exceptions to the filing requirement. First, filing is not required if the acquirer purchases less than 10 percent of the target's voting stock and intends only to be a passive investor. Second, the filing requirement does not apply to the purchase of options, warrants or other securities convertible into voting stock unless the purchase is deemed a device for the avoidance of filing.

Of course, the conversion of the securities into voting stock may trigger a later reporting responsibility. Third, certain acquisitions involving foreign targets or acquirers are also exempt from filing.

Finally, there is a loophole for newly formed partnerships and corporations. A partnership or corporation that has not yet prepared a balance sheet showing $10 million or more of assets need not file. The exception applies only if no single party controls 50 percent or more of the entity, measured by the right to assets or profits. Furthermore, there must be a business purpose for purchasing through the entity, other than just avoidance of the Hart-Scott filing requirement.

After notifying the government of an intended transaction, the parties are subject to a waiting period of thirty days (fifteen days for cash tender offers) before the deal can be consummated. Both companies involved in the deal must file notification forms. In the case of a tender offer, the target company must file a notification form within fifteen days of the acquirer's notice (or within ten days in the case of a cash tender offer). Included in the extensive information required by the notification form are a description of the transaction, all background studies relating to it, detailed product-line breakdowns, a listing of competitors and an analysis of sales patterns.

During the waiting period, the government may ask for additional material and, based on the responses, may request a twenty-day extension (ten days for cash tender offers) of the waiting period from a federal district court. In the event the government reacts adversely to the information it receives, the act sets up a procedure for facilitating the immediate federal court hearing of a preliminary injunction motion.

Implications These technical rules have important implications. The imposition of the $15 million reporting threshold and increased enforcement of the rules have changed the tactical playing field for hostile takeovers. In addition, executives have become wary of overstating the competitive case for a particular transaction and deal documents generally are drafted with an eye toward possible antitrust problems.

The $15 million reporting requirement has been a significant curb on hostile takeovers. During the 1980s, hostile bidders often used the passive investment and partnership exceptions to avoid filing under Hart-Scott. However, the government attacked many of the cases as abusive. As a result, hostile acquirers, particularly strategic acquirers, find it more difficult to secretly build a substantial stake in a company prior to a tender offer. Once the acquirer's interest becomes public knowledge through a Hart-Scott filing, the target's stock price usually jumps. The acquirer therefore has little room for profit if a white knight wins the target or if the target fends off an attack.

In the friendly-deal context, executives often feel pressured to overstate the case for a particular transaction, both internally and externally. Internally, certain executives may be in a position of lobbying ultimate decision makers, and in the process, may be tempted to use unrealistic superlatives to describe the potential benefits. Likewise, externally, an acquirer has an incentive to convince investors that a transaction is worthwhile.

Through the antitrust filing process, the government gains access to a great deal of information, including internal memos written by people who never thought their words would see the light of day. The result can be a classic smoking gun document.

For example, Microsoft's 1994 deal to merge with Intuit Corporation is a classic story of the self-inflicted wound. The deal followed closely on the heels of an antitrust settlement between Microsoft and the Justice Department. This settlement—which was the product of four years of haggling between Microsoft and Justice—was roundly criticized by Microsoft's competitors as too soft. So when Microsoft announced the Intuit deal, the Justice Department faced political pressure to toughen up.

Unfortunately for Microsoft, as part of their review, Justice Department officials came across several unfavorable documents. Naturally, the government became fond of quoting Scott Wood, Intuit's chief executive officer, who referred to Microsoft as "Godzilla" in internal memos. According to the government, Wood also predicted in writing that the combination of Microsoft and Intuit would leave financial institutions "one clear option" for financial software and would eliminate a "bloody [market] share war."

In a separate memo also cited by the government, a Microsoft executive wrote, "as a combination, [Intuit and Microsoft] would be dominant." Relying on these statements and more substantive arguments, the Justice Department challenged the Microsoft-Intuit transaction. Shortly thereafter, the deal collapsed. The lesson is that, even in internal, preliminary documents, salesmanship must be tempered with realism so that any materials that end up with the government present a balanced picture.

With regard to deal documents, the problems faced by Jimmy Ling demonstrate the importance of including what's known as an "antitrust out." Reacting in part to the howls of the other large steel manufacturers, the Justice Department challenged LTV's 1968 takeover of Jones & Laughlin, a large but sluggish steel company. Pending determination of the suit, LTV was not allowed to exercise control over J&L, tying up vast amounts of cash in J&L stock without offsetting cash flow from dividends. The LTV house of cards then began to topple. Cash to pay interest on LTV's pyramid of securities became scarce; everything was tied up in J&L. Finally, a negotiated settlement was reached with the Justice Department. LTV agreed to spin off some other subsidiaries but kept J&L. It was, however, too late; the time delay brought about the eventual downfall of Ling.

This kind of antitrust proceeding can be incredibly expensive, basically because it consumes so much time. Of course, if the transaction or the challenge to it is terminated at the preliminary injunction stage, the costs, though high, are not stunning because the time involved is limited. But disputes are not necessarily resolved at this level. For example, the FTC or Justice Department is perfectly free to challenge a merger after the notification period has run and the deal has been consummated. If fully litigated, a government merger suit can take eight to ten years to be finally resolved. Expense, however, cannot be thought of merely in terms of legal bills. The drain on management time and energy can dwarf those fees. In addition, if a private suit is brought, there is also the possibility of having to pay treble damages.

Antitrust litigation may result in the loss of corporate flexibility while the suit continues. Even assuming the lack of injunctions, it is difficult for a firm to do the most elementary planning when its asset structure is seriously in doubt. Furthermore, investors and creditors will naturally reflect the ambiguity of the situation in their decisions.

Although the risks are substantial, they can be exaggerated. First, even if sued, a company may well settle the case without a significant divestiture, or it may win in court. Even if an acquisition is lost after a suit, much of the economic benefit of a good investment will have accrued, and, probably, a sizable profit can be made on resale. Second, not that many suits are actually brought. So a theoretical antitrust problem may not be a real litigation risk.

However, given the uncertainty surrounding most antitrust issues, an acquirer typically demands that transaction documents contain a provision that allows the acquirer to pull out of the deal if it is challenged. Of course, a seller will attempt to limit the scope of this provision, which can be of varying strength. At the most pro-buyer extreme, the purchase agreement might give the buyer the right to scuttle a deal if an antitrust challenge is even threatened. The most pro-seller extreme would be to require the deal to go forward regardless of a challenge. An intermediate approach would allow the buyer to pull out in the presence of an adverse injunction or ruling.

In addition to negotiating an antitrust provision in the deal documents, an acquirer should be prepared to spend considerable time and energy on the review process. Like DuPont, an acquirer should not treat the review process as a black box that will take care of itself. Rather, the acquirer should seek to create an ongoing negotiation with the reviewing agency.

An alternative to the whole process under Hart-Scott-Rodino is for the parties to a deal to negotiate a voluntary settlement with the government. Such settlements typically are reached during the review process. The government then files a complaint together with a proposed consent decree. Though a consent decree must be approved by a federal judge, the court in most cases merely validates the terms of the existing agreement.

The government typically either requires the merging parties to divest overlapping businesses or restrict potentially anticompetitive conduct. So, for example, in the recent Time Warner–Turner consent decree, the government required the combined entity to guarantee competitors access to its cable systems. Understandably, buyers who are risk-averse often prefer to seek a consent decree rather than face a challenge. Otherwise, they bear the risk that one day after the deal is consummated, the acquisition will be challenged.

PROFILE

Robert Joffe

Bob Joffe, a partner at law firm Cravath, Swaine & Moore, is a master of the complicated antitrust process for mergers. Joffe has distinguished himself as an adept, smooth courtroom presence with an effective behind-the-scenes negotiating style. He has been selected to take over as Cravath's presiding partner when Sam Butler retires at the end of 1998.

Joffe graduated from Harvard Law School in 1966. He spent the next two years on a fellowship in the newly independent

African nation of Malawi, where his responsibilities included helping the country rewrite its laws. Joffe then joined Cravath in 1969.

Very quickly, Joffe gravitated toward antitrust matters. He
proved himself working on drawn-out cases for Kellogg and Westinghouse. By 1978, he was a partner at the firm and began to develop a relationship that would define much of his career. The
client was Time Inc.'s HBO subsidiary.

In 1980, four movie studios teamed up with Getty Oil to
launch a cable channel called Premiere. As part of the venture,
the studios agreed not to license their films to HBO. If allowed to
stand, the arrangement would have given Premiere a distinct
competitive advantage over HBO. Joffe convinced the government
that this constituted unacceptable anticompetitive behavior. The
Justice Department sued and Premiere fell apart.

Joffe's Premiere victory sealed his relationship with HBO.
Soon, he grew into the lead antitrust litigator for all of Time. In
1989, another triumph—largely outside the field of antitrust—
propelled Joffe to even greater prominence. The merger of Time
and Warner was the focus of action. First, Joffe successfully shepherded the deal through the Justice Department's antitrust review. Then, when Paramount tried to bust the deal apart, Joffe
teamed up with Herb Wachtell to defend the deal.

In a hearing broadcast live on CNN, Joffe made a widely ac-
claimed presentation defending the authority of Time's board to
make a strategic decision and stick to it. Of course, Time won the
case, and the deal was done.

Though less heralded, Joffe won another victory in 1996, when
he negotiated the settlement with the FTC that allowed the Time
Warner–Turner deal to proceed. At the outset, Joffe faced a
thicket of problems. The FTC's Pitofsky had an expressed concern
about large media deals. The Turner acquisition, bringing together two of the largest cable channel operators, one of which

(Time Warner) is also a major cable system operator, was just the kind of deal to excite Pitofsky.

TCI's partial ownership of Turner Broadcasting only exacerbated the situation. John Malone has a long history of run-ins with federal antitrust regulators. Not only was the government predisposed against TCI, but the combination arguably would give TCI an incentive to favor Time Warner–Turner channels on its cable systems.

On top of this, Time Warner's Jerry Levin publicly promised that the Turner deal would go through, putting pressure on Joffe to deliver. In addition, the terms of Malone's deal with Ted Turner allowed him to veto any settlement Joffe might negotiate with the government.

The process began with the Hart-Scott-Rodino filing and subsequent information requests. Joffe quarterbacked a huge document-review process. When the FTC expressed reservations about the deal, he opened negotiations on a settlement. The process dragged on for months. Joffe laid out an assertive position—he had a strong case and would go to court if need be. Time Warner was willing to work with the FTC, but would only go so far to settle. The trick, according to Joffe, is to "draw a line in the sand" only where a strong legal foundation exists for the position.

The approach paid off. Three days before the FTC was scheduled to vote on the deal, the government blinked. Time Warner and the FTC reached a settlement that amounted to a win for Joffe and his client but also allowed the FTC's Pitofsky to declare victory.

The Substantive Law

While procedural rules are important, the actual teeth of antitrust resides in the substantive law. Antitrust is probably one of the most uncertain areas of the law, and, therefore, one of the most frustrating to corporate executives. In the merger field, there are few bright-line rules, only guidelines from precedents.

For legal purposes, mergers are analyzed in three categories: horizontal (between competitors), vertical (between customers and suppliers) and conglomerate (between firms in unrelated industries). The law is most developed in the horizontal area and most uncertain as applied to conglomerates. However, because conglomerate mergers are relatively rare, most of the interplay surrounds horizontal and vertical deals.

In all three cases, Section 7 of the Clayton Act is the starting point for antitrust analysis. As amended by the Celler-Kefauver Act of 1950, Section 7 provides that "no corporation . . . shall acquire, directly or indirectly, the whole or any part of the stock . . . [or] the whole or any part of the assets of another corporation . . . where in any line of commerce in any section of the country the effect of such acquisition may be substantially to lessen competition, or to tend to create a monopoly."

In examining any merger, the scope of the relevant market must be defined both geographically and by product. The answer to this threshold question is often critical, as was demonstrated in the Staples–Office Depot case. Procter & Gamble's 1991 acquisition of Max Factor provides another example. Prior to the transaction, Procter & Gamble's Cover Girl—America's leading brand of mass-market cosmetics—controlled 23 percent of the mass cosmetics market. Max Factor had roughly 7 percent of the mass market.

So, in one sense, the deal concentrated the market, arguably reducing competition. However, the market can also be defined more broadly. If one includes cosmetics sold through department stores such as Estée Lauder, and direct sale products like Avon, the market shares plunge. Inevitably, market definition, therefore, involves a complex, multifactor inquiry. When the government embraced a broader definition, the deal sailed through.

Horizontal Mergers   The history of court decisions on horizontal deals is one of a movement during the 1960s and 1970s toward a tough quantitative test of illegality followed by the relaxation of that test in the 1980s and 1990s.

The early, quantitative approach to market definition began with the first major case decided by the U.S. Supreme Court under the amended Section 7, *Brown Shoe*. The case involved the merger of the Brown and Kinney shoe chains. Although the Court in its 1962 decision considered many factors, there was a primary emphasis on market share in the analysis of the impact of the merger at the horizontal level among competing retail branches. Significantly, the Court seemed to indicate that even a 5 percent level of market control after a merger could, under certain circumstances, be regarded as anticompetitive.

In its 1963 decision in *Philadelphia National Bank*, the Supreme Court went a step beyond *Brown Shoe* and articulated a presumption that high market shares resulting from a merger will reduce competition. The Court held that such an increase in concentration would be enjoined in the absence of evidence clearly showing the merger was not likely to have anticompetitive effects. *Brown* and *Philadelphia National Bank* were breakthrough cases because the Court spurned the "rule of reason," an analysis that considered and balanced all pertinent factors, and instead accepted the advantage of a bright-line presumption. The Court rejected the rule-of-reason approach in *Philadelphia National Bank* on the theory that permitting too broad an economic investigation would defeat the congressional intent of limiting the increase in concentration.

After *Philadelphia National Bank*, and until recently, courts became increasingly specific about what would be considered unacceptable concentration levels. In the 1964 *Alcoa-Rome* decision, the Court firmly established the principle hinted at in *Philadelphia National Bank*: in a concentrated industry even slight increases in market share may be considered illegal. Thus, Alcoa's acquisition of

Rome was deemed in violation of Section 7, even though it added only 1.3 percent to Alcoa's approximately 28 percent control of the national aluminum conductor market. A later appeals court case, *Stanley Works*, established the converse proposition: a firm with 1 percent market share could not acquire the leading firm with 24 percent of the market.

In *Von's Grocery*, the Supreme Court in 1966 expanded the *Philadelphia National Bank* quantitative standard to firms with relatively small market shares if the industry was exhibiting a trend toward concentration. Noting that the number of single-store groceries was declining in the Los Angeles area, the Court held that a merger resulting in a firm with a total of 7.5 percent of the Los Angeles market was illegal.

However, in more recent times, both the courts and the enforcement agencies have relaxed their tough quantitative approach to merger policy. While the courts continue to enjoin mergers on the basis of a projected increase in market share, they tend to do so only in cases where the existing market shares and the impact of the merger on concentration are considerable. Otherwise, courts have given increasing weight to evidence that merged firms will be unable to raise prices even though they may have an increased market share. This evidence generally relates to ease of market entry or projected efficiencies from the proposed merger.

The ease of entry into a defined market is important because firms will be less able to raise prices if new competitors can easily enter the market. For example, in *United States v. Gillette Co.*, a lower court in 1993 refused to enjoin the merger of two fountain pen manufacturers. The court reasoned that the combined entity would be unable to raise prices. This conclusion rested on a finding that the relevant manufacturing technology was readily available to potential competitors and no regulatory or legal barriers barred potential entrants from the market. Thus, no significant barriers to entry existed.

In other cases, courts have identified the following as potential barriers to entry: high capital expenditures, large sunk costs, long lead time, a large minimum scale for efficient production, the need for specialized knowledge or technology, regulatory barriers and brand loyalty.

Although early Supreme Court cases, including *Philadelphia National Bank* and *Brown Shoe*, imply that efficiencies should not be taken into account when analyzing a prospective merger, recent lower court decisions nonetheless have considered potential efficiencies. However, no court has relied solely on efficiency arguments to support the legality of a merger. On the contrary, courts have required strong evidence that proffered efficiencies will materialize and that such efficiencies could not be achieved by some means short of merger.

HORIZONTAL MERGERS — GOVERNMENT GUIDELINES   In the early days of the Clinton administration, joint guidelines were issued as to which mergers were likely to be challenged by the Justice Department and the Federal Trade Commission. Although they are not definitive, the guidelines do give a rough feel for the antitrust problems involved in a merger.

The calculation of a projected post-merger market share—based on either the total sales or the production capacity of all market participants—is the starting point for analysis under the guidelines. Both existing market concentration and the extent to which concentration will increase after a merger are stated in terms of something called the Herfindahl-Hirschman Index. The formula was selected as a measure of market concentration in part because it weighs firms with large market shares more heavily and is more sensitive to increases in the size differences between firms. To achieve rough justice to this concept, the post-merger market shares of the market participants are squared and then added up. This, in effect, gives extra weight to large market shares.

So, for example, under a pure market share approach, three companies with a combined 45 percent market share, split evenly, would be treated the same as three companies with a combined 45 percent share where one company had 43 percent and the other two had 1 percent each. The Herfindahl Index distinguishes between the two cases. In the first situation, the index would total 675 (15^2 times three); in the second situation, 1,851 ($43^2 + 1^2 + 1^2$). This attempt at high science is obviously, in fact, quite primitive, but it is important to be in on the jargon.

The guidelines indicate that a separate index will be calculated for each market in which either of the merging companies participates, both pre- and post-merger. The guidelines then provide the following decision rubric:

Post-Merger Market Concentration	Ordinarily Not Subject to Review	Potentially Anticompetitive	Presumed Anticompetitive
Unconcentrated (HHI<1,000)	Yes	N/A	N/A
Moderately concentrated (HHI between 1,000 and 1,800)	HHI increases less than 100 points	HHI increases more than 100 points	N/A
Highly concentrated (HHI>1,800)	HHI increases less than 50 points	HHI increases between 50 and 100 points	HHI increases more than 100 points

As the next step under the guidelines, the reviewing agency will conduct a broad analysis of a particular merger's anticompetitive effect. The guidelines describe two basic concerns. First, a merger may make coordinated interaction, such as price fixing, more likely or more successful. Second, a merger may create market conditions that allow participants to benefit from anticompetitive unilateral action such as raising prices.

Finally, the guidelines allow ease of entry and efficiency to counterbalance other negative merger effects. With regard to ease of entry, the guidelines provide three factors that will be considered: the timeliness of entry, the likelihood of entry and the sufficiency of entry. The efficiency analysis is free-ranging, but the guidelines indicate the government generally will reject claims of efficiencies if comparable savings could be achieved by some means short of a merger. Efficiency claims also must be substantiated.

HORIZONTAL MERGERS — MARKET DEFINITION   With the focus on market shares and the index, product and geographic market definitions are critical in the determination of the legality of a merger. *Brown Shoe* defines a product market as follows: "The outer boundaries of a product market are determined by the reasonable interchangeability of use or the cross-elasticity of demand between the product itself and substitutes for it."

The cross-elasticity of demand between two products posits a change in the price of one product and measures the impact on demand for the other product, whether one product would, in fact, be substituted for another.

With respect to geographic markets, the Supreme Court adopted a "pragmatic, factual approach" in *Brown Shoe*. Moreover, in that case, the Court indicated that every city with a population of 10,000 might be considered a geographic market. Subsequent decisions have split as to whether a particular small town fit the "section of the country" standard in Section 7, but the general principle remains true that geographic markets may be determined on quite a localized level.

More generally, in *Philadelphia National Bank*, the Supreme Court defined a geographic product market as "the 'area of effective competition . . . in which the seller operates, and to which the purchaser can practicably turn for supplies.'" Lower courts have identified a number of factors relevant to this inquiry: actual sales patterns (i.e., localized versus national), transportation cost, regulatory barriers and industry practice. As with product markets, the guidelines repeat the "small but significant" price increase analysis to define geographic markets.

In the case of both product and geographic markets, the courts have broken broad product categories down into more narrow submarkets. Starting with *Brown Shoe,* the Supreme Court indicated that in defining submarkets it would consider as important factors industry or public recognition of a submarket as an independent economic entity and the product's characteristics such as uses, required production facilities, customers and sensitivity to price changes in competing products. Thus, the Court in *Brown Shoe* held that there were separate submarkets in men's, women's and children's shoes; in *Alcoa-Rome,* aluminum and copper cable were treated distinctly; and in *Clorox,* household liquid bleach was deemed to be a product with no close substitutes.

Some federal lower courts have in the past extended the Court's narrow interpretations of markets even further: for example, florist aluminum foil has been recognized as distinct from other lines of aluminum foil, and paper-insulated power cable has been deemed different from other cables. Recently, however, some courts have examined more seriously assertions of cross-elasticity—that the supply, demand and pricing of one product, such as oil supplied to utilities, is necessarily related to the marketing of another product, such as coal.

However, despite some broadening of the definition of product and geographic markets, and the application of less strict quantitative standards, all in all, horizontal mergers are still judged by fairly tough criteria.

Lately, the government has advanced a so-called differentiated products theory to define markets. This was the theory used in *Staples* to limit the relevant market to just office superstores. Under the theory, merging companies are in the same market if a significant percentage of their customers would not switch suppliers in the face of a small but significant price increase.

The real-world impact of this theory was seen in *Staples:* narrow market definitions tailored to the parties in a deal. Once a narrow market is defined, a deal will significantly concentrate that market, almost by default.

Only time will tell whether the differentiated products theory gains widespread acceptance in the courts. However, in the modern regional, national and global economy these narrow definitions of market and of potential competition are increasingly archaic. Decades from now, the standards will become more sophisticated. The new reality of international trade is a looming presence over the 1950s world of antitrust market definitions.

Vertical Mergers   The law covering vertical mergers has undergone considerable change in recent years. Initially, the basic concern of the courts in vertical mergers was that an acquisition by a supplier of an outlet for its products would foreclose the supplier's competitors from a segment of the market.

Over the years, the line of cases on vertical transactions has evolved multiple criteria to determine whether a particular vertical merger potentially forecloses competition. The *Brown Shoe* decision itself stated that the size and nature of the market foreclosed to competitors by a supplier acquiring a customer was a significant but not dispositive factor in evaluating the legality of a vertical merger. Trends, the actual economic effect on competitors, the barriers to new entries, all should be considered in vertical integration situations, according to the *Brown Shoe* Court.

More recently, both courts and the Justice Department have reversed field somewhat and questioned the fundamental notion that vertical mergers are in fact anticompetitive. Several courts have highlighted the potential efficiency gains from a vertical combination and have rejected the idea that market foreclosure leads to increased market power. Picking up on this trend, the 1982 guidelines, which still govern vertical mergers, state that the Justice Department is unlikely to challenge a vertical merger unless the relevant market is highly concentrated (i.e., has an index above 1,800).

Following these standards, the government challenged relatively few vertical mergers during the Reagan-Bush years. However, the Clinton administration has demonstrated renewed concern about vertical mergers. Three major vertical telecommunications acquisitions were challenged by the Clinton administration in 1994: the AT&T–McCaw Cellular deal, the British Telecommunications–MCI deal and the TCI–Liberty Media deal. All three challenges resulted in agreements between the parties and the government designed to address potential anticompetitive effects. The message seems to be that vertical deals are permissible if the government can claim some concessions.

Conglomerate Mergers   The most vexing area of merger law concerns conglomerate deals. Piercing through the rhetoric of the cases, one key area of concern is simply the overall tendency toward economic concentration. Unfortunately for the sake of clarity, neither the statutes nor the cases explicitly cope with this problem; there is no clear legal basis for a position that bigness or overall concentration is per se bad. Instead, the few early cases overturning conglomerate transactions relied on two perceived problems: first, conglomerate mergers can entrench the position of a dominant firm, and second, conglomerate mergers create the opportunity for reciprocal dealing between business units.

Perhaps the leading case in the conglomerate field is the Supreme Court's 1967 *Clorox* decision. Clorox had some 48 percent of the national sales market for liquid bleach and was acquired by the nation's largest advertiser, Procter & Gamble. The Court found that Clorox had largely achieved its dominant position through advertising, since, in fact, liquid bleaches were chemically identical.

Holding that the acquisition was illegal, the Court reasoned it was more likely that potential new entrants to the market would be dissuaded from entering the bleach business and smaller competitors would fear to compete if Procter & Gamble kept Clorox than if Clorox remained independent. Furthermore, Procter & Gamble was regarded as the most likely potential entrant into the market, and the Court felt that this loss of potential competition exacerbated the entrenchment of Clorox's position. Procter & Gamble was therefore ordered to divest Clorox. Yet years later it was allowed to buy Max Factor with no challenge.

The 1965 *Consolidated Foods* decision is the leading reciprocity case. In *Consolidated*, the Supreme Court held that the acquisition by Consolidated, a wholesale and retail food marketer, of Gentry, a garlic and onion powder supplier, was illegal. The Court reasoned that buyers of garlic and onion in the food-processing business would favor Gentry in order to spur their sales to Consolidated, reinforcing Gentry's leading role in the market.

However, recently, conglomerate mergers have received little attention, perhaps because such mergers are no longer as fashionable and the implicit recognition is that the legal case against them was thin. The guidelines make no mention of conglomerate mergers.

Special Situations

The Failing Company   Although the guidelines clearly state that the economics of a transaction will not ordinarily be considered in evaluating a merger, there is one exception: the failing company doctrine. If a target company is clearly failing with no reasonable prospect of remaining viable and no offer of acquisition has come from a noncompetitor, the government may forgo a challenge to a deal it might otherwise attack.

This appears to have been one reason for the light review given to the Boeing–McDonnell Douglas merger of 1997. McDonnell Douglas had been routed by Boeing and Airbus in the commercial aircraft market. Though not on the verge of failing, the downward trend in this key overlap market made approval easier.

Private Suits   Under Section 16 of the Clayton Act, private parties are entitled to sue under Section 7 and recover treble damages.

Recently, private claims have become popular in defense of tender offers. Courts have questioned, however, whether competitors or target companies have standing to sue. Standing requires an antitrust injury, and the Supreme Court has emphasized that competitors often benefit from an anticompetitive merger, but litigators like the tactic anyway.

Cross-Border Deals

When a merger or acquisition crosses international boundaries, new layers of antitrust complexity result. The merger review processes of countries other than the United States may be implicated. Of course, the rules vary from jurisdiction to jurisdiction. Generalizations are difficult. However, a review of merger policy in Japan and Europe—the two most active sources of cross-border deals with a U.S. component—gives a flavor for the variations.

Japan The Japanese antitrust framework, created in the aftermath of World War II, was consciously modeled on the U.S. system but has evolved to include a few key differences. As in the United States, the parties to a merger must get consent from the Japanese equivalent of the FTC. A filing is required and the government initially has thirty days to review the antitrust implications of a planned merger. The period can be extended by another sixty days if required.

One of the differences between the Japanese and U.S. antitrust treatment involves stock purchases. In the United States, no distinction is made between mergers and stock purchases—both require a Hart-Scott filing. However, in Japan, the acquisition of shares is not reviewed in advance. The government will provide guidance but is rarely definitive before the purchase takes place. Essentially, the feeling is that a stock purchase can be easily unwound after the fact, making advance review unnecessary. After a stock purchase takes place, the government has ninety days to raise an antitrust challenge.

Substantively, the Japanese antitrust regulators focus on market share as the touchstone of their analysis. The basic rule of thumb is that a combined market share below 25 percent is acceptable. A market share above that threshold is not automatically disallowed but will draw more careful scrutiny.

This focus on market share makes the question of market definition crucial. Obviously, the larger the relevant market, the less likely there will be problems. Acquirers try to broaden the analysis to include somewhat similar products and international markets. Boxes of data are reviewed by the Japanese FTC. Ultimately, most deals above the 25 percent threshold come down to a negotiation between the parties and the government, and, as in the United States, the parties and the government reach a compromise.

Europe   The European antitrust regulation is a patchwork of an overarching European Union regulation and the various rules of individual states. However, most large cross-border deals are picked up under the EU Merger Regulation.

The EU Merger Regulation gives the European Commission exclusive authority to review the antitrust implications of deals with a "Community dimension." A merger or acquisition has a Community dimension if the aggregate worldwide sales of the resulting entity exceed roughly $4.5 billion per year and the aggregate EU sales of the parties, taken individually, each exceed $250 million. These rules will be expanded in 1998 to pick up certain smaller deals. However, a transaction is not covered if each party generates over two thirds of its Community revenues in a single country. A deal that impacts the "legitimate interests" of an EU country, such as national security or media diversity, may also be referred to the country's antitrust authorities.

As in the United States, the parties to a deal covered by the EU Merger Regulation must notify the EU's minister of competition before proceeding. A three-week waiting period is imposed, with a possibility for extension. The commission must decide whether to open an investigation within one month of receiving the notification, and must decide within five months whether to approve the deal.

The EU's standard of review is whether a deal is "compatible" with the European common market. A deal is incompatible if it would "create or strengthen a dominant position as a result of which effective competition would be significantly impeded in the common market or in a substantial part of it." The EU's antitrust case law is relatively underdeveloped but the commission seems to conduct a wide-ranging contextual economic analysis. With some notable exceptions, few deals have been challenged by the EU antitrust authority to date.

CORPORATE DIPLOMACY

The Boeing–McDonnell Douglas Deal

Over the past two decades, many industries have become global in focus and international in scope. As a result, international merger rules can be implicated even in a deal involving two "U.S." companies. This new reality was dramatically demonstrated in 1997 when the European Union challenged Boeing's plan to acquire McDonnell Douglas.

Boeing and McDonnell Douglas announced their $14 billion stock merger in December 1996. The deal was part of the wider post–Cold War implosion of the defense industry. Yet the concentration of the U.S. defense industry was not the main concern for EU regulators. The commercial aviation market was the real focus. The business has been dominated by three companies—Boeing, McDonnell Douglas and Europe's Airbus consortium. In 1996, Boeing captured roughly 65 percent of the market for commercial jets, Airbus 31 percent and McDonnell Douglas 4 percent.

Standing alone, the Boeing deal posed little realistic threat to Airbus. McDonnell Douglas already was a troubled competitor relegated to the margins of the commercial market. There was some question whether its effort would continue. However, the deal coincided with a new aggressive Boeing marketing campaign which had already raised European hackles. In the space of a few months, Boeing tied up long-term exclusive contracts with American Airlines and Delta Air Lines. Negotiations continued on a similar deal with Continental Airlines. These deals threatened to close Airbus out of the lucrative U.S. market for twenty years.

EU competition commissioner Karel Van Miert branded the Boeing–McDonnell Douglas deal as "totally unacceptable" under the European merger regulation. Despite howls from Boeing, the EU issued a "statement of objections" on May 21. Van Miert promised to block the deal unless concessions were made. He backed up the threat by pointing to a treaty that gives the EU the authority to block a deal where it finds "an abuse of market position." If Boeing had flouted the EU's concerns, Van Miert could have imposed fines of up to 10 percent of the combined companies' annual revenues, or $4 billion. The EU could seize Boeing planes in Europe to enforce any fine.

Boeing initially talked tough, calling the EU's antitrust position an inappropriate attempt to extend its reach outside the borders of its territory. President Clinton and other U.S. politicians lobbied for the deal. However, eventually Boeing settled the controversy rather than get sidetracked with an extended controversy.

The company agreed to forgo enforcement of the exclusive contracts with American Airlines and Delta Air Lines, and to keep Douglas Aircraft as a separate unit. But the contracts themselves were kept in place. As a result, the airlines had large outstanding orders with Boeing but could theoretically also purchase planes from other suppliers. The general expectation in the marketplace was that Boeing's relationship with the airlines would continue on an exclusive basis even without the exclusivity clause.

Of course, the subtext for the Boeing controversy was the ongoing struggle between the United States and Europe over the relative competitive positions of their state-supported aerospace companies. Still, the flare-up demonstrated the growing importance of international antitrust policy even for what might be thought of as purely domestic transactions.

Regulated Industries

Antitrust is not the only regulatory framework that is relevant to mergers. An array of U.S. federal agencies govern regulated industries such as broadcast communications and commercial banking. In each case, an agency is typically responsible both for ongoing oversight and for approval of any corporate combinations. The ostensible overlap of these other regulatory frameworks and the antitrust law raises two questions. First, with respect to the various regulated industries, there is the question of which agency or agencies have the authority to review a merger. Second, there is the question of what standard applies to the review of a merger in each particular industry.

Generally speaking, the existence of an industry-specific regulatory framework does not exempt industry participants from the antitrust laws. In rare cases, however, Congress has exempted a specific industry from antitrust oversight, supplanting an alternative framework. Rail mergers, for example, are subject to the exclusive supervision of the Surface Transportation Board (formerly the Interstate Commerce Commission).

The standards used in considering mergers generally mirror the statutory antitrust provisions. However, regulatory bodies are often specifically granted more flexibility to consider factors other than competitive effects in analyzing a proposed transaction.

Defense Industry   Over the past five years, the defense industry has gone through a domino-toppling consolidation, one deal after the next. More than $75 billion in defense-related transactions have taken place since 1992. Two factors triggered the sudden rush. The end of the Cold War brought defense cutbacks. As opportunities for revenue growth narrowed, cost savings became the critical profit driver. Then, in 1993, the new Clinton administration began to help matters along with relaxed antitrust review for defense deals and the consolidation began in earnest.

Lately, the defense merger wave has accelerated as the remaining properties dwindled. Lockheed and Martin Marietta joined in a 1995 merger agreement. The next year, the new company bought most of Loral for $7 billion. Boeing acquired the defense and aerospace businesses of Rockwell International. Raytheon bought the defense assets of Hughes Electronics and Texas Instruments for a combined $8 billion.

A contest developed between Boeing and Lockheed, each racing to be the largest defense contractor. Boeing's $13.3 billion deal for McDonnell Douglas raised the stakes. In July 1997, Lockheed followed with its own $11.6 billion Northrop Grumman acquisition.

The Pentagon played an active, behind-the-scenes role in bringing these deals together. In fact, the government actually agreed to pay part of the costs of consolidation on the theory that the government would benefit from cost reductions and should encourage the process. Lockheed Martin, for example, is set to receive about $1 billion in reimbursements related to the merger that created the company.

Government inducements in favor of consolidation have not been limited to the economic. The antitrust review process has played a part. Technically, defense mergers are governed by the antitrust laws and are subject to Hart-Scott review. However, from a practical standpoint, both the FTC and the Justice Department essentially have deferred to the Pentagon's view on many of the recent transactions. The Defense Department view was that a market with two or three strong contractors would generate more active, productive competition than a market with five or ten weaker contractors. Besides, in a world of declining budgets, there seemed to be little choice. Less defense infrastructure could be supported, and mergers are an effective way to squeeze out costs and redundancy.

Antitrust review of the defense industry is, therefore, rather cutting-edge. The major focus has been on costs and efficiency, with an undercurrent of political concern for layoffs. Transactions that the government might challenge in other sectors have passed muster largely because the government is paying the bills and any cost savings have a tangible political benefit.

Banks and Bank Holding Companies Banks are subject to both Section 7 and regulatory agency oversight. In reaction to the *Philadelphia National Bank* decision, Congress passed the Bank Merger Act of 1966, which, aside from legalizing past bank mergers, mandated that any merger not challenged by the attorney general within thirty days of its approval by the pertinent regulatory agency could not be challenged under Section 7. In addition, the 1966 act also stated that anticompetitive effects could be outweighed by a finding that the deal meets the "convenience and needs" of the community to be served. However, this defense is not applicable to the acquisition by banks of nonbanking businesses.

Three different agencies review banking mergers, depending on the parties involved. The comptroller of the currency has responsibility for transactions where the "acquiring, assuming or resulting bank" is a national bank. The Federal Deposit Insurance Corporation oversees mergers where the acquiring or resulting bank will be a federally insured state-chartered bank that operates outside the Federal Reserve System. Finally, the Board of Governors of the Federal Reserve System reviews transactions where the acquiring or resulting bank will be a state bank within the Federal Reserve System.

In all three cases, the relevant agency conducts its own review, but also considers a review provided by the Justice Department. The

Justice Department applies a slightly modified Herfindahl Index to bank mergers. Under this rubric, the Justice Department generally will not oppose a bank merger unless it results in an index over 1,800 and an increase of more than 200. Notwithstanding this input from the Justice Department, the parties involved in a transaction covered by the Bank Merger Act are not required to file notifications under Hart-Scott-Rodino.

Railroads   Railroad mergers are governed by the Surface Transportation Board, which is the direct descendant of the now defunct Interstate Commerce Commission. Under the ICC Termination Act of 1995, a transaction approved by the STB is exempt from the antitrust laws. The STB applies a multifactor test to determine whether a specific transaction should be approved. In particular, the STB at least will consider the five factors laid out in the act. They are:

- The effect of the proposed transaction on the adequacy of transportation to the public;
- The effect on the public interest of including, or failing to include, other rail carriers in the area involved in the proposed transaction;
- The total fixed charges that result from the proposed transaction;
- The interest of rail carrier employees affected by the proposed transaction; and
- Whether the proposed transaction would have an adverse effect on competition among rail carriers in the affected region or in the national rail system.

The fundamental question considered by the STB is whether the combination is "consistent with the public interest."

In exchange for approving a transaction, the STB may also impose conditions. Examples provided in the statute include the divestiture of parallel tracks or the granting of track access to competitors. When faced with conditions, the parties to a transaction may either accede or may forgo the deal. Hence, an interplay between the parties and the STB may result, with a negotiated settlement the outcome.

Despite the exclusive grant of authority to the STB, the Justice Department is not shut out of the review process. Rather, the parties and the STB must file notices with the Justice Department, which is given an opportunity to contest a deal at STB hearings. Standard antitrust principles therefore do carry some weight. Objections from the Justice Department are not, however, decisive, as was seen in the case of the Union Pacific–Southern Pacific merger. The combination of the two Western railroads was strongly and publicly opposed by officials from the Antitrust Division of the Justice Department. Even so, the STB approved the deal.

THE GOLDEN SPIKE

As the referee of railroad takeover fights, the STB has tremendous power to shape outcomes. The saga of the consolidation of the railroads has been part of American economic life since the Civil War. Finally, the country is on the edge of the creation of two national systems, in effect, designed by the STB.

The epic saga again flared publicly in October 1996 when our client CSX agreed to merge with Conrail. Under the terms of the original deal, CSX offered $92.50 in cash for 40 percent of Conrail and stock for the remainder. Less than a week later, Norfolk Southern declared war, launching a rival all-cash bid of $100 per share.

Reminiscent of Vanderbilt's pursuit of the Erie, the Conrail fight featured the three major East Coast roads. Conrail—in fact, a direct descendant of the Erie—was formed in 1973 out of the wreckage of the Penn Central bankruptcy. To ensure its health, the railroad was given a stranglehold on the valuable Northeastern market. Both CSX and Norfolk Southern saw parts of Conrail as the vital piece needed to form a competitive rail network.

Conrail had talked with both roads over a period of years about potential combinations, and CSX and Norfolk had extensive negotiations with each other. Essentially, CSX wanted the old New York Central and Norfolk wanted the old Pennsy plus half of the New York Central. Conrail wanted to stay in one piece.

CSX got the jump on Norfolk by persuading Conrail chairman David LeVan and the Conrail board that a deal with CSX offered greater benefits. CSX chairman John Snow had built a first-class network throughout the Southeast and Midwest. A combination of CSX and Conrail made strategic sense in a world of multiple transportation alternatives. Together, the two companies could offer shippers one-stop shopping for transportation services over a wider geographic region. Equally important, John Snow also promised to keep the company's headquarters in Philadelphia and minimize layoffs of Conrail employees. Although CSX was willing to split Conrail, neither Norfolk nor Conrail would do it in the manner CSX desired.

Knowing Norfolk Southern was a potential suitor, Snow and LeVan wanted a tight deal with strong breakup protections. We were brought in along with Marty Lipton to help package the deal. Conrail already had a poison pill in place. A $300 million breakup fee was added in the merger agreement, and Conrail granted CSX stock options at $92.50 a share. Finally, Conrail and CSX agreed to a no-shop provision under which neither side could talk to other potential merger partners.

Of course, these strong deal protections were subject to court challenge. But, based on Wachtell, Lipton's review of Pennsylvania corporate law, the parties were confident the protections would stand. The Pennsylvania law had been enacted in response to Boone Pickens' attack on home-state favorite Gulf Oil. Under the law, a board can weigh the interests of employees, the community and other constituencies, along with the effect on shareholders, in approving a merger. Essentially, the board has no obligation to auction a company to the highest bidder. The intent was to allow a company like Conrail to agree to a strategic merger without effectively putting itself in play.

Indeed, on the strength of the Pennsylvania law, a federal court judge upheld Conrail's agreement with CSX. However, another provision of Pennsylvania law limited the impact of the court victory. This provision requires an acquirer that purchases 20 percent or more of a target company's stock to provide the same consideration to all shareholders in a later acquisition of the whole company. Target company shareholders are permitted to waive this requirement in a shareholder vote.

Because the CSX offer included both cash and stock, the deal required shareholder approval to proceed. A shareholder meeting, originally scheduled for December 1996, was held in the middle of January.

A temporary stalemate resulted. CSX owned 19.9 percent of Conrail after completion of its first-stage tender offer. In a ploy to win the shareholder vote, Norfolk Southern had promised to buy 9.9 percent of Conrail for $115 after the vote. CSX calculated that it would lose the first vote because shareholders would have to vote no to get the $115. But after the first vote, CSX thought it would eventually win because the present value of Norfolk's offer was much lower for the remaining 90 percent of Conrail's stock. CSX had this view because the breakup provisions of its agreement were still in place and shareholders would probably not be allowed to receive Norfolk stock for two years, although Norfolk was vigorously squirming to fight this result.

Norfolk Southern was now offering $115 a share in cash, or $10.5 billion. CSX had raised its front-end offer to $110 cash and had included additional securities in the back end. Many arbs argued that the CSX offer was fundamentally inferior, but CSX and Conrail retained the winning position. Presumably, shareholders would eventually tire of the fight and take the CSX offer. Technically, CSX was poised to buy the company at a lower price once the court upheld the terms of the agreement.

At this point, the STB stepped into the fray. STB chairwoman Linda Morgan expressed a strong suggestion that all three parties to the fight sit down and negotiate a settlement. The preservation of balanced competition in the East was her stated goal. If either party captured all of Conrail, the winner might potentially dominate the market and limit the possibilities for creating two balanced East–West lines.

The result was that Conrail was split, with CSX buying the Grand Central, and Norfolk the Pennsy. In the end, Linda Morgan controlled the deal.

Cable Television   The cable television industry is an example of a federally regulated industry where the oversight agency—the Federal Communications Commission—has expressly stated it does not consider itself primarily responsible for antitrust enforcement. Consequently, the Justice Department and FTC retain primary responsibility for reviewing cable company transactions.

The Voting Trust   In the case of a stock purchase, an acquirer may wish to go ahead with the transaction while regulatory review is pending. This may be the case where the review process is extended, as with the STB and rail merger oversight, which typically takes more than six months, or where the acquirer is sure it will receive approval and is willing to contest any adverse ruling.

The voting trust mechanism is fairly simple. An acquirer purchases the securities in its target company, then places them in a trust with an independent trustee. The trustee often is required to vote the shares in proportion to the vote of all other shareholders, except the trustee must vote in favor of approving the transaction.

The advantages of a voting trust are several. First, it may give a bidder an edge in a competitive bidding situation because selling shareholders can be paid for their shares without contingencies.

The 1995 battle for Santa Fe Pacific railroad illustrates the importance of this tactical leverage. Union Pacific bid for the company in an effort to bust apart a deal with Burlington. However, the Street consensus was that the Union Pacific bid, though significantly higher than what Burlington promised, would not be enough. The regulatory concerns were too great. Shareholders feared the government would block the deal and were unwilling to give up the Burlington offer for a riskier Union Pacific deal.

To stay in the contest, Union Pacific lowered its offer but guaranteed the purchase with a voting trust mechanism. It would take all the risk that the deal might fall apart. Union Pacific ended up losing the fight anyway, but the voting trust kept it competitive longer than would have otherwise been the case.

Second, a voting trust may allow an acquirer to receive economic benefits from a target company. While the trustee retains the voting rights associated with the targeted securities, any economic benefits, such as dividend payments, can flow through to the acquirer as beneficiary.

The major and obvious disadvantage of a voting trust is that considerable capital can be tied up for an extended period during which the acquirer has no ability to control the target. This situation can cause severe problems in the case of a target company in need of restructuring, or in an acquisition premised on the assumption that target company assets will be sold to pay down debt.

Although antitrust is more vibrant today, the doctrines are clearly in need of modernization. The administrative structure, the definition of market share and the impact of globalization all impel timely reform.

Postscript

At the turn of the century, Admiral Alfred Mahan, a nineteenth-century naval historian, reflected on political events and concluded that seapower had a broad impact on the course of history. His seminal book, *The Influence of Seapower on History, 1660–1783*, stated an obvious but underappreciated thesis that changed the perception of the naval role.

The impact of mergers and acquisitions has a similar quality. While not claiming any exaggerated significance for the M&A process, the buying and selling of companies has been a critical and undervalued force in the history of American economic development.

Over the past two decades, the pace of economic change has been staggering, the volatility overwhelming. In industry after industry—media, telecommunications, health care, oil, financial services—fissures in the economic foundations have jolted the competitive landscape.

There have been pain, dislocations and blunders. Perhaps some of these jolts reduce the pressure along the fault lines of our system, without which the economy would spasm into more convulsive eruptions. The turbulence involved in running some of America's leading businesses is daunting. AT&T, one of America's most distinguished corporations, managed to make itself the butt of ridicule as it rocked from one debacle to another. Yet decisions have to be made in the face of tremendous uncertainty and some will inevitably be wrong.

Who would have thought ten years ago that the local and long-distance markets would be reunited? Or that oil prices would fall back to earth and stay there for over a decade? Or that computers, movies and phones would become a vast interrelated business? Or that our traditional banks would disappear? Or that the stock market would increase 400 percent?

The sweep of history may not have an inevitability, but there are discernible lessons. Flexibility and change are necessary for economic vitality. The capital market system is central to our country's ability to adapt, and it is fueled by the merger process. The net result is that America has prospered.

During our history, there has been a yin and yang, a balance of centrifugal forces, as to the role of mergers. Sometimes, the pace is too fast. Sometimes, the pain in adapting to industrial change is too much. Sometimes the process is subject to abuse. The government changes the antitrust laws, the states pass protective takeover statutes, the Delaware courts use their sense of smell and stop the greenmailers. But the discipline the process creates for the whole economic system and the incentive for innovation are immeasurably valuable.

More narrowly, there are some clear lessons on doing deals:

Fundamentals   The difference in a deal is never the intricacy of a computer model but rather a fundamental understanding of the business and industry, and a strategy for coping with the inevitable changes.

Management   The impact of strong management is not apparent when things are going well, but when the rain comes, as it will, it makes the difference. Ted Forstmann's role at Gulfstream comes to mind. Through sheer tenacity and hands-on control, he turned a bad investment around. Success is never guaranteed, and businesses do suffer fatal wounds, but consistent effort and management insight significantly add to the final return.

Sensible Financing   Looking at deals that did go wrong, many suffered a common problem—the mismatched book. In good times, it is possible to get away with financing long-term cash needs with short-term debt. Of course, one never knows when the good times will end, and the jolt can be sharp.

Even more difficult than analyzing the past is gazing into a Delphic crystal ball, prognosticating speculative profundities. Yet history is prologue and observations about the past do provide insight into the future course of events. Extrapolating, then, from the past, six trends in particular likely will continue to shape the future:

Cyclicality The deal business will continue to be cyclical with secular growth. We have experienced an unprecedented run of record-breaking years since the downturn of the early 1990s. However, the boom times will not last forever.

At the peak of the merger cycle, excesses will occur. There is a tendency to accept mediocrities into the ranks of takeover professionals, a dangerous indulgence. The nature of activity also varies with the financial circumstances and the mood of the times. Today there is a significant preponderance of stock deals. However, that will change again sometime in the next few years. Financial buyers alone have over $40 billion of committed capital to invest. The accounting gurus are considering revising the restrictive pooling rules which motivate strategic buyers in favor of stock deals. So the question is not whether there will be a resurgence of cash deals, but when.

The Danger of Belly Flops Of course, there is also a danger of belly flops. Poor strategic conception or tactical implementation can lead to problems with a merger or acquisition. The tribulations of AT&T in the computer sector, including the poorly executed NCR acquisition, Union Pacific's problems getting freight to run on time after the Southern Pacific takeover and alleged improprieties at Columbia/HCA all indicate the risks. As in all aspects of business, consistent follow-through, attention to details, quality leadership and sometimes a bit of luck are necessary to a successful merger process.

Increasing Sophistication   The evolution of takeovers through the years has been a process of increasing sophistication. The cash deals of the 1980s represented an implicit repudiation of prevailing corporate valuation methods. Valuing companies based on book earnings understated a target's capacity to generate cash. Financial buyers saw the embedded opportunity and acted on it.

The greater role taken on by institutional investors has been another aspect of the increasing sophistication of the deal business. With their significant ownership percentages of most large corporations, institutional investors have been the vehicle for reuniting ownership and control. By acting in concert, they can bring considerable pressure on a board to accept an offer or take other value-maximizing actions. This process has only accelerated since the recent revision of the proxy rules made coordinated action less cumbersome, and will continue into the future.

The Delaware Pendulum Swings   In crafting the basic rules of takeover law, the Delaware courts have attempted to balance the interests of shareholders and other constituencies. The excesses of the 1980s hostile deals have been muted with the acceptance of the poison pill and the *Time* strategic merger ruling.

Delaware takeover law swings back and forth over a fairly narrow range of middle ground. The pill redemption issue surely will continue to come up until the Delaware Supreme Court clarifies the responsibilities of a board.

Securities Law Revisions   The creation of clear, fair securities laws has been critical to protecting the deal process over the long run. A system with integrity is crucial to the market trust behind mergers and acquisitions, and the standards still need to be elevated.

Globalization The global strategic imperative is a thread running throughout this book. No matter the industry, the impact is universal. We have barely begun global consolidation, and the pace will accelerate.

Layered on top of these trends, the Five Pistons also will continue to shape the deal flow. Regulations, technology, financial fluctuations, leadership and the size-simplicity vortex will all drive change.

At this juncture, America is riding the crest of prosperity, and mergers are part of the story. It is largely an untold tale, a complex pattern missed because the focus is on individual transactions. Although conditions change, the time has come to take a realistic view of the merger process, not through rose-tinted lenses, but giving this important component of our economic development the recognition and sophisticated understanding it requires.

Bibliography

Much of the contemporary factual material in this book is drawn from memory, supplemented heavily by articles from leading business publications. Particularly important sources include *The Wall Street Journal, The New York Times, Business Week, Forbes* and *Fortune*. My avocation is business history, and I have also drawn on many fine books that I have read over the years. A partial list follows:

Part One

Anders, George. *Merchants of Debt: KKR and the Mortgaging of American Business.* Basic Books, 1992.

Auletta, Ken. *Greed and Glory on Wall Street: The Fall of the House of Lehman.* Warner Books, 1987.

Brooks, John. *The Takeover Game.* Truman Talley Books/Dutton, 1987.

_____. *Once in Golconda: A True Drama of Wall Street.* Watson-Guptill Publications, 1969.

Bruck, Connie. *The Predators' Ball: The Inside Story of Drexel Burnham and the Rise of the Junk Bond Raiders.* Penguin USA, 1989.

_____. *Master of the Game: Steve Ross and the Creation of Time Warner.* Penguin USA, 1989.

Chernow, Ron. *House of Morgan.* Atlantic Monthly Press, 1990.

Cray, Ed. *Chrome Colossus: General Motors and Its Times.* McGraw-Hill, 1980.

Fischel, Daniel. *Payback: The Conspiracy to Destroy Michael Milken and His Financial Revolution.* Harper Business, 1996.

Galbraith, John. *The Great Crash—1929.* Houghton Mifflin, 1988.

Groner, Alex. *The American Heritage History of American Business and Industry.* American Heritage, 1972.

Hearings Before the Subcommittee on Telecommunications, Consumer Protection, and Finance, of the Committee on Energy and Commerce, House of Representatives. U.S. Government Printing Office, 1984.

Hessen, Robert. *Steel Titan: The Life of Charles M. Schwab*. University of Pittsburgh Press, 1990.

Jacobs, Michael T. *Short-Term America: The Causes and Cures of Our Business Myopia*. Harvard Business School Press, 1991.

Johnston, Moira. *Takeover: The New Wall Street Warriors: The Men, the Money, the Impact*. Arbor House, 1986.

Josephson, Matthew. *The Robber Barons: The Great American Capitalists, 1861–1901*. Harcourt Brace, 1962.

Lacey, Robert. *Ford: The Men and the Machine*. Little, Brown, 1986.

Mair, George. *The Barry Diller Story: The Life and Times of America's Greatest Entertainment Mogul*. John Wiley & Sons, 1997.

McKee, Carl W. *Japanese Takeovers*. Harvard Business School Press, 1991.

Ravenscraft, David J. *Mergers, Sell-Offs and Economic Efficiency*. The Brookings Institution, 1987.

Salsbury, Stephen. *No Way to Run a Railroad: The Untold Story of the Penn Central Crisis*. McGraw-Hill, 1982.

Schoenberg, Robert J. *Geneen*. Norton, 1985.

Sloan, Alfred P. *My Years with General Motors*. Doubleday, 1996.

Smith, Roy C. *The Money Wars*. Truman Talley Books, 1990.

Sobel, Robert. *Dangerous Dreamers: The Financial Innovators from Charles Merrill to Michael Milken*. John Wiley & Sons, 1993.

_____. *The Great Bull Market: Wall Street in the 1920's*. W.W. Norton & Company, 1968.

_____. *ITT: The Management of Opportunity*. HarperCollins, 1982.

_____. *The Rise and Fall of the Conglomerate Kings*. Stein & Day, 1984.

Steiner, Peter O. *Mergers, Motives, Effects, Policies*. University of Michigan Press, 1975.

Stevens, Mark. *King Icahn: The Biography of a Renegade Capitalist*. Dutton, 1993.

Stewart, James B. *Den of Thieves*. Touchstone, 1992.

Stone, Dan G. *April Fools: An Insider's Account of the Rise and Collapse of Drexel Burnham*. Donald I. Fine, 1990.

Tarbell, Ida. *History of the Standard Oil Company*. Amereon Ltd., 1993.

Vanderbilt, Cornelius, Jr. *Farewell to Fifth Avenue*. Simon & Schuster, 1935.

Wall, Joseph Frazier. *Andrew Carnegie*. University of Pittsburgh Press, 1989.

Weidenbaum, Murray, and Kenneth Chilton. *Public Policy Toward Corporate Takeovers*. Transaction Books, 1988.

Part Two

Araskog, Rand V. *The ITT Wars*. Henry Holt, 1989.

Auletta, Ken. *The Highwaymen: Warriors of the Information Superhighway*. Random House, 1997.

Bollenbacher, George M. *The New Business of Banking: Transforming Challenges into Opportunities in Today's Financial Services Marketplace*. Irwin Professional Publications, 1995.

Brooks, John. *The Go-Go Years*. Dutton, 1984.

Brown, Stanley H. *Ling: The Rise, Fall, and Return of a Texas Titan*. Atheneum, 1972.

Chandler, Alfred D., and Herman Daems. *Managerial Hierarchies: Comparative Perspectives on the Rise of the Modern Industrial Enterprise*. Harvard University Press, 1980.

Clurman, Richard M. *To the End of Time: The Seduction and Conquest of a Media Empire*. Simon & Schuster, 1992.

Coll, Steve. *The Deal of the Century: The Breakup of AT&T*. Atheneum, 1986.

_____. *The Taking of Getty Oil: The Full Story of the Most Spectacular and Catastrophic Takeover of All Time*. Atheneum, 1987.

Gart, Alan. *Regulation, Deregulation, Reregulation: The Future of the Banking, Insurance and Securities Industries*. John Wiley & Sons, 1993.

Grover, Ron. *The Disney Touch: How a Daring Management Team Revived an Entertainment Empire*. Irwin Professional Publications, 1991.

Harvey, Thomas W. *The Banking Revolution: Positioning Your Bank in the New Financial Services Marketplace*. Irwin Professional Publications, 1996.

Mayer, Martin. *The Bankers: The Next Generation*. Dutton, 1997.

_____. *The Money Bazaars: Understanding the Banking Revolution Around Us*. Dutton, 1984.

O'Connor, Richard. *The Oil Barons*. Little, Brown, 1971.

Pickens, T. Boone. *Boone*. Random House, 1988.

Porter, Michael E. *Competitive Strategy: Techniques for Analyzing Industries and Competitors*. The Free Press, 1984.

Rogers, David. *The Future of American Banking: Managing for Change*. McGraw-Hill, 1992.

Slater, Robert. *The New GE: How Jack Welch Revived an American Institution*. Irwin Professional Publications, 1992.

_____. *Ovitz: The Inside Story of Hollywood's Most Controversial Power Broker*. McGraw-Hill, 1997.

Spiegal, John, Alan Gart, and Steven Gart. *Banking Redefined: How Superregional Powerhouses Are Reshaping Financial Services*. Irwin Professional Publications, 1996.

Wallace, James. *Overdrive: Bill Gates and the Race to Control Cyberspace.* John Wiley & Sons, 1997.

Wendel, Charles B. *The New Financiers: Profiles of the Leaders Who Are Reshaping the Financial Services Industry.* Irwin Professional Publications, 1996.

Yergin, Daniel. *The Prize: The Epic Quest for Oil, Money, and Power.* Simon & Schuster, 1991.

Part Three

Bernstein, Leopold. *Financial Statement Analysis: Theory, Application, and Interpretation.* Irwin Professional Publications, 1983.

Caplan, Lincoln. *Skadden: Power, Money, and the Rise of a Legal Empire.* Farrar Straus & Giroux, 1994.

Cohen, Herb. *You Can Negotiate Anything.* Bantam, 1989.

Copeland, Tom, Tim Koller, and Jack Murrin. *Valuation: Measuring and Managing the Value of Companies.* John Wiley & Sons, 1995.

Cottle, Sidney, Roger F. Murray, and Frank E. Block. *Graham and Dodd's Security Analysis.* McGraw-Hill, 1988.

Dunlap, Albert J., and Bob Andelman. *Mean Business: How I Save Bad Companies and Make Good Companies Great.* Simon & Schuster, 1997.

Ferrera, Ralph C., Meredith M. Brown, and John H. Hall. *Takeovers: Attack and Survival, a Strategist's Manual.* Michie Dullerworth, 1987.

Fisher, Roger, and William Ury. *Getting to Yes: How to Negotiate Agreement Without Giving In.* Simon & Schuster, 1987.

Fleischer Jr., Arthur, and Alexander R. Sussman. *Takeover Defense.* Aspen Law & Business, 1995.

Freund, James C. *Anatomy of a Merger: Strategies and Techniques for Negotiating Corporate Acquisitions.* Law Journal Seminars Press, 1975.

Gaughan, Patrick A. *Mergers, Acquisitions, and Corporate Restructurings.* John Wiley & Sons, 1996.

Hamel, Gary, and C.K. Prahalad. *Competing for the Future.* Harvard Business School Press, 1994.

Hartz, Peter F. *Merger: The Exclusive Inside Story of the Bendix-Martin Marietta Takeover War.* William Morrow, 1985.

Hayes, Samuel L., and Philip M. Hubbard. *Investment Banking: A Tale of Three Cities.* Harvard Business School, 1990.

Hoffman, Paul. *Lions in the Street: The Inside Story of the Great Wall Street Law Firms.* Dutton, 1973.

Lowenstein, Roger. *Buffett: The Making of an American Capitalist.* Doubleday, 1996.

Mark, Howard. *Financial Shenanigans: How to Detect Accounting Gimmicks and Fraud in Financial Reports.* McGraw-Hill, 1993.

Mayer, Martin. *Lawyers.* Greenwood Publishing, 1980.

O'glove, Thornton L., with Robert Sobel. *Quality of Earnings: The Investor's Guide to How Much Money a Company Is Really Making.* The Free Press, 1987.

Reich, Cary. *Financier, The Biography of André Meyer: A Story of Money, Power, and the Reshaping of American Business.* William Morrow, 1983.

Stewart III, G. Bennett. *The Quest for Value: The EVA™ Management Guide.* Harper Business, 1991.

Thornhill, William T. *Forensic Accounting: How to Investigate Financial Fraud.* Irwin Professional Publications, 1994.

Tom, Willard K., and Abbott B. Lipsky Jr. *Antitrust Law Developments,* 3rd edition, Volume I. American Bar Association, 1992.

Wasserstein, Bruce. *Corporate Finance Law: A Guide for the Executive.* McGraw-Hill, 1978.

Key Takeover Cases

Basic, Inc. v. Levinson, 485 U.S. 224 (1988) (obligation to issue nonmisleading disclosure regarding merger negotiations).

Brown Shoe Co. v. United States, 370 U.S. 294 (1962) (antitrust).

Brunswick Corp. v. Pueblo-Bowl-O-Mat, Inc., 429 U.S. 477 (1977) (antitrust).

Chiarella v. United States, 445 U.S. 222 (1980) (insider trading liability).

FTC v. Procter & Gamble Co. (Clorox), 386 U.S. 568 (1967) (antitrust).

Grand Metropolitan PLC v. The Pillsbury Company, 558 A.2d 1049 (Del. Ch. 1988) (court enjoins elements of defensive restructuring and orders pill redeemed).

Invacare Corporation v. Healthdyne Technologies, Inc., 968 F. Supp. 1578 (1997) (denying a bidder's motion to remove a "dead-hand" poison pill).

J.J. Case Co. v. Borak, 377 U.S. 426 (1964) (recognizing implied private right of action on behalf of shareholders for proxy violations).

Kennecott Copper Corp. v. FTC, 467 F.2d 67 (10th Cir. 1972) (antitrust).

Missouri Portland Cement v. H.K. Porter Co., CCH Securities Law Reporter, Para. 95,864 (S. Ct. 1977) (antitrust).

Moore Corporation v. Wallace Computer Services, Inc., 907 F. Supp 1545 (Del. 1995) ("just say no" defense approved).

Moran v. Household International Inc., 500 A.2d 1346 (Del. 1985) (poison pill is an acceptable preventive takeover defense).

Otis Elevator Co. v. United Technologies Corp., 405 F. Supp. 960 (S.D.N.Y. 1975) (antitrust).

Paramount Communications Inc. v. QVC Network Inc., 637 A.2d 34 (Del. 1994) (board may not unduly favor one party over another in a company sale).

Paramount Communications Inc. v. Time Incorporated, 571 A.2d 1140 (Del. 1990) (company need not forgo strategic merger in favor of a higher hostile bid).

Piper Aircraft Corp. v. Chris-Craft Industries, 430 U.S. 1 (1977) (bidder does not have standing to sue target for disclosure violations).

Revlon v. MacAndrews & Forbes, 506 A.2d 173 (Del. 1985) (board must maximize return to shareholders in a sale of company).

Smith v. Van Gorkom, 488 A.2d 858 (Del. 1985) (liability of directors for breaching duty of care).

Stanley Works v. FTC, 469 F.2d 498 (2d Cir. 1972) (antitrust).

TSC Industries, Inc. v. Northway, Inc., 426 U.S. 438 (1976) (defining materiality under securities laws).

United States v. International Tel. & Tel. Corp. (Grinnell), 306 F. Supp. 766 (D. Conn. 1969) (antitrust).

United States v. Philadelphia Nat'l Bank, 374 U.S. 321 (1963) (antitrust).

United States v. Von's Grocery Co., 384 U.S. 270 (1966) (antitrust).

United States v. Gillette Co., 828 F. Supp. 78 (D.D.C. 1993) (antitrust).

Unocal Corporation v. Mesa Petroleum Co., 493 A.2d 946 (Del. 1985) (discriminatory self-tender is a reasonable defensive response to a coercive hostile bid).

Index

Icahn, Carl, 80, 102, 107–11,
145–46; bear hug tactic,
605; congressional
testimony, 149, 150;
negotiation style, 570–71;
and Phillips, 135–37,
196, 479; and RJR
Nabisco, 615–16; Texaco
shares buyup, 203
ICC Termination Act of
1995, 780
ICI, 477
IC Industries, 217–18
IDB WorldCom, 342
Idei, Nobuyuki, 390–91
IDS. *See* Investors Diversified
Services
Illinois Central Industries,
461–62
Inco, 73–75, 458–59, 470
Income smoothing, 507–8
Increasing-rate note, 116
Indemnities, 579–80
Indentures, 541
Infinity Broadcasting, 227,
364, 366, 406–7
Inflated-value stock, 30
Ingersoll-Rand, 228
ING Group, 246, 247, 285
Initial public offering (IPO),
88, 92, 164, 513, 559;
AT&T as largest in
history, 673; of subsidiary,
645, 649–50, 670
InPhyNet Medical
Management, 426
Insider information, 46–47,
119–28, 237, 490
Institutional investors, 71,
141–42, 243; bear hug
approach, 604–5; and
Conoco takeover, 183;
growth and influence, 67,
790; and investment
banks, 241–42; as merger
advisers, 478–81; and
proxy fights, 617
Insull, Samuel, 53, 54
Insurance companies, 248;
consolidation, 277,
280–81, 286; health care
and, 408, 411–13;
institutional investors,
478; investment banks,
242; LBO financing by,

101; retail brokerage
business, 251
Integrated Resources, 129
Interest costs: bank loans,
592, 593; bridge loans,
592; and DCF model,
516, 519–21; drop in
early 1980s, 218; junk
bonds, 595; leveraged
buyouts, 94, 117, 147;
leveraged recapitalization,
729; tax-deductibility, 91,
153
InterMedia Partners, 360
Internal Revenue Service. *See*
Tax law
International Harvester Co.,
41
International Nickel Co. of
Canada. *See* Inco
International Telephone &
Telegraph. *See* ITT Corp.
Internet, 401–7; access
services, 322, 343, 344,
346, 405; online services,
302, 401, 402, 489
InterNorth, 207, 213
Interstate Commerce
Commission. *See* Surface
Transportation Board
Intuit Corp., 748, 757–58
*Invacare v. Healthdyne
Technologies* case, 695
Inventory sales, 506–7
Inventory turnover ratio, 510
Investigative Group, 476, 477
Investment banks, 241–51;
asset management, 283;
bridge loans, 592; creation
of, 248; fairness opinions,
659–61; foreign markets,
250; future trends, 286;
"highly confident letter,"
596–97; junk bond
underwriting fee, 83; LBO
financing, 96; as merger
advisers, 67, 456, 466–73;
mergers and acquisitions,
241–46, 247t, 251, 256;
"success" fee, 661;
takeover defenses, 139,
458–59, 725
Investors Diversified
Services, 253

IPO. *See* Initial public
offering
Iron Law, 177
IRS. *See* Tax law
ITT Corp., 28, 367, 604,
615; debt and turmoil,
64, 217–18, 219, 220–24;
as diversified conglom-
erate, 57, 60–65, 222,
224, 352, 469, 742;
divestiture program, 63,
221–24, 672, 674;
earnings management,
506; Hilton Hotels bid,
739–46; long-distance
phone market, 297;
Rohatyn and, 469

Jacobs, Irwin, 207, 221, 374,
375, 477
Jacobs, Jacob, 22–23
Jacobs, Michael, 150–51
Jacobs Suchard, 636
Japan, 68, 94, 111–12, 131,
389–90, 773–74
Jett, Joseph, 237–38
Joffe, Robert, 463, 760–62
Johnson, F. Ross, 113–15,
142–43, 154, 254, 486,
635, 736
Johnson & Johnson, 432,
436, 706–7
Johnston, Don, 610
Jones & Laughlin Steel Co.,
58, 60, 71, 74, 758
Jones, Day, Reavis & Pogue,
457, 465, 466
Jordan, Michael H., 226–27,
407
Joseph, Fred, 129, 130
J. Paul Getty Museum, 190,
191
J.P. Morgan & Co., 34–35,
47, 48–49, 274, 277, 282,
466
Junk bonds, 81–85, 595–97;
campaigns against, 117,
146–47; and Drexel
Burnham failure, 129,
131; insurance industry
effects, 278; LBO
financing, 94, 101, 104,
110, 115–16, 145–47,
595–97; market dry-up,
132; market over-

Leveraged buyouts (*cont.*)
and, 464; tax benefits,
153; three models,
87–91, 163–64, 591–97
Leveraged recapitalization,
559–60, 646–47, 726,
728–33, 737–38
Levin, Gerald (Jerry), 376,
397, 398, 762
Levine, Dennis, 120–21,
122–23
Levitt & Sons, 61, 63, 469
Levy, Gustave, 71
Liabilities: careful selection
of, 542; hidden, 508–9,
535; merger transfer,
534–35
Liberty Media Corp., 13, 17,
18, 21, 27, 332, 382, 771
LIBOR. *See* London
Interbank Offered Rate
Liedtke, J. Hugh, 190, 191
LIFO inventory valuation,
506–7, 510
Liman, Arthur, 465
LIN Broadcasting, 311–12,
314–15, 323, 349
Ling, Jimmy, 56, 57–59, 71,
72, 74, 139, 758; profile,
59
Ling Electric Co., 57
Ling-Temco-Voight. *See* LTV
Lipton, Martin (Marty),
9–10, 11, 79, 146, 190,
191, 461–62, 463, 465,
469, 782; negotiation
style, 565, 566; poison
pill development, 462,
690
Liquidation, partial or total,
731
Litigation: as corporate raider
tool, 31, 32, 456; for
fin/syn rules repeal,
393–94; as greenmail by-
product, 719–20; hostile
takeover, 22–23, 31,
80–81, 104, 588, 666,
714, 738–39; outside
bidder, 584–85, 587, 588;
tender offer definition,
621–22; trust-busting,
40–42; Unocal
antitakeover defense,
197–201 (*see also*

Antitrust; Law firms;
*specific cases and
companies*)
Little, Brian, 96, 119
Little, Royal, 57
Litton Industries, 64, 71,
217–18
Lobbyists, 79, 138, 139, 146,
198
Lockheed, 724, 778
Lockup, 23, 584–89, 606,
633, 645, 725, 731–32
Loewen, Raymond, 717–18
Loews Corp., 371, 384
Loews theaters, 381, 382,
383
London Electricity, 212
London Interbank Offered
Rate, 592
Long-Distance Discount
Service (LDDS). *See*
WorldCom
Long-distance phone
services, 289–99, 301,
302, 305, 318, 324–25;
bundled with local
service, 3–4, 322, 335,
337; competition, 325,
346–47; WorldCom deal,
342–46
Long Lines, 290
Loral, 778
L'Oréal, 581–82, 656–57
Lorenzo, Frank, 109–10
Lorillard, 382
Lotus Development, 487,
614, 615, 619, 633, 706
Low-grade debt bonds. *See*
Junk bonds
LTV, 57–59, 65, 82, 210,
218, 758
Lucent, 324, 325, 672–73
Lynch, Gary, 123

M&A. *See* Mergers and
acquisitions
MacAndrews & Forbes,
103–6
MAC clause, 573, 576
Mack, John, 241, 244–45
Macmillan Co., 154
Macy's, 132, 139, 148
Madison Square Garden, 17,
26, 28, 222, 352, 741
Magellan Fund, 283

Magness, Bob, 355, 356
Mahan, Alfred, 787
Malone, John, 13, 21, 349,
354, 360–61, 398, 708,
762; on digital revolution,
392; and Microsoft, 404;
profile, 354–56; vertical
mergers model, 381–82
Managed care. *See* Health
care industry
Management: and
arbitrageurs, 482; Baby
Bell, 303; and casual
bids, 688; conglomerate,
219–20; corporate
marriage, 668–69;
dealmakers as, 108;
deification of, 56; fight
against Phillips takeover,
135, 136; Geneen style,
60, 61–63; golden
parachutes, 711–12; Gulf
Oil problems, 193, 194;
and hostile takeovers, 74,
108–9; importance of
strong, 788; incentive
programs, 678; and
institutional investors,
479; as LBO critics, 146;
as LBO participants, 89,
154; and LBO strategy,
93, 95–96; MCI-
WorldCom merger, 345;
merger market as curb
on, 142–43, 151; as NCR
problem, 321–22;
negotiation leadership,
563, 565–66, 570–71;
Perelman enterprises,
106; personal excesses,
114, 142–43, 390; self-
interest, 154, 157;
stockholder pressure,
138, 481; strategic
thinking, 162–63; Time
Warner joint duties, 385;
Westinghouse resignation,
226–27 (*see also*
Directors)
Management fee, 101
Mancuso, Frank, 15, 379
Mandatorily convertible
preferred stock, 420–21
Mandl, Alex, 326